D1457667

SO-BPW-317

SECOND EDITION

POLITICS

AND

GEOGRAPHIC

RELATIONSHIPS

Toward a New Focus

Edited by

W. A. DOUGLAS JACKSON
University of Washington
and

MARWYN S. SAMUELS
University of Washington

PRENTICE-HALL, INC., Englewood Cliffs, New Jersey

Current printing (last digit):
10 9 8 7 6 5 4 3 2 1

13-685123-1

Library of Congress Catalog Card Number:
70-138481

Printed in the United States of America

Prentice-Hall International, Inc., London
Prentice-Hall of Australia, Pty. Ltd., Sydney
Prentice-Hall of Canada, Ltd., Toronto
Prentice-Hall of India Private Limited, New Delhi
Prentice-Hall of Japan, Inc., Tokyo

CONTENTS

INTRODUCTION: THE GEOGRAPHY OF POLITICAL SYSTEMS

I
THE FIELD OF POLITICAL GEOGRAPHY

AN HISTORICAL OVERVIEW

II
POLITICAL GEOGRAPHY AND POLITICAL SYSTEMS

FUNCTIONS AND SYSTEMS: A THEORETICAL FRAMEWORK

THE LIMITS OF THE POLITICAL SYSTEM

III
SYSTEM AND AREA: THE POLITICAL REGION

REGIONAL THESES IN POLITICAL GEOGRAPHY

ADMINISTRATIVE AND SPECIAL-PURPOSE REGIONS

REGIONALISM AND SECTIONALISM

IV
SYSTEM AND AREA : THE POLITICAL COMMUNITY

THE QUESTION OF COMMUNITY

COMMUNITY AND SPATIAL PERCEPTION

LEVELS OF POLITICAL COMMUNITY : LOCAL

LEVELS OF POLITICAL COMMUNITY : URBAN

LEVELS OF POLITICAL COMMUNITY : NATIONAL INTEGRATION

LEVELS OF POLITICAL COMMUNITY : SUPRANATIONAL

PREFACE

Definitions of political geography have changed over the years as the focus or emphasis within the field, as part of the larger geographic discipline, has been modified. In recent years, the status of political geographical work has come under close scrutiny.[1] Indeed, the field as a whole has been described by one prominent geographer in the United States as "moribund."[2] Criticism is a healthy condition for growth and in the case of political geography it seems, on the surface at least, justified. However, the increasing sophistication with which geographers have approached their study of political phenomena and the growing awareness of some political scientists of the total "environment of the political system" (apart from the purely regional aspect) suggest that there is fast emerging a framework for study, which augurs well for the future. It is hoped that the present collection, which draws heavily on the works of political scientists as well as of political geographers and other specialists, will demonstrate the direction political geography as a field of study in the modern world might take.

THE PROBLEM

Max Lerner reminds us that one of the common fallacies of intellectual effort and research in our time "is the belief that whatever is new or on the frontier must therefore be better, more profound or more exciting than what is traditional or somewhere near the center of [their] area."[3] The slow growth of political geographic thought and method, as critics have charged, is to be

---

[1] W.A. Douglas Jackson, "Whither Political Geography?" *Annals* of the Association of American Geographers, XLVIII, No. 2 (June 1958), 178–183.

[2] See Brian J.L. Berry in a review of *International Regions and the International System: A Study in Political Ecology* by Bruce M. Russett, *The Geographical Review*, LIX, No. 3 (July 1969), 450.

[3] Max Lerner, "The Frontiers of the Human Condition," *The American Scholar*, XXVII, No. 1 (Winter 1957–58).

regretted, but should it be ascribed to an inability among political geographers to open up new frontiers? Is it because they have not incorporated into their work methods of quantitative analysis to achieve more precise definitions of relationships? Although there may be elements of truth in both of these charges, the superficiality of such questions leaves much to be desired. The past weakness of political geography lies not in its techniques of analysis, even though they may have been imperfect; rather that weakness, like the weakness of systematic philosophy in Kant's age,[4] may be attributed to a failure to arrive at an understanding of the substance of political geography, a failure to determine its essential principles.

The economic geographer, in pursuit of understanding and concepts, has found the construct *homo economicus* useful, and has adopted from economics (and more recently from mathematics) techniques that have raised the level of his analytic and descriptive skills. But, as Aristotle suggested long ago, man may also be considered *homo politicus*, a political animal, a construct inherently less precise than *homo economicus*. For reasons that man himself has often little understood or perceived, he has formed (or been formed into) groups and associations that have organized territory for a wide array of purposes. The political geographer, in his attempt to analyze the process of man's political behavior on the earth's surface, has had difficulty in recognizing factors relevant to his task. In the past, political science offered few guidelines. Certainly, the geographer failed to grasp the fact that the event of organization was in itself a political act.

Traditional political science has embraced a wide range of topics with no generally accepted methodology. Indeed, there have been those who have questioned whether political science should rightly be thought of as an independent discipline at all, since it included not only the study of political institutions (in the narrow sense), but also political philosophy, the process of government at different levels, political power, and international relations. However, according to Hans Morgenthau, there has been a central core that has united the field: a common subject matter defined in most general terms as an "orientation toward the nature and activities of the state and toward activities which have in turn a direct bearing upon the state."[5] Clearly, the link between political science and political geography, where it existed in the past, was a sharing of interest in the political region, and specifically in the State.

---

[4] "We often hear complaints against the shallowness of thought in our own time, and the decay of sound knowledge. But I do not see that sciences which rest on a solid foundation, such as mathematics, physics, etc., deserve this reproach in the least. On the contrary, they maintain their old reputation of solidity, and with regard to physics, even surpass it. The same spirit would manifest itself in other branches of knowledge, if only their principles had first been properly determined. Till that is done, indifferentism and doubt, and ultimately severe criticism, are rather signs of honest thought...." Immanuel Kant, *Critique of Pure Reason* (1781) (Garden City, N.Y.: Doubleday & Company, Inc., Dolphin Books, 1961), p. 21.

[5] Hans J. Morgenthau, "Reflections on the State of Political Science," *The Review of Politics*, XVII, No. 4 (October 1955), 431–460.

As Jackson pointed out some years back,[6] political science, as a social science, was focused on man in society, organized for the purposes of promoting and carrying on political activities, of establishing a government, of creating a State; above all, the political scientist was concerned with institutional relationships. Political geography, as a branch of geography generally assumed to have had its roots in the natural sciences, tended to concentrate on the territorial aspect: what territory, how organized, and, to some extent, why. However, the division of labor between the political geographer and the political scientist relative to the political-territorial unit or the State was quite unrealistic. If the geographer ventured very far into what was regarded as essentially "political" and "not geographical," he was charged with trespassing on the domain of the political scientist. On the other hand, prior to World War II it was argued, particularly by Harold Sprout, that political geography "should become an established political science field," since political science, he believed, was founded on the bedrock of regional geography.[7] This matter could be discussed at length. Indeed, it may have been a factor prompting Richard Hartshorne's appeal in 1950 for "a more geographical political geography,"[8] reaffirming geography's claim to an interest in politics. Whatever the truth, the issue no longer appears relevant. When our thinking adhered to the quite arbitrary division of knowledge into disciplines, arguments over discipline content had validity. Today these divisions have lost much of their revered status through a growing awareness on the part of scientists, philosophers, and theologians of the unity of all studies of man.

When geography was essentially chorology,[9] the State, identified on the ordinary political map as a section of the earth, obviously offered a given framework or focus for the geographer's attention. But political geographers in their treatment of politics progressed only as rapidly as their understanding of the State developed, and in practice their study frequently represented little more than a tedious encyclopedic collection of facts, often irrelevant and clumsily strung together. When geography moved away from regional description, as it tended to do after World War II, political geography for the most part remained attached to the region. In particular, its attention remained focused on the State as the quintessence of political geographical concern.

Along with that, the simultaneous involvement of geographers in geopolitics, which developed primarily in the Western World after Versailles, further enhanced the difficulties that political geographers later faced in seeking a new direction or orientation. Though the implications of geopolitics—especially the

---

6 Jackson, *op. cit.*

7 Harold H. Sprout, "Political Geography as a Political Science Field," *The American Political Science Review*, XXV, No. 2 (May 1931), 439–442.

8 Richard Hartshorne, "The Functional Approach in Political Geography," *Annals* of the Association of American Geographers, XI, No. 2 (June 1950), 95–130.

9 The terms *chorology* and *chorography* are often used interchangeably, although strictly speaking the former means the science of areas or places and the latter the description of areas and places.

German variant—were decried after World War II as much of Europe and parts of Asia lay in ruins, the influence of the pseudoscience lingered on.[10] Attempts to use the term "geopolitics" with new meaning only led to greater confusion.

The most comprehensive statement of this continuing interest may be found in Ladis Kristof's "The Origins and Evolution of Geopolitics,"[11] published in 1960. A political scientist by training, Kristof stated that "geopolitics should cover all the field parallel to, and intermediate between, political science and political geography...." But at the outset, Kristof refused to give a precise definition of the field of study he contemplated on the grounds that it would be both difficult and premature; there is no universally accepted definition of geography, and political scientists have seldom even tried to define their field. Ultimately, however, he did define it as follows:

> Geopolitics is the study of political phenomena (1) in their spatial relationship and (2) in their relationship with, dependence upon, and influence on earth as well as on all those cultural factors which constitute the subject matter of human geography ... broadly defined. In other words, geopolitics is what the word itself suggests etymologically: geographical politics, that is politics and not geography—politics geographically interpreted and analyzed for its geographical content. Being an intermediary (or subsidiary) science, it has no independent field of study but one that is defined in terms of the fields of geography and political science and their mutual interrelation.

Still, Kristof noted that

> there is not any fundamental difference, either in method or in the field of study, between geopolitics and political geography—at least insofar as political geography is understood and practiced today in America and in most of the West.... The only real difference between political geography and geopolitics is in emphasis—in the focus of attention. Political geography qua geography tends to focus its attention on the geographical phenomena; it gives a political interpretation and studies the political aspects of geographic phenomena. Geopolitics qua politics, on the contrary, tends to focus on the political phenomena and attempts to give a geographical interpretation and study the geographical aspects of these phenomena....[12]

Kristof's statement was unfortunate, because it was misleading. It distinguished between geographic phenomena and political phenomena where no distinction need or should be made. And it seemingly showed a lack of understanding of what was transpiring in the field of geography generally, as well as of the new trends in political science.

---

10 See S. Leszczycki, "Nowsze kierunki i prądy w geografii," *Przegląd geograficzny*, No. 4 (1958), 549.

11 Ladis K.D. Kristof, "The Origins and Evolution of Geopolitics," *The Journal of Conflict Resolution*, IV, No. 1 (March 1960), 15–51.

12 *Ibid.*, 36–37.

TOWARD A NEW ORIENTATION

The phenomenon known as the State is the most formal manifestation of political activity and, in an age of nationalism, the focus of many of our most intense loyalties and the source of our strongest political control. However, it is *only one* manifestation of political activity. There are others within the sphere of politics, often but not necessarily less formal than that of the State, which in the past have largely gone unnoticed by geographers and political scientists alike. Indeed, the poor performance of political geography is not so much that geographers should have remained interested in the State, and especially the Nation-State, together with its attendant features, i.e., boundaries, capital cities, electoral divisions, and so forth, but that they should have done so to the exclusion of other equally important phenomena. In short, it can be said that geographers have been slow to recognize what constitutes politics as a generic object of concern and, with the exception of environmentalism and geopolitics, what aspects of politics treated spatially might properly belong within the geographic discipline.

With a broader definition of what constitutes politics, particularly a definition that cuts across institutional (not to mention disciplinary) boundaries and emerges as a more humanistic subject, political geographers and political scientists may more clearly recognize their common concern—a concern that revolves about human beings interacting to form, institutionalize, and change their political systems.

INTRODUCTION:
THE GEOGRAPHY OF
POLITICAL SYSTEMS

PART I: THE FIELD OF POLITICAL GEOGRAPHY

An historical overview

Political geography as a distinct branch of geographical study is said to have begun with the publication of *Politische Geographie* by Friedrich Ratzel in Munich in 1897. Indeed, Ratzel is generally described as the founder of modern political geography. His work did much to influence the direction of political geographical writing up to and immediately following World War II. Much of the work of this period has been described in considerable detail by W.G. East in Great Britain[1] and Richard Hartshorne in the United States (*Recent Developments in Political Geography*).

Actually, during this half century political geographers—at least in the Western World—followed not one but three paths. These may be described as environmental, geopolitical, and chorological.

The environmental path may be characterized as one by means of which political geographers were searching, as were geographers generally, for a final determinant. Together with Ratzel, Mackinder in Great Britain and Hunting-

---

[1] W.G. East, "The Nature of Political Geography," *Politica*, II, No. 7 (1937), 259–286.

ton, Barrows, and Semple in the United States were its most distinguished representatives. While their environmentalism differed in the degree of determinism—and none should be accused out of context of a naive expression of that—all were interested in the relationship between human activity, particularly historical political events, and specific features of the physical geographic environment. As Hartshorne succinctly observed: "Formerly, most geographers defined human geography in terms of relationships between earth features, or the natural environment on the one hand, and man with his activities on the other."

There was a tendency, however, toward the occasional exaggerated statement or conclusion that this hypothesis encouraged. Many geographers, especially in France, Britain, and the United States, sought to free their field from extremes and, in stressing geographic possibilities, lessened the emphasis on the deterministic role of the physical environment. With "possibilism" came a recognition that, while the environment placed certain limitations on human activities, the decision ultimately lay with man. As Harold and Margaret Sprout were to note,[2] possibilist analysis was conceived in terms of those opportunities present in the milieu but latent until man makes a decision and acts toward some chosen end.

In Germany, at the same time, other geographers who had become interested in the political aspect of their field sought to direct and determine the course of history, particularly as it involved the Third Reich. They drew upon Ratzel's concept of the state as an organism,[3] but wrapped it in strong emotional overtones. In its simplest form, the concept portrayed the State as an organism sprung from a cell; although not identical with a biological organism, it had nevertheless its own laws of development. As generalized by Otto Maull,[4] the State possessed two attributes: *Raumwesen and Raumorganismus.* The former constituted the liaison between man as part of an organic group and the territory the group occupied; the latter involved the intense feeling generated in the relationship between group and territory.

The roots of German geopolitics lie deep in German history and thought, but the active emergence of a school of *Geopolitik* under Karl Haushofer in the 1920's was due essentially to frustration over the terms of the Versailles settlement. Whether or not *Geopolitik* actually had an influence on Nazi policy in Europe is of little concern here; the pseudoscience, however, did influence geographic thinking elsewhere in the world.

[2] Harold and Margaret Sprout, *Man-Milieu Relationship Hypotheses in the Context of International Politics,* Center of International Studies (Princeton, N.J.: Princeton University Press, 1956), pp. 39 ff.

[3] For a detailed discussion of theories pertaining to the State as an organism, see F.W. Coker, *Organismic Theories of the State: Nineteenth Century Interpretations of the State as Organism or as Person,* Studies in History, Economics and Public Law, XXXVIII, No. 2 (New York: Columbia University Press; London: Longmans, Green, and Co., agents, 1910), pp. 5–209; see also the discussion in Hartshorne, "The Nature of Geography," *Annals of the Association of American Geographers,* XXIX, Nos. 3, 4 (1939), 256 ff.

[4] Otto Maull, *Politische Geographie* (Berlin: Safari, 1956).

Apart from the contribution that Germany's collapse in World War I made in the evolution of geopolitical thinking, the Versailles settlement itself created a number of political geographical problems. Most notable among these were the problems associated with the drawing of State boundaries according to the rationale of the "right of national self-determination." While the organismic concept was given little adherence, geographers in the Allied countries focused on the State, and particularly the Nation-State, as the most important political feature of the landscape; the most vital political geographical problems were understood to be those involving the boundaries of the State.

The importance of the State was, after all, long recognized, having its roots in the French revolution and in the work of Rousseau. As Nisbet has pointed out:

> After Rousseau, the State would be regarded by many men as the most implicative of all forms of association. Inevitably the charms of kinship, religion, and cultural association would pale before the brilliance of the new State. No longer would the political relationship be regarded as but *one* of society's bonds. It would be seen as synonymous with society, as the culmination of man's long struggle for a just social order. The new State would be more than an abstract legal framework of rights and duties. It would be community itself, the Political Community.[5]

This emphasis on the State contributed to the advance of regional political geography, or chorology. Among the leading exponents of the latter were Isaiah Bowman and, somewhat later, Richard Hartshorne in the United States; C.B. Fawcett in Great Britain; and Jean Brunhes in France. From the mid-1930's on, it was primarily Hartshorne's definition of the field as "the study of the State as a characteristic of areas in relation to the other characteristics of areas" that tended to prevail (at least in the United States), a logical outcome of his viewing geography as the study of areal differentiation.

Following World War II, a way was sought out of the impasse created by the collapse of German *Geopolitik* and the disrepute into which political geography generally had fallen. In the United States an attempt was made to give regional morphological studies a new direction and purpose. Of the latter, the best illustration may be found in the work of Hartshorne and Jean Gottmann.[6] Hartshorne, harking back to Ratzel, noted that the latter had recognized that the State was organized as a single unit in terms of a particular, distinctive idea. Ratzel had perceived that those states are strongest "in which the political idea of the State fills the entire body of the State, extends to all its parts." Accordingly, Hartshorne believed that the first step in the study of the State, should be to determine its raison d'être. From that base could follow logically an assessment of the State's viability through a weighing of centripetal and

---

[5] Robert A. Nisbet, *Community and Power* (New York: Oxford University Press, 1962), p. 155.

[6] Jean Gottman, *La Politique des états et leur géographie* (Paris: Libraire Armand Colin, 1952).

centrifugal forces—forces making for cohesion and unity in the State and forces making for disunity and the possible ultimate disintegration of the State.

Gottmann's approach to the State, on the other hand, tended to stress the role of "iconography," or the system of symbols in which a nation believes, and of "circulation," or the movement factor, the forces shaping or modifying the iconography. The emphasis placed by Hartshorne and Gottmann on the functioning of the State marked a turning point in the development of political geography.

Though not ignoring the State as the essential focus of study, others, best represented by John Wright and Stephen Jones, sought to expand the scope of the field to include group political activity at any level, Nation-State or otherwise. Though Wright's study (*Training for Research in Political Geography*) was required reading for every budding political geographer, much of its message seemed to go unnoticed. Not so with Jones. His "unified field theory" has constituted a major contribution to the evolution of a more sophisticated political geography. Gottmann's concept of "circulation" became what Jones called "movement," one of the links in the chain from the conception of a political idea to its ultimate manifestation in a political organization or in a political-territorial unit. According to Jones (see footnote 13), the

> idea-area chain may unite in one concept two main parts of geographical theory, the possibilist and regionalist views. Possibilism focuses on man's choices among environmental possibilities. Choices are decisions. They imply ideas and must lead to movements. The regional or chorological approach, beginning with the study of areas, can lead through movement to decisions and ideas.

In short, Jones demonstrated an interest in political ideas that come to fruition in spatial political phenomena, their associations and relationships.

PART II: POLITICAL GEOGRAPHY AND POLITICAL SYSTEMS[7]

Functions and systems: A theoretical framework

It was almost 40 years ago that George Catlin complained that "political science has too long paraded about in the gorgeous uniform of state pomp; it is time it wore a more humble khaki which utility and the hope of scientific results dictate."[8] Like Harold Lasswell and others, Catlin recognized the need for a shift away from the State as the political articulation of society to a focus

---

[7] The literature on the nature of political systems is by now fairly substantial. The following, however, provide useful and essential guides to the theoretical literature on political systems: David Easton, *The Political System* (New York: Alfred A. Knopf, Inc., 1953); *A Framework for Political Analysis* (Englewood Cliffs, N.J.: Prentice-Hall, Inc., 1965); *A Systems Analysis of Political Life* (New York: John Wiley & Sons, Inc., 1965); Robert A. Dahl, *Modern Political Analysis* (Englewood Cliffs, N.J.: Prentice-Hall, Inc., 1963); and James C. Charlesworth, ed., *Contemporary Political Analysis* (New York: The Free Press, 1967).

[8] George Catlin, *A Study of the Principles of Politics* (London: George Allen and Unwin Ltd., 1930), p. 103.

on the political behavior of society as a whole. What these early behavioralists were calling for was a thorough reinterpretation of politics, based in effect on the functional lines of society. This shift in focus required a new framework to depict society as a network of social action and human interaction.

The historical and philosophical sources of this new framework were wide-ranging. Indeed, the intellectual process of formulating a general theory of social action began at least as early as Leibnitz and was increasingly explicit in the work of such social theorists as Saint-Simon, Hegel, and Karl Marx. Other sources might just as easily be traced to Max Weber, Sigmund Freud, and C.G. Jung. In the realm of philosophy and physics, the process of deriving a theory of social action might also be related to the impact of the Quantum Theory of Max Planck and especially of the Einsteinian theory of relativity. All of this is mentioned simply to emphasize the long evolutionary process through which social theory passed in order to arrive at a "general action frame of reference" for the study of society.[9]

In broad outline this "general action frame of reference," as D.F. Aberle suggested, emphasized *what* gets done in society rather than *how* it gets done, an emphasis on social functions rather than social structures or institutions per se. This emphasis did not necessitate a dichotomy between social structures and functions, but simply asserted that institutions must be understood and ana-lyzed in terms of their functions and functioning.[10] This implies that society is to be recognized as nothing less than a system of

individual actors interacting with each other in a situation which has at least a physical or environmental aspect, actors ... whose relation to their situations, in-cluding each other, is defined and mediated in terms of a system of culturally structured and shared symbols.[11]

The patterns of human interaction constitute the system.[12] *Hence, society repre-sents a system of human interaction, a system that is enforced and reinforced by cultural, political, economic, social, and physical supports, a system that has*

---

[9] For a fairly comprehensive theoretical grounding, see the following: Alfred Kuhn, *The Study of Society, A Multidisciplinary Approach* (London: Tavistock Publications, 1966); Tal-cott Parsons and R.F. Bales, *Working Papers in the Theory of Action* (New York: The Free Press, 1953); Talcott Parsons and E. Shils, eds., *Toward A General Theory of Action* (Cam-bridge: Harvard University Press, 1951). In a more philosophical vein, the following are of particular interest: J.M. Blaut, "Space and Process," *The Professional Geographer*, XIII, No. 4 (July 1961), 1–7; Alexandre Koyré, *From the Closed World to the Infinite Universe* (New York: Harper & Row, 1958); Albert Einstein and Leopold Infeld, *The Evolution of Physics* (New York: Simon and Schuster, Inc., 1942); Lincoln Barnett, *The Universe and Dr. Einstein* (New York: Harper & Row, 1948).

[10] D.F. Aberle, A.K. Cohen, A.K. Davis, M.J. Levy, Jr., and F.X. Sutton, "The Functional Prerequisites of a Society," *Ethics*, LX, (January 1950), 100–111. See also Robert Merton, *Social Theory and Social Structure* (New York: The Free Press, 1957); Talcott Parsons, *Struc-ture and Process in Modern Society* (New York: The Free Press, 1960); Talcott Parsons, *The Structure of Social Action* (New York: The Free Press, 1949); Karl W. Deutsch, *The Nerves of Government* (New York: The Free Press, 1966), pp. 39–50.

[11] Talcott Parsons, *The Social System* (New York: The Free Press 1951), pp. 5–6.

[12] Systems and interaction theory in the social sciences has had a long history. As em-ployed in general systems analysis, the following are useful guides: Ludwig von Bertalanffy,

a spatial dimension and that operates within a particular situation, milieu, or environment.

It is here that the "action frame of reference" has value for the geographer. As noted above, social interaction involves man's relationship with his total environment, a relationship that has a spatial dimension. This spatial dimension "describes" the situation and the system, while at the same time it enters the system as a motivational factor usually described as the friction of distance and the problem of access. These aspects of space have long been recognized by geographers. Stated briefly, the area of interaction forms essentially a functional region, "draining" into a node; the spatial dimension constitutes the distance between the node and periphery over which and through which interaction occurs. Following Stephen Jones and Peter Haggett,[13] we may refer to this region as an *activity field*, the spatial expression of the system of human interaction.

Aberle further defines society as a group of human beings sharing a *self-sufficient system of action*.[14] Society remains a system of human interaction, *but it is also something more*, for it must have internal coherence, and this entails organization and control. Essential to society are a number of prerequisites that ensure its formation, maintenance, and survival. Among them, as listed by Aberle, are membership recruitment, role differentiation and role assignment, communication, shared cognitive orientations and articulated goals, regulation of the means to achieve the goals, regulation of effective expression, integration (socialization), and effective control of disruptive forces. These prerequisites, and perhaps others as well, are essential to the internal coherence of society, i.e., they provide the means for the formation and maintenance of a self-sufficient system of action. The degree of self-sufficiency may be interpreted here as the ability to carry out the regulative functions of society, functions that make possible control, order, and coherence.

Although Aberle did not differentiate between the social system as a whole and the political system, it is clear that, with some reservations, these regulative

---

"Outline of General Systems Theory," *British Journal for the Philosophy of Science* (1950–51), 134–165; P.G. Herbst, "Situation Dynamics and the Theory of Behavior Systems," *Behavioral Science*, II, No. 1 (January 1957), 13–29; R.F. Bales, *Interaction Process Analysis* (Cambridge: Addison-Wesley Press, 1950); Kuhn, *The Study of Society*, pp. 13–25, 55–75; Charles E. Osgood, "Behavioral Theory and the Social Sciences," *Behavioral Science*, I, No. 3 (July 1956), 167–185; "Systems Analysis," *International Encyclopedia of the Social Sciences*, XV (1968), 452–495, esp. "Political Systems" by William C. Mitchell, pp. 473–479. In geography see Edward A. Ackerman, "Where is the Research Frontier?" *Annals of the Association of American Geographers*, LIII, No. 4 (December 1963), 429–440; Allen Pred, *Behavior and Location, Foundations for a Geographic and Dynamic Location Theory* (Sweden: Lund Series, 1967); and Peter Haggett, *Locational Analysis in Human Geography* (New York: St. Martins Press, Inc., 1966).

[13] Stephen B. Jones, "A Unified Field Theory of Political Geography," *Annals of the Association of American Geographers*, XLIV, No. 2 (1954), 111–123; Haggett, *Locational Analysis in Human Geography*, pp. 31–60.

[14] Aberle, *et al., op. cit.* See also the refinement of these prerequisites in Amitai Etzioni, *Studies in Social Change* (New York: Holt, Rinehart and Winston, Inc., 1966).

functions serve to define what political scientists have come to consider the *political system*.

Traditional definitions of politics have taken into account the element of power, but they have been applied primarily to the State and its formal institutions. Once it is understood, however, that the role of government is affected by political attitudes, informal groups and associations, and a multitude of transactions, then the concept of power inherent in such definitions requires modification. In 1936, Harold Lasswell defined politics as power, but in 1950 with Abraham Kaplan he expanded this notion to include all forms of influence and (the threat of) severe deprivation.[15] For political scientists such as David Easton, however, these definitions were too broad, for they took into account all the regulative functions of society and made no distinction between politics and other aspects of society. Still, even with Easton's qualification that the political system embraces those activities that pertain to "the authoritative allocation of values,"[16] there remains a wide range of functions that are socially regulative. Politics may be defined as the study of those functions of society whereby the latter is regulated, organized, and maintained. As expressed by Gabriel Almond and G.B. Powell, "legitimate force is the thread that runs through the action of the political system, giving it its special quality and importance and coherence as a system."[17] In short, the action of the political system is defined by the regulative functions of a society. In this sense, therefore, *the political system represents that pattern of human interaction wherein power and authority are generated, allocated, influenced, and changed—the pattern whereby society is organized, whether that organization is formal or informal, differentiated or undifferentiated.*

Like society as a whole, the political system should have some staying power and a measure of self-sufficiency. It must be able to regulate the behavior or activities of its constituents. This is not to suggest that political systems cannot change. They do change, of course, along with other aspects of society. The change may be accomplished slowly, as it was in Great Britain after the American Revolution, or rapidly, as in Russia in 1917 and in China in 1911 and 1949. Similarly, a political system may simply die out as the society of which it is a

---

15 Harold Lasswell, *Politics: Who Gets What, When, How?* (New York: McGraw Hill, 1936). See also Harold D. Lasswell and Abraham Kaplan, *Power and Society* (New Haven: Yale University Press, 1950); Franz Neumann, "Approaches to the Study of Political Power," *Political Science Quarterly*, LXV, No. 2 (June 1950), 161–171; David B. Truman, "The Impact on Political Science of the Revolution in the Behavioral Sciences," in *Research Frontiers in Politics and Government* (Washington, D.C.: The Brookings Institution, 1955), pp. 202–231; Heinz Eulau, "Recent Developments in the Behavioral Study of Politics," paper read at the annual meeting of the Northern California Political Science Association, University of San Francisco, May 31, 1961; W.J.M. Mackenzie, *Politics and Social Science* (Baltimore: Penguin Books, 1967); Robert A. Dahl, "The Behavioral Approach in Political Science: Epitaph for a Monument to a Successful Protest," *American Political Science Review*, LX (December 1961), 763–772.

16 Easton, *The Political System*, pp. 130 ff.

17 Gabriel A. Almond and G.B. Powell, Jr., *Comparative Politics: A Developmental Approach* (Boston: Little, Brown and Company, 1966), pp. 17–18.

part is dispersed (e.g., the tenth-century Khazar state) or suffers biological extinction (e.g., the indigenous tribal units of Tasmania). Political systems, too, may disappear for a period of time only to reemerge in altered form. Thus Poland, following the final partition of its territory among Russia, Prussia, and Austria at the end of the eighteenth century, disappeared from Europe as an independent political system for over a century.

Whatever else we might say about political systems, it should be made absolutely clear that the political system need not refer *only* to the modern State and its particular set of formal institutions. This is what Catlin was suggesting some four decades ago. In fact, it was in this context, before the notion of a political system had been thoroughly formulated, that such anthropologists as M. Fortes and E.E. Evans-Pritchard were led to study clan and tribal units in Africa as legitimate political systems in a preliterate, nonstate environment.[18] Their efforts eventually provided the foundation for the growth of what has become known as political anthropology.[19] Though no direct connection need be established, it was only a short intellectual distance between Catlin's argument, Fortes' and Evans-Pritchard's efforts in anthropology, and David Easton's conclusion that "political systems may be identified at different levels of inclusiveness, from the paramilitary system of a voluntary organization, to a municipality, province, state, national unit and various kinds of international units."[20] The underlying premise for each of these views is that wherever and by whatever means power and authority are generated, allocated, influenced, and changed in society, there lies the outline of the political system.

In this context, the League of Women Voters represents a type of political system whose internal coherence is maintained by virtue of the regulation of authority within the League. So, too, does the lineage system of the Hazara Mongols of Afghanistan, for it is through the lineage system that Hazara society is regulated.[21]

Easton's recognition that "political systems may be identified at different levels of inclusiveness" is an admission that power and authority need not necessarily have one source or pattern of distribution. This is especially true in complex or pluralistic societies, where compromises within the political system are common and lead to or result in the formation of subsystems.

The Constitution of the United States offers perhaps the best, though most

18 M. Fortes and E.E. Evans-Pritchard, eds., *African Political Systems* (London: Oxford University Press, 1940), pp. 1–24. In this connection it would also be useful to see Walter Goldschmidt, *Comparative Functionalism, An Essay in Anthropological Theory* (Berkeley: University of California Press, 1966).

19 In addition to the work of Fortes and Evans-Pritchard, see the following: Marc Swartz, Victor W. Turner, and Arthur Tuden, eds., *Political Anthropology* (Chicago: Aldine Publishing Co., 1966); Marc Swartz, ed., *Local-Level Politics* (Chicago: Aldine Publishing Co., 1968); Lucy Mair, *Primitive Government* (Baltimore: Penguin Books, 1967); E.R. Leach, *Political Systems of Highland Burma* (Boston: Beacon Press, 1965); *Political Systems and the Distribution of Power*, Conferences on New Approaches in Social Anthropology, Association of Social Anthropologists, Monograph 2 (London: Tavistock Publications, 1965).

20 Easton, *A Systems Analysis of Political Life*, p. 181.

21 On the Hazara Mongols see Elizabeth Bacon, *Obok, A Study of Social Structure in Eurasia* (New York: Wenner-Gren Foundation for Anthropological Research, Inc., 1958).

formal, example of political subsystems, i.e., the 50 states of the union, operating within a larger political system.[22] Of importance, too, are the numerous political subsystems not specifically described in the Constitution and identifiable at nongovernmental levels. These include political parties, interest groups such as the League of Women Voters referred to above, labor unions, and political cliques and factions, as well as various types of regional political associations.

By definition, each of these subsystems is a part of the larger political system. However, in its own context, the subsystem is self-sufficient in that it regulates the behavior of its own immediate members or constituents. The degree of self-sufficiency may vary from case to case, and the variation may determine how effectively or ineffectively the subsystem may function or operate. Though self-sufficient in their own context, subsystems are obviously not independent; as part of, or having become part of, larger political systems, they are consequently subordinate or dependent. Political subsystems may then be seen to have two roles: as self-sufficient systems in their own contexts, and as subordinate or dependent systems within larger systems.

History is replete with examples of formerly independent political systems reduced to subsystem status within a larger political system. During the period of eighteenth to nineteenth century European imperialism, independent indigenous political systems in Asia and Africa became colonies, protectorates, or provinces of the United Kingdom, France, Belgium, The Netherlands, Germany, Russia, and so forth. In many instances, especially in British Africa, domestic systems, though reduced to subordinate status, continued to regulate their own societies, often with little interference from the Colonial Office.

Occasionally political subsystems may move toward independence, or the constituents (often the elites) of subsystems may interpret their situation as having potential for independence and, accordingly, attempt to secede. The attempt of antebellum Southern society to secede from the American Union was an abortive act directed toward the formation of a new political system. The Thirteen Colonies of the Atlantic Seaboard, on the other hand, were essentially successful in ending their subsystem status vis-à-vis Great Britain. The dissolution of colonial empires and imperial political systems under the impetus of rising nationalist aspirations after World War II may thus be seen as the transformation of dependent political subsystems into independent political systems. The process may be an easy one, but, as recent events have shown, it may also be very painful. Nigeria, for example, became independent of Great Britain with little bloodshed. The Biafran attempt to secede from Nigeria, however, led to a devastating civil war. What will be achieved by the separatists of Quebec Province, the Black nationalists in the United States, or the Welsh nationalists in the United Kingdom, to cite a few potential transformations, remains to be seen.

The Lebanese crisis in the early fall of 1969 revealed how patently complex

---

[22] Studies on American federalism abound. For a highly readable collection of essays see Robert A. Goldwin, ed., *A Nation of States* (Chicago: Rand McNally & Co., 1961).

the overlapping of political systems or subsystems can become. A paramilitary organization such as Al Fatah may be conceived as a subsystem within specific Arab states—apparently the Israeli view. On the other hand, because of the difficulty that both Lebanon and Jordan have had in controlling the activities of the revolutionary movement, the latter may be deemed a self-sufficient and seemingly independent transnational political system.

Potential and actual revolutionary political situations almost by definition reflect highly complex political processes in the growth of subsystems and systems. The reactions of other political systems to such complex situations are usually based on the way in which the overlapping processes are understood. The struggle in South Vietnam, for example, might be viewed as a loss of control by the Saigon government of part of South Vietnamese society. Communist states, however, would regard the Viet Cong as an independent and self-sufficient political system, representing a higher social order that inevitably must supplant the existing system in Saigon.

The most complex form of political system yet obtained is that of the State, especially the Nation-State.[23] Not only are Nation-States theoretically self-sufficient in their own contexts, but they have also achieved the highest degree of independence. In reality, the degree of self-sufficiency or internal coherence possessed by States varies greatly. Indeed, today very few States appear to be free of internal or external threats to their ability to regulate their own societies. Moreover, even the most powerful, such as the United States and the Soviet Union, are not able to impose their will everywhere in the world without inviting some reaction that would seek to curtail their freedom of action. Modern technology requires that States surrender some of their sovereignty and consequently their independence. Still, the twentieth century political map represents the partitioning of the world into more than 120 political systems, each with its own pattern of human and political interaction. Unfortunately, that same map does not reveal the nature of that interaction, or the extent to which the sovereign territory of the State is an adequate representation of the scope or effectiveness of the State's political system.

The difficulties associated with the development of political systems are prominently displayed in the failure of mankind to evolve an international system, despite enormous efforts to that end. Such institutional frameworks as

---

23 The Nation-State is a phenomenon about which no brief statement may suffice. It is questionable at this juncture in modern history whether the term "Nation-State" is an adequate description of the currently predominant State system. Still, no other form of political system has been given as much attention. The following studies are of particular value: Hans Kohn, *The Idea of Nationalism* (New York: The Macmillan Company, 1967), first published in 1949; *Nationalism, Its Meaniing and History* (Princeton, N.J.: D. Van Nostrand Co., Inc., 1955); *The Age of Nationalism, The First Era of Global History* (New York: Harper & Row, 1962); also Ernst Cassier, *The Myth of the State* (New Haven: Yale University Press, 1946); Lawrence Krader, *Formation of the State* (Englewood Cliffs, N.J.: Prentice-Hall, Inc., 1968); Karl W. Deutsch, *Interdisciplinary Bibliography on Nationalism, 1935–1953* (Cambridge, Mass.: M.I.T. Press, 1956); Karl W. Deutsch, *Nationalism and Social Communication, An Inquiry into the Foundations of Nationality* (Cambridge, Mass.: M.I.T. Press; New York: John Wiley & Sons, Inc., 1953).

the Commonwealth of Nations and the United Nations do not in themselves constitute political systems, for they lack the ability to regulate the behavior of their constituents. Both the Commonwealth and the United Nations do, however, represent efforts *toward* the establishment of coherent international political systems, and they may be studied in that vein. Similarly, history is replete with efforts to create large trans-State or transnational political systems, such as the Third Reich and the Empire of the Mongols. Indeed, imperial systems, even where they were of short duration, more adequately represented international political systems than do either the Commonwealth or the United Nations.[24] The same might be said for the type of trans-State political systems represented by international corporate businesses, for here the constituents are regulated from within. There is, however, evidence to suggest that in the modern era trans-State political systems are taking shape, as reflected in the development of regional treaty organizations and regional economic associations.[25] Invariably, both of these entail some measure of political interaction and the allocation of power. To the extent that these trans-State systems function to generate and allocate power, to the extent that they perform regulative functions, they may be said to constitute political systems.

The limits of the political system

Political systems form regions, the limits or boundaries of which are defined by their functions. These limits may be viewed either as separating the political system from the rest of the social system or as separating one political system from another. Both views are discussed in depth by David Easton in *The Environment of a Political System*. While the geographic literature is rich in studies of boundaries and frontiers (S.W. Boggs, Hartshorne, Jones, Kristof, and Julian Minghi),[26] the geographic concern has traditionally been with boundaries

---

[24] Studies on the nature of imperial systems are no doubt as prolific as those dealing with the Nation-State, and usually the two are related. On the coherence or lack of coherence of imperial systems, see especially: S.N. Eisenstadt, *The Political Systems of Empires* (New York: The Free Press, 1963); S.N. Eisenstadt, ed., *The Decline of Empires* (Englewood Cliffs, N.J.: Prentice-Hall, Inc., 1967); Karl A. Wittfogel, *Oriental Despotism* (New Haven: Yale University Press, 1957); Rupert Emerson, *From Empire to Nation* (Boston: Beacon Press, 1962); Adda B. Bozeman, *Politics and Culture in International History* (Princeton: Princeton University Press, 1960).

[25] G. Modelski, "The Corporation in World Society," *The Yearbook of World Affairs*, XXII (1968), 64–79; see also David S. Collier and Kurt Glasser, eds., *Western Integration and the Future of Eastern Europe* (Chicago: Henry Regnery Co., 1964); Karl W. Deutsch, L.J. Edinger, R.C. Macridis, and R.L. Merritt, *France, Germany and the Western Alliance* (New York: Charles Scribner's Sons, 1967); Karl W. Deutsch, *Political Community at the International Level* (Garden City, N.Y.: Doubleday & Company, Inc., 1954); Andrew M. Scott, *The Functioning of the International Political System* (New York: The Macmillan Company, 1967); Charles A. McClelland, *Theory and the International System* (New York: The Macmillan Company, 1966).

[26] See, among others: S. Whittemore Boggs, *International Boundaries: A Study of Boundary Functions and Problems* (New York: Columbia University Press, 1940); Stephen B. Jones, *Boundary Making: A Handbook for Statesmen, Treaty Editors and Boundary Commissioners* (Washington, D.C.: Carnegie Endowment for International Peace, 1945); and Julian V. Minghi, "Boundary Studies in Political Geography," *Annals of the Association of American Geographers*, LIII, No. 3 (1963), 407–428.

between States as depicted on the political-administrative map. In practice, such boundaries have frequently given rise to problems of delineation and demarcation, to disputes and wars. It should be borne in mind, however, that the boundaries shown on the map and recognized in international agreement do not tell us much about political reality. In other words, the boundaries of the State do not necessarily, or always, coincide with those of the political system.

If the limits of the political system extend beyond the boundaries of the State, the latter may be said to be expansionist or imperialistic, or to have vital interests beyond its sovereign territory. When President John F. Kennedy said in Berlin, "Ich bin ein Berliner," he was voicing what he believed to be a political fact of life—that the security of West Berlin was essential to that of the United States, as vital perhaps as any U.S. territorial outpost. Much of the discussion in the United States concerning the war in Indo-China reflects a basic disagreement over the extent to which that part of Southeast Asia is critical to the defense of American interests, and whether South Vietnam should, in effect, be included, as is South Korea, within the defense perimeter of the U.S. political system.

Conversely, a political system may not encompass the entire area of a sovereign State and, consequently, the functional region will fall short of the international territorial boundaries of the State. This was especially true of Republican and Nationalist China after the Revolution of 1911. Consider Outer Mongolia, which was recognized de jure as part of China. As the Mongolian People's Republic (after 1924) it had some of the trappings of independence, although in practice it was a satellite of the Soviet Union and virtually included within the Soviet political system. Indeed, it is generally believed that before World War II the Soviet Union intended to annex the region, as it was to do a few years later with the adjacent Tuvinian People's Republic. At any rate, the Chinese political system did not include Outer Mongolia even though it remained legally a part of the Chinese State. In effect, it was a frontier zone over which the Chinese system did not function but over which the Soviet, as a de facto integrating force, did.

Relative to the social system or to the rest of the environment, it is difficult, if not impossible, to determine precisely the limits of the political system.[27] The complexity of this problem can be better understood, perhaps, if one looks at role assignment in society. A chief in a tribal system, for example, has many roles to play. He may head the council and be politically paramount, but he may also be the principal economic decision maker, the primary link to the real or mythical lineal heritage of the tribe, as well as the head of his own family. Role combinations such as these are not limited to primitive societies.

---

[27] Spiro argues that the political system is larger than the State and, therefore, "is more important, more encompassing, and 'greater' than the social system." For an elaboration of this theme, see Herbert J. Spiro, "An Evaluation of Systems Theory," in *Contemporary Political Analysis*, pp. 164–174.

One need only think of the roles played out by any mature individual in modern urban industrial society. Without changing his physical location, he can be *homo politicus* or *homo economicus,* and have other roles as well. Consider the functions of the Pope. When speaking *ex cathedra,* the Pope acts as spiritual head of the Roman Catholic Church; under other circumstances he may serve as administrative head of the church hierarchy or as political ruler of the Vatican State. The functional differences among these roles may be difficult to determine.

Focus of the political system

Just as political systems have limits, so, too, do they possess a focus of political authority. In tribal societies that focus usually resides with the chief or chieftains, but it may also be interpreted to include major and minor clan centers. In pluralistic or differentiated societies, authority and power, except in the most totalitarian of systems, are not concentrated in a single individual, but are shared among individuals and groups of individuals located in one or a number of places.

Ordinarily, the source of political authority in societies that are unitary in governmental form and not highly pluralistic is concentrated in the capital city. This is true of Sweden, Italy, France, and, to a lesser extent, the United Kingdom. In the latter case, although the central parliament is situated in London, not all of the political authority is resident there. Authority within Northern Ireland, for example, is shared with the local parliament sitting in Belfast. On the other hand, despite the seemingly federative nature of the USSR and Communist China, political authority is highly centralized and concentrated in Moscow and Peking, respectively.

The examples cited above indicate that not only is the capital city often the locus of all or most of the political power of the system; it is also often the locus of economic power and sets the "pace" for the society as a whole.

In more highly pluralistic societies, political authority is usually shared or dispersed. This is especially true of States with federal constitutions, such as the United States, Canada, Australia, and India. At Canada's confederation in 1867 very specific powers were given to the provinces, while all remaining authority, as conceived at the time, was granted to the central government in Ottawa. In the United States and Australia, on the other hand, specific powers were granted to the federal government, with all remaining authority resting in the constitutions of the state governments. In the case of the Union of South Africa, the legislative, executive, and judicial functions of the political system are shared among Cape Town, Pretoria, and Bloemfontein. The principle of "checks and balances" in the United States Constitution has insured that, in addition to the division of authority between state and federal governments, there are additional guarantees that no one branch of government in the federal system can usurp all authority.

In political systems such as these, the locus of political power is usually not the same as that of economic power. Indeed, not only is the political capital often removed from the economic core—or is at most on its periphery—but its location may represent a compromise between competing socioeconomic regions or ethnic groups; it may be located so as to be removed from undesirable (commercial, cultural, and political) elements. Peter the Great founded St. Petersburg as his capital on the Gulf of Finland to minimize Muscovite influence and maximize Western influence; the Bolsheviks returned the capital to Moscow to emphasize an identification with some aspects of past history *and* to minimize the effects of Western anti-Bolshevism. The capitals of most states within the American Union are ordinarily in towns or cities whose only function is political.

Political power and authority, however, are not abstract things. They run through the entire fabric of the political system and must be thought of in operational terms. Power and authority are, in the final analysis, resident in the men who wield them, whether the society is primitive and undifferentiated or complex and differentiated. This situation is well demonstrated in the example of Regional City provided by Floyd Hunter (*Location of Power in Regional City*).

Hunter selected some 40 persons who belonged to the possible power elite of a typical regional city. The largest number of these people directed or administered major portions of the activities of large commercial enterprises; some represented the government, some the labor unions. It was a group whose interests and employment set them apart from the rest of the community. They generally lived in the same residential area, belonged to and met in the same clubs, and had frequent contact. Because of these characteristics, they tended to be isolated from the mass of less powerful citizens and from community problems at large. Their views of issues affecting the community tended to be similar because of their own work and social habits.

The point that Hunter makes is that where and how the leaders of a community meet is of importance structurally because it affects their relationships with the rest of the community. It is clear that it is here, within the elite, that decisions affecting the community are made—it is here that power in Regional City resides.

The focus of power and authority in the political system must then be understood in terms of how it operates. Electoral geography, especially where it traces voting behavior, for example, is one way of analyzing the processes whereby power and authority derive from the people. The "people," however, are not an amorphous mass, and power that derives from "the people" is no more uniform throughout the political landscape of the system than are the physicogeographic elements. Indeed, the importance of voting may be overestimated as a factor of political behavior. Maurice Duverger and Lionel Tiger have noted the disparities that exist between men and women in the voting mechanism, and as Tiger pointed out, "voting as a behavior is of little account in the actual emergence of a dominance hierarchy in most societies."[28] Moreover, as a result of different population densities, economic wealth, and so forth, there may be regional inequalities in electoral strength leading to essential disparities in political power and influence. This is especially true in the United States. Indeed, the greater the degree of pluralism in societies, the more likely we are to find a wide array (or disarray) of political cores and foci (Sayre and Kaufman, *The Diffusion of Power in New York City*). An analysis of political systems must entail some understanding of the way in which these foci and the boundaries of subsystems are arranged, together with the impact of these foci and subsystems on the larger political system of which they are a part.

Supports of the political system

Certain supports are necessary in order for the political system to have some staying power and internal coherence. These may vary in quality and quantity from system to system, but without them no system can survive. Moreover, without careful assessment of the supports, calculations concerning the viability of a system cannot be made. This assessment is what Hartshorne sought by defining the patterns of interaction within the State system as "centrifugal and centripetal forces" (*The Functional Approach in Political Geography*). However, the weakness of this approach is that a balance between the centripetal forces (those that tend to integrate the system) and the centrifugal forces (those that tend to tear the system apart) cannot be determined with any degree of precision, especially when the theory neglects to inform us as to the connections between sets of supports. Nor does it provide a means whereby systems can be compared.

Almond and Powell noted that an analysis of a political system must consist not only of observation of its actual patterns over a period of time, but also of those subtle propensities within the system (as well as those in the society as a whole). They illustrate their point with the example of Italy under Fascism, which appeared formidable and powerful until the retreat and surrender of whole army divisions in North Africa. With the advantage of hindsight, it is apparent that estimates of the strength of Mussolini's Italy were based on outer appearances, especially after the Ethiopian campaign, rather than on its internal system and society. However difficult it may be to estimate a society's propensities, they are essential to a realistic appraisal of a political system.

Despite the manifold differences among political systems, it would seem that a number of supports are basic and have universal application. Some of these have been suggested, at least by implication in the preceding discussion. Perhaps the most obvious supports are those that relate to Almond and Powell's "thread of legitimate force," namely the *support of the participants*

---

[28] Lionel Tiger, *Men in Groups* (New York: Random House, Inc., 1969), p. 68. See also Maurice Duverger, *The Political Role of Women* (Paris: UNESCO, 1955).

of the system. Whether by virtue of recognized legitimacy or simply by reason of compliance, the political system, by definition, must have the support of its participants. Furthermore, as a system of human interaction, the political system is also supported by the various modes of social communication that facilitate interaction. These modes may be interpreted as anything from common language(s) to the number of television sets in use. The practical importance of these modes of social communication is recognized not only by candidates for office in democratic systems, but also by regimes of mass mobilization systems such as prevail in the USSR and the People's Republic of China. In either case, the *modes of social communication* serve as a basic support to the system.

Directly associated with these modes of social communication is the support of a *set of shared cultural and political symbols* (essentially Gottmann's "iconography"). The modes of social communication are irrelevant to the political system unless they carry "messages" of political significance. It is this set of shared cultural and political symbols, perhaps more than anything else, that provides the framework for the interpretation of these "messages." While this is most clearly seen in "movement or mass mobilization systems" whose sources of support are directly linked to philosophical ideals and ideological commitments, it holds true for other political systems as well, whether these are represented by a set of recognized lineage associations in a tribal society, more complex historical symbols embodied in such documents as the Constitution of the United States, or the accumulated myths and legends associated with the experiences of the nation. Moreover, these shared cultural and political symbols provide the premise for another major support of political systems, the *sense of belonging or community.* As will be shown in a later section, this sense of community makes an *interactive political system* an *integrated political system.* For the moment, however, it is sufficient to note that the sense of belonging to the community is a basic support to political systems.

In addition to the above, a vast number of other supports derive from the *physical and human resources of the system.* As suggested earlier, the social system and its constituent political system must be able to adapt to the environment and be capable of carrying out activities essential to survival. The internal coherence of a political system is invariably linked to the quantity and quality of the physical and human resources at its command. The precise nature of these requisite resources is, however, a subject for considerable debate, although there may be some general agreement that, at a minimum, the political system must be able to command those resources essential to its survival (Jones, *The Power Inventory and National Strategy*). Even more difficult than questions about requisite physical resources are those relating to human resources, for here subjectivity is inevitable. What represents one system's population explosion may be another system's human resource base.

Estimates of both the quantity and quality of resources necessary for the formation and maintenance of political systems invariably seem to fail. In part, this failure may be attributed to the subjective interpretation usually given the idea of *essential* resources. How essential a given resource may be at any particular time or place is, of course, highly relative. There is no reason to suspect that assumed stages in economic growth can alone serve as a substitute for the coherence of political systems. Highly advanced technological societies, even those that have obtained a large measure of self-sustained economic growth, may find that both society and the political system are being eroded by other conditions within the society (e.g., race or communal riots, urban blight, and environmental deterioration). Demands on the system relative to these other requirements may entail a reevaluation of what is and what is not essential to the effective functioning of a political system.

Although an adequate measure of the resources necessary to the formation and maintenance of political systems is lacking, an understanding of the support functions of these resources, a type of minimum base requirement, is not necessarily precluded. If there are no objective measures of the resources essential to the survival of political systems, there are nonetheless subjective measures of what resources the political system *deems* to be essential. The performance of different political systems might be judged in part by *their* interpretation of what is an essential resource support, and the degree to which that interpretation is translated into action.

All questions pertaining to resources share this dilemma. Still, we may agree that all societies and political systems regard certain resources as being essential to their survival. We need then to measure the degree to which a certain resource is regarded as being essential against the actual performance of the system in obtaining the support of that resource. Questions about the objective importance of resources may help to define the problem of resources generally, but may not add to an understanding of the performance of political systems.

In the broad sense that the term has been used here, *the supports of the political system may be regarded as those aspects of the social and physical environment that have an impact upon and lend coherence to the system.* In systems' theory parlance, these supports represent the inputs of the system, i.e., anything that enters into the system and functions to help generate, allocate, influence, and change power and authority in society.

The concept of systems' supports needs to be qualified in terms of the *degree* to which the supports have an impact on the political system. The degree of impact is especially important with reference to social supports, for the latter are to some extent determined by the type of political system extant. Obviously, the impact of social supports may vary considerably, depending on whether the system is *open* or *closed*. While no system is totally open or closed, these categories typify two essentially different types of political systems. The patterns of activity in an open system may trace sources of support to a wide variety of social and physical inputs, whereas the patterns of support in closed systems are relatively circumscribed in terms of the number and quality of inputs. In either case, it is important to note that the impact of the social inputs of the political system will vary according to the degree that the system is open or closed.

Such a definition may be refined, as Easton has done, by separating *inputs of support* from *inputs of demand*.[29] However, once the inputs of demand are made with the expectation of a response, demands may be included under the general category of a system's supports.

Finally, while geographers have most commonly thought of the supports of political systems in terms of the resource base, the supports may also be interpreted in terms of the ways in which they function to modify the distance between the locus of power and authority and the limits of the political system. This may be visualized most clearly in the operational patterns of social communication and the densities of social transactions. Whether we think of these social processes as the use of common languages and adherence to political values and symbols, as commodity flows, or in terms of the distribution of television sets, the supports of the political system function to make the system more coherent. *In a spatial context they function to minimize the distance between the sources of power and authority and the objects of that power and authority*. In this sense the supports of a political system can tell us something about the framework through which the system must operate, as well as something about the *possibilities* of political integration. They must, however, be thought of as *supports* to the system, and not as being synonymous with the system itself.

Impact of the political system

One of the most obvious observations to be made about political systems is that they have an impact on the societies that they serve to regulate. As Easton points out in *The Environment of a Political System*, changes from within society (*the intrasocietal environment*) as well as changes from without (*the extrasocietal environment*) modify, alter, or affect in varying degrees the nature and functioning of the political system. But there is a reverse impact as well. Indeed, as has been noted above, there is a broad pattern of interrelationships or exchanges between the political system and the society, exchanges that are in continual operation.

The nature of a society, as William Livingston has pointed out,[30] is *roughly* reflected in the external forms of its political and constitutional arrangements. The extent to which a society is federal, for example, can be approximated by the extent to which the external forms are federal. As K.W. Robinson has observed in his study of the Australian Federation, however, forms of govern-

---

[29] Easton, *A Systems Analysis of Political Life*, pp. 26, 36–246.
[30] William S. Livingston, "A Note on the Nature of Federalism," *Political Science Quarterly*, LXVII, No. 1 (March 1952), 81–95.

ment are causes as well as effects.[31] A careful appraisal of developments in Australia over the past six decades or so "supports the contention that the states are, in some respects, more geographically distinct than they were at the time of federation." A federal structure was implanted in Australia in 1900–1901 largely as a result of economic pressure groups, but over the years the states have acquired a sufficiently distinctive character, or "personality," for them to be treated as geographical units.

The impact of the system is discussed in a somewhat broader context by Derwent Whittelsey (*The Impress of Effective Central Authority Upon Landscape*). Charles McKinley's study (*The Impact of American Federalism Upon the Management of Land Resources*) also provides a detailed account of a topic that has gained wide attention and promoted much concern in the modern world. Still other examples that illustrate the nature of a system's impact might be cited: August Lösch, in *The Economics of Location*[32] wherein the role of national boundaries in economic location is demonstrated; and Roy Wolfe, in *Transportation and Politics*[33] wherein the process of nation-building in Canada is shown to have a bearing on the construction, location, and function of transcontinental railways. Similarly, we may refer to the work of David Reynolds and Michael McNulty (*On the Analysis of Political Boundaries as Barriers*).

The impact of the political system in the most fundamental sense, however, should be regarded as a measure of the internal coherence of the system itself. Through its institutions, agencies, and relevant personnel, the system reaches a decision, issues an order, or implements a chain of activities; society in turn reacts. Depending largely on the type of political system, the societal reactions may constitute simple compliance, active support, or rejection. If the latter occurs, questions concerning the internal coherence of the system may be raised.

The impact that systems have on societies, however, is seldom—if ever—expressed in such a direct or simple fashion. Where the system is open, that is, highly responsive to intrasocietal supports and demands as well as to extrasocietal influences and forces, the exchange process between the system and the total environment is relatively effective. Such a process may be referred to as *feedback*. The idea of feedback into the political system simply attests to the physicists' rule that action is accompanied by reaction, although the two need not be coequal. The output of the political system (power and authority) has an impact on society, which in turn leaves its imprint on the patterns of support and demands that enter into the system. In time the reaction of the system

---

[31] K.W. Robinson, "Sixty Years of Federation in Australia," *Geographical Review,* LI, No. 2 (1961), 1–20.

[32] August Lösch, *The Economics of Location* (New Haven: Yale University Press, 1954), especially pp. 382–388.

[33] Roy Wolfe, *Transportation and Politics* (Princeton, N.J.: D. Van Nostrand Co., Inc., 1963).

may make a 360 degree turn and lead to changes in the political system itself. This may be referred to as a *feedback loop*.

In open systems that are at least theoretically responsive to social supports and demands, the complex process of feedback is evident. As Charles Frankel recently stated in referring to modern American political development: "The government is surrounded by instruments of all sorts intended to interrupt its waking dream—electoral processes, an opposition party, a separate Congress, a rambunctious press, a scholarly community with no deficiency of mavericks, a nation full of prodders and organizers and demonstrators."[34] Yet the social crisis, as it has unfolded in recent years, is as much a consequence of political policies and decisions as it is of the nature and quality of American society and of the historic patterns of American social organization. Prodders, organizers, and demonstrators have been motivated to take to the streets and to initiate other forms of dissent as consequences of decisions made and actions taken in Washington, D.C., the Gulf of Tonkin, Saigon, Chicago, Los Angeles, Harlem, and the forests of the Cascade Mountains. Whether an open political system can endure the pressures of such an immense feedback and still remain open is a subject for much debate and concern, for there are few precedents.

The impact of feedback in a closed political system is more difficult to assess, simply because, if the system is really closed, its degree of responsiveness cannot be adequately measured. The truly closed political system is fully unresponsive. Power here is held in the hands of a few—either a small clique, or by one individual who rules by fiat. The impact of such a system is fundamentally direct, pervasive, and devastating in terms of the values associated with open societies and systems. Feedback, if it can be said to exist at all in such a system, is itself direct, involving either compliance or rejection. If the latter, feedback invariably entails further repression; if the former, it entails the further extension of power.

These observations on the closed system are not conclusive, for there are no empirical models of fully closed systems. There are approximations—some closer than others. Perhaps the Duvalier regime of Haiti most explicitly approximates the gross model of a closed system. The Soviet political system, as well as that of the People's Republic of China, less clearly approximate the model we have suggested, not only in form (i.e., in view of the structure of democratic centralism), but also in practice.[35] Closed political systems may also operate in nominally democratic environments, especially where constitutionally democratic structures are controlled or manipulated by capable elites. In these and similar cases, analysis of the impact of the political system, especially as it

34 Charles Frankel, "Out of Touch in Washington," *Saturday Review*, November 1, 1969, p. 22.

35 See James Townsend, *Political Participation in Communist China* (Berkeley: University of California Press, 1968); Lucian W. Pye, *The Spirit of Chinese Politics* (Cambridge, Mass.: The M.I.T. Press, 1968); Frederick C. Barghoorn, *Politics in USSR* (Boston: Little, Brown and Company, 1966).

involves the question of feedback and internal coherence, is subject to the most subtle of interpretations.

PART III: SYSTEM AND AREA—THE POLITICAL REGION

Regional theses in political geography

Geography owes much of its enduring worth to its role as the art and science of regions. Political geography, as a branch of the larger discipline, shares fully in this essential interest, having devoted much of its attention to the study of political regions. As was noted earlier, however, the region with which political geographers have been concerned has been the large territorial administrative region or the State. Even as late as 1960, Hartshorne in his "Political Geography in the Modern World" stated that:

> The ultimate goal of geography is to provide scientific description of the way in which the originally unorganized areas of the earth are organized into various kinds of functioning regions. . . . Of areas larger than a city, the most complete and precise forms of functioning units are those organized by the political forces of government.[36]

In his functional approach, Hartshorne (*The Functional Approach in Political Geography*) attempted through an assessment of centrifugal and centripetal forces to determine the patterns of interaction that contribute to or detract from the ability of a government to function throughout the organized territory.

Since 1950 geographers have attempted to examine the centrifugal and centripetal forces operative in other than State areas.[37] But implicit in Hartshorne's thought is the notion that unless a territory possessed formal governmental organization—along lines familiar to the Western scholar—a functioning region did not exist.

Despite an effort to inject an even more dynamic element into political geographical study, Gottmann (*The Political Partitioning of Our World*) fell victim to the same assumption. He argued that the world was cut up as the continents beyond Europe were opened up, made accessible, explored, and mapped. Organized political units (colonies, protectorates, and ultimately independent States) thus appeared in Asia, Africa, and the Americas. Although the organization of the non-European world by Europeans did reflect a momentous political process, it ignored the reality both of already extant political systems (no matter how "primitive" they may have appeared to the imperial European powers) and of political regions (no matter how indeterminate they

---

[36] Richard Hartshorne, "Political Geography in the Modern World," *The Journal of Conflict Resolution*, IV, No. 1 (March 1960), 53 ff.

[37] Robert B. McNee, "Centrifugal–Centripetal Forces in International Petroleum Company Regions," *Annals of the Association of American Geographers*, LI, No. 1 (1961), 124–382.

were). This view of the non-European world ignored the universality of socio-political organization and the fact that, wherever there are human beings, there also is organization. Indeed, there cannot truly be unorganized areas so long as man is present. The indigenous peoples of the so-called colonial world did not need to be discovered, and their tribal and village territories did not need to be partitioned and "organized" in order that they could constitute functioning units or systems.

On the other hand, it should be pointed out that, despite his traditional focus on the State, Hartshorne *was* aware that the area of effective political activity did not always coincide with the formal or legal limits of governmental jurisdiction. In a little known essay published in 1941 he stated that:

> Ordinary political maps represent only legally recognized distinctions in political control of areas and thus hide the reality of essential differences in character . . . we need a more realistic classification of areas in terms of their political organization. In particular we need to distinguish between those areas that are actually organized as integral parts of states and those that are essentially controlled by outside states of which they are not, politically, integral parts.[38]

Unfortunately, Hartshorne did not carry the logic of his argument to its ulti-mate conclusion.

Gottmann's use of the concept of *circulation* provided an intellectual prism through which the processes of political activity might be viewed. But, how-ever exciting these ideas may be, he failed to illustrate nomothetically how circulation brings about the formation or reformation of political organiza-tions, systems, or regions.

In concentrating on political activity rather than on the organized territory, Stephen Jones (*A Unified Field Theory of Political Geography*) was able to explore the larger implications of the work of Hartshorne and Gottmann. The political activity field that Jones posited as the political region was defined not by the formal institutions of government, but by the function of politics, by the generation and allocation of power, whether institutionalized or not.[39]

---

[38] See, for example, the map, p. 46, in his "The Politico-Geographic Pattern of the World," *Annals of the American Academy of Political and Social Science*, CCXVIII (November 1941), 45–57.

[39] The geographic literature on functional regions is as extensive as the literature on gen-eral interaction theory, the two often going hand in hand. See the following: William Warntz, "Global Science and the Tyranny of Space," *Papers, Regional Science Association*, XIX (1967), 7–19; Edward A. Ackerman, "Where Is the Research Frontier?" *Annals of the Association of American Geographers*, LIII, No. 4 (December 1963), 429–440; M. Weber, "Culture, Terri-toriality, and the Elastic Mile," *Papers, Regional Science Association*, XIII (1964), 59–69; Haggett, *Locational Analysis in Human Geography*, especially pp. 31–60; Gunner Olson, *Dis-tance and Human Interaction, A Review and Bibliography*, Bibliographic Series, No. 2 (Phila-delphia: Regional Science Research Institute, 1965). See also Pitirim A. Sorokin, *Sociocultural Causality, Space, Time, A Study of Referential Principles of Sociology and Social Science* (Durham, North Carolina: Duke University Press, 1943), especially pp. 97–157. Jones' activity field is, of course, not unique to the social science literature. See Borje Hanssen, "Fields of Social Activity and Their Dynamics," *Translations of the Westermarck Society*, 2 (Copen-hagen: Ejar Munksgaard, 1953), 99–133.

For illustration, Jones refers in passing to the movements of a state highway patrolman who, in enforcing the law, produces a field. The focus of the field is, of course, the patrolman's movements or activities. (Since the patrolman is mobile, the focus, the center of immediate law enforcement, may shift within the field.) The patrolman possesses considerable discretionary power as to how and to what degree he will enforce the law under various circumstances. In reality, the enforcement of the law may not be uniform; the patrolman may elect to be more rigid in one place and with one group of violators than in another place and with another group. Thus, although the patrolman's movements or actions may not be uniformly experienced or identical on every occasion, his activity field constitutes something of a functional region.

This example, as elaborated above, serves a useful purpose, but it tends also to be misleading. In the final analysis, the activities of the patrolman are confined by state boundaries; he has no authority to enforce the law on the highway beyond. Moreover, the stretch of highway to which he is assigned *within* state boundaries is predetermined *not* by the patrolman himself or by his capacity to act, but rather by his supervisor in the police department. It is his duty, however, to see that his field of movement corresponds to the given area or stretch of highway.

Administrative and special-purpose regions

When there is a lack of coincidence between area and field, problems may arise, as Jones suggests, in reference to the growing city. Strictly speaking, the administration of the city is confined within legal, territorial limits. With an increase in urban settlement, the legal limits of the city are soon bypassed, but vested interests tend to prevent any significant change in political boundaries. Hence, the field—one based on urban function—becomes more extensive than the legal city and may entail a host of other administrations and agencies. This problem is discussed at length by V. Ostrom, C.M. Tiebout, and R. Warren (*The Organization of Government in Metropolitan Areas*). What is required is a resolution of field-area discontinuity or, as James Fesler notes, a reconciliation of function and area (*The Reconciliation of Function and Area*). Either the legal political area must be expanded to fit the field or special purpose regional administrations must be established in order to handle some of the functions that transcend existing boundaries. The establishment in 1953 in Greater Toronto (Canada) of a metropolitan government represents one of the more successful attempts to concentrate jurisdiction over a number of basic services, rather than to leave them to be provided by 13 local municipalities.[40] The New York Port Authority, TVA, and the Puget Sound Governmental Conference are similar types of special-purpose regional organizations, commanding

---

[40] Frank Smallwood, *Metro Toronto: A Decade Later*, Bureau of Municipal Research, Toronto (November 1963), pp. 1 ff; *Report of the Royal Commission on Metropolitan Toronto*, Toronto (June 1965).

varying degrees of influence and authority. In the United States, the tendency
has been to move in the direction of more (and often overlapping) administration to resolve the problems that arise from population growth and resettlement or economic change, rather than to alter existing political boundaries or
enlarge existing political regions.

In the final analysis, the resolution of field-area discontinuity or the reconciliation of function and area requires a clear understanding of the nature and
extent of the field. Once this is achieved, the delineation of area to fit the field
depends upon effective regionalization.

Regionalism and sectionalism

Regionalism and sectionalism, as discussed by Howard Odum and Harry
Moore (*Exploring the Region: The Political Scientists*), constitute essentially
different types of political processes, although the terms are often used interchangeably. Correctly speaking, regionalism "sees the differing areas from the
point of view of the nation," whereas sectionalism "sees the nation from the
point of view of the differing areas." In short, the one comes down from the top
of the political spectrum; the other comes up from the bottom.

Regionalism involves the superimposition of boundaries on the system, the
creation of fields from above. Sectionalism entails a growth of local attachments
and, consequently, of *de facto* boundaries within the system, the spontaneous
emergence of fields from within. Sectionalism has been a common phenomenon
in American history. In 1860 it led to the secession of southern states from the
Union; it led in 1863 to the secession of the western part of Virginia and the
formation of a new political region, West Virginia. In many instances, the
differences between the two processes have become blurred. The division of the
Australian continent into states early in the twentieth century represented a
fairly clear-cut illustration of regionalism. The consequent growth of loyalties
to the states and to state boundaries has reflected the emergence of sectional
feelings. If such feelings transcend state boundaries, a new set of regions might
conceivably be called into being. There is some evidence that such a process is
at work in modern Canada, which not only could result in a redrawing of
regional boundaries, but also might destroy the country altogether.

Clearly, the emergence of sectionalism suggests the growth of regional
consciousness. It may be understood, therefore, to be the spatial expression of
community formation and development.

PART IV: SYSTEM AND AREA—THE POLITICAL COMMUNITY

The question of community

Discussion in preceding sections has focused on the nature of the political
system and its relationship to society. Both the political system and society are

characterized by patterns of human interaction through time and space. To function effectively, each political system requires a number of supports, one of the most important of which is the presence within society of community, of the participants' awareness of belonging to a system. The question of community provides, therefore, another dimension that must be taken into consideration if the attempt to understand and analyze the nature, function, and viability of political systems is to be meaningful.

Over the centuries, social philosophers and critics have distinguished between two sets of human relationships, one that represents social interaction and one that represents social integration; between human relationships that are essentially contractual and those that are binding through a deeper sense of commitment. In China, for example, this distinction provided the fundamental philosophical difference between the Confucian and Legalist schools of social ethics.[41] The Confucian school insisted that society ought to be based upon those human relationships that mark family ties and close friendships. The Legalists, led by Hsun Tzu and Han Fei-tzu, rejected the Confucian concept and saw merit in a system based on contract, on rewards and punishment. The history of Chinese social thought and institutions, in effect, represented a compromise between these two schools. For example, while the Legalists helped create the bureaucratic system so characteristic of the Chinese imperial order, the Confucianists helped ensure that the bureaucrats were scholars and possessed of higher virtue.

In the West, Plato also drew a distinction between the binding relationships that support the ideal republic and the merely contractual links within the polis. At another level of interpretation, St. Augustine saw in the "City of God" a quality of relationship not to be found in the "society of men." Centuries later, such writers and thinkers as Thomas Hooker, Thomas Hobbes, Baruch Spinoza, John Locke, and Jean Jacques Rousseau defined civil society in terms of a social contract.[42] Whether motivated by fear or force as Hobbes suggested, or by economic gain, as Locke maintained, the relationships between men were contractual, entailing with some measure of consent a system of rewards and punishment or of obedience and submission. Some thinkers, like David Hume, went one step further and insisted that all social groupings, including the family, were held together by the threat of force and obedience to that threat.[43]

With Auguste Comte and the rise of scientific sociology in the late eighteenth and early nineteenth centuries, the notion that society derived from the social contract was replaced by one that viewed society as an organism.[44] The Orga-

41 See A.C. Graham, "The Place of Reason in Chinese Philosophical Tradition," in *The Legacy of China*, ed. Raymond Dawson (London: Oxford University Press, 1964), pp. 28–56; H.G. Creel, *Confucius and the Chinese Way* (New York: Harper & Row, 1960).

42 Howard Becker and Harry E. Barnes, *Social Thought From Lore to Science* (New York: Dover Publications, Inc., 1961), pp. 370–405; Pitirim Sorokin, *Contemporary Sociological Theories* (New York: Harper & Row, 1964), pp. 3–62.

43 Becker and Barnes, *Social Thought from Lore to Science*, pp. 396–404.

44 *Ibid.*, pp. 560–594; Sorokin, *Contemporary Sociological Theories*, pp. 194–218.

nismic school that came to be epitomized by the work of Herbert Spencer (1820–1903) held that society was characterized by some *consensus universel* that produced a collective and integrated organism.[45] Human relationships, therefore, were not defined by, or based on, contract.

From the above examples, it is clear that history contains a record of philosophic distinction between a society based on social contract and one based on something subliminally more binding. This distinction has been carried over into modern social science and forms the foundation on which society per se is differentiated from that which is called community. An already classic contribution in this area is that of Ferdinand Tönnies (1855–1935), who devised a system of antithetical types, defined as *gemeinschaft* (community) and *gesellschaft* (society).[46] In a similar vein, Pitirim Sorokin recognized the difference between community and society in terms of "familistic" and "contractual" relationships,[47] the former entailing a qualitatively deeper binding force than the latter. Emile Durkheim interpreted this significant difference to be an *organic* solidarity, as contrasted with the *mechanical* solidarity of society.[48] Similar to these are Charles Cooley's *primary* and *secondary* groups, R.M. MacIver's *communal* and *associational* relations, Carl Zimmerman's *localistic* and *cosmopolitan* communities, Robert Redfield's *folk-urban continuum*, and Becker's *sacred* and *secular* societies.[49] Harvey Cox' notion of the secular city may be included here, too, since it also suggests that basic qualitative differences exist between community and society.[50]

Paradoxically, the human condition underlying the existence of community has most frequently been demonstrated empirically when and where community is lacking or has been lost. Durkheim's study of suicide, for example, indicated a direct connection between the loss or lack of strong and intimate social ties and the rates of suicide among urban industrial workers.[51] Studies by Elton

---

[45] Becker and Barnes, *Social Thought from Lore to Science,* pp. 664–792; Herbert Spencer, *Principles of Sociology* (3rd ed.; New York: Appleton Century Crofts, 1910), Vol. 1, Part 2, Chaps. ii–ix. See also Karl R. Popper, *The Poverty of Historicism* (New York: Harper & Row, 1964), pp. 17–19.

[46] Ferdinand Tönnies, *Community and Society (Gemeinschaft und Gesellschaft),* trans. and ed. Charles P. Loomis (New York: Harper & Row, 1963). *Gemeinschaft und Gesellschaft* was originally published in Germany in 1887, and the first English edition was published in 1957 by the Michigan State University Press.

[47] Pitirim A. Sorokin, *Social and Cultural Dynamics* (New York: American Book Company, 1937), Vol. 3; *The Crisis of Our Age* (New York: E.P. Dutton & Co., Inc., 1942), Chap. V; *Contemporary Sociological Theories,* pp. 491 ff.

[48] Emile Durkheim, *The Division of Labor in Society,* trans. G. Simpson (New York: The Free Press, 1933), especially Bk. 2, Chaps. i–ii; Sorokin, *Contemporary Sociological Theories,* pp. 463–480.

[49] Charles Cooley, *Social Organization,* (New York: Scribner, 1924), pp. 23–31; Robert Redfield, "The Folk Society," *American Journal of Sociology,* LII, No. 4 (January 1947), 293–308; Howard Becker, "Sacred and Secular Societies: Considered with Reference to Folk-State and Similar Classifications," *Social Forces,* XXVIII, No. 4 (May 1950), 361–376.

[50] Harvey Cox, *The Secular City* (New York: The Macmillan Company, 1965).

[51] Emile Durkheim, *Suicide,* trans. John A. Spaulding and George Simpson (New York: The Free Press, 1951).

Mayo and associates of workers in the United States further confirmed a connection between the lack of community attachment and levels of insecurity.[52] Indeed, it would seem that the greatest price twentieth century man has paid for technological progress has been the progressive secularization of his human relationships and the further diminution of his awareness of immediate community. Such is the view of modern social critics, one of the most articulate of whom is C. Wright Mills. As he summarized it,

> The uneasiness, the malaise of our time is due to this root fact: in our politics and economy, in family life and religion . . . the certainties of the eighteenth and nineteenth centuries have disintegrated or been destroyed and, at the same time no new sanctions or justifications for the new routines we live and must live have taken hold. . . . Newly created in a harsh time of creation, white collar man has no culture to lean upon except the content of mass society. . . . For security's sake he must attach himself somewhere, but no communities or organizations seem to be thoroughly his.[53]

Mills may be guilty of some exaggeration and may even have been remiss in one sense, in neglecting to note an enduring human propensity to create or recreate community. In one way or another, clubs, associations, fraternities, even communes, still find their place within mass society. Moreover, the content of mass society itself has provided the foundations for a new order or level of community, the Nation-State. Indeed, disintegration of the certainties of the eighteenth and nineteenth centuries in the West was accompanied by the birth of new certainties, associated with nationalism, the State, and various other political ideologies focusing upon the State. Modern man has replaced the *ancien regime* with a new order that draws its inspiration from the Nation; he has supplanted direct and obvious local attachments with complex or abstract and more distant attachments. Faith in the Prince and the Priest have yielded to faith in ideology, which seeks to enthrone and deify State power. The appeal of National Socialism to millions of disenchanted and alienated Germans in the 1920's and 1930's, for example, would remain inexplicable without some recognition of their need for a sense of belonging. The initial appeal of Marxist Socialism may be attributed to its view of a new society based on revolutionized human relationships.[54]

Still, Mills' appraisal of the dilemma of modern man contains much that is valid. Even the State has not been able to provide for all men that sense of purpose, of direction, of community that men seek. Indeed, those Germans who put their faith in National Socialism, the Leader, and the State found them-

---

[52] Elton Mayo, *The Social Problems of an Industrial Civilization* (Cambridge: Harvard University Press, 1945).

[53] C. Wright Mills, *White Collar: The American Middle Class* (New York: Oxford University Press, 1951), p. xvi.

[54] Richard Crossman, ed., *The God That Failed* (New York: Harper & Row, 1950); also see Gabriel A. Almond, *The Appeals of Communism* (Princeton: Princeton University Press, 1954).

selves by 1944–45 caught in a funeral pyre. Still others, whether in the Soviet Union or in the United States, remain in opposition to a state system in which they cannot or can no longer believe, alienated from fellow men still further by the quickening pace of postindustrial society.[55]

What Mills and others have characterized as a crisis in modern capitalist society appears to be nothing less than a universal crisis. It is associated with the *gesellschaft* type of society wherein human relationships are based on little more than contract, and where the binding, cohesive, or integrative relationships characteristic of the *gemeinschaft* type of society, i.e., community, are found to be lacking or have been lost.

Community as opposed to society, or the notion of the political community as distinguished from the political system, entails, in short, a greater degree of social bonding than is implicit in the concept of human interaction. The existence of political community must include processes of social integration. Like many such terms, integration means different things to different people, with the result that there is no universally accepted or acceptable definition. Used in relation to community, integration is commonly thought to embrace the growth and emergence of strong ties within social groups. Even allowing for so broad a definition, how is the growth of the degree of social cohesiveness to be measured?

For some modern students of community, the only adequate measure of social cohesiveness is to be found in the quantitative analysis of the densities of human interaction.[56] The underlying assumption is that the greater the density, the stronger the existence of community or, at the very least, the greater the propensity for the formation of community. Such an assumption, however, is misleading. Quantitative analysis, though useful, measures *only* densities and *not* the quality of such densities. To be sure, densities of human interaction (i.e., freight flows between producer and consumer) may be thought to represent something essentially more profound, but such a conclusion is highly speculative. A map of the density of shells exchanged on a battlefield may tell us something of the relationship between two armies, but that interaction, however intense, is hardly a reflection of the existence of community. While human interaction may be regarded as a prerequisite for human integration (in the same sense that communication entails some mutually understandable language), interaction and integration are not synonymous. Nor do we have any idea as to how much interaction is required to ensure that integration will follow. On the other hand, too much interaction, as in too heavy a flow of communication, could have the reverse effect; it could lead to satura-

---

55 See Jacques Ellul, *The Technological Society*, trans. John Wilkinson (New York: Alfred A. Knopf, Inc., 1964), originally published in French as *La Technique ou l'enjeu du siècle* (1954).

56 Karl W. Deutsch, *Nationalism and Social Communication* (New York: John Wiley & Sons, Inc., 1953), pp. 60–80, 97–138; Karl W. Deutsch, "Transaction Flows As Indicators of Political Cohesion," in *The Integration of Political Communities*, ed. P.E. Jacob and J.V. Toscano (Philadelphia: J.B. Lippincott Co., 1964), pp. 75–97.

tion, with a consequent breakdown in the entire interactive process.[57] The simple interaction hypothesis, in short, will not suffice to explain how and why social groups and units become integrated to function as communities.

Some social scientists, following the lead of writers like Talcott Parsons, have qualified the interactance hypothesis and have suggested that it is the degree of interdependence within the densities of interaction that accounts for the formation of community, rather than densities per se.[58] According to this interpretation, integration implies functional interdependence, as in the division of labor. A society becomes integrated as social functions become specialized and participants become interdependent. As Karl Deutsch has phrased it, "the essence of the integrative relationship is seen as a collective action to promote mutual interest." In terms of the political community, "cohesion is politically integrative if the political unit, acting through its governing organs, adopts public policies that commit the resources of the community to common purposes."[59] Integration would thus entail collective action to promote mutual interest, political integration being the process whereby political systems direct their policies to the common good (commonwealth).

The above view of social and political integration, however, does not fully resolve the problem. To what extent, one may ask, is functional interdependence a measure of community attachment? Managerial personnel and workers on a production line are functionally interdependent, but do they constitute a community? They do represent an interdependent system of action and, insofar as power is generated and a chain of command exists, they form a type of system. The history of labor-management relations and of labor union activity would suggest, however, that this system of action based on functional interdependence would not alone account for the formation here of community. The Blacks and Whites in South Africa are functionally interdependent, but they do not form a community. Indeed, it is the deliberate policy of the government of South Africa to maintain not only different social communities to accommodate the ethnic and racial diversification in that land, but different political communities as well (apartheid). Thus, it may be possible to suggest that type and quality of interdependence, and not simply degree, are essential to the process of societal integration and community formation.

Deutsch's concept of community as "collective action to promote mutual interest" amounts in effect to social contract. His type of community is essentially "a community of interest" wherein members resolve to limit their competition or hostility in the mutual interest. If such a definition were to stand, members of a treaty organization, or for that matter parties to a legal contract, would represent a community.[60] But, as noted earlier, this concept fails to pro-

---

57 Sometimes referred to as "overloading" the system. See Amitai Etzioni, *Studies in Social Change* (New York: Holt, Rinehart and Winston, Inc., 1966), p. 35.

58 *Ibid.*, pp. 14–16, 180–181.

59 Karl W. Deutsch, "The Integrative Process: Guidelines for Analysis of the Bases of Political Community," in *The Integration of Political Communities*, p. 5.

60 *Ibid.*, pp. 4–5. See also Karl W. Deutsch *et al.*, *Political Community in the North Atlantic Area* (Princeton: Princeton University Press, 1957).

vide for that qualitative distinction between pervasive social bonding and simple covenants. It may be adequate as a definition of "society," but it fails with respect to "community."

If community (especially political community) cannot be defined simply in terms of interaction or functional interdependence, how then may it be defined? David Easton, as was pointed out earlier, has suggested that community be treated as a support to the political system. As such, it is to be regarded as that sense of attachment or belonging whereby individuals identify with each other; in political terms, community may be thought of as that sense of belonging whereby loyalties are attached to the political system. Whatever its source or cause, the sense of belonging is a primary cement that lends coherence to the system. Thus, community should not be regarded so much as a social entity, but as an on-going psychological process. Community comes into being when the sense of belonging is translated into loyalty and action. *The political community may, therefore, be understood to represent an integrated political system in which human relationships are interdependent, in which transactions between the participants in the system are understood to be decisive and not simply incidental to their identity as a community, and in which attachment to the system is translated into loyalty and political action.*

A political system that has functioned as a cohesive unit (maintaining law and order and its legitimate threat of authority) often seems to be transformed, under the threat of external attack, into a political community, functioning as an integrated unit with a maximum of loyalty and a minimum of dissent. At other times (also under conditions of stress), what was assumed to be political community is found to be little more than a political system. This might suggest that political community is a fragile thing, subject to emerge or fall if pressure is applied at the right time. The attainment or loss of community is usually a complex process which external threat, wars, or other crises only tend to intensify.

The strength of the ties or transactions that determine the degree of social bonding is seldom left subject to chance. Part of the function of any political system is to ensure its survival, and this it ultimately seeks through compliance and consent. Relationships between the participants and between the participants and the system are thus maintained and reinforced by the process commonly referred to as *political socialization*. It is the basic process, so well demonstrated in the history of the nineteenth and early twentieth century United States, by which the political system attempts through the media of communication and the symbols at its disposal to shape, increase, and consolidate loyalty and, hence, its own legitimacy.[61]

---

[61] See especially Richard E. Dawson and Kenneth Prewitt, *Political Socialization* (Boston: Little, Brown and Company, 1969); Lewis A. Coser, ed., *Political Sociology* (New York: Harper & Row, 1967), pp. 9–47; Gabriel Almond and Sidney Verba, *The Civic Culture* (Boston: Little, Brown and Company, 1965), pp. 1–44, 266–306.

In the "open system," political socialization theoretically entails "feedback." The goals, ideals, and symbols of the system are not monolithic in nature and may change as society changes. In the "closed system," political socialization is based less on "feedback" and more on the goals of the system (the goals being essentially those of the ruling elite). In many cases the process of socialization seeks to integrate and to assimilate, and to achieve conformity. Without it, community or the sense of belonging remains weakly developed. Not all systems are equally successful in the process; Canada, for example, never was the "melting pot" that supposedly characterized the United States. Nor are all systems equally successful throughout the territory over which they function, with the consequence that portions of territory or regions remain unassimilated. The inhabitants of such regions may see themselves as members of another community from which they have been separated, or they may simply not have been totally integrated into the system of which politically they are a part.

Community and spatial perception

The concept of community as a support to the political system recognizes that community itself is an ongoing psychological process. This entails, in brief, the way in which individuals perceive their relationships with one another and identify with the group.

In spite of the widespread interest in perception (or environmental perception) demonstrated by geographers and other social scientists in recent years, the study of perception is not new to our era, although procedural techniques are undoubtedly more refined. Throughout the centuries, philosophers have concerned themselves with the problem of existence and the ways in which knowledge about existence is rendered comprehensible to man. Indeed, the study of perception in Western thought is as old as Plato's *Republic* and the allegory of the cave (Book VII).[62] In more modern times, philosophers such as David Hume, Bishop Berkeley, and Immanuel Kant have speculated on the problem, not to mention the focus of such schools of thought as British empiricism and logical positivism. The more immediate source of much of contemporary thinking about human perception, however, may be traced to the development of two schools of psychology, the "behaviorist" and the "behavioralist."[63]

Behaviorism, developed and fostered by scientists among whom was the Russian physiologist Pavlov, asserted the proposition that human behavior

---

[62] In the allegory, Plato confined a group of human beings to a den where, being chained, they could not move. They could see only their own shadows and the shadows of one another on the opposite wall. To them, said Plato, the truth would be literally nothing but the shadows of the images. When freed, however, the prisoners found that their shadows were in reality clearer than the objects shown them in the bright sun.

[63] See Charles E. Osgood, "Behavior Theory and the Social Science," *Behavioral Science*, I (1965), 167–185; Heinz Eulau, *Recent Developments in the Behavioral Study of Politics;*

could be traced directly to external stimuli. Perception, if it could be said to exist at all, was essentially the reception of stimuli, the entire process constituting a stimulus-response (S-R) chain of "pure perception." The behaviorist thesis, however, has been largely discredited as an oversimplification of the process of human perception, consciousness, and behavior. Much of the criticism directed at behaviorism notes the failure of its adherents to account for the causal link between stimulus and response, and their insistence that perception itself was not a proper subject for study.

The behavioralists, on the other hand, recognize the legitimacy of such study. Behavioralism accepts the phenomenological assertion—which is accepted in this treatise—that whenever one deals with human perception and the effects on behavioral patterns, value must be added over and beyond the simple S-R chain. Hence it is argued that "perception is not a passive activity, which only requires the opening of the eyes; it is a transaction with the environment. . . ."[64] Individuals possess not only immediate perception in the sense that they perceive an object (are open to stimuli), but also "meaning perception" whereby the object perceived is interpreted, internalized, and made real and meaningful to the psyche. As Colin Wilson has stated: "Perception is at least 50 per cent *assumptions*, and these assumptions depend on the total circumstances in which perception takes place."[65] Whatever the ratio of assumptions, the "total circumstances" (environment) are not only "external stimuli"; they also include the internal consciousness of the individual through which new stimuli are sifted. Experience, not merely stimuli, is the "stuff" of perception and, once taken within oneself or internalized, it is interpreted, modified, and reshaped to make it real and meaningful. Moreover, as Michael Novak has recently observed:

> Because men are symbol-making animals, they can structure their superabundant, polymorphous experiences and assimilate them in perceptual forms. They can gain insight into the unities, identities, and wholes among the data of experience. They can articulate criteria and procedures of evaluation. And they can devise strategies and tactics to direct the effects of their actions. The symbol-making drive establishes the possibility of orderly and intellectually manageable development.[66]

David B. Truman, "The Impact on Political Science of the Revolution in the Behavioral Sciences," in *Research Frontiers in Politics and Government* (Washington, D.C.: The Brookings Institution, 1955), pp. 202–231. A well-written critique of the behavioral approach in political science may be found in Robert A. Dahl, "The Behavioral Approach in Political Science: Epitaph for a Monument to a Successful Protest," *American Political Science Review*, LV, No. 4 (December 1961), 763–772.

[64] Colin Wilson, *Introduction to the New Existentialism* (Boston: Houghton Mifflin Company, 1966), p. 65. Wilson provides an excellent introduction to phenomenology. For a more thorough study see Quentin Lauer, *Phenomenology: Its Genesis and Prospect* (New York: Harper & Row, 1965); Edmund Husserl, *Ideas, General Introduction to Pure Phenomenology*, trans. W.R. Boyce Gibson (New York: Crowell Collier and Macmillan, Inc., 1962).

[65] Colin Wilson, *Introduction to the New Existentialism*, p. 66.

[66] Michael Novak, *The Experience of Nothingness* (New York: Harper & Row, 1970), p. 27.

In a somewhat similar vein, Alfred North Whitehead argued that perception is largely a matter of symbols and language.[67]

The internalization of experience is part of the perceptual process, or, as some have termed it, the apperceptive process: the response to external stimulus is reshaped by the residuum of past experience, all of which comes to constitute a new whole, a new gestalt. In this way human consciousness constitutes a wide-ranging perceptive field, or, to use Professor Novak's term, a "horizon," in which experience is not only immediate, but residual. According to Novak:

> The value of the concept of horizon is twofold. If each man has his own unique horizon, then the self-awareness of each must include a pervasive sense of the relativity of views of reality. To work with the concept of horizon as a fundamental tool is to be constantly reminded of the central role of myth-making in all acting and knowing. Secondly, the concept of horizon is sweeping and all-inclusive; elements in the subject or in the range of his activities presently undifferentiated may at a later time be more carefully articulated.
>
> In particular, the concept of horizon is intended to pierce the rationalistic bias by calling attention to the fundamental role of undifferentiated, inexhaustible experience. Thus, dreams and fantasies and zany impressions and impulses of all sorts, which quite clearly play a role in ethical action, cannot a priori be excluded from consideration. Secondly, the notion of horizon emphasizes that social and institutional forces structure the perceptions, feelings and intentions of the would be rationalist agent.
>
> ... The concept of horizon emphasizes that the self and its world interpenetrate at every point. There is no part that is purely self or purely world. It may well be the case that both reality and the self are social constructs....[68]

The term "experience" should not, therefore, be taken too literally, for the consciousness of the individual may be filled not only with the residue of external encounters (lived experience) but also with the residue of that which has been learned in other ways. Indeed, symbols and myths inherited from the past may prove more vital in the apperceptive process than any other phenomena. It is possible that the courage associated with the ancient defense of Masada, for example, may be as essential to a comprehension of contemporary Israeli political behavior as it was centuries ago to the Jewish defenders who were intent on resisting Roman control to the death. The memory of Masada may have become part of the Israeli's horizon and of Israel's national iconography.

Not all human perception can be considered relevant to the question of politics, the political system, or the political community. Cognitive maps, such as the one depicting the New Yorker's view of the United States, are interesting (and sometimes amusing), but their revelance to political behavior or political

---

[67] Alfred North Whitehead, *Symbolism, Its Meaning and Effect* (New York: The Macmillan Company, 1955).

[68] Novak, *op. cit.,* pp. 28 ff.

community needs to be demonstrated. Do all New Yorkers view the United States in the same way? If so, what do they do politically to reflect their view? Peter Gould's study of student spatial perception in and of certain sections of the United States provides, more concretely than the New Yorker's view of the United States, an interesting cartographic representation of sectional identities and spatial preferences.[69] Unless these can be correlated with political behavior (such as voting habits) or with political identities and preferences, the relevance to the political geographer of such an exercise remains at best indirect and intangible. The following example may serve to focus the problem. One may speak of a Hindu, Buddhist, or Jewish view of the world without reference to any political context and within the realm of transcendent metaphysics. Once, however, Hinduism, Buddhism, or Judaism becomes a political force— as the first has become in India, the second in South Vietnam and Japan, and the third in Israel—their respective views of the world become immediately relevant to the question of political systems and communities. The mere assertion that each individual carries in his head a cognitive map which influences his decisions and actions is nothing short of a platitude.

The identifiable link between spatial perception and political behavior, the articulation of ideas and their translation into political activity, remains a complex and elusive process to analyze.[70] Perception, as was noted above, is essentially an individual process; groups as groups do not perceive. Yet an acceptance of the Spencerian thesis that groups are nothing more than the sum total of the participants leaves us with a dilemma, since the thesis is not particularly helpful in telling us how the perceptions of individuals merge to form group awareness, or why individuals live and die for the group or otherwise play out their lives as a coherent "we." This dilemma is compounded when we remember that "politics is by definition an intensely social process which must be seen

[69] Peter R. Gould, *On Mental Maps,* Michigan Inter-University Community of Mathematical Geographers, Discussion Paper No. 9 (Ann Arbor: University of Michigan, 1966).

[70] It is even more so when the context of the perceptions and ideas are themselves non-political, especially when the learned perceptions and ideas are embedded in the long cultural history of mankind. See the following: Mircae Eliade, *Cosmos and History, The Myth of the Eternal Return* (New York: Harper & Row, 1959), especially pp. 3–17; *The Sacred and the Profane* (New York: Harper & Row, 1961), especially pp. 20–65; Robert Redfield, *The Primitive World and Its Transformation* (Ithaca, New York: Cornell University Press, 1957), pp. 26–53, 84–110. On the State and nationalism see especially: Hans Kohn, *The Idea of Nationalism* (New York: The Macmillan Company, 1967); Ernst Cassier, *The Myth of the State* (New Haven: Yale University Press, 1946). An interesting interpretation of the perception-action chain is provided by Jose Ortega y Gasset's "The Sportive Origin of the State," in his *History as a System and Other Essays Toward A Philosophy of History* (New York: W.W. Norton & Company, Inc., 1962), pp. 13–40. On the international order see: Inis L. Claude, *Swords Into Plowshares, The Problems and Progress of International Organization* (New York: Random House, Inc., 1959), pp. 407–432; George Catlin, "The Atlantic Idea: Beginnings," in his *The Stronger Community* (New York: Hawthorn Books, Inc., 1966), pp. 119–132; Adda B. Bozeman, *Politics and Culture in International History,* especially pp. 238–297, 389–522. An interesting perspective on American attitudes toward the world order is provided by Roger D. Masters, "The Lockean Tradition in American Foreign Policy," *Journal of International Affairs,* XXI, No. 2 (1967), 253–277.

as a group and not as an individual phenomena; in which, therefore, the importance of bonding is paramount."[71]

In geographic terms, individual perception is basically a consciousness of place. Indeed, what has been termed "spatial perception" is nothing more than an individual's understanding of his place in the group (obviously involving territory) or a nation's consciousness of its place and role in the world (usually articulated by its leaders). It is in this respect that spatial perception entails the process of community formation and development.

"Spatial perception" is, however, not an entirely satisfactory term to describe the process. Unless one wishes to abide by the philosophical anachronism of Newtonian absolute space, it is not space that is perceived, but rather relationships within a spatial framework.[72] Abstract space, like abstract time, has no attributes apart from reference points, whether they be human, animal, or physical.

If this qualification is kept in mind, the term may be retained to indicate that process whereby individuals perceive of their relationships to other phenomena, whether human or otherwise. The "spatial" aspect of these relationships consists in the fact that the subject and object entering into the relationship are located; that is, they are removed from one another. Place then becomes a surrogate for both the perceiver and the perceived. The intervening space or distance (which, after all, is time) helps to condition the relationships, provides the spatio-temporal environment of the relationships, and influences the nature of the perceptions about those relationships. Consciousness, however, is always relative to the reference points afforded by the circumstances, milieu, or environment in which perception takes place. Hence, the American view of continental unity is in part a function of the American view of itself and of the world as a whole (Connor, *Myths of Hemispheric, Continental, Regional,* and *State Unity*). The Maoist view of the world order is equally a reflection of the Maoist (or Mao's) view of China itself (Schwartz, *The Maoist Image of the World Order*).

An individual's place entails a perception of another individual's place. The much maligned geopolitical perspective is, in essence, an assertion by a political community of "our place" as opposed to the "their place" of another community. In reality, all political communities have some geopolitical perspective although it need not be as fully articulated (however unsystematic) as that of German *lebensraum* in the Nazi era. American isolationism in the 1930's was equally a case of a geopolitical perspective on the role of the United States in the world.[73] Manifest destiny, the Monroe Doctrine, and the politics of containment enunciated by John Foster Dulles—all reflect geopolitical calculation and space perception.

---

[71] Tiger, *Men in Groups,* p. 92 .

[72] Blaut, "Space and Process"; Koyré, *From the Closed World to the Infinite Universe.*

[73] Bernard Fensterwald, "The Anatomy of American Isolationism and Expansionism," *The Journal of Conflict Resolution,* II, No. 2 (1958), 111–139.

Spatial perception entails the perception of distance, but, since distance is itself a subjective phenomenon, the perception of distance involves a thoroughly internal process. Still, since distance may be measured in discrete spatial and temporal units, its perception may be said to represent the perception of these units as they have an impact upon the relationships between subject and object. In the field of political geography, an awareness of the impact of perceived distances has come down to us largely in terms of the problem of access, although a somewhat broader context may have been implied by Mackinder's statement that ". . . political geography seems to be founded on the fact that man travels and man settles."[74] In recent years, political geographers have sought more systematic ways of defining the impact of perceived distance on political behavior. One such effort is that of Kevin Cox on the impact of perceived distance and movement on voting patterns in the United States.[75]

Much work remains to be done. Edward Hall's studies of animal perception of critical distance is a milestone, but the relationship between human perception and political behavior remains something of an enigma.[76] The resurgence of interest in the whole question of environmental perception, through the efforts of Hall, Robert Sommer, Kevin Lynch, David Lowenthal, Robert Kates, and others[77] has helped focus interest on the broader framework, but little of this work has had any direct bearing on distance perception, or even on the wider topic of environmental perception and political behavior.

Levels of political community: Local, urban, national, and supranational

The spatial aspect of community has often been thought of only in physical terms. As Christian Jonassen noted, a survey of social scientists on the question

---

[74] H.J. Mackinder, "The Physical Basis of Political Geography," *The Scottish Geographical Magazine*, VI (February 1890), 78.

[75] Kevin Cox, "A Spatial Interactional Model for Political Geography," *The East Lakes Geographer*, IV (December 1968), 58–76.

[76] Edward Hall, *The Hidden Dimension* (Garden City, New York: Doubleday and Company, Inc., 1966).

[77] In addition to Hall's work, see the following: Robert Sommer, "Studies in Personal Space," *Sociometry*, XXII, No. 3, (September 1959), 247–260; *Personal Space, The Behavioral Basis of Design* (Englewood Cliffs, N.J.: Prentice-Hall, Inc., 1966); Kevin Lynch, *The Image of the City* (Cambridge: M.I.T. Press, 1960); David Lowenthal, "Geography, Experience and Imagination: Towards A Geographical Epistomology," *Annals of the Association of American Geographers*, LI, No. 3 (1961), 241–260; David Lowenthal, ed., *Environmental Perception and Behavior* (Chicago: University of Chicago, Department of Geography Research Paper No. 109, 1967); R.W. Kates and J.F. Wohlwill, eds., "Man's Response to the Physical Environment," *The Journal of Social Issues*, XXII (1966); Thomas F. Saarinen, *Perception of Environment*, Commission on College Geography, Resource Paper No. 5 (Washington, D.C.: Association of American Geographers, 1969); James D. Harrison, *An Annotated Bibliography on Environmental Perception*, Exchange Bibliography No. 93 (Monticello, Illinois: Council of Planning Librarians, August 1969).

of community revealed that a general consensus among them existed on at least one point—that communities are spatial entities.[78] They agreed that communities have "spatial structure," "possess an area," or "have a territorial base." Members belonging to the community must, accordingly, live in relative proximity to one another.

Relative proximity, however, entails more than simple physical proximity. Whether we deal with the cognitive aspects of community identity or more simply with the degree to which people relate to one another, it is not so much physical proximity that underlies social bonding as it is social proximity or ideational proximity.[79] Physical proximity may shape the bonding process, and geographers have, no doubt, been in the vanguard of those who have attempted to measure that impact. Except in highly localized cases, however, the impact of physical distance has been greatly lessened by the evolution of rapid transportation and mass communication. Where once local area and physical proximity were virtually synonymous with community, technological change has undermined these assumed imperatives.[80]

This is not to say that local community—that type of community which is often described or appears as a closely-knit settlement—has been thoroughly destroyed. In many parts of the world the hamlet, the village, the small town, the clan, the tribal unit, and so forth, not only continue to persist but also constitute the main level of community attachment (Mair, *Government Without the State*). They may be subsumed within the Nation-State, but they still retain their function as the more dominant community type. A large part of the nation-building process in the so-called underdeveloped world entails the transfer of these local community attachments to the State. Having to share an identity with the State, local community attachments compete vigorously with the latter's efforts toward national political socialization (Silverman, *The Community-Nation Mediator in Traditional Central Italy*). Even where the State has been most successful in the socialization process, local community attachments persist, not only in the form of small towns or villages, but also in such forms as local clubs and neighborhood associations. While much of small town America may have lost its political and social vitality, the demand for neighborhood schools, local control over many facets of life (including problems

[78] Christen T. Jonassen, "Community Typology," in *Community Structure and Analysis,* ed. Marvin B. Sussman (New York: Crowell Collier and Macmillan Inc., 1959), pp. 15–36.

[79] Pitirim Sorokin, *Sociocultural Causality, Space Time: A Study of Referential Principles of Sociology and Social Science* (Durham, North Carolina: Duke University Press, 1943), pp. 141–157.

[80] The loss of community through urbanization and technological change has long been a recognized phenomenon, and one not necessarily associated simply with the advent of mass society in the industrial and postindustrial eras. Hence, we have the Roman proverb, *Magna civitas, magna solitudo* ("A great city, a great desert") to which Francis Bacon (1568–1626) added, "because in a great town friends are scattered, so there is not that fellowship for the most part which is in less neighborhoods." See Becker and Barnes, *Social Thought from Lore to Science,* p. 312.

in the environment), and efforts to reestablish police precinct stations in many American cities reflect the desire and longing to retain direct links with the system and ensure some participation in community political action.[81]

The modern urban environment represents to a large degree a complex overlay of political systems and communities. Neighborhood residential subdivisions, often entailing a sense of community, are characteristic of the suburbs. Most cities in America have ethnic or racial ghettoes. However, one should not always assume that, whatever the subdivision, neighborhood, or ghetto, the residents identify as members of a community. Nor is it always true that a political community exists wherever strong community loyalty is evident. In New York, for example, the subdivision of Harlem into political wards had the effect of hindering or preventing the emergence of a single Black political community.[82] It is true that electoral boundaries in many cities in the United States have been drawn in such a manner as to divide actual or potential ethnic power blocs.[83] The emergence of "Black Power" is a reflection not only of growing pride on the part of many Afro-Americans in their own unique heritage, but also of an awareness that through community identification and ghetto organization they may participate effectively in the American political system. When the ethnic group is not necessarily concentrated in any one area, it is usually impossible to gerrymander electoral boundaries to capitalize on ethnic power; still, the minority group may wield considerable power, as in the case of the New York Jewish community or the Irish of Boston.

Nonresidential communities also operate politically within most modern urban settings. They may, as in the case of the Junior Chamber of Commerce, function both socially and economically to exert political pressure for objectives of their own (which may or may not coincide with the welfare of the urban community as a whole). Still other examples may be found in the secret or semisecret lodges, clubs, and religious and other charitable and social organizations that may attempt to influence the political behavior not only of their own membership but of nonmembers as well.

The high mobility of the population and the rapid growth in the size of the modern city tend to mitigate the establishment of a real sense of loyalty or belonging. Where a community exists, it may be found, as indicated above, in special organizations, neighborhoods, suburban subdivisions, or neighboring towns or villages. Indeed, it is often the stronger attachment to the immediate community that seriously inhibits the political unification of the metropolitan area and the formation of a metropolitan community (Hawley and Zimmer, *Resistance to Unification in a Metropolitan Community*).

---

[81] See Henry M. Levin, ed., *Community Control of Schools* (Washington, D.C.: The Brookings Institution, 1970).

[82] Gilbert Osofsky, *Harlem, The Making of a Ghetto: Negro New York, 1890–1930* (New York: Harper & Row, 1968), pp. 159–178.

[83] One of the most comprehensive studies of the problem of electoral subdivisions is that by Robert W. Teshera, "The Territorial Organization of American Internal Governmental Jurisdictions" Ph. D. diss., Department of Geography, University of Washington, 1970).

National integration, which provides an essential support to the State, has received more attention than possibly any of the other levels of political community referred to above. One possible exception might be the quest for universal peace and supranational community. For centuries, as Nisbet has pointed out, the very term "political community" was literally synonymous with "national community" (Nisbet, *The Political Community*). Deutsch, too, has suggested that "political integration" is the quintessential task confronting the Nation-State (Deutsch, *Nationalism and Social Communication*). Not all of the new political-territorial units which have appeared on the map of the world over the past quarter century are truly national, in the sense that their inhabitants form a single nation, defined in the classical manner. Many of the lesser-developed States in Asia, Africa, and South America are, in effect, engaged in the difficult task of nation-building, an intense and costly process. Where community formation, as in Nigeria, differs from that in Metropolitan America, is in the degree, nature, and quality of socialization.

Despite the fact that the State remains the focus of our most intense loyalties, the human propensity toward a larger community has demonstrated itself throughout history. In the twentieth century, efforts to establish an effective League of Nations or a United Nations have failed to provide the machinery essential to ensure the peace and create a transnational community. The successful organization of trans-State regional associations, however, suggests a path that may offer more realistic opportunity. The High Authority of the European Coal and Steel Community is one such example.[84] Unlike the international associations mentioned above, the High Authority has powers in particular areas of economic development which are binding on the constituent members. It approximates, therefore, a coherent political system, or a community of interest (Haas, *The Challenge of Regionalism*). It represents what Amitai Etzioni refers to as "sectoral integration," as in the joint management of resources, the joint control of commodity prices, or unified military commands.[85] Assuming that integration in one sector might result in further integration (e.g., the German Zollverein) and ultimately political community, one might ask, as does Etzioni, if there is a particular sequence leading to total unification. Deutsch has suggested that conditions of integration "may be assembled in almost any sequence, so long as all of them come into being and take effect,"[86] but Etzioni and Haas believe that the process moves from integration of adaptive functions (i.e., specific environmental control measures) to the economic, political, and finally normative (ideational) sectors, or vice versa.[87] Whatever the sequence of sectoral integration, it is clear that integration must be multisectoral.

---

[84] Etzioni, *Studies in Social Change*, pp. 36–78.

[85] *Ibid.*, pp. 46–47.

[86] Karl Keutsch *et al.*, *Political Community and the North Atlantic Area* (Princeton: Princeton University Press, 1957), p. 70.

[87] Etzioni, *op. cit.*, pp. 42–51; Haas, "The Challenge of Regionalism," *International Organization*, XII, No. 4 (Autumn 1958), 448.

The movement of commodities, or the density of telephone calls and mail flow among different States, although helpful in demonstrating sectoral relationships, will not alone suffice either to denote the establishment of political community or even the propensity for political community (Soja, *Communications and Territorial Integration in East Africa;* Nye, *Patterns and Catalysts in Regional Integration*). In the first place, it is necessary to know what such densities mean; whether or not, for example, the individuals engaged in telephone conversations are communicating in a way that would essentially promote the development of community. Not only must other sectors contribute to the integrative process, but there may be a particular sequence or stage of sectoral integration destined to be more successful than another sequence. Thus, Etzioni argues that "industrialized societies might tend to merge in an adaptive-first, normative-last sequence," whereas "non-industrialized ones [might tend to do so] in a normative-first, adaptive-last sequence."[88] In either case, the integrative process is understood to entail more than the density of social or political interaction, and to involve, at a minimum, all the crucial sectors of the merging societies.

Despite their essential qualitative difference, the ideas of both the political system and the political community share the common premise that the significance of any particular phenomenon is relative to its relationship with other phenomena. Meaning, and especially social meaning, are defined in terms of the extent to which people or things are connected to or associated with one another in some functional relationship. The relationship itself is defined as *process,* and, as Hannah Arendt argues, "what the concept of process implies is that the concrete and the general, the single thing or event and the universal meaning, have parted company. The process, which alone makes meaningful whatever it happens to carry along, has thus acquired a monopoly of universality and significance."[89]

---

[88] Etzioni, *op. cit.,* p. 47.
[89] Hannah Arendt, *Between Past and Future, Eight Exercises in Political Thought* (New York: The Viking Press, Inc., 1968), p. 64.

1

THE FIELD OF
POLITICAL GEOGRAPHY

RICHARD HARTSHORNE

Recent Developments in
Political Geography

I. HISTORY OF THE FIELD

Political geography before the world war (I)

While it is true that the greatest developments in this field owe their stimulus to the changes caused by the World War, it is incorrect to consider political geography as a new field of knowledge first opened up at that time. In a sense, it is as old as the science of geography itself.

If Herodotus was a geographer, he was also a political geographer; Strabo certainly was both, as his description of the geographic basis of the Roman Empire shows. The relation of states to the natural conditions of their areas has been a subject of speculation of historians and philosophers as well as geographers from Plato through Montesquieu and Kant[1] to the present time. These speculative students developed a great wealth of hypotheses which they were not in a position to prove, but which provide a stimulating body of ideas for present students in the field, and which should make it unnecessary for them to spend much effort in that phase of investigation.

In contrast to the hypothetical work of the philosophic writers, Carl Ritter, often called the founder of modern geography in Germany, first attempted (1817) to base conclusions of political geography on the growing body of material of physical geography. Since then, a whole host of geographers have con-

---

From *American Political Science Review*, XXIX, No. 5 (1935), Part I, 785–804. Reprinted by permission.

[1] In his discussion of geography, Immanuel Kant provides for a political geography "founded entirely on physical geography." "Kant's Physische Geographie," *Philos. Bibl.*, B.A. 51, 2 Aufl. (Leipzig, 1904), p. 17 (after Maull).

sidered this subject, chiefly in terms of the relation of physical geography to political and military history.

Among the earlier workers were two of Ritter's disciples, the Swiss-American, Guyot (1849), and the early master of French geography, Elisée Réclus (*L'Homme et la terre*, 6 vols., 1905–8); the Russian geographer Metchnikoff, who wrote on the relation of civilization to the great river valleys (1889); a group of German writers headed by H. F. Helmolt, who published nine volumes of geographic history under the title of *Weltgeschichte* (1889, later translated into English); two English geographers, Mackinder (1890) and Hereford George (1901); and three American geographers who studied the relation of geography to American history: Shaler (1891), Brigham (1903), and Semple (1903).[2]

More recently, there have been significant contributions by Fairgrieve, Cornish, and Kermack in England, and by Semple and Wright in America, not to mention the works in foreign languages.[3] Huntington's special studies of the relation of climate to history are well-known.[4] In addition, the standard geographies of major world regions, such as those of Lyde, Mackinder, Partsch, Hettner, etc., have usually included sections on historical or political geography.[5]

In the field of political geography as distinct from the more general historical geography, the foundations were laid by Friedrich Ratzel, whose *Politische Geographie*,[6] published in 1897, is universally recognized as the first systematic

---

[2] These and a number of similar works may be found in the bibliography in Franklin Thomas, *The Environmental Basis of Society; A Study in the History of Sociological Thought* (New York, 1925). Two have recently been republished: Hereford B. George, *The Relations of Geography and History* (rev. and enl. by Howarth and Fawcett, Oxford, 1924); Ellen C. Semple, *American History and Its Geographic Conditions* (rev. by C.F. Jones, Boston, 1933). Mackinder enlarged upon his earlier papers, notably "The Geographical Pivot of History" (*Geog. Jour.*, April 1904), in which Haushofer finds much of the world's history of 1914–1924 correctly predicted, in *Democratic Ideals and Reality* (London, 1919).

[3] James Fairgrieve, *Geography and World Power* (London, 1915, 1921); V. Cornish, *The Great Capitals; An Historical Geography* (London and New York, 1922); W.R. Kermack, *Human Environment and Progress: The Outline of World Historical Geography* (chiefly the British Isles) (Edinburgh and London, 1927), and two previous studies of Scotland and the British Empire; Ellen C. Semple, *Geography of the Mediterranean Region: Its Relation to Ancient History* (New York, 1931); J.K. Wright, *The Geographical Basis of European History* (New York, 1928). To these should be added the study of this continent by the English geographer, Rodwell Jones, Part 1 of Llewelyn R. Jones and P.W. Bryan, *North America; An Historical, Economic, and Regional Geography* (New York, 1924), and especially C.O. Paullin (J.K. Wright, ed.), *Atlas of the Historical Geography of the United States* (New York, 1932), abstract by Wright: "Sections and the National Growth," *Geog. Rev.*, 1932, pp. 353–360.

[4] Of Ellsworth Huntington's many publications, the most significant in this connection are *World Power and Evolution* (New Haven, 1919), and two studies of the geography of Biblical history: *Palestine and Its Transformation* (Boston, 1911) and Chaps. XII–XVII in *The Pulse of Progress, Including a Sketch of Jewish History* (New York, 1926).

[5] Aside from these well-known works, mention might be made of two early ones: C. Naumann and Josef Partsch, *Physikalische Geographie von Griechenland, mit besonderer Rücksicht auf das Altertum* (Breslau, 1895), pp. 97 ff.; Theobald Fischer, "Die iberische Halbinsel," in Kirchhoff's *Länderkunde von Europa* (Vienna, 1893), pt. 2, 2nd half; and of two more recent: Alfred Hettner, *Russland, eine geographische Betrachtung von Volk, Staat, und Kultur* (Leipzig, 1916); and I. Bowman, *Desert Trails of Atacama* (New York, 1924), Chap. V.

[6] Fr. Ratzel, *Politische Geographie* (Munich, 1897); 2nd ed. with additional title *oder die*

treatment of the subject. In France, where his *Anthropogeographie* was already well-known, this volume was discussed at great length by Vidal de la Blache,[7] a condensed article by Ratzel was published in French,[8] and Vallaux later used the *Politische Geographie* as the basis, at least for departure, of his two volumes in the same field.[9]

Unfortunately, Miss Semple, on whom geographers in England and America have largely depended for their knowledge of Ratzel's ideas, did little with his political geography.[10] In this field, a more important follower was the Swedish political scientist Kjellén, whose work was to have such a profound influence on the development of the subject in Germany after the World War. But for a generation Ratzel's work was almost the only major authority in the field, the framework for studies by Hassert, Schöne,[11] Sieger, Maull, Haushofer, and a few others.

On the whole, however, Ratzel's study did not have the effect that he expected. Geography was for some time carried along in the general upswing of the physical sciences (especially in America under the leadership of W.M. Davis). It was not until the World War emphasized the need for development of social sciences in general, and in particular stimulated popular as well as academic interest in political geography, that that part of their subject attracted the attention of many geographers.[12]

Summarizing for the century preceding the World War, the work in the border area between history and political science on the one hand and geography on the other was in large part that of geographers. Although historians have frequently had good reason to object to exaggerated conclusions or too simple generalizations in some of these geographic interpretations of history (compare with the school of economic interpretation), many historians have appreciated the value of the new point of view and methods offered. Thus, the French historian, Febvre, in his masterly examination of the work of his period

---

Geographie der Staaten, der Verkehrs, und des Krieges, 1903; 3rd ed. rev. with chapter on the historical development of the subject by E. Oberhummer (Munich and Berlin, 1923). In addition should be listed: *Das Meer als Quelle der Völkergrösse* (Munich, 1900); *Die Vereinigten Staaten von Nordamerika,* Bd. 2, *Politische Geographie* (Munich, 1893); and various special studies in *Kleine Schriften,* 2 vols. (Munich, 1906).

7 Vidal de la Blache, "La géographie politique d'après les écrits de M. Fr. Ratzel," abstract and rev. in *Ann. de Geog.* (March, 1898), pp. 97–111.

8 Ratzel, "Le sol, la societé, et l'état," *Année Sociol.,* 1898–99.

9 See the preface to each of Camille Vallaux, *Géographie sociale: le mer* (1908), and *Le sol et l'état* (Paris, 1911).

10 Though in her great treatise which is derived in large part from his *Anthropogeographie* she devotes a chapter or so to political geography. E.C. Semple, *Influences of Geographic Environment* (New York, 1911), Chap. III and parts of Chap. VII.

11 Emil Schöne's little book was intended as "a popularization of the ideas of Ratzel," *Politische Geographie* (Aus Natur- und Geisteswelt series, Leipzig, 1911).

12 Nevertheless, Haushofer feels that the subject, as developed by Ratzel, Vallaux, and Mackinder did have a notable influence on political thought and action in England and France—in the latter through the École de Politique—but unfortunately little or none in Germany. "Politische Erdkunde und Geopolitik," in *Freie Wege Vergleichender Erdkunde* (Festgabe, E.V. Drysgalski, Munich, 1925), pp. 94 ff.

—especially that of Ratzel, Vallaux, and Vidal de la Blache—pays this tribute: "Anyone nowadays who wants instruction on the relation between the land and history—I mean conscientiously and with guarantees—must apply to them (the geographers) first."

. . .

The world war and political geography

The changes in the political map of Europe which were discussed in all countries during and after the war drew the attention of geographers in America, as well as in Europe, to specific problems in political geography. Many were drawn into active work for their governments, and the following, in particular, functioned as experts at the Peace Conference: Ogilvie for England, de Martonne for France, Romer for Poland, Cvijić for Serbia, and Bowman and Douglas Johnson for the United States. A large number of others made special studies of particular boundary problems.[13] Several geographers published somewhat general studies of world political problems for non-academic readers, which expressed purely personal points of view but included much expert information.[14]

Most of these geographers have returned to their former areas of work. On the whole, the products of this period reflect the lack of adequate development of political geography as a discipline, as well as a lack of sufficient grounding of most of the writers in the subject, even so far as it had been developed. Their problems were too complex for either their training or their information, and the nationalist spirit was usually the dominating influence. There were, however, notable exceptions—not only men like Sieger and Maull, who had long been studying political geography, but also others like the physiographers Supan and Penck, who, in spite of intense nationalism, were able to make valuable contributions to the development of theory on the subject.[15]

---

[13] Including Partsch, Penck, Krebs, Sapper, Volz, Sölch, Teleki, Gallois, Holdich, and Lyde.

[14] Alfred Hettner, *England's Weltherrschaft* (Leipzig, 1915, revised 1928); G. Wegener, *Die geographische Ursachen des Weltkrieges* (Berlin, 1920), summarized in "Erdraum und Shicksal," *Z. f. Geopolitik*, 1931, pp. 542–557; H.J. Mackinder, *Democratic Ideals and Reality* (London, 1919); A. Demangeon, *Le declin de l'Europe* (Paris, 1920, trans. as *America and the Race for World Dominion*, New York, 1921); O.D. Von Engeln, *Inheriting the Earth; or the Geographical Factor in National Development* (New York, 1922).

[15] Penck, *Über politische Grenzen* (Rektoratsrede, Berlin, 1917). (Only the theoretical discussion, the major part, is of value now; it is unfortunate that the applications suggested for Europe, given in an address made during the heat of the war, could not have been omitted in publication.) Supan's work will be noted later. For other work in political geography in Europe during this period, notably that of Fleure, Newbigin, Cvijić, and Teleki, see the full list in W.L.G. Joerg, "Recent Geographical Work in Europe," *Geog. Rev.*, 1922, pp. 431–784. In America, the most important—other than Bowman, *The New World*—were Leon Dominian, *The Frontiers of Language and Nationality in Europe* (New York, 1917), and Douglas Johnson's studies in the special field of military geography: *Topography and Strategy in the War* (New York, 1917), and *Battlefields of the World War*, 2 vols. (New York, 1921).

Political geography since the period of the world war

The stimulus of the war and post-war period had, moreover, its more permanent effects. Especially in Germany, where dissatisfaction with the territorial settlements of the Peace Conference greatly increased popular as well as academic interest in the subject, has political geography developed. Systematic treatises of the field, based fundamentally on Ratzel, have been published by Supan, Dove, Vogel, Dix, and Maull.[16] Of these, the most important is Maull's strikingly objective and scholarly, if somewhat too encyclopedic, work. In addition to a great wealth of factual material, the author provides a comparative study of the various points of view of nearly all his predecessors.[17] Unfortunately, Sieger's plans for a full treatment of the subject were cancelled by his death (1926); his keen analysis and development of precise terminology are available only in a dozen or more articles scattered through various periodicals, some difficult to obtain.[18]

Of special studies in the political geography of certain regions and boundary areas, there have been a great number by Obst, Passarge, Uhlig, Volz, Sölch, and others.[19]

But increasingly the younger German geographers interested in the political aspect of the subject have taken their lead from Karl Haushofer,[20] the founder (with Obst) and editor of the *Zeitschrift fur Geopolitik*. The work of this school is based in part directly on Ratzel, but particularly on the system of the Swed-

---

[16] Alexander Supan, *Leitlinien der allgemeinen politischen Geographie: Naturlehre des Staates* (Berlin and Leipzig, 1918, 1922); K. Dove, *Allgemeine politische Geographie* (Leipzig, 1920); Walther Vogel, *Politische Geographie* (Leipzig, 1922); Arthur Dix, *Politische Geographie: Weltpolitisches Handbuch* (Munich, 1922, 1923); Otto Maull, *Politische Geographie* (Berlin, 1925).

[17] "Without doubt it deserves a distinctly prominent place in the modern geographic literature." J. Sölch, review in *Geografiska Annaler*, 1925, pp. 251–255. Other reviews by Sieger in *Geog. Z.*, 1926, p. 379, and Schluter in *Geog. Anz.*, 1926, pp. 62–66.

[18] For an appreciation, with full bibliography, see J. Sölch, "Robert Sieger," *Geog. Z.*, 1927, pp. 305–313. Perhaps the most valuable single reference is "Zur politische-geographischen Terminologie," *Z. Ges. f. Erdkunde Berlin*, 1917, pp. 497–529; 1918, pp. 48–69.

[19] Erich Obst, *England, Europe, und die Welt: eine geopolitische-, weltwirtschaftliche Studie* (Berlin, 1927); Johann Sölch, various articles on the Tyrol, including "The Brenner Region," in *Sociol. Review*, October 1927, pp. 1–17; S. Passarge, "Ägypten und der Arabische Orient: eine politische-geographische Studie* (Weltpol. Bücherei, Bd., 28, Berlin, 1931). Special mention should be made of the cartographic work, as applied to political geography, in W. Volz and H. Schwalm, *Die deutsche Ostgrenze, Unterlagen zur Erfassung der Grenzzerreisungsschäden* (Leipzig, 1927), and H. Overbeck and G.W. Saute, *Saar-Atlas* (Gotha, 1934); see my review in *Geog. Rev.*, October 1934, 680–682.

[20] Formerly a regular officer of the German army, Haushofer's intention to transfer to academic life was postponed by the War to 1920, when he retired as a major-general. Now professor at the University of Munich, his best work is on Japan, where he was stationed as a military attache in 1908–1911. Karl Haushofer, *Dai Nihon: Betrachtungen über Gross-Japans Wehrkraft, Weltstellung and Zukunft* (Berlin, 1913); *Das Japanische Reich in seiner geographischen Entwicklung* (Vienna, 1921); *Japan und die Japaner, eine Landes- und Volkskunde* (Leipzig, 1923, 1933). For an appreciation of the work of this significant leader, see "Karl Haushofer, zum 60 Geburtstag," *Z. f. Geopolitik*, 1929, pp. 709–725.

ish political scientist Kjellén,[21] whose concept of the state as an organism was taken from Ratzel.[22] Taking the name of *Geopolitik* from Kjellén, and ultimately enlarging its scope greatly, the members of this group,[23] publishing in their monthly magazine as well as in numerous pamphlets and books, have met with enthusiastic response among the nationalistic reading public in Germany, if not in academic circles. In the reconstruction of education in Nazi Germany, the subject of Geopolitik will apparently occupy that place of importance which its proponents have long been claiming for it. Whether this is properly to be considered a part of geography, and not rather a part of political science, will be discussed later; at any rate, the work to date has largely been carried on by geographers.

While French geographers have not shown anything like the same interest, there have been many studies of boundaries and border areas by Gallois, Demangeon, de Martonne, and others, as well as two works of major importance. Demangeon wrote on the British Empire as a type study in "colonial geography, an independent branch of knowledge" which should "study the effects arising from the contact between the two types of people who are called upon to associate in a colony, the one civilized . . . the other isolated and self-centered."[24] For such a purpose, it seems unfortunate to have selected the very empire in which self-governing dominions are so important, areas that hardly fit the concept of "colony" from which the author starts.

More important is the theoretical treatise in which Vallaux, whose earlier work has already been mentioned, joined with Brunhes to write *La géographie de l'histoire*,[25] which includes a general survey of the field of political geography, based chiefly on Vallaux' earlier *Le sol et l'état*. Unfortunately, little cognizance is taken of the work done in Germany since Ratzel and foreign

---

21 Rudolf Kjellén (1864–1922). For an appreciation of his work, see "Kjellén" (by Vogel) in *Encyc. Soc. Sciences*, or, in more detail, by Sieger in *Z. f. Geopolitik*, 1924, pp. 339–346. Most important of his studies were: *Stormakterna*, 4 vols. (Stockholm, 1910–14, trans. *Die Grossmächte der Gegenwart, Leipzig*, 1915, 22nd ed., ed. by K. Haushofer, *Die Grossmächte vor und nach dem Weltkriege*, Berlin and Leipzig, 1930); *Staten som lifsform* (Stockholm, 1916, trans. *Der Staat als Lebensform*, Berlin, 1917, 1924); *Grundriss zu einem System der Politik* (Berlin, 1920).

22 In addition to the work of Ratzel and Kjellén, Haushofer lays particular emphasis on Fairgrieve's study, *op. cit.*, which he has had published in German (trans. by Martha Haushofer, his wife) with an introduction by himself: J. Fairgrieve, *Geographie und Weltmacht, eine Einleitung in die Geopolitik* (Berlin, 1925).

23 Of the original group, Obst and Maull, formerly co-editors with Haushofer of the *Zeitschrift*, seem to have dropped out. Most prominent now are Lautenach, Albrecht Haushofer (son), and Baumann.

24 Albert Demangeon, *L'Empire britannique: étude de géographie coloniale* (Paris, 1923), trans. as *The British Empire: A Study in Colonial Geography* (New York and London, 1925, German trans., Berlin, 1926).

25 J. Brunhes and C. Vallaux, *La géographie de l'histoire: Géographie de la paix et de la guerre sur terre et sur mer* (Paris, 1921). Abstract and review by Douglas Johnson, *Geog. Rev.* 1922, pp. 278–293. Mention may be made also of J. Brunhes and Deffontaines, "Géographie politique," Pt. 3 of *Géographie humaine de la France* (Vol. II of G. Hanotaux, *Histoire de la nation francaise*, Paris, 1926).

students are disturbed by the marked national prejudice in the second half of the book dealing with the World War and its settlement.

Recent publications in the English-speaking countries have been equally out of touch with the development of the subject in Germany. In England, the chief workers have been Mackinder, whose earliest work was contemporaneous with Ratzel, and Cornish, and Fawcett.[26] In American geography, Bowman's by-product of the Peace Conference stands alone as a major work. Wright's brief but excellent outline for the historical geography of Europe has already been mentioned. Other publications have been limited to periodical articles by Bowman, Wright, Whittlesey, and others.

II. DEFINITION OF THE FIELD

Our brief survey of the history of political geography shows it to be a field in which geographers have not merely laid out claims, but have done a very considerable amount of valuable work. Nevertheless, there is wide divergence of opinion, not only among geographers in general, but also among those working in political geography itself, as to the proper nature of that field and the scope that it should include.

Political geography defined as a study of relationships

If political geography is to be oriented properly in the general field of geography as a part of human geography, any definition of it must be based on a definition of the field of human geography.[27] Formerly, most geographers defined human geography in terms of relationships between earth features, or natural environment, on the one hand, and man with his activities on the other. Expressed in terms of "geographical control" or "geographic influences," this was, in part, derived from Ratzel's *Anthropogeographie*, though as Febvre (following Durkheim) shows, it represented only a part of Ratzel's view of the field. That this concept of "environmentalism" has largely dominated the subject for a generation may well be a result, in part, of the fact that geography occupied no independent position in universities outside of Germany, but was

---

26 H.J. Mackinder, "The Physical Basis of Political Geography," *Scott. Geog. Mag.*, VI (1890), p. 73 ff.: *Democratic Ideals and Reality* (London, 1919); Vaughan Cornish, *The Great Capitals; An Historical Geography* (London, 1922), very largely political geography: *Geography of Imperial Defense* (London, 1922); C.B. Fawcett, *Frontiers; A Study in Political Geography* (Oxford, 1918); *A Political Geography of the British Empire* (London and New York, 1933).

27 For a discussion of changing concepts of geography, see Alfred Hettner, *Die Geographie; ihre Geschichte, ihr Wesen, und ihre Methoden* (Breslau, 1927, pp. 73–109, 121–131); Febvre, *op. cit.*, 1–67; Carl Sauer, "Recent Developments in Cultural Geography," *op. cit.*; I. Bowman, *Geography in Relation to the Social Sciences*, Chap. I; and "Geography" in *Encyclopedia of the Social Sciences*, Vol. 6, pp. 621 ff., sections by Sauer, Vallaux, and Sapper. Brunhes' chapter in *History and Prospects of the Social Sciences* contributes little beyond a detailed discussion of the points of view of Ratzel and Brunhes.

either the handmaiden of history, as in France and Belgium, or of economics, as in England, or was a side-line of geology, as in America.[28] The students of geography were constantly endeavoring to demonstrate its significance in terms of established fields, and so the subject was defined not so much in its own terms as in terms of its relations to other fields.

Although it is a gross error to assume that Ratzel tried to prove all human activities were geographically determined, his terminology did lead easily to exaggeration, which Vidal de la Blache, the founder of modern geography in France, met by substituting the concept of "geographic possibilities." Many other geographers have criticized the extremist point of view as vigorously as have critics from the outside, and geographers in general feel justified in being a little weary of the continued attack on the straw-man of "geographic determinism."

A decade ago, Barrows sought to free geography from the danger of exaggerated claims, which the terms "control" or "influence" had inspired, and which had aroused the attack of the social scientists. Reversing the approach, he spoke of man's adjustments to the natural environment, but he maintained the fundamental idea of geography as a "science of relationships."[29]

Whichever way the definition is stated, the field for political geography as part of the main field can easily be derived from it: the study of the relations between man's political activities and organizations (including the state, but also parties, etc.) and the natural environment or earth conditions, whether stated directly or conversely. This is clearly the basis, either stated or implied, for the work of Vallaux, Fairgrieve, Newbigin, Fawcett, Brigham, and Semple. As Vallaux puts it, the essential problem of political geography is to determine whether "the life of political societies is determined, in part at least, by the natural frame in which they develop; in what manner the soil, air, and water ... relate themselves to the collective action of men."[30]

With this concept of human geography in mind, Fawcett, in his recent study of the British Empire, states as his object: "to set out and examine those geographical facts which are of direct importance in their influence on the development and organization of the British Empire and its component parts." With such a definition (Fawcett, *op.cit.*, p.v.), it is not surprising to find the excellent material of this book presented in a confused mixture of general and political geography.

At the present time, much of the work in Geopolitik in Germany is pursued on a very similar basis. According to the founder, Haushofer, "Geopolitik is

---

28 Douglas Johnson describes these differences in development in "The Geographic Prospect," *Annals Assoc. Amer. Geog.*, 1929, pp. 170–190.

29 H.H. Barrows, "Geography as Human Ecology," in *Annals Assoc. Amer. Geog.*, 1922, pp. 1–16; for a favorable response in England, see P.M. Roxby, "The Scope and Aims of Human Geography," *Brit. Assoc. Ad. Sc.* (Sec. E. Bristol, 1930); also published in *Scot. Geog. Mag.*, 1930, pp. 276–290.

30 *Le sol et l'état*, pp. 7–8. Similarly in Brunhes and Vallaux, *op. cit.*, pp. 24–25, 267.

the study of the earth relations (*Erdgebundenheit*) of political occurrences. . . . The character of the earth's surfaces . . . gives to Geopolitik its frame within which the course of political events *must* [italics mine] take place if they are to have permanent success."[31]

Clearly, such definitions provide the political geographer a wide range for his activities, so wide that it need not surprise one if he reaches far into the area of political science, where his lack of complete training betrays him into fallacious and exaggerated conclusions, to say nothing of gross national partisanship. No wonder then, that in spite of the fruitful work of many of these students, their critics within the field of geography have often wanted to ban political geography completely.

An alternative definition

Bowman presents a more practical, and at the same time less controversial, definition by suggesting that geography "is also and chiefly a study of living conditions of mankind as affected by regional combinations of specific soil types . . . (and other environmental conditions), together with production habits and possibilities, and landscape effects that give every area its characteristic stamp."[32] Geography, then, "has political implications because it helps to provide an understanding of the adaptations of group life to the environment of a given area of political control," it ". . . helps indicate the scope of national limitations and possibilities."[33] Further, from his critique of Maull's *Politische Geographie*, we may infer that geography should "offer organized expert knowledge of what we may call the original set-up of the world," and "judgments respecting the political set-up of the world today . . . ; rational information of use to policy-makers in government."[34]

That the geographer should be able and ready to supply expert knowledge is not to be questioned. But what is the field within which his knowledge may be presumed to be, in fact, "expert"? Few geographers will be in a position to pass judgments on all of the questions which these statements might include. In his own treatment of world problems, Bowman clearly does not intend to keep within any definite limitation of the field.

Geography as the science of earth-areas

In recent decades, many geographers, notably in Germany and Belgium, more recently in this country, have defined their field in terms not of relationships between things, but in terms of the things themselves, namely, the individual areas or regions of the earth, with all the elements, both natural and otherwise, which in their varied combinations, form the character of those

---

31 Haushofer, Obst, Maull, and Lautensach, *Bausteine zur Geopolitik* (Berlin, 1928).
32 *Op. cit.*, p. 13.
33 *Ibid.*, p. 205.
34 *Geog. Rev.*, pp. 511–512.

areas. Hettner shows that this "chorological" conception of geography is far from new.[35] Based on the concept, as well as the term itself, of Ptolemy and Strabo, it reappeared in the geography of Humboldt and Ritter and was definitely expressed by F. Von Richthofen, who first among modern geographers used the classical term. Ratzel, from whom Semple and others derived their concept of "influences," in fact maintained, both in principle and in practice, in much of his work, the character of geography as the science of areas.

* * *

That American geographers have become more interested in the developments in Germany than have either their French or English colleagues is due largely to the vigorous efforts of Carl Sauer,[36] whose influence has been particularly marked among the younger workers.[37]

First in rank among the geographers who have concerned themselves with the epistemology of their subject is Alfred Hettner. For him geography is "the science of the earth surfaces, studied according to their local differences, of the continents, lands, regions (*Landschaften*), and localities." In addition to the study of individual areas, he includes the general comparative study of areas (*Länderkunde*). In the general system of the sciences, geography is analogous to history; the latter is concerned with the arrangement of phenomena in relation to time, the former in relation to place. One may say that the guiding principle for history is chronology; for geography, it is chorology. Hettner tells us that the philosopher Kant had come to essentially the same conclusion in his analysis of the field of knowledge.[38]

It must not be supposed that the chorographical concept of geography involves an abandonment of interest in relationships between "earth" and "man".... The difference involved in the new, or rather, resumed definition is essentially a difference in focus of attention, in the location of the central goal of the science. Geography is again fundamentally a science of places or areas rather than of supposed relations, but in its study of places it is concerned with the casual relations that may be found between the different elements that go to make up the landscape, or the "character," of the place or area. The study of the relationship then is subordinate to, and geographically significant only as a part of, the study of the area.... On this basis, Vidal accepts "historical

[35] *Op. cit.*, pp. 121–132. See also Sauer, *op. cit.*, pp. 175–182.

[36] Carl Sauer, "The Morphology of Landscape," *Univ. of Calif. Pub. in Geog.*, 1925, pp. 19–53; and the articles, previously cited, in *Recent Developments in the Social Sciences* and the *Encycl. of the Social Sciences*. As Sauer has noted in several places, Fenneman, in his presidential address in 1918, emphasized "the study of areas as the center of geography:" Nevin M. Fenneman, "The Circumference of Geography," *Annals Assoc. Amer. Geog.*, 1919, pp. 3–11.

[37] The current view of many of these is reflected by Preston James in "The Terminology of Regional Description," *Annals Assoc. Amer. Geog.*, July 1934, pp. 78–86, in particular pp. 81–82.

[38] *Kant's Werke* (pub. by Schubert and Rosenkranz), Bd. 2, pp. 425 ff. (after Hettner, *op. cit.* p. 115).

events, in so far as they reveal qualities or potentialities of the countries where they occur, which would otherwise remain latent."[39]

Apparently all of these students recognize as a part of geography the comparative study of any particular element of the landscape in its relations to the remainder of the landscape, as found in the different regions of the world. Hettner, indeed, emphasizes the weakness of individual studies when the student has failed to study this "general geography," as the French and Germans call it, or "systematic geography," as most American geographers prefer to call it.

Political geography according to the chorographers

Applying Hettner's definition of the general field, the division, political geography, is the branch of systematic or general geography which concerns itself with those political phenomena of regions differing from place to place and bearing significant relations to other regional phenomena. For those who insist on the limitation to "observational facts," whatever that may mean, the field is rather narrowly restricted.... However, we might well say with Maull that the state itself constitutes a fact in the cultural landscape as observable as humidity or temperature in the natural landscape, though by many Americans commonly overlooked because of not having observed the differences in another state. ("State" is used throughout in its original sense, as the independent political area, not as one of the United States, for example.) Many German geographers have pointed to the effect of the state on a wide range of cultural landscape elements: farms, houses, roads, railroads, trade areas, etc. Conversely, as Maull and many other political geographers have pointed out, the states develop more or less in lands and land types, and constitute in fact "one of the most striking expressions of the effect of landscape [or region—'Landschaft'] on the development of the earthy life."

Schlüter[40] objects to Maull's concept of the state as a space-organism, on the ground that it is a form of human society that is invisible and spiritual. Consequently, political geography, in his view, while an important outlying field of geography, is not a part of geography proper. Brunhes' viewpoint appears on the whole to be similar, though his somewhat illusive discussions are difficult to interpret. The facts of political geography apparently lie "beyond the essential facts,"[41] but are included in the purpose of study of human geography;[42] on the other hand, "political geography is properly only a part of the geography of history," which as a whole belongs to history rather than to geography.

---

39 Vidal de la Blache, "Les caractères distinctifs de la géographie," *Annales de Geog.*, 1913, p. 299.

40 In his review of Maull's *Politische Geographie*, *Geog. Anz.*, 1926, pp. 62–66. Maull replies in the same volume, pp. 245–253.

41 *Human Geography*, pp. 543–568.

42 Brunhes, in *History and Prospects of the Social Sciences*, p. 55.

What then is the value in defining narrowly the "proper" field for geography, or its "essential facts," if one recognizes outlying areas of apparently indefinite extent? If geographers may "follow the influence of human geography into the very midst of history" with the sole provision that "they strive never to lose sight of those 'essential facts' which are the 'touchstones' of true geography,"[43] there would seem to be no corner of the whole realm of social science in which a somewhat far-sighted geographer might not feel free to work. . . .

Consequently we return to the conviction that a proper field for political geography should be found within the confines of geography. But a political geography of any major importance cannot accept the limitation of "observational features" narrowly interpreted to mean features directly and physically observable. The fundamental concept of *Landschaft*, as Passarge or Hettner understand it (or "landscape" as James re-defines the word), justifies the following conclusions: political boundaries are a proper object of study by geographers regardless of whether marked by stones or not; and a division into states is one of the major cultural facts of an area (of its *Kulturlandschaften*), significantly related to many other facts of the cultural and also natural landscape, regardless of whether or not that division is physically observable.

Hettner defines political geography as the study of space relations of states and their characters, in so far as those are related to other regional phenomena. Passarge similarly says it is the study of the reciprocal relations between space and political organizations.[44] Vogel's definition is essentially the same, except for the use of "earth" or "earth surfaces" instead of "space."[45] According to Maull, it is the study of "geographic nature (*Wesen*) and geographic forms of the state or the study of the state in its geographic association (*Gebundenheit*), in its dependence on the natural and cultural landscape."[46]

Disregarding the minor differences between these definitions, we may arrive at a somewhat simpler formulation. If geography according to the "chorologists" is the science of areas, *then political geography is the science of political areas*, or more specifically, *the study of the state as a characteristic of areas in relation to the other characteristics of areas.* . . .

---

43 Brunhes, *Human Geography*, p. 552.
44 S. Passarge, "Aufgaben und Methoden der Politische Geographie," in *Z. f. Politik*, 1931, p. 444.
45 Vogel, *Politische Geographie*, pp. 6–7.
46 *Op. cit.* p. 44.

RICHARD HARTSHORNE

What is Political Geography?

Political geography . . . has long been recognized as an essential part of geography. It remains nevertheless one of the less-developed parts. Perhaps this is a result of the desire of geographers of the 18th and early 19th centuries to escape from the complete domination of political areas as the sole framework of what was called regional geography. Furthermore, to escape from subordination to history or to statecraft they emphasized the physical or natural factors that make for significant differences between areas, and, becoming increasingly imbued with the spirit of the rapidly developing natural sciences, they tended to ignore political boundaries almost completely.

European geographers found a much more congenial spirit of international scientific cooperation when they concentrated on aspects of geography in which differences of opinion did not arouse nationalist sentiments. Geographers in the United States, on the other hand, living and studying within the huge territory of their single nation, rightly regarded its division into forty-eight more or less arbitrary units as of minor importance, but failed to recognize that this was far from true of the differences among the areas of independent states.

A more realistic viewpoint was forced upon geographers by the events of World War I. Several geographers of the United States were called upon by the government to make studies of European territorial problems, both in preliminary work carried on at the American Geographical Society in New York and as members of President Wilson's staff at the Peace Conference. None of them had had specific training in political geography and none had published in this field. Essentially a new subject to them, they applied their geo-

---

"Political Geography," *American Geography: Inventory and Prospect,* Preston E. James and Clarence F. Jones, eds. (Syracuse, N.Y.: Syracuse University Press, 1954), pp. 169–178. Reprinted by permission.

graphic training to it, but without being able to draw upon any system of methods, terminology, or objectives.

Some of the geographers who participated in that work were stimulated thereby to publish studies in political geography, but none of them turned to this field as an area of specialization. In the two decades that followed, only a few younger geographers concentrated attention on political geography. At one time, H.H. Sprout suggested that political geography should be developed as a part of the field of political science.[1] Many more geographers, however, though not specializing in this field, made studies of problems in political geography as aspects of the broad treatment of specific areas of the world in which they were specializing. In texts dealing with major areas of the world, such as the well-known volumes by George B. Cressey, Preston E. James, and Robert S. Platt, attention was paid to the political geography of the individual countries studied.

World War II led to the introduction of many more courses in political geography in graduate schools, liberal arts colleges, and teacher's colleges. Interest in political geography at the secondary level is reflected in the appearance of a school text on geography and world affairs,[2] written under the direction of a scholar of standing in political geography. The number of scholars engaged primarily in research in this field, however, remains small. In perhaps no other branch of geography has the attempt to teach others gone so far ahead of the pursuit of learning by the teachers.

Since much of what has been published in political geography has resulted less from concern to develop a field of scholarship, and more from a desire to contribute to an understanding of international problems, it is not surprising that there has been little agreement on the nature and scope of the field. At the time Isaiah Bowman wrote the first important work on this subject in America there was no "body of principles or body of doctrine with respect to political geography," nor did he attempt to construct one.[3] Rather his book, *The New World*,[4] represented a study of international relations as viewed by a geographer. In that field its methods of examining specific territorial problems of the world, country by country, opened a new path which contrasted with the methods of both diplomatic history and studies of the principles of international law and international relations. In the discussions of the specific problems, however, students found here no method or system demonstrating a distinctive character for political geography, with the important exception, generally recognized as the most outstanding contribution of the work, that an extraordinarily large amount of material was presented on maps.

In his review of the field early in the 1930's, Richard Hartshorne found in

---

1 H.H. Sprout, "Political Geography as a Political Science Field," *Amer. Polit. Sci. Rev.*, XXV (1931), 439–442.

2 S.B. Jones and M.F. Murphy, *Geography and World Affairs* (Chicago, 1950).

3 From a letter written by Isaiah Bowman in 1937, in which he added that "there were political geographies, a bundle of nationalistic philosophies outside the scope of science."

4 Bowman, *The New World: Problems in Political Geography* (New York, 1921; 4th ed. rev., 1928).

the publications of American or English geographers no clear basis for determining the purpose and scope of political geography. He sought to establish such a basis by introducing the system developed by contemporary German geographers on the foundations laid down a generation earlier by Friedrich Ratzel. In the meantime, Derwent Whittlesey, who first among the geographers of the United States developed political geography as an academic subject of teaching and research, had released himself from the domination of the historical environmentalism of Ellen C. Semple and Harlan H. Barrows, a domination which was reflected in his earlier study of the historical relations of the United States and Cuba.[5] Whittlesey presented political geography as a study of areal differentiation based on political phenomena, a viewpoint that was in accord with the approach to geography as a whole then being adopted in the United States. Illustrated in various substantive writings, this view was outlined in a short article in 1935,[6] and a few years later in the introductory pages of his major work, *The Earth and the State*.[7] At the same time Samuel Van Valkenburg's *Elements of Political Geography*[8] presented a quite different view of the field.

GEOPOLITICS

With the outbreak of World War II, the interest in political geography was again focused on the immediate problems of international relations, particularly that of the geography of power. Many American geographers, as well as the general public and many military leaders, were impressed by exaggerated reports of the influence purportedly exerted in German strategic planning by the school of geopolitics which Karl Haushofer had developed in Germany. Consequently it became difficult to distinguish between political geography and the supposedly new field of geopolitics.[9]

The difficulty in determining the distinction between the two fields was intensified by lack of any clear statement by the followers of geopolitics, whether in Germany or later in this country, as to the purpose and scope of that field. Haushofer's statements of his own views tended to add confusion rather than to clarify, though his basic purposes ultimately became quite clear.[10]

In his early attempt to analyze the German work in geopolitics, in 1935, Hartshorne discussed these difficulties, but concluded that geopolitics, as viewed

---

[5] D. Whittlesey, "Geographic Factors in the Relation of the United States and Cuba," *Geographical Review*, XII (1922), 241–256.

[6] Whittlesey, "Political Geography: A Complex Aspect of Geography," *Education*, L (1935), 293–298.

[7] Whittlesey, *The Earth and the State* (New York, 1939).

[8] S. Van Valkenburg, *Elements of Political Geography* (New York, 1939).

[9] Whittlesey and others following him used the adjective form "geopolitical" not in the sense used by the German students of geopolitics, but simply as a useful abbreviation of the cumbersome phrase "political-geographic."

[10] Haushofer, whom the writer of this section found quite able to speak simple and clear German, wrote in a style extremely difficult for German as well as foreign readers, perhaps because of inability to write clear prose or possibly with the intention of obfuscating his reasoning while impressing his conclusions.

by the more conservative members of the group, represented simply the application of the knowledge and techniques of political geography to the problems of international relations. But as it was soon evident that these problems require many other kinds of knowledge, geopolitics, having gained popular success as a catchword, became both broader in scope and narrower in purpose: namely, to apply all kinds of knowledge about foreign areas to the problems of foreign policy of the German state.

Whittlesey demonstrated a considerable correspondence between the conclusions presented in scattered writings of Haushofer and others of the group on the one hand and the actual strategy subsequently followed by Hitler on the other.[11] The German geographer Carl Troll, however, in his post-mortem on the school of geopolitics[12] makes it at least doubtful that this correspondence represented a direct cause and effect relationship. Further, if such a relationship did result, from early personal contact between Hitler and Haushofer, it is not clear which of the two had the greater influence on the other. There can be no question, however, that Haushofer and his group, through publication and by teaching of young journalists, made very important contributions to internal propaganda, supplying a pseudo-scientific rationalization for the Nazi policy of expansion.

Nevertheless, many students in this country, both geographers and political scientists, urged the development of a field of geopolitics purified of its nationalistic German ingredients. They sought to look back to H.J. Mackinder and A.T. Mahan rather than to Haushofer, but they overlooked the fact that neither of those individuals had attempted, any more than had Haushofer, to provide a conceptual framework for a field of study, but had merely used what knowledge and techniques were available to them to draw conclusions for action on certain problems of power. N.J. Spykman, who had previously presented to his colleagues in political science detailed discussions of the importance of geography to foreign policy,[13] adopted the term, and applied many of the concepts of geopolitics to his war-time studies of the situation and needs of the United States.[14] His conclusions as well as those of less influential students were strongly opposed by various critics. Hans Weigert concluded his analysis of the German school with an emphatic warning lest the American prophets of geopolitics should indoctrinate both military leaders and the public in this country with doctrines no less dangerous than those that had been propagated in Germany.[15]

---

[11] Whittlesey, *German Strategy of World Conquest* (New York, 1942).

[12] C. Troll, "Geographic Science in Germany During the Period 1933 to 1945," *Annals Assn. Amer. Geogrs.*, XXXIX (1949), 128–135.

[13] N.J. Spykman, "Geography and Foreign Policy," *Amer. Polit. Sci. Rev.*, XXXII (1938), 28–50, 213–236; Spykman and A.A. Rollins, "Geographic Objectives in Foreign Policy," *ibid.*, XXXIII (1939), 391–410, 591–614.

[14] Spykman, *America's Strategy in World Politics* (New York, 1942); *idem, The Geography of Peace* (New York, 1944).

[15] H.W. Weigert, *Generals and Geographers: The Twilight of Geopolitics* (New York, 1942).

The disagreements that arose were not of the kind commonly involved in the attempt to determine facts and relationships. Rather, they stemmed from differences in fundamental assumptions of purpose and aspiration, assumptions seldom stated clearly either by the writer who held them or the opposing critics. Such failure to recognize basic assumptions is perhaps to be expected in a field whose nature and scope remain nebulous. One proponent, E.A. Walsh, while urging the development of "a future geopolitics, born of sanity and law and equity" provided no more definite concept of the field than "geopolitics, by which is meant a combined study of human geography and applied political sciences."[16]

The last statement reflects the intellectual difficulty involved in defining any applied field. The economic geographer who attempts to apply his knowledge to any practical problem finds that his problem demands the consideration of matters not commonly regarded as included in geography. In the application of knowledge to concrete problems, the problems determine what shall be studied; definitions of fields of study as divisions of the whole field of knowledge become "academic" in the sense of not useful to the immediate purpose.

Thus the erection of a single bridge may involve problems not only of the physics and chemistry of metals and the aesthetics of architectural design, but also problems of hydrography, geology, economics of transportation, and labor. Bridge construction and statecraft both require the integration of information, principles, and techniques from many disciplines; it does not follow that either can be made into a discipline itself.

Finally, in the application of knowledge to concrete problems, the question of purpose is always involved. If the purpose can be assumed as accepted by all students concerned in the development of an applied field—as is commonly true in such cases as the application of medical knowledge to the prevention of disease, or the application of engineering knowledge to the construction of bridges —the answer to the question is universal and no problem arises. Just the opposite is the case in the application of knowledge to the concrete problems of international relations: every state concerned has a different purpose and these are most often in conflict. As an applied field concerned with specific problems, geopolitics would appear inevitably to be divided into as many different schools as there are independent states.

CONVERGENCE OF POLITICAL GEOGRAPHY AND POLITICAL SCIENCE

Nevertheless the convergence of students from geography and from other social sciences on the problems of war and peace must be welcomed and encouraged, not only for the aid it may give to statesmen in reaching tolerable conclusions on international problems, but also for the sake of the increasing depth of understanding in all fields that should result from such cross-fertilization.

---

16 E.A. Walsh, "Geopolitics and International Morals," Weigert and Stefansson, eds., *Compass of the World: A Symposium on Political Geography* (New York, 1944), pp. 12–39.

The geographer, concerned with regions . . . has found in the political unit an example of an area that is homogeneous and cohesive in political terms, yet heterogeneous and perhaps not even cohesive in other terms. He studies the structure and functions of that area as a region homogeneous in political organization, heterogeneous in other respects. The political scientist, concerned with political processes, has found he must do more than develop generalizations independent of differences in different areas; the processes, which can only be partially described and analyzed in generalizations, must be studied as they operate in particular areas; he has been led increasingly to the study of what may be called regional politics.

Likewise in the field of international relations, grim reality has compelled students from all disciplines to focus on what may be called power analysis, the analysis of political units of power and the relations among them. Since these political units are defined by area and the relations among them are conditioned by space relations, geographers have long shown an interest in such problems. H.J. Mackinder presented nearly half a century ago a thesis of world power analysis and prognosis which for better or worse has become the most famous contribution of modern geography to man's view of his political world.[17] Mackinder's interest and purpose, it may be noted, were primarily political and practical and it is not surprising therefore that his hypothesis is much less firmly grounded than, for example, his more academic and geographic analysis of the foundation of Britain's seapower in the relation of Great Britain to "the British seas."[18]

Though many geographers have quoted and used Mackinder's thesis of the "heartland," Weigert is one of the few who have examined it critically.[19] It would appear to have greater interest for students of world politics, like Spykman, who not only examined it critically but also attempted a major revision. The influence of Mackinder's thinking is likewise notable in the studies of the Atlantic Ocean and of the problems of national power by H.H. Sprout and M. Sprout.[20] In these examinations of regional politics a substantial amount of geography has been included. Owen Lattimore's war-time and postwar studies of regional politics in the Far East are focused on the search for solutions to current problems and are based on a specialized knowledge of the area.[21] Of a different kind, dealing with strategic problems of a single area of strategic unity, is the study of the Mediteranean by W. Reitzel.[22]

---

[17] H.J. Mackinder, "The Geographical Pivot of History," *Geog. Journ.*, XXII (1904), 421–437; *idem, Democratic Ideals and Reality* (New York, 1919, 1942).

[18] Mackinder, *Britain and the British Seas* (Oxford, 1906, 1930).

[19] H. W. Weigert, "Mackinder's Heartland," Weigert, Stefansson, and Harrison, eds., *New Compass of the World* (New York, 1949).

[20] Sprout and Sprout, "Command of the Atlantic Ocean," *Encyclopedia Britannica* (1946), II, 637; *idem, Foundations of National Power* (New York, 1951).

[21] O. Lattimore, *The Situation in Asia* (Boston, 1949).

[22] W. Reitzel, *The Mediterranean: Its Role in America's Foreign Policy* (New York, 1948).

An examination of these works reveals the almost unlimited variety of things that may have to be assessed if one is to reach a thorough evaluation of national power, a list that may quite literally include "shoes and ships and sealing wax, cabbages and kings."

Geographers can and have contributed information and techniques for the evaluation of many of these factors. In greatest volume, perhaps, have been studies of the physical and economic conditions within particular countries, studies prepared for governmental use and, therefore, unfortunately not published. One important aspect of production for national power, the occurrence and development of mineral resources essential for modern industry and war, has been most intensively studied and presented in well-known works of economic geologists.

. . .

Geographers have also studied the strategic situation of major world areas, demonstrating the geographic technique of viewing power distribution in terms of space relationships. A number of such studies are included in the two symposia edited by Weigert, V. Stefansson, and R.E. Harrison;[23] and Stephen B. Jones has published several in the series of memoranda of the Yale Institute of International Studies.

Many other factors of national power, however, may be unfamiliar to the geographer. For the evaluation, say, of the strength or weakness inherent in the one-party dictatorship of the Soviet Union versus the two-party democracy supporting a strong executive in Great Britain, or the multi-party legislature dominating the executive in France, the knowledge and techniques of the student of government are essential. Therefore it is of the utmost practical importance that problems of international relations should be studied by the convergence of students from all of the disciplines that can contribute to their solution. Workers from various fields will and should seek to integrate the findings from the several disciplines in relation to specific problems, whether they seek this integration jointly in research teams or individually. The analysis of national power represents a distinct area of convergence, not only of geography and political science, but also of economics, anthropology, and psychology. It would seem well to identify this area of joint interest with a clear and simple name, such as "power analysis" rather than to obscure it by the all-embracing term, geopolitics, the origin of which is steeped in error, exaggeration, and intellectual poison.

Experience from the history of science indicates that each discipline participating in such a joint undertaking will be able to render its maximum contribution if it develops to the utmost its own body of principles and techniques. The formulation of concepts cannot be done in isolation, to be sure; but such formulations must be done independently. In the remainder of this chapter,

---

23 Weigert and Stefansson, eds., *op. cit.;* Weigert, Stefansson, and Harrison, eds., *op. cit.*

therefore, attention is concentrated on political geography as an integral part of the whole field of geography.

POLITICAL GEOGRAPHY AS A BRANCH
OF GEOGRAPHY

Even when the opinion of geographers concerning the nature and scope of political geography is examined there is still a wide divergence. This divergence is illustrated by the great variety of methods followed by the numerous geographers who contributed to the symposia edited by Weigert, Stefansson, and Harrison. The divergence is even more striking in the book on *World Political Geography* by G.E. Pearcy, R.H. Fifield and associates.[24] In the introductory chapters by George T. Renner and Etzel Pearcy, political geography is identified with geopolitics purified of its irrelevant Nazi aspects. Renner attempts to summarize the different viewpoints of American political geographers in terms of three schools, but one may doubt whether the scholars he names would accept his interpretation of their writings. However, there is little indication that the writers of the subsequent chapters were guided by the views expressed in the introductory chapter.

The earlier attempts of Whittlesey and Hartshorne to determine the nature of the field have been mentioned previously. Somewhat different views have been offered by Stephen B. Jones[25] and J.K. Wright.[26] More recently, and partly as a result of preliminary discussions of the committee . . . ,[27] Hartshorne presented in his presidential address to the Association of American Geographers in 1949 an appeal for "a more geographical political geography" in a paper which emphasized the "functional approach" to the subject, thereby marking a major change as compared with the views he had published in 1935.

Discussions in the committee demonstrated not merely the existence of a variety of views regarding the scope of this field, which might well be a healthy situation. These discussions also demonstrated that geographers have tended to nibble at the more obvious aspects, such as boundaries, capitals, or international waterways, or, on the other hand, when endeavoring to cover the political geography of a whole state or larger area they have had in mind no systematic concept of what topics should be included, of what questions should be posed or which answers are to be sought.

The committee therefore felt that, in reviewing the work that has been done and in seeking to offer guidance for future work, it was desirable not merely to

---

24 G.E. Pearcy, R.H. Fifield and associates, *World Political Geography* (New York, 1948).
25 S.B. Jones, "Field Geography and Postwar Political Problems," *Geog. Rev.*, XXXIII (1943), 446–456.
26 J.K. Wright, "Training for Research in Political Geography," *Annals Assn. Amer. Geogrs.*, XXXIV (1944), 190–201.
27 Committee on Political Geography, including (in addition to Richard Hartshorne) J.O.M. Broek, George Kish, Robert S. Platt, Malcolm J. Proudfoot, Stephen B. Jones, and Samuel Van Valkenburg.

determine the major topics that have been studied in political geography, but also to arrange these in an organized system that would make clear the relation of each topic to the whole and reveal gaps that need development. With such a framework any geographer interested in examining particular topics in political geography could see the relationship of his topic to the field as a whole and to the overall study of areal likenesses and differences—that is, to geography.

It is appropriate for geographers to begin, not with a verbal definition, but with a map. The primary facts in political geography are presented in the common political map. . . . Such a map presents an important degree of reality in showing each sovereign state with a distinctive symbol covering the whole of its area; but . . . also . . . such a map conceals important differences. We know that, in any particular case, some parts of a state may consist of barren mountains, others of fertile lowlands; some parts may be highly industrialized with primarily urban populations, others are largely rural and agricultural; there may be different languages spoken in different parts of the same state and diverse religions followed; portions of the state area may have recently belonged to another state and their populations may still feel themselves attached to the former state rather than to the one in which, as a result of war, they have been assigned; or indeed areas long recognized as parts of the state may be largely wilderness inhabited by scattered tribes who hardly know even the name of the state in which they are included on the political map.

While these cases refer to sovereign states, similar conditions may be found in political divisions at lower ranks. Thus the State of Tennessee is presented on the common political map as a homogeneous unit, and, on maps purporting to show political attitudes, it has appeared in the past as a part of "the solid South," blanketed as a terrain of one political party. Closer inspection, however, shows that over a third of the counties may have majorities of the opposing party, and the regions revealed by mapping these data show marked correspondence to the economic and racial differences in the several portions of the State: the Mississippi lowlands, the Nashville Basin, the Tennessee Valley, and the mountain region. These contrasts are significant not merely for those interested in interpreting or predicting election returns; the political differences, and the cultural, economic, and physical differences which underlie them, present serious problems to the operation of the State of Tennessee as a coherent unit.[28]

In each of the cases cited in the previous paragraphs, the geographer analyzes the area concerned by the regional method. On the basis of a series of criteria relevant to political problems, he determines the regional differences and similarities within the area and, by comparative study of the different regional systems revealed by each criterion, seeks for evidence of accordant areal relationships. By studies in historical geography he seeks the cause-and-effect relationships that are suggested by the application of the regional method. . . .

---

[28] L.C. Glenn, "Physiographic Influences in the Development of Tennessee," *The Resources of Tennessee,* April 1915, pp. 44–63.

Political geography, then, may be defined as the study of areal differences and similarities in political character as an interrelated part of the total complex of areal differences and similarities. The interpretation of area differences in political features involves the study of their interrelations with all other relevant areal variations, whether physical, biotic, or cultural in origin. . . .

JOHN K. WRIGHT

Training for Research in
Political Geography

Political geography is perhaps the most "human" phase of geography, since it deals so largely with the strengths, weaknesses, and ambitions of men. If political geography itself had reached a more mature stage of development, it would be easier to discuss the problem of training for research in it. As things stand, so much of the field is still virgin that the pioneers who venture into it will receive the better part of their training through actual cultivation of its soil. One might, of course, select a number of the most urgent political problems facing humanity today—collective security versus balance of power, or the future international position of China, or what not—and try to figure out how persons should be trained to investigate them from the geographical point of view, but any such selection could represent only a small fraction of the many types of problem with which political geography might potentially deal, and furthermore no two individuals would ever agree on what are the "most urgent problems." My approach will be more general.

Obviously those responsible for training others to undertake research in political geography should, first, have as clear a notion as possible of the various topics with which such research might deal in a useful manner, and then try to develop in their students the proficiencies needed for conducting such research. In this paper, accordingly, the potential scope of political geography and the question of training will be discussed separately.

Reproduced by permission from the *Annals* of the Association of American Geographers, Volume 34, No. 4 (1944), 190–201.

THE SCOPE OF POLITICAL GEOGRAPHY

The diagram (Fig. 1) illustrates a conception of political geography. The two boxes at the upper corners of the triangle stand for any two or more political groups. The box at the lower corner stands for "the earth"—i.e., the earth's surface and associated terrestrial phenomena. The sloping lines represent relationships between "the earth" and political groups considered as separate units (such, for example, as the relationships disclosed by ordinary "political" maps showing states, provinces, and other governmental units, or maps of the distribution of coal, iron, or other natural resources in relation to such units). The two solid horizontal lines stand for "political contacts" between the groups, either of conflict or of cooperation. As distinguished from purely areal or spatial contacts, political contacts involve action, such as conducting election campaigns, waging wars, or concluding treaties. The heavy vertical line stands for the relationship of these contacts to the earth.

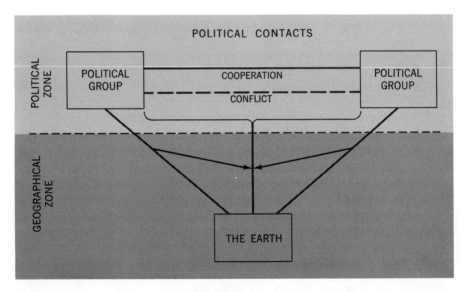

FIG. 1

For "political groups" we might substitute "any human groups" in the diagram. The triangle would then suggest a wider realm of study, of which political geography would be only a part (though perhaps the most important part): "the geography of active human contacts." This immense field would embrace the whole great triangle of Men, Other Men, and Earth—a triangle as old and fully as perplexing as the proverbial one that is commonly called "eternal."

However this may be, most geographers would doubtless agree that the heavy vertical line stands for the central core of political geography, and that, while studies of the facts represented by the sloping lines are essential, they are merely contributory to studies of the contacts between political groups as symbolized by this line. This central core, of course, has been and might be investigated in a great many different ways, ranging from the quest for principles or generalizations of worldwide application to the detailed factual examination of specific regional or even local contacts. The focus may be upon the contacts of the political groups within a particular area, such as a continent or a county, or on those of a particular political group, such as a nation. Geopolitics, I take it, is the geographical study of the contacts of a specific political group, usually a nation, when such study is pursued for the purpose of promoting the interests of that group. Another approach is to concentrate on the analysis of a particular type or manifestation of political action (e.g., plebiscites, arbitration, war), or the relationship of political contacts to a particular aspect of the environment (e.g., the sea, as exemplified by Mahan; or mineral resources, etc.). The present global war has stimulated many studies of political contacts in terms of the purely geometrical relationships of position and direction on the earth's surface. (Such relationships are, of course, geographical as well as geometrical, but they fall far short of being the *only* geographical relationships, as some recent popular writers might lead one to think.) But, whatever may be the actual subject of his research, the political geographer must know his way about in two zones of knowledge.

The broken horizontal line in our diagram is the boundary between these zones—the "political" one above and the "geographical" one below. As this paper is addressed to professional geographers, it hardly seems necessary to discuss the geographical zone in any detail. This is familiar ground, and the reader's imagination may be counted upon to suggest the nature both of the pertinent terrestrial facts and of the various geographical techniques that might be used in correlating them with the political facts. In the upper zone, the "stamping ground" of politicians and political scientists, most geographers are less at home. The political geographer, however, might do well to conceive of the configuration of this political zone as systematically as he presumably conceives of the geographical zone, and, furthermore, his conception of it ought to be adapted to the purpose of correlating its features and processes with those of the geographical zone, a purpose that ordinarily differs considerably from that of the political scientist or politician.

In the following paragraphs I shall present a tentative classification of the main features of the political zone, followed by a few hints as to how the facts of the political zone might be studied geographically.

Nature of political groups

Any combination of people which *as a group* acts politically is a "political group." In this discussion "political action" will be regarded as action connected solely with political government, though it could, of course, be conceived as any action that savors of "politics" in the broadest sense of the term. Non-governmental politics of the kind that is known, for example, sometimes to rage in universities, is not normally considered a subject for research in political geography. Military action, however, is governmental political action carried to its furthest extreme, and hence military geography may properly be deemed a highly specialized branch of political geography.

For the purposes of political geography, useful criteria for the classification of political groups are those of *size, essential function,* and *relative power.*

Political groups form hierarchies of lesser within larger groups. They vary enormously in *size*—e.g., from factions within villages to the whole populations of huge coalitions of nations.

In terms of *essential function* they fall into two main categories: 1) primary or territorial groups, and 2) secondary groups. In the hierarchies of primary groups the most important units are nations. Other primary groups comprise the entire populations of such combinations or subdivisions of national states as alliances and coalitions, empires, provinces, colonies, municipalities, wards, precincts, etc., and for convenience these entities themselves will sometimes be referred to as political groups (e.g., "province" instead of "provincial group"). The political action of primary groups consists in maintaining, in submitting to, and sometimes in rebelling against the governments in authority over them.

The secondary groups comprise parts only of the whole populations of primary groups. They also form hierarchies, but these are not organized along such definite and clean-cut lines as those of the primary groups. Functionally, the most important secondary groups are political parties; other groups consist of factions within parties, "pressure groups," lobbies, etc., and sometimes even of unorganized mobs. The political action of the secondary groups consists in efforts to gain influence or control over, or to resist control by, the governments of the primary groups. Most secondary groups operate largely in the interests of various non-political groups—linguistic, religious, industrial, agricultural, commercial, and the like.

Political groups differ profoundly from one another in the *relative degree* of *political power* at their command. In this regard there are two modes of comparison. One is "horizontal"—that is, the relative power of coordinate groups is considered: nations in comparison with nations, provinces with provinces, or parties with parties. The other is "vertical," the power of lesser groups being compared with that of the larger groups of which they form component parts —municipalities with provinces, provinces with nations, factions with parties, parties with nations. In a loose federation of states, the political power of the smaller component groups is greater in relation to that of the whole federation than in a highly centralized state. In a totalitarian state a single secondary group, a political party, dominates the whole nation.

Political power is derived from the inherent energy of political groups and from the material means that they possess for giving effect to this energy. We shall come to the matter of means a little later. The inherent energy of a group is largely a function of its cohesion. Cohesion may be achieved voluntarily by the component elements, as in a democracy, or else it may be enforced upon them by dominant elements, as in an autocracy. Frequently it is maintained by fear of aggression from without. Enforced cohesion brought about by repression or cohesion due to fear may at times give rise temporarily to mighty political power, as the recent examples of Germany and of the United Nations show. Such cohesion, however, may suddenly dissolve when the dominant elements lose their grip or the causes of fear are removed.

The nature of the political action of groups

Political groups are to political geography what landforms are to geomorphology. Geomorphology aims to describe, classify, and map the distribution of landforms and to explain the processes that create, mold, and destroy them. Political geography aims not only to describe, classify and map political groups, but to explain the processes that affect them in terms of the relationships of these processes to "the earth." Most of the processes with which geomorphology deals are due to forces that originate outside of the landforms themselves—in the atmosphere, the ocean, streams and lakes, and the depths of the earth. The forces and processes with which political geography is concerned, on the other hand, originate largely within political groups themselves, in an immense complex of human desires and needs.

In geomorphology it has long been an instructive practice to differentiate between the physical forces and processes that build up and those that wear down landforms—between constructive and destructive processes. This distinction can usually be made in a clean-cut manner. Weathering and erosion are clearly destructive; uplift and alluvial deposition are clearly constructive. Political processes also are both destructive and constructive, but here it is not so easy to make the distinction. Most of the political processes of which one usually thinks are comparable to such geomorphic processes as stream action or wave action, which are constructive of certain landforms and destructive of others. It is, however, entirely feasible to make a precise distinction between two major categories of political process, a distinction based on the nature of political action itself rather than on its more debatable results. *This distinction is between processes of cooperation and those of conflict.* Indeed, political action that does not involve either cooperation or conflict is inconceivable. All political activities in which individuals or groups work together toward common purposes—the establishment and maintenance of governments, of law and order within nations, and of peace between them—are cooperative. All political activities in which individuals or groups work against each other are processes of conflict. As long as peace prevails the processes of conflict are subordinated to and operate within a larger framework of cooperation. In war the reverse is true. Then the subordinate cooperative processes are often enormously intensified to subserve the dominant processes of conflict.

The distinction between cooperation and conflict is not wholly unconnected with that between constructive and destructive political processes. The specific processes which may be assigned to these categories are usually, like stream action, destructive in certain places and constructive in others. The cooperation of certain groups, while constructive in respect to those groups themselves, may be destructive of their enemies or rivals, and conflict, while destructive of the losing side, may be constructive from the winners' point of view. The terms "constructive" and "destructive" can also be used in a more absolute sense, with reference to human civilization as a whole. Only extreme militarists deny that the processes of human cooperation throughout the ages have been constructive and those of conflict destructive of the things and ideals that men cherish the most.

Indeed, the greater evils that afflict human beings today have sprung from political conflict, and one of the most urgent of the tasks that confront men of science today is to seek for a better understanding of the processes of conflict that produce these evils and of the cooperative processes that tend to counteract them. This is why there is value in the conception of political geography as concerned fundamentally with the nature of political cooperation and conflict and why researches in this field might well be consciously oriented to shed a maximum amount of direct light on these two modes of political action.

If this were a rounded treatise instead of a short paper, I should go on from here to discuss both modes. Some comments on the matter of conflict, however, will have to suffice. I trust that they may suggest to the reader comparable ideas regarding cooperation.

Political confict

There are many kinds of human conflict. My ideas or interests may be in conflict with yours without either of us doing anything about it. This is static conflict. If we argue or fight it is dynamic conflict. If our ideas and interests continue to conflict over a long period with occasional outbursts of argument or fighting, it is chronic static conflict punctuated by acute dynamic conflict. If we merely argue, it is non-physical, or verbal, conflict, but if we fight it is physical. When I make my ideas or my interests prevail over yours the conflict is resolved, but if neither prevails it is unresolved.

These distinctions apply to political as well as to personal conflict, and political geography potentially embraces all types of political conflict. It may be concerned with the chronic, long-lasting, static conflict of ideas and interests between political groups or with specific instances of dynamic conflict. In either case it considers the causes and results of conflicts, the means employed in conducting them, and their manifestations at particular times and in particular areas.

Causes and results

If all men were equally satisfied with their destiny and did not strive to get the better of one another, there would be no political conflict. Nature and human ambitions, however, have given certain groups advantages, which they seek to preserve and enlarge and which rival groups seek to overcome. These differential advantages are the root causes of political conflict. They show themselves in the possession of, or the control over, those things and conditions that contribute to the enjoyment of life and power—tangible things such as resources in materials and men, geometrical circumstances such as the occupation of advantageous positions on the earth's surface, and intangibles such as technological skill, political cohesion, energy, etc. The specific issues of conflict in its acute form are almost invariably connected in one way or another with these differential advantages, and the end results of conflict can invariably be summed up in terms of the change brought about in such relative advantages.

Means

The means of political conflict consist in the *measures* and the *instruments* used by political groups in applying force. The force itself may be either non-physical or physical. Non-physical—or we might call it "verbal"—force is applied in electioneering, in legislative debates, in diplomatic meetings, in legal arguments, through newspaper editorials, and in political propaganda. It is given effect through such *measures* as court injunctions and decisions, treaties, embargoes, economic sanctions, the enactment of laws, etc. It is force exerted in the first instance against the minds rather than directly upon the bodies or possessions of those toward whom it is directed. These minds may resist it; or they may yield to it either through fear of the consequences or because of inner conviction that to yield is reasonable or in the best interests of society. Physical force is resorted to only when verbal force does not suffice, or it is believed that it may not suffice, to accomplish the desired purposes.

The *instruments* of political conflict comprise the various human and material resources, institutions, and mechanisms that are either actually employed or could potentially be employed in the application of force of either kind. Frequently verbal force is applied in the form of threats that the potential instruments of physical force will be used. The instruments do not consist of material things alone. They include intangibles, such as having a case that is, or can be made to appear, the more just. Possession or lack of the instruments of political conflict add to or diminish the differential advantages of political groups, and hence such instruments may constitute both the causes and the means of conflict.

In war a large fraction of the potential instruments of conflict are converted into immediate instruments—manpower into armies and navies, natural resources into guns and ships and planes, advantageous positions and boundaries into the direct utilization of the advantages associated with them; and a just or plausible case into active propaganda for that case.

Manifestations

Precisely how, where, and when does political conflict occur? One might regard it as occurring only at those points where the opposing forces collide. In the case of physical conflict these points and what happens at them can usually be definitely identified in place and time, in most instances on battlefields. In the case of non-physical conflict the nature, time, and place of the actual collision of forces are not always so readily recognized. Where, when, and how does the collision occur that is resolved in a political election? It occurs in the minds of individuals scattered over large areas and it may last over many months or years. In a political conflict resolved by legal or diplomatic means the collision may occur in a conference hall or courtroom far from the areas where the issues of the conflict have arisen. Hence, except in so far as physical conflict is concerned, the actual place of collision may be of little significance in political geography, and the manifestations of conflict might better be regarded as occurring over the period of time during which the maneuvers and movements unfold that bring the issues to the point of collision and that follow immediately after. Obviously no sharp lines can be drawn between this period and the longer preceding and succeeding periods in which the factors of cause and effect alone might be considered as operative.

THE GEOGRAPHICAL STUDY OF POLITICAL GROUPS AND OF POLITICAL CONFLICT

What does the foregoing classification suggest with regard to geographical research? One way of considering this is to allow the imagination to roam over the various facts for which the classification provides a frame of reference—to roam in an exploring expedition into new possibilities of employing existing maps to illuminate these facts and of mapping some of those facts for which no maps now exist. While research in geography is by no means a matter solely of making and interpreting maps, a good preliminary test of the potentialities of almost any set of facts as subjects of geographical investigation is whether or not they are capable of cartographic expression.

If maps of any one type could be said to occupy the same basic position in political geography as that of topographic maps in geomorphology, they would be maps disclosing the distribution of population in relation to political boundaries. Maps of this kind reveal the fundamental geographical anatomy of the primary political groups.

We have seen that political groups vary enormously in size. Any and all political groups are proper subjects of research in political geography. The fact that such research has for the most part been devoted to national groups as represented by sovereign states, is no reason why studies could not be profitably pursued with respect to very much smaller groups. Thus the "micro-political geography" of local or regional groups might well be developed along interesting and original lines. Especially worthwhile would seem to be studies in the micro-political geography of regions that are critical from either the national or international points of view (e.g., the "core areas" of Whittlesey or certain frontier areas). Such studies, although on the micro-scale in their immediate scope, bear upon what might be called "meso-" and "macro-political geography" by those who like such terms, the "meso-" type having to do with nationwide and the "macro-" type with international affairs.

Some political phenomena lend themselves much more readily to geographical analysis and interpretation than do others. This is because maps, statistics, and other information are already easily available regarding the geographical distribution of these facts. A good deal of this information has already been exploited in political-geographical studies. It consists in general of facts concerning the distribution of population in terms of primary political groups, and the distribution of certain non-political groups—linguistic, religious, and occupational, for which census data are available—also of facts concerning material things (natural resources and manpower), and geometrical relationships (including political boundaries) which contribute to the differential advantages of nations and constitute instruments of conflict; and, finally, of facts concerning the manifestations of physical, particularly of military, conflict.

The more virgin parts of political geography are those concerning the more intangible facts and concepts. Take, for example, the "vertical" relationships of the power of primary groups. If satisfactory criteria could be established on which they could be based—and this might be possible—maps showing the degree of self-government enjoyed nominally and actually by primary groups of various ranks would be revealing indeed. Together with the geographical study of secondary political groups, they would illumine the matter of political cohesion and help to establish the geographical lines of cleavage along which political groups tend to split apart. In this country historians rather than geographers have taken the lead in studying these lines of cleavage and in the geographical analysis of secondary groups—witness the work of Turner and others. A good many maps already exist relating to secondary groups (e.g., the distribution of votes in elections and upon Congressional measures). On the other hand, some of the most powerful non-political groups, in whose behalf the secondary groups act or which seek to exert direct influence on governments and their policies, have largely escaped geographical study—for example, cartels, and other industrial groups, and also agricultural, commercial, and labor groups. The competitive nature of most of these organizations causes them to keep to themselves many of the data on which maps and other geographical studies could be based.

When we turn to political processes, we see that here, too, certain types of process have been neglected—the more intangible factors operating among the causes and instruments of conflict, the measures by which non-physical force is applied and many of the results of its application, and the manifestations of non-physical conflict. A great deal of unexplored geography underlies and helps to explain the political processes connected, for example, with political campaigns, with the conclusion of certain treaties, or the settlement of certain disputes in the United States Supreme Court, even where the immediate issues may not appear to possess any distinctively geographical characteristics.

For an understanding of political contacts and of the good or evil that they may cause, the elusive facts and concepts are as much needed as are the accessible ones and as closely connected with terrestrial circumstances. It is not because they are non-geographical but because they are hard to get at and to study in geographical terms that they constitute terrain still largely virgin. The cultivation of this terrain, because it presents difficulties, may be all the more attractive to those whose purposes in research are other than to follow lines of least resistance.

TRAINING FOR RESEARCH

Two qualities are requisite for successful research: enthusiasm and technical proficiency. Enthusiasm springs partly from confidence in one's ability to carry on research and partly from a vision of its pursuit as leading into fascinating domains of knowledge where challenging problems await solution. The ideal trainer for research is one who himself has such vision and the skill to project it in clear and colorful form before his students.

Research in political geography may be pursued with either one of two main purposes in view: principally for what it may contribute to an understanding of the political behavior of mankind, or principally for what it may contribute to geography. In the first case, the end purpose is to explain from the geographical point of view the nature of political groups and of the processes that affect them. In the second, it is to explain how other things, such as the distribution of economic, social, or cultural conditions, or the general character of regions, are affected by the nature of political phenomena. Toward whichever of these goals research in political geography be directed, those techniques that seek to establish the patterns of the distribution of things and conditions on the earth's surface are indispensable tools, and all training programs should be designed to give proficiency in these fundamental techniques. They consist in the critical interpretation of existing maps, in the making of new maps, and in the ability to correlate given political data with given terrestrial data in terms of their areal relationships.

The larger problems of research, however, are connected with the explanation of the data so correlated—with the more hypothetical and controversial matters that involve not merely showing how things exist together in space but how they affect each other. Presumably, training programs in this respect should be so organized as to afford opportunities alike for those whose purpose it is to use political geography as an auxiliary to geography of other kinds, and for those who aim to apply geographical techniques toward a better understanding of political phenomena. These two goals are both worthy and meritorious. The geographical goal will be selected by students wishing to become well-rounded teachers of or scholars in geography. The political goal will allure many in the confusing postwar period, and the public demand for studies leading in its direction will doubtless be greater than it ever has been before. Man's political behavior has assumed such terrible forms of late that research in which it is made the center of analysis may well yield greater personal satisfaction to many students than studies that might appear to deal with problems of lesser human urgency.

As was pointed out at the beginning of this paper, the political geographer must know his way about in both the georaphical and political zones of his subject. He must have a grounding in physical and economic geography such as that which our better university courses might be expected to give him. On the political side, he should doubtless be required to take courses and do some reading in political science. Geography and political science, however, are not the only essentials. History is also needed. The history presented incidentally in political science courses will not suffice and should be supplemented by broader historical study of a kind that I assume is required of advanced students in political science itself. Without the perspectives that historical study should give, research in political geography can produce misleading results. If based too exclusively on consideration of contemporary facts, however skilful the use may be of maps and statistics, political geography is a thing of shallow geometrical designs. Maps and statistics, valuable tools though they are, disclose momentary and partial aspects only of the dynamic forces and processes that must be taken into account. Except possibly for historical geography itself, there is no other branch of geography in which historical-mindedness is more indispensable than in political geography.

Historical-mindedness should put the political geographer on his guard against oversimplification. The forces and processes with which he deals are of a very different and far more complex order than those with which the geomorphologist, for example, has to do. The geomorphologist studies forces over which he personally has little or no control and in which his interest is purely scientific. While he may harbor prejudices against certain theories regarding these forces, his judgment is not affected by personal loyalty to any particular geomorphic force or landform. He classifies delta building as constructive and glacial scouring as destructive, but he does not regard the one as thereby good and the other as evil. After having described, classified, and sought the explanation for peneplains, coral reefs, and the like, he does not feel impelled to advocate measures designed to alter them, because such alteration, except within very narrow limits, is beyond the power of man. The political geographer, on the other hand, cannot approach his subject in quite such an objective manner. Political processes and forces are definitely good or evil, though it is sometimes difficult to know which. The political geographer to some considerable degree has it in his power to alter or deflect them, both as a citizen and as a scholar. Through his vote and through his teachings and writings he can give support to forces that he regards as good. Furthermore, even if he thinks his studies are strictly impartial and coldly "scientific" and he refrains from the advocacy of specific measures of political action, his whole thought is affected by his political environment. He cannot avoid feeling partiality for or against different political groups and processes, and this inevitably colors and is reflected in his researches. Except on some of its purely descriptive levels, research in political geography is inextricably concerned with problems in political ethics—with good and evil—and any training for such research that failed to take this into account would be worth very little indeed.

II

POLITICAL GEOGRAPHY
AND
POLITICAL SYSTEMS

GABRIEL A. ALMOND

A Developmental Approach
to Political Systems

I. SYSTEM AND FUNCTION

The term "system" has become increasingly common in the titles of texts and monographs in the field of comparative politics. Older texts tended to use such terms as "governments" or "foreign powers." Something more is involved here than mere style in nomenclature. The use of the concept of system reflects the penetration into political theory of the anthropological and sociological theory of functionalism. The chief social theorists whose names are associated with functionalism are the anthropologists Malinowski and Radcliffe-Brown and the sociologists Parsons, Merton, and Marion Levy.[1] Though they differ substantially in their concepts of system and function, what these men have been saying is that our capacity for explanation and prediction in the social sciences is enhanced when we think of social structures and institutions as performing *functions* in *systems*.

The point being made here is both simple and important. A circulatory system in an organism makes little sense by itself. When we view it as serving a purpose or set of purposes for the functioning of the organism as a whole, we can begin to comprehend its significance. Similarly, political parties or administrative agencies mean little by themselves. Their significance becomes clear

From Gabriel Almond, *World Politics*, Volume XVII, No. 2 (January 1965), 183–214. Reprinted by permission of Princeton University Press.

[1] Bronislaw Malinowski, *Magic, Science, and Religion* (Anchor Books: Garden City, N.Y., 1954); A.R. Radcliffe-Brown, *Structure and Function in Primitive Society* (Glencoe, 1957); Talcott Parsons, *Essays in Sociological Theory Pure and Applied* (Glencoe, 1949); Parsons, *The Social System* (Glencoe, 1951); Talcott Parsons and Edward Shils, eds., *Toward a General Theory of Action* (Cambridge, Mass., 1951); R.K. Merton, *Social Theory and Social Structure* (Glencoe, 1957); Marion Levy, Jr., *The Structure of Society* (Princeton, 1952).

when we see them as interacting with other institutions to produce public policies and enforcements of public policies in the domestic or international environments.

Functional-system theory as formulated by such writers as Talcott Parsons and Marion Levy implies three conditions: functional requisites, interdependence, and equilibrium. A particular system, whether it be an organism, a machine, or a family, has to behave in particular ways, perform a set of tasks, in order to "be" the particular organism, machine, or family. Levy calls these requirements "functional requisites," and lists nine activities as essential to the existence of any society. To illustrate, Levy includes among these requisites adaptation to the natural environment, differentiation of and recruitment to social roles, the maintenance of a common body of knowledge and beliefs, the socialization of the young, and the control of disruptive behavior.[2] Parsons speaks of four "imperatives of any system of action," including adaptation, goal gratification, integration, and latent pattern maintenance and tension management.[3] These and other writers also make the point that, for a system to continue in operation, these functions must be performed in certain ways. When a function is performed in such a way as to maintain the equilibrium of the system, the performance of the function by the agency or structure is referred to as "functional" (or *eufunctional*, in Marion Levy's formulation). When the performance upsets the equilibrium, then it is referred to as "dysfunctional." We shall come back to this concept of functionality-dysfunctionality at a later point.

We need to elaborate a little on the other two assumptions of systems theory —*interdependence* and *equilibrium*. By the interdependence of the parts of a system, we mean that when the properties of one component in a system change, all the others, and the system as a whole, are affected. Thus if the rings of an automobile erode, we speak of the car as "burning oil"; the functioning of other systems deteriorates; and the power of the car declines. Or, in the growth of organisms there are points, for example, when some change in the endocrine system affects the overall pattern of growth, the functioning of all the parts, and the general behavior of the organism. In political systems, the emergence of mass parties or mass media of communication changes the performance of all the other structures of the political system, and affects the general capabilities of the system in its domestic and foreign environments. In other words, when one variable in a system changes in magnitude or in quality, the others are subjected to strains and are transformed, and the system changes its pattern of performance; or the dysfunctional component is disciplined by regulatory mechanisms, and the equilibrium of the system is reestablished. Parsons and Shils argue that social systems tend toward equilibrium;[4] i.e., families, economies, churches, politics tend to preserve their character through time, or to

---

2 Levy, *Structure of Society*, 149 ff.
3 Talcott Parsons, *Economy and Society* (Glencoe, 1956), 16 ff.
4 Parsons and Shils, eds., *Toward a General Theory of Action*, 107 ff.

change slowly. Hence the analytical scheme which they propose for generalized use in the social sciences is this concept of system, implying the interdependent interaction of structures performing functions in such a way as to maintain the social system in equilibrium.

Even in this starkly simple form, the generic system model has value for the study of politics. The concept of function pushes us into realism and away from normative or ideological definitions. To answer functional questions we have to observe what a particular social system actually is and does. The concepts of functionality and dysfunctionality sensitize us to the factors making for social stability and social change, and enable us to perceive them in an orderly and thorough way. The concept of interdependence forces us to examine the performance of any structure or institution systemically; i.e., in all of its ramifications and interdependences. We can no longer be contented with describing a single institution or looking at bilateral interactions. Our research must assume interdependence and interaction among all components.

II. CRITIQUE OF FUNCTIONAL THEORY

The introduction of functionalism into the social sciences has stirred up a good deal of controversy and polemic.[5] Among the critics of functional theory, the logician Hempel has raised questions about the scientific status of functionalism, arguing that its exponents fail to provide operational criteria of function and dysfunction, and of the kind of interaction among variables which maintain a system in equilibrium. Gouldner's principal criticism is that the concept of system and function has come from biology and mechanics, and that there has been a tendency to attribute the properties of organismic and mechanical systems to social systems. He points out that interdependence and equilibrium may be of a radically different character in social systems. The autonomy of the components of social systems—i.e., the extent to which they may vary without significantly affecting other variables and the system as a whole—may be far greater than in mechanical and organismic systems.

Gouldner also argues that there is a static tendency in systems theory, a tendency to stress the functionality of institutions and the equilibrium of social systems. The distinction as formulated in anthropological and sociological theory tends to be dichotomous; i.e., structures perform either functionally or dysfunctionally. He argues that they should be viewed as continua, since without specification and measurement it is impossible to say what kind and degree of performance by given structures and institutions produce what kind of social equilibrium. Here Gouldner and Hempel would agree that what we need is a model of interaction of components in which the relations among variables

---

5 See *inter alia* Carl G. Hempel, "The Logic of Functional Analysis," and Alvin W. Gouldner, "Reciprocity and Autonomy in Functional Theory," in Llewellyn Gross, ed., *Symposium in Sociological Theory* (New York, 1959), 241 ff.

and their consequences for system performance are left open to empirical investigation.

A further valuable criticism is Gouldner's argument that there is a tendency to treat each component in a social system as having a value equal to each of the others. Actually the significance and autonomy of the various parts of social systems may be quite unequal. Thus one may argue that the bureaucracy in differentiated political systems is in some sense the central structure of these systems, and that all other structures are significant by virtue of the way in which they affect the performance of the bureaucracy. Here again we need system models more appropriate for social and political phenomena.

Finally Gouldner argues that such a social system theorist as Parsons does not give sufficient stress to the special character of the interaction of social systems with their environments. He may attribute too great an impermeability to the boundaries of social systems. Thus political systems are quite porous, so to speak. The exchanges and movements which take place between political systems and their societies or their international environments, particularly in the modern world, are quite massive. It is impossible to account for either equilibrium or change in political systems without observing the volume and kind of their interactions with their social and international environments.

The main burden of these criticisms is that social system theory is still too much under the influence of biological and mechanical analogies, and that it fails to specify operational indices for such concepts as functionality, interdependence, and equilibrium. The criticisms have merit, but they should not obscure the importance of the original insights of the social system theorists. What we are engaged in here is simply an elaboration and adaptation of their work.

Before we drop the generic system concept and turn to the special characteristics of political systems, we need to deal with one or two other terms. Intrinsic to the concept of system is the notion of boundary and of exchanges or actions across boundaries. A system starts somewhere and stops somewhere. In dealing with an organism or a machine, it is relatively easy to locate the boundary and specify the interactions between it and its environment. The gas goes into the tank; the motor converts it into revolutions of the crankshaft and the driving wheels; and the car moves on the highway. In dealing with social systems, of which political systems are a class, the problem of boundary is not that easy. We may speak of what separates a social system from its environment as a boundary, but what we mean by this is not at all clear. Social systems are not made up of individuals but of roles; i.e., a family consists of the roles of mother and father, husband and wife, sibling and sibling, and the like. The family is only one set of interacting roles for a group of individuals who also may have extra-familial roles, and hence be involved in other social systems. In the same sense, a political system consists of the roles of nationals, subjects, voters, interacting—as the case may be—with legislators, bureaucrats, judges, and the like. The same individuals who perform roles in the political system perform roles in other social systems, such as the economy, religious community, family, and voluntary associations. As individuals expose themselves to political communication, vote, demonstrate, they shift from non-political to political roles. One might say that on election day as citizens leave their farms, plants, and offices to go to the polling places, they are crossing the boundary from the economy to the polity. It is crossing the boundary in both an objective and a subjective sense. In the objective sense, a man leaves his assembly line, where he is performing a role in a manufacturing process, to enter the polling booth, where he is performing a role in a political process. In a psychological sense, some shift of norms, values, expectations, and cognitions takes place as well.

The concept of boundary as we apply it to social and political systems is, of course, an analogy. What we really mean by this analogy can be specified only if we examine empirically the actual exchanges which take place between one system and another. Thus, when we speak of the interaction of personalities and the political system, we are thinking of the impulses, attitudes, and values entering into the performance of political roles by the individuals who make up the political system. At some point in this interactive process, properties which we associate with personality, such as hostility and rigidity, get converted into attitudes toward or choices of particular foreign or defense policies or candidates for public office. In other words, there are boundaries here between general affective and value tendencies, and political attitudes and choices.

There is a boundary between the polity and the economy. For example, an inflation may reduce the real income of certain groups in the population. When these changes in the economic situations of particular groups get converted into demands for public policy or changes in political personnel, there is an interaction between the economy and the polity. What really happens in the empirical sense is that certain psychic states resulting from changes in the economic capabilities of groups are converted into demands on the political system, demands on trade union or other pressure group leaders that they lobby for particular actions by the legislative or executive agencies, and the like. Somewhere along the line here a boundary is passed from one system to another, from the economic system to the political system.

That we are using an analogy when we speak of the boundaries of political systems, and a misleadingly simple analogy at that, becomes clear when we consider the variety of phenomena we include under it. We use it in a simple physical sense, as when we speak of the boundaries of nations or of subnational political jurisdictions. We use it in a behavioral sense, as when we refer to the interactions of voters and candidates, governmental officials and citizens, as these are separated from the interactions of these same individuals in their roles as workers and employers, parishioners and clergy. We use it in a psychological sense, as when we refer to attitudes toward politics, politicians, public officials, and public policies, as these are differentiated from the other contents of the psyches of the members of a polity. Whenever we use the term we need to be clear just which one, or which combination, of these phenomena we have in mind.

Another way of thinking about the interaction of political systems with their environments is to divide the process into three phases, as is usually done in systems theory—input, conversion, output. The inputs and outputs which involve the political system with other social systems are transactions between the system and its environment; the conversion processes are internal to the political system. When we talk about the sources of inputs and how they enter the political system, and how outputs leave the political system and affect other social systems, we shall in effect be talking about the boundaries of the political system.

III. THREE TYPES OF FUNCTIONS

One further thought before we leave this generic concept of system and turn to political systems, properly speaking. We have talked about the functions of systems and how they give the system its identity. Actually, we need to think of systems as functioning at different *levels*. One level of functioning involves the unit as a whole in its environment. An animal moves, while plants do not. Some machines process data; others produce power. An economy produces and distributes physical goods and services. Families produce children and socialize them into adult roles and disciplines. Religious systems regulate the relations of their members with authorities and norms to which supernatural qualities are attributed. What we focus on at this level is the behavior of the system as a unit in its relations with other social systems and the environment.

The second kind of functioning is internal to the system. Here we refer to "conversion processes," such as the digestion of food, the elimination of waste, the circulation of the blood, the transmission of impulses through the nervous system. The conversion processes or functions are the ways particular systems transform inputs into outputs. Obviously the two levels of behavior are related. In order for an animal to be able to move, hunt, dig, and the like, energy must be created in the organism and the use of the energy controlled and directed. The level and kind of performance of the system in its environment are tied up with a particular kind of structural-functional performance inside the system.

In talking about politics, we shall speak of the performance of the political system in its environment as the political system's "capabilities." What happens inside the political system we shall refer to as "conversion functions." To illustrate, we shall speak here of the "responsive capability" of political systems, meaning by the term the openness of the political system to demands coming from various groups in the society, or from the international political system. This capacity to respond is associated with the performance inside the political system of such functions as communication, interest articulation, aggregation, and rule-making.

Finally, we shall speak of "system-maintenance and adaptation functions."

For an automobile to perform efficiently on the road, parts must be lubricated, repaired, replaced. New parts may perform stiffly; they must be "broken in." In a political system the incumbents of the various roles (diplomats, military officers, tax officials, and the like) must be recruited to these roles and learn how to perform them. New roles are created and new personnel "broken in." These functions (in machines, maintenance and replacement of parts; in politics, *recruitment* and *socialization*) do not directly enter into the conversion processes of the system; they affect the internal efficiency and operations of the system, and hence condition its performance.

When we compare classes of political systems with each other, or individual political systems with each other, we need to make these comparisons in terms of *capabilities, conversion functions,* and *system-maintenance and adaptation functions,* and the interrelations among these three kinds of functions. And when we talk about political development, it will also be in terms of the interrelations of these three kinds of political functions. A change in capability will be associated with changes in the performance of the conversion functions, and these changes in turn will be related to changes in political socialization and recruitment.

While the individual categories that we use may, on empirical test, turn out to be inappropriate, this threefold classification of functions is important for political analysis, and we believe it will hold up under testing and examination.[6] The theory of the political system will consist of the discovery of the relations among these different levels of functioning—capabilities, conversion functions, and system-maintenance and adaptation functions—and of the interrelations of the functions at each level. The theory of political change deals with those transactions between the political system and its environment that affect changes in general system performance, or capabilities that in turn are associated with changes in the performance of the system-adaptation functions and the conversion functions.

IV. THE POLITICAL SYSTEM: INPUTS AND OUTPUTS

This discussion of the concept of system has been useful, but we shall be open to the criticism of being carried away by an analogy if we fail to bring these analytical tools into the world of politics. What is the political system? What gives it its special identity? Much has been written on this subject, and it is difficult to get agreement among political theorists on the precise language of

---

6 This approach to functional requisites analysis is related to earlier work but differs in its explicit differentiaton of these three classes of functon. For other application of functional theory to the study of political systems, see in particular David Apter, *The Gold Coast in Transition* (Princeton, 1955), 325 ff.; Apter, "A Comparative Method for the Study of Politics," *American Journal of Sociology,* LXIV (November 1958), 221–37; and Apter's contribution to Harry Eckstein and David Apter, eds., *Comparative Politics* (New York, 1963), 723 ff.; also William C. Mitchell, *The American Polity* (New York, 1962), 7 ff.

their definitions. Common to most of these definitions is the association of the political system with the use of legitimate physical coercion in societies. Easton speaks of *authoritative allocation of values*, Lasswell and Kaplan of *severe deprivations*, Dahl of *power, rule, and authority*.[7] Common to all of these definitions is their association of politics with legitimate heavy sanctions.[8] We have suggested elsewhere that "Legitimate force is the thread that runs through the inputs and outputs of the political system, giving it its special quality and salience and its coherence as a system. The inputs into the political system are all in some way related to claims for the employment of legitimate physical compulsion, whether these are demands for war or for recreational facilities. The outputs of the political system are also all in some way related to legitimate physical compulsion, however remote the relationship may be. Thus public recreational facilities are usually supported by taxation, and any violation of the regulations governing their use is a legal offense. . . ."[9] When we speak of the political system, we include all of the interactions—inputs as well as outputs—which affect the use or threat of use of physical coercion. "We mean to include not just the structures based on law, like parliaments, executives, bureaucracies, and courts, or just the associational or formally organized units, like parties, interest groups, and media of communication, but *all of the structures in their political aspects*, including undifferentiated structures like kinship and lineage, status and caste groups, as well as anomic phenomena like riots, street demonstrations, and the like."[10]

This is not the same thing as saying that the political system is solely concerned with force, violence, or compulsion, but only that its relation to coercion is its distinctive quality. Political elites may be concerned with peace, social welfare, individual freedom and self-realization, but their concern with these values as politicians is somehow related to compulsory actions such as taxation, law-making and law enforcement, foreign and defense policy. The political system is not the only system that makes rules and enforces them, but its rules and enforcements go "all the way" in compelling obedience or performance.

David Easton, who was the first political scientist to write about politics in explicit "system" terms, distinguishes two classes of inputs into the political system—*demands* and *supports*.[11] Demand inputs may be subclassified in a variety of ways. We suggest that they may be classified under four headings: (1) demands for goods and services, such as wage and hour laws, educational

7 David Easton, *The Political System* (New York, 1953), 130 ff.; Harold Lasswell and Abraham Kaplan, *Power and Society* (New Haven, 1950), 176; Robert Dahl, *Modern Political Analysis* (Englewood Cliffs; N.J., 1963), 5 ff.

8 See Max Weber, "Politics as a Vocation," in Hans Gerth and C. Wright Mills, eds., *From Max Weber* (New York, 1964), 78.

9 Almond and Coleman, eds., *Politics of the Developing Areas*, 7.

10 *Ibid.*, 8.

11 "An Approach to the Analysis of Political Systems," *World Politics,* IX (April 1957), 383–400.

opportunities, recreational facilities, roads and transportation; (2) demands for the regulation of behavior, such as provision of public safety, control over markets and labor relations, rules pertaining to marriage and the family; (3) demands for participation in the political system, for the right to vote, hold office, petition governmental bodies and officials, organize political associations, and the like; and (4) symbolic inputs, such as demands for the display of the majesty and power of the political system in periods of threat or on ceremonial occasions, or demands for the affirmation of norms, or the communication of policy intent from political elites.

Support inputs may be classified under four headings: (1) material supports, such as the payment of taxes or other levies, and the provision of services, such as labor contributions or military service; (2) obedience to laws and regulations; (3) participation, such as voting, joining organizations, and communicating about politics; and (4) manifestation of deference to public authority, symbols, and ceremonials.

On the output side, we may speak of four classes of transactions initiated by the political system that tend to match up with the supports we have listed above and may or may not be responsive to demands, depending on the kind of political system that is involved. These are: (1) extractions, which may take the form of tribute, booty, taxes, or personal services: (2) regulations of behavior, which may take a variety of forms and affect some subset of the whole gamut of human behavior and relations; (3) allocations or distributions of goods and services, opportunities, honors, statuses, and the like; and (4) symbolic outputs, including affirmations of values, displays of political symbols, statements of policies and intents.

When we speak of a stable political system, what we usually have in mind is a particular pattern of flow into and out of the political system, a particular kind of input-output flow. In the political system, properly speaking, the inputs of demands and supports are *converted* into extractive, regulative, distributive, and symbolic outputs. The demands can be handled by the political system; the strains which they impose are bearable without any basic change in structure or culture. The outputs are responsive to the demands in expected or legitimate ways; and the supports are responsive to the outputs again in expected or legitimate ways. When these conditions obtain, the political system may be said to be in a state of equilibrium both internally (in the performance of conversion functions by political structures) and in its relations with its environments.

One last point should be made about the flow of inputs and outputs. This is the question of the source of the inputs. We do not wish to leave the impression that inputs necessarily come only from the society of which the political system is a part, and that the political system must be viewed only in "conversion" terms. It is typical of political systems that inputs are generated internally by political elites—kings, presidents, ministers, legislators, and judges. Similarly, inputs may come from the international system in the form of demands and supports from foreign political systems. The flow of inputs and outputs includes transactions between the political system and the components of its domestic and foreign environments, and inputs may come from any one of these three sources—the domestic society, the political elites, and the international environment.

Something should be said about the relations between demands and supports. Generally speaking, demands stemming from inside or outside of the political system affect the policies or goals of the system, whether they be responsive, distributive, regulative, or the like, while supports of goods and services, obedience, deference, and the like provide the resources available to the political system which enable it to extract, regulate, and distribute—in other words, to carry out these goals.

V. THE CONVERSION FUNCTIONS

This brings us to the events which occur in the political system, properly speaking, or to what we have called the conversion functions. In every political system there is a set of political structures which initiates or processes inputs, and converts them into outputs. The demands entering the political system are articulated, aggregated or combined; converted into policies, rules, regulations; applied, enforced, adjudicated. These kinds of conversion events occur in all political systems; they are incidental to any political process, no matter how simple or undifferentiated it may be. But the kinds of structures, institutions, or roles which perform these functions, and the way they perform them, vary from the intermittent political structure of a primitive band hardly distinguishable from the family, religious, and economic system, to the highly differentiated political systems of modern societies, with their complex interactions between domestic social and international systems, and the internal interaction of electorates, interest groups, political parties, media of communication, parliaments, bureaucracies, and courts. This conceptual language in regard to the political system enables us to discriminate effectively among these systems, to talk intelligently about their performance and prospects.

This list of political conversion functions is not derived from generic system theory, or from concepts in use in sociological theory. Whatever virtue this classification of functions has results from the fact that it is derived from the observation of political systems. In other words, we are not forcing our data into categories that fit system concepts formulated in other disciplines, but developing concepts which can help us codify and classify political events.

The problem of developing categories to compare the conversion processes in different kinds of political systems is not unlike the problem of comparative anatomy and physiology. Surely the anatomical structure of a unicellular organism differs radically from that of a vertebrate, but something like the functions which in the vertebrate are performed by a specialized nervous system, a gastro-intestinal tract, a circulatory system, are performed in the amoeba by intermittent adaptations of its single cell. Hence we may say that the amoeba performs the same physiological functions as does the vertebrate. In addition we use the functional concepts which we derive from the study of more advanced biological forms to compare them with the less differentiated forms. Indeed, it is only by using the categories of physiological functioning derived from the analysis of differentiated organisms that we can compare them with the more simple ones.

In the same sense, if we look at complex political systems, we can observe specialized structures performing distinctive tasks. We observe electorates, media of communication, pressure groups, parties, parliaments, bureaucracies, and courts. By observing these structures and their interactions, we can explicate what distinctive jobs are being done in the process of converting political inputs into outputs. And we can use these functional categories to compare complex political systems with one another, and these with the less differentiated ones.

We suggest a sixfold classification of political conversion functions: (1) the articulation of interests or demands, (2) the aggregation or combination of interests into policy proposals, (3) the conversion of policy proposals into authoritative rules, (4) the application of general rules to particular cases, (5) the adjudication of rules in individual cases, and (6) the transmission of information about these events within the political system from structure to structure and between the political system and its social and international environments.

VI. THE CAPABILITIES OF POLITICAL SYSTEMS

More than four decades ago when Max Weber delivered his lecture on "Politics as a Calling," he discouraged us from thinking of politics in terms of performance. He told us: ". . . The state cannot be defined in terms of its ends. There is scarcely any task that some political association has not taken in hand, and there is no task that has always been exclusive and peculiar to political associations. . . . Ultimately, we can define the modern state only in terms of the specific means peculiar to it . . . namely, the use of physical force."[12] Contemporary empirical political theory tends to follow Weber in its stress on power and process, the "who" and the "how" of politics. It emphasizes two questions: (1) Who makes decisions? (2) How are decisions made?[13] The performance of political systems tends to be inferred from structure and process or evaluated according to moral and ideological norms. When we introduce the concept of capabilities, their development and transformation, we explicitly add two more questions to the "who?" and the "how?" The first of these is what impact does the political system have, what does it do, in its domestic and international

---

12 Gerth and Mills, eds., *From Max Weber*, 77.
13 See, for example, Harold D. Lasswell, *Politics: Who Gets What, When and How* (Glencoe, 1959); Dahl, *Modern Political Analysis*.

environments? And the second question is, what impact does the society and the international environment have on the political system?

Parsons comes closer to meeting the needs of the contemporary political theorist when he speaks of the function of the polity as that of the ". . . mobilization of societal resources and their commitment for the attainment of collective goals, for the formation and implementation of 'public policy.' "[14] Francis Sutton similarly emphasizes the importance of the functions of political systems in their social and international environments, stressing integration for the internal environment and representation for the international.[15] The development of the concept of the capabilities of political systems represents a pursuit of these leads, but we have had to go farther in specifying types of relationships between the political system and its environments, for "goal attainment," "integration," and "representation" must be broken down into their components, and these elements treated as continua, if we are to be able to code the performance of political systems in the environment in a discriminating way.

The concept of capabilities, then, is a way of characterizing the performance of the political system and of changes in performance, and of comparing political systems according to their performance. Our particular classification of capabilities is a coding scheme, derived from a kind of informal pre-testing operation. We have to try it out to determine whether it helps us discriminate among political systems, or handle political development in a meaningful way.

We suggest five categories of capability derived from our classification of inputs and outputs proposed at an earlier point. These are: (1) extractive, (2) regulative, (3) distributive, (4) symbolic, and (5) responsive. These five categories of capability may be viewed as functional requisites; that is, any political system—simple or complex—must in some measure extract resources from, regulate behavior in, distribute values in, respond to demands from, and communicate with other systems in its environments. There are surely other ways of categorizing the functional requisites of political systems at the system-environment level,[16] but this particular classification is presented as a useful starting point. It is the product of an informal coding of historical and contemporary political systems. A rigorous test of their usefulness can be made only by formal and explicit employment of these categories in coding historical and contemporary data.

But to say that these are functional requisites of any political system is only the beginning, since we are not interested in defining the minimal political system. We are concerned with characterizing real political systems both historical and contemporary, comparing them with one another at the system-environment level, dividing them into meaningful classes, and discovering their developmental properties.

---

14 Talcott Parsons, *Structure and Process in Modern Societies* (Glencoe, 1960), 181.

15 "Social Theory and Comparative Politics," in Eckstein and Apter, eds., *Comparative Politics*, 77.

16 See, for example, David Apter, "A Comparative Method for the Study of Politics," in *ibid.*, 82 ff.

For these purposes, we need to treat capabilities as performance magnitudes, either actual performance or potential performance. We stress that capability refers to performance and has to be separated from the institutions and agencies involved in the performance. To relate the institutions and structures to performance is one of the central problems of political analysis, and we ought not to confuse rates of performance with the means or instruments of performance.

Perhaps capabilities may be best thought of as ranges of particular kinds of performance. An examination of a particular political system may show variation in its rate of resource extraction over time. In war situations, the rate may be high; in normal periods, the rate may be substantially lower. But the problem of ascertaining the range of capability is more complex than examining rates of performance in normal and crisis situations. We may need to specify the extractive *potential* of a political system. What rate of extraction is this system capable of and under what conditions? This is only partly inferable from past record of performance. To get at this aspect of the range of capability we need to look at the support aspects of capabilities.

It is also necessary to distinguish between capabilities and elite policies and goals. Elite policies and goals may and usually do involve more than one capability. For example, a policy of economic development will require increases in resource extraction, and regulation, perhaps holding the line on distribution, and coping with demand inputs by increasing the symbolic capability. From this point of view capabilities may be viewed as ends intermediate to the policy goals of the elites. Since policies are made up of different doses of the different classes of outputs, capabilities analysis is essential to rigorous comparative policy analysis. It may enable us to distinguish sharply and operationally among different kinds of economic development, welfare, and other kinds of public policies.

It may also be in order to point to the implications of capabilities analysis for normative political theory. The inclusion of the performance or capabilities aspect of political systems may help bridge the gap which has been developing between the scientific and normative study of political systems. Questions regarding the "proper ends" of the state need to be grounded on empirical evidence of the different ways different kinds of political systems interact with individuals and groups in their domestic societies, and with political and social systems in the international environment. Empirical studies of the *performance* of political systems, of the *what* of politics (in addition to the *who* and *how*), should enable us to grapple operationally with what we mean when we speak of good and evil, just and unjust, political systems.

We may turn now to definitions of the five categories of capability. By the *extractive* capability, we mean measures of the range of performance of the political system in drawing material and human resources from the domestic and international environment. We separate this capability out because there have been political systems like the Mongol Empire, the warlords in China, guerrilla chieftains in Mexico, which have had little more than an extractive capability. Thus it makes sense to treat it separately, since it is to be found in all political systems, and is the distinguishing mark of a particular class of political systems. The extractive capability may be estimated quantitatively as a proportion of the national product; and its variations may be estimated quantitatively over time.

The *regulative* capability refers to the flow of control over behavior and of individual and group relations stemming from the political system. It is even more difficult to express it in quantitative terms than is the extractive capability, though aspects of it are measurable, and in a general way its magnitude, its pattern, and changes in its magnitude and pattern can be estimated. Here we have to concern ourselves with the objects of regulation, the frequency and intensity of regulation, and the limits of tolerance of regulation. While formulating indices to measure changes in this capability is a complex problem, the utility of this concept as an approach to political classification and development is evident. With these two capability concepts we can distinguish between primarily extractive political systems such as those referred to above, and extractive-regulative ones such as the historic bureaucratic political systems described by Eisenstadt in his recent book.[17] Furthermore, we can chart the developmental process from the one to the other, as regulative outputs cease being primarily unintended consequences of or instrumental to extraction and acquire goals of their own, such as some conception of social justice, order, economic advantage, or religious conformity.

The *distributive* capability refers to the allocation of goods, services, honors, statuses, and opportunities of various kinds from the political system to individuals and groups in the society. It is the flow of activity of the political system as dispenser of values or as redistributor of values among individuals and groups. Some aspects of this capability are more readily measurable than others. The structure of taxation may be viewed in its distributive aspects. The magnitude of welfare and educational programs can be expressed quantitatively, as proportions, and in terms of the social strata affected. Thus, while the general impact of public policy on social stratification is difficult to express quantitatively, there are aspects of it which are measurable, and the total pattern may be characterized for comparative and developmental purposes.

What we have said about political capabilities suggests a logic of capability analysis. An extractive capability implies some regulation and distribution, though these consequences may be unintended. A regulative capability implies an extractive capability, if only to gain the resources essential to regulation; and it is difficult to conceive of a regulative capability which would not in some way affect the distribution of values and opportunities. They are not only logically related. They suggest an order of development. Thus political systems which are primarily extractive in character would appear to be the simplest ones of all. They do not require the degree of role differentiation and specialized orientations that extractive-regulative systems or extractive-regulative-distributive ones do. Regulative systems cannot develop without extractive

---

17 S.N. Eisenstadt, *The Political Systems of Empires* (Glencoe, 1963).

capabilities; thus the development of the one implies the development of the other. Increasing the extractive capability implies an increase in the regulative capability, as when, for example, political systems move from intermittent collection of tribute or raids to some form of regularized taxation. Similarly, a distributive system implies an extractive capability, and obviously can reach a higher distributive level if it is associated with a regulative capability as well.

At an earlier point we spoke of *symbolic* inputs, referring to demands for symbolic behavior on the part of political elites—displays of the majesty and power of the state in periods of threat or on ceremonial occasions, affirmations of norms, or communication of policy intent from political elites. We referred to symbolic supports, meaning such behavior as showing respect for, pride in, or enthusiasm for political elites, physical symbols of the state such as flags and monuments, and political ceremonials. And we spoke of symbolic outputs, including affirmations of values by elites, displays of physical symbols, displays of incumbents of sacred or honored offices, or statements of policies and intents. Thus we need to deal with the *symbolic capability* of political systems and treat its relations to the other forms of capability. Surely we do not mean by symbolic capability simply the quantitative flow of symbolic events into and out of the political system. If capability is a profile of rates of performance— e.g., rates of extraction, regulation, and distribution—then symbolic capability is a rate of *effective symbol flow*, from the political system into the society and the international environment. The displays of flags, troops, and ships, the conduct of ceremonies on the occasion of anniversaries, or on the birth, marriage, coronation, and death of princes, kings, presidents, and the like, the construction of monuments, visits by royalty or high officials, are symbolic outputs either in response to demands or independently initiated by elites. The effectiveness of symbolic outputs of this kind is difficult to measure, but political elites (and journalists and scholars) often attempt to do so by counting crowds and audiences, recording the decibels and duration of applause, examining reports on the demeanor of audiences, or conducting surveys of attitudes. Similarly, affirmations of values by elites may be effective or ineffective. They may create or mobilize reserves of support, as did Churchill's speeches during World War II. Statements of policies may facilitate other kinds of system capability, increasing the rate of acquiescence in extraction, obedience to regulation, acceptance of distribution, and reducing the input of demands.

Symbolic output is not the same thing as symbolic capability. The output of symbols may cease to be edifying, menacing, stirring, credible, or even observed, listened to, or read. Royalty or high officials may be spat upon, pelted with rotten vegetables, statues thrown down from high places, pamphlets cast aside, television and radio sets turned off. Or, as in the case of new nations, the symbolism may have little if any resonance. Symbolic messages may be transmitted but not received. The symbols of local authority may be the only ones granted legitimacy, while the central symbolic output may have little, if any, meaning or effect.

While extractive, regulative, distributive, and symbolic capabilities are ways of describing the pattern of *outputs* of the political system into the internal and external environments, the *responsive* capability is a relationship between *inputs*, coming from the society or the international political system, and *outputs*. The responsive capability is an estimate of the degree to which outgoing activity is the consequence of demands arising in the environments of the political system. Again, the usefulness of this concept is suggested by the fact that it implies operational measures, i.e., a given quantity of responses to demands over the total of the demands. We are not minimizing the difficulties in translating this concept of responsiveness into specific measurable relationships. Obviously, in reality we shall have to settle for approximations for measurement of aspects of the relationship between inputs and outputs.

The reader must forgive the crudeness of this provisional formulation of the concept of political capability. It is the logical next step from treating the political system in terms of interaction with its foreign and domestic environments, in input-conversion-output terms. The capabilities of a political system are a particular patterning of input and output, particular performance profiles of political systems. We are more interested in demonstrating the importance of this level of analysis than in making claims for the effectiveness of this particular schema, more concerned with focusing and directing theoretical speculation and research than in presenting what would be a prematurely formalized theory. The truth of the matter is that we shall only arrive at a good capabilities theory through historical and contemporary studies in which we test out these and other coding schemes.

.   .   .

... The aims of research on political systems must be: (1) to discover and compare capabilities profiles summarizing the flows of inputs and outputs between these political systems and their domestic and international environments; (2) to discover and compare the structures and processes which convert these inputs into outputs; and (3) to discover and compare the recruitment and socialization processes which maintain these systems in equilibrium or enable them to adapt to environmental or self-initiated changes.

We have also to speak of the capabilities of other social systems. Just as the political system has a particular level and range of performance which we can summarize in terms of a capabilities profile, so also do other social systems in the society of which the political system is a part, and the international political system of which it is a member, have capabilities. Such social systems as the economy, the religious community, or family, kinship, and tribal structures also extract resources from the environment, regulate behavior, distribute values, display and transmit symbols, and respond to demands. Similarly, political systems in the international environment have capabilities, and the international political system may have some extractive, regulative, distributive, symbolic, and responsive capability. The flow of inputs into political systems, the kinds of problems they confront, and the pressure on them to develop capabilities will vary with the performance patterns or the capabilities of these other social systems. The distributive capability of an economy will affect the rate and intensity of demands for distribution, regulation, and the like entering into the political system. The need for developing the regulative capability of a political system will vary with the regulative capability of other social systems, including the international political system. When we think of the factors affecting the capabilities of a particular political system, we must see this problem in the context of interacting social systems, of which the political system is only one.

VII. THE SUPPORT ASPECTS OF CAPABILITY

Thus far we have stressed the performance aspect of capability, the rates which may be computed from the volume of particular kinds of output over time. We have already suggested that the range of capability can only partly be inferred from these performance rates, since political systems may operate at "less than capacity," or they may be drawing on reserves which in time will be exhausted. To get at this aspect of capability we need to deal with the question of supports. If we undertook the task of estimating the extractive capability of a political system, we would look for measures of the quantity or value of the money receipts, goods, and services drawn from the society in proportion to the total product of the society. But there are two aspects of political extraction which such a measure of the extractive capability would leave out. The first of these is the relation between the quantities "levied" by the political system, and the quantities delivered. How much tax evasion is there? How much evasion of military service, desertion? Is a day's work given for a day's pay? Do troops stand under fire? We speak of French and Italian *incivisme*, meaning by that a tendency toward non-performance, evasion, unresponsiveness, desertion. In other words, we need some way of estimating social performance in response to the outputs of the political system. Does the population pay its taxes, obey the laws, accept the reallocation of values, opportunities, and wealth stemming from the political system, respond to symbolic displays and appeals?

Related to this support performance is the idea of "support potential." The tax receipts of a political system, the proportion of taxes paid to taxes levied, will not tell us what the tax potential of a political system is. In the same sense, measures of the output of obedience to regulations will not tell us what the obedience potential of a political system is.

The support aspect of capability has to be measured, therefore, in terms of the resources delivered in relation to the resources levied, the obedience accorded in proportion to the obedience required, the allocations accepted in relation to the allocations imposed, the responsiveness of the population to symbolic outputs in relation to that which is expected. And in addition to these support performance measures, we need to know what rate of extraction, regulation, distribution, and symbol receptivity a society might accept, under varying conditions, from its political system without fundamental structural change in the relations between the political system and the society.

This may appear to be a needless conceptual complication, but we are constantly making judgments of this kind about political systems, estimating loyalty, morale, and commitment in relation to the performance and stability of political systems. What we are suggesting is that the support aspect of capability may be measured in two ways, by estimates of support performance—in other words, of behavior—and by probing the political culture in order to ascertain what the support possibilities are, the depth of the loyalty, the intensity of the commitment, the availability of support for various purposes, and the like. These constitute a kind of political system "reserve," and we need to know something about this reserve in comparing political systems, or in speculating about developmental prospects. . . .

.   .   .

VIII. DYSFUNCTIONAL INPUTS

.   .   .

An analysis of the capabilities of a political system will enable us to characterize the kind of development a political system has attained, but it does not tell us what factors affect political change or development, what produces change in capabilities.

Changes in capability are the consequence of the interaction of *certain kinds* of inputs with the political system. Consider, for a moment, a political system in equilibrium. There are flows of demands and supports from various groupings in the society; flows of demands and supports from the international political system; and inputs from the political elites (within the political system itself). There are flows of output—extractions, regulations, allocations, communications—from the political system into the society and the international political system. Within the political system the demand and support inputs are converted into extractions, regulations, allocations, communications. When all these flows have a particular range of content and level of magnitude, such that the existing structure and culture of the political system can cope with them, we may speak of the political system as being in equilibrium. But suppose there is a change in the content or magnitude of any one or combination of these input flows.

Suppose there is a depression and the unemployed in a political system demand jobs and food from the government, or a war breaks out and a neighboring power threatens its territory. Or suppose a new dynasty in a political system wants to engage in large-scale construction of temples, palaces, and tombs. Or suppose a political elite embarks on a radical departure in taxation; or requires religious conformity of its entire population and suppresses other religions; or embarks on a large-scale program of welfare. Any one of these input flows may be innovative, dysfunctional—i.e., they may require significant changes in the magnitude and kind of performance of the political system. These dysfunctional input flows are what "cause" changes in the capabilities of political systems, in the conversion patterns and structures of the political system, and in the performance of the socialization and recruitment functions. What we need to know is how these dysfunctional flows affect political development, what kinds of dysfunctional flows affect what kinds of capability patterns.

To cope with this question operationally we need to lay out the dimensions in which the flow of inputs may vary. We suggest that they may vary (1) quantitatively, (2) in their substance or content, (3) in their intensity, (4) in their source, and (5) in the *number of kinds* of dysfunctional inputs affecting the political system at a given point in time. We also need to keep in mind, in considering the significance of these flows for political development, the reactions of elites to dysfunctional inputs from the domestic and international environments, and the capabilities of systems other than the one we are examining—other social systems in the same society and the international political system—as they affect or are affected by the processes of the political system.

. . .

IX. SYSTEM ADAPTATION, RECRUITMENT, AND SOCIALIZATION

New roles and new attitudes are the essence of system change. New capabilities or levels of capability, new political institutions and processes, call for new elites, changes in elite training and indoctrination, and changes in expectation, commitment, values, and beliefs among the various strata of the population. The socialization and recruitment processes of a political system have a special relation to political change. We need to consider the different ways in which these system adaptation functions can become involved in the process of political change.

One common way in which recruitment and socialization patterns affect political development is through changes occurring in other social systems. Consider, for example, the process of industrialization. The spread of industrial technology and associated phenomena such as urbanization and the spread of mass communication tend to mobilize (in Karl Deutsch's terms) new strata of the population, recruit them into new economic and social roles and attitudes. These changes in activity and attitude may spill over into political orientations and stimulate new demands for participation and welfare. New elites (middle- or working-class demagogues and organizers) may be recruited and constitute the source of demands for structural change in the political system. Adults recruited into the industrial economy will be resocialized; children raised in urban-industrial families will be socialized differently from children in rural-agricultural families. This illustrates a sequence in which industrialization affects general socialization, role differentiation, and recruitment, which affects political socialization and recruitment, which in turn builds up innovative pressure on the political system.

Changes in the religious system may have similar consequences. The Protestant Reformation and the rise of individual sects, such as Methodism, changed the content and form of socialization and recruitment in England. New religious elites—clerical and lay—were recruited and came to constitute a stratum from which political elites were drawn. In the case of Methodism, the early British trade union and labor leaders were in many cases recruited from the Methodist subculture, just as the "radical" middle-class elites of the first part of the nineteenth century were recruited in part from the earlier nonconformist sects.

A second way in which recruitment and socialization may affect political change is through actions originating with the political elites themselves. Thus a political elite may directly manipulate the socialization and recruitment processes. This is dramatically illustrated in the policies of totalitarian countries, where the whole social infrastructure of family, community, church, and school is infiltrated, and where the party sets up an organizational system to indoctrinate and recruit among the younger generations. Resocialization of adults through party and party-controlled organizations and control of the mass media is also a totalitarian tactic. While this pattern is more deliberately manipulative in totalitarian countries, it is common in many others. The introduction of civic training in the schools is a common practice in democratic countries; and in clerico-authoritarian countries the church and its schools are self-consciously used as a device for political socialization.

A third pattern is one in which elite reaction to innovative pressures may affect socialization and recruitment in an indirect way. An adaptive reaction by political elites to demands for participation and welfare will not only produce immediate changes in political culture, structure, and capabilities. It may also have the longer-run consequences of affecting family and community socialization processes, producing young adults committed to the political system, providing it with support in the form of goods, services, and loyalty. Passive or alienated adults may be resocialized by adaptive and responsive behavior among the political elites, changing from alienated to allegiant orientations. Rejective reactions among political elites may have the contrary effect, transforming allegiant to alienative orientations and affecting the flow of support into, and the support potential of, the political system.

The consequences for political socialization and recruitment of aggressive foreign policies and frequent warfare should also be stressed. If successful, an aggressive foreign policy may increase support and introduce a nationalist-militarist content into family, community, and school socialization. If unsuccessful or excessively costly, it may produce a withdrawal of support and alienative tendencies in a population. French and German political history is instructive in these connections. The radicalization and alienative tendencies of French political culture during the life of the Third and Fourth Republics have often been attributed in part to the humiliating defeats and costly victories of the Franco-Prussian War and World Wars I and II. The rapid growth of the French Communist Party has been attributed in part to the strong pacifist currents set in motion by the enormous casualties of World War I. The fall of the Fourth Republic was triggered off by army officers who had experienced military defeat and the collapse of the French colonial empire.

The failure of efforts to democratize Germany has been attributed to the bureaucratization and militarization of Prussian and German society in the course of their aggressive expansion in recent centuries. The German educational system and family life were shaped in this military-authoritarian society and tended to produce obedient subjects lacking in "civil courage." The National Socialist elites recruited heavily among the "irregulars" of World War I, the men who could not adjust to peaceful routines after years of battlefield life.

The sequence here involves a particular pattern of foreign policy which produces a feedback of socialization and recruitment consequences, which in turn affects the flow of demands and supports into the political system. In our efforts to relate political development to dysfunctional interaction among political systems and their social and international environments, we need particularly to illuminate the recruitment and socialization processes as they reflect social change and stimulate political change, as they are the direct instruments of political change, or as they become the instruments of political change through a particular pattern of public policy.

What we have been suggesting here is that the performance of a political system (e.g., its "immobilism" or "mobilism"), its conversion characteristics (e.g., the congruence or incongruence of its structures, the cohesion or fragmentation of its culture), the operations of its recruitment and socialization processes, are explainable in terms of a particular history of interaction between the political system and its social and international environments.

We are not simply making the obvious point that we can learn much about political development from the study of history. What we are proposing is an approach to political development in terms of systematic comparative history. This has to be done with a common coding scheme, a set of categories, and hypotheses about their interrelations. The adaptation of political systems theory proposed here may serve as a starting point. We need to meet both prongs of the critique of recent tendencies in comparative politics at the same time—by formulating a conception of the political system which is developmental, and by testing and elaborating this conception against the richness of knowledge of man's historical experience with politics.

DAVID EASTON

The Environment of a
Political System

. . . if we are to entertain the notion that there are things outside of a system, latent in our minds must be the complementary idea that there are boundaries of some kind that demarcate a political system from whatever is not included within it. If that is so, in one way or another we must be able to indicate the nature of the boundary that tells us when something is happening in the environment or nonpolitical sphere. At the very least, such a boundary should not be conceptually ambiguous. It should have sufficient empirical referents so that positive clues are available to tell us when a person is acting as a member of a political system and when his interactions occur outside this area.

Furthermore, once the idea of a boundary between systems is introduced, it should make sense to say that if something happens in the nonpolitical arena, it may influence the political system. An exchange will have taken place across the boundaries of the two systems. Except for this possibility, there would be little point in seeking conceptual clarity with respect to the environment of a political system.

AMBIGUITIES IN THE CONCEPT "SYSTEM BOUNDARIES"

It seems reasonable to impose conceptual requirements such as these in connection with systems terminology. Yet when we look at the phenomenal systems, we encounter certain apparent difficulties and ambiguities. To consider a relatively simple obstacle, by way of illustration, are families, as structural units, to be excluded from political systems? If we were considering solely primitive, nonliterate societies, we might not be predisposed to do so too hastily. There, interactions within and between both nuclear families and extended kinship groups are highly charged with political content; this was equally true in earlier days among the aristocratic classes of many European societies. In at least two ways most families in modern societies continue to play a part in politics: through the contribution they make to the socialization of their own maturing members with respect to political attitudes, knowledge, and values; and in a diffuse way through the continued molding of the political attitudes and opinions of adult members. But the bulk of a family's activities relates to matters that cannot be labeled political. Yet because of its transparent participation in the vital area of political socialization and attitude formation, does this suggest that the family as a structure should normally be placed within the boundaries of the political system? To do so would be counter to common sense.

In a like vein, we might point to the investment policies and other activities of powerful financial houses in an industrialized society. These have at times been critical for the political destinies of a political party and government, as in the case of the influence presumably exercised by the Bank of England during the financial crisis of the Ramsay MacDonald Government in the thirties.[1] For that time are we to consider that the Bank of England and its specific actions lay inside the boundaries of the English political system? We would probably decide against inclusion of this structure on the grounds that the Bank was primarily an economic institution and therefore fundamentally part of the economy, especially since at the time it was privately dominated. Does this signify that if we are to be consistent, we must view a structure like this as part of two systems or that we at least ought to see it as oscillating between the political and economic systems?

At worst, this imagery seems to invite excessive reification or unpalatable analogizing; at best it confronts us with the real difficulty of deciding how we are to describe the boundaries of a political system so that we know what we can usefully include and exclude. For that matter, it raises the even more serious question as to whether we can intelligibly continue to speak of the boundaries of a system of interactions and of movement or exchanges across such boundaries.

THE SIGNIFICANCE OF SYSTEM BOUNDARIES

If the questions as to whether boundaries were real or mythical, simplifying or complicating, had little consequence or relevance for our subsequent analysis, there would be little point in pursuing the discussion any further. We shall find, however, that the idea of exchanges between a political system and its

---

[1] R. Basset, *Nineteen Thirty-One: Political Crisis* (London: Macmillan & Co., Ltd., 1958), Chap. 4, especially p. 62.

environment plays a critical role in the theoretical approach being developed. The concept "boundaries" will represent an essential analytic tool, and this for two reasons.

Closed and open systems

In the first place, an explicit conception of boundaries will aid us immeasurably in simplifying, interpreting, and understanding the way in which changes in the environment are communicated to a political system and the way in which a system seeks to cope with these influences. It is obvious that many changes in a political system may be owing to factors internal to it. Its own form of organization may be the source of major difficulties, such as those attributed to the separation of powers in the American political system.

Other significant kinds of stress may derive from the fact that a system is open to influences from its environment. Although this is an inescapable observation, an empirical truism need not always provide the groundwork for a theoretical analysis. For some purposes it is often necessary and useful to violate what is known, temporarily at least, in order to build a simplified model even if it bears only a remote resemblance to reality. It is entirely possible to conceive of a mode of analysis that would follow some models of physical systems and interpret political life as a closed system, one that conceived it to be isolated from the influences of its environment. Such an interpretation would require us to account for what happens in a political system solely in terms of its internal activities.

This is not quite so farfetched as it may seem. In the past considerable research with respect to political life did leave the impression that insufficient account was being taken of the parameters of political behavior. Personality, culture, and social structure, three of the major parametric systems, have only episodically been used as central explanatory variables until recent years. But no political scientist could neglect the obvious effects of at least some of the nonpolitical aspects of social life.

Nevertheless, if for initial analytic purposes we were to adopt the assumption that a political system is entirely closed, we would be forced to conclude that the system would have to move toward what could be called maximal social entropy. We would be rather hard put, however, to describe just what is implied in the notion of a political system "running down" in any sense comparable to its use in the physical sciences from which the ideas of closed system and entropy are borrowed.

As meaningless as the term might be for a political system, it does serve the vital purpose of forcing us to conceptualize the nature of the relationship between a system and its environment. That is, it raises what has been a latent assumption to a conscious level so that we recognize that we have indeed been conceiving of political life as an open system. Because this notion has been latent, its implications have not been fully understood nor has its theoretical significance been clear or fully exploited.

Once we raise the notion of an open system to the level of theoretical consciousness, it impels us to clarify the meaning conveyed by the idea of a system as distinct from its environment. To say that a system is open to outside influences makes sense only if we can distinguish inside from outside. But we cannot do this satisfactorily except by examining the properties of a presumed boundary that separates the two. At a later point the logic behind the idea of an open system will also make it necessary to seek to develop concepts that will enable us to handle an analysis of the exchanges between a system and its environment. At that time we shall find the ideas of inputs and outputs invaluable for this purpose. Here again the idea of exchanges or flows of effects would make little sense unless we were able to think of boundaries across which such transactions took place.

Identification of dependent variables

In the second place, the adoption of boundaries as a concept will also represent a strategic step toward the simplification of reality, an essential condition for any scientific research. It will provide us with a criterion for determining which politically important elements need to be explored in depth as our major dependent variables and which may be accepted as given in the form of external variables. Each of these types of elements, the internal and the external, will be crucial for an understanding of our problems concerning political systems, but each will have a different theoretical status in the conceptual model that we are in the process of constructing.

THE GENERAL PROPERTIES OF SYSTEM BOUNDARIES

How are we to distinguish between a political system and its setting? Does it make empirical as well as theoretic sense to say that a political system has a boundary dividing it from its environment? If so, how are we to define the line of demarcation?

The difficulties that beset us in seeking to answer these questions can be exposed, if not fully clarified, if we briefly consider other types of behaving or empirical systems with respect to which the existence of system boundaries is in much less doubt. By examining these systems and discovering the true significance of boundaries as a concept, we shall be in a better position to appreciate the utility and reality of attributing apparently similar boundaries to systems of social interaction, such as political systems.

The boundaries of physical and biological systems

All types of systems that have been found useful for research in the natural sciences are alike at least in that none of them functions in a vacuum in the phenomenal world. They are all imbedded in some kind of environment in fact, even though for heuristic purposes it may be necessary to exclude the influence of the setting temporarily, as in the case of the study of gravity under conditions of a frictionless world. Yet even though all systems are to be found in some kind of setting, they are able to maintain their identity with sufficient distinctiveness so that it is relatively easy for us to distinguish them from their environment.

From this perspective a boulder is one of the simplest of physical systems. Its density separates it from the surrounding air, and its parts share a common destiny as long as it retains its character as a boulder. Thereby we are able to distinguish it from adjacent boulders and the ground upon which it rests. The boundary between the boulder and other things is clear and unmistakable.

Our solar system, consisting of the sun and its satellites, similarly represents by its very designation a physical system of interest. Imaginatively and literally, given the technology, we could draw a line around it to designate its physical boundary. We can even consider the interaction of its parts as though, for the moment, it were not affected by the gravitational field of its own galaxy or even larger segments of the universe. Yet we know that the destiny of the solar system is irrevocably linked to the broader environment outside its spatial boundaries.

A waterfall as well may be considered a system of behavior, even though in this instance there is the complication that after a brief stay each drop of water constantly leaves the system never to appear again. This rapid flow of the water through the system does not lead us to confuse the waterfall with the precipice over which it cascades, the river feeding the water and drawing it away, or the winds contributing to its turbulence. Indeed, even though disturbances to the system may change the rate of flow of the water, the boundaries will usually change only marginally. They tend to be quite stable during short intervals of time.

An apple is an organic system isolated from its environment by a skin. We take it for granted that if our task is to understand the processes occurring within the apple itself as it matures and decays, we need to take into consideration factors outside of the skin itself. The soil in which the apple tree grows, the nature of the tree itself, and when parted from this, the humidity, temperature, and circulation of the atmosphere in which the apple is stored are all of decisive importance for the life of the apple as a system. Yet, from the point of view of the horticulturalist, these elements are variables external to the apple as an organic system. The boundary is well defined by the skin.

The human body is another biological system whose boundaries consist not of an imaginary line but of an epidermis that seems to mark it off unambiguously from its environment. In the maturation process we quickly learn not to confuse things bounded by our skin and those outside.

In each of these examples of physical or biological systems the boundaries seem simple enough to perceive. They form the spatial or material limits to the collection of variables in which we are interested. Either they in fact contain these variables, like an envelope, as the skin of an apple or of the human body, or it requires very little stretching of the imagination to conceive of some kind of shell surrounding them, as for the boulder, waterfall, or solar system. Such a container would decisively mark off the relevant variables from their surroundings.

But a system of social interactions, such as a political system, is normally so diffused throughout a society that we have considerable difficulty in accommodating the same imagery to these actions, taken collectively, that we apply so easily to physical and biological systems. A system of social interaction need not and usually does not include all of the actions of the person or group. Of course, if we were thinking of a specific political organization, such as a legislature, political party, interest group, or court, it is not beyond the bounds of our imagination to think of each of these organizations as possessing a physical boundary. At least we could think of scooping up all the members identified with these organizations and containing them within the walls of one building, if it could be built large enough.

We know that political interactions do not occur only within such well-defined goal-oriented structures. Much behavior occurs in other contexts, entirely outside a political organization, as in the illustrations mentioned earlier with regard to the family or an economic organization such as a bank. Furthermore, persons may act in political roles only intermittently, in the course of behaving economically or religiously, so that they may well seem to be popping in and out of a political system, as it were. We often talk politics at work, at social gatherings, and the like. When we take into account all kinds of political behavior, suffused as they are throughout society, it certainly seems to put a considerable strain on language as well as imagery to think of containing political interactions in some sort of envelope or within spatial boundary lines.

The general character of all boundaries

The circumscribing of boundaries for physical and biological systems seems to be simple enough. They do not seem to depend upon a decision on the part of the investigator but appear to be given in nature as though the systems were indeed purely natural in kind. But the simplicity in conceptualization of the boundaries is quite deceptive. These boundaries are, in fact, not phenomenally out there waiting to be identified. They conform to our general conclusion about the character of systems, that they are products of analytic selection; this is also true with regard to the boundaries of political systems.

We select the density of a boulder, the imaginary celestial line around our solar system, the form of the waterfall, and the skin of the apple and of the human being because we are particularly interested in understanding what happens to a set of variables defined by these limits. Although these are boundaries that we have become habituated to accepting, they stem from decisions that indicate the nature and limits of the theoretical or, for the layman, the practical interests on the part of the observer. If we had so wished, we could have ignored these boundaries and drawn entirely different ones. We could have considered each of these systems to be subsystems of a broader suprasystem consisting respectively of all rock formations constituting, say, the Pre-Cambrian shield, the Milky Way Galaxy, a river system, an orchard, and (with Patrick Geddes) the human biological organism as part of the ecological system. In fact, with regard to the human skin, as cytologists move in the opposite direction and reduce it to its component cells, at a given point of refinement in analysis they have difficulty in differentiating the epidermal cells from the surrounding air. The skin as an apparently natural boundary disappears.

In many cases, therefore, we may be able to draw a physical line to represent a boundary for a system, but this is an accidental although useful empirical property of some systems only. Conceptually a boundary is something quite different from its possible physical representation. A boundary line stands rather as a symbol or spatial embodiment of the criteria of inclusion-exclusion with respect to a system. It is a summary way of referring phenomenally to what we have included in or left out of a system. If, for systems in which space is a significant dimension, we can point to a line or a container, we know immediately that what is inside is part of the system and what is outside may belong to other systems.

For systems in which spatial location is not well defined or highly differentiated with regard to other systems and in which there may be considerable interlacing of behavior from different systems, we need other ways of describing or identifying the boundaries. Since the systems cannot be spatially and wholly separated from each other, the boundaries can be identified by the criteria in terms of which we can for each interaction determine whether it falls inside or outside the system. For the political system, as I have indicated, the test is whether the interactions are more or less directly related to the authoritative allocations of values for a society.

Accordingly, what we choose to put inside our system, to consider within its boundaries, will depend upon what we wish to examine in detail; for scientific purposes we also expect that these variables will show considerable interrelationship and coherence. What we leave outside, as part of its environment, will be those factors that we can accept as givens. They represent the independent variables or parameters of the system. In identifying them we thereby relieve ourselves of the need to go into detail about how they arise and what induces them to take the values that they do.

The external as compared to the internal or dependent variables may well have major consequences for the operation of the system. The fact that we consider them to be parameters of the system is not to be interpreted as indicating their irrelevance or lesser significance for understanding the functioning of the system. Their exclusion from the system for purposes of analysis says nothing at all about their contribution to the persistence or transformation of the system. All that it indicates is that the interrelationship of those elements or variables included in the system is what we wish to understand. They are the strictly political variables. We leave the explanation of variations in the parameters to others who are specialists in those areas. We need to know how the parameters vary, but we usually accept these variations as "givens" and seek to trace out their impact on the dependent internal or political variables.

Here we are fundamentally in no different a methodological position than those who study the physical or biological systems already mentioned. The gravitational forces of the universe compose part of the relevant environment of the solar system; large changes in these forces may destroy this system. In the analysis of the functioning of the solar system, however, it is quite satisfactory to assume these changes, to ignore their causes, and to confine our interest exclusively to the behavior of our solar system.

Similarly with regard to the human organism as a biological system, inadequate provision of nourishment can lead to its destruction. Yet in order to be able to cope with the unique range of problems that confront them as specialists, biologists are not called upon to become professional students of agriculture or of the system of distribution and exchange within a society.

We do not need to conclude from this generalized description of what is involved in the delineation of boundaries that, once established, they are eternally fixed. If it should turn out that owing to some mistaken interpretation or lack of insight, in order to improve our understanding of the political system we must include within it some element previously assigned to the environment, we are faced with no crisis. We simply redefine the system to meet our analytic needs. Each time that we enlarge our system we simultaneously shrink the environment. If this seems to introduce an element of indeterminacy into our conceptualization, I can only refer to our discussion of what we mean by a system. It is a device to help us to understand a defined and redefinable area of human behavior, not a strait jacket to imprison analysis permanently within a preconceived mold or model.

The deceptive character of geographic boundaries

It might appear that I am overstating the case against the spatial delineation of a political system. After all, we do have maps of societies and the boundaries on these maps represent positive constraints on the behavior of persons in the society. Are these not the physical boundaries of a political system? They are often referred to as geopolitical boundaries.

On the surface it may seem plausible to utilize geographic boundaries as coincident with our analytic ones. In fact, these are not the kind of limits which I am speaking of here. Geopolitical boundaries have important and obvious consequences for a political system and to that extent form an important variable. They do help to define the claims to and acceptance of the jurisdiction of a particular set of authorities, but they stand as the politically defined boundaries for the whole society, not solely of the political system in that

society. Geopolitical boundaries do not help us to differentiate those interactions *within* the society that are political from those that are economic,
religious, educational, or the like. They tell us when a person moves from the
jurisdictional claims of one set of authorities into those of another; they do not
help us to understand when this person moves from an economic setting to a
political one. The geopolitical boundaries circumscribe all interlaced social
systems of the society, not any specific social system.

From this discussion we must conclude that, in their theoretical status,
boundaries of systems need not always be spatial in nature. Analytically, the
boundaries of all systems may be interpreted as the criteria of inclusion in or
exclusion from the systems forming the focus of interest. The fact that empirically a system of political interaction cannot be contained, unmixed with other
social systems, by a line drawn on a map or cannot symbolically be put within
an envelope of some sort that separates it unmistakably from other systems of
social interaction does not weaken the utility of the concept "boundaries" as an
analytic tool. It just compels us to recognize that physical boundaries are only
one way of empirically separating systems.

EMPIRICAL INDICATORS OF BOUNDARIES
OF POLITICAL SYSTEMS

Although empirically there is no physical line across which we might step as
we move from one system to another, experience, nevertheless, lends reality to
the existence of a boundary between political and other systems in a society.
Most societies provide some clues as to when we move from one system of
behavior to another, although the absence of manifest telltales need not be
conclusive proof that an exchange between systems has not taken place.

The most distinctive indications of such exchanges occur in societies with a
high degree of structural differentiation, as in modernized social systems. In
such societies there is usually a sharp demarcation of many political roles from
other kinds of roles. Members of a society will have different expectations with
regard to the way persons will behave in political as compared with religious
or familial roles, for example. As we move from a strictly religious or family
setting to a political one, we are expected to change our rules of behavior in
some known degree. If we did not, we would be looked upon as odd or ignorant. In other words, in a structurally highly differentiated society regularized
patterns of expectations with regard to how we act in different situations provides one empirical test of the existence of boundaries between systems. This is
so clearly the case that in ordinary conversation we often speak of a person
"stepping out" of his role, say, as a religious leader or scientist and undertaking
to act as a political prophet or politician.

In many societies, though, the analytically distinguishable kinds of behavior
may be empirically fused. In various traditional, nonliterate societies, for
example, a few structures may perform all the major tasks. Through the kin-

ship structure alone all of the activities necessary for the persistence of the society may be carried out, such as the production of goods and services, transmission of cultural norms, inculcation of motivations, and the making of binding allocations. Under these conditions the political system would be completely embedded in this major structure and its components. A chief might act not only as the political chief, but as the ceremonial leader, the main economic decision maker, and the ultimate head of the kinship unit in its familial aspects. And in practice he might perform these varied kinds of actions virtually simultaneously. That is to say, a person might act in any analytically differentiated role without changing his setting or empirical role.

Under conditions such as these, empirical indicators of the boundary between the political and other social systems would be considerably more obscure than in modern societies. Even here, the society is not entirely devoid of empirical clues corresponding to the analytically distinguished kinds of behavior. A meeting of the elders of the clan, a council of war, or the introduction of a wand of authority in a ritual, cue the participants to the change of setting or of activity. In that sense, these cues provide evidence that the boundary into the political system of the society has been crossed.

It has been suggested that the degree of differentiation of political systems from other social systems and therefore, we may add, the clarity of the boundary between them is signalized by the following properties: (1) the extent of distinction of political roles and activities from other roles and activities, or conversely the extent to which they are all imbedded in limited structures such as the family or kinship groups; (2) the extent to which occupants of political roles form a separate group in the society and possess a sense of internal solidarity and cohesion; (3) the extent to which political roles take the shape of a hierarchy which is distinguishable from other hierarchies based upon wealth, prestige, or other nonpolitical criteria; and (4) the extent to which the recruitment processes and criteria of selection differ for the occupants of political as contrasted with other roles.[2] If we used indicators such as these, it would be possible to rank societies on a continuum with regard to the sharpness of definition and empirical delineation of intersystem boundaries.

THE ENVIRONMENT OF POLITICAL SYSTEMS

The intrasocietal systems

Those aspects of a society that fall outside the boundaries of a political system can be generalized by stating that they consist of all the other subsystems of the society. They constitute the environment of the political system. Environment embraces the social as well as the physical environment. Unless the context indicates otherwise, the concept will be used, henceforth, in both senses.

---

2 See S.N. Eisenstadt, *The Political System of Empires* (New York: Free Press, Inc., 1963).

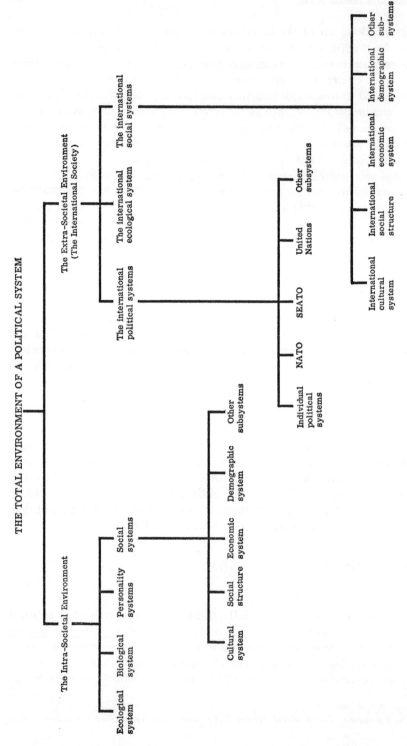

TABLE 1   Components of the total environment of a political system.

But this universal environment, with its variety of differentiable systems, has two major aspects: that is, the numerous systems external to a political system are composed of two basically different types, intrasocietal and extrasocietal. Table 1 depicts this dichotomy and indicates the various kinds of systems that are included within each of these two major types.

Let us consider the classification scheme. By the environment we may be referring to that part of the social and physical environment that lies *outside* the boundaries of a political system and yet *within* the same society. This is the intrasocietal part of the environment. In examining the impact of the environmental changes on a political system, we would be referring to changes that occur in these other social systems. A depression in the economy, a change of values and aspirations in the culture, or a shift in the class structure may each have consequences for a political system. These changes occur in areas outside of what is normally conceived to be the political system; yet they take place within the same society as the one that contains the political system. This part of the total environment will engage a considerable share of our attention. When we move beyond it into the extrasocietal systems, we are in effect dealing with what we normally call the international political system.

This intrasocietal part of the environment of a political system may be classified in many ways, but it will be helpful to simplify and order it by dividing it into several systems. The following may be identified as some of the major external intrasocietal systems of importance to the persistence and change of political systems: the ecological, biological, personality, and social systems.

There is nothing predetermined or sacrosanct about this classification scheme. Alternative formulations could be easily visualized. Since the mode of analysis to be explored does not rest definitively on the specific categorization of the environment of the political system, we do not need to pause very long over it. The important point, rather, requires that we recognize the fact of the environment and the theoretical problems it occasions. Without this, we could not proceed to suggest a kind of analysis designed to shed light on the way in which political systems are able to persist and change or cope with the stresses to which they are constantly exposed.

To indicate what is involved in the major intrasocietal environmental systems, we shall examine each in turn, but only very briefly. The ecological system encompasses the physical environment and the nonhuman organic conditions of human existence. In the physical part of the ecological system may be included geographical or spatial characteristics such as the nature of the physical resources, topography, size of territory, climate, and similar properties that influence the conditions of all existence including the political. The nonhuman organic aspects of the environmental systems refer to the nature, location, and accessibility of food supply and other flora and fauna that can be utilized by members of a political system. Variations in food supply, both for nomadic and sedentary societies, are known to affect the structure and processes of political systems, if technology is accepted as a constant.[3]

The biological system in the environment draws attention to the fact that in seeking to understand political processes, it is easy to neglect the hereditary properties that may help to determine human motivation in political as well as other social contexts. It refers to that aspect of political interactions that is determined or influenced by the biological make-up of human beings. To the extent that genetic characteristics impose limits upon the behavior of individuals, this may have implications for political life. Capacities for pacific or rational behavior, for cooperation as compared to conflict, are said to be related to the genetic inheritance of human beings. Orthodox Freudians have insisted on the inherent aggressive drives which all social arrangements, including the political, can ignore only at their peril.[4] The validity of this proposition is not at stake here; rather the only point is that politically relevant biological traits cannot be neglected as part of the total environment in which a political system operates. The fact that political science tends to do so, does not, of course, reduce either their theoretical or empirical importance.

Personality and social systems have received the widest and most detailed attention in the traditional literature. Social systems may be classified into several types: cultural, social structural, economic, and demographic. Here again the precise subdivision is not crucial.

Variations in the nature of the personalities and acquired motivations of members of a political system have long drawn the attention of students of politics. The science of ethology toward which John Stuart Mill was reaching and recent efforts around the theme of national character and variable kinds of political behavior presumed to be associated with different types of personalities reflect a firm recognition of the role of this major parameter.[5]

Fluctuations in the social culture by which personalities are shaped and in the economy, shifts in the general structure of society or in specific aspects of it (as in the number and size of group formations or of social classes) and changes in the size, rate of growth, composition, and distribution of populations are known to have high significance for what happens in the relevant political system. A great deal of the effort of political research has gone into

----

[3] E.R. Leach, *Political System of Highland Burma* (Cambridge: Harvard University Press, 1954), in which political structure seems to shift with movement from plains to hill agriculture; I. Schapera, *Government and Politics in Tribal Societies* (London: C.A. Watts & Co., Ltd., 1956), especially Chaps. I and VI and p. 219.

[4] See S. Freud, *Group Psychology and the Analysis of the Ego* (New York: Liveright Publishing Corp., 1951) and *Civilization and Its Discontents* (New York: Doubleday & Company, Inc., 1958); E.F.M. Durbin and J. Bowlby, *Personal Aggressiveness and War* (New York: Columbia University Press, 1939), and the same authors with others, *War and Democracy* (London: Routledge & Kegan Paul, Ltd., 1938).

[5] See N.J. Smelser and W.T. Smelser, eds., *Personality and Social System* (New York: John Wiley & Sons, Inc. 1963); J.S. Mill, *A System of Logic*, Book VI, especially Chap. V which is significantly entitled "Of Ethology, of the Science of the Formation of Character"; L.W. Pye, *Politics, Personality and Nation Building* (New Haven: Yale University Press, 1962); Lipset and Lowenthal, eds., *Culture and Social Character* (New York: Free Press, Inc.,

seeking to trace out, informally at least, the relationships between the political system and these environmental or parametric systems. Although I shall not interpret it as the task of an introduction to systems analysis to seek to extract systematically the actual relationships that exist between any of these parametric systems and the political system, nevertheless, a major effort will be directed toward devising a satisfactory set of categories for doing so.

Extrasocietal systems

The systems just identified are part of the same society of which the political system itself is a social subsystem. In this sense, these systems are external to the political system. Any influence they exert on the political system must derive from the fact that actions bridge the boundary between one or another of them and of the political system. This is the first sense in which a system may be said to be external to or in the environment of a political system.

But a system is external to a political system in a second and different sense. It may lie outside the society of which the political system itself is a social subsystem; yet it may have important consequences for the persistence or change of a political system. Instances of this are societies and political systems that are different from the society and political system under consideration. From the point of view of the United States, France is a society and contains a political system the consequences of the actions of which may cross the boundary of the American political system and help to shape its destinies.

We can broaden considerably this image of the external environment if we also view the whole international society as a unit external to any given political system. We may consider it a vital part of the extrasocietal environment. In fact, it is a summary way of referring to the whole of this environment, including the individual societies as subsystems of the international society. From this point of view, as components of the international society, we would find an international ecological system, an international political system, and such international social systems as an international culture, an international economy, an international demographic system, and so forth, just as in the case of the domestic societies. The international society as a whole or any of its subsystems would constitute parameters in the extrasocietal environment of a given political system and would have to be taken into account as possible sources of influence upon what happens within the given system. Among the

1961); R.E. Lane, *Political Life* (New York: Free Press of Glencoe, Inc., 1959), especially Part III and the many references found there, and *Political Ideology* (New York: Free Press of Glencoe, Inc., 1962), especially p. 400 ff.; A. Inkeles and D.J. Levinson, "National Character: The Study of Modal Personality and Sociocultural Systems," in *Handbook of Social Psychology*, G. Lindzey, ed. (Cambridge, Mass.: Addison-Wesley, 1954), II, 977–1020, and an extensive bibliography therein; D. Tomašić, *Personality and Culture in Eastern European Politics* (New York: George W. Stewart, Publisher, Inc., 1948); F.L.K. Hsu, ed., *Psychological Anthropology: Approaches to Culture and Personality* (Homewood, Ill.: The Dorsey Press, Inc., 1961), especially the essay by A. Inkeles, "National Character and Modern Political Systems," pp. 172–207.

international subsystems would also be found various collections of political subsystems such as NATO, SEATO, the United Nations, or the Soviet bloc, and each of these might have separate effects on a given political system.

The task will be to devise a conceptual structure for systematically and economically tracing out the exchanges of the extra- and intrasocietal parameters with a given political system. Diagram 1 provides a highly and inexpressibly oversimplified version of the relationships just discussed. It is presented here as another way of interpreting the classification shown in Table 1 and offers a simple spatial representation of the exchange between a system and the various components of its environment. At a later point I shall be able to modify this diagram so as to show, first, the dynamic relationship of a political system to its environment and, second, the flow of the influences of the environment through the system.

In reply to the questions with which we began this discussion, we have seen that political life may be described as a set or system of interactions defined by the fact that they are more or less directly related to the authoritative allocation of values for a society. Although similar allocations occur within other organizations, I shall find it useful to include within our range of theoretical concern only societal political systems rather than parapolitical systems. How-

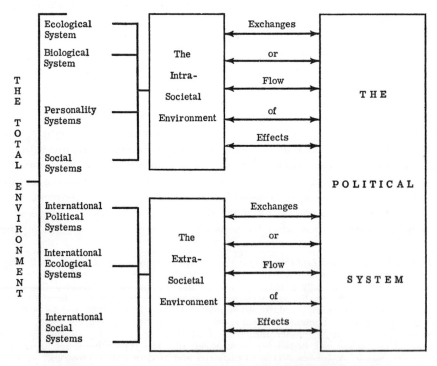

DIAGRAM 1 Exchanges between the political system and the total environment.

ever, much of our conceptual structure might apply equally well, with the necessary modifications, to the parapolitical systems of organizations.

What happens to a political system, its stability or change, will in part be a function of the operations of internal variables, the elements we are primarily concerned with understanding and explaining. The way in which they function, the stresses imposed upon them, and the behavior that occurs as a response to such stress will also be a product of what takes place in the total environment of the political system. A political system is an open one in the sense that it is exposed, in varying degrees, to the events that occur in its environment. The concepts "boundary" and "environment" help to order our analysis with these desiderata in mind. . . .

STEPHEN B. JONES

Boundary Concepts in the Setting of Place and Time

...Ideas about boundaries are related to their geographical and historical milieu. This theme is implicit in many writings about boundaries. It has been clearly exemplified for a particular area and era in Norman Pounds's two papers on the concept of natural frontiers.... It is my aim to extend the study backward and forward in time and expand it in space and to a variety of boundary concepts....

TRIBAL BOUNDARY CONCEPTS

I begin with the boundary concepts of people we call "primitive," whose political system we loosely call "tribal." ... It is easy to assume that primitive men have primitive ideas about boundaries, and that these are more or less alike around the world. A common assumption has been that primitive men have no linear boundaries but only zones. As Ratzel neatly puts it, "Not lines but positions are the essentials for this concept."[1] He describes many such cases, and they undoubtedly are common, but there certainly are exceptions. Forde says that the Boro, a people of the western Amazon, may set up fences and other boundary marks in the forest and use stream courses to delimit territories.[2] Both the Maidu of California and the Vedda of Ceylon had boundaries that

---

Reproduced by permission from the *Annals* of the Association of American Geographers, Volume 49, No. 3 (1959), 241–255.

[1] Friedrich Ratzel, "Die Gesetze des räumlichen Wachstums der Staaten," *Petermanns Mitteilungen*, XLII (1869), 103.

[2] C. Daryll Forde, *Habit, Economy and Society, A Geographical Introduction to Ethnology* (New York: Harcourt, Brace & World, Inc., 1934), p. 145.

were sometimes patrolled by sentries, according to Lowie.[3] Sharp describes the region of the Cape York peninsula of Australia inhabited by the Yir Yoront and their neighbors as divided into thousands of small, named tracts. These are clan property, the clan being "the only corporate entity," and are clustered to form larger, unnamed tracts, "the boundaries of which are well defined."[4] Pospisil spent a year in a part of New Guinea where European influence was virtually nil. Politically, the people among whom he lived formed a confederacy with four subdivisions. Boundaries, both internal and external, were clear-cut.[5]

Definite boundaries are compatible with depopulated defensive zones. Ratzel cites examples described by Barth and others from the Sudan, while Fischer mentions similar sharply bounded no-man's-lands between Germanic tribes.[6]

Barton's book on the Kalingas is an interesting anthropological study that touches upon political geography.[7] This people of the Luzon mountains inhabits much the same sort of environment as do the Ifugaos, and makes its living in much the same way. But the Kalingas developed the more definite concept of territory and boundaries. The Ifugaos have a zonal concept. The home region is surrounded by a neutral zone, with the people of which there is generally peace and intermarriage. Around this is a feudist zone with which there is more strife and less marriage. Outside all is a war zone, where hostility is the normal expectation. The Kalingas, on the contrary, present "a hard crustacean shell with respect to foreign affairs." "The bounds are vague and shifting in Ifugao, definite and stable in Kalinga." Barton further states that, although kinship is more often in the people's consciousness than is territory, territorial units are dominating the kinship groups, a process "considerably more advanced among the Kalingas than among the Ifugaos."

Kinship and territory have been major principles of political organization, sometimes competing, sometimes cooperating or compromising. Lowie argues convincingly that the territorial principle is never absent, even where kinship appears to be of overwhelming importance.[8] The territorial principle has tended to dominate as political development has progressed, though relics of kinship appear, as in the conflict of *jus sanguinis* and *jus soli*. It is permissible,

3 Robert H. Lowie, *Social Organization* (New York: Holt, Rinehart & Winston, Inc., 1948), p. 139.

4 R. Lauriston Sharp, "People Without Politics," *Systems of Political Control and Bureaucracy in Human Societies, Proceedings* American Ethnological Society (Seattle: American Ethnological Society, 1958), pp. 3–4.

5 Leopold Pospisil, *Kapauku Papuans and Their Law* (New Haven: Yale University Publications in Anthropology, 1958), No. 54, pp. 96–97.

6 Ratzel, *op. cit.*, p. 103; Eric Fischer, personal communication.

7 R.F. Barton, *The Kalingas, Their Institutions and Custom Law* (University of Chicago Press, 1949).

8 Lowie, *The Origin of the State* (New York: Harcourt, Brace & World, Inc., 1927), pp. 51–73.

I think, to say that the problem of racial segregation in the United States today is a form of kinship-territory conflict. The issue can be stated as, Shall there be two grades of citizenship based on so-called "blood" or only one based on territory? Residential segregation is a more or less conscious attempt to maintain the racial system by forcing it into the more viable territorial form. But if there is anything in historical trends, one should bet on the ultimate triumph of the territorial principle pure and simple.

Barton's study of the Kalingas illustrates the kinship-territory interaction in another way. Two men of different Ifugao home regions may enter into a trading partnership, which involves ceremonies and obligations, even to avenging the death of the partner's kin if it occurs in certain places. These Ifugao partnerships are usually not stable. Among the Kalingas, similar pacts have developed into "one of the most admirable and efficient primitive institutions I have ever seen or read about." These peace pacts, as they are called, are "held" by an individual and his kin and can be inherited. Only a man with numerous kin can muster the strength to enforce such a pact. The people of a region sometimes speak of themselves as "owned" by the pact-holders, although there is general social equality. As a mere hypothesis, I suggest that, in the absence of outside forces, Kalinga peace pacts might presage the development of a sort of feudalism and the emergence of strong territorial concepts. They could represent the incipient merger of the kinship and territorial principles, with the commoner's kinship bonds politically sublimated, so to speak, to those of the pact-holding families.

The foregoing are only samples of the possibilities that are open to the political geographer who delves into anthropology. The man who enters this field will find, however, that anthropologists have by no means supplied all the data he desires. The anthropologist who studies the politics of primitive peoples is likely to stop just where the political geographer becomes most interested. Tribal customs are described in detail, but the areal aspects of politics are likely to be given only vaguely, if at all.[9] There may be more on what may be called political ecology—for example, on the relation of customary law to agriculture—but even here, the things the geographer wants to know in detail are often the things that the anthropologist records only generally. This is of course no criticism of anthropologists. They do their research in terms of their own disciplinary goals. Rather it is an appeal to political geographers to do field work among primitive peoples. The results may be highly significant, for the political geography of tribes may shed light on that of national states.

SOME ASIAN BOUNDARY CONCEPTS AND PRACTICES

China can hardly be said to have had international boundaries, in the strict sense, until modern times. Like the Romans, the Chinese considered themselves

---

[9] George P. Murdock et al., Outline of Cultural Materials (3rd ed.; New Haven: Human Relations Area Files, 1950).

to be surrounded by barbarians, not by nations of equal rank. The Chinese did, according to, Lattimore, conceive of and desire precise limits between themselves and the barbarians. "The idea of a stable and exact Frontier—a Great Wall Frontier—was inherent in the structure of China as a whole. What could not be included must be excluded."[10] This was especially true on the north, vis-à-vis the peoples of the steppes. China's southern frontier was one on which the Chinese mode of agriculture could expand; that on the north could be crossed only by adopting another mode of life. The Chinese state was built on the base of irrigated agriculture. In Wittfogel's terminology, it was an agro-managerial despotism, ruling a hydraulic society.[11] Its organization was inapplicable to the steppes. But the ideal of a linear boundary between China and the steppes was never fully realized in practice. "That which was politically conceived as a sharp edge was persistently spread by the ebb and flow of history into a relatively broad and vague margin."[12]

Wall-building, according to Lattimore, was an expression of the desire for linear frontiers. It was, he says, a characteristic of the age. There were many Chinese walls before the Great Wall was built.[13] He calls the concept of a Great Wall "a product of the kind of state created within China"—a centralized state based on irrigated agriculture. In this connection, it may be noted that the steppe frontier of China parallels and flanks the irrigated valleys of the Hwang Ho, exposing it to invasion at many points. In contrast, Egypt's steppe frontier is transverse to the Nile.

Americans, conditioned by their own westward expansion, commonly think of frontiers as advancing and eventually disappearing, but only in recent times has Chinese expansion beyond the Great Wall been of that character. The historical purpose was to control the frontier rather than to obliterate it. The wall itself is evidence that further conquest was not strongly desired. Expansion beyond it was essentially defensive, to control border peoples, to suppress embryonic march-states.

In the steppes, the Chinese could not use their power in a normal way. At the risk of a strained analogy, one may suggest that this expresses a difficulty facing the United States along its "ideological frontier" today. The normal American way combines what we call "democracy" and "free enterprise." We understand that these words are simplifications of a complex way of life that has grown up in Europe and North America, chiefly, over many generations. We have found it difficult to operate in this way in lands of very different histories. At times even the most liberal of us must dream of a Great Wall— military, political, and economic—shutting out those whose ways we do not

10 Owen Lattimore, *Inner Asian Frontiers of China* (2nd ed.; New York: American Geographical Society, 1951), pp. 482–483.

11 Karl A. Wittfogel, *Oriental Despotism, A Comparative Study of Total Power* (New Haven: Yale University Press, 1957).

12 Lattimore, *op. cit.*, p. 238.

13 Lattimore, "Origins of the Great Wall of China: A Frontier Concept in Theory and Practice," *The Geog. Rev.*, XXVII (1937), 529–549.

understand. It is fortunate that orbiting sputniks remind us of the impossibility of such a boundary concept in this age.

China's southern frontier has been studied by my colleague, Herold Wiens.[14] In this region, a sort of indirect rule was maintained over some border peoples. Wiens quotes a statesman of the Ming Dynasty as follows:

> These barbarians are like the wild deer. To institute direct civil administration by Han-Chinese magistrates would be like herding deer into the hall of a house and trying to tame them. . . . On the other hand, to leave these tribal chieftains to themselves to conduct their own alliances or split up the domains, is like releasing deer into the wilderness without enclosing fences. . . . However, to fragment these domains under separate chieftains is to follow the policy of erecting restraining fences and is consonant with the policy of gelding the stallion and castrating the boar.[15]

But the Ming Court did not consistently follow this policy and the Ch'ing Dynasty was even more negligent. "Far from maintaining peace in the frontier area, [the chieftains] became the instigator of strife, and their capacity for protecting the frontier was negligible."[16]

One would expect to find waterpartings in common use as internal boundaries in lands of irrigated agriculture, to preserve the unity of drainage basins. Such in fact is often the case, Japan and Hawaii being exceptionally good examples. But the relationship of boundary to waterparting is incompletely explained by the assumption that it is inevitable. One must consider the relative role of pastoralism, for instance. Pastoralism was lacking in Japan and Hawaii. Where it is important, as in Tibet, waterpartings may not be the obvious boundaries. Kingdon Ward says of the Tibetan:

> His frontier is the verge of the grassland, the fringe of the Pine forest, the 50-inch rainfall contour beyond which no salt is. . . . The barrier may be invisible, but it is a far more formidable one to a Tibetan than the Great Himalayan range.[17]

Chinese statesmen, many centuries B.C., recognized the virtues of highlands and the defects of rivers as boundary sites for their civilization. The ideal of waterpartings as boundaries can be found in Japanese writings of the eighth century A.D. Indeed, the Japanese word for boundary is *sakai*, which means crest or divide. Where the Japanese boundaries cross or follow streams, they nearly always do so in parts of the course where there is little or no irrigated land.

In the third century B.C., China first became a unified state and was divided into districts. The formal subdivision of Japan into provinces or *kuni* dates

---

14 Herold J. Wiens, *China's March Toward the Tropics* (New Haven: The Shoestring Press, 1954).

15 *Ibid.*, p. 219.

16 *Ibid.*, pp. 220, 240.

17 F. Kingdon Ward, "Explorations of the Burma-Tibet Frontier," *Geog. Journ.*, LXXX (1932), 469.

from the seventh and eighth centuries A.D. The Chinese and Japanese languages use several of the same characters for territorial subdivisions, though the size of the division to which a given character applies may be quite different.

The general uniformity in size of the subdivisions of Japan is notable. This bespeaks not merely a naive use of waterpartings as obvious features but also a concept and a plan. The basic pattern is long-lived. The modern prefectures resemble the ancient *kuni* very closely, though consolidations have reduced the number. In the intervening centuries, the *kuni* boundaries were much used, though at times they "served merely as a geographical frame of reference."[18]

The pattern of water control in present-day Japan is exceedingly complex, says Eyre, with over one hundred thousand irrigation cooperatives and no general code of water law.[19] There is little central control; indeed there is marked aversion to it, though the central government has in recent years taken over some major constructions. The small size of the river basins favors local control. Moreover, there is generally a good deal of rain in Japan. Eyre quotes an old saying, "When rain falls, water disputes turn to bubbles." Wittfogel holds that the absence of large-scale irrigation works was a reason that a full-fledged hydraulic society, with its agromanagerial bureaucracy, did not develop in Japan.[20]

For India, "from Asoka to Aurenzeb," Spate has synthesized much information in the form of a map of boundary permanence.[21] The "skirt of the hills," both along the northwest frontier and in the jungles below the Himalayas, shows up prominently on this map, as does the line of the Narbada River across the northern Deccan. The *Arthaśāstra*, a manual of Indian statecraft perhaps dating from the fourth century B.C., recommends strong boundary defenses, with fortifications on sites naturally fitted for the purpose.[22] There appears to be a mine of rich ore, little touched as yet, from which significant geography can be smelted, in the historical records of India. Spate's chapter on "Historical Outlines" gives one an idea of both the possibilities and the difficulties.[23] The linguistic obstacles are great, but some day our graduate schools may consider the mastery of one difficult language at least equivalent to a smattering of two easier ones. If so, the learning of an Asian tongue may prove more attractive to language-shy Americans.

The partition of India in 1947 is described by Spate as "the expression of

---

18 Personal communication, John D. Eyre. For maps of *kuni*, see J. and R.K. Reischauer, *Early Japanese History* (Princeton University Press, 1937), Part B, pp. 10–37.

19 Eyre, "Water Controls in a Japanese Irrigation System," *The Geog. Rev.*, XLV (1955), 197–216.

20 Wittfogel, *op. cit.*, pp.197–200.

21 O.H.K. Spate, *India and Pakistan, A General and Regional Geography* (2nd ed.; New York: E. P. Dutton & Co., Inc., 1957), p. 147.

22 *Kautilya's Arthasastra*, trans. R. Shamasastry (4th ed.; Mysore: Sri Raghuveer Press, 1951), pp. 45–50.

23 Spate, *op. cit.*, pp. 144–170.

a new economic nationalism that has inevitably taken into its hands the immensely powerful weapon of immemorial religious and social differentiation." It left in its wake problems of water supply. The land drained by the Indus and its tributaries is one of the most ancient homes of a hydraulic society, and the great modern irrigation works have likewise been directed by the central government. Water supply is an immediate issue in the Punjab and potentially one in Kashmir.

ROMAN BOUNDARY CONCEPTS

As suggested above, there was considerable similarity between the frontier problems and policies of Rome and China. "The Roman Republic," wrote Pelham, "can scarcely be said to have had any frontiers. It certainly had no system of frontier delimitation or defence."[24] (It is obvious the "frontier" is here used in the sense of "boundary.") The Roman of the Republic "disdained to set any bounds to Roman dominion." The Rhine and the Euphrates were first suggested as boundaries not by the Romans but by barbarian rulers, and the suggestions fell on deaf ears.

> The foundations of a frontier system were laid by Augustus. It was he who organized the Roman army as a standing force, who stationed the greater part of it in the frontier districts, and who first established permanent camps; and though in the earlier years of his reign the old ideas of universal empire found expression in literature, and were possibly shared by himself, he left as a legacy to his successors the advice "to keep the bounds of the empire within fixed limits."

The centralizing and organizing zeal of the emperors, coupled with increasing anxiety about the barbarians, led to the elaboration of a frontier administrative and defensive system. Although the immensely long boundary cannot properly be treated as a unit, the basic desire seems to have been security within definite limits. Adami says that the Romans habitually laid down natural boundaries—rivers, mountain tops, watersheds. "Large rivers make essentially the best military boundaries. The Romans knew this well."[25] Given the military technology of the time, this was probably true. Moreover, the rivers were natural lines of communication along the frontier. And, of course, the Roman state was not based on irrigation, as was the Chinese, so river boundaries were less inconvenient.

But there were stretches of the Roman frontier where no rivers or other natural strong lines existed, and other stretches where, for one reason or another, the Romans overpassed the natural lines that did exist. Although the Romans did dig ditches and erect palisades and even walls in such places, they were less inclined to continuous fortifications than were the Chinese. *Limes,*

---

24 Henry Francis, *Essays*, ed. by F. Haverfield (Oxford: The Clarendon Press, 1911), p. 164.
25 Vittorio Adami, *National Frontiers in Relation to International Law*, trans. T.T. Behrens (Oxford University Press, 1927), pp. 4, 13.

the word commonly applied to such frontiers, originally meant a road along a property line. It came to have the military meaning of a fortified road in a frontier zone, and, by extension, the frontier zone itself. It was "a zone where all is organized for the protection of the empire."[26] The general map in Poidebard's atlas shows well the network of forts, watchtowers, and roads on the Syrian frontier. In North Africa, many miles of trench and wall exist, but Baradez believes these did not delimit the territories of Romans and barbarians but were rather the last line of a defense in depth.[27]

One of the best-known of the Roman *limes* was that across the reentrant formed by the upper courses of the Rhine and Danube. In this area, according to Pelham, a true barrier was erected only near the end of Roman rule, earlier constructions having been apparently for administrative convenience rather than defense. One stretch of nearly forty-eight miles was laid out in a straight line—perhaps the earliest example of a major straight-line boundary. Farther north, in the Taunus, a chain of posts was built beyond the Rhine in order to surround and isolate a formidable German tribe.

The Romans, like the Chinese, sought to stabilize frontiers and cut military costs by means of self-sustaining border forces. In the rear of the Roman defense lines was a zone called *terra limitanea* or *agri limitanei*. Those given land here were in general obligated to assist in defense. The system developed faults, however. The frontier militiamen became inferior in status to the soldiers of the regular army and were relatively immobile, "many of them indeed being little better than armed peasants."

BOUNDARY CONCEPTS OF MEDIEVAL EUROPE

The Middle Ages in Europe, speaking very generally, saw feudalism evolve into absolute monarchy, though, to be sure, there were kings in the feudal system and noblemen under the monarchies. The basic change, of course, was in the degree of central power. The salient characteristic of these ages, in respect to territory, was inheritance, not by the group but by individuals, and especially by eldest sons. Church lands were of course not transmitted in this wise, but we do observe the association of church lands with individuals for their lifetimes.

Yet, oddly, European feudalism did not begin as a hereditary system. Neither kinship nor territory was an original principle. Rather, feudalism began as a personal bond between two individuals, a lord offering protection and favor, a vassal offering loyalty and service. But this personal bond acquired both hereditary and territorial nature in many cases. Technically, the death of either lord or vassal ended the bond, but it became common practice to renew the bond with the successor, until this became customary. As Bloch puts

---

[26] Jean Baradez, *Fossatum Africae* (Paris: Arts et Métiers Graphiques, 1949), p. 134.
[27] *Ibid.*, p. 358.

it, the ties of kinship tended to pattern themselves after those of the feudal relationship.

Since the lord was responsible for the maintenance of his vassals, he commonly granted them land, and these fiefs tended to become hereditary. The combination of territorial and hereditary principles eventually obscured the purely personal bond. A nobleman might hold fiefs from a number of lords. The Count of Champagne held lands from the King of France, the German Emperor, the Duke of Burgundy, two archbishops, four bishops, and the Abbot of St. Denis. Obviously, he could not pledge complete loyalty to all of them. The concept of *liege homage*, or first loyalty, arose, but it was clear that the purity of feudal tenure was gone.

In the feudal system, each noble was largely autonomous at his own level. The power of the king was restricted. The obligations of inferior to superior were definite and limited. The limited nature of feudal rule was, Pounds points out, a reason that river boundaries often functioned smoothly. "The life of market and farm was one thing; the homage of the seigneur another."

A well-known feature of feudalism is that it produced a patchwork political map. Discontinuous holdings were common, and were tolerable because of the decentralized nature of feudal rule and warfare. Some of this discontinuity persisted into the period of monarchies, but with increasing dissatisfaction. The discontinuous nature of Brandenburg-Prussia is a well-known case. The two principal parts of this domain were separated by a band of Polish territory for a century and a half. This was slowly whittled away. Frederick the Great, who made Prussia a major power, was concerned for the unification and "rounding out" of his territory. By his time, of course, government and defense were strongly centralized.

The hereditary principle remained powerful after the feudal system had effectively been swallowed by centralism. Louis XIV, the monarch who did so much to emasculate feudalism in France, went to great pains to justify his territorial designs by claiming hereditary rights. Such claims were a factor in the War of Devolution (1667–68), the War of the League of Augsburg (1688–97), and the War of the Spanish Succession (1701–14).

Relics of feudalism still exist in Europe. Andorra's autonomy is legally a dual feudal tenure. The continued independence of Monaco hinged on the birth of an heir. This in the age of nationalism and ideology rampant!

THE CONCEPT OF NATURAL BOUNDARIES

Perhaps the clearest example of my theme in all history is the rise of the concept of natural boundaries, discussed by Pounds.... Some, perhaps many, of those who read this address were taught in school that there are two kinds of boundaries, natural and artificial. The concept of natural boundaries retained enough vitality to stimulate critical discussion at least as recently as 1940.

Natural marks were of course used for boundaries for millenia before there arose a doctrine about them. They are still being adopted—for example, the Oder-Neisse line. The virtues and defects of natural boundaries and the several meanings of the term have been well discussed by Broek[28] and need not be recapitulated here. It is the rise of the doctrine that concerns us, for it accompanied a change in *Zeitgeist*.

The doctrine of natural boundaries was a product of the Age of Reason and of nationalism chafing at old restraints. Its origin, according to Pounds, was largely French. Philosophers of the Age of Reason appealed to Nature for guidance, at least when it was convenient. . . .

When the revolution swept away the remnants of French feudalism, the concept of natural boundaries took predominance over historical claims. But such claims were not completely dropped, especially if they could be identified with those of natural law. Thus Carnot is quoted as desiring "the ancient and natural boundaries of France," combining the appeals of history and nature.

NATIONALITY AND BOUNDARY CONCEPTS

A German reaction to the concept of natural frontiers was the concept of boundaries based on folk or nationality. Actually, nationality was often confused with the related but not identical fact of language. Fichte said that one born where German was spoken could consider himself not only a citizen of that state but of "the whole common fatherland of the German nation." But most interestingly, Fichte did not discard the notion of natural law. He simply said that common language and culture constitute a natural law higher than that of rivers and mountains. The French reply, Pounds says, was to emphasize culture rather than language: ". . . what marks out a nation is neither race nor language. Men feel it in their hearts when they have in common thoughts and interests, affections, remembrances and aspirations." With this, most would now agree, but we know how difficult it is to determine such facts objectively and to translate them into boundaries.

It is understandable that the Germans of the early nineteenth century, not having attained a national state, should idealize it, and needing a criterion for German nationality, should turn to the seemingly simple one of language. We see something similar currently at work in India. Leaders of that federal republic have had to yield to the demand for states based on language, though fearing the divisive effect. The problems of the near but imperfect correlation of speech and nationality, of dovetailing along linguistic frontiers, and of imperfect censuses of languages plagued boundary makers after both World Wars.

Cobban states that national self-determination is inherent in nationalism— "the Divine Right of Peoples."[29] But the problem of determining nations by self-determination has been a difficult one. Its application has proved to be an

---

28 Jan O.M. Broek, "The Problem of 'Natural Frontiers,' " *Frontiers of the Future* (Berkeley and Los Angeles: University of California Press, 1941), pp. 3–20.

29 Alfred Cobban, *National Self-Determination* (University of Chicago Press, 1951), pp. 5–6.

art rather than a science. It has been particularly difficult to apply this concept
to the drawing of boundaries; yet this is precisely where nationality is a most
acute question.

The theme of self-determination was heard in chorus in the fateful years of
1917 and 1918. The Central Powers, the Provisional and the Bolshevik governments of Russia, and the Western Powers all sang in praise. Wilson made a
most broad and explicit statement on July 4, 1918, calling for "the settlement
of every question, whether of territory, of sovereignty, of economic arrangement, or of political relationship, upon the basis of the free acceptance of that
settlement by the people immediately concerned."[30]

The Paris treaties reflected Wilsonian idealism in part, in part power-
politics. The statesmen at Paris felt themselves competent to determine "self-
determination" in most cases. Plebiscites were held in a number of questionable areas, with varied success. All in all, it is one of the surprises of history that
the map of Europe of today bears so much resemblance to that established at
Paris in 1919. But some of the resemblance is superficial. There has been wholesale transfer of populations, making peoples fit boundaries instead of boundaries fit people.

Although nationality is basically a "we-feeling" in a group of people, it
embodies a strong territorial bond. The desire for territorial contiguity seems
to be intensified by nationalism. After Waterloo, France was reduced to its
pre-Napoleonic bounds, but, significantly, the Avignon enclave was not taken
away. Of all the territorial clauses of the Treaty of Versailles, none angered the
Germans more than that establishing, or reestablishing, the Polish Corridor,
even though there was some ethnic basis for it. The increasing activity of
central governments in all phases of life may be a reason for this dislike of discontiguity, but sometimes it seems almost mystical. One occasionally hears
Canadians object to the odd but inconsequential projection of Minnesota
north of the forty-ninth parallel. Discontiguity was used as an argument
against statehood for Alaska and Hawaii.

IMPERIALISM AND BOUNDARY CONCEPTS

European overseas imperialism followed the voyages of discovery that ... gave
a world-wide sense of space and opened up an immense exploitable world. It
was late in this era of imperalism—when, however, European flags still floated
bravely over much of the world—that Friedrich Ratzel promulgated his seven
laws of state expansion. Ratzel's laws refer to the growth of states as well as of
empires, but because the emphasis is on expansion, and expansion has usually
at least a flavor of imperialism, I am mentioning them at this point.

Only one of Ratzel's laws deals specifically with frontiers or boundaries.

---

30 Samuel Flagg Bemis, *A Diplomatic History of the United States* (New York: Holt,
Rinehart & Winston, Inc., 1936), p. 635.

This is the fourth: "The frontier is, as a peripheric organ of the state, the bearer of its growth and its security, conforming to all changes of the state organism." Not feudal tenure or natural law is the principle, but the character of the state as an organism. It is true that Ratzel used organismic terms as analogies and felt the state to be incomplete as an organism. Semple in fact said that the organismic aspect of his thought was only a scaffolding that could be removed without injuring the main structure. There is certainly much that is substantial in Ratzel's work. Nevertheless, the organismic aspect exists, and the geopoliticians later made use of it.

The organismic concept sees an analogy between such biological frontiers as timberline and the frontiers between human groups. As a descriptive device this may be effective, but an analogy is neither analysis nor proof. Stripped of its organismic terminology, Ratzel's fourth law is little more than a truism so far as it refers to territorial growth. Moreover, it is difficult to keep analogies in the role of servant. It is easy to use them as props for further analogies. This is what happened in the writings of Maull and Haushofer, acquiring with the latter a dynamism that is well-known. With the geopoliticians, boundary stability was denigrated as an effort to limit the growth of a living thing.

Lord Curzon's ideas on boundaries are well-known through his lecture on frontiers.[31] In this lecture, Curzon set forth his own frontier conditioning:

> It happened that a large part of my younger days had been spent in travel upon the boundaries of the British Empire in Asia, which had always exercized upon me a peculiar fascination. A little later, at the India Office and at the Foreign Office, I had had official cognizance of a period of great anxiety, when the main sources of diplomatic preoccupation, and sometimes of international danger, had been the determination of the Frontiers of the Empire in Central Asia, in every part of Africa, and in South America. Further, I had just returned from a continent where I had been responsible for the security and defence of a Land Frontier 5,700 miles in length, certainly the most diversified, the most important, and the most delicately poised in the world; and I had there, as Viceroy, been called upon to organize, and to conduct the proceedings of, as many as five Boundary Commissions.

Curzon looked upon his career as an imperial administrator with satisfaction. The peroration of his lecture is too long to quote, but it extolled the courage and skill of the frontier officer and called upon the English universities to furnish such men. Here, then, was a most explicit statement of the political climate as Curzon felt it, in which his boundary concepts grew. A similar feeling of successful work on the frontiers permeates the writings of Thomas Holdich, the great demarcator of about the same period.[32]

---

[31] Lord Curzon of Kedleston, *Frontiers*, The Romanes Lecture, 1907 (2nd ed.; Oxford: The Clarendon Press, 1908).

[32] For bibliography, see S. Whittemore Boggs, *International Boundaries, A Study of Boundary Functions and Problems* (New York: Columbia University Press, 1940), pp. 253–254.

Curzon did not sharply distinguish between "frontier" and "boundary," but he recognized the process by which a frontier may become a demarcated line. In contrast to the organismicists, he regarded this as progress, not as an artificial restraint. Curzon spoke respectfully of Science, which by this time had replaced Nature and Reason as an object of veneration:

> It would be futile to assert that an exact Science of Frontiers had been or is ever likely to be evolved: for no one law can possibly apply to all nations or peoples, to all Governments, all territories, or all climates.... But the general tendency is forward, not backward; neither arrogance nor ignorance is any longer supreme; precedence is given to scientific knowledge; ethnological and topographical considerations are fairly weighed; jurisprudence plays an increasing part; the conscience of nations is more and more involved. Thus Frontiers, which have so frequently and recently been the cause of war, are capable of being converted into the instruments and evidences of peace.

Curzon stood somewhere between what I shall call the power-political and the contractual concepts of boundaries. He knew the need for force along frontiers. He described the use of protectorates and spheres of influence in bland words but with callous realism. But he at least dreamed of boundaries as "instruments and evidences of peace." I think anyone will agree, after reading the lecture, that the imperialist was the core of the man. Boundary-making, to him, was to a great extent unilateral—a strong, wise, just, imperial power establishing good boundaries. He speaks of "what is known as the Scientific Frontier, i.e., a Frontier which unites natural and strategical strength, and, by placing both the entrance and the exit of the passes in the hands of the defending Power, compels the enemy to conquer the approach before he can use the passage." Science is thus military science and the Scientific Frontier gives an advantage to one side that obviously cannot be given to both. If frontiers were to be "the instruments and evidences of peace," preferably it was *Pax Britannica*.

THE CONTRACTUAL CONCEPT OF BOUNDARIES

The theory that government is, or should be, a contract between rulers and ruled has a long history and has been used to explain or justify a wide variety of institutions, from absolutism to democracy. This theory of government, in its democratic form, has been congenial to Americans, whose Declaration of Independence holds that governments derive their just powers from the consent of the governed. The American faith in written constitutions reflects the contractual concept.

The essence of the contractual concept of boundaries is that two countries should agree on a line and stick to it, as individuals agree on property lines. In contrast, an organismic state could hardly consider its "peripheric organ" to be the proper subject of a contract. Please note that, in distinguishing between power-political and contractual concepts of boundaries, I do not mean that practices necessarily follow one or the other. The contract may be a mere facade to hide power-politics.

Although I shall, for convenience, illustrate the contractual concept mainly with American examples, it would be hypocritical as well as incorrect to call it the American concept. American territorial expansion was basically power-political. Yet the steps in acquiring much of this territory had also some of the nature of real-estate transactions. Many of the Atlantic seaboard colonies began essentially as land ventures. Louisiana, Florida, Alaska, and the Gadsden strip were purchased and a payment was made to Mexico after the Mexican War. These steps seem to show a desire to establish a sort of contractual title. That the Indians might claim a prior title was seldom considered seriously, though sometimes this title was expunged, to American satisfaction at least, by purchase or treaty. That these treaties were repeatedly broken shows that the contractual concept was not allowed to stand in the way of "destiny." Yet it is possible that lip-service given this concept in time affects practice.

The increasing divergence between the usage of "frontier" and "boundary" is congruent with the contractual concept. Other languages than English permit a distinction between the two ideas, but in American usage the difference is now so great that they are essentially unrelated. In the United States and other new lands, a framework of boundaries was laid down before the land was densely settled or even effectively controlled in many cases. "Frontier" came to mean the advancing fringe of settlement rather than of territorial acquisition. Indeed, "frontier" has come to mean the locus of a way of life rather than a specific geographical location. There was still a frontier long after the Pacific Ocean became the western boundary of the United States. The Mexico-United States boundary lies in what most Europeans would call a frontier, but I have never heard an American so describe it.

We are not justified in attributing superiority to the contractual concept just because it has to work with us. Perhaps this concept, if raised to the level of a general principle, would be an attempt to apply "one law," and that law based heavily on the unusual American experience, to "all nations and peoples." Americans have quite correctly been charged with not understanding European politics....

The contractual concept has certainly colored the views of American writers on boundaries. We find it expressed in S.W. Boggs's *International Boundaries*. Boggs was both idealistic and practical. He sought to reduce friction along boundaries by changing functions rather than locations—by functional contracts, so to speak. Your present speaker mentioned the boundary concepts of Curzon, Haushofer, and Spykman in the opening chapter of his book, *Boundary-Making*, but it is clear that he thought the contractual concept was the desirable one.[33] This book was written during the war, expressly for use in

---

[33] Stephen B. Jones, *Boundary-Making, A Handbook for Statesmen, Treaty Editors, and Boundary Commissioners* (Washington: Carnegie Endowment for International Peace, 1945), pp. 4–11.

postwar treaty-making and boundary demarcation. With the wisdom of hind-sight, it can be called a case of "preparing for the last peace." We thought in terms of formal peace conferences. We hoped the victors would unite in seek-ing a lasting peace and would frame territorial settlements with that in view. We were strangely blind to the tumult of forces—the madness of the Nazis, the Communists' vested interest in disorder (outside their own domain), and the power vacuums created by destruction.

THE CONCEPT OF GEOMETRICAL BOUNDARIES

There is in the United States, Canada, Australia, and to a lesser degree in some other parts of the world, a massive simplicity in boundary pattern. Probably any governments occupying or claiming vast, poorly mapped, lightly settled areas would be inclined to adopt simple boundaries. The common use of rivers as boundaries in such cases was not respect for "the Law of Nature" but for the practical matters of exploration, transportation, and cartography. Rivers were conspicuous and seemingly precise on maps that showed mountains only vaguely.

The use of long geometrical lines as boundaries required some geodetic sophistication. Their application to America was of European origin. The Papal Line of Demarcation—really a "line of allocation" and not a boundary—was the earliest. The charters of English colonies specified geometrical bounda-ries in many cases. The conflicting western land claims of these colonies arose largely from the extrapolation of their geometrical boundaries. The parallel of forty-nine degrees was first suggested by the Hudson's Bay Company, as a boundary between French and English possessions in eastern Canada, as early as 1714.[34]

Thomas Jefferson played a leading part in applying geometry to the American landscape.[35] A neo-classical love of order, symmetry, and simplicity permeated his career. In 1784, Jefferson chairmanned a congressional commit-tee to plan for the western lands, between the Appalachians and the Mississippi, that had become federal property when the seaboard states gave up their con-flicting claims. This committee presented a plan for fourteen new states. Lines of latitude and longitude were to be boundaries wherever possible. The Ohio River was admitted as a boundary for part of its length, with the apology that it nearly coincided with the parallel of thirty-nine degrees. This is indeed an about-face from the concept of natural boundaries. Needless to say, this plan was not followed literally. Only a few state boundaries conform to the com-mittee's recommendations; yet the general pattern certainly reflects the geo-metrical ideal. In the new west, across the Mississippi, the geometers came into their own, creating two rectangular and many nearly rectangular states, with

---

34 Max Savelle, "The Forty-Nine Degree of North Latitude as an International Boundary, 1719, The Origin of an Idea," *The Canadian Historical Review*, XXXVIII (1957), 183–201.
35 William D. Pattison, *Beginnings of the American Rectangular Land Survey System, 1784–1800* (University of Chicago, Department of Geography, 1957).

sublime disregard for mountains and canyons. That Americans and Canadians adapted themselves to such boundaries with relative ease reflects their acceptance of the contractual concept.

POWER-POLITICAL BOUNDARY CONCEPTS

Boggs's *International Boundaries* and the second edition of Haushofer's *Grenzen* appeared at about the same time.[36] Boggs's America and Haushofer's Germany were divergent in their climates of political thought. The environment in which Haushofer evolved his boundary concepts needs little description. He was an officer in a proud army that had suffered defeat. His country had been forced to accept peace terms that he and many of his fellow citizens felt to be humiliating. Economic depression led him to think that Germany lacked *Lebensraum*. He read widely, drawing on such writers as Kjellén, Mahan, and Mackinder. His knowledge was vast but he "overinterpreted" it.

Haushofer's basic boundary concept is perhaps best summed in his own words: "a biological battlefield in the life of peoples."[37] To be more precise, this was his concept of frontiers, the boundary being but a truce line in the battlefield. If we grant his organismic postulate, his frontier concept follows as the night the day. To be sure, few of us have ever granted the postulate, even in the heyday of American interest in *Geopolitik*. But the mistake we made was failing to see that many in Germany did accept such a postulate or at least acted as if they did. The climate of thought that produced *Geopolitik* produced Nazism. Many of us believed Hitler when he said that the Sudetenland was his last territorial demand and felt that Chamberlain's scrap of paper was a valid contract.

The full impact of *Geopolitik* did not hit the United States until the war years. . . . Nearly all of those who played prominent roles in familiarizing Americans with *Geopolitik* were strongly critical. Gyorgy, Mattern, Strausz-Hupé, Walsh, Weigert, and Whittlesey come to mind. Spykman wrote critically of Haushofer's "geographical metaphysics" but said that "the fact that certain writers have distorted the meaning of the term geopolitics is no valid reason for condemning its method and material. . . ."

Spykman's concept of boundaries was derived from his ideas on power. A boundary is not only a line demarcating legal systems but also a line of contact of territorial power structures. "Specific boundaries at any given historical period become then merely the political geographic expression of the existing balance of forces at that period."[38] Now and then Spykman came close to organismicism: The power of a state is "like the dynamic force of every organic

---

36 Karl Haushofer, *Grenzen in ihrer geographischen und politischen Bedeutung* (2nd ed.; Heidelberg-Berlin-Magdeburg: Vowinckel, 1939).

37 Haushofer, "Das Wissen von der Grenze und die Grenzen des deutschen Volkes," *Deutsche Rundschau*, L (1924), 237. Haushofer calls this a German concept of boundaries and attributes it to Ratzel.

38 Nicholas John Spykman and Abbie A. Rollins, "Geographic Objectives in Foreign Policy," *Amer. Polit. Sci. Rev.*, XXXIII (1939), 391.

entity" and "other things being equal, all states have a tendency to expand." There is no doubt that his boundary concept is power-political rather than contractual. He would not have denied this or apologized for it.

Spykman evaluated power in terms of resources and strategy, both on a grand scale. Peacemakers, he argued, must think of the geography of power, for "interest in the frontier is now no longer in terms of the strategic value of the border zone but in terms of the power potential of the territory it surrounds." In the United States of 1941 this was a more startling statement than it seems today.

BOUNDARIES SINCE THE SECOND WORLD WAR

I shall not attempt to discuss the climate of political thought of recent years but will call attention to some aspects of it that are pertinent. . . . One is the concern with national power, or, as the Sprouts have suggested, state capabilities. National power has been conceived as having two dimensions, inventory and strategy, or what one has and what one does. Thoughts on the power inventory have considered population, natural resources, and industries, primarily. Thoughts on strategy have been dominated by spectacular advances in nuclear weapons and space technology, but the importance of diplomacy and economic activity and the possible menace of "limited wars" is now of widespread concern. Population and resources have been of concern not only as factors of state capability but also in respect to the maintenance of existing industrial civilization and its spread to the underdeveloped areas.

Important among the intangible aspects of the postwar *Zeitgeist* is the strength of nationalism and its spread to new parts of the world. Accompanying this is an increasing feeling of the need for international or even supranational organizations that is finding expression in a number of ways. Then there is, of course, the ideological factor that, with the concomitant activation of the resources of the Soviet Union and China, has divided the world into hostile camps of relatively equal power.

An awareness, though somewhat myopic, of the problem of power led to the focussing of much thought in the last years of the war on the containment (a word not then used) of Germany and Japan. Mackinder and Spykman were rather optimistic about Soviet-Allied cooperation for the control of unruly "Rimland" countries. In fact, of course, Soviet-Allied cooperation was a bit mythical even during the war and dissolved completely soon after. Welles and Morgenthau advocated the reduction of German power, the former by partition, the latter by both partition and deindustrialization.[39] Germany and Japan were temporarily deindustrialized by air attack and Germany was partitioned by the freezing of occupation zones, but this negative approach to power back-

---

[39] Summer Welles, *The Time for Decision* (New York and London: Harper & Row, Publishers, 1944), pp. 336–361. Henry Morgenthau, Jr., *Germany is Our Problem* (New York and London: Harper & Row, Publishers, 1945).

fired. It was the Communist Bloc, not the erstwhile enemies, that had to be contained, and both Germany and Japan have reindustrialized and are slowly rearming, with the blessing of former conquerors. A more positive approach to the power needs of the present has been the system of alliances that the United States, once wedded to the doctrine of "no entangling alliances," has taken the lead in forming, though some of these may still be no more than "Paper Curtains."

Some actual boundary settlements after the war were a restoration of the *status quo ante*. Some conformed to a degree with linguistic borderlands. Considerations of power underlay most of these decisions. The ideal of self-determination, which had been reaffirmed in an article of the Atlantic Charter, was not much heard in the actual war settlements but has influenced the postwar devolution of overseas empires.

As is well known, population transfers took place on a colossal scale, both during and after the war. . . . [The] transfer of populations [has] indicated the bankruptcy of nationalism as a form of human organization . . . [yet] its hold on the human mind is stronger than that of ideology. Nevertheless, it is possible that nationalism is near its zenith. As the national map of the world approaches completion, its colors may begin to lose their luster. . . .

LADIS D. KRISTOF

The Nature of
Frontiers and Boundaries

THE ORIGINS AND EVOLUTION OF TERMS

... In common speech we use the words "frontier" and "boundary" with the implication that these have not only a quite well-defined meaning but also that they are (or almost) interchangeable. However, it does not take much reading in pertinent literature to discover that the problem is not so simple.[1]

Frontier

Historically, the word "frontier" implied what it suggests etymologically, that is, that which is "in front." The frontier was not an abstract term or line; on the contrary, it designated an area which was part of a whole, specifically that part which was ahead of the hinterland. Hence it was often called the foreland, or borderland, or march. For the purpose of our discussion it must be stressed that in its historical origin the frontier was (1) not a legal concept, and (2) not, or at least not essentially, a political or intellectual concept. It was rather a phenomenon of "the facts of life"—a manifestation of the spontaneous tendency for growth of the ecumene. In antiquity, and later too, the

Reproduced by permission from the *Annals* of the Association of American Geographers, Volume 49, No. 3 (1959), 269–282.

[1] It may be of interest to cite the following definitions on which the British Association Geographical Glossary Committee has agreed: "*Frontier*. 1. A border region, zone, or tract which forms a belt of separation, contact, or transition between political units. 2. A delimited or demarcated boundary between States (more properly a frontier line).—*Boundary*. 1. Synonymous with frontier (in sense 2). 2. The line of delimitation or demarcation between administrative units or between geographical regions of various types, whether physical or human." "Some Definitions in the Vocabulary of Geography," *The Geographical Journal*, CXVII, No. 4 (December 1951), 458–459.

frontier was on the margin of the inhabited world, but each particular ecumene, for instance, that of the agricultural society as opposed to the nomad society, also had a frontier. The *limes* of the Roman empire were those of the ecumene of Western civilization.

With the development of patterns of civilization above the level of mere subsistence strictly adapted to particular environmental conditions, the frontiers between ecumene became meeting places not merely of different ways of physical survival, but also of different concepts of the good life, and hence increasingly political in character. But even at this stage the frontier was something very different from what a modern boundary is. It had not the connotation of an area or zone which marks a definite limit or end of a political unit. On the contrary, given the theory that there can (or should) be only one state —a universal state—the frontier meant quite literally "the front": the *frons* of the *imperium mundi* which expands to the only limits it can acknowledge, namely, the limits of the world. Thus the frontier was not the end ("tail") but rather the beginning ("forehead") of the state; it was the spearhead of light and knowledge expanding into the realm of darkness and of the unknown. The borderlands—the marches—were areas of dawn; they were frontiers in the sense of Turner's agricultural frontier: pioneer settlements of a forward-moving culture bent on occupying the whole area.

Boundary

The etymology of the word "boundary" immediately points to the primary function of the boundary: the boundary indicates certain well-established limits (the bounds) of the given political unit, and all that which is within the boundary is bound together, that is, it is fastened by an internal bond.

"Boundary" is a term appropriate to the present-day concept of the state, that is, the state as a sovereign (or autonomous) spatial unit, one among many. Since the transition from tribal law to territorial law the essentials of statehood both from the functional and legal point of view are: territory, people, and a government in effective control internally, independent externally, and willing and able to assume obligations under international (or federal) law. Sovereignty is territorial; hence it must have a certain known extent: a territory under exclusive jurisdiction limited by state boundaries. The borderlands, the old marchlands, are defined more and more exactly until there is, in principle, an exact borderline. The modern sovereign state is bound within and confined to its legal limits. The boundaries bind together an area and a people which live under one sovereign government and law and are, at least presumably, integrated not only administratively and economically but also by means of a state idea or "creed." At the same time "the state is marked off from its neighbors by political boundaries." In an age in which we (with exceptions) do not think in terms of universal empires but accept the co-existence of many creeds and states, it is important to have the spheres of the several centripetal, integrating forces legally delimited.

THE DIFFERENCES BETWEEN FRONTIERS AND BOUNDARIES

There are some difficulties in trying to distinguish between frontiers and boundaries. First, not all languages have separate words for the two. Then, the historical transition from one to another in many regions tends to diminish the awareness of the essential differences. Still, this does not change the fact that frontiers and boundaries are in their very nature two different things.

The *frontier* is *outer-oriented*. Its main attention is directed toward the outlying areas which are both a source of danger and a coveted prize. The hinterland—the motherland—is seldom the directing force behind the pulsations of frontier life. As history, American, Russian, or Chinese, well illustrates, the borderlands often develop their own interests quite different from those of the central government. They feel neither bound by the center nor binding its realm. Rather, they represent runaway elements and interests of the state's corporate body.

The *boundary*, on the contrary, is *inner-oriented*. It is created and maintained by the will of the central government. It has no life of its own, not even a material existence. Boundary stones are not the boundary itself. They are not coeval with it, only its visible symbols. Also, the boundary is not tied inextricably to people—people teeming, spontaneous, and unmediated in their daily activities on, along, or athwart the border. It is the mediated will of the people: abstracted and generalized in the national law, subjected to the tests of international law, it is far removed from the changing desires and aspirations of the inhabitants of the borderlands.

While the frontier is inconceivable without frontiersmen—an "empty frontier" would be merely a desert—the boundary seems often to be happiest, and have the best chances of long survival, when it is not bothered by border men. Yet the boundary line is not merely an abstraction. Still less can it be a legal fiction. It must be reality, or, rather, reflect reality. In other words, it must be co-ordinated with an empirical force actually present and asserting itself in the terrain. The boundary is, in fact, the outer line of *effective* control exercised by the central government.

The *frontier* is a manifestation of *centrifugal forces*. On the other hand, the range and vigor of *centripetal forces* is indicated by the *boundary*. True, the frontier has, and always had, also a strategic meaning—the defensive line which keeps enemies out—and in this it depends on support from the hinterland. But precisely in order to be able to maximize its strategic forces the central government must mobilize and integrate all the available resources. All efforts and loyalties must be concentrated and co-ordinated under the banner of the state idea and interest. Consequently, the frontier lands, too, have to be controlled and bound to the state; they must be subordinated to the imperative and overriding demands of the sovereign *raison d'être* of the state as a whole. In other words, an effort is made to draw somewhere a line of effective control over both ingress and egress; not only the enemy has to be kept out but one's own citizens and resources have to be kept in. It is in the interest of the central government to substitute a boundary for the frontier.

The *frontier* is an *integrating factor*. Being a zone of transition from the sphere (ecumene) of one way of life to another, and representing forces which are neither fully assimilated to nor satisfied with either, it provides an excellent opportunity for mutual interpenetration and sway. Along the frontier life constantly manipulates the settled patterns of the pivotally organized sociopolitical and cultural structures. It is precisely this watering down of loyalties and blurring of differences that the central governments attempt to forestall by substituting the semi-autonomous frontiers with a controlled and exact borderline.

The *boundary* is, on the contrary, a separating factor. ... The boundary separates the sovereign (or federal, or autonomous, or any other) political units from one another. However much physical-geographical, cultural, or certain political factors may tend to make it inconspicuous, it remains always a fixed obstacle; it impedes integration across the borderline. ...

In general, discussing the differences between frontiers and boundaries, one faces a grave dilemma: to what degree is it possible to generalize about the frontier? The boundary is defined and regulated by law, national and international, and as such its status and characteristics are more uniform and can be defined with some precision. But the frontier is a phenomenon of history; like history it may repeat itself, but, again like history, it is always unique. It is difficult to pinpoint essential features of the frontier which are universally valid. For instance, the degree to which the frontier is an integrating factor depends on the attractiveness to the frontiersman of the way of life of his opposite number. This way of life usually seems attractive if the adoption of it promises better chances of survival in the given environment or if it appears generally "superior." On the American frontier both the white settler and the Indian were willing to learn from each other certain techniques, but on the broader cultural level each considered his way of life as definitely preferable ("superior"). Consequently, the integrating process along the American frontier touched only upon the externals—the internal lives of the two social groups remained incompatible; witness the fact that intermarriages were rather rare and almost no white American ever really "became" an Indian or vice versa. The Spanish and the native Mexican culture were relatively more compatible; hence much more integration occurred along the frontier in Mexico, and the result is a genuinely composite culture, especially outside the cities.

The importance of the relative compatibility of cultures which meet on a given frontier can be illustrated by comparing the advance of the Russian and the northern Chinese frontier. Both of these frontiers have been biting into the heritage of the Mongol Empire. But the Russian way of life, based on an extensive agriculture, was much less different from that of the pastoral nomad subjects of the Mongol khan than was the Chinese culture which was based on an intensive and irrigated agriculture. This helps to explain why the Russians succeeded in taking such a lion's bite of the Mongol Empire, and in integrating, even absorbing to a large extent, the natives, while the Chinese pushed their frontier only a few hundred miles or less into Extra-Mural China. Since the Russians did not, like the Americans, steam-roll the native cultures, or even the natives themselves, out of existence, the Russian expansion was not merely a *frontier of conquest* but also a *frontier of integration*: the new culture was the result of a fusion. There are historians who think that the Russians paid a heavy price for integrating so many "barbarians": in the process they ceased to be Europeans and became Eur-Asiatics.

BOUNDARIES AS LEGAL-POLITICAL PHENOMENA PAR EXCELLENCE

We have said that boundaries are fixed by law. There is, however, often confusion as to what a law is and what kind of laws determine the limits of states. The misunderstandings which arose from the use of the terms "natural boundaries" and "artificial boundaries" are at least partly due to this confusion. Thus, it will be helpful if we make the distinction among three types of law:

(1) *Law of nature, i.e., scientific law,* is a creature of facts. . . . It is ruled by the empirical world. We observe the natural phenomena . . . and deduce from our observations certain generalizations about the behavior of elements and call them laws, e.g., the law of gravity. But these laws have no coercive power over nature. On the contrary, if facts do not conform to the laws, the latter are adjusted to conform to reality. The concordance between what *is* and the law must be absolute.

(2) *Natural law, i.e., moral law,* is as strict as the scientific law but in an exactly opposite sense. It is not the *is* but the *ought* which is sovereign. The status of the moral law is not affected by the facts. All Jews and Christians ought to obey the Ten Commandments, yet even if not a single one of them did, the Law would still be there; unchanged, categorical, and as binding as ever. The moral law exists in itself, that is, in the justice of "thou shalt" and not in the empirical world in which it may or may not be observed. While in the natural world a law which does not conform to facts is no law at all, in the moral world only that is a "fact," i.e., a moral fact, which conforms to the moral law.

(3) *Jural law (lex)* is a formal verbalization and particularization of the moral standards of a given socio-political order in respect to the practical (or at least observable) behavior of the members of the society. It is an attempt to bring the spiritual and empirical realms together, to make the moral standards "efficient." Three characteristics of jural law are important for our discussion: it is coercive, it may be violated, and its ultimate source is public opinion about values. Imperfect both in its moral substance and enforcing procedure, the jural law is, as all political phenomena are, the result of compromises reflecting the complexity of the social forces interacting on the given scene.

Boundaries are supported by jural laws. They are one of the spatial expressions of the given legal order. As distinguished from "boundaries" between phenomena of the physical geographical or natural history world, they are man-made geographical occurrences. A boundary does not exist in nature or by itself. It always owes its existence to man.

True, the "boundary" in the natural world, e.g., an orographic line, or the limit of the habitat of certain species of flora and fauna in the desert, steppe, or forest zone, also may occasionally be man-fixed, but it is not man created. It *is* in nature, and all man does is to shift and reshuffle it in space as he transforms the natural environment into a cultural environment.

The limit in the political world is not a matter of *is*; like everything political it is of the domain of *ought*. Man chooses among certain priorities and values—of faith, philosophy, or civilization—and decides according to them where the boundary ought to be: follow the line of religious divisions, extend to where "might made it right," or separate the peoples according to their tongues and customs. And the life span of the boundary is coeval with the pre-eminence of the forces stemming from the given "ought," for it is a function of human will. Human will brings it to life and must sustain it continuously in the terrain or at least within the legal framework on which it rests.

The "boundaries" in the natural world rest on physical laws which are self-enforcing and cannot be broken. A water divide always conforms to the law of gravity, and it must always exist in nature. It does not need to and cannot be willed because it is independent of human will. Man may want to know where it is, but he does not create it. In any given environment the watershed is automatically traced by immutable physical laws. The boundaries in the political world are, on the contrary, built on jural laws, and thus, in the ultimate instance, on the moral laws accepted by the lawmakers. Given certain values the boundary ought to be here or there, but it may be elsewhere. Moral laws are not absolute rulers. They are, like all wisdom, only advisory.

If we understand the political nature of boundaries we shall never commit the mistake of speaking, like Lapradelle, of an objective as opposed to a subjective (that is, one leaving room for choices and preferences) conception of boundary making. Even if we reject the currently fashionable theories of cultural relativism and adhere to the classic philosophical concept of objective truths, problems of boundaries will always remain a matter of the particular—an application of general principles to specific cases—and thus *par excellence* political. To say that there is an "objective conception" of politics which eliminates choices reminds us of the often advocated "depolitical politics." Politics without alternatives and choices is a contradiction in terms, like dehydrated water.

In fact, not only boundaries but all limits ascribed to an area—any compound area, also a nonpolitical purely physical geographical and wholly uninhabited area—are always subjective. They are defined anthropocentrically: both the area and its limits are viewed through the eyes of man and conceived in terms of human concepts of life. "Any attempt to divide the world involves subjective judgment. . . . A map of 'natural regions' or of 'regions based solely

on natural elements' with reference to mosquitoes, would be entirely different
from one made with reference to sequoias.... Needless to say, all such divisions by geographers have been made with reference to man's point of view—
nature as man is concerned with it."[2] Moreover, man's judgments of areas are
colored by his particular culture. The criteria of definition for "natural"
regions or landscapes are of one kind in an industrial society, of another in a
society of primitive food gatherers, and again different among pastoralists,
peasants, etc.[3]

The political nature of boundaries, and the nature of politics itself, is much
better understood by Haushofer than by Lapradelle. We may disagree with
Haushofer's classification of boundaries and boundary problems, or with the
solutions he envisages, but this is a political disagreement, one which has its
roots in the values we cherish and the concepts of state we hold. It is not possible to deny the validity of his assertion that boundaries are zones of frictions.[4]

The boundary is a meeting place of two socio-political bodies, each having
its particular interests, structure, and ideology. Each generates loyalties and
also imposes duties and constraints for the sake of internal harmony and compactness and of external separateness and individuality. Two neighboring
states do not need to be engaged continuously, or at any time, in a struggle for
life and death. They may compete peacefully and, in general, minimize their
conflicts of interest. Still, the very existence of the boundary is proof that there
are some differences in ideology and goals, if not of a virulent present-day
character then at least imbedded in the historical heritage. The French-Swiss
boundary is certainly very peaceful. Yet, the political ideas and ideals, the

---

[2] Richard Hartshorne, *The Nature of Geography* (reprinted by the Association of American Geographers from the *Annals Assoc. Amer. Geogrs.*, XXIX, No. 3 and 4 (1939), 296, 300.
See also Jean Brunhes and Camille Vallaux, *La Geographie de l'Histoire* (Paris: Felix Alcan,
1921), pp. 61–62: "A river or a mountain are frontiers [boundaries] only in so far as we have
this or that economic and political conception of the frontiers—conception which is subject
to change with the course of history.... There are in nature only those frontiers which we
seek.... According to times and places the same phenomena of nature have been, or have
ceased to be limits."... For a recent, very exhaustive, discussion of the problem of subjectivity in man's concept of landscape—subjectivity conditioned by value systems, specific
interest, or individual preference, see Otto Wernli, "Die neuere Entwicklung des Landschaftsbegriffes," *Geographica Helvetica*, XIII, No. 1 (March 1958), 1–59, especially 17–22, 35–
46. See also Hans Carol, "Zur Diskussion um Landschaft und Geographie," *Geographica
Helvetica*, XI, No. 2 (June 1956), 111–133.

[3] It is this cultural (technological or ideological) differentiation and subjectively or judgments which, in this writer's opinion, justifies the use of the terms "ecumene" and "frontiers
of ecumene" not only in all-human but also in a particular human sense: it may be sometimes meaningful to speak of the ecumene of the human race as a whole, but it may, at
other times, be equally meaningful to differentiate between the ecumene of the Pygmies, of
the Eskimos, of the Chinese civilization, of the Islamic faith, etc. In fact, such differentiation
was already at least implied in the use of the term by the Greeks and early Christians when
they contrasted their *oikumene* with the lands of the barbarians or the *partibus infidelium*.
Contemporary writers who speak of cultural blocs are also implying such a differentiation.
See Donald W. Meinig, "Cultural Blocs and Political Blocs: Emergent Patterns in World
Affairs," *Western Humanities Review*, X, No. 3 (Summer 1956), 203–222.

[4] Nicholas John Spykman, "Frontiers, Security, and International Organization," *Geographical Review*, XXXII, No. 3 (July 1942), 436–447.

ways of life, and the structure of society are very different in the two countries, and consequently no one advocates a Franco-Swiss merger or even federal union. If two neighboring political units pursue both theoretically and practically identical goals, then the intellectual and physical communication across the boundary will be so intensive as to sweep it away. When Malta voted to join Great Britain, or Syria and Egypt merged, the community of thought and interest was able to overcome even geographical separation. The two Germanys are, in their own political will, one, but remain separated by a boundary which is that of superimposed political entities and supranational integrating forces.

FRONTIERS IN THE CONTEMPORARY WORLD

The example of Germany brings us face to face with the problem of the current reappearance of the phenomena of frontiers and frontier lands, but in a novel, less earthbound, form. Whether we like it or not, boundary disputes, so dominant in international politics a generation ago, are fading away from diplomatic agenda. They are replaced in both urgency and importance by problems of a new kind of frontiers—frontiers of ideological worlds.

During the Middle Ages the development of clear-cut concepts of political entities and boundaries was hampered by two factors: one, the hierarchical system of feudal authority with its overlapping, divided, and often conflicting loyalties, and, two, the still lingering idea of the supremacy of a universal *imperium* (or *sacerdotium*) over the particular *regnum*—the lingering hope for a Christian *Monarchia*, a true *Civitas Maxima*. But after the fiasco of the religious wars the idea of sovereignty, combined later with the rising tide of nationalism, favored the emergence of national states with sovereign territory bound by an internationally recognized and inviolable boundary. With the adoption in 1918 of the principle of national self-determination, it was hoped that a stable international order with rule of law might be realized. However, any legal order is possible only if a certain socio-political maturity is attained, that is, if there is a general understanding as to the underlying values. Laws reflect the crystallization of the political community around a value system.

The Versailles-created system of quasi-law-regulated international order was based on a Western concept of justice, and, among others, on the assumption that loyalty to the nation and the nation state is the overriding loyalty. Today, not only is the old consensus undermined, but the very concept of territorial law is challenged. "Proletarians have no fatherland" and "proletarians of all countries unite" are the best known but not by any means the only ideas which try to transgress on the territorially organized socio-political order. In the resulting confusion friends are sought in enemy territory, and enemies discovered among fellow citizens of the homeland.[5]

Under such circumstances the whole situation on the international scene,

---

[5] See Ladis K.D. Kristof, "Political Laws in International Relations," *Western Political Quarterly*, XXI, No. 3 (September 1958), 598–606.

and often even on the national scene, retrogresses from a state of relative maturity, indispensable for the rule of law, into a state of unpredictability and fluidity. The concepts of sovereignty and boundary often become meaningless. The French Communist parliamentarians openly boast that "France is our country, but the Soviet Union is our fatherland." The Soviet Union exercises, for all practical purposes, full sovereign rights in certain, not even contiguous, territories, e.g., Albania. Just as in premodern times all members of a tribe obeyed their tribal law regardless of which and whose territory they inhabited, so today all adherents of an ideology are urged to obey their ideological, and not the territorial law. Our national and international law system was possible because *jus sanguinis* was superseded by *jus soli*. It cannot survive if allegiance to a *jus ideae* (*jus idealogi*) takes roots.

One of the great difficulties of American foreign policy is that it tries to enforce clear-cut loyalties and territorial divisions in a world which is in flux. Those who accuse the State Department of being legalistically minded point out that law and order do not precede but follow from a certain general agreement as to the desired legal order. As long as such a consensus is wanting, politics are necessarily in a more primary, that is, prerule of law stage. Given the existing conditions, it is wiser to recognize that between the two great ideological ecumene certain "grey areas" of frontier lands, equivocal loyalties, and undefined allegiances, are unavoidable; perhaps not only unavoidable but even desirable: they permit mutual influencing and interpenetration in a broad border zone in which either of the two centripetal forces is too weak to integrate. The detachment of Yugoslavia or India is an offspring of centrifugal forces reacting against colonialism—of the Eastern and Western variety, respectively—but the two countries, having integrated into their systems certain characteristics from both camps, are areas of transition often much more valuable in our quest for international peace than the old buffer states.

Buffer states were a purely mechanical device of international politics: they separated physically two potential warriors, making it more difficult for them to exchange blows. The "grey areas" of the ideological frontiers of today are capable of a more sophisticated intellectual-political role. In contact with and willing to internalize currents from both poles, they are not merely transitive but also transformative: like an electrical transformer they adjust tensions of the two political voltages to permit at least some flow of current without danger that flying sparks will fire the whole house.

A clear-cut boundary between East and West would, on the contrary, accentuate and underline the differences and divisions, and tend thus to heighten the existing tensions. Besides, it could not prevent ideological influences from jumping a border line, however well-armored. The chain of military alliances from Greece to Pakistan—the so-called southern tier—was intended to seal off all of the Middle East from the Russians. But it has not. Sparks between Moscow and Cairo jumped our earthbound defense line and established Soviet influence right in the center of the area. It is for this reason that the British would like to substitute for our legalistic and centralizing "boundary-seeking" foreign policy, a more pragmatic and looser "frontier-tolerating" foreign policy. . . .

The British are "less pessimistic" because they believe that a zone of inter-penetration—a frontier of mutual influence—will not necessarily lead to Soviet gains; it may also work to our advantage. The British seem to have greater faith in the vigor and potential strength of the West, and in the attraction it may exercise.

Soviet leaders boast that Communist ideology spreads throughout the world "without visas and fingerprints" and that "revolutionary ideas know no boundaries." This may be true, but, as we know, it does not mean that the Soviets do not have to face knotty problems on the frontiers of their own ideological ecumene. The case of Tito is most obvious. It is also most illuminating of the dilemma frontier *versus* boundary.

Though frontier conditions may sometimes be deliberately created by governments, the state tends to view frontiers and frontiersmen as a temporary expedient, as appropriate to a period of transition. The ultimate goal is a boundary, not a frontier. This is what the Chinese frontier policy of keeping the Chinese in and the barbarians out aimed at. Since frontier conditions affect, and unsettle, the internal order and quiet, the state must, ultimately, *either* make an effort to integrate the frontier lands within its socio-economic-political system—to enclose them within the state boundary—*or*, if it cannot be done economically or at all, to exclude them from its realm: put them beyond the pale of its community. This is something of the dilemma that has confronted the Soviet Union in its dealings with the satellites China and, especially, Yugoslavia.

On the one hand, it was desirable to keep Tito within the bounds of the Communist camp; on the other, given the fact that he was not willing, and could not be forced, to consider himself integrated within and bound to this camp, it was not possible to include him. Hence, despite all the disadvantages of having such a "barbarian" with ways of life (or, rather, ways of thinking) "Chinese" enough to attract not too loyal border elements, he had to be shut without the "Great Wall." Putting him outside the "boundary" Moscow acknowledged that Tito is a chieftain with whom one has to negotiate: he is beyond the line of control and command. In relation to the Iron Curtain, the Yugoslavians are like the semi-nomadic and semi-Chinese tribes which did not fit either within or without the Great Wall: they are the Hsiugnu of the Soviet empire.

CONCLUSION

The nature of frontiers differs greatly from the nature of boundaries. Frontiers are a characteristic of rudimentary socio-political relations and/or absence of laws. The presence of boundaries is a sign that the political community has reached a relative degree of maturity and orderliness, the stage of law abidance. The international society in a frontier era is like the American West during open-range ranching: limits, if any, are ill-defined and resented; there is little law and still less respect for law; and men afield do not always worry on whose territory or under whose jurisdiction they nominally are. Under a boundary regime the international society resembles rather fenced ranching: each rancher holds a legal title to his land, knows and guards its limits, and manages and surveys it with a view to some over-all end.

Both frontiers and boundaries are manifestations of socio-political forces, and as such are subjective, not objective. But while the former are the result of rather spontaneous, or at least *ad hoc*, solutions and movements, the latter are fixed and enforced through a more rational and centrally co-ordinated effort after a conscious choice is made among the several preferences and opportunities at hand.

Boundaries are not boundaries of all political power. They are the limits of *internal* political power, that is, of the power which integrates the given political unit in the name of certain values and loyalties within the bounds of its territory as delimited under international law. *External* political power does not know territorial limits; it operates on the international scene. However, orderly international intercourse is possible only if it is, on the whole, a relation between legal governments: an encounter between the external governmental political powers. In other words, in order to have some stability in the political structure, both on the national and international level, a clear distinction between the spheres of foreign and domestic politics is necessary. The boundary helps to maintain this distinction.

It is a characteristic of contemporary, so-called ideological politics that it deliberately tends to blur the difference between foreign and domestic territory, and between internal and external politics, weakening thus the status and importance of boundaries. Governments, and nongovernmental organizations, bypass the legal channels in order to deal directly with peoples inhabiting territories under the jurisdiction of other governments. Supranational, nonnational, and other loyalties and interests are promoted which integrate socio-political forces into unofficial or semi-official groupings and blocks transgressing upon the existing formal territorial arrangements.

These groupings and blocks are neither fully incadrated by, nor responsible for, the upholdings of law. On their fringes—the edges of communities of thought and culture—there are borderlands, frontiers, and frontiersmen. On the fringes of the ideological ecumene of our divided world unintegrated elements occupy shifting frontier zones. These zones are not the cause of international instability; they reflect the unsettledness of the contemporary human society.

FLOYD HUNTER

Location of Power
in Regional City

In order to keep the discussion of power in operational terms, it is necessary to locate power as resident in a community, and—more important still—as resident in the men who wield power in the community. Thus, in describing the physical setting in which Regional City leaders operate, it should be stressed that the physical community is dominated by the men in it, rather than that the men are dominated by topography, climate, or any other physical element.

Regional City's geographical location makes it a focal point for transportation operations and financial transactions both within and beyond its region. Commercial transactions supply goods to an extensive hinterland through storage, assembly, and distribution activities. Raw materials supplied by the hinterland make possible many branches of both light and heavy industry. The position of Regional City makes it a center devoted to finance, commerce, and industry, in about that order of importance. The activities centered in these areas of activity engross most men of Regional City from Monday through Saturday of each week. To paraphrase a president of the United States, "The business of Regional City is business," and if the world business is put in its original form, "busy-ness," the community is well described.

By day there is a constant roar of traffic over the congested streets carrying goods and people to their destinations. By night the great diesel trucks and busses blast the air with their exhausts, telling those who may hear that Regional City never sleeps. The all-night restaurants thrive in the commercial and warehouse areas, catering to men and women who ply their trades through

From Community Power Structure (Garden City, New York: Doubleday & Company, Inc., 1963), pp. 11–25. Reprinted by permission of The University of North Carolina Press.

the night shift. The whistles of trains and the "revving up" of airline motors add to the sounds made when men move goods and people. Regional City is always moving. It never stops. And it is filled with activity, more, perhaps, than many other cities, because of its strategic geographical location.

Twelve major highway trunks converge on the city. Ten air routes and eight major rail lines radiate from it. The volume of traffic over these routes is heavy. More than 500 passenger cars a day go over the rail lines. Nearly 400 busses run daily along the highways leading to and from the city. More than 150 scheduled planes operate daily from the municipal airport. The motor truck lines and private passenger cars traveling the highways and streets add an unestimated volume of traffic to the city's transportation load.

Because of all this physical activity involved in moving goods and services in the complex system designated as Regional City, it is obvious that a social order, or system, must be maintained there. Broadly speaking, the maintenance of this order falls to the lot of almost every man in the community, but the *establishment of changes* in the old order falls to the lot of relatively few. In a city as old and as large as Regional City, the existing order has been a cumulative process. It has been handed down to the present generation by the past. Consequently, the men in power in Regional City may be said to have inherited its present order. But new times bring new problems, and decisions have to be made concerning changed conditions. Policies have to be formulated and made effective.

The physical community plays a vital part in maintaining the existing order by helping to differentiate men from one another. The men of power and policy decision in Regional City have definite places in which they are active. There are certain places in which they make decisions and formulate policies to meet the many changing conditions that confront them. In locating these men of power in a community one finds them, when not at home or at work, dividing their time between their clubs, the hotel luncheon and committee rooms, and other public and semi-public meeting places. And the appearance of a man's surroundings is very considerably determined by the kind of work he does, the money he is paid for it, and the status his occupation has in the community.

A description, therefore, of the physical features which surround the men of power, such as their offices, industrial plants, or commercial establishments, as well as their clubs, homes, and other personal living quarters, seems more pertinent to the present discusion than do facts about most other parts of the physical community. Men are ranked and classified by other men, in some degree, by the physical elements around them. An office with soft carpeting, wood-panelled walls, and rich draperies immediately suggests that the man occupying it is more influential than the man who walks on composition concrete floors and looks at plaster-board walls each day, and whose only window decoration is a fifty-cent pull-down shade. Such physical characteristics may not give a completely accurate picture of power and influence, but they are indicative of power, position, and status in our culture. They are a part of the power structure in any community, in its physical aspects. As will be developed later, where men locate their homes is another measure of status on a class basis.

Within the physical setting of the community, power itself is resident in the men who inhabit it. To locate power in Regional City, it is therefore necessary to identify some of the men who wield power, as well as to describe the physical setting in which they operate. In Regional City the men of power were located by finding persons in prominent positions in four groups that may be assumed to have power connections. These groups were identified with business, government, civic associations, and "society" activities. From the recognized, or nominal, leaders of the groups mentioned, lists of persons presumed to have power in community affairs were obtained. Through a process of selection, utilizing a cross section of "judges" in determining leadership rank, and finally by a further process of self-selection, a rather long list of possible power leadership candidates was cut down to manageable size for the specific purpose of this study. Forty persons in the top levels of power in Regional City were selected from more than 175 names. Many more persons were interviewed than the basic forty, but they were interviewed in relation to the forty. The whole method will unfold as the analysis proceeds. . . .

. . .

We shall know more about Regional City when we know where these persons are in relation to each other, and what they do in relation to each other so far as policy-making and policy-execution are concerned.

What men do for a living, as already suggested, locates them in a community setting. The occupations of the men studied in Regional City tended to fall into groupings commensurate with the physical location of the city and its functions as a regional center of activities. In an occupational array of the kinds of activities in which the forty men named were engaged, one finds certain clusterings.

Of the forty persons studied, the largest number are to be found directing or administering major portions of the activities of large commercial enterprises. There are eleven such men in the list. Since Regional City has been described as a commercial center, this fact is not surprising. Financial direction and supervision of banking and investment operations are represented by the next largest number, namely, seven persons. Again, the occupations of the leaders turned up in the study follow one of the major functions of the community activities concerned with finance. Regional City is a "service" city also, and its service functions are represented on the list by six professional persons, five lawyers and one dentist. Five persons have major industrial responsibilities. Governmental personnel are represented on the list by four persons, which also fits into the functional scheme of the community, since it is both a regional and a state center for many important governmental activities. Two labor leaders are on the list, representing large unions. The five remaining persons in the list of forty leaders may be classified as leisure personnel. They are persons who have social or civic organization leadership capacities and yet do not have business offices or similar places in which they conduct their day-by-day affairs. One of these persons is a woman who actually spends very little time in Regional City, but who contributes approximately $100,000 annually to charitable purposes in the community and is looked upon by many as a leader.

These occupational groupings are mentioned at this time merely to indicate that the leaders are a differentiated group as a whole, and their differences in work or leisure activities set them apart physically from other members of the community. The places in which the different groups work vary in appearance, luxury, and comfort of appointments. Even the meeting places of the different groups may vary. These facts seem to be of structural significance.

. . .

Meetings in Regional City are generally held in the hotels, in several civic centers, in private clubs, or in fraternal halls. The "top flight" meetings—those of a high policy nature—are held in the private clubs or in private homes. The club meetings are famous in Regional City, and the leaders of the community are often referred to as "that Grandview Club crowd," this organization being the most exclusive athletic club in the community and a place where many decisions affecting the future course of events in the community take root. Only select community leaders may enter the Club for luncheons upon invitation by members. It does not cater to the general public in any sense. Private homes also serve as places where decision of considerable consequence are reached. One leader, when asked about his social contacts, stated, "I have no purely social contacts. All my contacts relate to business. Generally I have people with whom I want to do business visit my home, whether that business concerns only me or the community at large." Homes were mentioned by others as being important places of contact for informal decisions.

The hotels cater to the Chamber of Commerce type of meeting. Many leaders may be involved in the endless luncheons that go on in the hotels. One leader described the men who attend the hotel meetings regularly, whether they be the like of Rotary, Kiwanis, or privately sponsored gatherings, as men who belong to the "luncheon circuit." It is common knowledge that the same men are seen over and over again in the same places. This frequency of contact makes for community solidarity among the leaders, a solidarity which springs partially out of carefully selected meeting locations. Places tend to center activities. Luncheons and meetings differ in their fundamental purposes, and those devoted to policy matters are usually held in the places already described.

. . .

There tends to be a clustering of residential quarters of the leaders, and a rough evaluation of the "desirable" areas of Regional City was made to see

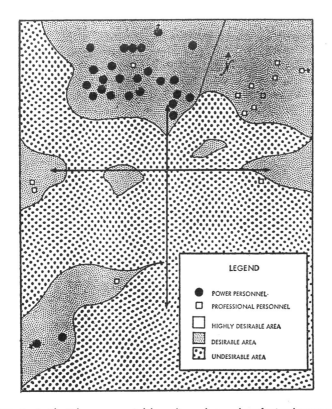

FIG. 1   Residential areas occupied by policy-makers and professional personnel.

where the men of power live in relation to these neighborhoods. The "A-1" areas of the community zoning maps, and so on down the scale, were used as an estimate of desirability. The map in Figure 1 indicates approximately where the leaders reside. Obviously there is a clustering of professional personnel in one section of the city and of power leaders in another.

· · ·

... The labor organizers included in this analysis are not found in the exclusive area but near each other at the opposite end of the community. They represent competing unions but live in close range of each other in an area occupied pretty largely by production managers and other highly skilled employees. They do not live in the districts inhabited by the rank and file in their unions.

Office space occupied by the union leaders, particularly by one of the newer union groups, has undergone an interesting transformation in Regional City within the last decade. In the late 1930's the writer visited the union head-quarters of one of the newer unions. The building was a ramshackle structure, poorly lighted, and badly ventilated. The stairs were wooden, creaky conveyances leading from the building entrance into a large open hall which was used as an informal and formal meeting place. There was a constant stream of traffic up and down the stairs, and groups of labor representatives would gather in buzzing knots to discuss their organization plans. Doors to the small offices flanked the open hall, and there was a steady shuffling of men in and out of these offices. Most visitors and union officials were in their shirt sleeves.

On a recent field trip to Regional City it was found that the newer union had moved its headquarters to a better building and one more centrally located. An elevator carried visitors to the main offices. The walls were painted in light colors. Fluorescent lighting was utilized. The office interiors were furnished with new furniture, rugs, and draperies. The leader of one of the largest unions had a large hardwood "conference type" desk. Leather-upholstered chairs flanked the desk. Visits from sub-officials of the union were held in scheduled conferences. There was no shuffling and milling of men in the outer office. The leaders interviewed were conservatively dressed. In short, the atmosphere was one of subdued orderliness. Labor in Regional City is in the process of arriving, and the physical surroundings of the leaders reflect this fact.

The older union group in the community has long occupied space in a building that is on a par with the surroundings of the present quarters of the newer union. The furnishings are not new, but they are substantial. Scheduled conferences in adequate meeting rooms have been the general rule with the older union. The leaders have been noted for their correct dress and for their public-relations programs, which take into account physical factors.

The Negro population of Regional City is largely segregated and concentrated in the center of the metropolitan area. A belt of Negro population extends eastward and westward from the center of the city with the westward area tending toward better living facilities for its inhabitants. The leaders in the Negro community, in locating their homes, have followed the westward trend of population movement. Thus, the pattern of residential differentiation between leaders and followers among Negroes themselves parallels that of the larger community....

The office buildings and the offices of the Negro leaders are of relatively inferior construction and design. With three exceptions the buildings are apparently twenty-five to thirty years old. They are drab in appearance and poorly maintained. Space in all of the offices seems to be at a premium, and even in the newer buildings the private offices of the power leaders appear as cubicles compared with the offices of some of the leaders in the larger community. Meeting places for Negroes, with the possible exception of places in local Negro colleges, tend to be as colorless as the meeting places of the professional, civic, and social personnel in the larger community.

It may be said, then, that the leaders selected for study in the larger community meet in common places and live in close proximity to each other. This is structurally significant.

The location of the men of power in Regional City tends to isolate them from the mass of people in that community. Consequently they are isolated from many of the problems which affect the average citizen. They daily shuttle by automobile between their homes, their work, and their meeting places. The streets over which they travel pass through many "blighted areas," but the sights of poverty are hidden from view, along most of the routes, by relatively new store fronts, neon signs, and the gleaming chromium of the new cars on display along "automobile row." This is not to say that the men of power in Regional City are unaware of the many social problems behind the façade of their daily route, Commercial Avenue. These problems are a constant causal background of many of the meetings attended by the leaders, brought to them secondhand, in many instances, by the professional men who are less isolated from the problems. It can only be said that location tends to isolate the men of power from the mass of citizens less powerful than themselves and from community problems.

The professional men, used as a contrasting group in this study, take different routes from home to work. Their way runs through an industrial and warehouse area. The store fronts are painted in sombre colors which are smoke-faded, giving the impression of dominant browns and grays. There are loan shops, feed stores, tool shops, small neighborhood grocery stores, and many other struggling small business establishments crowded into blocks of unpainted, rotting, wooden dwellings off Independence Boulevard. It is true that the professional men turn into pleasanter suburban streets at the end of their homeward journey, but most of the route is depressing to anyone sensitive to social disorder. The smoke pall, grassless yards, unwashed children rolling abandoned automobile tires as hoops, gray dogs, and the bargain clothing emporiums are constant reminders of decisions which press for attention on the leaders and their executors of power in the community.

Only two men among our power leaders travel a route comparable to the one described for the professionals. They are . . . the labor leaders. The other power leaders travel at high speeds along Pine Grove expressway to their homes and to their work. The image held by groups residing in different parts of the physical community may consequently vary. Physical structure may thus affect social structure and its functioning.

One other spatial feature of Regional City must be mentioned. The city spreads over a large area. It is a metropolitan community. Its growth has pushed its natural bounds into large portions of the County of Hilldale and two outlying counties in which, and near which, the original city was located. The city boundaries have never caught up with the ever-widening population distribution of the metropolis. As population moved into the outlying areas, city services such as water supply, gas supply, fire and police protection, and road construction and maintenance were demanded of the local units of government. The city charter did not allow the city government to go beyond its corporate limits in providing such services, and consequently the county government was called upon to take on functions which are normally considered within the jurisdiction of a city.

Differing tax rates in the three counties making up the metropolitan area of Regional City, overlapping jurisdictions of governmental units of city and county administrations, and other related matters have brought a cumulative set of problems to the attention of the general community within recent years and to the leaders of Regional City specifically. The ... spatial arrangements of the community are prominent in the discussions ... in organized groups and between individuals in the city and in the outlying areas. Decisions of grave import, revolving around these space problems, are being demanded of the men of decision.

The concern here has been with the physical structure of the community studied. It is obviously impossible to talk about structure without becoming concerned with action. In describing the physical structure of Regional City in some of its aspects related to power personnel, one notes movement. Men move over highways to and from their homes. They attend meetings. They talk about one another. The community is a locus of action—a structured, organized entity that can be measured, charted, plotted. It has "reality" in a stronger sense than many other materials with which social scientists must work. Men create the structure of Regional City's physical plants, its streets, and its dormitory areas, and in the creation they bring into being social structures. The physical structures are a part of the social structure in that they help to regularize and routinize the behavior patterns of the men around which physical features are built. There is, therefore, an interaction between the physical characteristics of the community and the patterned actions of men. The physical structures, once created, act as passive barriers or channels for the dynamic actions of men.

... It should be borne in mind that most of the leaders are persons of power status. In some cases they have the machinery of government at their bidding. In many cases they control large industries in which they reign supreme in matters of decision affecting large numbers of the citizenry. They are persons of dominance, prestige, and influence. They are, in part, the decision-makers for the total community. They are able to enforce their decisions by persuasion, intimidation, coercion, and, if necessary, force. Because of these elements of compulsion, power-wielding is a hidden process. ...

WALLACE S. SAYRE AND
HERBERT KAUFMAN

The Diffusion of Power in
New York City

A full view and a fair judgment of New York City's many-faceted political and governmental system has been a matter of national as well as local debate for at least a century and a half. Historians and journalists, statesmen and politicians, social scientists and other analysts, writers in verse and prose have all been fascinated by the power, the variety, the size, and the significance of the city, its politics, and its government. But they have not achieved consensus. The city in the nation, the city in the state, the city in its metropolitan region, the city as a city, the quality of its political and governmental life—all these remain, and will continue, as matters of debate and discussion, of interest and concern—for the nation as well as for the city.

The most striking characteristic of the city's politics and government is one of scale. No other American city approaches the magnitude, scope, variety, and complexity of the city's governmental tasks and accomplishments. Nor does any other city represent so important a political prize, in its electorate and its government, in the national party contest. Nor can any other city match the drama, the color, and the special style of the city's own politics. In all these respects the city is imperial, if not unique, among American cities.

. . .

The city's political system is, in fact, vigorously and incessantly competitive. The stakes of the city's politics are large, the contestants are numerous

Extracted from Chapter XIX, "Risks, Rewards, and Remedies," from *Governing New York City* by Wallace S. Sayre and Herbert Kaufman, © 1960 by Russell Sage Foundation, New York.

and determined, the rules of the competition are known to and enforced against each other by the competitors themselves, and the city's electorate is so uncommitted to any particular contestant as to heighten the competition for the electorate's support or consent. No single ruling élite dominates the political and governmental system of New York City.

CHARACTERISTICS OF THE CITY'S SYSTEM

A multiplicity of decision centers

The decisions that distribute the prizes of politics in New York City issue from a large number of sources.

Each source consists of two parts: a "core group" at the center, invested by the rules with the formal authority to legitimize decisions (that is, to promulgate them in the prescribed forms and according to the specified procedures that make them binding under the rules) and a constellation of "satellite groups," seeking to influence the authoritative issuances of the core group. The five large categories of participants in the city's political contest . . . —the party leaders, the elected and appointed public officials, the organized bureaucracies, the numerous nongovernmental associations (including the mass media of communication), the officials and agencies of other governments—play their parts upon the many stages the city provides. The most visible of these stages are those provided by the formal decision centers in each of which a core group and its satellite groups occupy the middle of the stage. Every center (every core group and its satellite groups), whatever its stage, must also continuously acknowledge the supervising presence of the city's electorate, possessing the propensity and the capacity to intervene decisively in the contest on the side of one contestant or the other.

Party leaders are core groups for nominations. They function as satellites, however, in many decisions about appointments, and in connection with substantive program and policy decisions in their role as brokers for other claimants. The city's electorate is the core group for electoral decisions, where it has a virtual monopoly. Other participants in the contest for the stakes of politics may exert considerable influence on the electorate, but only in the same fashion as satellite groups in other special areas influence each appropriate core group.

In all other decision centers the core groups are composed of officials. Most prominent among these core groups are the officials presiding over the decision centers of the general organs of government—the Mayor, the Board of Estimate, the Council, and the legislators and executives at the higher levels of government. Their decisions spread across the entire spectrum of the city's governmental functions and activities; consequently, all the other participants in the political process are, at one time or another and in varying combinations, satellite groups to these central core groups, trying to influence their actions.

Each of their decisions, it is true, evokes active responses only from those participants particularly interested in the affected sphere of governmental activity, but most of their decisions prove to be of interest to some participants in all the five major categories (though rarely to all participants in all categories). In the course of time, most groups taking part in the city's politics apply leverage to the core groups in the general governmental institutions in efforts to secure favorable decisions. The courts are also general organs, and therefore the judges as the core group in that arena are of interest to most contestants at one time or another, but the modes of influence exerted on them are somewhat more restricted and institutionalized than those exerted on the core groups of other general organs.

Functionally specialized officials constitute the core groups for decisions in particular functional areas of governmental action, whether these are in line agencies (such as the Board of Education, the Department of Welfare, the Police Department, the Fire Department, the Department of Health), in special authorities (Transit, Housing, Triborough Bridge and Tunnel, or the Port of New York Authority), or in overhead agencies (the Budget Bureau, the Personnel Department, the Law Department, the City Planning Department, for example). Each of these decision centers is surrounded by satellite groups especially concerned with its decisions—the leaders of the interests served, the interests regulated, professional societies and associations, organized bureaucracies, labor unions, suppliers of revenue and materials, and others. Usually, the groups concerned chiefly with particular functions are uninterested in decisions in other, unrelated functional areas, so that most of the decisions (about appointments as well as programs and policies) in each decision center are worked out by an interplay among the specialized core and its satellite groups.

Most officials have a dual role. They appear not merely in core groups but also as satellites of other officials. From the point of view of the general organs, for instance, the agency heads are claimants endeavoring to influence decisions in the city's central governmental institutions. From the point of view of a department head, the general organs are satellites making demands. Although the general organs' influence on agency leaders is especially strong, it is not by any measure complete domination; the agency leaders commonly preserve a region of autonomy free from invasion by the central organs as well as from other groups and institutions. Department heads also often see their own official colleagues (particularly the heads of overhead agencies), as well as the leaders of the organized bureaucracies, acting as satellite groups, as wielders of influence, and as competitors. Their counterparts in other governments tend to appear in the same light. Other officials (themselves core groups in their own respective areas) are thus likely to appear among the satellites of any particular official core group.

The leaders of the city's organized bureaucracies are, strictly speaking, never members of a core group but always a satellite group seeking to exert influence over one or more core groups. Their role is not without ambiguity in this respect, however, for many bureaucrats also occupy significant decision-making posts in the city government. As members or leaders in their organized bureaucratic groups, these bureaucrats thus occasionally play a dual part; as leaders or members of satellite groups they engage in efforts to influence the actions of a core group in which they are also members. But these are not yet typical situations. In most instances, the leaders of the organized bureaucracies are satellite groups.

The leaders of the city's nongovernmental groups never formally constitute core groups, but appear instead as satellites. Functionally specialized groups, being close to the agency officials whose decisions affect them, are not far from the center of the particular arena in which they operate. But, except when they are coopted into what amounts to a part of officialdom, they cannot do what the core groups do: issue authoritative, official, binding decisions. As satellites, some of the civic groups, and the communication media, are active and frequently highly influential in a broad range of functional spheres. In any specific functional area of governmental activity, however, it is the specialized, well-organized, persistent, professionally staffed nongovernmental organizations that continuously affect the pattern of decisions. Core groups of officials tend to estimate the reactions of other nongovernmental groups that might be galvanized to action by specific decisions, and the officials respond to the representations of such groups when these groups are sufficiently provoked to exert pressure. But the impact of these organizations is more intermittent and uncertain than that of those with sustained and specialized programs of influence. Yet even the specialized are compelled by the nature of the rules to accept roles as satellites.

.   .   .

Partial self-containment of decision centers

The decisions that flow from each constellation of groups active in each of the city's decision centers are ordinarily formulated and carried out without much calculated consideration of the decisions emanating from the other centers. They are usually made in terms of the special perspectives and values of the groups with particular interests in the governmental functions or activities affecting them. Only occasionally are they formulated in a broader frame of reference.

This fragmentation of governmental decision-making in the city is partially offset by features of the system tending to introduce more or less common premises of decision into the centers. A major "balance wheel" has been noted by David B. Truman: the overlapping memberships of many groups in society. The same individuals turn up in many contexts and in many guises, carrying to each the viewpoints and information acquired in the others. A second balance wheel is the frequency with which the core groups of one center operate as satellite groups in other centers; no center is completely isolated from the others. Overhead agencies serve as a third unifying element, for they cut across the whole range of governmental functions and activities introducing, within the limits of their own specialties, a commonset of assumptions and goals into many of the decisions of other centers. A fourth unifying factor is represented by the civic groups and the press, which exert their influence on a wide variety of decision centers without regard to the subject-matter specialties of the centers. They are not equally effective everywhere, and they are seldom so effective in any given center as the more specialized participants in it, but they help to relate what happens in every center to what goes on in others. Finally, the central institutions of government (including the courts) operate under relatively few functional restrictions and therefore make decisions with respect to all phases of the city's government and politics. Collectively, their perspectives are broad, their interests are inclusive, their desire to rationalize and balance the actions in all decision centers are strong, and their formal authority to impose a common basis for decisions is superior to that of other groups. These five factors help to keep the system from flying apart.

Yet the autonomous nature of the core group and its satellite groups in each decision center is striking. Although the leaders may belong to many groups, they behave, when particular decisions are at issue, with a remarkable lack of ambivalence. The interests immediately at stake provide the criteria of action, and they often seem unambiguous; at any given moment, group leaders and members act as though they had only one interest, one membership, at that moment. Most participants are galvanized to action by only a relatively narrow range of issues and ignore most others no matter where they occur; as a result, most of the actors in any center share very special interests in the problems at hand, and the casual outsider or the intermittent satellite group has much less effect on the decisions made there than do the strongly motivated "regulars." As modes of integrating the decisions of the city's whole governmental system, the balance wheels have therefore not been spectacularly successful.

What is perhaps most surprising is the failure of the central organs of government to provide a high level of integration for the city's system. The Council has been weak, the Board of Estimate inert, the Mayor handicapped. The government at Albany cannot do the job of pulling the decision centers of the city together, even if it were so inclined. This would mean running the city, a task the state is unable and unwilling to assume, a task that would not win it the thanks of the city's residents or of other residents of the state. Moreover, the state government has not been inclined to strengthen the central institutions of the city, but has enacted legislation and created agencies that intensify the independence of many local officials. State administrative supervision of city agencies has encouraged many city officers and employees to develop close links with their functional counterparts in the state capital, and to rely on these to buttress their resistance to leadership from the city's central institutions. The nature of the judicial process renders the courts incapable of performing an integrative function. Thus, despite the opportunities for integration presented by the formal powers of the city's central institutions, they have generally either officially ratified the agreements reached by the active participants in each decision center, which are offered to them as the consensus of experts and interested groups, or, on an *ad hoc* basis, have chosen one or another alternative suggested when the experts and interested groups have been divided on an issue. It is in the latter role that the city's central institutions have had their greatest significance. Seldom have they imposed, on their own initiative, a common set of objectives on all the centers of decision. The central institutions are important participants in all the decision-making in the contest for the stakes of politics in the city, but they are rarely the prime movers or the overriding forces.

As a result, most individual decisions are shaped by a small percentage of the city's population—indeed, by a small percentage of those who engage actively in its politics—because only the participants directly concerned have the time, energy, skill, and motivation to do much about them. The city government is most accurately visualized as a series of semiautonomous little worlds, each of which brings forth official programs and policies through the interaction of its own inhabitants. There are commentators who assert that Tammany, or Wall Street, or the Cathedral, or the labor czars, or the bureaucracy, or even the underworld rules New York. Some of these, it is true, are especially influential in shaping some decisions in some specialized areas. Taking the system over-all, however, none, nor all combined, can be said to be in command; large segments of the city's government do not attract their attention at all. New York's huge and diverse system of government and politics is a loose-knit and multicentered network in which decisions are reached by ceaseless bargaining and fluctuating alliances among the major categories of participants in each center, and in which the centers are partially but strikingly isolated from one another.

THE PERILS OF A MULTICENTERED SYSTEM

Tendencies toward stasis

One consequence of this ordering of the city's political relationships is that every proposal for change must run a gantlet that is often fatal. The system is more favorable to defenders of the *status quo* than to innovators. It is inherently conservative. The reasons for this are threefold.

No Change Without Cost. In the first place, every modification of the existing state of affairs—of the rules, of personnel, of governmental or administrative structure or procedure, or of public policies and programs—entails the fear of cost for some participants as well as hope of gain for the proponents. Any proposed increase in dollar costs, for example, stirs up the revenue-providing nongovernmental groups and their allies among the core groups. Proposals to change regulatory policies arouse quick opposition from the regulated groups and their core group allies if the proposal is to tighten regulation; from the protected groups and their official allies if the proposal is to relax regulation. Curtailed service angers those served and alarms the core groups of officials, as well as the bureaucracies, whose status, jurisdiction, and jobs are threatened, while expanded service alerts those who must pay the dollar costs as well as those who are competing for dollars to be expended for other purposes. Proposals for public works represent threats of displacement for some groups, risks in property values and neighborhood amenities for others. Proposals to reorganize agencies or other governmental and political institutions change adversely the lines of access to decision centers for some groups, affect adversely the career ladders of others, reduce the status and prestige of some others. In most instances, the costs of change are more intensely perceived by participants close to the center of decisions than are the benefits of innovation.

Those who perceive the costs of change in the city's going system have strategies and weapons with which to resist. They ordinarily have prizes to withhold, inducements to offer, sanctions to impose. The core groups of party leaders, for example, have nominations to confer or deny; they have, in addition, experience and skill in the exercise of influence in campaigns, elections, and appointments to office. The core groups of officials have their formal authority of decision with which to bargain with other groups. The organized bureaucracies can resist change by dragging their feet, the issuance of threats to strike or to "demonstrate," or appeals to allies or to the general public. Nongovernmental groups can use their special knowledge and skills, mobilize their members, resort to publicity in criticism of a proposed change. Almost all the participants have allies at other levels of government to whom they may turn for help in their opposition to a proposal. And most participants can threaten to withdraw from existing alliances as a sanction against change. The prospects for any advocate of change are intense opposition: lengthy, costly, wearing maneuvering and negotiation, and uncertainty about results until the last battle is won. If the *anticipation* of such a struggle, with all its costs in money, time, energy, and the possible disruption of longstanding friendships and alliances, is not enough to discourage campaigns in support of many proposed innovations, the strain and the drain of the *actual* fight may well exhaust the supporters and induced them to abandon their causes before they have come near their goals.

Official Hesitancy. In the second place, public officers and employees, whose action is required to make official the decisions reached by the participants in the specialized centers in which they operate, are ordinarily reluctant to move vigorously when there is extensive opposition within the constellation of interested individuals and groups. For they, as the formal authors of changes, are most likely to bear the brunt of enmities and retaliations provoked by adverse consequences of departure from established practice. They are the visible and vulnerable targets of blame for failures, though they must often share with others any credit for achievements. If they yield to demands of economy groups to curtail services or expenditures, the groups that are hurt direct their retribution against the officials in the decision centers and not against the originators of the reductions (who may have virtually compelled the decisions) or the less salient officials in other decision centers who may have cooperated with the economy groups (the Comptroller, for example, or the Director of the Budget). On the other hand, if officials yield to service-demanding groups or other groups (such as the bureaucracies) urging increased service and expenditures that are followed by fiscal crisis and rises in taxation, they may feel the wrath of those affected. If fluorine is added to the city's drinking water at the behest of health and dental groups and their allies in the Health Department, and if there should be later charges of fluorine poisoning attributed to engineering difficulties connected with keeping the fluorine content of the water within safe tolerances, it is the elected members of the Board of Estimate and the water supply engineers who will pay the penalty; hence their unwillingness to go ahead with this program despite the impressive array of advocates behind it. Indeed, officials are understandably wary even when there is a general consensus on the desirability of a particular novelty, for they must try to take into account consequences unanticipated by the assenters. They are doubly cautious when an important and highly vocal segment of their constituency stresses the dangers and costs. So the world of officialdom is often prudent when confronted by recommendations for innovation.

Incentives to Delay. When the specialists and other groups immediately interested in decisions disagree sharply among themselves about the wisdom or soundness of a proposed measure, or when the participants in one decision center line up in opposition to an action taken or projected in another decision center, the controversy is likely to find its way to the general organs of government, usually to the Mayor and the Board of Estimate, but frequently to the Governor and the state legislature. These governmental leaders then find they must choose between courses of action on which the experts and other informed interests are themselves divided. They must weigh the possible consequences of the choices they face—the possibilities of serious errors of judgment, of alienation of substantial blocs of voters, or repercussions on contributions to their parties and their campaigns. The course of prudence for them, therefore, is to temporize in the hope that the disagreements will work themselves out, or that they will have time enough to inform themselves more fully about the situations, or that the circumstances giving rise to the clashes will pass and obviate the need for their action, or that one side or the other will lose heart and abandon its fight. Sometimes they simply defer decision; this is the characteristic strategy of the Board of Estimate. Sometimes they set up study commissions to investigate and bring in recommendations. Rarely do they leap eagerly into the fray.

If some of the participants resort to litigation as part of their strategy, they may find the judges less hesitant to decide (because of the insulation of the courts, designed to encourage judicial independence). They also discover that legal proceedings are often protracted, costly, and time-consuming. This lends to litigation a special attraction and utility for the opponents of change.

The Tortuous Path. Changes of any magnitude thus encounter a long, rocky, twisting path from conception to realization. They are likely to be blocked almost at the start unless their authors revise and modify them to appease strong opponents, and to win the active and enthusiastic support of their allies. At the outset, the authors are likely to be the only zealous advocates in any decision center, and their proposals will face a group of equally zealous critics and a large number of relatively indifferent (that is, unaffected) observers. To overcome the objections and to stimulate the indifferent, plans must be adjusted—altered here, modified there, strengthened in another place. After all the bargaining and concessions, a plan may well have lost much of its substance, much of its novelty. If plans are radical, they seldom survive; if they survive, they seldom work major changes in the going system.

There is nothing intrinsically desirable about change. But it becomes a problem of major importance to the well-being of the city if the governmental system has such a built-in resistance to change, such a tendency to suppress innovation, that it cannot keep up with the problems that confront it in a constantly and rapidly changing world. A city in stasis faces the potential fate of many of the great urban centers of the past, whose glories are all in archives and museums, whose significance is solely historical.

Neglect of communitywide perspectives

Another risk inherent in the multicentered system of New York City's government and politics is the subordination of widely shared community values to the special interests of the separate and numerous "islands of power" within it. The tendencies of each core group and its attendant satellite groups to arrive at decisions maximizing their own special interests, including the comfort and convenience of officials and bureaucrats, are sometimes described as characteristic products of the system.

The fact is clear that only a few central institutions in the city produce decisions made on the basis of premises relevant to the entire community. Moreover, these central institutions often actually possess no more than the role of satellite groups with respect to the core groups in each decision center; although they may have theoretical, formal superiority over all the other groups, the central institutions often function, in fact, merely as additional participants in the decision-making processes rather than as masters of the system. They most often appear vulnerable to, and anxious about, the capacity of "lesser" contestants to extract concessions from them. If communitywide perspectives are introduced into the governmental decision-making system, this is usually an incidental by-product of the interaction of special interests.

.   .   .

ACHIEVEMENTS OF THE SYSTEM

Openness, responsiveness, and tolerance

Because the city's system is multicentered, then, it harbors traits that may be serious risks to its own continued existence. But it also has qualities richly rewarding to all the inhabitants of the city and particularly to the active participants in the contest for the stakes of politics.

One of these qualities is its openness. No part of the city's large and varied population is alienated from participation in the system. The channels of access to the points of decision are numerous, and most of them are open to any group alert to the opportunities offered and persistent in pursuit of its objectives. All the diverse elements in the city, in competition with each other, can and do partake of the stakes of politics; if none gets all it wants, neither is any excluded.

Consequently, no group is helpless to defend itself, powerless to prevent others from riding roughshod over it, or unable to assert its claims and protect its rights. The great number of *de facto* vetoes built into the system intensifies the tendencies toward immobilization that constitute one of the hazards of the system, but these vetoes also enable every group to obstruct governmental decisions that fail to take its interests into account, to restrain governmental actions that ignore its rights or its aspirations, and to employ its possession of veto power as a basis from which to bargain for recognition and concessions. Furthermore, the abundance of decision centers enables each group to concentrate on selected arenas of special importance to it instead of being cast into a broader environment in which it might have far more difficulty making its voice heard. Some inhabitants of the city have been slower than others to make use of the weapons the political system places within their grasp, but most— even immigrants from lands with altogether different traditions—have learned quickly, and there are not many who accept passively whatever the system deals out. They have learned that governmental decisions of every kind in the city are responsive to the demands upon the decision centers.

The city's system is, at the very least, tolerant of differences of every kind, and usually is even more than that: it engenders official respect for differences. That is not to say the forces working everywhere for orthodoxy and conformity are not at work in New York, or that the city is free from racial, religious, and ethnic prejudices. It does not mean that dissenters and minorities of all kinds are welcomed, or that their claims are immediately and warmly acknowledged and fulfilled. It does mean, however, that they are not suppressed, and that in official and party circles they will generally receive respectful attention. It does mean that personal antagonisms to groups or creeds will generally be stifled by officials. It does mean that candidates and party leaders will not only recognize, but will court the favor of, groups of every kind. And it does mean that third parties and insurgent factions in the major parties cannot be prevented (in spite of the roadblocks often thrown in their paths) from challenging the dominant political parties and factions. There are too many points of entry, too many opportunities for retaliation, too many methods of self-protection and self-assertion, for bigotry or intolerance or fear of heterodoxy to become major elements of official decisions or behavior.

If these attributes are measures of the democratic qualities of a governmental system, then New York City's system must be rated highly democratic. It may run the serious risks noted above, and it may pay a cost in terms of engineering concepts of efficiency, but the system can justly claim to possess openness, responsiveness, and tolerance as essential characteristics of its democracy.

STEPHEN B. JONES

The Power Inventory and National Strategy

A familiar sight in the newspapers and weekly magazines is a world map (often, I regret to say, on the Mercator projection) on which population, oil production, or similar information is shown by rows of small men, barrels, or other appropriate symbols. These maps are often interpreted in caption or accompanying text as indices of national power. No one denies that such information is relevant to power, but ... such information is only a first step toward an evaluation. An estimate of national power has two aspects which are related, in a figurative way, like the two rays of a triangulation. Either ray gives direction, but it takes the two to give distance. A better analogy, perhaps, is that of two searchlight beams groping through the dark until they intersect on the target. One ray or beam is the conventional inventory of the elements or factors of power. It gives the power resources of a nation, using "resource" in a broad sense. The other ray is here called "national strategy."

This thesis is not fundamentally original, except perhaps in presentation. Clausewitz (thinking only of military strategy, of course) wrote of superiority as a function of absolute strength and of the skillful use of that strength.[1] The Sprouts differentiate between the tools and techniques of statecraft,[2] and the distinction is implicit in other books.

From *World Politics*, Vol. VI, No. 4 (1954), 421–452. Reprinted by permission.

[1] Karl von Clausewitz, *On War*, trans. O.J.M. Jolles, Infantry Journal Press edition (Washington, 1950), pp. 137–141.

[2] Harold and Margaret Sprout, *Foundations of National Power* (2nd ed.; New York, 1951), p. 40.

DEFINITION OF TERMS

"Power" is here defined as "that which permits participation in the making of decisions," a slight modification of the Lasswell-Kaplan definition.[3] This is perhaps not truly a definition; it tells not what power is, but what it makes possible. It has the virtues of including constructive uses and of saying that power is not solely material or possessed only by those who have a lot of it. Power, like radiant energy, can move in many directions at once. The interplay of British, American, and Russian power on Iran and the counter-radiation of Iranian power, through its ability to tantalize, frustrate, and play one great rival against another, shows that even a state that comes near to being a vacuum, militarily, can exert a significant force.

"Strategy" is used with some misgivings, since the word has many meanings, from the strictly military one of the conduct of campaigns to such figurative usages as "the strategy of raw materials." It is defined here as "the art of using power for the attainment of goals in competition."[4] (The subordinate clause is perhaps implied by the main one.) The extension to other forms of power and other types of competition than military seems justified in this age of cold war and total effort. "Strategy" is preferred to "policy" for present purposes. Policy is more concerned with setting goals than with the art of attaining them—a distinction brought out by a modern revision of the ant-and-grasshopper story.

"National strategy"[5] has been adopted in preference to "grand strategy" or "global strategy," for a nation's strategy may be neither grand nor global.[6] To speak of national strategy does not imply a genre of strategy peculiar to a state, though, to be sure, no two states can have identical national strategies, if for no other reason than that they are geographically distinct. The national strategy is not necessarily wrought with logic. It may contain as much prejudice as plan. If a plan exists, rarely will it be consistently followed.

We use the term "resources" in a very broad sense, somewhat like the familiar reference to a man "calling up all his resources." In discussions of power, there may be some confusion among the terms "resources," "natural resources," "sources," "reserves," and "raw materials." "Resources" is the broadest of these terms. We use it to mean anything a nation has, can obtain, or can conjure up to support its strategy. The items of an inventory of power resources are commonly called either "elements" or "factors." There is, we

---

[3] Harold D. Lasswell and Abraham Kaplan, *Power and Society: A Framework for Political Inquiry* (New Haven, 1950), p. 75.

[4] "Strategy" is also used in the sense of "a strategy" or, as the dictionary puts it, "a kind or instance of it." The phrases "strategic plan" or "strategic program" would be more precise, but also more cumbersome, and the specific usage is well established.

[5] The following definition of national strategy is used by the armed forces: "The art and science of developing and using the political, economic, and psychological powers of a nation, together with its armed forces, during peace and during war, to secure national objectives" (*Dictionary of United States Military Terms for Joint Usage,* 2nd revision, April 1953).

[6] "Geostrategy"—a word of uncertain meaning—has also been avoided.

believe, a shade of difference between these two terms. The distinction may not be important and probably will not be adopted by others, but in making it we may clarify a concept that will be useful later. An element is a basic, separable part, commonly thought of in terms of its own properties. A factor, in the words of the dictionary, is "one of the elements that contribute to produce a result." A factor is commonly thought of in terms of the specific whole of which it is a part, of what it does rather than what it is. One might say loosely that there are elements of potential power, factors of actual power, but both "potential" and "actual" need to be subdivided and clarified, as we attempt to do on a later page.

The concept we are endeavoring to establish is simply that inventories of power resources may contain items at several levels of organization. Morgenthau, for example, lists natural resources, industrial capacity, and military preparedness among his eight elements of national power.[7] This is no sin, of course. A manufacturing firm would include in its inventory raw materials, semi-finished goods, and finished merchandise. The important point is that estimates of national power are made for comparative purposes and that valid comparisons are possible only if levels of organization are taken into account.

An inventory of power resources, or, briefly, a power inventory, could be a few lines or many pages in length. Taxonomists divide themselves into "lumpers" and "splitters" and the terms are appropriate here. An extreme lumper could compress the whole inventory into the familiar three factors of production of economics: land, labor, and capital. This is not to say that all power is economic. Even the older term, "political economy," is not broad enough to cover all the items of power, such as military competence and morale. But these items, though outside the conventional bounds of economics, may be considered either attributes of labor (using that term for all useful population) or mental capital.

The splitter will immediately go to work on this basic group. Land includes two categories of resources. One might be called "area resources," including the size and the shape of the country and immobile resources like landforms, soils, and climates. The other is the mobile mineral and biological resources. Location, sometimes considered an attribute of land by economists, will be treated later in another manner.

The factor of labor is perhaps better called "human resources." There are likewise two parts. First is population, considered as to number, age structure, and so forth. Second is what might be called "mental resources," the social, political, economic, and military systems of a country and the stock of skills, leadership, and patriotism.

Capital is better called "equipment resources," since it includes not only economic capital goods but also military equipment and the material apparatus of government. An additional item is supplies or stockpiles of consumable

---

[7] Hans J. Morgenthau, *Politics Among Nations* (New York, 1951), pp. 80–108.

materials and goods—foods, metals, merchandise, munitions, etc.—and the financial stockpile of precious metals and credit.

There is of course a high degree of relationship among the items mentioned. Equipment is produced by organized skill operating on mobile natural resources. In turn, it may be used to extract further natural resources. Whether an ore deposit of marginal tenor is usable or not depends on skill, organization, and equipment. Leadership and patriotism are like enzymes in metabolism. In the final analysis, without them there is no power.

The foregoing paragraphs list resources as tangible as soil, as intangible as leadership, as measurable as population, as difficult to measure as patriotism. There is no common unit and no statistical summation is possible. Cost has been suggested as a measure of tangible items. Because of the importance of the budget in national housekeeping, there is a tendency to express many problems in terms of cost, but even as a measure of armaments it has its limitations. That a carrier might cost twenty times as much as a destroyer does not mean that twenty destroyers equal one carrier, in the operational sense. "Power value" rather than cost would be the significant figure if it could be measured, as sales value rather than cost is the real criterion for the inventory of a store. The Maginot line was costly, but its power value turned out to be nil. Cost is therefore not an adequate index of power. It does have its use as a "modifier" of inventory items, as will be discussed on a later page.

Even though one must give up the seductive hope that the power inventory can be summed up in dollars, kilowatt hours, or some other common unit, there remains the possibility that some key items may be used as rough indices of the probable total. The hope, of course, is to find measurable items that will so serve. Manpower of military age or the output of fuels, steel, or all heavy industry are some of the possibilities. Such data unquestionably are basic and under some conditions give a correct estimate of relative power. The longer a war lasts, the more likely are such data to be significant. They are particularly applicable when a country has limited access to external supplies. One could write a history of World War II in terms of supplies, with a measure of truth. But with far less than the whole truth: equally important is what was done with the supplies. Poverty of resources correlates with the weakness of Italy but does not explain the military failures against Greece or, for that matter, against the British at sea and in North Africa. Too little oil and too much intuition were long-run handicaps for Hitler, and it would be difficult to say which was the greater. Had his long-range strategy been sounder, he might have created a sufficient synthetic oil industry. Even in estimating potentials one must consider the strategic ray. To be sure, our analogy does not imply that the strategic ray is the more important, but only that *both* rays are important.

National income and its close relative, gross national product, have been considered possible indices of national power. They are operational in nature, rather than being inventory items, but this would be no disadvantage if they measure what can be done with a given inventory. For one thing, they give an idea of the dislocations to be expected from the diversion of resources from civil to military purposes. Their chief value is as tools, not as indices, however. Sherman Kent has commented adversely upon the search for indices of national power, and upon this use of national income data in particular.[8] He stresses the importance of fat, slack, and flexibility in the national economy.

That quantifiable items like manpower or the output of heavy industry or economic aggregates like national income cannot serve as indices of national power does not, of course, mean that quantification is useless. Much of science consists of efforts to narrow the range of guessing. Since there is, inevitably, a large element of guesswork in an estimate of national power, quantitative information is highly desirable for all items for which it is obtainable. But, for the same reason, there is no use refining quantitative data to a high degree.

MODIFIERS OF THE POWER INVENTORY

If the power inventory is thus essentially a check-list, with some quantifiable items, it becomes desirable to run through the concepts that must be kept in mind when the check-list is used. It can be qualified almost without limit. We might start with population for example, and find ourselves many pages later discussing the rate of training of civil defense workers in the use of Geiger counters. Such thoroughness may be necessary and desirable for some purposes —for a detailed mobilization program, for example. For general thinking about power, more generic concepts are desirable. These generic concepts we shall call "modifiers" of the power inventory. Not all the modifiers are applicable to every item of the power inventory, though with some imagination most of them can be applied. It may seem absurd to apply "motivation" to petroleum, for instance, but the motivation of the investors, management, and workers determines whether oil is produced or not. To return to the earlier attempt to distinguish between an element and a factor, motivation is essential to the petroleum industry as a factor of power.

One of the most obvious modifiers of the power inventory is quantity. In some commentaries on national power, quantity is the only modifier considered. That the United States produces three times as much steel as the Soviet Union closes the argument for some people. But quantity is a whole family of modifiers. Its principal genera are availability and change. Availability has two subdivisions, the space and time aspects. Spatial availability is summed up in the term "location." The effect of location on steel supplies is shown by the fact that the United States during World War II needed a third more steel for shipbuilding than for ordnance and other direct military uses. Location has two subspecies, accessibility and mobility. To illustrate, Mackenzie River oil is highly inaccessible but highly mobile. The Canol pipe-

---

[8] Sherman Kent, *Strategic Intelligence for American World Policy* (Princeton, 1949), p. 51 and n.

line (another non-combatant use of steel) did not improve the accessibility until after the need had passed. "Tonnage" ores like iron are less mobile than ores that can usefully be measured in pounds. Labrador iron ore probably could not have been made accessible during World War II even had the need arisen. Manpower is relatively mobile and with a man move his skills, but the mobility of manpower varies with culture. Aboriginal natives need fewer supplies than do more civilized troops and workers, but at the same time they may be more essential to the economy of their villages, which have no labor-replacing machinery.

The time aspect of availability appears in the familiar phrase "lead-time," which stands for the period required to convert plans into production.[9] Lead-time is a phase of the problem of potential power. That there is a difference between actual and potential power is obvious, but these two terms are too vague to be of much service. A geographer is likely to think of ore and fuel reserves when he hears the word "potential." An economist is likely to think of factories convertible to war production. A military man may think of the reserve corps or of mothballed ships. A fivefold classification of states of availability is here proposed: (1) power resources available immediately; (2) power resources available after activation; (3) power resources available after conversion; (4) power resources available after development; and (5) power resources available hypothetically.

Immediately available resources include such things as armed forces in being, munition in depots, money or credit at hand. (There is of course a locational immediacy as well. A division in Germany and one in Texas are not equally immediate in availability for a given emergency.) Resources available after activation include such things as reserve troops and officers, mothballed ships, money, and credit requiring legislation before use. Resources available after conversion include such things as factories suited for war production, and manpower untrained but adaptable to military or industrial service. This category is one that the United States has banked on heavily in the past, thanks to Britain, France, and the Atlantic Ocean. Resources available after development form another group that has given much comfort to Americans in the past but which is less comforting now. Such things as minerals known to exist but not in production and products known to be practical but not available in quantity, like synthetic rubber in 1942, are included. Hypothetical power resources remind one of the story of the diplomat who spoke most feelingly of his country's claims to some tropical territory. "It is full of rich resources," he exclaimed, "all undiscovered!" But hypothetical power should not be laughed at. The atomic bomb was hypothetical until 1945.

---

[9] Lead-time has a range of meanings. An artilleryman might think of it as the interval between placing an order and receiving the ammunition. An airman is more likely to think of the longer interval between conceiving a new airplane and the mass production of the final model. There is a different lead-time for each of the availability states discussed in this article, *infra*.

These availability states are of course not rigidly separated pigeonholes, but they do differ in kind as well as in degree. They should permit sharper thinking than do "actual" and "potential." A given power resource is not confined to one category. Many exist in all five states. Oil, for instance, may be immediately available in storage tanks. Idle wells and refineries may be activated. Non-essential use can be curtailed—this would be conversion. New wells may be drilled in proven fields—this is development—and favorable structures may be wildcatted on the hypothesis that oil exists in them. Intangibles like leadership can exist in all five states. How power resources are distributed through the availability series reflects the national strategy. The United States traditionally has left as much of its power as possible in the convertible and developable states. The trend is to push many items into higher states and to step up the pace of conversion and development. Not even the most spartan of nations could keep all its resources in a condition of immediate availability, but simple trust in "the power and potential of American mass production" goes the way of the faith that a million Americans would spring to arms overnight if their country were attacked.

The term "potential" has another connotation than that of availability. It also implies the maximum sustainable rate of production, or, more precisely, of expenditure, of a given item of power. Maximum sustainable rates follow different rules, depending upon the nature of the resource, the time element, and national strategy. Where natural resources are ample and the rate of production depends largely upon capital and labor, long-continued increases are possible, though perhaps at the cost of diverting capital and labor from other items. American steel production, for example, is capable of much further growth, if low-grade and foreign ores are utilized. In other cases, the maximum sustainable rate may vary with the period of time involved. The expenditure of manpower, if in excess of natural replacement, is an obvious example. To estimate the maximum sustainable rates of power expenditure therefore requires knowledge of both resources and their probable strategic use.

The availability states discussed above are closely related to three aspects of the national economy discussed by Sherman Kent: fat, slack, and flexibility. Kent defines these terms as follows:

> By *fat,* I mean such things as some of the things Britain had at the start of World War II: extensive external assets, a large merchant marine, access to necessary raw material and the credits to buy them without going into current production, a large and up-to-date supply of capital equipment, a large inventory of finished goods, a national diet of three to four thousand calories per day, etc. Important elements of German fat may be said to have existed in the excess capacity of machine tools, a large amount of brand new plant and new housing. The Italians had practically no fat, indeed little enough lean.
>
> By *slack,* I mean such things as the 40-hour week, twelve to sixteen years of education for youth, small proportion of women in the labor force, unemployment of both labor and capital, only partial utilization of equipment, etc.

By *flexibility,* I mean the capacity of the economy to beat plow-shares and pruning hooks into swords, and that in jig time. I mean the ability of technicians to make typewriter factories over into machine gun factories, and put the manufacturers of dry breakfast food into the shell-fuse business. I mean the ability to make synthetics from scratch where the natural sources have dried up.

"Fat" and "slack" correspond to "resources available after activation." Steel production, for example, is expansible in several ways. Plants may be operating below capacity. To activate this unused capacity would be taking up slack. Or they may be operated temporarily above capacity by postponing repairs. This would be using up fat. "Flexibility" covers the two concepts of "conversion" and "development." The quotation from Kent illustrates both. Making war goods in typewriter and cereal factories is conversion. Making synthetics from scratch (if the basic processes are known and not hypothetical) is development. The difference is significant because the lead-time of change is likely to be greater for development than for conversion and the investment of money, manpower, and materials larger. The expansion of steel production by building new mills is development, and involves the temporary diversion of steel from other uses.

These terms can be applied to persons as well as to commodities or plants. The conversion of clerks into soldiers, of housewives into welders, is familiar. The longer process of producing physicians, physicists, or general officers is more appropriately called development. The population factor as a whole can be developed, as by the importation of labor, alliances, and public health measures. The long-term effect of pro-natalist policies on the birth rate is still somewhat hypothetical.

The importance of change in relation to quantity needs no emphasis. Change has two aspects, rate and range. Rates of production, mobilization, conversion, expansion, etc., need no discussion. Changes of rates, or accelerations and decelerations, are also important, and one may need to consider changes in the changes of rates. The higher derivatives of change are significant in demography, where one wishes to know not only the death rate, for instance, but whether it is rising or falling and how the rate of rise or fall is changing. Rates of resource accumulation or wastage are important. Secular changes of vast consequence may be taking place almost unperceived by untrained observers, such as soil erosion, climatic alteration, or the aging of the population. The range of change obviously applies to fluctuating quantities like temperatures or harvests. Better knowledge of the range of Russian winter temperatures would have aided Hitler in 1941–1942. Range may also apply to rates. There is an upper limit to the rate of oil production from a given field, for instance, beyond which recovery declines and salt water may intrude.

Rates and ranges of expansion are major considerations in estimating power. The expansion of American production during World War II surprised even optimists, though whether time will be available in a future conflict for similar expansion is debatable. Soviet recovery after World War II was also surprisingly rapid. Expansion has its converse, contraction. The ability to do without may be important in war. Many contractions are effected for the purpose of expanding or maintaining supply or effort in other lines or places. Rationing of gasoline to civilians permitted expanded military consumption. But expansion without concomitant contraction is of course possible, as in the activation of unused plants. Use of the electrolytic process of tin plating instead of the dipping process gave more plate from less tin, so that a reduced supply of a raw material was not reflected in an equivalent contraction of the product.

Substitution is another modifier of quantity. Substitution can be looked at from two sides. One can ask if an item in short supply can be replaced by a more abundant or a synthetic product, or one can ask if some item which is abundant may have other uses. We usually think of the former—glass for tin plate, synthetic for natural rubber—but the latter may be significant when weighing the power resources of other countries. An American thinks of potatoes as food, primarily, but they are an important source of industrial alcohol in the Soviet Union. Substitution of machines for men is a favorite American occupation. The high degree of automation possible in peace may be deceptive as to the possibilities in war, when destruction and disruption may make muscle-power indispensable. The reverse substitution of men for machines has its limitations also.

The doctrine of limiting factors in biology means, for example, that a plant needing nitrogen is not helped by an excess of phosphate. Man's ingenuity in finding substitutes makes this doctrine only loosely applicable to human affairs. Nevertheless, limiting factors do appear, particularly in war and under conditions of blockade and attrition. Substitution very often requires time and imports, which may not be available. The limiting factors may be rates. For instance, there was no doubt that the United States could create a synthetic rubber industry adequate for its needs. The question was whether it could be created in time.

THE QUALITY MODIFIERS

Quality is a second family of modifiers. The two main branches of the quality family are the quality of materials and goods on the one hand, and of operation on the other. These terms are meant to apply very broadly. American schoolboys or African natives are materials in the present sense, having certain qualities in that condition. Trained as workers, soldiers, professional men, etc., they might be called goods, their qualities in that state depending not only on inherent vigor and intelligence and childhood environment but upon specific training. Operation is also used broadly, to include business management, military organization, and government.

Quality of course connotes the question, "How good?" For our study, the question really is, how well does something serve its strategic purpose? An example of the distinction is the use by the Communists in Korea of obsolete wooden-frame airplanes for night bombing, because these old planes give poor radar echoes.

Quality is often placed in opposition to quantity, the ideal of "the mostest of the bestest" being difficult to attain. It is not necessarily unattainable, however, and quality often has been improved while quantity was being increased. The *a priori* opposition of quality and quantity possibly dates from handicraft days. The Battle of Britain is often cited as a triumph of quality over quantity, British planes, pilots, and operations being considered superior to the German. Because of these qualitative superiorities and the fact that fighting took place over British soil, the Royal Air Force sometimes obtained local quantitative superiority.[10] A different relationship of quality and quantity can be illustrated by a famine-struck area. The difference between high- and low-grade wheat would mean little. Quality would be negligible in comparison with quantity and availability.

Change of quality must also be considered. This has three aspects, durability, obsolescence, and variation. Durability and obsolescence might be lumped as life expectancy of materials or goods. The significance of durability needs little elaboration. The United States was able to get through four years of war with its initial stock of private automobiles, in part because the cars proved durable beyond customary expectation. (Gasoline and tire rationing of course lengthened car life by reducing use.) The durability of railroad equipment, machine tools, and the like was important. Materials and labor needed for maintenance and replacement of non-combatant equipment of course must be drawn from the supply available for military use. Durability can be obtained at excessive cost and can be offset by obsolescence. Military equipment, however, is subject to very hard usage, and expenditures to increase its durability usually are justified. Breakdowns are likely to occur at the worst possible time and place when the equipment is overworked during an emergency.

High durability and low rate of obsolescence are major criteria of materials and goods that are to be stockpiled or mothballed. To judge when obsolescence has so reduced power value that goods should be scrapped requires something like clairvoyance. Brodie argues cogently against prematurely scrapping obsolescent naval ships, on the grounds that quantity may offset a modern qualitative inferiority.[11] The destroyer-for-bases deal of 1940 is a supporting illustration. Whether the great stock of slow Liberty ships is a real or an illusory asset in event of war is a question currently debated. Rommel repeatedly refers to the gradual obsolescence of his tanks relatively to those of the British.[12] Rommel's victories actually increased his problems, for the Germans came to think him a miracle worker who could win with any weapons, while

---

[10] Chester Wilmot, *The Struggle for Europe* (London, 1952), pp. 51–53.
[11] Bernard Brodie, *Sea Power in the Machine Age* (Princeton, 1943), pp. 203, 334, 442–445.
[12] *The Rommel Papers,* ed. B.H. Liddell Hart (New York, 1953), p. 245 and elsewhere.

the British were compelled to replace lost equipment and had fewer competing demands for their best tanks. There is perhaps more danger that obsolescent items will be rated too highly in terms of power than that they will be scrapped prematurely, but pruning the power tree of its fading branches does not strengthen it unless there is concomitant new growth. In the inorganic world of ships, tanks, and the like, new growth does not come spontaneously.

Variation in quality may involve the familiar phenomenon of "the weakest link." Ships in line of battle can steam no faster than the slowest vessels. One defective shell can jam a gun. All troops in combat may have to fall back if one unit gives way. In the first battle of El Alamein, Auchinleck directed major counter-attacks at Italian divisions, forcing the Germans to limit their own drives. On the other hand, the phenomenon of "the strongest link" sometimes is encountered. Rommel's crack Afrika Korps saved many critical situations and kept the Italian army in battle long after it would otherwise have collapsed.

Variations in the quality of leadership—economic, political, military—are important modifiers of the power inventory and of course are difficult to assess. A change of leaders may change the power value of a military unit almost overnight. Even push-button warfare will require not only a man to push the button but, more important, a man to say when to push the button. This ineluctable individual factor may be overlooked in the power inventory because it cannot be treated statistically. It is apt to be neglected in the economist's or the geographer's approach to the study of power. Uncritical historians, on the other hand, may give too much attention to individuals. "The Gauls were not conquered by the Roman legions but by Caesar," said Napoleon, whose own history showed the potency of genius, but also that manpower, weather, and nationalism were not to be ignored.

OPERATION: FOCUS OF INVENTORY AND STRATEGY

When we speak of operation and of the quality of operation, we are at or near the common focus of the inventory and strategic beams of our opening analogy. We use "operation" in the broad sense of "the way things work."[13] How well things work is a major modifier of the power inventory. We can apply this concept of working quality to items in wide variety—a squad of soldiers, a mine, a factory, an army, the whole of an economic or political system. This aspect of quality may be illustrated by Russian experience in the first five-year

---

13 "Operation" has the narrow military meaning of "a military action" and the broader one of any strategic, tactical, service, training, or administrative action. "Administration" was considered as a substitute for "operation" in the present paper, but was rejected because of its bureaucratic connotation and because, in military usage, it does not apply to strategic or tactical activities.

plan, when modern factories were built but sometimes nothing came off the assembly lines.

Operation has two main parts, motivation and organization. Motivation—involving reward, punishment, loyalty, leadership—is essential even for the most prosaic effort. To return to the example of petroleum as a factor of power, the motivation of the seamen on tankers may be a critical matter. Motivation for the long-haul usually demands pecuniary or other material rewards. But material motivation is not enough; it has proved insufficient for high quality of work even in purely economic activities. In this respect, however, states may go to the other extreme. As has been said, without patriotism there is no power, but one cannot expect patriotism to replace pay checks year after year. Americans seem particularly reluctant to admit that political and military operation really works from the top down, though checked and criticized (in both senses of criticism) from below. Patriotism, luck, or *le bon Dieu* may not provide administrators of high quality if pay is inadequate.

Organization may be divided into control and integration. Control is essential in government, industry, or battle. Loss of control is a nightmare of the military commander and all sorts of communication devices are used to provide a mechanical guard against it. Control involves motivation. A General Patton might control where a weaker man might lose control. Control is necessary for a rationing system and for maintaining secrecy in government and the armed forces. Integration means how the parts of an organization mesh together. One aspect is illustrated by the integration of Negro troops into white units in the United States Army. This step multiplied manyfold the power value of the Negro soldiers and removed from them the stigma of "the weakest link." The operations of alliances are generally hampered by imperfect integration. The faulty integration of American railroads early in World War I led to intolerable congestion. The converse of congestion—shortages—may also arise from faulty integration, even when ample materials or goods are available.

The pace of operations is an important aspect of their quality. Equipment of high quality is necessary but not sufficient for fast pace. Whittlesey has pointed out that the time-dimension of human activities has three derivatives, velocity, pace, and timing.[14] A jet airplane may have a velocity near the speed of sound. The pace of air operations depends on many other velocities than those of airplanes. It depends, among other things, on the rate at which intelligence reaches the commander, on the rapidity with which plans are formulated and orders issued, upon the speed of servicing and repair. Pace—"the average tempo of trajections in a specified area"—may thus be more significant than velocity. The sluggishness of bureaucratic pace is notorious. Fortunately, it is also world-wide, though this does not permit us to be complacent about it.

---

14 Derwent Whittlesey, "The Horizon of Geography," *Annals Assoc. Amer. Geogrs.,* XXXV (March 1945), 23–24.

One purpose of war games is to step up the pace of operations that may some day be performed in the face of the enemy. Perhaps all branches of administration should hold war games.

Operational quality is roughly synonymous with some meanings of "efficiency" but not necessarily with that which relates output to input, if we measure output and input in conventional ways. Diplomatic operations of high quality are not necessarily economical of time or money. It is debatable whether the decision of 1953 to concentrate war production in the most efficient factories was wise or unwise as a long-run policy, since dispersal among more plants not only might decrease vulnerability but might permit faster acceleration of production in event of war.

VULNERABILITY AND COST

Vulnerability is a modifier of the power inventory that of course now affects the innermost parts of the home front. The power value of two factories may depend, after war begins, more on their vulnerability than on their efficiency. The vulnerability of Britain to air attack weakened Chamberlain's hand at Munich. Theoretically, the states with atomic weapons have the power virtually to blow each other to bits. Whether they will do so is debatable. Atomic warfare might resemble the strategy of the fleet-in-being, the threat of atomic weapons being used to tie up the resources of the opponent. Vulnerability will nevertheless be a factor, for the side that has attained the best defense against atomic weapons can make the most aggressive threats. Distressingly little attention has been paid to the reduction of vulnerability during the period of rapid construction since World War II. Some records have been stored in underground vaults, but little has been done to safeguard the really essential resources of labor and equipment, without which records have little meaning.

Simplicity is one of the classical principles of war. A major reason is the vulnerability of complicated operations, especially in the face of an active enemy. Simplicity is difficult to attain in industrialized war, in spite of modern methods of communication and control. Simplicity in plan may be obtainable only through complexity of control, as in assembly-line manufacturing. In industry, simplicity is not sought for itself but only if costs can be reduced or sales increased. In fact, the search for cheaper supplies or more extensive markets often results in complicated cross-hauling of materials and goods[15] and in duplication of delivery and marketing systems. Much of this complexity, efficient though it may be in a capitalistic economy in peace, would have to be eliminated in time of war, especially if the home front were heavily bombarded.

Cost as an index of power or a measure of power value has been discussed on an earlier page. In spite of its limitations in these respects, it remains a

---

15 Edward L. Ullman, "The Railroad Pattern of the United States," *Geog. Rev.*, XXXIX (April 1949), 254–255.

significant modifier. In part, this is because of the subjective importance given to the cost of national defense by taxpayers and their Congressional representatives. There is a persistent clamor for social security and insurance sells steadily, but that national power is the most basic form of social security and insurance, without which the others are illusory, is commonly forgotten in time of peace. The subjective importance of cost is of course greatest in the democracies where public opinion is most effective in government.

Cost has objective as well as subjective importance. Cost, in relation to national power, implies the question, "How much of our resources are required to increase our supply of a given item, or its readiness for use?" Japan, for example, could build warships with cheaper labor than could the United States, but the cost in terms of available steel was proportionately greater to Japan. Japan could man a warship for a small part of the payroll of its American counterpart, but the oil for fuel came from a much more limited resource. World War II showed that most nations can sacrifice living standards for war to a degree hardly thought possible and that national bankruptcy can be staved off for years. Nevertheless, drain on resources is a reality, if replacement does not keep up with use. The attrition on manpower is perhaps the most obvious form, but drain on equipment, if there is insufficient reinvestment to maintain or replace it, may be serious.

THE STRATEGIC BEAM

The power inventory has now been provided with a set of modifiers—a checklist for a check-list, so to speak. A question may arise: Are the modifiers so numerous and so indeterminate that they reduce the inventory to a pulp? This thought can be dismissed with little comment. So long as there is politics among sovereign states, there will be estimation of power. Even though the best estimates are only rough, they are better than reliance on intuition or emotion. It is true that the modifiers are warning signs rather than guideposts, that they point out traps rather than show where the path lies. Nevertheless, insofar as they conform to realities they should be useful. It may be significant that Klaus Knorr, in a parallel but completely independent study of war potential ... uses a basic methodology that might be called that of inventory and modifier, though the resemblance to the present paper may not be obvious to anyone but the present writer. In this book, Knorr presents certain major factors in war potential and discusses the conditions and qualifications that govern their evaluation.

One of the most serious of the problems that beset the student of national power is how to avoid encyclopedism. The modifiers of the power inventory are no protection against this. In fact, the mechanical application of a check-list to a check-list would yield compound encyclopedism. Encyclopedism is likewise a problem in basic intelligence research. What facts to collect, in how much detail to present them, how far to go in evaluation without treading on the sacred ground of policy-making? These and similar questions plague the intelligence research worker. Roger Hilsman has challenged the encyclopedic method in intelligence and calls for workers to be "manipulative, instrumental, action-conscious, policy-oriented."[16] In terms of our analogy, what Hilsman appears to desire is that the intelligence worker get more light from the strategic beam and not work only by the inventory beam, where he is forever stepping into shadows. The aptness of this analogy will be attested by many who have worked in intelligence, though they may not be optimistic about the practical solution of the problem.

If one looks at power along the inventory beam, one is asking, "What have I?" If one looks along the strategic beam, one is asking, "What do I need?" Each question of course connotes the other, but most will agree that, as in personal finances needs run ahead of funds, among nations it is strategic needs rather than love of statistics that sets us counting our power resources. This analogy can easily be strained, however. In the first place, neither the power inventory nor strategic needs can be expressed completely in monetary or even statistical terms. Second, the public purse is much more elastic than the personal one. A nation does not live on a fixed income, and it is production rather than the budget that really counts. Third, it is not so much a case of shifting one's line of sight from the inventory to the strategic beam as of looking along both. It takes binocular vision, so to speak, to see national power in full relief. What one can do is influenced by what one has, but what one has is influenced by what one does, in world politics at least.

This paradox, if it is one, will be discussed under four heads: (1) the harmony of resources and national strategy; (2) the augmentation, or reduction, of resources by national strategy; (3) the allocation of resources in relation to national strategy; and (4) the relativity of power in the light of national strategies.

HARMONY OF INVENTORY AND STRATEGY

That national strategy must be in harmony with national resources may seem like a truism, but the statement is true only in a very general sense. It can be a very misleading doctrine if resources are considered to be a fixed sum and if national strategy is conceived in strictly military terms and only in isolation. The doctrine has been used by some isolationists, who argue not that the United States *can* isolate itself (by means of some wonder-weapon, perhaps), but that it *must* isolate itself because it cannot afford a broader strategy. One possible answer, of course, is to say that the broader strategy may be the cheaper in the long run. Walter Lippmann took a different tack: he held that a state must balance its commitments and its power,[17] but he goes on to say

---

16 Roger Hilsman, Jr., "Intelligence and Policy-making in Foreign Affairs," *World Politics,* V (October 1952), 44.

17 Walter Lippmann, *U.S. Foreign Policy: Shield of the Republic* (Boston, 1943), pp. 9–10. He adds, "with a comfortable surplus of power in reserve."

of the "true statesman": "Having determined the foreign commitments which are vitally necessary to his people, he will never rest until he has mustered the force to cover them." In other words, if two strategies appear equally good, we many choose the cheaper, but if it is penicillin we need, aspirin will not do.[18]

Harmony of resources and needs may be all very well, but what if a state cannot muster the force to cover its vitally necessary commitments? One answer, too popular with Americans, is to recalculate the risks and cut the commitments. Another answer, popular with Americans and justifiably so if the limitations are realized, is to turn to science. The development of wonderful new weapons is much in mind, but should the brunt of war remain on the shoulders of the ground forces, even more important may be the use of science to augment natural resources. A kinder deity might have given this country limitless high-grade iron ore and never-failing oil wells, but we know of other ways to meet our needs, such as beneficiation of lean ores and the distillation of oil shales. But such expansion of resources does not come about automatically or with the ease of comic-strip art. It requires research, capital, labor, and time, all of which must be comprehended in the long-term national strategy.

Import and stockpiling programs are of course another way of augmenting a state's resources or of conserving domestic supplies. Since the United States has traditionally discouraged imports and since large stockpiles are uneconomic, in a business sense, such programs require a consciously strategic viewpoint.

A state may augment its resources through the acquisition of colonies or the formation of alliances. An alliance may be the only resort of a small state, short of outright annexation to a great power, by which it can "muster the force to cover its vitally necessary commitments." In estimating the power of an alliance, due consideration must be given to strategic aspects. The power of an alliance is never the simple sum of the power inventories of its members. The total may be much less than the sum if organization is weak or if the members cannot easily support each other. On the other hand, the joint power of the United States and Canada is potentially more than the sum of their separate resources, because together they form a coherent block of North America reaching into the Arctic instead of splitting the continent along a long, weak boundary.

A state may augment its power by building up the power of its allies or, without an alliance, of its presumptive friends. This of course is an objective of American foreign aid programs. The motivation of foreign aid programs ranges from pure humanitarianism through the belief that sound independent nations are "safe" to the strictly military desire to build up foreign facilities and sources of supply. This last is sometimes called "geologistics" and aug-

---

18 This analogy, while sound in principle, is difficult to apply. The choice of strategies may be more like the choice among medicines of uncertain therapeutic value for a disease not definitely diagnosed.

ments resources by cutting down "transmission losses" and taking advantage of lower wages and prices.

Power resources can be reduced instead of augmented if the national strategy is unsound or obsolete. Clumsy diplomacy or a speech or act that is stupid in relation to foreign policy may cut national power, or looked at another way, may require an increased use of resources to achieve a given end. Wishful thinking plays a role in national strategy. A State's resources may be as effectively reduced by it as by the drainage of an oil field or a drop in the birth rate. Two ingrained American habits of mind are faith in machinery and a desire to pull back from overseas commitments. Any strategic theory that embodies or seems to embody these ideas is sure to find advocates. The popular enthusiasm for wonder-weapons finds support in these mental habits. Wishful thinking is by no means confined to the man-in-the-street and the professor-in-the-tower. The fateful conferences of Munich and Yalta show that statesmen are not immune.

THE PROBLEM OF ALLOCATION

One of the knottiest problems of national strategy is the allocation of resources, between private and governmental demands and among the various branches of the government. In a democratic country, such allocations are strongly influenced by habits, moods, and political pressures held or generated by the public. Certain clichés crop up. For instance, it becomes said that the civilian economy can bear only so much military or foreign aid expense. At bottom, this is a rationalization of American hedonism. Pushed to the test, a state must pay the price of victory or lose. If there is sufficient solidarity, spontaneous or enforced, civilian consumption can be pared to the bone.

The division of resources among the armed forces may bring up the cliché of "balance," which usually means that increases and cuts in the budget shall be equally shared. Certain criticisms of "balance" are, however, not without cliché themselves. The argument is heard that air power has the greatest inherent capabilities of any arm, because of the velocity of its vehicles and their global, three-dimensional medium of operation; the air arm should therefore receive the lion's share of appropriations. The conclusion may be true, but it does not follow from the premise as stated in general terms. Capability, like balance and allocation, is a vague word unless we are told, capability for *what*. Even within an armed service we find arguments about allocation of resources. Hitler's navy was torn between the submariners and the advocates of a balanced fleet, with each side claiming that the war would be lost if its counsels were disregarded.

Allocation of resources therefore can be discussed rationally only in the light of given national strategies. National strategy is to the power inventory as management is to the materials inventory of a factory. What is produced, and when, depends on the judgment of the management. The decisions of course are not free or unlimited. They depend not only on the resources of the factory but upon the milieu—the cultural and natural environments offering possibilities and imposing limitations. It hardly needs to be said that national strategy usually is less logical and consistent than industrial management. The play of interests makes the national strategy a sort of vector sum of ideas that are often divergent and sometimes diametrically opposed. The struggle between isolationists and interventionists in the United States in the interwar period is an obvious example. The single vote in the House of Representatives that renewed the selective service act might be called the vector sum in that case.

The strategy of industrial management is tested promptly. The statement of profit and loss gives the answer. There is no such easy test for national strategy. That a state has survived thus far may be all that we can claim, and we may not know for sure whether this is because of, or in spite of, its national strategy. Even the lessons of war are not conclusive. Witness the different conclusions that have been drawn from strategic bombardment in World War II.[19]

Generally speaking, there are two philosophies of resource allocation. One holds that a country should cleave to the strategy that seems best in terms of its own resources. The other holds that the "best" strategy is always relative to opposing strategies and calls for more flexibility, or for less complete commitment to one program. Strategic air power provides an illustration. Advocates of concentration on this arm have a number of arguments. There is the "inherent capabilities" doctrine: the long range and great pay-load of a strategic bomber. There is the argument from American strengths and weaknesses: the United States has a lively technology but not unlimited manpower; Americans like machinery and speed; they detest infantry service but will take any risk if they can do it sitting down. The Soviet Union is the most important enemy, and the doctrine of hitting the core rather than the extremities of enemy power has much to recommend it. But there are three terms of the equation of power that weigh against the foregoing: first, the unexpectedly rapid Soviet development of atomic bombs, making it unlikely that the United States will initiate their strategic use again; second, the Soviet strategy of limited risks and aggression by satellite; and third, American reluctance and unreadiness to turn a limited war into a general one. The evaluation of all these terms necessarily changes with time, technology, and national mood. Flexibility currently is dominant, and strategic thought seems to be seeking in tactical atomic missiles a means of combining flexibility, relatively conventional three-arm warfare, and American predilections for small armies and mechanization.

Neither the "one-basket" nor the "flexibility" philosophy of resource allocation can guard against obsolescence. As cavalrymen loved horses, so sailors

---

19 E.g., Alexander de Seversky, *Air Power: Key to Survival* (New York, 1950); and Marshall Andrews, *Disaster Through Air Power* (New York, 1950). There were divergent opinions in the Strategic Bombing Survey (*Summary Report, Pacific War* [Washington, 1964], and *Air Campaigns of the Pacific War* [Washington, 1947]).

love ships and airmen love airplanes. Whether anybody but a scientist can love an intercontinental rocket is a question, yet conceivably it might make other military implements obsolete. Steel and oil are sinews of war, as everyone knows, but one can imagine a titanium-hulled, uranium-powered missile that would make no great demand for steel or oil even in the manufacturing stage. This is of course dream-stuff today, but it shows that the projection of the inventory ray into the future must be checked against possible projections of the strategic ray.

National power must constantly be re-evaluated in terms of the methods and instruments available to national strategy. If Lower Slobbovia plans war on Upper Denturia, relative power is not determined solely by the fact that the former has bigger piles of rocks and more men to throw them. Can it bring its power to bear? If a wide, swift river separates these two countries, does Lower Slobbovia have the needed vehicles for crossing? Is its organization good enough to land its rock-throwers en masse, not in driblets? Are its emissaries loud braggarts who infuriate the Denturians or shrewd operators who may settle the dispute without fighting? All this bears on such questions of allocation as whether the Slobbovian *Führer* should put some of his rock-gatherers to canoe-building and send some of his rock-throwers to a school of diplomacy.

ALLOCATION IN SPACE AND TIME

Power resources exist in space and time. This may seem an obvious statement, yet it is an aspect that may be neglected. In the language of physics, there are space and time dimensions of the field of power. Strategy is the art of movement in such a field.

In a sense, space and time are resources. The nation that has them can adopt strategies that would be suicidal without them. Space consumes more than time; it consumes fuel, supplies, and manpower. Yet trading space for all of these is generally a sign of unpreparedness rather than of wisdom. But space and time are more than resources. They are conditions of resource allocation and use. Here, again, the strategic ray of the power triangle is valuable. Space and time aspects may be left out of an inventory. They are integral parts of national strategy.

The Sprouts made use of space as a strategic condition when they compared British sea power, based on an island close to the continent where the main rivals lay, with American sea power, facing two broad oceans.[20] Whittlesey, we have said, lists three derivatives of time: velocity, pace, and timing.[21] Velocity and pace have been touched on above, under operational quality. Timing was implicit in the discussion of the five availability states. Availability is strate-

---

[20] Harold and Margaret Sprout, *Toward a New Order of Sea Power* (Princeton, 1940), pp. 14–15 and 19–22.
[21] "The Horizon of Geography," *op. cit.,* pp. 23–24.

gically meaningful only in terms of how long it takes to bring a given item to the state of "immediately available." Locational availability also can be translated into terms of time and timing. Thomas' discussion of the "railway revolution" in war shows that even a century ago mobilization was not something that just happened.[22] In the Battle of Britain, radar helped the British get their planes to the right place at the right moment. One might say that radar gave the RAF a complete picture of the space-time field which helped offset the fact that the Luftwaffe was the larger force and held the strategic initiative.

THE PROBLEM OF RELATIVE POWER

That national power is always relative is almost axiomatic. In the eyes of Lichtenstein, Switzerland is a great power. A superficial approach to the relativity of power has been to compare the power inventories of the states or alliances under discussion, with emphasis upon actual or potential power according to the purpose or leanings of the writer. Such a simple method has of course long been rejected by those more deeply concerned with the problem. No substitute formula, simple or complex, will come from the present paper. The emphasis upon the interplay of the inventory and strategic beams leads only to greater uncertainties, when two or more states are considered.

Emphasis upon the strategic aspect of relative power does not render the power inventory useless. Basic data on such fundamentals as manpower, steel production, and the like are indispensable, and it is generally true in world politics as in pugilism that a good big man is better than a good little man. What the strategic approach does is to ask how good the man is, as well as how big. If strategic considerations make the estimation of relative power more complex, they may compensate by making it less fatalistic. It is less necessary to kneel before statistical superiority, unless the margin be great. The free world has had no reason to fear the Soviet Union—statistically. But generally the Soviet Union has held the initiative in world affairs. If the statistically weaker country has often called the tune for the statistically stronger, a reversal of roles is at least theoretically possible.

The simplest statement about relative power is that the margin of power between A and B is more significant than the absolute power of A or B. Unfortunately, we cannot express a margin of power statistically any more accurately than we can measure absolute power. We must make the best informed guess possible.

Relative power is sometimes discussed as if a state had only its own resources. But tight blockade is rare. Alliances, trade with neutrals, conquests of territory, scientific substitution, all may increase relative power. On the other hand, we cannot assume that a state necessarily commands all its own resources. Some may be highly vulnerable (like the French coal fields in both

---

22 Thomas H. Thomas, "Armies and the Railway Revolution," *War as a Social Institution* (New York, 1941), pp. 88–94.

world wars); some may be withheld by public unwillingness to sacrifice; administrative clumsiness may prevent full employment of resources. In short, the modifiers we have discussed apply to the calculus of relative power.

Power relations are never simply between A and B. They take place in the configuration of international politics. Even in the so-called bipolar world of today, many states are involved. The shift of China from the non-Soviet to the Soviet camp profoundly affected the relative power of the United States and the Soviet Union, without changing the absolute power of either of these countries by itself. The relative power of the United States and Communist China in Korea was profoundly affected by the mere existence of the Soviet Union in the background. Even weak states affect relative power if they influence when or where competitive crises arise. The weakness of the states of the Eurasian rimland is the despair of the American strategist.

If it is the margin of power that really counts, one must ask for how long a period the margin must be maintained and what sort of competition is taking place. In a short war, margins of skill and readiness may count for more than relative potentials. There are some who hold that a little more skill (especially in handling Soviet minority peoples) and a little more readiness (for Russian winters) might have given Germany military victory over the Soviet Union. In long wars, relative potentials obviously become more significant, if the disparity in skills is not too great. In short crises not leading to war, relative diplomatic skill may be decisive. The long-term competition called the Cold War has demanded skills and other resources in combinations of unusual nature. The Cold War is a competition for entire peoples. Diplomacy is no longer merely the communing of diplomat with diplomat but a problem of mass communication of many kinds. Skill in communicating ideas and methods on a wide range of topics—government, subversion, farming, birth control, etc. —may tip a country like China or India to an extent that military power is almost incapable of offsetting.

Relative power, considered item by item, must be evaluated differently if the given item is scarce or abundant. If some element is scarce, the margin between just enough and not enough may be very significant. If both parties to a competition have some item in plenty, some derivative factor may be significant. Both the United States and the Soviet Union have large coal reserves, for instance. Whether they will last four hundred or four thousand years makes no immediate difference; they suffice for the present. Much more important are such derivatives as the rate of production, how much it could be increased, the manpower requirements of coal-mining in the two countries, and the speed with which a hydrogenation industry might be developed if liquid fuels run short.

Our opening analogy stated that the power inventory must be triangulated by national strategy. To extend the analogy to relative power, not only a state's own inventory and strategy must be considered but also the inventories and strategies of the other state or states involved in the political configuration.

Theoretically, in this age of global competition, this would mean sixty or more strategic beams sweeping the international skies—with an effect more dazzling than illuminating. And, actually, it is in such a spider-web of beams that we are caught, when Germany and China, Iran and Guatemala, Indochina and British Guiana may hit the headlines the same day. The speed of communication and reaction in world politics, as well as the global scope, calls for more background in strategic thought than has been the American custom. Otherwise we are repeatedly surprised, "for, to the blind, all things are sudden."[23]

The complicated interrelationships of national strategies and relative power may be somewhat simplified if we consider national strategy to have two aspects, one of which we may call "autonomous," the other "responsive." There is not a dichotomy between these but, rather, a gradation. For example, England was not forced to adopt sea power as its principal weapon. In fact, there was little attempt to employ sea power independently until the reign of Henry III. Insularity permitted the British to rely on sea power but did not command it. Similarly, the decision of Britain to maintain a fleet equal to the two closest rivals was an autonomous decision, for Britain was free to adopt a smaller or greater ratio, limited only by the willingness to risk and the willingness to sacrifice. The location of the principal British naval bases was less autonomous; it depended on the probable enemy of the period and that enemy's resources and possible strategy. The distribution of British ships among the fleets and bases was also not fully autonomous; it was responsive to the political changes and the moves of the opponents.

A state faced with rising unemployment might make autonomous decisions on combating it. It might widen military training, thus tightening the labor market by removing young men and increasing economic activity by orders for military equipment and supplies. Or it might pay men for raking leaves or expand unemployment insurance. One policy enhances available power, the other doesn't, though the theoretical potentials remain unchanged. If, having failed to train its men, the second state is attacked, it is forced to make a convulsive responsive effort. Enemy power must be matched if possible, when and where and however it is used.

The autonomous aspects of national strategy are extremely important. They are the main aspects about which decisions are made in advance of conflict. These decisions are likely to be swayed by factors extraneous to the true problem. These decisions may weigh heavily in the scales when one comes face to face with an opponent and must respond to his moves. The decision of the Truman administration to take a stand on immigration to Palestine was autonomous. Extraneous factors of domestic politics played an important part. The effect of this and subsequent decisions on American power in the Middle East was and continues to be significant.

The last aspect of relative power that we shall discuss might inelegantly be

---

[23] Carlyle, *History of the French Revolution*, I, Bk. 7, chap. 8.

called "historical peristalsis." In both politics and technology, change is endless but not continuous. Nor is the phase always the same from one country to another. The peristaltic changes in naval technology, the political responses to such changes, and the relative power relations resulting from both are so well brought out in Bernard Brodie's *Sea Power in the Machine Age* that no discussion here is needed. Similar processes take place in diplomacy, propaganda, and all the other implements and methods of national strategy. To use a more refined but less apt analogy, the light of the strategic beam fluctuates. Hence the evaluation of the power inventory must change.

Thought is subject to many kinds of distortions, many of them quite unintentional. One common distortion is polarization. One polarization that is germane here is the tendency to place in opposition the long and the short views. The phenomenon of "historical peristalsis" indicates that both long and short views are necessary and complementary. A statement about national power really should carry a date.

Another form of polarization also is germane: The "and/or/versus" distortion. If one mentions, for example, "the spirit and the sword," it takes the merest twist of the tongue to change it to "the spirit or the sword" and but an intonation to give "or" the meaning of "versus." When we have spoken of power inventory and national strategy, *and* means *and*, not *or* or *versus*. Especially is it not intended to polarize material and imponderable aspects of power. There are non-material as well as material items in the power inventory and national strategy requires the availability of both. Even a national strategy of complete pacifism requires for inventory a stock of Grade A martyrs, as complete militarism requires a stock of Grade A brutes. Though a sound national strategy should reduce the wastage of resources, strategy is not a substitute for resources but is the art of using them.

HAROLD AND
MARGARET SPROUT

Environmental Factors in the Study of International Politics

Those who practice statecraft, as well as those who study and write about it, seem generally to take it for granted that the phenomenon called "international politics" is meaningfully related to the setting or environment or milieu in which political decisions are taken and executed.

Let us start with some illustrative examples. First, the words of a German diplomat, Richard von Kühlmann, that "geographical position and historical development are so largely *determining* factors of foreign policy that, regardless of the kaleidoscopic change of contemporary events, and no matter what form of government has been instituted or what political party may be in power, the foreign policy of a country has a *natural tendency* to return again and again to the same general and fundamental alignment. . . ."[1]

Next, the French diplomat, Jules Cambon: "The geographical position of a nation . . . is the principal factor *conditioning* its foreign policy—the principal reason why it must have a foreign policy at all. . . ."[2]

Third, from a recent text on sea power: "England *driven* to the sea by her sparse resources to seek a livelihood and to find homes for her burgeoning population, and sitting athwart the main sea routes of Western Europe, seemed *destined by geography* to command the seas. . . ."[3]

From *The Journal of Conflict Resolution*, I, No. 4 (1957), 309–328. Reprinted by permission.

[1] R. von Kühlmann, "The Permanent Bases of German Foreign Policy," *Foreign Affairs*, IX (1931), 179.

[2] J. Cambon, "The Permanent Bases of French Foreign Policy," *Foreign Affairs*, VIII (1930), 174.

[3] E.B. Potter *et al.*, *The United States and World Sea Power* (Englewood Cliffs, N.J.: Prentice-Hall, Inc., 1955), p. 44.

Fourth, from a highly regarded work on Japan: "The mountains of Japan have *pushed* the Japanese out upon the seas, *making* them the greatest seafaring people of Asia. . . . Sea routes have *beckoned* the Japanese abroad. . . . The factor of geographic isolation during . . . two thousand years has *helped fashion* national traits which eventually, and *almost inevitably, led* Japan to political isolation and to crushing defeat in war. . . ."[4]

Fifth, from a standard treatise on resources, the assertion that invention of the basic steel furnace (which made it possible to produce good steel from the acidic ores of Alsace-Lorraine) "*led inevitably* to Germany's industrial hegemoney on the continent [of Europe]."[5]

In all such statements (and one could extend the list indefinitely), a causal relationship is asserted between some environmental factor or set of factors, on the one hand, and some attitude, action, or state of affairs, on the other. Some of the statements are phrased in deterministic language—"determined," "drove," "led inevitably," etc. Others, probably more numerous, are phrased in terms compatible with some degree of choice—"influence," "pressure," etc.

Such forms of speech and the causal relationship which they state or imply delineate the main issues with which this study is concerned: How are environmental factors related to political phenomena? And what forms of speech are most fruitful in expressing such relationships?

In approaching these questions, it will be helpful to draw a distinction between political attitudes and policy decisions, on the one hand, and, on the other hand, the layouts in space or other states of affairs which we shall call the "operational results of decisions." We regard this distinction as important, indeed as prerequisite to fruitful investigation of ecological viewpoints, concepts, and theories, in connection with politics in general and international politics in particular.

Within these terms of reference, we shall attempt to establish the following propositions or theses:

1. Environmental factors become related to the attitudes and decisions which, in the aggregate, comprise a state's foreign policy *only* by being apperceived and taken into account by those who participate in the policy-forming process.
2. Conclusions as to the manner in which apperceived environmental factors are dealt with in foreign-policy-making depend on the theory or theories of decision-making which the analyst brings to bear on the case under consideration.
3. Hypotheses as to the manner in which apperceived environmental factors enter into the decision-making process can provide fruitful linkages between ecological and behavioral approaches to the study of international poliitcs.
4. Environmental factors can be significantly related to the operational results of policy decisions, even though such factors are not apperceived and taken into account in the policy-forming process.

---

[4] E.O. Reischauer, *Japan: Past and Present* (New York: Alfred A. Knopf, Inc., 1946), pp. 5, 8.

[5] E.W. Zimmermann, *World Resources and Industries* (rev. ed.: New York: Harper & Row, Publishers, 1951), p. 648.

5. What is called analysis of state power or international power relations or (preferably, in our view) analysis of state capabilities consists essentially of calculating opportunities and limitations latent, or implicit, in the milieu of the state under consideration.

6. Capability calculations or estimates are always carried out within some framework of assumptions regarding the policy objectives, operational strategy, and political relations of the state under consideration.

7. Conclusions as to the opportunities and limitations which are implicit in a state's milieu and which may affect the operational results of its policy decisions depend on the ecological theory and the topical explanatory premises which the analyst brings to bear in the specific case under consideration.

THE PROBLEM IN GENERAL

In the preceding paragraphs we have used numerous ecological terms— "environment," "milieu," "environmental factors," "man-milieu relationship hypotheses," etc. This terminology suffers from ambiguous and conflicting usage in the special vocabularies of ecological and behavioral sciences and in the vocabulary of human geography, which has ecological aspects but is not regarded by its principal spokesmen as primarily in ecological science.

We have attempted to straighten out this semantic tangle in a previous study.[6] Because "environment" has come to mean different things to different specialists, we have substituted the French word *milieu*, to designate the general concept. Since there is no corresponding French adjective, we have retained the English adjective "environmental." But we have restricted the noun "environment" (modified by qualifying adjectives) to limited aspects of the milieu, as for example, "physical environment," "social environment," "non-human environment," "psychological environment," "operational environment," etc.

We define the general concept of "milieu" to include all phenomena (excepting only the environed unit's own hereditary factors) to which the environed unit's activities may be related. So defined, milieu includes both tangible objects, non-human and human, at rest and in motion, and the whole complex of social patterns, some embodied in formal enactments, others manifest in more or less stereotyped expectations regarding the behavior of human beings and the movements and mutations of non-human phenomena. This definition of milieu includes the environed unit's own ideas or images of the milieu, a concept designated herein as "psychological environment."

This aggregate of physical objects and social patterns is conceived as comprising the potential maximum set of environmental factors that might be deemed relevant to any given human state of affairs. What specific components of this aggregate are judged to be significantly relevant in a particular context depends on how the analyst defines the problem in hand and on the relationship of the theory, or theories, which he brings to bear.

---

[6] H. and M. Sprout, *Man-Milieu Relationship Hypotheses in the Context of International Politics* (Princeton: Center of International Studies, 1956).

Environment, or milieu, connotes some idea of relationship, both in popular usage and in technical vocabularies of special fields. Something is conceived to be encompassed—that is to say, environed—by something else in some meaningful relationship. In the discusion of human affairs, the "something environed" may be defined as a single human being or as some human group. In the context of diplomacy and other aspects of international politics, the environed unit may be conceived as a single policy-making agent of the state, as some *ad hoc* policy-making group, as a formal agency of government, as some non-official group within the body politic, as the population of the state as a whole, as the state itself viewed as a corporate entity, or as some supra-state grouping, such as, for example, the "Atlantic Community."

What phenomena are included in the milieu depends in part on how one defines the environed unit. If, for example, the unit is a formal agency of government or some *ad hoc* policy-making group in the government, a great many factors physically internal to the state as well as factors external thereto may be significantly relevant elements of the milieu of such policy-making units. On the other hand, if the environed unit is conceived as the corporate entity of the state, only factors external to that entity are components of that milieu. For certain purposes—for example, the analysis of policy decisions—it may be more fruitful to proceed in terms of the concepts of decisional unit and internal and external setting. For other purposes—for example, analysis of certain aspects of state capability—it may be more fruitful to conceive the state as an entity in relation to its external setting alone.

All too often in discussions of foreign policy and state capability, the precise referent is obscure. But some concept of environed unit there must be. Otherwise, by definition, there is no concept of milieu, no ascertainable set of relevant factors, no concept of environmental relationship.

Relationships between man and milieu have been hypothesized in various ways. In our earlier study, cited above, we identified and discussed five more or less distinct relationship theories: environmental determinism, free-will environmentalism, environmental possibilism, cognitive behaviorism, and environmental probabilism.

Environmental determinism hypothesizes an invariable correlation between some set of environmental "causes" and environing "effects." Man, by this hypothesis, has no choice; indeed, he is, by definition, incapable of choice. The properties of the milieu determine his activities. Hence his past activities are explicable and his future activities predictable by reference to the variation of some set of environmental causes.

Construed literally, two of the statements quoted at the beginning of this essay would appear to be exhibits of environmental determinism: the quotations regarding British sea power (Potter *et al.*), and regarding Germany's "industrial hegemony" (Zimmermann). The authors of these statements, we are confident, would deny that they are environmental determinists.

Looking at the matter more broadly, one notes that the determinist label has been pinned on numerous interpretations of history. Such names as Demolins, Ratzel, Semple, and Huntington immediately come to mind. Huntington, for example, has been called a determinist because he claimed to discover regular correlations between climatic variables and "civilization."

Neither Huntington nor any other alleged determinist known to us has denied man's capacity to choose among alternative courses of action. We have never discovered any interpretation of history that even closely approaches rigorous environmental determinism. We would contend that both general interpretations of history and specific statements phrased in deterministic rhetoric are simply rhetoric and nothing more. A little later on, we shall attempt to show that most man-milieu relationships expressed in deterministic rhetoric are also and more fruitfully explicable in non-deterministic terms.

Free-will environmentalism, or simply environmentalism, represented in its origin a retreat from strict determinism. The environmentalist substituted, in place of "determine," "control," and other deterministic verbs, such verbs as "influence," "push," "beckon," etc., which admit the concept of choice among alternatives.

Most environmentalists have concerned themselves mainly with man's relations to the physical environment. Environmentalist discourse often displays a certain teleological coloration. "Nature" is conceived as a wise and purposeful entity guiding human destiny. Man is the target of Nature's signals. If he is wise, he heeds them. But the environmentalist conceives man as capable of choosing the "wrong road"—albeit to his future sorrow and frustration.

One encounters environmentalist rhetoric in many fields. We have quoted several examples. We are confident that the authors of those passages would reject the teleology implicit in a literal interpretation of their words. Again, we suspect, these authors have indulged in a poetic license which, in our view, has no justification in serious explanations of human activities. At any rate, environmentalist rhetoric explains nothing that is not more satisfactorily explicable in terms of other relationship theories yet to be considered.

Environmental possibilism is the relationship theory that took form in reaction against determinism and environmentalism. In the possibilist theory, the issue of choice is bypassed. The milieu as a whole or some set of environmental factors is conceived as a sort of matrix which limits the operational results of whatever is attempted.

These environmental limits are conceived to vary from place to place and from time to time. The limits implicit in one set of factors (for example, Atlantic winds and currents) may vary with changes in other factors (for example, changes in ship design and mode of propulsion). But, at any given place and time, possibilism postulates some set of limits that affect the outcome of any attempted course of action.

A particular set of limits may circumscribe broadly or narrowly; that is to say, they may leave room for considerable, or very little, range of effective choice. Under conditions of primitive technology, the range tends to be narrow. As men attain more efficient tools and skills, accumulate capital, and perfect their social organization, the limits may be pushed back, and the range of effective choice widens.

In the possibilist hypothesis, environmental limitations on accomplishment are assumed to be discoverable. But methodological discussion of possibilism is rarely explicit as to how one goes about discovering them. One may assume that a hypothetical omniscient observer could identify and delineate *all* the interrelations between milieu and environed unit. But, of course, no observer is in fact omniscient. The most that one can do is to frame hypotheses as to what environmental factors are significantly relevant to the action under consideration and how these set limits to the operational results thereof.

Thus the example just above rests upon some such set of hypotheses or premises, as follows: north of about 40° north latitude, Atlantic winds and currents move generally toward the east. These westerly winds and currents presented formidable obstacles to westbound sailing ships unable to sail close to the wind. In that state of marine technology, the normal westbound course across the Atlantic included a long detour southward to the latitudes of the northeasterly trade winds. Development of sailing ships capable of sailing closer to the wind reduced somewhat the limiting effects of headwinds and adverse currents. The development of externally powered ships eventually reduced the wind-current limitation to a level where it no longer substantially affected the westbound movement of ships across the Atlantic.

In possibilist theory, *environmental limitations* may exist and be operative irrespective of human knowledge and decisions. In the example just cited, Atlantic winds and currents indubitably limited certain movements of a fifteenth-century ship, irrespective of the desires and decisions of the ship's master. But *hypotheses to account for this state of affairs* do not exist apart from human observation and thought. Such hypotheses are formulated by someone. They have been called acts of creative imagination. Generally, though not necessarily, they are generalizations derived from observed events. But there is no certainty that any two observers will formulate identical explanatory hypotheses. However, in any given society and period, there is likely to be considerable agreement as to how things work and why.

Environmental possibilism carries no built-in assumption that a given environed unit will discover the limits of fruitful choice prior to reaching a decision. Nor is there any assumption that prior discovery would necessarily affect the decision taken. In the possibilist frame of reference, motives and decisions are *always taken as given*, not as phenomena to be explained or predicted.

Broadly speaking, environmental possibilism is the frame of reference within which the capabilities of states are calculated. But possibilism provides no basis for analyzing environmental factors in the context of policy formation. We shall return to this point later.

Cognitive behaviorism is the label that we have selected to designate the simple and familiar principle that a person reacts to his milieu as he apperceives it—that is, as he perceives and interprets it in the light of past experience. This concept of milieu is variously designated in the special vocabularies of psychological science: "life-space," "psychological field," "behavioral environment," "psychological environment," etc.

Cognitive behaviorism per se postulates no particular theory and no particular mode of utilizing environmental knowledge. It simply draws a sharp distinction between the *psychological environment* (with reference to which an individual defines choices and takes decisions) and the *operational environment* (which sets limits to what can happen when the decision is executed).

This distinction was at issue in a recent rejoinder to a familiar passage in R.C. Collingwood's work on *The Idea of History*. Collingwood argued that "the fact that certain people live . . . on an island has in itself no effect on their history; what has an effect is the way they conceive of that position."[7] To this the geographer, O.H.K. Spate, replied that "people cannot conceive of their insular position in any way unless they live on an island."[8]

Spate's rejoinder plainly runs contrary to a great deal of well-authenticated human experience. From time immemorial, men have formed opinions and taken decisions on some inaccurate image of the milieu. One thoroughly investigated demonstration of this phenomenon and its operational consequences was the now all-but-forgotten panic that was triggered off in New Jersey in 1938 by Orson Welles's rather too realistic radio description of the landing, near Princeton, of imaginary invaders from Mars. To contend that "people cannot conceive of their insular position in any way unless they live on an island" is equivalent to insisting that they cannot perceive non-existent "flying saucers."

Cognitive behaviorism simply affirms the elementary first principle that what matters in decision-making is not how the milieu is but how the decision-maker imagines it to be. The next step in linking environmental factors to decisions involves application of some hypothesis as to the decision-maker's environmental knowledge and his mode of using it.

Environmental probabilism is a general label for various behavioral models by which choices and decisions are explained or predicted on the basis of probable conformity to a hypothetical norm. Such a model may be simple or complex. It may be set forth explicitly or (what is more likely) left implicit. The analyst may even deny that he has any behavioral model in mind at all. But such denials are largely quibbles over terminology; for every explanation of past action and every prediction that is more than a throw of the dice are based on some set of assumptions regarding what is normally expectable behavior in the situation under consideration.

---

[7] R.C. Collingwood, *The Idea of History* (New York: Oxford University Press, 1946), p. 200.
[8] O.H.K. Spate, "Toynbee and Huntington: A Study in Determinism," *Geog. Journ.*, CXVIII (1952), 406, 423.

Some historians, geographers, and political scientists contend that every human being is unique and hence that human decisions are unpredictable. But such persons generally do not hesitate, for example, to cross a busy street when the traffic light turns green. In stepping from the curb, they are making a prediction that adverse traffic will obey the signal. In effect, such a prediction is simply an inference (generally subconscious) from a generalized model (rarely articulated) of how a "typical" motorcar driver behaves in the milieu under consideration. The pedestrian generally knows nothing about the lives of the specific drivers of oncoming cars. Nor does he usually know anything about their specific individual driving behavior. But he does have some notion of how drivers generally behave in that city and country; and he predicts driving behavior on the expectation of probable conformity to that hypothetical norm. That is all any behavioral model provides.

Before considering some of the assumptions incorporated into models of decision-making, we should like to stress a little further the probabilistic nature of such a model. The model is not a description of any specific person's behavior, and it carries no built-in assumption that the generalized description of "typical" behavior fits any particular person. In the present state of knowledge, no behavioral model can possibly anticipate idiosyncratic deviations from the hypothetical norm.

Norms are derived by generalization of past experience. Such a generalization is initially a trial hypothesis to be tested. When (in the example cited above) further observation confirms that car drivers almost invariably obey traffic signals, the hypothesis is said to be confirmed to a high degree of probability. In due course, the hypothesis evolves into an assumption accepted without further proof and eventually hardens into a firm expectation. At any stage in the evolution from trial hypothesis to firm expectation, the proposition may constitute the general premise (also called "explanatory hypothesis," "principle," "law") from which future decisions are predicted by logical deduction.

No model can eliminate uncertainty from the prediction of decisions. This holds with special force for decisions formulated in complex organizations. One's closest approach to certainty can be expressed by some such sentence as "A will almost certainly choose x." Generally, if deliberation is involved in the decision-making process, the most one is justified in predicting is that A will probably choose x. Often one can find no justification for more than "The odds are about even that A will choose x." In every graduation of certainty to uncertainty, prediction consists essentially of making rough estimates of the betting odds for or against a certain choice being made.

Probabilistic behavioral models generally include at least three categories of assumptions: (1) assumptions regarding motivation; (2) assumptions regarding environmental knowledge; and (3) assumptions regarding the mode of utilizing such knowledge in defining alternatives and taking decisions.

Ideological or other characteristics of the model depend, it is clear, on the content of these assumptions. The assumption regarding motivation, for example, can have an acquisitive, power-seeking, self-denying, Marxist, racist, or other content. The assumption regarding the extent of the decision-maker's environmental knowledge can range anywhere between total ignorance and omniscience of relevant factors. The assumption regarding the mode of utilizing environmental knowledge in making decisions can be that the hypothetical "typical" person is predominantly rational or that his behavior is explicable by the "theory of games" or by "Freudian theory" or by some other theory of human behavior.

A very familiar American version of the decision-making model is one that might be called "common-sense probabilism." In this model, men are presumed to be predominantly acquisitive, adequately knowledgeable, and generally rational. In the context of daily living, the assumption of acquisitiveness usually shows a strong pecuniary coloration. People are assumed to want money and the things money buys. Common-sense probabilism further assumes that men generally have environmental knowledge that is adequate for their purposes. That is to say, the actor's psychological environment is assumed to correspond in essential respects to the operational environment in which his decisions are executed. Third, common-sense probabilism assumes that the individual applies his environmental knowledge rationally to the choice of ends achievable with the means at his command and to the choice of appropriate means to achieve possible ends. That is to say, he calculates rationally the opportunities and limitations implicit in his operational environment. Finally, built into common-sense probabilism is the implicit assumption that the actor upon the stage and the analyst who observes and interprets from the sidelines both perceive and evaluate the milieu of the actor in substantially the same way.

Some such behavioral model, we submit, is implicit in Griffith Taylor's so-called "scientific determinism" and in the rhetoric of all those who employ deterministic or environmentalistic modes of speaking. Let us consider Taylor's familiar example of Antarctica as a milieu which largely determines man's choices and actions with reference to it. The purport of what he says appears to be about as follow: *If* the choice of fruitful means to a desired end in a given milieu is narrowly circumscribed (as in establishing a permanent settlement in Antarctica), and *if* (as Taylor clearly assumes) persons involved in the enterprise are adequately cognizant of limitations set by that milieu, and *if* (as he also appears to assume) such persons take their environmental knowledge rationally into account in making choices, *then* it follows that there will be close correlation between environmental limits and human action.

If, as the common-sense probabilist also appears to assume, his (the analyst's) own knowledge of the milieu in question and his mode of thinking about it correspond in essential respects to his subject's, the analyst can explain the subject's past choices and predict his probable future choices simply by informing himself as to the milieu and by imagining how a "rational man" like himself would react to it. Thus, starting with a given action and the set

of environmental factors which he deems relevant, the common-sense probabilist reasons backward to an explanation of the action, as indicated above.
Starting with a set of environmental factors, he reasons forward to the probable
correlated behavior. This, we submit, is substantially what underlies most
statements in which environmental factors are asserted to "determine" or to
"influence" choices and other actions.

Now, in the light of this discussion, let us re-examine some of the statements quoted in the opening paragraphs. Von Kühlmann, it is recalled, cited
"geographical position" as one of the factors "determining" a state's foreign
policy. Reischauer contended that the "mountains of Japan pushed the Japanese abroad." The sea-power text spoke of England "driven to the sea by her
sparse resources. . . ."

How should one construe such rhetoric? One possibility is to brand it as
pure teleology. Read in context, however, such seemingly teleological statements as those just quoted rarely appear to justify the conclusion that the
author intended to ascribe human-like purposes and behavior to non-human
phenomena. Sometimes, it would appear, teleological rhetoric represents simply
a sort of poetic license, designed perhaps to infuse an atmosphere of struggle
and drama into the subject at hand.

However, there is still a third way of interpreting such rhetoric. Quite
often, it would appear, authors employ action-verbs with an environmental
factor or set of factors as the grammatical subject, but in a sense neither teleological nor poetic. Take the verb "influence," for example. This is probably
the most commonly used verb in seemingly teleological environmentalistic
rhetoric. The essence of dictionary definitions of influence is "Some *activity*
on the part of a person or thing, that produces without apparent force an
effect on another person or thing." The father speaks and thereby influences
the child. The traffic officer blows his whistle and thereby influences the
motorist. Then, by a sort of analogical extension, an author speaks of geographical location or climate or a new machine or some other non-human
factor influencing people to do so-and-so.

Construed in context, such seemingly teleological statements appear frequently to be a sort of verbal shorthand to connote that the "influenced"
person or group perceived the environmental factor or aggregate in question;
that he, or they, evaluated it with reference to their purposes; and that he, or
they, acted in the light of the conclusions reached. One could similarly construe the whole battery of action-verbs when employed with environmental
subjects. In such usage, the force of the verb—ranging from determine, or
control, to influence—may be construed merely as expressing the speaker's
estimate of the odds that the environed unit would recognize and heed the
limitations implicit in the environmental factors in question.

When one reads in the Reischauer book that "sea routes have beckoned
the Japanese abroad," perhaps all that the passage was intended to communicate is that, at a certain stage in Japanese history, substantial numbers of

Japanese envisaged more attractive opportunities in seafaring than in farming or other pursuits ashore.

Our conclusion is that these and other examples of environmentalistic rhetoric, when not construed as teleology or poetic license, are equivalent to saying that the environed persons *envisaged* certain ends; that they *perceived and comprehended* adequately the opportunities and limitations latent in their milieu: and that they applied such knowledge *rationally* in choosing ends that were possible and in formulating means appropriate to the ends selected.

All the probabilistic models with which we are here concerned carry an assumption that the environed unit is capable of choosing among alternatives. But that is *not* equivalent to assuming that *all* choices which, by definition, are *possible* choices are equally *probable* choices. The essence of such a model is that some choices are more probable than others. The function of the model is to enable the analyst to arrange a set of possible choices on a sort of continuum of estimated degrees of probability. By reference to the assumptions of normally expectable behavior, incorporated into the model, the analyst eliminates as very improbable or less improbable those choices which would represent greater or lesser deviations from the hypothetical norm.

Probabilistic models, it may be argued, are manifestly better suited to predicting the odds of occurrence in a large aggregate of units than to "pinpointing" the actions of a specific unit. A market analyst, for example, may be able to predict within a more or less calculable range of error how many persons in a given society will buy new automobiles next year. But if the analyst should attempt to identify the specific prospective purchasers, the incidence of error would increase greatly, and the statistical methods employed in handling large aggregates of data might prove quite fruitless for predicting the behavior of particular individuals.

From this position it is an easy step to skepticism concerning all models for predicting the behavior of specific individuals and small groups. But, as previously emphasized, a recurrent and inescapable feature of our day-by-day living in society is precisely that kind of prediction. Hardly anyone would contend that the scores of predictive judgments which each of us makes every day are merely blind guesses, like pulling numbers out of a hat. We argued from the street-crossing example that such predictions consist essentially of deductions from assumptions of typical, or normally expectable, behavior respecting particular aspects of the total behavior of our fellow men. . . .

ENVIRONMENTAL FACTORS IN FOREIGN-POLICY ANALYSIS

Our thesis, as stated at the outset, is that environmental factors become related to the attitudes and decisions which comprise a state's foreign policy only by being perceived and taken into account in the policy-forming process. The stateman's *psychological* environment (that is, his image, or estimate, of the situation, setting, or milieu) may or may not correspond to the *operational* environment (in which his decisions are executed). But in policy-making, as we have stressed before, what matters is how the policy-maker imagines the milieu to be, not how it actually is.

The American debacle at Pearl Harbor is a historic example of this principle. The American commanders there remained totally ignorant of the approaching Japanese task force. Their psychological environment contained no hostile force readying its planes for a dawn attack on the great American base. Hence that force, though indubitably part of the operational environment, was *not related* in any way whatsoever to the *decisions* of the American commanders to the moment the attack began.

Many other examples come to mind. The United States-Canadian boundary was originally drawn in ignorance of the geographic layout and had subsequently to be corrected. The Battle of New Orleans was fought in January, 1815, in the erroneous belief that a state of war still continued. The Battle of the Bulge caught the Allied Command unprepared in December, 1944, because of faulty evaluation of intelligence reports. The Monroe Doctrine was promulgated in 1823, with reference to a threat of aggression that had largely subsided. American missile and satellite research after World War II proceeded on a widely held, but erroneous, assumption of a comfortable margin of superiority over Russian technology. Attitudes are formed and decisions of foreign policy are constantly being taken on fragmentary and often quite defective estimates of the situation.

The British Cabinet's decision to occupy the Suez Canal, in October, 1956, illustrates the same principle, but with a complicating dimension. Let us assume, for purposes of this discussion, that the decision to intervene was predicated on some such set of assumptions as these: that the operation could be executed swiftly; that the Egyptians would be unable to either offer effective resistance or to block the canal; that other Arab peoples would not disrupt the production and flow of oil to Europe contrary to their manifest economic interest; that the Soviet government would keep its hands off; that the United States and Commonwealth governments would accept a *fait accompli*; that the United Nations would offer no serious opposition; and that public opposition, which was dividing Britain internally, would speedily collapse as soon as British forces were re-established in the Canal Zone.

In the Suez case the significant environmental factors included potential human responses to the decision under consideration. These responses, when they did occur, became part of the operational environment in which the British decision was executed. That they did not exist prior to the decision added a complicating element of uncertainty to the decision-makers' problem. But that in no way invalidates the thesis that environmental factors are related to policy decisions only to the extent that they are taken into account in the decision-making process. The Suez example rather emphasizes that the decision-maker's estimate of the situation may frequently (perhaps generally) have to include not merely phenomena existent prior to the decision but also his predictions as to how the situation will develop as the decision is carried into execution.

Discrepancies between the policy-maker's estimate of the situation (that is, his psychological environment) and the operational environment become highly significant when the problem is to explain or to predict the results of a given decision. We shall consider that issue further in the next section. For the present it is sufficient to emphasize once again that what matters in policy-making is how the milieu appears to the policy-maker, not how it appears to some sideline analyst or how it might appear to some hypothetical omniscient observer. Hence, excluding the special problem of self-analysis by the policy-maker himself, the first step in linking environmental factors to policy decisions is to find out how the given policy-maker, or policy-making group, conceives the milieu to be and how that unit interprets the opportunities and limitations implicit therein with respect to the ends to be accomplished.

This task presents formidable difficulties. The task is to construct at second hand, from what the decision-maker says and does, a description of his image, or estimate, of the situation and his orientation to it. The analyst functions at some distance, often at a great distance, from his subject. He may have to contend with linguistic, ideological, or other social barriers to communication and understanding. As a rule he has to work with insufficient, incomplete, and often contradictory evidence. At best, the analyst's inferences regarding his subject's image of the milieu and his orientation to it rest invariably and inescapably on more or less arbitrary decisions as to the relevance and weight to be given to various kinds of evidence perceived and filtered through the analyst's own (and usually several intermediaries') culture-based spectacles.

Even when one comes to grips in some fashion with the methodological difficulties inherent in imagining the "universe of the decision-makers"—or, in less technical idiom, the "pictures in their heads"—he is still only on the threshold of explaining or predicting how environmental factors enter into the policy-forming process. In order to take another step, he must apply some theory of decision-making; and, in order to be relevant for this purpose, the theory must include assumptions as to (a) the purposes or ends toward which the policy-maker's efforts are oriented; (b) the environmental data which the policy-maker deems relevant to his purposes and from which he derives his estimate of the situation; and (c) his mode of utilizing such data in deciding what ends are feasible and in formulating strategy calculated to attain the ends envisaged.

Discussion of the relation of environmental factors to policy decisions has tended in the past to follow more or less in the pattern which we have called "common-sense probabilism." Rarely have the guiding assumptions been clearly articulated. Often they have been obscured by environmentalistic rhetoric, as in the examples quoted early in this essay. But scratch the surface of almost any discussion of foreign policy, and one is apt to discover the famil-

iar assumptions that men are predominantly acquisitive, adequately knowledgeable, and generally rational.

In the specific context of foreign policy, the assumption of acquisitiveness
typically appears as power orientation. Politics is defined as a struggle for
power. Desire to enhance the power of one's own state over other states is said
to be the paramount objective of the foreign policies of all states. At a lower
level of generality, this struggle for power is described in terms of expansion
and protection—expansion at the expense of other states, protection of things
previously acquired against encroachment by other states.

Whether this assumption is adequately descriptive of the typical orientation
of policy-makers in all countries and whether the assumption is a fruitful one
at still more specific levels of policy definition are both debatable. But these
issues are marginal to the present discussion. The point here is that *some*
concept of ends to be accomplished underlies all foreign-policy analysis and
that the analyst's assumptions as to the general orientation and specific objectives envisaged by the policy-makers in a given situation will affect his conclusions as to what environmental factors probably were (or probably will be)
taken into account in the deliberations under consideration.

Turning, now, to the issue of the policy-maker's environmental knowledge,
the common-sense model assumes that policy-making units normally command
data that are sufficiently complete and accurate for their purposes. This assumption is implicit in the venerable cliché that "politics is the art of the possible."
That cliché is sometimes quoted as a description of typical policy-making
behavior, sometimes as a precept for policy-makers. In either context, it implies
that those who make decisions for the state can be assumed, in general, to
know what is possible. That is to say, their estimates of a situation can be
assumed to represent close enough approximations of opportunities and limitations implicit in their operational environment.

This is a dubious assumption. It is one thing, for example, to assume that
farmers generally know the elements of good farming in a given milieu. It is
something else again to assume that a specific individual farmer commands
such knowledge. It is still more dubious, in our judgment, to assume that a
head of state or a foreign minister or a legislative committee commands *effectively* the vastly greater range of environmental data required to conduct
adequately the foreign relations of a modern state.

The higher one moves in the hierarchy of a great power's government, the
more one is impressed by the remoteness of executives from the operational
environment in which their decisions are executed. What passes for knowledge
of the situation at the higher levels consists mainly of generalized descriptions
and abstracts, several degrees removed from on-the-spot observations. On most
issues the individual or group responsible for decisions will have little time
and only the most general knowledge for checking what is prepared at lower
working levels of the organization.

Let us assume (and we think it is a reasonable assumption) that the British Cabinet's decision to send military forces in to re-occupy Suez was predicated on a firm expectation that the job could be finished quickly. How did Eden and his colleagues come to such a conclusion? One can only speculate, of course. They probably received estimates of the situation prepared by civil servants and military staffs. Such estimates probably included statements regarding the strength and deployment of land, sea, and air forces, their state of readiness, landing craft and other transportation and handling equipment on hand, liaison arrangements with the French Command, the condition of Egyptian defenses, the morale of Egyptian troops and civil population, etc. In addition, we may perhaps assume that Eden and his immediate associates had some general notions of their own about British military power, conditions in the Arab countries, and what it would take to re-occupy the canal. But is it likely that they had much fresh knowledge of these matters or the time necessary to check up on their experts?

These questions immediately pose others. To what extent is a top-level executive a virtual prisoner of the civil and military officials who provide data for him? On the other hand, how may his known preferences affect the substance and coloration of what his staffs decide to tell him? To what extent may their own attitudes and preferences bias their observations and calculations? In other words, to what extent is the "wish father to the thought" in statecraft as in other walks of life? And to what extent do such considerations affect the whole chain of communications in a complex foreign-policy-making situation?

Such questions raise doubts as to the common-sense assumption of adequate environmental knowledge. The proposition that a head of state, foreign minister, legislative committee, or other decision-making unit in a complex modern government commands such knowledge effectively is no more than a hypothesis to be confirmed—rarely, if ever, an assumption to be taken for granted.

With reference to past actions, it is sometimes possible for the historian to discover what environmental data were actually available, recognized as relevant, and taken into account. But with reference to past actions about which evidence is scanty and untrustworthy and with reference to all future contingencies, the analyst has no alternative but to supplement empirical research with some hypothesis or model as to the manner in which information is "normally" or "typically" gathered, interpreted, and communicated upward through the organization under consideration.

We come finally to the closely related issue of how environmental data are utilized in foreign-policy-making. Here one encounters a wide range of opinions. At one pole stand those who are generally sceptical of all explicit models for explaining or predicting how individuals or groups are likely to *react* to a perceived state of affairs. This scepticism is especially marked with respect to interpreting the behavior of persons functioning in a milieu radically different from the analyst's own. This view is reflected in the argument that it is useless to try to understand or forecast the reactions of Chinese or Russians or other "inscrutable" foreigners. The classic expression of this pessimism is Churchill's description of Soviet foreign policy as a "riddle wrapped in an enigma."

At the opposite pole one hears it optimistically contended that "human nature" is everywhere the same and that one can (within limits, to be sure) intuit how other people (even the "inscrutable foreigners") are likely to react. The analyst has simply to imagine how he himself would react to the state of affairs in question. This intuitive hypothesis rests upon assumptions previously discussed in connection with the difficulty of reconstructing another's image of the milieu. It involves assuming that persons of different social class, different educational background, different functional role, different nationality, etc., will nevertheless perceive *and react* in substantially similar ways. When doubts are voiced, these are resolved by assuming that analyst and subjct analyzed, alike, function rationally in according with universal principles of "human nature."

Some such view seems to be implicit in much of the environmentalistic rhetoric which encumbers the literature of foreign policy. We opened this discussion by quoting numerous examples of such rhetoric. Later on, we contended that environmentalistic statements in the context of foreign affairs can be construed as teleology or as poetic license but that such statements are just as likely to be no more than a sort of shorthand for longer and more cumbersome descriptions of human *reactions* to *perceived* environmental conditions. We concluded, it will be recalled, that when an author speaks of some environmental factor or set of factors influencing foreign policy or the makers of foreign policy, what he seems generally to be saying is that the policy-makers desired to achieve certain ends; that they imagined the milieu to be so-and-so; that their image of the milieu corresponded substantially with the operational environment; and that they employed their environmental knowledge rationally in framing a strategy to accomplish the desired end.

In general, this concept of man-milieu relationship takes for granted that policy-making is a deliberative process and that it is carried on within an intellectual framework of rationality and logic. There is much evidence to confirm these assumptions. But they do present difficulties, for there is also evidence that policy decisions may reflect not only defective environmental knowledge but also illogical reasoning as well. For example, how often do executives discount overtones of caution, warning, or pessimism in staff advice which casts a shadow on the choice to which they are predisposed? What are the odds that the top-level decision-maker will disregard, for quite illogical reasons, the estimates and recommendations prepared for his guidance?

Such questions go to the heart of systematic foreign-policy analysis. They raise the issue whether attempting to forecast the choices of a single individual or decision-making group by means of assumptions regarding "typical," or normally expectable, behavior is any more fruitful than throwing the dice. Analogies drawn from various kinds of macro-prediction are not especially helpful. The economic geographer predicting crop distributions, the demographer projecting population trends, the market analyst, or the election forecaster rarely, if ever, attempt to predict reactions of specific individuals but only the odds that certain choices will recur in large aggregates of behavior. The foreign-policy analyst, on the contrary, deals (by definition) with the choices of specific individuals or relatively small organized groups.

Nor is it very helpful to compare street-crossing behavior (see preceding section) and foreign-policy analysis. In the street-crossing example, it is true, the analyst drew a predictive inference from assumptions as to what he regarded as normally expectable behavior. But the significant variables involved in predicting when a man will cross a busy street are probably much fewer and simpler than those involved in predicting what a foreign minister will do about disarmament, nuclear-bomb tests, technical assistance to underdeveloped countries, etc.

Even though it may be generally unfruitful (in the present state of knowledge about human behavior) to attempt to "pinpoint" the *specific* choices of *specific* decision-making *units* operating in *complex* situations, it does not necessarily follow that throwing the dice is the only alternative. Under these conditions, negative prediction can become a useful product of analysis. By applying suitable premises regarding what is "typical," or normally expectable, behavior in the kind of situation under consideration, the analyst attempts to narrow the range within which specific choices will probably fall. By this method (described in the preceding section), the foreign-policy analyst eliminates as *very* improbable or as *quite* improbable those choices which would represent greater or lesser deviation from the hypothetical norm. If he cannot forecast precisely what the British Cabinet will do about the European "common market" during the next five years, the foreign-policy analyst can perhaps reach fruitful conclusions as to what they are more or less likely *not* to do.

Negative prediction to narrow the range of probable choice, no less than positive prediction of specific choice, involves the application of general hypotheses, or premises, of typical or normally expectable behavior. The value of such premises will depend, in part, on the analyst's knowledge of the setting and functions under consideration, in part on the imagination he displays in drawing generalizations from such knowledge that are relevant and significant for the problem in hand. If the problem is to compare the collection, communication, and utilization of environmental data in all governmental systems, the model would obviously have to be pitched at the highest level of generality. But the problem may be to compare the effective command and use of such data in all totalitarian governments or in all democratic governments or in all democratic governments of the parliamentary type. Or the problem may be to compare democratic and totalitarian types, Western and non-Western types, or more specifically, for example, the British and Chinese systems of foreign-policy-making. Or the problem may be to form conclusions regarding the command and use of environmental data within a single form of government or even within a single specific system.

In every case the issue is what set of premises (hypotheses or assumptions) will yield the most fruitful insights as to the way in which environmental data are related to policy decisions. Such premises, we emphasized previously, are not found in "nature"; they are formulated. In the main, they are generalized descriptions of typical, or normally expectable behavior either at the level of a single system or at the level of two or more systems. In the context of foreign-policy analysis, premises regarding man-milieu relationships focus mainly on the policy-maker's knowledge of the milieu and the uses he makes of that knowledge. At these two points of focus, the ecological approach gives way to behavioral concepts and theories for the further developmnt of knowledge and understanding of the relation of environmental factors to the foreign policies of states.

ENVIRONMENTAL FACTORS IN CAPABILITY ANALYSIS

We drew a distinction at the outset between capability analysis and foreign-policy analysis. The latter consists essentially of explaining or predicting policy decisions. Capability analysis, on the other hand, is directed to the calculation of the opportunities and limitations implicit in the milieu, which will affect the operational results of whatever is attempted, irrespective of whether such factors are known and heeded by the decision-makers in question.

The Japanese task-force approaching Pearl Harbor, for example, was unknown to, and hence formed no part of the psychological environment of, the American commanders there. But that hostile fleet was indubitably part of their operational environment and (though not related in any way to their decisions) affected the results of those decisions.

Put in general terms, the distinction is this. If the problem is to explain or to predict a policy decision, the analyst has to answer such questions as: What environmental factors (or aspects of the situation) did the decision-maker recognize and consider to be significant? What *use* did he make of his environmental *knowledge* in defining what was to be attempted and the means to be employed? If, on the other hand, the problem is to explain or to predict the operational results of a *given* policy decision or set of decisions (actual or hypothetical), the question he must answer is: How may the properties present or latent in the milieu affect the operational results of that decision, even though these factors are not known or taken into account in the decision-making process?

Capability analysis, so defined, involves the application of the frame of reference and ecological theory commonly known in geographic science as "environmental possibilism," whereas foreign-policy analysis involves application of the theory which we have called "environmental probabilism."

Statements about state capabilities, like statements about foreign policy, are frequently couched in deterministic or environmentalistic rhetoric. Zimmermann (quoted earlier) asserted that the invention of the basic steel furnace "*led inevitably* to Germany's industrial hegemony" on the Continent. The sea-power text spoke of England being *"destined by geography* to command the seas. . . ."

In reviewing the sea-power book, we contended that "geography did not destine England to command the seas." We construed the passage to mean simply that "available resources ashore, configuration of lands and seas, and other conditions in the milieu *enabled* Englishmen to achieve the kind of history which they did in fact make for themselves."[9]

One could similarly recast the Zimmermann statement in non-deterministic terms. The invention of the basic steel furnace *made it possible* to produce good steel out of acidic ores. A lot of such ore *was present* inside Germany (that is, latent in the German milieu). German industrialists *took advantage* of the new process to expand steel production. Thus a change in one environmental factor (steel-making process) enabled German industrialists to make use of another environmental factor (acidic iron ore) and thereby to outstrip the steel production of other European countries and achieve the "industrial hegemony" which they did, in fact, achieve.

One can analyze state capabilities either historically or predictively. In the former context, the task is to formulate an explanation of how it was possible for certain functions to be performed, which were in fact performed, as exemplified above. In a predictive context (and most capability analysis is predictive), the task is to calculate the odds for or against ability to perform certain functions in the future.

At this point, some analytical distinctions should be made. Capability calculations normally enter into the policy-making process. A foreign-policy analyst (who studies the process from the sidelines) will normally attempt to find out how the policy-makers and their staff themselves envisage the opportunities and limitations implicit in their milieu. Such an inquiry is *not* capability analysis but rather an aspect of foreign-policy analysis, considered in the preceding section. But the operation becomes capability analysis when the sideline observer makes an *independent* judgement as to what those opportunities and limitations are and how they will affect the course of events, irrespective of whether or how these factors are conceived or taken into account by the decision-makers in question.

Perhaps an analogy from medicine will help to make this distinction clearer. The physician may ask the patient to describe his symptoms. From the latter's responses, the physician learns how the patient conceives his illness. The physician may also deduce from the patient's description of symptoms some conclusions as to what the illness really is. But he may also make various laboratory tests—blood pressure, metabolism, etc.—from which to confirm or modify the inferences drawn from the patient's verbalization. Similarly, the capability analyst may make his own independent assessment of the opportunities and limitations implicit in the milieu of the state under consideration.

---

9 H. Sprout, Review of Potter *et. al., op. cit.,* in *United States Naval Institute Proceedings,* February 1956, p. 213.

It should be clear by now that we conceive capabilities to be calculable only with reference to some set of policies and some operational situation. It is utterly meaningless to speak of capabilities in the abstract. Capability is always capability to do something, to bring about or to perpetuate some state of affairs. Policy assumptions may be left implicit. But, unless some set of ends and means is envisaged, no calculation is possible, no inventory of environmental factors has any significance.

Failure to keep discussion of state capabilities within some policy frame of reference is one of the reasons why a good deal that has been said about the so-called "elements" or "foundations" of national power is footless and unconvincing. The data of physical geography have no intrinsic political significance whatever. Nor have demographic, technological, economic, or other environmental data. Such factors acquire political significance only when related to some frame of assumptions as to what is to be attempted, by what means, when and where, and vis-à-vis what adversaries, associates, and bystanders.

The policy framework may be short-term and rather specific. What factors, for example, will set limits to the results of the declared American intention to regain ground lost to the Russians in science and military technology? What factors will affect the outcome of the French policy of holding the line in Algeria? What factors will limit British military expenditures during the next five years? By what criteria may one judge the proposition asserted in the British Defense Statement of 1957, that "there is at present no means of providing adequate protection for the people of (Britain) against the consequences of an attack with nuclear weapons"?

Such relatively short-term capability questions shade off into longer-term and more general questions. By what criteria, for example, may one evaluate the thesis, propounded by a prominent geographer, that "permanent environmental restrictions of cold, drought, and continentality will never permit [the Soviet Union] to achieve strictly first-class rank"? Or Sir Halford Mackinder's historic thesis that "the grouping of lands and seas, and of fertility and natural pathways, is such as to lend itself to the growth of empires, and in the end of a single world empire"?

Putting the problem within a suitable policy framework constitutes only the first step in capability analysis. Given the most explicit policy assumptions —as to what is to be attempted, by what means, when and where, etc.—one still has very little basis for judging the significance of a state's geographical position, material resources, population, economic plant, social structure, and similar data regarding other states. Such data acquire significance for capability analysis only when subjected to the criteria of appropriate explanatory propositions or hypotheses.

What do we mean by explanatory capability hypotheses? We mean such propositions as, for example: The growth of air power has progressively diminished the military value of insular bases. Or: In the present state of military technology there is no effective tactical defense against nuclear missiles.

Or: Democratic systems of government are less able than dictatorships to execute quick changes of policy. Or: Size of population is not per se an index of military or economic capacity. Such hypotheses, which are the essence of capability calculations, comprise the logical premises from which the analyst deduces what environmental factors are significantly relevant and what they signify with respect to the policy objectives and strategy under consideration.

Like models of normally expectable policy-making behavior, discussed in the preceding section, capability hypotheses or premises are not found full-blown in nature. They are creative acts of imagination, generally, though not necessarily, derived by generalization from observed events. Many of the premises employed in capability analysis have been so repeatedly confirmed as to be accepted as truisms. But in our era of rapid technological and other social changes, most capability premises have become more or less debatable. Take, for example, the thesis that scientists in a totalitarian communist state operate under ideological and other handicaps that prevent them from keeping pace with their counterparts in a "free society." Only yesterday that proposition seemed as sound as the Rock of Gibraltar. Today it is at most no more than a working hypothesis to be confirmed.

The propositions which an analyst adjudges confirmed and fruitful depend, as a rule, on his previous experience with the problem's antecedents or on generalizations derived from other problems which, in his judgment, exhibit fruitful analogies. There is no guaranty whatever that any two analysts will reason from exactly the same premises or reach the same conclusions. The most that one can expect is that explanatory premises will be made explicit, that environmental factors considered significantly relevant will be so designated, and that logical procedures will be observed. Only thus is it possible for one analyst to check the work of another, to identify the sources of conflicting conclusions regarding the capabilities of states.

Consider, for example, the prediction quoted above, that "permanent environmental restriction of cold, drought, and continentality will never permit [the Soviet Union] to achieve strictly first-class rank." Read in context, that prediction seems to be derived from a number of hypotheses—regarding future trends in science and technology, regarding the Russian people's tolerance of austerity, regarding the pace of development of other nations, etc. But these strategic hypotheses are not explicitly articulated. Greater explicitness would have rendered the exposition more fruitful, by removing doubt and uncertainty as to the premises from which the final conclusion was derived.

This is not a plea for elaboration of the obvious. It is rather a plea for more sophisticated discrimination between what is obvious and non-controversial and what is significant and controversial. It might be instructive to re-examine from this point of view some of the many disconfirmed capability predictions of our time. One might reflect, for example, on the generally implicit assumptions from which observers predicted that Nazi Germany could not stand the financial and moral strains of a long war; that the Red Army would collapse in a few weeks under the hammer-blows of the Wehrmacht; that it would take Russian scientists and engineers twenty years or more to produce an atomic bomb, etc.

It is easy to be wise after the event. Some degree of uncertainty is probably inherent in all complex capability calculations, at least in the present state of knowledge. But the burden of our argument in this section is that clearer understanding of the steps involved in capability analysis, more sophistication in formulation of capability premises, more explicitness in articulating strategic premises, and more rigor in their application to environmental data should help to avoid such gross miscalculations as have characterized capability predictions in the past.

CONCLUSIONS

The first conclusion that emerges from this discussion is our conviction that the ecological viewpoint and frame of reference—the concept of man-milieu relationship and certain relationship theories—provide a fruitful approach to the analysis of foreign policy and the estimation of state capabilities.

Our second conclusion is that it is fruitful to distinguish analytically between the relation of environmental factors to policy decisions, on the one hand, and to the operational results of decisions, on the other. With respect to policy-making and the content of policy decisions, our position is that what matters is not how the policy-maker imagines the milieu to be, but how it actually is. With respect to the operational results of decisions, what matters is how things are, not how the policy-maker imagines them to be. In our judgment, a good deal of confusion which has clouded the discussion of environmental factors in international politics derives from failure to keep this distinction explicit and to observe it rigorously.

Third, we conceive of the ecological approach as a system of concepts and theory that is useful to a student of international politics not as a substitute for, but as a complement to, the behavioral and other approaches to the study of foreign policy and the international capabilities of states.

Finally, we see in the ecological approach a useful bridge for bringing to the study of international politics relevant theories and data from geography, psychology, sociology, and other systems of learning.

DAVID R. REYNOLDS AND
MICHAEL L. McNULTY

On the Analysis of Political Boundaries as Barriers: A Perceptual Approach

The principle purpose of this paper is to suggest possible spatio-behavioral approaches to model building in research directed toward the explication of the impact of political boundaries on human interaction. In order to achieve this, we will (1) briefly review some of the studies which have dealt with the analysis and measurement of boundary effects on patterns of human interaction, (2) present several concepts of general importance to the study of spatial behavior, (3) extend and relate these concepts to analyses of selected behavioral activities in boundary zones, and (4) suggest research incorporating these concepts. Although the focus is primarily upon international boundaries, many of the concepts apply to internal boundaries as well.

One approach to understanding the nature of political boundaries as barriers to movement is indicated by Mackay:

> The inhabitants separated by a boundary do not, except in very unusual circumstances, live in complete isolation from each other.... If we can estimate, with reasonable precision, the effect of physical and cultural boundaries (e.g., a river or political boundary) upon each type of interaction, we will possess a powerful tool for regional analysis and boundary studies.[1]

Reprinted from the *East Lakes Geographer*, Henry L. Hunker, Editor, Vol. 4 (December 1968), 21–38, with permission of the author and editor.
[1] J. Ross Mackay, "The Interaction Hypothesis and Boundaries in Canada," *Canadian Geographer*, 11 (1958), pp. 1–8.

Yuill carries this thinking a step further: ". . . if the effect of a barrier is to be understood, then this effect must be viewed within the context of the activity to which the barrier is supposedly an impediment. The barrier then may be actually defined in terms of the activity; a functional relationship. The concept of a dynamic process appears to be crucial to the study of barriers in a spatial context. If barriers are studies only in relation to static distribution, then the whole character of the barrier may be easily misinterpreted or distorted."[2] More recently Nystuen has addressed himself to the possible consequences of boundary properties (e.g., shape, length, permeability) upon the spatial outcome of different processes and to the difficult task of measuring the boundary properties themselves, particularly the length, edge, and domain of a boundary.[3] Unlike some investigators, Nystuen does not attempt an *ex post facto* explanation of the spatial effects of boundaries on "fixed facilities." Instead, he attempts explanation by mathematically deducing the effects of boundary properties upon spatial processes in boundary zones. Unfortunately, most of his constructs have not yet been tested in a rigorous manner; nevertheless, this approach holds some promise.

Actual attempts to measure the relative barrier effects of boundaries on various types of interaction have been few and infrequent. Two well known studies are those of Lösch and Mackay.[4] Lösch demonstrated that the areal extent of the financial sphere of El Paso, Texas, was roughly similar to that which could be deduced for physical goods by considering customs duties as additional transportation costs, over zero distance, at the boundary crossing.[5] However, if Lösch's transport cost interpretation of boundary effects were to be extended to human interaction, it must be recognized that it is predicated on the rather stringent assumptions of man's economic rationality and his perception of travel costs. These assumptions have increasingly been subjected to criticism by geographers and other behavioral scientists.[6]

Mackay, in his pioneering study on the measurement of the effect of political boundaries on telephone interactions, was cognizant of a basic dilemma encountered in ascertaining barrier effects—namely, the problem of existence.[7] Patterns of interaction across a boundary can be determined, but how does the investigator "remove" the boundary so as to measure the barrier effects?

---

2 Robert S. Yuill, *A Simulation Study of Barrier Effects in Spatial Diffusion Problems* (Evanston, Ill.: Department of Geography, Northwestern University, Research Report No. 5, 1964).

3 John D. Nystuen, "Boundary Shapes and Boundary Problems," Paper presented at the Fourth North American Peace Research Conference, Peace Research Society (International) (Chicago, Illinois, November 1966).

4 August Lösch, *The Economics of Location*, trans. W.H. Woglom and W.F. Stolper (New Haven, Conn.: Yale University Press, 1954); Mackay, *op. cit.*

5 Edgar M. Hoover, *The Location of Economic Activity* (New York: McGraw Hill Book Co., 1963); Lösch, *op. cit.*

6 W. Edwards, "The Theory of Decision-Making," *Psychological Bulletin*, 51 (1954), pp. 380–411; Herbert A. Simon, "Economics and Psychology," in Sigmund Koch (ed.), *Psychology: A Study of a Science*, 6 (New York: McGraw-Hill Book Co., 1963).

7 Mackay, *op. cit.*

Against what criteria is an interaction pattern compared? Mackay overcame this problem in a statistical sense. He regressed "demographic potentials"[8] against telephone calls between a selected city and all other cities and by then comparing the elevations of the regression lines for intra-Canada calls and U.S.-Canadian calls. Therefore, he, like Lösch, measured the relative barrier effects of political boundaries by imputing an additional distance factor to them.

Even though Mackay did not attempt to identify the variables contributing to the diminution of interaction in his model, he did measure boundary effects in a relative sense. While information provided by the application of social gravity models is perhaps valuable input for spatial diffusion models, it does not provide sufficient theoretical insights contributing towards an explanation of how and why political boundaries function as barriers to certain behavioral activities. We think that the approaches suggested below contribute toward this end.

In developing models of human behavior, Herbert Simon and a number of other authors have drawn attention to the necessity for distinguishing between the objective environment (the geographer's "real world") and an individual's subjective environment or psychological "image" of that environment.[9] For the most part, it is the former which has generally been used by geographers and other social scientists as the setting for their research. However, there is evidence of an increasing awareness that it is the latter to which man responds.

The disparity between the objective and subjective environments can be attributed to the nature of the perceptual and cognitive processes. Although consideration of these processes has been rare in the geographical literature, a number of writers have recently espoused behavioral notions in examining their respective problems.[10] These and other writers have begun to examine the importance of the individual's subjective or psychological image of the objective world in affecting his behavior.[11] Occasionally, geographers have

---

8 See Walter Isard, *Methods of Regional Analysis* (New York: John Wiley and Sons, 1960) for a discussion of this concept.

9 Kenneth E. Boulding, *The Image* (Ann Arbor, Michigan: University of Michigan Press, 1956); David Lowenthal, "Geography, Experience, and Imagination: Towards a Geographical Epistemology," *Annals, Association of American Geographers*, 51 (September 1961), pp. 241–261; Simon, *op. cit.*; Harold and Margaret Sprout, *The Ecological Perspective on Human Affairs* (Princeton, N.J.: Princeton University Press, 1956).

10 Kevin R. Cox, "Social Relational Analysis as a Behavioral Model in Geographical Research" (Columbus, Ohio: Department of Geography, The Ohio State University) (Mimeographed); Peter Gould, "On Mental Maps," Michigan Intercommunity of Mathematical Geographers, Discussion Paper No. 9 (University of Michigan, September 1966); Robert W. Kates, *Hazard and Choice Perception in Flood Plain Management*, Research Paper No. 78 (Chicago: Department of Geography, University of Chicago, 1962); Donald L. Thompson, "Future Directions in Retail Area Research," *Economic Geography* (January 1966), pp. 1–18; and Julian Wolpert, "Behavioral Aspects of the Decision to Migrate," *Papers*, Regional Science Association, 15 (1965), pp. 159–169.

11 Boulding, *op. cit.*; Kevin Lynch, *The Image of the City* (Cambridge, Mass.: M.I.T. Press, 1960).

found it necessary to employ various transformations of distance (e.g., time-distance) when the objective or geographical distances failed to account for a given pattern.[12] These transformations are, of course, no more than attempts to obtain closer approximations to the "subjective" distances to which people react.

Isard and others have on several occasions exhorted researchers to consider sociological and psychological variables as they relate to behavior over space.[13] In the context of central place models, when behavior patterns of consumers appear as "irrational," geographers have attempted to account for this behavior with reference to cultural factors or other personal or "subjective" variables.[14] In this instance, the geographer has encountered the differences between the subjective environment of the individual and the objective environment of distances to places, numbers of functions, square feet of shops, etc.

Perhaps the geographer has too long been satisfied with being able to obtain adequate "fits" to aggregate patterns of behavior with the concepts and models at hand. Therefore, an approach which explicitly examines the relevant processes generating these patterns (i.e., the patterns of individual behavior) might better provide the requisite theoretical insights with which to account for them.

The highly complex perceptual and cognitive processes of the individual involve the gathering of information through the senses, and the selecting, weighing, evaluating, and interpreting (or generally organizing) of this information against past experience. Since no two individuals can perceive things from exactly the same place at the same time, and since each interprets the information from the external world against his past experience, the subjective images of the external or objective environment vary considerably from individual to individual. Nevertheless, there is reason to posit that images are to a large extent shared by various groups of people.[15]

While perception is almost certainly affected by the group memberships of the individual, or by his position and role in networks of social interaction, it will also be affected by his location in space. Through personal observation the individual is likely to be more familiar with local areas than those places at some distances from him and about which the information available is

---

12 Gunnar Olsson, *Distance and Human Interaction,* Bibliography Series, No. 2 (Philadelphia: Regional Science Institute, 1965).

13 Karl W. Deutsch and Walter Isard, "A Note on a Generalized Concept of Effective Distance," *Behavioral Science* (October 1961), pp. 308–311; Walter Isard, *Location and Space Economy* (New York: John Wiley and Sons, 1956); Donald L. Thompson, "New Concept: Subjective Distance," *Journal of Retailing,* 39 (1963), pp. 1–6; and Melvin M. Webber, "Culture, Territoriality, and the Elastic Mile," *Papers,* Regional Science Association, 13 (1964), pp. 59–69.

14 Robert A. Murdie, "Cultural Differences in Consumer Travel," *Economic Geography,* 4 (July 1965), pp. 211–233.

15 Boulding, *op. cit.;* Robert K. Merton, *Social Theory and Social Structure* (rev. ed., New York: The Free Press, 1957); and Webber, *op cit.*

limited.[16] Thus, while a person's perception is conditioned by the nature of the objective world, it is also affected by a number of other factors, including his particular experiences, culture, values, etc., as well as location in space and within social networks.

One way of conceptualizing behavior in terms of these factors is suggested by Lewin's notion of the psychological life space.[17] Wolpert provides an interesting geographical analogue to life space when he suggests that the "action space" of an individual may be considered "to include the range of choice or the individual's area of movement which is defined by both his personal attributes and environment." He further contends that "most prominent among the determinants of the alternatives in this action space which are conspicuous to the individual is his position on one of divergent life cycles and location in terms of the communication networks linking his position to other places."[18] Just as with perception, the extent of the action space will differ from individual to individual and will not be independent of the particular purpose or activity of the individual at a given time.

Conceptually, Wolpert's analogy is very attractive. Yet Wolpert is one of the few geographers who has attempted to investigate systematically the formation of individual action spaces relative to various types of behavior. His investigations into the relationship between action space and the decision to migrate would seem to provide a useful framework for research into other areas of spatial behavior. Similarly, the work of other social scientists, sociologists and social psychologists in particular, contains useful insights into the formation of the individual action space and the extent to which these are shared by groups of people.[19] The importance of social or cohort groups in affecting an individual's behavior has been especially well studied.[20] Studies of the networks of interpersonal contacts have also provided empirical information which suggests a close relationship between social and spatial propinquity.[21] This body of research likewise contains concepts of use to the geographer. An important example is Festinger's distinction between physical and functional

---

16 Wolpert, *op. cit.*; G. Boult and C.G. Janson, "Distance and Social Relations," *Acta Sociologica*, 2 (1956), pp. 73–98.

17 Kurt Lewin, *Principles of Topological Psychology* (New York: McGraw-Hill Book Co., 1936); Kurt Lewin, *Field Theory in Social Science* (New York: Harper & Row, 1951).

18 Wolpert, *op. cit.*

19 Sigmund Koch (ed.), *Psychology: A Study of Science*, Vol. 6 (New York: McGraw-Hill Book Co., 1962); John H. Kolb, *Emerging Rural Communities* (Madison, Wisconsin: University of Wisconsin Press, 1959); C.P. Loomis and J.A. Beegle, *Rural Sociology* (Englewood Cliffs, N.J.: Prentice-Hall, Inc., 1957); Albert H. Rubenstein and Chadwick J. Haberstrol, *Some Theories of Organization* (Homewood, Illinois: Richard D. Irwin, Inc., and the Dorsey Press, 1964); and Roland Warren (ed.), *Perspectives on the American Community* (Chicago: Rand McNally and Co., 1966).

20 Leon Festinger, Stanley Schachter, and Kurt Back, *Social Pressures in Informal Groups* (New York: Harper and Brothers, 1950); Loomis and Beegle, *ibid.*; Merton, *op. cit.*

21 Festinger, Schachter, and Back, *ibid.*; and Robert K. Merton, "The Social Psychology of Housing," *Current Trends in Social Psychology* (Pittsburgh: University of Pittsburgh Press, 1951).

distance.[22] Two individuals may reside within a few feet of one another, yet, if their apartment entrances face onto opposite streets, the probability of their confronting one another may be low. Thus while the physical or geographical distance separating them may be slight, the functional distance (taking into account positional and directional components) may be great. This concept is particularly relevant to studies of human interaction in boundary zones.

Interest in information theory has also served to illustrate the importance of interpersonal communication in affecting behavior and to focus attention upon the communicative process as an important channel of information about the objective environment.[23] It is this flow of information through the network of interpersonal communications which is the basis for the images shared by individuals in social networks. Formation of the individual's image of the environment will therefore be greatly affected by the groups to which he belongs. Although group membership fosters the development of shared images, it may also inhibit the flow of information to the individual from other sources. In this regard Deutsch has commented on the manner in which people may be "marked off from each other by communicative barriers, by 'marked gaps' in the efficiency of communications."[24]

It is suggested, then, that the subjective environment of an individual and therefore the extent of his action space will be dependent in large measure upon his position and role in social and interpersonal communication networks. Evidence suggests that the extent of one's social-net is of more consequence to behavior than models in geography have previously allowed. Future studies should be designed so as to incorporate aspects of the subjective, as well as the objective, environment.

.   .   .

In the preceding section, the importance of information flows and social network development to the formation of an individual's action space and to his perception of his environment was stressed. Therefore, perhaps the first task of the researcher is to ascertain the extent of which a political boundary impedes the flow of information. This was the objective of Mackay in his aforementioned study. However, the satisfactory measurement of the "interruptive" effect of a boundary is only *one* aspect of a considerably larger problem. Deutsch cogently points this out by stating that "barriers are more or less effective not only according to the difficulty of communication across them but also according to the relative ease and attractiveness of alternative channels of communication available to the individual."[25] This notion has particular relevance for

---

22 Festinger, Schachter, and Back, *ibid.*
23 Stanford Goldman, *Information Theory* (Englewood Cliffs, N.J.: Prentice-Hall, Inc., 1953).
24 Karl W. Deutsch, *Nationalism and Social Communication* (Cambridge, Mass.: M.I.T. Press, 1953).
25 Deutsch, *ibid.*

the study of human interaction in boundary zones. We now wish to conceptualize how the presence of a political boundary in an objective environment may *indirectly* affect information flows between individuals and groups of individuals by influencing the areal extent, shape, and connectivity of social groups or communities of interest.

It is well documented that transportation and other communication networks and channels in boundary zones are often constructed so as to facilitate the integration of inhabitants (both actual and potential) into the economic, social, and political structure of the state exercising sovereignty over the territory in question.[26] Wolfe provides an example of this phenomenon with reference to the 49th parallel portion of the U.S.–Canadian boundary:

> ...Canadian statesmen were determined that Canada would span the continent no matter what the obstacles, and that transportation links would be the agents ensuring nationhood. By insisting that those links would be wholly within the Canadian domain, they went against economic logic, but they demonstrated their topological shrewdness. Once a railroad crossed an international boundary, they understood, it did violence to the "insideness" of their nation, artificial as that insideness might be.[27]

The development of communication facilities along nationalistic lines is one source of the "gaps" in communication to which Deutsch alludes, in that it usually facilitates intra-zone communication at the expense of inter-zone communication. This can best be illustrated by viewing boundaries, regions, and groups topologically. In topology, boundaries (which are actually boundary points) always serve to *separate* "regions," but they can also *connect* regions. This dual function of "boundaries" is of considerable theoretical importance in topological psychology;[28] its theoretical significance for boundary studies in geography is also considerable.

Assume that two social groups, X and Y, have been delimited spatially and that each has its geometric center on different sides of a political boundary. If groups X and Y are conterminous along the boundary, it both separates and connects the two groups. However, when the bounds of X and/or Y do not

---

26 Hoover, *op. cit.;* Lösch, *op. cit.*, A.E. Moodie, *Geography Behind Politics* (London: Hutchinson, 1961); and Roy I. Wolfe, *Transportation and Politics* (Princeton, N.J.: D. Van Nostrand, 1963).
27 Wolfe, *ibid.*
28 J.E. Brown, "Topology and Hodological Space," in Melvin H. Marx, *Psychological Theory* (New York: Macmillan Co., 1951); Lewin, *op. cit.*

reach the boundary (as below, if we assume that it represents the metricized spaces of the two groups), both "regions" and "boundaries" separate the groups. If physical communication networks (such as highways, telephone exchanges, etc.) have fostered the development of two *social* networks, as above, the existence of the political boundary has reinforced or *indirectly* resulted in spatial gaps to communication between the two social groups.[29]

In the many instances where internal communication channels have been constructed to the detriment of trans-boundary communication (and therefore serve as easy and attractive alternatives to trans-boundary channels), it would appear that the spatial extent of social-nets or communities is less likely to extend across the boundary.

What, however, are the implications of the above discussion with respect to individuals' perceptions of the objective environment and their action spaces? We suggest that when social groups or other communities do not extend across a political boundary, one extremely important source and method of spreading information concerning opportunities in and characteristics of the area across the boundary is greatly circumscribed with the result that personal action spaces may well be skewed in directions along or away from the boundary. To be sure, individuals within social groups hold images of the area across the boundary, yet the congruence between their subjective images of it and those held by the residents of the other area in question may be slight. Some empirical evidence of these phenomena is provided by Form and Rivera,[30] Lynch,[31] and the results of in-depth interviews by Reynolds with householders along the Maine-New Brunswick boundary. In a study of work contacts and shared perceptions in areas along the U.S.-Mexican boundary, Form and Rivera found that in those groups of Mexican laborers which included some members who had worked in the United States, individuals evidenced much greater subjective knowledge of the United States than did individuals who were not members of such groups.[32] One of the most striking findings of Lynch in his study of several urban areas is that for many of the individuals interviewed, boundaries or "edges" are important organizing features of their subjective environments. It was also found that individuals have more difficulty in relating the position of a boundary to the spatial structure of areas on the "opposite" side of a boundary than to the spatial structure of areas on "their" side.[33] These two findings of Lynch are particularly significant since they tend to imply the degree of spatial congruence between features in the objective environment and the same features on an individual's "cognitive map" changes

---

[29] This, of course, is dependent upon whether the boundary was demarcated prior to the settlement and development of the transportation infrastructure.

[30] W.H. Form and Julius Rivera, "Work Contacts and International Evaluations: The Case of a Mexican Border Village," *Social Forces*, 37 (May 1959), pp. 334–339.

[31] Lynch, *op. cit.*

[32] Form and Rivera, *op. cit.*

[33] Lynch, *op. cit.*

markedly at certain perceived boundaries. If this is the general case, it would also lend support to our hypothesis that action spaces are skewed along boundaries or at least restricted by such boundaries.

One other finding of Lynch's study deserves mention since it was also observed by one of the authors in a boundary zone context. Here we refer to Lynch's suggestion that people do not perceive highway routes as paths or channels of interaction unless the routes have clearly perceived and well-known destinations. During the field interviewing portion of Reynolds' investigation of shopping behavior along the Maine-New Brunswick international boundary,[34] New Brunswick respondents located on routes crossing the boundary were asked to (1) indicate where the route led (in the direction of the boundary) and (2) elaborate on and evaluate the shopping opportunities that can be reached by traveling in either direction. Of the 63 respondents so located, approximately 75 per cent indicated that the route led either "to the boundary" or "to the States." All respondents in the New Brunswick sample of householders (not just the 63 mentioned above) clearly evidenced that they possessed more information concerning shopping opportunities in New Brunswick, but, interestingly enough, all perceived the opportunities to be greater in Maine. This appears to be evidence of a shift in the scale of perception occurring at the boundary: a finer articulation on the side of residence and a general, more crudely articulated conception of the other side.

· · ·

In those instances when *actual* restrictions are imposed on a certain trans-boundary interaction, there may be *de facto* "restrictions" extending to the types of interaction typically linked to that which is restricted *de jure*. The importance and typical occurrence of linked travel patterns and multiple purpose trips in economic, urban and transportation geography have been illustrated by a number of writers.[35] The significance of interdependent travel patterns in the study of human interaction in boundary zones appears to have been overlooked. For example, if individuals on one side of a political boundary are not permitted employment on the other side, activities typically linked to the journey to and from work, such as the purchasing of gasoline and convenience goods, will largely be absent in trans-boundary interactions. Although this example pertains to aspects of consumer behavior, the concept extends to other behavioral activities. This phenomenon can be termed the "spill-over" effect of a boundary.

The above suggests that behaviors which are typically linked in the absence of boundary restrictions must become unlinked in the presence of restriction

---

34 David R. Reynolds, "Shopping Trip Inputs in a Boundary Zone," Ph.D. Dissertation, Department of Geography, Northwestern University, 1966.

35 William Bunge, *Theoretical Geography*, Lund Studies in Geography, Series C, General and Mathematical Geography, No. 1 (1966 edition); Thompson, *Economic Geography, op. cit.;* and Thompson, *Journal of Retailing, op. cit.*

on one of the linked behaviors, if certain cross-boundary interactions take place. Thus, behavioral spill-over effects stemming from the interrelatedness of behavior patterns can be particularly important in the formation of an individual's action space and subjective environment. It can be hypothesized that when boundary restrictions impinge upon an individual's action space for one activity, they will likewise impinge upon those for related activities, resulting in a further reduction in the boundary zone resident's sources of information about areas across the boundary and/or resulting in aggregate spatial behavior patterns with considerably more variability than those in areas more remote from the boundary.

Unless a state wishes to isolate itself completely from contiguous states, it must provide points of access at intervals along the boundary. These boundary crossings necessarily function as funnels, concentrating the traffic from wide areas on both sides of the boundary. Not surprisingly, the spacing of these points of access can have important consequences upon the subjective environments of boundary zone residents and will be manifested in their spatial behavior patterns.

.   .   .

In large measure, the problem of detour is analogous to the situation confronting boundary zone residents. Those individuals who live near the boundary but far from a crossing point are less likely to include areas on the opposite side of the boundary within their action spaces than individuals located near a crossing point because they are "functionally" farther from the opposite area and are less accessible to the interpersonal spread of information concerning it. Furthermore, the functional distance separating such individuals from the opposite area will probably be greater than the actual highway mileage (or travel time) because of the availability of more adequately perceived and accessible destinations in the area of residence. To the former persons, the boundary is likely to be perceived as an "impassable" barrier, whereas to the latter it may only be viewed as "troublesome." Empirical evidence is again provided by Lynch who suggests that the lack of accessibility to areas within the cities he examined was the most important factor contributing to whole areas of cities being excluded from peoples' subjective environments.

.   .   .

DERWENT WHITTLESEY

The Impress of Effective Central Authority upon the Landscape

Political activities leave their impress upon the landscape, just as economic pursuits do. Many acts of government become apparent in the landscape only as phenomena of economic geography; others express themselves directly. Deep and widely ramified impress upon the landscape is stamped by the functioning of effective central authority.

By "central authority" is meant sovereignty over an area of marked diversity. To be "effective" the central government must exert more than nominal control over its area. Today "effective central authority" is a function of the national state.[1]

EXPRESSIONS OF SECURITY

Security is one of the most valued products of effective central authority—the guarantee against molestation within the state and the assurance of resistance to invasion from without.

In the state which feels itself secure, habitations are disseminated wherever this mode of settlement suits the economic life. In new countries (by "new" is meant those which have been settled in the current age of central authority), farmsteads are dispersed in most types of agricultural occupance. Even where the agricultural mode favors clustering, as in irrigated districts and on plantations and market gardens, the farmsteads commonly line up as stringtowns along roads, so that each may be centrally located in the midst of its farmland.

Reproduced by permission from the *Annals* of the Association of American Geographers, Volume 25, No. 2 (1935), 85–97.
1 Unless capitalized, "state" is used throughout in its generic sense of "sovereign power."

This is in marked contrast to the farm villages in similar agricultural units of old countries. There the houses may cluster in tight knots. A good many are perched on defensible hills or protected by water, and are therefore inconveniently remote from the farmland. A comparison of the settlement patterns of Southern California and Southern Italy illustrates this distinction. In countries which were settled in eras of insecurity, defense points have now been to some degree abandoned in favor of more convenient sites. Crowded hills are deserted for open plains, as at Les Baux in Provence. Or hill villages expand downhill, but remain their ancient centers on the defense point; Spain supplies numerous examples of this shifting. In extreme cases, the crest is denuded of buildings and reclaimed for gardening (e.g., Loudon, France). Sicilian villages which formerly hugged the coast and its protecting waters are pushing tentacles of farmsteads into the rolling, open uplands, now that the Mafia has been deprived of its threat to life and property. Where artificial defenses were formerly maintained, moated granges and villages free themselves for expansion by filling their encircling waters with their encircling walls. Where the agricultural system cogently favors scattered habitations, isolated farmsteads appear, concomitant with security.

Urban centers are precluded by their function from dispersing in the way farm villages do, but they may and do spread out. Security not only permits them to occupy more space, but it stimulates both trade and manufacturing, their two chief reasons for existing. Flourishing economic life demands land for port facilities, rail and road terminals, and wide thorofares; space must be provided for retailing on a large scale and for wholesaling; professions and other services multiply; new largeness of ideas sets up new space requirements for residence and recreation. All these call for acreage undreamed of in days of straitened insecurity.

Trade follows security, and trade has forced walled seaports to burst their bonds. All of La Rochelle but its port lies on land which was outside the walls in the seventeenth century; so also with San Juan, Puerto Rico. The easily defended *calanque* which has fixed the Rhône Valley seaport of Marseilles for at least 2800 years has been turned over to the fishing fleet, and a new commercial port filched from the open Mediterranean by jetties. London, Antwerp, Rotterdam, Hamburg, and many another estuary city has dug a new harbor in soft alluvium adjacent to but below the ancient constricted port. To obtain space for new business, nearly every commercial city in continental Europe, and the larger ones in Japan, have converted their moated walls into boulevards. Paris and Vienna are the most famous examples, but Toulouse, Cologne, Seville, Milan, and hundreds of others, large and small, disclose the same history in their street patterns. Less spectacular, but more costly, is the widening and straightening of countless streets and the substitution of modern streets for medieval rookeries. Of all the square miles pierced only by ten- or fifteen-foot streets and still narrower culs-de-sac, which made up fourteenth-century Paris, only one small fragment survives today. The dead-end and zigzag alleys

of Japanese cities are giving way to more regular plats of streets. Three centuries ago, hardly a cathedral in Europe stood free from a parasitic congeries
of habitations; today their plazas are open. The cluttered and congested urban
landscape which expressed the day when political security lagged behind
expanding business has all but disappeared. New functions, particularly large-
scale manufacturing and the manifold business of rail terminals, have grown
up outside the "ring" boulevards which mark ancient fortifications.

The spacious residential suburb is likewise the product of an age of security
as well as an age of fast transport. It has nothing but location in common with
its precursor, the medieval faubourg, which was a slum huddled for protection
against the walls of a city. Residents in most European and Asiatic cities retain
the walled-in character of their predecessors. In the new countries of British
origin, and even in Great Britain itself, dwelling houses are likely to face the
street across the open lawn, with no barrier except rarely a fence of wood or
wire, or at most a low wall. The spacious habit of building each town house
detached and not walled-off from its neighbors, seems to be the ultimate landscape expression of generations of security, beginning in Europe and transplanted to the colonies. At any rate, it is practiced almost exclusively in the
newer parts of them. But even there, some time has generally elasped between
the abandonment of the stockade and the adoption of the detached house. The
residential streets of little cities along the Atlantic seaboard of North America,
such as Portsmouth (N.H.) and Charleston (S.C.), as well as the older sections
of all the large seaboard centers, present solid ranks of abutting facades. West
of the Appalachians, only the most congested sections of the largest cities are
built in solid blocks; in small cities and in residential sections of large ones,
the detached dwelling reigns, even where it is built with the intention of
housing two or three families in "flats."

SPECIAL FEATURES OF BOUNDARIES

Expansiveness does not everywhere accompany security. Along international
boundaries, the landscape may be strewn with features intended by central
authority to maintain security. At the least, a customs-house and immigration
post (often housed in the officer's home) stand sentinel at every major route
crossing. On some European borders, a gate, usually a heavy balanced pole,
stands ready to be lowered at night and for any emergency. On minor roads a
single military official is in sole charge. On main thorofares, several men are
stationed, often both civilian and military authorities. Even the undefended
border between the United States and Canada is studded with official buildings
where a few men are kept on duty. Along boundaries where acute tension is
felt, either because of smuggling, antipathy between political systems which
face each other across the line, or recent boundary displacements, the soldier
guard may amount to a military encampment, although only at crucial pass-
ways. At the exit of the Vall d'Arán in the Pyrenees, where the temptation to

smuggle is powerful, the border is controlled by a small company of soldiers. On the Carso, the new frontier between Italy and Yugoslavia near the strategic Peartree Pass is marked by a made-to-order garrison city, regiments of soldiers, airplane landing fields, ammunition dumps along the railroad, and freshly made military roads—all in a karst region almost bare of vegetation and apparently devoid of human inhabitants other than the garrison and its entourage. Even the St. Gotthard Pass on the border of peaceable Switzerland is heavily fortified.[2]

At railroad crossings there are, in addition to the usual officials, terminal facilities for trains which technically do not cross the border. In practice, the terminal is generally in the town nearest the boundary, and not on the line. Whether the gauge differs or not, the terminal exists, because only a few of the trains go through, and in any event, the locomotives and crews are changed. Many boundaries are closed to aircraft, except along specified lanes, which are as definite routes as roads and rails, although they are invisible.

Definition of boundary lines, i.e., replacement of boundary zones by boundary lines, follows upon the establishment of effective central authority. When central authority is weak, border districts, event if legally subordinate, are in practice at liberty to carry on their life pretty much as they please. They usually work out intimate economic reciprocity with neighboring political units, which themselves may be independent or nominally subordinate to some other inclusive state. Inhabitants of such harmoniously functioning border regions feel foreign to the people of their respective distant capitals, but not to their neighbors across the political boundary. When power is concentrated in a central locus, border zones are subordinated. Whenever the local interests clash with interests of the state as a whole, the border interests suffer. Central authority, to be effective, must proclaim fixed linear boundaries which can be defended against military aggression and economic penetration. Where political borders coincide with population deserts, such as oceans or large lakes, expanses of dunes without oases, perpetual ice, or dense forests, local life is little or not at all affected by fixing a linear boundary. In new countries, where a linear boundary has been drawn antecedent to settlement, the economic life conforms to it without strain, although tariffs often induce branch factories in border towns, and thus modify the landscape. Where manufacturing plants are built beyond the line to take advantage of tariffs, workers commute from their established homes across the boundary, or if distance prevents this, they may move to new "line" towns on the frontier of their homeland. Rarely, a double town bestrides the line. In most regions, the substitution of linear for zonal boundaries cuts off kinsmen from each other, parts business associates, and severs chorologic units. This is true even along mountains which are commonly thought of as barriers (e.g., the Pyrenees), and populous plains such as

---

[2] For details of border phenomena, especially those along the Franco-German boundary, see Hassinger, H.: "Der Staat als Landschaftsgestalter," *Zeitschrift für Geopolitik 9* (1932), pp. 117–22, 182–7.

the Flanders, Lorraine, Posen, Silesia, have repeatedly seen towns lopped off from part of their upland, and have occasionally suffered the arbitrary dissection of cities.

Boundaries recently displaced are likely to make zones of personal risk. On borders of the Polish Corridor and Upper Silesia, transgression without the proper papers makes one liable to arrest and confinement, even though the culprit has not left his own property. Since boundaries are often arbitrarily drawn cross-country through farms and even through towns, this surveillance annoys the individual and so adds increments of personal hatred to the general enmity.

To guard against aggression, many boundaries are lined with defenses, e.g., the Franco-German border. Such defenses are linked by strategic roads and railroads, such as the Stelvio Pass road, the high-level bridge across the Kiel Canal, and certain railroads in pre-war Poland (many of which are now useless). The land thus used is withdrawn from other occupance. Towns along the boundary are semi-military, being differentiated from ordinary commercial towns by barracks, fortifications, and a general air of being supported by government rather than by business.

Boundary displacements may be followed by political acts which directly or indirectly modify the landscape. Slight changes, such as the substitution of one language for another on public buildings and street signs, are common. Even stores and offices are required by law to display only the official language. Perhaps the extreme case at the moment is the Lower Vistula valley. There an important railroad bridge across the river was first closed, and later moved to another site. A fishing hamlet among the dunes has been elevated into a modern port by the construction of costly harbor works, and linked to the interior of Poland by new stretches of railroad. Indirect pressure, such as government contracts, is exerted to deflect goods and people into this new all-Polish channel of ingress and egress. As a result, Danzig, the ancient port city of the Vistula Valley, has to share the trade with its politically fostered rival. By treaty, Danzig has accepted the smaller share—45 per cent to Gdynia's 55 per cent.[3] Routes and other communication patterns are frequently altered after a boundary displacement; at first certain connections are closed or so restricted by inspections at the border that they fall into disuse; then new connecting links, suited to the new alignment of territory, are built. All this in the name of security.

EXPRESSIONS OF GOVERNMENTAL ACTIVITY

Central authority usually undertakes to act for the whole of its territory in specified matters. This tends to produce uniformity in cultural impress, even where the natural landscape is diverse.

---

[3] Other modifications of Germanic border regions since 1914 are discussed by Hassinger, *op. cit.*

Public buildings of uniform function and form are commonplace examples. The post-offices in France, army posts in all countries, the state capitols in the United States (these by imitation rather than by prescription), are easily recognized types. In a very heterogeneous country, such as the United States, regionalism may be given recognition. Generally nowadays the federal government builds its post-offices in conformity to local tradition. In New England, they are "colonial"; in California, Spanish; and in the Middle West, either classical or modernistic.

In many new countries, a uniform land survey, including routes, has been sketched upon the landscape antecedent to settlement. This is notably true of English-speaking North America, except for the colonial settlements and the Old South. It also applies, but much more locally, to parts of Latin America and other new countries, including settlements made centuries ago in eastern Germany, when it was "new." Perhaps the system of Roman roads, still conspicuous features of the route pattern in Romanized Europe, may be cited as an additional and still earlier example of a pattern of communication ordained by central authority.

In the Roman permanent "camps" of Western Europe, and in towns laid out by Germans as they pushed eastward after the tenth century, rectilinear street patterns within circular or elliptical walls are common, although blocks are likely to be unequal and streets not quite straight. Modern national governments began to sponsor fiat towns early in the seventeenth century. The gridiron patterns of streets was seized upon as convenient since the new towns were generally laid out on plains and defense was not necessary. Richelieu in western France, laid out by an officer of the Church, and Mannheim on the Rhine, laid out by a military officer of the state, are samples. The grid proved to be an equally handy pattern for mushroom towns in new countries. Nearly every municipality of the Pampa, except Buenos Aires, is an example. Philadelphia is an early case (1682) in North America. The Dutch followed the scheme in Batavia. In these cases, the orientation is rarely due north-south and east-west. Compass orientation of city streets fits naturally into the coarser grid of the rectilinear survey, adopted in many new countries. Melbourne is an example from the Antipodes. Chicago is the outstanding case of the very large city oriented north-south and east-west, and monotonously and regularly extended. The almost featureless lacustrine plain on which it lies has neither compelled nor encouraged deviation from the ideal plan. The offsets which accommodate the straight-line survey to the spherical earth appear as jogs in the street pattern. Numerous new suburbs of old cities throughout the world have been similarly platted. Where no rectilinear survey exists, grids may have any conceivable orientation, e.g., along streams, country roads, or railroads, or hinged to a stretch of fortifications-turned-boulevard.

Most gridiron street plans have not been directly imposed by governments. The appeal of convenience, however, has been irresistible in an age when new cities and new suburbs of old cities have been multiplying on open plains, thanks to increased trade and manufacturing made possible by powerful government.

Governments often stimulate migration into newly acquired areas by offering landholdings larger than those current in regions from which settlers are drawn. This distinction tends to disappear in time, unless it is reinforced by the natural environment. In the Pampa, large holdings, originally stock ranches, persist because they carry social prestige, but much of the land is now under the plow, being tilled by tenants on short-term leases. Eastern Germany, wrested from the Slavs, was blocked out by the invaders from the west in large, uninterrupted units, strikingly in contrast to the crazy-quilt of both holdings and fields in parent Germany. These very large units persist today chiefly in rugged, marshy, sterile districts where small farmers cannot make a living, and horse-raising affords a genteel occupation.

As the United States approaches demographic maturity, the average size of landholdings is undergoing progressive change toward harmony with the environment. In the Corn Belt, the typical patent from the government granted 160 acres, a figure not far from the unit which in that region can most effectively be worked by a single farm family. Farther west, in the semi-arid and desert country, this unit early proved too small, and homestead allotments double and later quadruple this size came to be permitted by law. Where grazing or dry-farming dominates, even 640 acres is too small a unit, and holdings are being merged to form adequate ranches. In the irrigable areas of "Mediterranean" California and "Egyptian" Arizona, on the contrary, the original large holdings, many of them stock ranches dating from Spanish times, are being morselled into twenty-, ten-, and even five-acre lots.

The existence of effective central authority implies the power to collect taxes and distribute funds throughout the whole territory of the state. Notable modifications of the landscape have resulted from the habit governments have of distributing to backward and pioneer sections money collected from prosperous districts. This is, in other terms, a transfer from regions favored by the natural environment to regions laboring under temporary or permanent environmental handicaps. The Tennessee Valley Authority of the moment is a spectacular example, but the principle has long been in operation in the United States, thanks to loose construction of the Constitution. Much of the irrigation of land in the western states has been paid for from federal funds; the federal government provides aid in building roads, especially in sparsely populated regions; and many of the railroads in North America (and in every other continent) have been similarly aided, wherever they have been trajected through difficult or unpeopled territory. In North America and Australia, at least, the States and the Provinces have carried this redistribution of funds further. The southern half of Michigan, Wisconsin, Minnesota, and Ontario each supports schools and roads in the northern quarters; in like fashion, the eastern part of each Great Plains State contributes to the maintenance of its western part, and humid Australia to the arid ends of the several States.

Lowlands in mountainous middle latitude countries spend a part of their taxes for objects which make habitation of the highlands possible. Forests and recreational preserves in handicapped regions are likely to be maintained by central government. From this viewpoint, the study of pioneer areas, as undertaken recently by the American Geographical Society, resolves itself into these problems: first, how much government aid is needed; and second, how much it is socially wise to disburse in any given area.

A number of regions, prosperous enough to support themselves in local affairs, can benefit greatly if given aid from the central government on specific problems which transcend a single region. Flood prevention in the Mississippi Basin is too comprehensive a task to be dealt with effectively, by any existing political unit smaller than the United States. Reclamation of the Zuyder Zee by the Netherlands, reforestation in Alpine Europe and elsewhere, the construction of autostrade by the Italian state and similar national road systems wherever automobiles are important, the Canadian policy of supporting intersectional railroads, hydro-electric installations in Ireland and Russia—all these are examples of comprehensive undertakings which only central authority can handle.

Public funds available for regional redistribution may be misdirected. Some unwise expenditure results from necessary experimentation, since governments have had relatively little experience in enterprises of this nature. Political favor and "long-rolling" cause other and lamentable leaks. The federal appropriation for "rivers and harbors" in the United States has been notorious for a century. Every country no doubt has counterparts of our "pork barrel." An abuse hard to eliminate arises naturally, as useful institutions become outdated or cease to satisfy the needs of the community. Vested interests, often supported by law, prolong customary expenditure for indefinite periods. The continuance of army posts in the United States Indian Country, the support of the established church in England, are cases in point.

Government lays hands in a special way upon its capitals. The focusing of roads, railroads, and canals upon the seat of government is partly the result of economic evolution, but it is often encouraged by political aid. Berlin, for instance, is not the center of Germany to the degree indicated by its hub of communication lines. The location of some capitals has been shifted in harmony with migrating political power. Nearly every one of the original United States moved its capital from the seaboard to the interior, as population increased in the back country. The reverse process occurs when overseas powers impose their rule upon settled communities. The seat of administration may then be brought to the coast, as from Cuzco to Lima, from Kandy to Colombo, and from Delhi to Calcutta.

Once fixed, capitals become the pets of government. On them public money is frequently lavished beyond present needs, even beyond the natural desire of the people to dress up their capital city. Delhi, Peiping, Berlin, Rome (both ancient and modern) are notable examples of generous expenditure. All these cities are splendid to look at, and each looks very different from the ordinary commercial city. Minor capitals have been garnished in proportion to their funds. Every German quondam state has an imitation Versailles, and the forty-eight democratic United States of America have spent staggering sums to house their governments. Washington and Canberra, as purely political fiat towns, are the clearest beneficiaries of political favor, but even London, primarily a world port and the leading manufacturing city of Britain, is impressively the capital of a nation and an empire. The spaciousness of modern capitals— "Washington, city of magnificent distances," Paris with its broad boulevards, Rome, roomy enough to accommodate both the modern capital and its exhumed predecessor of antiquity, are made possible by the security which central authority affords. Some governments which have spent overmuch on dressing up their capital cities have been overthrown not long after. Athens of Pericles and Versailles of the later Bourbons by their very splendor contributed to the undoing of their sponsors.

Outside the capital city, the hand of government puts its stamp on many places. Universities may form the nuclei of small cities. Prisons strikingly modify the landscape, and in places, as at Princetown in Dartmoor, dominate it. Experimental farms may occupy large acreage. All these are exceptional. Most government agencies are housed in buildings more or less lost in ordinary towns and cities—district courts and police registration bureaus, central banks, port headquarters, and the like. Yet they are likely to bear clear evidence of their official character. If built of costly materials in a massive or pretentious style, as is commonly the case, they stand out among their neighbors. The site too is likely to enhance their distinction. It may be a conspicuous hill, a plaza, or a park, such as only government can afford. On the other hand, it may be an out-of-the-way spot or an obscure block on a mean street which people would never search out, but for government compulsion. A government building erected in a poor neighborhood improves surrounding values. Conversely, if the site happens to be in a retail shopping section, the government building, lacking windows and shops, no matter how fine a piece of architecture, serves as a damper to trade, and surrounding land values are thereby lessened.

LAWS RESULTING IN LANDSCAPE MODIFICATIONS

Tariffs imposed by central authority set their mark on widely separated regions. The incidence of tariffs is determined largely by economic geography. Those which fence out foreign manufactured goods lead to the creation of new manufactural districts, as in Montreal, Toronto, Hamilton, and Windsor in Canada. Budapest and Ljubljana are creating factory districts to supply people formerly served by Vienna. Tariffs or subsidies applying to agricultural produce favor agricultural systems different from those which would exist with free trade. Examples: the large acreage of wheat in France, a cool, moist land;

the intensive spots of tobacco and sugar beets in nearly every country of Western Europe; sugar-cane as the dominant crop in Hawaii, Puerto Rico, the Philippines, and a crop of moderate importance in Louisiana.

Embargoes of other sorts alter the location of items in the landscape. The refusal of the State of Maine to permit the exportation of its water power leads to the building of a large pulp-mill on the Lower Penobscot to use Kennebec power and imported pulpwood. Power developed in New Hampshire on the Upper Connecticut in the same year, is shipped to populous Boston and vicinity for miscellaneous manufacturing and lighting. Dissatisfaction with Mexican participation in an irrigation canal which crosses the international boundary in the Imperial Valley spurs on the construction of an all-American canal on less advantageous terrain.

Laws affect both the tempo and the direction of settlement in all new countries, although in the process, the law itself is much modified, or where it conflicts too stridently with its new-found environment, abrogated.

The early European settlements in the New World, made in the fifteenth century, were launched under franchise from European governments; in many cases, the present political subdivisions are bounded by the terms of those franchises. Sea-to-sea grants in British North America account for the east-west boundaries of several States on the Atlantic seaboard and in the Middle West, boundaries which run counter to the grain of the country. The Papal Line of Demarcation of 1493–4 accounts for Portuguese Brazil in Spanish America and for four centuries of Spanish rule in the Philippines.

As settlement progressed inland from toeholds on harbors, it was protected or hampered or deflected by the aegis of the law. At the outset, the seigneurial system dominant throughout Europe was transplanted to the new continents. It suited the plantation system of agriculture and has never been modified where that mode of land use still prevails. For centuries it suited the Pampa, a remote grassland where livestock ranching paid better than any other agricultural system. With increasing demand for grain, all the more humid Pampa has recently become potential wheat or mixed farming country. Thus far, the social prestige of immense estates, fortified by the law, has retarded their subdivision, although more and more land is being tilled under a wasteful system of tenantry. In contrast to the Pampa stand Canada and the United States. In New England particularly, the seigneurial system never took root; elsewhere, it was abandoned because the small farm better fitted the environmental conditions. As settlement swept inland from the humid seaboard into the humid Middle West, homestead laws fixed the size of individual's claims to unappropriated public land at a figure which had proved satisfactory in the parent States. In sub-humid regions, where tillage has to be extensive, and still more in regions so dry that only grazing can prosper without irrigation, application of these laws predestined homesteaders to hopelessly inadequate holdings. The common practice of allotting alternate sections of the land to railroad companies as an inducement to extend the rails, further complicated the pattern of land holdings. Successive laws increased the acreage allowed, but they came too late to benefit most of the stock-raising country. It has been found difficult, often impossible, to piece together from abandoned claims and the rigid checkerboard of railroad holdings, enough land with the proper balance between winter and summer pasture, and with suitably spaced waterholes, to make a successful stock ranch. As a result, some land is overgrazed, while other land is not used to its capacity, or is occupied without legal right.

The general progression of settlement in new countries of British origin has been from humid to arid. The English Common Law did not require much modification to serve for the humid parts of the United States and the British Dominions, but when it began to be applied indiscriminately to dry regions, some sections of the code were found to run so sharply counter to local needs that they had to be abrogated. To cite a notable example: riparian rights, if adhered to, would have prevented the installation of irrigation works, without serving any useful purpose in regions devoid of navigable streams. Conversely, laws had to be drafted to safeguard rights of irrigation farming, since the Common Law, a native of the humid English climate, incorporated no such rules. In the San Joaquin Valley of California, litigation between landholders who wished to maintain riparian rights and those who desired to divert water for irrigation, retarded the evolution of "Mediterranean" agriculture for decades. Even today, not all the irrigable land is under ditch, and in each irrigated district the crops grown are dominantly those which promised profit at the time when legal controversies happened to be settled.

Laws affecting the use of land and natural resources are not confined to new countries. Every considerable social revolution produces its crop of laws affecting land holdings. Generally, such laws are calculated to break up or prevent the rise of large estates, to restrict holdings to small acreage, and to limit the agricultural occupance to those modes in which small holdings pay. In Rumania, Russia, Ireland, and other parts of Europe where estates have been subdivided during and since the World War, subsistence farming has generally replaced commercial farming, crude tools have replaced machinery, fields have been reduced in size, the percentages of crops grown and stock reared have changed, and in places, soil fertility has decreased. In general, small holdings in Europe favor stock raising at the expense of grain production, since the small proprietor can pay careful attention to his animals, whereas he may not be able to afford the machinery needed for economical grain growing on a commercial scale.

In the Philippines, plantations large enough to attract foreign capital may not be owned by outsiders. In Java, laws imposed by the Dutch have the effect of maintaining a fixed ratio in the acreage of the major crops. This restricts unbridled planting of commercial crops and reserves adequate acreage for the food crops on which the natives subsist. In Cuba and Brazil, laws forbid or limit new plantations of certain cash crops produced in excess of the market demand.

GOVERNMENT AND REGIONAL GEOGRAPHY

Examples of cultural impress of effective central authority upon the landscape can be multiplied indefinitely. The cases cited suffice, however, to point to a group of geographic phenomena often overlooked. Each deserves more detailed study, particularly in its regional setting. Phenomena engendered by political forces should have a recognized place as elements in the geographic structure of every region.

CHARLES MCKINLEY

The Impact of American
Federalism upon the
Management of Land Resources

A sense of urgency is abroad lest the natural resource base for our American civilization fail us. This anxiety, aroused by events, discussion, and public policies during the days of the New and Fair Deals, has been heightened by the war-revealed critical shortages in the domestic supplies of strategic materials and the approaching depletion of high quality domestic deposits of base minerals like iron, copper, lead, and bauxite ores. The dramatic reversal of the prewar birth rate revives the prospect for a burgeoning population. These new Americans will greatly expand the demand for all the materials essential to a high level economy. Finally, we take seriously our front rank position in the resistance of the noncommunist world to the revolutionary expansionism of Russian-led world communism. Whether or not we teeter on the brink of a third world war, the present world rearmament race and the competition between the United States and Russia in material aid to other peoples seem to make unprecedented demands upon our physical as well as cultural resources.

This new resource situation has . . . been outlined in the reports of the President's Water Resources Policy Commission released early in 1951, and in the so-called Paley Commission's report on material resources published in 1952. While they reveal that our problems are not primarily those of resource exhaustion, they do indicate shortages of particular minerals and of water in a number of areas. The mineral resource problems that lie ahead are principally those of higher cost, unless technology improves more rapidly than

From *Federalism, Mature and Emergent*, ed. Arthur W. McMahon (Garden City, N.Y.: Doubleday & Company, Inc., 1955), pp. 305–327. Reprinted by permission of the Trustees of Columbia University in the City of New York.

seems assured. Water policy issues center around comprehensive river basin multiple purpose planning, proper watershed management, deficiencies of water data, questions of who shall administer, who shall pay, and the adequacy of state laws governing the use of water. Neither study was directed primarily toward the problems of agricultural land but neither could avoid them. Here again the basic issue is not imminent shortage but wise management of what we have and improved agricultural technology.

The mere statement of these problems suggests the need for public authority on a national or international scale. Here the American federal system of divided powers confronts a crucial test. For if, in general, the bulk of our best land and most important minerals has passed to private ownership, then the role of the American states which in legal theory monopolize the police power over the use of private property must be made to harmonize with national policy. Similarly the division of legal authority which recognizes the states' title to the appropriation of water for beneficial use while the nation controls its use for navigation and interstate commerce, poses another set of key problems for governance under our federal system. Even the apparently simple question of the proper management of publicly owned land, which in the western states is predominantly retained in federal ownership, includes many complex relations with states, counties, and private owners.

I. FEDERALISM AND THE MANAGEMENT OF PUBLIC LAND RESOURCES

I turn first to the impact of our federal system upon the management of our public "wild land" resources, though it will be quickly apparent that this is in many respects interlocked with important private land policies and operating relationships. In this matter I shall confine my attention to situations found in the public land states of the West; even there I shall omit consideration of the limited though important acreages within the National Parks, the national game refuges, and the Indian reservations, and include only the vaster areas comprising the National Forests and the picked-over but extensive residue of the public domain. . . .

The fact that conservation management by the national government of its landed estate really started with the National Forests under Gifford Pinchot needs no belaboring here. But it is well to recall that until recent years national forest management was centered around the functions of fires, insect and disease protection, and grazing management.

The prevention of fire or its prompt suppression has been an elemental requirement vital to all owners of timber land as well as to the dependent public. Nevertheless, it was not until the disastrous fires on the west slope of the Cascades in the summer of 1902 swept over at least seven hundred thousand acres of green timber and snuffed out the lives of thirty-five people that private timber owners and the states of the Pacific Northwest awoke to the need of organized, cooperative fire protection, compulsory patrol laws, and a code of forest fire practices. From 1905 to 1912 private protective associations sprang up throughout the timbered areas of Washington, Oregon, California, and the panhandle of Idaho, and took the lead in forest fire protection.[1] This coincided with the transformation of the old Bureau of Forestry into the U.S. Forest Service and the dispatch by Gifford Pinchot of his young forester disciples of conservation to the National Forests to begin a vigorous management program, with special stress on fire control. An even greater disaster which struck in the summer of 1910 in the Bitter Roots and Coeur D'Alenes of northern Idaho, and which took a toll of three million acres of timber and eighty-five lives, finally awakened national, state, local, and larger private timber owners to the realization that they must either hang together in furnishing fire protection or burn together.[2] As a consequence in part Congress in 1911 passed the Weeks Act which offered national grants-in-aid to protect state and private timber. Since many state governments not only had large public forest acreages of their own (today estimated in the neighborhood of twenty-seven million)[3] but also monopolized the legal power to compel private owners to join in a fire protective program, they had perforce to be part of any effective protection programs. On the foundation laid by the Weeks Act and the McNary Act of 1924 (with its 1944 amendment) has been built an increasingly efficient three-way partnership between the Forest Service, state forestry departments, and associations of private timber owners.[4] Thus has been bridged the legal gap inherent in a federal system of divided powers.

This program has also been of great and increasing value to all the timbered states, though those of the southeast were slow to take full advantage of it. By 1950, forty-three states and Hawaii had joined this partnership, leaving only the five timberless prairie-plateau states of Kansas, Nebraska, North Dakota, Wyoming, and Arizona outside the program. Out of approximately 426 million acres of state and private forest and watershed lands needing fire protection, more than 360 million were by 1952 under organized protection.

It is to the leadership and supervision of the U.S. Forest Service that this fire protection system owes its stimulus, its improvements in fire planning, personnel training and management, and the application of improved suppression techniques. . . .

Building on this successful pioneer cooperative scheme came other facets of national-state, public-private forest collaborative land management. A program of federal subsidizing of the state production and distribution of trees at

---

1 William B. Greeley, *Forests and Men,* Garden City, Doubleday, 1951, pp. 19–20.

2 Stewart H. Holbrook, *Burning on Empire,* New York, Macmillan, 1952, pp. 132 ff.

3 Luther H. Gulick, *American Forest Policy,* New York, Duell, Sloan & Pearce, 1951, p. 145.

4 The Weeks Act restricted the fire protection program to the watersheds of navigable streams but the Clark-McNary Act took a broader view of national constitutional power by extending the grant system to all forested and cut-over land. See the 1950 report of the Chief of the U.S. Forest Service, p. 3.

nominal cost for reforestation on state land and on farm wood lots soon followed and was expanded in 1951 to include any timberland owners. At present forty-three states and two territories are in this program.[5]

Forty-five states aided by federal funds and Forest Service guidance now employ trained extension foresters to bring the gospel of good wood lot management to farmers and small timber tract owners. Nearly three fourths of the private forest land is owned by about 3,500,000 farmers and 750,000 small-town business and professional men. Potentially these lands are highly productive but they universally suffer from neglect or bad management.

The Norris-Dixey Act of 1937 was intended to bring direct case work assistance to the management of farm wood lots. This was included in the farm planning program of the Soil Conservation Service. Since 1945 the Forest Service has supervised this program. It works through the state foresters who, with the approval of the Forest Service, now hire and supervise about two hundred and fifty farm foresters who work directly with farmers in selected counties in thirty-eight states. This program was expanded to included direct assistance to all small timber land owners and small mill owners by the Cooperative Forest Management Act of 1950.[6]

·   ·   ·

The research programs of the Forest Service were for many years the principal sources of information for improved forest management for all types of owners. This was also true at first for wood utilization research. However, private industry soon expanded this activity, and in recent years the states have added their efforts to improve both utilization and forest management knowledge. Nearly one-half of the estimated three and a half million dollars spent in 1951 for forest research by states and private agencies goes into projects planned and organized jointly with the Forest Service, "with mutual agreement on what the program will be, how the work will be done and how the financial load will be shared. In cooperative research some problems are attacked jointly, the cooperators merging their facilities and personnel; others are divided into segments under correlated arrangements."

The toll of timber taken by insects and plant pests often exceeds even that of fires. Because these biological menaces are likewise blind to ownership boundary lines, mastery of pest control must also be a cooperative undertaking. Hence come frequent appeals from the states and private owners for federal funds and administrative leadership to deal with special pest problems. In 1947 Congress put forest pest control on a basis similar to that of fire control, with the federal Bureau of Entomology and Plant Quarantine in the role of technical leader, with the four federal agencies having timber management responsibilities participating, and with financial aid to encourage private-owner

5 1951 Report of the Chief of the Forest Service, U.S. Dept. of Agriculture, p. 56.
6 1952 Report of the Chief of the Forest Service, pp. 37–38.

cooperation. The precise arrangements for participation vary from one pest infestation problem to another, but in the three years after the enactment of the national pest control law, eight states centered responsibility for their part in these programs upon their state foresters.

The interlevel operation of this program as illustrated by experiences in the Pacific Northwest has been very close knit and highly successful.

While the current retreat from national leadership in resource development may change the intergovernmental relationships in some of the forest land programs, none of those reviewed above is likely to be greatly modified. They have become too fully embedded in a web of interlocking practices, buttressed by the consensus of the forestry profession and the timber industry.

When we inquire into other aspects of the forest resource problem the federalism answer is not so clear. First let us note the quality of management of state owned timber lands. Here the situation seems very uneven, though careful studies of state management operations are few and precise information is hard to obtain.[7] Of the three Pacific Northwest states, most rapid headway has probably been made in Oregon which, however, had the smallest forested estate left to manage. By the time forest conservation had found an appreciative public, Oregon had squandered most of its valuable timber holdings. Nevertheless, it still had a sufficient number of isolated school land sections within National Forest boundaries to permit an exchange during the thirties for a solid block of about seventy thousand acres on the edge of one of the National Forests.

.   .   .

Statehood came to Idaho and Washington nearly a half century later than to Oregon. The improvident disposal policies pursued by the older states made some impression upon the early law makers of these two states, who specified either in the state constitution or in statutes a minimum acre sale price of ten dollars for their land endowments. This requirement so throttled sales that each state still has large, though dispersed, acreages of virgin, burned-over, and cut-over timber lands for permanent management. The areal dispersion is not so great as in the older public land states because, in addition to the two-section gift out of every township for public school support, other sizeable acreage allotments for the support of institutions of higher education, the penitentiary, charitable institutions, public buildings, and so forth, were given to the states for their later selection. As a result since 1950 about half of Idaho's

---

7 The Conservation Foundation, in its 1952 publication, "Forests for the Future," p. 15, estimates that on the state and locally owned commercial forest lands totaling about twenty-seven and a half million acres cutting practices are good or better on 47 per cent, are fair on 10 per cent, and poor or worse on 43 per cent. This is a much better situation than exists on private lands but much inferior to that of the National Forests. No overall estimates of other management practices of state and community forests or of their use for grazing purposes are available.

state owned timber lands, totaling more than four hundred thousand acres, has been grouped under its state forester into five state forest blocks for full scale management. Approximately the same amount of timber land is so scattered as to defy continuous economic management.

Yet aside from fire control, Idaho state forest management until very recently was minimal. The first professionally trained state forester was appointed only five years ago. Under his leadership, backed by better state financial support, with the forward looking cooperation of the state land commissioner (under whose jurisdiction come all state timber sales), forestry on the state's property in Idaho has been making rapid strides. Yet because there is no formal merit system in Idaho state service, except for the Social Security-aided agencies and the State Game Department, the quality of personnel depends upon the changing agency heads.

The state of Washington, which owns approximately 18 per cent of all standing timber in the state, still denies to its state forester management functions other than fire control, reforestation, and the supervision of the tax-reverted county lands held in trust by the state. The constitutionally elected state land commissioner, flanked with an ex-officio state land board with which he is often politically in conflict, "manages" the state's school and most other grant lands. The atmosphere of county court house politics, not untainted by scandal and operational laxness in handling timber sales, still surrounds these agencies. As in Idaho, no statutory merit system protects the personnel of the land commissioner's department, nor has custom yet furnished alternative safeguards. Other management duties on state forest lands are split between the land commissioner and several boards, so that responsibility is thoroughly confused. No classification of the state's lands has been made to guide sale and harvest policies. While fire control on state and private lands and the enforcement of the recently adopted act regulating a few of the cutting practices on private timber lands are handled by the state forester's trained staff, elsewhere the job of managing state owned lands in Washington has not attained a high standard.

The hottest spot in the relationships between state and national forest agencies and policies has to do with the control of private forest cutting practices. For some years the U.S. Forest Service, backed by the Secretary of Agriculture, has been pushing for public regulation of private timber harvesting as essential to a sufficient national timber supply and to watershed protection. In private hands lie 75 per cent of the nation's forest lands and 90 per cent of its timber production. The most recent proposals of the Forest Service call for national laws setting the harvesting standards, with administration by those states choosing to enforce them, but with federal control in states unwilling or unable to provide adequate administration. Beginning with the Oregon Forest Conservation Act of 1941, as subsequently amended, a start toward the state regulation of private harvesting practices has been made. This law established an annual permit system for loggers and timber owners as condition for harvesting timber; it required the leaving of seed trees sufficient to restock the land and the disposal of slash without injury to the trees left standing or to young growth. The act as defined by regulations laid down by the state forester and approved by his forestry board would allow that officer to reforest the land and assess the costs against any violator. Undoubtedly this law, like its counterpart statutes later adopted by Washington, Maryland, and California, was enacted to forestall federal regulation. It was not enforced until the end of the war. Since then, and partly as a consequence of penalty amendments which facilitate enforcement, the Oregon state forester's organization has begun to give reality to these cutting regulations.

. . .

The adjustment of National Forest Wildlife programs to our scheme of divided powers may be noted here. Gifford Pinchot clearly included wildlife conservation programs in his plans for management. He took the position that if the states did not develop proper fish and game policies the Forest Service, as the agent for the national sovereign, might do so within the National Forests. But in practice this right has not been asserted. Instead the states have been encouraged to improve their wildlife activities and the Forest Service field men have become highly valuable collaborators in the analysis of problems of management, in the enforcement of state game laws, and in the application of the many management improvement programs.

There have been long-standing difficulties in obtaining state action to keep some species of wildlife—particularly deer—which have multiplied rapidly in recent years, in balance with the supply of forage. This has been especially hard to solve where the game habitat cycle crosses state boundary lines. One example is the interstate deer herd that winters in the forests of northern California and summers in the Fremont forest in Oregon. For years this constituted a problem of bistate and interlevel disharmony. The United States Forest Service, whose browse was being injured, has been the chief catalytic agent in finally precipitating an agreement that promises a solution.

The adoption of improved wildlife management practices by the states in recent years is probably the most striking achievement in state conservation efforts. This is in part the result of federal grant-in-aid assistance under the Pittman-Robertson Act which is administered by the U.S. Fish and Wildlife Service. This program, financed jointly by national and state funds, has stepped up the use of research in state management; it has improved the quality and increased the number of state wildlife staff; and it has greatly expanded the facilities, land and structures, for effective wildlife programs.

National-state-private relationships in range management reveal a less successful operation of our complex federal system. At the time the National Forests were first placed under management, the grass, browse, and soil on many of the high mountain meadows had been terribly depleted, especially in the more arid parts of the West. Earlier unregulated use of the livestock men left a heritage of problem areas with depleted forage and eroding soil. While improved management since 1905 has alleviated this situation there are still many "sore spots." Some of these will not heal until grazing is prohibited or greatly reduced. Time after time rehabilitation efforts have been checked or rendered less than adequate by the intervention of special circumstances: two world wars which emphasized all-out production of meat; financial hardship resulting from over-commitment of the industry during the first World War and sudden price deflation thereafter; and prolonged drought accompanied by economic collapse.

Despite these impediments the greatest headway toward sustained yield range management made by the public land agencies is to be found on the National Forests and on the pastures created from the dry-farm repurchase areas by the Soil Conservation Service. This constructive improvement has required as a tool the extensive development of range research. Thus the Forest Service has become the principal center of information for improved range management available to all range land owners, national, state, and private. . . .

As in the case of forests, there is an interlocking management relationship between the national, state, and private range lands. Domestic livestock, and to a lesser degree the browse-eating big game, move back and forth in accordance with the seasons, from the valley and low-bench privately owned lands to the intermingled state and national grazing district lands, on to the summer mountain meadows of the National Forests. Depletion on one kind of grazing land, resulting from mismanagement or natural causes, has a definite and sometimes immediate impact upon the other range ownerships and their freedom to pursue their own programs. Division of the national range lands between the Forest Service and the Bureau of Land Management makes this situation even more difficult of successful administration.

Operation under differing congressional and administrative policies concerning permittee user rights, fees for forage, the administrative influence of livestock advisory boards, standards of grazing management, participation by the states in range improvements, etc., has furnished excellent opportunity for private livestock interests, through their well organized national associations, to play the laxer or more favorable policies of one national agency against the other, and to use as a weapon the demand to transfer federal grazing lands to the states. The cry of states' rights in the controversy over public range land management is a thinly veiled disguise for the abandonment of range conservation, though it is not only in the public interest but also in the *long run* interest of the livestock industry. This is pretty evident in view of the kind of management practiced thus far by most of the western states in the handling of their own grazing lands.[8]

---

8 When the comprehensive report on the condition of the Western Range was made (Sen. Doc. No. 199, 74th Cong., 2nd Sess.) the states owned in excess of 58 million acres and the counties had foreclosed on an additional seven million acres of range land. Since these lands had been administered with the object of sale or lease, concern over conservation of the

Until the enactment of the Taylor Grazing Act the states had paid virtually no attention to sustained yield management of their remaining grazing lands. Though some of it was leased to private operators, most of it, like the federal domain public ranges, was left to the tender mercies of those private livestock operators who were the most successful at aggressive and illegal range preemption.

The Taylor Grazing Act as amended by the Pierce Act permitted the states to incorporate their range lands into the district management program and to receive rental payments in return. While considerable state land was thus early incorporated into the district program, most of it (at least in the Pacific Northwest) has been withdrawn in late years because (as a result of the rising values of forage after 1940) the states have been able to make more money by direct leases to stockmen. Their concern has been immediate income, not range land restoration, long run productivity, or watershed protection.

This short run crowding of the forage by the states is partly the result of long established habit; but it is also partly excusable by the terms of federal grants to the states. The school lands were given to provide endowment income. Hence state sales and leases have in most instances been made with an eye to immediate cash return. The state agencies supervising these range properties have too often thought of themselves as investment organizations and have had little or no interest in or experience for a land management job. Thus the state land board in Oregon has spent no money for conservation practices or for range improvements, although in the early forties it had nearly seven hundred thousand acres of range land under its jurisdiction.

. . .

One other illuminating experience for federalism in range management is the spread of grazing associations in the northern Great Plains states, beginning with organization in 1928 by the stockmen of Custer County, Montana, of the historic Mizpah-Pumpkin Creek Association. It took a special act of Congress to transfer to the association for joint management purposes twenty-five thousand acres of public domain land needed to round out this first venture in pooling private, state, county, and national grazing land for sustained yield management. This advance in range management has been the fruit of state laws (first enacted in 1933 by Montana) in the Great Plains region and of cooperative national administrative policies followed by the Resettlement Administration (or its successors), the Soil Conservation Service, the Grazing

---

basic resource had been absent. "It is estimated that the grazing capacity has been depleted approximately one half from virgin conditions and that about 28 million acres are severely eroded and an equal amount is materially eroded." (p. 477) No general summary of the present situation is available. Consequently the factual conclusions contained herein are based on limited first hand observations in states of the Pacific Northwest and in Utah, on the judgement of federal range and forest officers who have worked on range management in a number of western states, and on a few studies of limited aspects of the range situation.

Service and its successor, the Bureau of Land Management. By 1940 Montana had forty such associations to which had been entrusted the management of nearly thirteen million acres of pooled private, state, county, and federal grass lands. In Montana but not in all the other states a state agency (the Grass Conservation Commission) has supervised the creation of grazing districts and the organization of the cooperative associations.

The Montana law in effect gave "legislative endorsement of the range management policies of the Grazing Service and the Soil Conservation Service, and the individual operator using district-controlled lands is usually subject to the same type of regulations set up by those agencies." The federal range management agencies turned over in trust to these associations the management in accordance with their carrying capacities of national range lands (including the large acreages repurchased as submarginal for cash cropping) on generous rental terms. The Soil Conservation Service, as the administrative heir of the repurchased farm lands and the special agent of the nation for spreading the gospel of conservation farm land management, also lent the associations its technical assistance in range problems and in spreading interest among livestock men and the local public in the use of this cooperative, collective tenure method of range management. In a few cases the Farm Security Administration made loans to the associations for constructing range improvements or land purchases. Where the associations operated largely on national public domain lands, as many in Montana have done, their management relations with the Bureau of Land Management and the Soil Conservation Service have been particularly intimate.

II. FEDERALISM AND THE MANAGEMENT OF
PRIVATELY OWNED NON-URBAN LAND RESOURCES

While publicly owned lands greatly contribute to the protection of our watersheds and to the production of timber, wildlife, livestock, and minerals, it is the privately owned farming lands upon which our American civilization chiefly depends for its principal supplies of food and much of its fibre. But the use of these lands is only indirectly the subject of central governmental action. Under our federal system any public interference with a private owner's use of his land is the function of the states.

Even though many still regard as absolute the right to do as one pleases with his own property, the states have for many years recognized the legitimacy of drastic controls to meet such urgent threats or emergencies as the spread of insect pests, noxious weeds, and plant diseases, or the ravages of forest fires. Public intervention to regulate private land management in these cases has been fully accepted as a proper function of the states. Even such exceedingly drastic actions by public agents as the destruction of diseased orchard trees without compensation, or the performance of weed eradication or fire suppression with the costs charged against the private owner, are universally approved as justifiable state or local regulations and have been sustained by the courts. In many of the timbered states, the private owner of timber land or wood lots has long been compelled by taxation or by the threat of state intervention for which he must pay, or both, to protect his trees against fire.

But such acquiescence in public interference with private ownership rests upon the idea of a temporary emergency or of imminent irreparable damage to adjacent private owners. Intervention by the state or its local agents in private land use meets stronger resistance when the benefits of such interference are much more diffused in time or incidence. It is to the "cheek by jowl" life in urban communities that we must turn for the origin of the recent, broader proposals to regulate private agricultural and forest land. Rural land zoning laws and land use regulations are the legal offspring, perhaps one should say the step-children, of urban zoning statutes.

Rural zoning is of many varieties and serves diverse purposes but our concern is primarily with what Erling Solberg in his recent analysis of state enabling acts and local zoning ordinances has called "open-country-use" rural zoning,[9] that is, the effort to encourage the best long run treatment of those vast areas that produce our major supplies of agricultural and timber raw materials.

The pioneer regulation was made by Wisconsin. The cut-over timber lands of the sandy soiled areas between the Great Lakes were submarginal for farming, even under good price conditions. The decline of agricultural prices during the twenties, accentuated after the financial crash of 1929, created such human distress and such havoc in local government finance and services that private decisions about land use could not longer be left uncontrolled. So the state adopted a rural zoning statute permitting county or town boards to create forestry or recreational zones and general agricultural zones—along with other zoning restrictions—as one means to bring the use of land into line with its basic potentialities. Forest and recreation zones were drawn which prohibited farming and year-long residence in those regions where such uses were incompatible with the capabilities of the land and would result in individual and public bankruptcy.

The Wisconsin example has been followed, with some changes, in Michigan, Minnesota, and to a much more limited extent in Washington. At least one ordinance in Colorado also provides for forest conservation districts.[10] There are also several states in which "rural communities concerned about the destruction or impairment of agricultural soils by strip mining have adopted ordinances prohibiting or regulating such operations."

Despite the fact that by 1949 one hundred and seventy-three counties in twenty-three states had rural zoning ordinances, the evidence indicates that

---

[9] Erling D. Solberg, *Rural Zoning in the United States*, Bureau of Agricultural Economics, U.S. Dept. of Agriculture, Agricultural Information Bulletin No. 59, Jan. 1952, Washington, D.C. The information in this publication is the principal source of facts used in the discussion of this topic.

[10] Solberg, *op. cit.*, pp. 34 ff.

except for areas along the Great Lakes in northern Minnesota, Wisconsin, and Michigan, in the unorganized towns of Maine, and a few scattered locations in other parts of the nation, rural land zoning has done little toward bringing privately owned agricultural and forest land into adjustment with its best sustained use.[11] The large volume of discussion and study during the thirties which pointed toward land classification and rural zoning as one of the principal devices to be relied upon seems to have produced very modest results.

So it is to the initiative and support of the national government that we must look for most of the headway that has been made in stimulating private owners of agricultural and forest land toward a more provident use of these resources.[12] To be sure the states have been drawn into the programs as essential collaborators, and, however reluctant some of them were in the beginning, a wholehearted mood of cooperative effort seems now to be firmly established.

.   .   .

. . . While the latest available count shows 2,570 [state-created soil conservation districts] of local government, which include nearly six-sevenths of the entire agricultural area of the United States, it should at once be added that "basic" farm plans are in effect for only about one-fifth of the district farms, including about a fifth of the total farm and ranch acreage.[13] Additional conservation treatment is being given land on farms without "basic" plans.

Even though a close scrutiny might modify these statistics (since practices once established may be abandoned without penalty), this rapid spread across the nation's private farmland of so much in the way of improved management practices geared to perpetual productivity is a great achievement. That it has not been as fast, complete, or assuredly permanent as desired does not alter this conclusion. Nor is it the result solely of this one program of intergovernmental collaboration between the Soil Conservation Service, the states, and the local soil conservation districts. Once the evangel of soil conservation had begun to win popular acceptance, many private institutions embraced the faith,

---

[11] The raw statistics about "rural zoning" seem very impressive. But most of the 175 enabling statutes are designed chiefly to prevent building development of an urban character from encroaching upon the countryside along the highways or to bring some order into the suburban accretion beyond the city limits. Most of them have little or nothing to do with the management of agricultural or forest lands. Thirty-one laws in seventeen states exempt all agricultural activities from zoning, and in many of the other states in which agricultural zones are permitted the ordinances are directed toward the regulation of such activities as hog ranches, livestock feed and sales yards, etc., which might be offensive to suburban or town dwellers. See *Ibid.*, pp. 30–31, 43–44, 46.

[12] The state creation of conservation agencies in the Theodore Roosevelt era never entered the province of private resource regulation.

[13] These data rest in part on 1953 estimates furnished the Portland, Oregon, regional office of the Soil Conservation Service. In part they are taken from page 8 of the recent study by W. Robert Parks, *Soil Conservation Districts in Action*, Ames, Iowa, Iowa State College Press, 1952. In summarizing the work of the Soil Conservation Service and its relations with the soil conservation districts in the quest for securing conservation practice on private land, I have relied principally on this study of Professor Parks.

particularly when the faith was buttressed by sound business considerations. The banks handling agricultural paper or mortgages, the insurance companies owning large numbers of farms, the creditors of farm borrowers, the farm machinery companies finding new demand for conservation equipment, the mail order houses which prosper when farmer incomes are high and stable, and other private citizens have added support to the official programs.

Included in the impact of our national system on this resource management change were several other bureaus in the U.S. Department of Agriculture, namely: the Farm Security Administration (which survives vestigially as the Farmers Home Administration), the Farm Credit Administration, and the Production and Marketing Administration. The first two agencies brought many of their borrowers into the district programs, but the PMA—the most ubiquitous, affluent, and charitable agency of the departmental family—has probably exercised the strongest supplementing influence.

It was the intention of the national department as reflected in its "standard" act that the local soil conservation district should perform two major tasks: (1) induce farmers to adopt plans to modify practices and land use so that every acre would be used in accordance with its capability, thus stopping accelerated erosion and conserving fertility; and (2) adopt compulsory land use regulations that would prevent or control erosion. To achieve these purposes the districts were to contract with farmers to furnish them technical, financial, and material assistance. In addition they might conduct research in erosion control, develop land use plans and programs for their districts, conduct demonstration projects, build and maintain structures, and the like. But they were not to have taxing or bonding power. These financial limitations compelled the districts to seek gifts in the form of technical assistance, equipment, labor, or money. The first three the Soil Conservation Service was prepared to give, but it was hoped that other national, state, or local agencies might augment its assistance. In fact the SCS became the principal and in most cases the sole source of effective aid so that the district were soon regarded, even by district supervisors, as "Soil Conservation Service" districts. The whole administrative organization of the SCS was realigned to suit the district aspect of its work.

Why did the Department of Agriculture assume the role of local government procreator instead of using the county government as the vehicle for its attack upon the problem of private land management? No doubt the Wallace regime was unwilling to draft the county agent-extension service organization for another action program as it had done for the crop restriction program in 1933. To use the county for the SCS work might have seemed to make that inevitable. Other reasons were the general backwardness of the county as an efficient or responsible unit of local government; the preoccupation of its officials with matters not related to soil conservation; the desire to lodge local control with that vocational group primarily affected by the program; and (most frequently voiced) the conviction that conservation farm planning and operation could succeed only if geared into unified watershed treatment.

Obviously county boundaries had only accidental relationships to this physical area concept.[14]

Though the district was undoubtedly conceived as the federal government's chosen instrument the "standard act" did not bypass the state government. It provided for a state committee to assist in the organization of the districts, select two of the five board members, and, after a district was established, act as an advisory and informational agency.

While the early state laws followed this general design, later statutes and amendments have tended to increase the operational influence of the state body over the districts. The Missouri, Wisconsin, and Pennsylvania state committees have a tight administrative rein over their districts, acting as buffers between the districts and the national agencies.

In modifying the "standard act" conceptions the most tight-reining states like Missouri doubtless responded to the political influence of the land-grant colleges with their suspicion of the Soil Conservation Service and of "federal domination." Until recently the representatives of the state colleges plus their Farm Bureau or Extension farmer friends have dominated the state committees.

. . . A counterpoise to this tendency and to the influence of the SCS bureaucrats is the organization of Soil Conservation District Supervisors and their farmer friends. These associations are not only carrying the ball for state appropriations for the districts and for federal appropriations for the SCS (as well as supporting the latter against hostile administrative rearrangements at the hands of Congress or the Department of Agriculture) but also they are taking the farmer member places on the state committees which originally went to the Farm Bureau or the Grange (or in some Great Plains states, to the Farmers' Union), sometimes by explicit direction of the legislature.

.   .   .

The field organization of the Soil Conservation Service has of course been designed to facilitate its relations with the state committee and the state colleges. The latter have inevitably been drawn into the program, whether they liked it or not, since their experimental work and technical skills as well as the Extension Service educational facilities had to be utilized even if with ill grace —and the response was often cordial.

Yet the regional structure of the agency was intended to resolve both policy and technical questions at the regional level where pressure from state agencies was least. This pattern of regional control of the lower units in the field structure and of decentralization from Washington to the region, while disliked by the land-grant colleges and their farm pressure group friends, illustrates the kind of administrative adaptation to our federal constitutional system that

---

[14] The actual application of this area justification has been honored in the breach. More than half the districts consist of a county or group of counties. See Charles, M. Hardin, *The Politics of Agriculture,* Glencoe, The Free Press, 1952, p. 71.

after 1933 became characteristic of national land and water programs.[15] While it was in part a structural response to the inadequacy of state boundaries for field supervision (due to work load-cost, span of control, and other operating characteristics) it was also one means of easing and adjusting the pressures of state officialdom.

In the case of the Soil Conservation Service, however, regionalization has also functioned, probably without intention, as a device for modifying the application of national agency policy to meet not only the great variability in physio-agronomic conditions in so vast a country but also the variable political conditions.

.   .   .

The early national policy emphasis on "complete" farm planning was stated by Service Chief Bennett in 1937 as follows:

> ...a partial program for a given farm does not meet the essential requirements of a good soil conservation program and is, therefore, not acceptable. The program for each farm...must call for the *full* treatment of *every* acre affected and for the employment of *all* measures and practices needed to provide that treatment. Otherwise the Soil Conservation Service fails to discharge its full responsibility.

But district supervisors, responsive to local farmer sentiment, were prone to push the type of program that was immediately profitable and popular and were, moreover, convinced that acceptance of the whole program would come later if not all practice changes were required simultaneously. There was also the constant example of the AAA which after 1937 was handing out cash payments for single or limited conservation practices. No farm plan to guide that program was required.

.   .   .

The culmination of this relaxing process came in 1951 and 1952 when Secretary Brannan ended the competition between the SCS and the PMA by reorganizing their relationships so as to harmonize the two conservation programs at the county level and by making the SCS responsible for the technical phases of both of them. SCS field technicians now assist PMA farmers in their limited practices even though they do not become district cooperators and are thus not committed to complete farm planning and conservation management. Yet the Secretary of Agriculture as late as April 1952 reemphasized the national goal of embracing "every acre of farm land...in soil conservation districts." He also asserted as the ultimate objective a scientifically developed, technically sound conservation plan for each farm.

---

[15] It is true that the PMA, and the AAA before it, never succeeded in making this structural adjustment, though the latter took the first steps in that direction by regionalizing within the Washington organization. The Eisenhower administration in 1954 was attempting to reverse this process, and was dismantling the regional offices of the SCS. State field headquarters were to be the centers for field supervision.

The second half of the original soil conservation district task was the adoption and enforcement of land use regulations to prevent erosion. Even if farmers rejected the program of affirmative assistance or failed to live up to the district-farmer agreement, they would still have to so treat their lands as to preserve the top soil. By the end of 1951, however, only eight districts in the entire United States were enforcing land use ordinances. Six of these were in the "dust bowl" section of southeast Colorado, one was a sandy-soiled district in southwest North Dakota, and the eighth was in the shifting sand-dune Pacific littoral west of Astoria, Oregon. Seven other Colorado districts had at some time adopted such ordinances but these are no longer in effect because of a 1945 amendment to the state law requiring reenactment by a greatly increased majority or because of changes in local sentiment. Those regulations, however, which require the owners to perform certain practices to abate soil blowing have been so successful that the Colorado legislature in 1951 applied them to the entire state, to be enforced by the boards of county commissioners.

Despite the emphasis that the "standard act" placed on the right of the district to issue and enforce land use regulations, the early state legislative acquiescence in this policy has been sharply reversed. Today sixteen states deny all regulatory authority to the districts. It is clear from the Colorado experience that absentee land owners and their local representatives and the real estate speculators, when beaten by local sentiment, have been able to exert such powerful influence upon the state legislature as to render the exercise of regulatory authority over land use by the districts very difficult or precarious. The climate of farmer and public opinion has so changed since the distressed thirties that there is no appreciable public support for the police power mode of obtaining better land management even for the most badly adjusted lands.

It would be too simple to explain the weakening of these national standards and policies solely by the division of our constitutional system of powers between nation and states. The war brought a reversal of earlier national agricultural policies. Emphasis shifted from restrictive policies, favorable to many conservation practices, to all-out production and to a price policy designed to bring in much formerly submarginal land. The gospel of soil and fertility conservation so strenuously preached during the thirties was drowned out after Pearl Harbor by the evangel of patriotism to which clung seductively the certain prospect of returns beyond anything farmers had experienced since the days of World War I. No wonder that farm plans went by the board as farmer after farmer broke his conservation rotations to reap the golden harvest offered by returning moisture and high guaranteed prices. From this jettisoning of farm planning standards the original SCS policies never recovered.

· · ·

Our federal political system, as it has related to the task of bringing conservation practices to the management of private agricultural lands, has thus not only stimulated the elaboration of a strong bureaucracy but likewise has generated parallel semipublic or private federations of political influence. What persists and gets itself applied in the way of national land resource policies depends in considerable part therefore on the efficiency of these associations, their breadth of membership, their economic and social status, their ability to attach to themselves influential "friends" from other segments of the farm and urban population, and the skill of their leaders. They have had the basic political advantages inherent in the divorce of legal authority from national will as well as those which flow from the contradictions within the national willing process, so much accentuated by checks and balances.

Nor does the different type of organization under the aegis of the Tennessee Valley Authority for similar national purposes within the counties of the seven-state valley tell a tale of greater national policy penetration. Quite the contrary.... There the existing state and county organizations were employed to administer the farm land use program. TVA controls over state and county performance were so gossamer thin that no accurate quantitative summary of conservation achieved by federal expenditure for these national objectives has been possible. Both experiences suggest the insubstantiality of the fear of "federal dictatorship" insofar as private agricultural land management is concerned.

III

SYSTEM AND AREA:
THE POLITICAL REGION

RICHARD HARTSHORNE

The Functional Approach
in Political Geography

ANALYSIS OF THE POLITICAL GEOGRAPHY
OF A STATE: INTERNAL

... The fundamental purpose of any state, as an organization of a section of land and a section of people, as Ratzel first put it, is to bring all the varied territorial parts, the diverse regions of the state-area, into a single organized area.

What does the state attempt to organize, in all regions of the state-area?

In all cases, it attempts to establish complete and exclusive control over internal political relations—in simplest terms, the creation and maintenance of law and order. Local political institutions must conform with the concepts and institutions of the central, overall, political organization.

In many social aspects—class structure, family organization, religion, and education—a state may tolerate considerable variation in its different regions. But because of the significance of these factors to political life, there is a tendency—in some states a very marked effort—to exert unifying control even over these institutions.

In the economic field, every modern state tends to develop some degree of unity of economic organization. At the minimum, it establishes uniform currency, some uniformity in economic institutions, and some degree of control over external economic relations. Beyond that, states of course vary greatly in the degree to which all aspects of production and trade—price and wage levels, etc.—are placed under uniform control.

Finally, and most importantly, because we live in a world in which the continued existence of every state-unit is subject to the threat of destruction

Reproduced by permission from the *Annals* of the Association of American Geographers, Volume 40, No. 2 (1950), 95–130.

by other states, every state must strive to secure the supreme loyalty of the people in all its regions, in competition with any local or provincial loyalties, and in definite opposition to any outside state-unit.

Throughout this statement of the organization of the state-area as a unit, the geographer is primarily concerned with emphasis on regional differences. The state of course is no less concerned to establish unity of control over all classes of population at a single place. In political geography, our interest is in the problem of unification of diverse regions into a single whole; the degree of vertical unification within any horizontal segment concerns us only as a factor aiding or handicapping regional unification.

Parenthetically, we may also note the ways in which this primary function of the state affects the general field of geography. Land-use, industrial development, trade, and a countless list of social aspects of human geography in any region will differ in greater or less degree as a result of the efforts of the state in which it is included to control its development as part of a single whole. Only the peculiarity of geographic study in such a large country as the United States, where we are usually forced to do most of our work within the territory of our single state, has permitted us to study geography as though we could ignore political geography.

Our analysis of the primary function of any state leads directly to the primary problem of political geography. For no state-area constitutes by the nature of its land and people a natural unit for a state, in which one merely needs to create a government which shall proceed to operate it as a unit. The primary and continuing problem of every state is how to bind together more or less separate and diverse areas into an effective whole.

For the political geographer, this presents a wide range of specific problems for analysis. In every state area, larger than such anomalies as Andorra or Liechtenstein, the geographer finds: (1) regions that are more or less separated from each other by physical or human barriers; (2) regions that in greater or lesser degree diverge in their relations with outside states; and (3) regions that differ among themselves in character of population, economic interests, and political attitudes. Let us look briefly at each of these types of problems.

CENTRIFUGAL FORCES

Geographers are familiar with the effect of particular types of physical features in handicapping communication between regions. Semple and others have described for our own early history the political consequences of the forested Appalachians and later of the mountain and desert barrier of the west. Whittlesey's study of the Val d'Aran depicts in detail the problem in that bit of Spain north of the Pyrenees.[1] In most modern states, however, these prob-

---

[1] Derwent Whittlesey, "Trans-Pyrenean Spain: The Val d'Aran," *Scot. Geog. Mag.* (1933), pp. 217–228.

lems have largely been overcome by the development of the telegraph and the railroad. They continue of importance, however, in parts of the Balkans, in the highland states of Latin America, and in China.

Since state-organization requires communication not only from one region to the next, but from a central point to each peripheral region, distance itself is a centrifugal factor. Obviously, distance within a state depends on its size and shape. Size and shape are significant to the state in other, quite different respects, but I suggest we wait until we have determined that in our analysis, rather than attempt to proceed deductively from size and shape to consequences.

Of human barriers, the most common is the absence of humans. Uninhabited or sparsely inhabited areas were, until recently, difficult and dangerous to cross. It was primarily on this account that relatively low mountains, in central Europe or the Appalachians, long functioned as dividing zones. Even in the Alps, the problem of surmounting high elevations was less serious, in the Middle Ages, than the difficulty of securing supplies along the way and the ever-present danger of attack from "robber barons."

Further, the presence of such relatively empty areas created, and still creates, a feeling of separation in the regions on either side. Both on this account and because of distance, oceans continue to function as the strongest separating factors, other than Arctic ice, even though they have long been crossed with relative ease.

France has first inaugurated the interesting experiment of incorporating trans-oceanic areas into the organization of its state. Its West Indian islands and the island of Réunion in the Indian Ocean are now departments of metropolitan France, sending delegates to its national assembly. We may be about to do the same with Hawaii.

Perhaps the most difficult barrier to overcome is separation by a zone populated by a different people, especially an unfriendly people. The Germans have apparently convinced the world that the separation of East Prussia by the Polish Corridor was an experiment that is never to be repeated. (They overlooked the fact that there were not one but two alternatives to that device.)[2]

Serious difficulties may arise for a state, if any of its regions have closer relations with regions of outside states than with those within the state. This is commonly the case where a boundary has been changed so that it now cuts across an area formerly within a single state. The partition of Upper Silesia, in 1922, presented a particularly intense case.[3] But there are many cases, not dependent on boundary changes, in which a region has closer connections, particularly economic connections, with regions of other countries than with regions of its own state. We are familiar with the political importance of this

---

2 Richard Hartshorne, "The Polish Corridor," *Journal of Geography*, XXXVI (1937), 161–176.

3 Hartshorne, "Geographic and Political Boundaries in Upper Silesia," *Annals Assn. Amer. Geogrs.*, XXIII (1933), 195–228.

factor in each of the major regions of Canada, each more closely related in certain respects with the adjacent areas of the United States than with the other regions within the Dominion. In some cases, mutual interdependence among the regions of the state-area is less than the dependence of individual regions on remote, overseas countries. This is a major problem of the Australian Commonwealth, in which each state unit is primarily dependent on separate trade with Great Britain. In Western Australia, this factor, together with notable physical and human separation, has led at times to demand for secession from the Commonwealth. Northeastern Brazil offers a somewhat similar problem for study.

The geographer, however, must beware of drawing conclusions from the physical map, or, on the other hand, of assuming that an economic situation to which we are accustomed represents a "normal" development in economic geography, independent of a particular political framework. Consider southern California, separated by thousands of miles of desert and mountain from the main body of the United States, facing the Pacific highway to densely populated lands of the Orient. And yet which region of the United States is more completely bound into the economy of the country as a whole?

All the previous examples are relatively extreme cases. In most instances, the potentialities are highly flexible. The plain of Alsace, separated from the rest of France by the rugged heights of the Vosges, facing southern Germany across the narrow band of the Rhine flood-plain and easily connected with northern Germany by that navigable river—with which state does it fit in terms of economic geography? Surely the answer must be that in terms of modern technology, all these features are of minor importance, and in terms of economic potentialities of the area, it can be associated almost equally well in either the French or the German economic unit.

Separation of regions by barriers or by divergence of outside connections is commonly less important than the centrifugal forces that result from diversity of character of the population. To secure voluntary acceptance of a single common organization requires some degree of mutual understanding; obviously this is easier in a population homogeneous in character. Further, where regions differ in social character, the tendency of the state to force some degree of uniformity of social life meets with resistance. Thus the very attempt to produce unity may intensify disunity. Hungary, before 1918, was the classic example; since then, Yugoslavia has perhaps been the leader among several successors.

What particular social characteristics may be important depends on the particular state. Everyone thinks of language and religion. I suggest, also, education and standards of living, types of economic attitudes and institutions, attitudes toward class and racial distinctions, and, especially, political philosophy.

For materials on these topics, we look to that branch of geography that has been least developed—social geography. In most cases, what materials we have provide only the raw data, the facts about the distribution of, say, religions or races, rather than the regional differences in social attitudes toward these facts; it is the latter that we need.

Thus, the fact that Alsace was predominantly Roman Catholic, like France but unlike most of Germany, was less important than the fact that its attitude toward the relation of church and state was similar to that in the German Empire of 1871–1918, and was in conflict with the anti-clerical attitude of the French Republic.

Racial differences, in the terms studied by the physical anthropologist, may be of no relevance to our problem. The distribution, percentagewise, in the different countries of Europe, of blondes and brunettes, dolichocephalic versus brachycephalic—what does it matter? These facts have no reflection in social or political attitudes in those countries. Though standard material in most geographies of Europe, I submit that they have no significance to political geography, or for that matter, to geography in general.

In contrast, the United States is a country in which regional differences in attitudes of people toward the racial components of the regional group—as indicated by skin color—are of tremendous importance in social, economic, and political life. We have mapped and studied the underlying differences in racial composition,[4] but we have not studied the phenomenon itself—namely the differences in attitudes. We need a map, a series of maps, portraying different kinds and degrees of Jim Crowism in the United States. These I would rate as a first requirement for an understanding of the internal political geography of the United States, for in no other factor do we find such marked regional cleavages, such disruption to the national unity of our state. For geography in general, in one quarter of our country, these attitudes are fundamental factors in every aspect of the human geography and are significantly related to its physical geography.

Geographers are more familiar with differences in economic interests, since these are more closely bound to the land. But these are seldom seriously disrupting to national unity. It is true that almost every modern state has experienced marked political tension between the divergent interests of highly industrialized regions and those of primarily agricultural areas. But these very differences tend to lead to interlocking, rather than competing, interests. Even when competing, economic differences, Marx to the contrary notwithstanding, are easier to compromise than differences in social and political attitudes.

Furthermore, the state is only in partial degree an economic unit. Since it is basically a political unit, the state necessarily imposes the greatest degree of uniformity in political life. Political attitudes are peculiarly inflexible. If a region is accustomed to one set of political concepts, ideals, and institutions —most especially if its people feel that they have fought in the past to establish those political values—it may be extremely difficult to bring them under

---

4 Hartshorne, "Racial Maps of the United States," *Geog. Rev.*, XXVIII (1938), 267–288.

the common cloak of a quite different system. Even where regions formerly in separate states have voluntarily joined together to form a state, on the basis of common ethnic character—for example, the three Polish areas in 1918 or the Czech and Slovak areas—the marked difference in past political education led to difficult problems.

In times and areas of relatively primitive political development, such factors were no doubt of minor importance. In long-settled areas of relatively mature political development, they may be of first importance. The classic example is, again, Alsace. Thanks particularly to the French Revolution, the people of that province had become strong supporters of political concepts, ideals, and institutions that could not be harmonized within the semi-feudal, authoritarian monarchy of Hohenzollern Germany.

Conversely, one may understand on this basis the negative reaction of the Swiss in 1919 to the proposal that the adjacent Austrian province of Vorarlberg should be added to their state.

CENTRIPETAL FORCES

The preceding discussion of political attitudes points to an essential ingredient that has been lacking in the discussion up to this point. We have been considering a variety of centrifugal factors in the regional geography of a state-area, which make it difficult to bind those regions together into an effective unit. In considering how such difficulties may be overcome, we have not asked whether there was any force working to overcome the difficulties, anything tending to pull these regions together into a state.

This omission, I suggest, has been the single greatest weakness in our thinking in political geography. If we see an area marked clearly on both physical and ethnic maps as suitable for a state, but which for many centuries was not integrated as a state—as in the Spanish peninsula, the Italian peninsula, or the German area—we cudgel our heads to find factors in its internal geography that will explain the failure. We forget that before we speak of failure, we must ask what was attempted.

The Italian peninsula, together with the northern plain attached to the mainland but isolated by the Alps, with a settled population speaking approximately a common tongue since the Middle Ages, has offered one of the most obvious geographic units of Europe for the development of a state. Yet Italy, as an Austrian minister jeered, was only a geographic expression; there was nothing that could be called even the beginnings of a state of Italy. For no one of importance had any idea of producing an Italian state, and, had anyone tried, his purpose would have shattered in conflict with two opposing ideas: one, the concept of the Papal States, the secular control of mid-Italy by the Pope in order to secure his undivided domination of Rome as the spiritual capital of Western Christendom; the other, the concept of a single great empire in the heart of Europe, extending from northern Germany to northern Italy.

Only after the power of these centuries-old ideas had been irrevocably destroyed by the ferment of the French Revolution, was it possible for any Italian leader to consider seriously the unification of Italy.

One of the concepts that prevented integration in Italy is likewise the key to the failure of medieval Germany to develop a unified state, at the time when the kingdoms of France and England were being effectively established. For centuries, the persons holding the title of King of Germany, and whatever opportunity that might give, were far more affected by the higher title of Emperor. Inspired by the grander idea of reincarnating the empire of Rome, they fought to build up a state straddling the Alps, uniting many different peoples. The sacrifices made in the vain attempt to accomplish the greater idea destroyed the possibility of achieving the lesser, when later emperors finally were reduced to considering German unity.

The fact that a country has a name and a government, that an international treaty recognizes its existence as a state and defines its territorial limits—all that does not produce a state. To accomplish that, it is necessary to establish centripetal forces that will bind together the regions of that state, in spite of centrifugal forces that are always present.

THE STATE-IDEA

The basic centripetal force must be some concept or idea justifying the existence of this particular state incorporating these particular regions; the state must have a *raison d'être*—reason for existing.

Although ignored in much of the literature of political geography, this is not a new thought. Ratzel defined the state as a section of land and a section of humanity, organized as a single unit in terms of a particular, distinctive idea.[5] Maull, among other German geographers, has discussed the concept at some length.[6] It was presented to this Association a decade ago.[7]

At the primitive level, Ratzel explained, this idea may be no more than the will of a ruler, to which, for whatever reasons, all the regional parts through their local leaders grant their loyalty. In such a case, as in the empire of Charlemagne or that of Genghis Khan, the state may endure hardly longer than the lifetime of the individual ruler. In the attempt to perpetuate the binding idea of loyalty to a personal ruler, there evolved the concept of hereditary monarchy. Where that succeeded, however, we find there was always something more—politically-minded people in the various parts of the kingdom came to regard the state, for reasons independent of the monarch, as representing something of value to them. Today the monarchical institution is safe only in

5 Friedrich Ratzel, *Politische Geographie* (3rd ed.; Munich and Berlin, 1923), pp. 2–6.

6 O. Maull, *Politische Geographie* (Berlin, 1925), pp. 112–115.

7 Hartshorne, "The Concepts of 'Raison d'Être' and 'Maturity of States,'" (abstract), *Annals Assn. Amer. Geogrs.*, XXX (1940), 59.

those states in which the monarch has exchanged the active power to rule for the passive role of personification of the national heritage.

To be sure, a state in which the original idea has lost its validity will not fall apart at once. The forces of inertia, vested interests, and fear of the consequences of change may keep it going more or less effectively for some time. But inevitably a structure that has lost its original *raison d'être*, without evolving a new one, cannot hope to stand the storms of external strife or internal revolt that sooner or later will attack it. For when that day comes, the state, to survive, must be able to count on the loyalty, even to the death, of the population of all its regions.

It is not mere coincidence that the terms I have been using came to me from a Viennese geographer, in his analysis of the failure of the Hapsburg monarchy. Unless Austria-Hungary, Hassinger wrote after the first World War, had been able to discover and establish a *raison d'être*, a justification for existence, even without the calamity of the war, it could not long have continued to exist.[8]

Those states are strongest, Ratzel had concluded, "in which the political idea of the state fills the entire body of the state, extends to all its parts."[9]

What does this mean for our study of the political geography of a state? It means, I am convinced, that before we can begin to study the problems presented by the centrifugal forces I have previously outlined, we must first discover the motivating centripetal force, the basic political idea of the state. Under what concept, for what purposes, are these particular regions to be bound together into one political unit, absolutely separated from every other political territory?

Does this seem too remote from geography? Too much like political science? The student of geography of climates must understand the nature of air-masses, as analyzed by the meteorologist. We cannot intelligently study the geography of soils until we have grasped the soil scientist's analysis of soil types. In agricultural geography, it is not sufficient, we now know, to study crops and animals; we are concerned with the farm unit of organization of crops from fields, livestock in barns and pasture, all directed toward ultimate production of food for the farmer and products to be sold from his farms. We are not ready to begin the study of farm geography, until we have analyzed the farmer's purpose—the idea under which his piece of land is organized.

Geographers generally know quite a bit about farming, so they may know beforehand what is in the farmer's mind, or perhaps they can infer that from observation of the visible facts—the fields, silo, corncrib, or cow-barn. But to know for certain, you must ask the farmer.

Whom shall we ask concerning the idea of a particular state? Obviously,

---

[8] Hugo Hassinger, in R. Kjellén and K. Haushofer, *Die Grossmächte vor und nach dem Weltkriege* (Berlin and Leipzig, 1930), p. 34.
[9] Ratzel, *op. cit.*, p. 6.

one must go to those who actually operate the state in question. This is not so easy as in the case of the farm or factory. A modern state is an organization operated, in greater or less degree, by all the politically-minded people included in it—ideally its entire adult population.

One might logically suppose that geographers should be able to find the answer to this question in studies in political science. Unfortunately, from our point of view, political scientists seem to have concerned themselves solely with the idea and purpose of the generic state—the purposes, that is, that are common to all states. This ignores the very thing that is of direct concern to the geographer—namely, the idea that is distinct for the particular state in contrast with that of other states, that which makes for significant differences from country to country. Perhaps that means that it is logically a problem for the geographer.

In any case, unless we can find the answer to this fundamental question in the works of other students—perhaps of the historians, if not the political scientists—we are apparently forced to work it out for ourselves. We must discover and establish the unique distinctive idea under which a particular section of area and of humanity is organized into a unit state.

I realize that the problem is remote from the geographer's training and knowledge. But years of stumbling effort have convinced me that there is no circumventing it. Until we can determine for any particular state the idea under which it is organized, we shall have no basis on which to analyze its political geography; we shall not have started on the significant contribution that geography can make to the study of states.

Perhaps we exaggerate the difficulty of the problem because it is unfamiliar. To pin down precisely the particular idea on which any state is based is certainly very difficult, but study of the essential historical documents may enable one to come fairly quickly to a rough statement sufficiently close to the mark to be usable.

Let me give you a case in which one of my advanced graduate students had particular difficulty—the state of Iraq. He finally arrived at something like this: the idea of an Iraqi state sprang from two factors: (1) the recognition by the Great Powers of the strategic and economic significance of the Mesopotamian region, and (2) the need to provide a *pied à terre* for Arab nationalism banished from Syria. On the basis of these two considerations, there was established a territory embracing the settled Arab region of the Tigris-Euphrates plain, together with adjacent but dissimilar regions of mountain and desert tribes, the whole to be developed as a separate Arab state.

You note that the idea of this state was a compound of purposes, and those external: foreign diplomacy and transported nationalist fire. That was the case in 1919. One would need to determine whether the Iraqi have since evolved a truly native concept.

In much older states, we may expect to find that an indigenous *raison d'être* has evolved that may have little or no relation to the original genesis. To determine the distinctive idea of such a state, therefore, we must study the current situation, rather than the remote past. In the well-developed modern state, politically-minded people in all regions of the state-area are conscious of their loyalty to the state, and have some common understanding, even though not clearly phrased, of what that state means to them. In such a case, we may recognize, I think, the existence of a *nation*—as something distinct from the state itself. . . .

THE APPLICATION OF THE STATE-IDEA
IN POLITICAL GEOGRAPHY

Whatever is found to be the *raison d'être*, the underlying idea of the state, it is with this concept, I submit, that the geographer should start in his analysis of the state-area. What use is he then to make of it? His first concern is to determine the area to which the idea applies; then the degree to which it operates in the different regions, and finally the extent of correspondence of those regions to the territory actually included within the state.

On this basis, we may approach the most elementary problem in political geography—namely, that of distinguishing within the legal confines of its territory, those regions that form integral parts of the state-area in terms of its basic idea, and those parts that must be recognized as held under control, in the face of either indifference or of opposition on the part of the regional population.

The vast areas of the subarctic lands, whether in Alaska, Canada, Sweden, or the Soviet Union, sparsely populated by primitive tribes, with a few scattered settlements of civilized peoples, are organized politically as though they were colonies of an outside state, even where there is no break in the extent of territory under the same flag. The same is true of tropical lowland areas, in almost all the Latin American countries. In most of the latter, these essentially unorganized territories constitute over half the total area officially credited to the country.[10]

A more difficult question for definition is raised in examining the areas of long-settled Indian population in the highlands of tropical America—both in Central American states and in the Andes. Are these areas of native languages and culture to be considered as integral parts of states, or are they not still colonial areas subject to outside control, even though the center of control is not in Spain, but in the neighboring districts of Spanish-American culture?

A similar situation may be found in more highly developed countries. Thus during the centuries in which all of Ireland was recognized in international law as part of the United Kingdom, its greater part was certainly operated in fact as a subject area, distinct from the controlling state. Much the same may

---

[10] For more complete discussion, with an attempt to map these areas, see Hartshorne, "The Politico-Geographic Pattern of the World," *Annals Amer. Acad. Polit. Soc. Sci.*, CCXVIII (November 1941), 45 ff.

be true today of certain portions of the Soviet Union, notably the so-called republics of Central Asia—but the difficulty of determining the actual operations of the Soviet government make definite statement impossible. On the other hand, we have in the United States clearcut though tiny relics of internal colonialism in the Indian reservations.

If the idea of the state is based on the recognition of the existence of a nation, then the major geographic question to consider is whether there is close correspondence between that area of the nation and that of the state. Are there regions within the state whose population do not feel themselves part of the nation? Are there regions of the nation that are not included within the state—the issue of irredentism?

It is not easy to measure the area to be included in a particular national group. In many cases, we must approach the question indirectly. If we can determine the essential factors involved in the particular nationality, we may be able to measure the area over which each of these factors exists. On this basis, we may establish certain areas that are clearly included in the given nation, and other areas that adhere in terms of some factors, but not in terms of others.

The entire area over which the nation extends, but in varying degree of intensity, may then be compared with the area presently included in the state. We have thus determined not only the areal correspondence of state and nation, but also the regions in which the national character is partial rather than complete. We shall thereby have presented, in part in map form, the basic factors and relationships involved in the primary problem of political geography—the analysis of the degree to which the diverse regions of the state constitute a unity.

INTERNAL ORGANIZATION

At this point, we reach one other problem for analysis—the relation of the internal territorial organization of the state-area to the regional diversities we have analyzed. Though all the regions of a state are clearly included under the state-idea and have complete loyalty to the overall concepts of the national unit, regional differences inevitably cause some differences in interpretation and implementation of those concepts.

If those differences are relatively minor, as in most of France or, I presume, in Uruguay, the regions may accept unitary government from a single central authority. If the differences are great, the attempt to impose such a uniform system may provoke opposition endangering the national unity. Since such regional differences are important in most countries, but most states attempt to operate under a uniform, centralized government, the number of examples of this type of problem is very large. Spain, at the moment, provides one of the most striking.

Certain states recognize openly the need to permit diverging interpretations of the overall concepts of that state, and hence significant differences in the institutions and law thereunder. This is the system of the federal state, of which Switzerland provides the oldest example, the United States the largest. In both cases, a notable degree of regional heterogeneity is guaranteed by the constitutional division of powers.

In this country, we are at the moment engaged in one of our periodic crises in determining just how much social and political autonomy is to be permitted the regions that are crudely represented by our so-called States. This crisis, incidentally, causes the Congress of the United States to work for the social and political geographer, producing raw material useful to us in measuring differences in intensity of regional attitudes toward the facts of racial composition.

The possible ways of organizing the state-area are not limited to the unitary and the federal systems. The United Kingdom, for example, has evolved in the course of its long history a most complicated system, under which Wales, Scotland, Northern Ireland, the Isle of Man, and the Channel Islands each has a different degree of autonomy adjusted to its particular linguistic, religious, economic, and political geography.

In determining the method of state-organization of a country, the student must study the actual method of government, not merely the words written into a constitution. He will recognize that while the constitution of the Soviet Union grants on paper more independence to its member republics than is true of the individual states of this country, and even though it encourages and exploits a great variety of languages and folk cultures, in every other respect of economic and political life, it operates its vast area of radically different regions as a highly centralized monolithic state.

ANALYSIS OF EXTERNAL FUNCTIONS

In a functional approach to the analysis of the political geography of a state, our first half was concerned with the internal problems of the state-area. The second half is concerned with the external relations of the state-area to the other areas of the world, whether those are also organized as states, controlled by outside states, or unorganized. For convenience, we may group these relations as territorial, economic, political, and strategic.

TERRITORIAL RELATIONS

Under territorial relations, we are of course concerned in the first instance with the degree to which adjacent states are in agreement concerning the extent of territory which each includes. Whether the area in question is large or small, agreement ultimately requires the determination of a precise boundary.

Of all the problems of international relations, those concerning the allocation of territories and hence the determination of boundaries are the most obviously geographic. . . .

If we start with what we are studying—the state-areas—we can recognize the essential function of the boundary from its name: it is that line which is to be accepted by all concerned as *bounding* the area in which everything is under the jurisdiction of one state, as against areas under different jurisdiction. (Consideration of the functions of a boundary zone, as an element of military defense, for example, is a separate question to be considered elsewhere.)

The first thing to know about an international boundary, therefore, is the degree to which it is accepted by all the parties concerned—i.e., the adjacent states and the population whose statehood is determined by the location of the boundary.

Consider the following cases of international boundaries: the boundary between Great Britain and France (including the Channel Islands with Great Britain); that between France and Spain; that between Switzerland and Italy (including the Ticino boundary that reaches far down the Alpine slopes almost to the Po Plain); and, finally, the boundary between the United States and Mexico both east and west of El Paso. These run through radically different types of physical zones. Some correspond closely with ethnic divisions, others do not. But from the point of view of the primary function of an international boundary, all are in the same category, namely that of boundaries completely accepted as final by the states themselves and the people of the border areas.

In a different category is the Franco-German boundary (considered as of 1930). Though this was fully accepted by France and officially so by Germany in the Treaty of Locarno, one could not assume that the German leaders intended that acceptance to be final, and by imprisoning some of the local leaders in Alsace, the French government demonstrated its lack of faith in the complete acceptance by the Alsatian people of their inclusion in the French state.

Still different is the case of the German-Polish boundary of the inter-war period, which neither state accepted as more than a temporary division of territory claimed by both sides.

Where boundaries run through primitive, essentially colonial, regions which at present have very slight productive value, but offer possibilities for future importance, we may need to recognize a different set of categories. Thus we may find cases in which for a time the states concerned, while not committing themselves to an ultimate boundary, raise no question concerning the line lost in the wilderness, but may at any moment challenge, with the force of arms, the line that had apparently been accepted. . . .[11]

---

[11] Dr. Robert S. Platt, "Conflicting Territorial Claims in the Upper Amazon," *Geographic Aspects of International Problems,* C.C. Colby, ed. (Chicago: University of Chicago Press, 1938), pp. 243–278.

The second question concerning any international boundary (whether or not it is fully accepted) is the degree to which its bounding function is maintained by the bordering states; the degree, that is, to which all movements of goods and persons across the line are effectively controlled by the boundary officials. In examining that, the geographer will of course observe the ways in which the control is made easier or more difficult by the character of the zone through which the boundary line is drawn.

A special aspect of boundary problems emerges where the territory of a state reaches to the sea. Though open to use by all, the seas are in fact little used by anyone. Hence, it is sufficient for most purposes to define the boundary simply as following the coast, as most treaties do. But for certain purposes, notably fishing, border control, and naval warfare, the exact determination of the line in the waters may be critical. There is no overall agreement in international law, either as to the width of territorial waters—the zone of sea included as part of the possession of the bordering state—or as to the manner in which the off-shore line bounding those waters follows the indentations of the coast. . . .

The use of territorial waters by merchant ships of a foreign state, commonly for the purpose of entering the ports of the country concerned, represents the most common occurrence of use of territory of one state for the purposes of another state. In this case, the purpose is mutual. In other, more special cases, problems arise from the desire or need of the people of one state to utilize the territory of a foreign country in order to have access to still other countries, or in some cases to a different part of their own state. Both Canada and the United States have permitted the construction of railroads across portions of their territories, whose major purpose was to connect regions of the other country—e.g., the Michigan Central across Ontario from Detroit to Buffalo, or the Canadian Pacific across the State of Maine from Montreal to St. John, New Brunswick. European countries commonly will not tolerate foreign railroads across their territories, but the Polish railroads in the interwar period operated, for Germany, through trains between East Prussia and the main part of Germany.

Nearly all states recognize the need of providing transit service for trade across their territories between states on either side, though this involves a multiplicity of minor problems of control. Most important are provisions for transit from an inland state to the seacoast, in order to have access to the countries of the world accessible by sea routes. The Grand Trunk Railroad of Canada, now a part of the Canadian National Railways, not only crosses New Hampshire and Maine to reach the sea, but, when the winter ice closes the St. Lawrence, uses the harbor of Portland, Maine, as its port of shipment for foreign trade of interior Canada, which constitutes most of the total traffic of that American port. In certain European cases more specific arrangements seem necessary: a section of a port, as at Trieste or Hamburg, may be allocated exclusively to handle the transit trade of a foreign country.

ECONOMIC RELATIONS

... In the analysis of a state-area, the need to consider its economic relations with outside areas arises from the fact that in many respects, a state operates, must operate, as a unit economy in relation with other unit economies in the world. The difficulties arise because, while it must operate completely as a political unit, a state-area operates only partially as an economic unit.

The first problem is to determine to what extent the economy of one state-area is dependent on that of others, though the mere analysis of self-sufficiency is only a beginning. If one says that the United States produces a surplus of coal and iron, but is dependent on foreign countries for much of its supply of tin, nickel, and manganese, of sugar and rubber—such a statement, even in precise percentage figures, tells us directly little of importance. If a country has plenty of coal and iron, it can normally secure the other metals mentioned from wherever in the world they are produced. Under abnormal conditions of war, or threat of war, it is essential to know that the manganese normally comes from the Transcaucasus in the Soviet Union, the tin from British Malaya (but can be obtained from Bolivia), whereas the nickel comes from adjacent Canada. Natural rubber supplies are available in adequate amounts only in one remote region—Malaya-East Indies—but nearby Cuba can supply most of our sugar needs.

In general, the geographer will analyze the economic dependence of one state-area in terms of the specific countries concerned, and their location and political association in relation to the state he is studying.

Since all sound trading is of mutual advantage to both parties, to say that one state is economically dependent on any other necessarily implies also the converse. But the degree to which any particular commodity trade, shipping service, or investment is critically important varies in terms of the total economy of each of the two states concerned. It is only in this sense that the common question, "Is a particular state economically viable?" has any validity, since every state above the most primitive level is in some respects critically dependent on others.

The problem is far from simple, but perhaps we can suggest two generalizations. As between two countries that differ greatly in the size of their total national economy, the economic relationships between them are more critically important for the lesser country (though this might not be true under war conditions). This is true because these economic relationships, which may be taken as equalized through international balance of payments, will form a larger proportion of the total economy of the lesser state. An obvious example is found in the relation of Eire to Great Britain, of Cuba to the United States.

The second generalization rests on the fact that the critical significance of the trade depends on the possibility of alternatives, of finding other sources for needed supplies or other markets for products which must be sold to maintain the national economy. Most popular discussions tend to think only of the former, whereas under the capitalist profit-system under which most international trade operates, it is the latter that is more significant. The reason for this is that for most commodities of world production, there are alternate sources of supply at moderate increase in cost; there may not be alternative markets even at greatly reduced selling prices.

Finally, we may note that relatively few areas of the world now produce a surplus of manufactured goods requiring a high degree of technological development, and these constitute therefore a relatively limited market for the surplus of primary products of farm, forest, and mine, which can be produced widely over the world. Consequently, the countries producing primary products, even the very necessities of life, may find it more difficult to find alternative markets for their products than the industrial countries producing articles less essential to life. With wider spread of industrialization over the world, this situation would of course be altered, conceivably reversed.

It should not be assumed, however, that these rough generalizations will provide the answer in any given case. Consider the problem posed by the independence of Austria after the dissolution of the Hapsburg empire—a problem which Austria still faces. To survive as a viable economic unit, Austria needed to maintain with the adjacent regions, re-organized as independent states, a high degree of economic relationship. Its position in competition with otherwise more favored regions of industrial Europe made it peculiarly dependent on markets immediately to the east. For these eastern neighbors, such relationships were also necessary for the maximum economic progress, but were not vitally necessary to economic life. If, for political reasons, and to develop their own industries at greater cost, they preferred not to trade freely with Austria, they had the choice of the less profitable plan, whereas for Austria the alternative was economic collapse.

In the nineteenth century, international economic relations, though both supported and retarded by state action, were generally operated as the private business of individuals and corporations. With the depression of the 1930's, the rise of totalitarian states, and the last war, there has been an increasing tendency for the state itself to direct the operations of international trade and investment. In these respects, states function increasingly as economic units, so that the economic relations among them become increasingly important in the politico-geographic analysis of the state.

POLITICAL RELATIONS

The most obvious form of political relation of a state to any outside territory is that of effective political control—as a colony, possession, dependency, or "protectorate." Commonly, we recognize only a small number of states as colonial, or imperial, powers: eight or nine in western Europe, together with the United States, Japan, Australia, and New Zealand (the latter two functioning in islands of the Southwest Pacific). Germany was eliminated from the list by the First World War, Japan by the Second. If, however, we recognize the colonial reality of areas adjacent to a state and legally included in its territory, but actually not forming an integral part of that state (as discussed earlier in this paper), the list is far longer—including Canada, Norway, Sweden, the Soviet Union, China, the Union of South Africa, and most of the Latin American states. A new-comer to this list is the Indonesian Republic, with large territories subject to it, in the primitive areas of Borneo, Celebes, etc.

The legal forms of colonial relationship vary widely—even within a single empire, such as that of Great Britain. Further, these legal forms may or may not express the reality of the relationship, the degrees to which political organization is imposed and operated by the outside state. It is the latter, I presume, that is our concern in political geography.

One characteristic of colonial areas that is of particular concern from our present point of view is the degree to which the governmental system of the home state is extended over the colonial territory. France is in the process of fully incorporating certain formerly colonial areas into metropolitan France, but others only partially. Many imperial powers have always extended their legal systems into colonial areas, so far as citizens from the home country are concerned, so that within any colonial area there may be an overlapping of two authorities—one having jurisdiction over citizens of the home state, the other over native people.

Many countries recognized by treaty as independent states, and functioning in large degree as such, are nonetheless under some particular degree of political control by an outside power. This may be limited to utilization of small fractions of the territory of one state by the government, usually the armed services, of the other—e.g., Great Britain in military control of the Canal Zone of Egypt, the United States Navy at Guantanamo Bay. The most important, relatively, is the American control, for essentially an indefinite period, of the Panama Canal Zone, across the most populous part of the Republic of Panama. In other cases, the outside country may control directly no part of the territory, but rather exercise limited control, as through an adviser, over major aspects of government, especially foreign relations, customs, or the national budget. The United States has in the past exercized such control for limited periods over small states in the Caribbean area; a group of outside powers for years operated the tariff customs of China to raise money to pay the Chinese foreign debts. The clearest case of political domination of supposedly independent states by an outside state today is found in the obvious control by the Soviet Union over the internal policies as well as foreign policy of the "satellite" states on its west, from Poland to Bulgaria, even though this relationship is expressed in no formal treaties.

Generally speaking, recognition of independent sovereignty of a state by the other states of the world presumes that that state will maintain similar political relations with all friendly states, will not be bound by special political associations with any particular states. Numerous exceptions, however, are widely recognized. Thus the dominions of the British Commonwealth are recognized as having emerged from colonial to independent status, even though they continue to be held together in continuously voluntary confederation with the United Kingdom, extending to one another numerous political and economic privileges not extended to other states. Likewise outside states have long recognized the special political concern of the United States for the Latin American republics, a concern now finally expressed in treaty as a mutual policy of association.

Likewise they have recognized the longstanding political interest of the United States in the Negro state of Liberia. The recent North Atlantic Pact, though intended primarily for military purposes, contains political clauses which, if implemented, would tend to create a special political association of the United States, Canada, and the states of western Europe.

Finally, of course, nearly all the states of the world have accepted certain political commitments in joining the United Nations; insofar as this applies to all states, such commitments are universal, rather than geographically distinctive. . . .

JEAN GOTTMANN

The Political Partitioning of Our World: An Attempt at Analysis

Our political world is a limited one: it extends only over the space accessible to men. Accessibility is the determining factor: areas to which men have no access do not have any political standing or problems. The sovereignty of the moon has no importance whatsoever today, because men cannot reach it nor obtain anything from it. The Antarctic had no political standing before navigators began going there, but since it was made accessible by its discoverers, the icy continent has been divided into portions like an apple pie—and all these portions are distinct political compartments in which a number of international incidents have occurred. When the first explorers land on the moon, the earth's satellite will pass from the field of astronomy to the geography textbooks and lunar political problems will appear and grow steadily. As, with improved techniques, men got within their reach the riches of the ocean's depths beyond territorial waters, the sovereignty and legislation of these abysmal spaces became a matter of concern for political authorities; new partitions were legally established deep in the sea and in the ground beneath it.

Partitioning thus results from accessibility; all the vast globe was partitioned as it was discovered and mapped. The political units or territories, as they emerged, acquired a "position in space" which became and remained a major characteristic of each unit. A position is not a simple thing, easily describable. The latitude and longitude of the points forming a territory provide a mathematical means of placing it on a map; these coordinates also indicate the relation of a position to the equator, the poles, the meridian zero of Greenwich or Paris, according to the mapmaker's choice. But there are a great many other relations, definable according to other systems of coordinates, that

From *World Politics*, Vol. IV, No. 4 (1952), 512–519. Reprinted by permission.

describe a position in space. These relations are sometimes determined by physical features, such as seacoasts, rivers, and mountains. All these features are important chiefly as they influence the accessibility of the position.

Much more numerous are the features of a position which result from the choices made by its inhabitants as to the relations they want to maintain with the outside; and some features also result from the attitudes of the peoples outside toward that particular territory and the local inhabitants. The system of relations is highly complicated because *every position in our partitioned space can be termed unique*. This means that no one position has much chance of having a network of relations with the outside similar to the network of relations of another position. There could not be two positions exactly alike. There is a simple mathematical reason for this: given one point or area in a limited space of definite shape, is there another point or area the relations of which to other points of the space considered would be similar to the system of relations of the first chosen point or area? The answer depends on the uniformity of the space considered and on the elements of symmetry with which it is endowed. When the elements of symmetry are few and the elements differentiating that space many, as is the case for our earth, the probability of finding two similar positions appears practically negligible.[1]

The uniqueness of its territory's position provides each country with a unique historical background. We have arrived at this statement by simple deduction, starting from the existence of a differentiated and partitioned space available to mankind. It is the people and not the territory of a country who establish the network of outside relations, who choose among the diverse facilities offered by physical conditions the way that they intend to follow. It is the people also who record the past and choose the form in which this historical background is conveyed to growing generations. The uniqueness of a "geographical position" is indeed essentially a political product, which means a work of man—all the more so as it is the accessibility of space to man which causes its political partitioning and makes of it organized, differentiated space.

Relations between one compartment of this space and the others cannot exist unless there is movement across the limits of the territory considered. We have already noted in [an] earlier article ("Geography and International Relations") the decisive importance of traffic, trade, transportation, and all the different exchanges existing between countries to an understanding of how closely geography and international relations are intertwined. The extent of accessibility is determined by an analysis of the existing status of traffic, communications, transportation, and trade. The French language describes this set of movements across space by the very useful word *circulation*—which is without an actual equivalent in English. It encompasses all the variety, the

---

[1] We are indebted to Professor Paul Montel of the Sorbonne and to Dr. Maurice Levy of the Institute for Advanced Study for discussing this point with us.

complexity, and the fluidity of the exchanges developing throughout the world. "Movement" seems too vague and general to cover the flow of people, armies, material goods, capital, messages, and ideas across the space open to men's activities, in all directions and for all purposes. For the sake of brevity and for lack of a better word in English, let us use the expression "movement factor" to describe all these processes. It is as a major influence in shaping the value of a position and the external relations of an area that the concept is necessary to the purpose of this paper.

Analysis of the movement factor as it applies to a position, whether point or area, helps us to understand easily the motives and imperatives of the policies and political problems focused on or emanating from that position. Movement, however, makes for fluidity and change. The life of relations between the various political units in the world produces constant changes in each of them: the briefest glance at history demonstrates how migration, travel, trade relations, evolution of transportation techniques, cultural relations, and so forth, have constantly brought about changes inside the countries participating in them. These changes inevitably create fluidity and instability in the comparative standing of these countries in terms of power, wealth, and resources. We understand better, therefore, why international relations have been in a state of turmoil throughout history.

If the movement factor has made for change and instability, it has always encountered an established order as well, favoring a certain pattern of flow and resisting change. What lies at the foundation of such resistance? Economic vested interests? That would be difficult to demonstrate: no actual economic interest can be proved theoretically to be developed to its full, ideal optimum. Even if such a marvel were achieved somewhere, it could not last, for the evolution of technique, financing, and politics would continue elsewhere in the world. An economic optimum is a relative situation, evolving with the flow of time and movement on earth.

An established order, however, normally has a tendency to defend itself, insofar as it is a structure within which those at the upper levels are afraid change may bring them to a different, less enjoyable level. Moreover, any social and political structure has some abstract values to preserve: those on which it is founded. Few political regimes have ever remained based on sheer force. Force may have often been used at critical moments—and with variable success —but it was always in the name and for the sake of some principle, however hypocritical it may have seemed at times.

The abstract strength of an existing order is rooted in the spirit of the nations involved. "Spirit" is another difficult notion, the use of which may appear rather unscientific. What it signifies here is a psychological attitude resulting from a combination of actual events with beliefs deeply rooted in the people's mind. In our previous article we used the word "iconography" to describe the whole system of symbols in which a people believes. These symbols are many and varied. A national "iconography" in our sense encompasses the national flag, the proud memories of past history as well as the principles of the prevailing religion, the generally accepted rules of economics, the established social hierarchy, the heroes quoted in the schools, the classic authors, and so forth and so on. A national iconography usually stops at a boundary; the frontier line is in grave danger when such is not the case. For any group of people, the iconography is the common cherished heritage. It is a powerful factor and it fights for stability and resists change, except for short periods in every nation's life when claims for change—i.e., for expansion—are raised, supported by a special interpretation of the iconography.

We have now brought to the fore two main factors or groups of factors— movement and iconography—which oppose one another in the play of forces constantly shaping and reshaping the political map. The importance of both these factors was stressed a year ago in our article on geography and international relations. Subsequent study has been devoted to a search for the ways and means by which these two factors combine themselves in order to bring about the political partitioning of space.[2]

It seemed to us worth while to go back far enough into the past to attempt an analysis of this play of forces at a time when partitioning was even less clear and politics more primitive than they have grown to be. Some studies by specialists of pre-history interested in the early establishment of routes of traffic provided us with an invaluable lead. It appears that early man liked to travel a great deal, but that he was afraid of leaving behind him a track which could be followed. To camouflage his itinerary and still be able to find his way back, he usually followed the paths of migrant animals. In every case, he would choose, of course, the path of those animals with which he was most familiar. But grave danger threatened him—or so at least he thought—at the intersection of his track with any other followed by animals or men with which he was less familiar. The crossroad seems to have been one of the earliest and perhaps one of the most permanent fears of mankind. For it is alarming for anyone who knows his own weakness to contemplate whom he might be meeting at the next crossroad—friend or foe, weaker or stronger than he.

At every crossroad the traveler still feels some need of protection. The modern motorist gets such protection from the red and green lights and the number of signs and regulations controlling traffic at intersections. But a long time elapsed before such a traffic system was devised. It does not yet exist, in fact, on the larger part of the earth's surface.

In almost all countries settled for a long time, it is customary to find monuments at the crossroads. Often these are religious in nature: chapels, or simply

---

[2] These problems have been studied at greater length in Jean Gottmann, *La politique des états et leur géographie* (Paris: Armand Colin, 1952). For the study of prehistoric routes, we are much indebted to the materials supplied by Professor A. Varagnac of Paris.

monumental crosses, are still frequently placed at the crossroads of Europe and Latin America; in Moslem countries, it is often the grave of a holy man, a Marabout, or even a stone endowed with religious significance. White and black stones in particular seem to have had an important significance for early man, and they have often been set up at places of meeting chosen for their accessibility. The Kaaba at Mecca is a huge black stone; and Mecca was an important center of caravan trade before Mohammed. The French pilgrimage center of Le Puy on the central plateau of France still has enframed inside the main stairway leading to the basilica a piece of stone known as the "Stone of Fevers," which popular belief has endowed with special curative powers. This stone is thought to have been there since prehistoric times. The region of Le Puy was apparently one of the main hubs of the trade routes through Central France in early times.

One could cite a great many examples of close association between the distribution of religious monuments and the early geography of trade and transportation. It is easy to understand why early travelers wished for a higher spiritual authority to protect them against their own fears and sometimes against the real possibility of danger at the crossroads. When political authority began to rise, one of its earliest and most imperative functions was to insure order along the main arteries of traffic. That so many castles were built in positions dominating navigable rivers, narrow passes in the mountains, or maritime straits was not only a matter of military strategy but also a means of controlling important routes of passage. The lord—and sometimes he was a bishop—would maintain order and insure safe travel and at the same time collect a fee or toll from the passing merchants. The more historians study the economics of past centuries, the more they perceive the growth of the complicated network of tollhouses and monopoly regulations which have formed the backbone of the political organization of the spaces considered.

Thus, from the black stones, and later the crosses erected at the crossroads, to the highway policeman in white gloves directing traffic at an intersection, we find an unbroken thread woven through the history of practically every region of the world which shows how the movement factor and the local iconography combined to support the establishment of political authority over a certain area.

The fluidity of the political map shaped with the help of such complicated and varied forces may be easier to understand once a method of analysis is applied which follows these two determinant leads: what we have called the movement factor and the iconography. The geographer ought to add in conclusion that such an approach to the study of the forces and ways of evolution of political partitioning in the world need no longer be based heavily on the physical obstacles that nature has put in man's path. Physical geography has not worked only for division. The vast oceanic spaces which seem to break the continuity of land masses may well have provided the realm where man

traveled and mixed the most easily and freely. The development of the traditions of freedom seems to have been associated with sea trade in a great many
ways in history.

The real partitions, those which are the most stable and the least flexible,
are in the minds of men. The worst barriers stem from the diversity of the
historical past. This field of national psychologies is one of the most difficult
and most delicate to study; that is probably why scholars of all kinds have tried
so hard to go around it. An understanding of how iconography and movement
combine to shape political authority and limit it in space may perhaps help
in the further analysis of the world's partitioning.

STEPHEN B. JONES

A Unified Field Theory
of Political Geography

... [The] unified field theory of political geography ... simply states that "idea" and "state" are two ends of a chain. The hyphen with which Hartshorne connects them represents the three other links of the chain. One of the links is Gottmann's circulation, which I shall call movement.

The chain is as follows: Political Idea—Decision—Movement—Field—Political Area. This "chain" should be visualized as a chain of lakes or basins, not an iron chain of separate links. The basins interconnect at one level, so that whatever enters one will spread to all the others.

Political idea, in this sequence, means more than just the state-idea. It means any political idea. It might be the idea of the state or it might be the idea of a speed limit on a country road. It might merely be a gregarious instinct, not consciously expressed. "War begins in the minds of men" and so does all other politics. But there are many political ideas that never reach the state of action. They die aborning, remain in the realm of pure thought, or are rejected by the powers-that-be. A favorable decision is a necessary prerequisite to action. A formal, parliamentary decision is not necessarily meant. Much current research in political science is focussed on the informal or unconscious aspects of the idea-decision end of the chain, through studies of political behavior. Though most of the fishermen in the basins of idea and decision are political scientists, Gottmann and Hartshorne, both geographers, enter them when they speak of iconography and the idea of state.

Both political scientists and geographers have studied the phenomena at the other end of the chain—political areas. This term is used very inclusively

Reproduced by permission from the *Annals* of the Association of American Geographers, Volume 44, No. 2 (1954), 111–123.

to mean any politically organized area, whether a national state, a dependent area, a subdivision of a state, or an administrative region or district. It includes all three categories of areas listed by Fesler:[1] general governmental areas, special or limited-purpose governmental areas, and field service areas. The one common characteristic of all political areas is that they have recognized limits, though not necessarily linear or permanent. An administrative center within the area is common, but not universal.

Movement, I have said, is essentially Gottmann's circulation. What new twist it is given comes from placing it in a chain of concepts relating it to decisions. Every political decision involves movement in one way or another. There may be exceptions, but I have been unable to think of any. Some decisions create movement, some change it, some restrict it. Some create a new kind of movement to replace or to control the old. The movement may not involve great numbers of men or great quantities of matter—it may consist only of radio waves—but usually persons and things move as a result of political decisions. These politically-induced movements may be thought of as "circulation fields." The movements of state highway patrolmen produce a field, shipments of military-aid materials produce a field, the despatch and delivery of farm-subsidy checks produce a field.

A concrete example may clarify the thought behind this chain of terms. National prohibition had a long history as an idea. The Eighteenth Amendment and the Volstead Act were the final decisions that took national prohibition from the realm of ideas to that of action, though, to be sure, many smaller decisions had preceded these or were necessary later to implement them. The prompt effect of the Volstead Act was to inaugurate sweeping changes in movement. Legal shipment of liquor ceased, raw materials no longer flowed to distilleries, illicit movements were organized along new lines, enforcement officers were patrolling and prowling. The fields of these movements were not of uniform density, nor did they exactly coincide with the boundaries of the United States. City slums and Appalachian valleys became centers of activity. Zones near the international frontiers were heavily policed. Enforcement reached twelve miles to sea. The effect on movement was felt overseas. No change in national territory resulted, but new administrative areas were set up. Had the law remained and been rigidly enforced, it is conceivable that our concept of the marginal sea might have changed, as later it was changed by the expanding field of activity of oil exploration. An earlier and more successful attempt at compulsory reform—the suppression of the slave trade—produced a field of enforcement on the high seas and led to the establishment of colonial areas in West Africa. Similarly, the idea-to-area chain is beautifully illustrated by the founding of Liberia.

In the case of prohibition, the existence of the political area of the United States gave general shape to the major fields produced by the Volstead Act, for obvious reasons. A political area in being is a condition of political ideas,

---

[1] James W. Fesler, *Area and Administration* (University, Alabama, 1949), p. 6.

decisions, and movements. Our linked basins, I have said, lie at one level. Add something to one, and it spreads to others. There is a general distinction, however, between flow from idea towards area and in the reverse direction. The former is essentially a process of controlling or creating. The prohibition law controlled some movements and created others. The idea of colonizing free Negroes created a migration to Liberia. The reverse spread is more correctly described as conditioning. The existence of a political area, field, movement, or decision conditions what may take place in the basins lying idea-ward.

Eric Fischer's paper, "On Boundaries," is full of good examples of such conditioning.[2] Benjamin Thomas has shown how the political area of Idaho, created upon a flimsy and essentially negative idea in the first place, conditioned further political thoughts and decisions until the present Idaho-idea is as firm as any.[3]

The essential characteristic of a field, in physics, is not movement, but spatial variation in force. The gravitational field exists even when no apples fall. Since we are not bound to a physical analogy, this distinction need not greatly concern us. However, it may sometime be important to keep in mind that movements and fields are not necessarily identical. A higher percentage of Democrats goes to the polls where the party is neck-and-neck with the Republicans than where the party is overwhelmingly strong. Movement to polls creates a field, but it is not identical with the field of party power.

In a recent publication,[4] Karl Deutsch has suggested a "field" approach to the study of political community. "According to this view, every individual is conceived as a point in a field consisting of his communications or other interactions with all other individuals." Deutsch suggests that this concept may be applied to both small and large "clusters," including families, villages, towns, countries, regions, peoples, nations, and federations. Some clusters are political areas, some are geographical but not political areas, others, like families and peoples, are not necessarily found in definable areas. Thus Deutsch's "interaction field" may be the general case of which the present writer's concept may be the politico-geographical subtype. On later pages of the same publication,[5] Deutsch gives fourteen tests of integration and a check-list of thirty-two possible indicators of social or political community, which should prove of value to the geographer as well as the political scientist.

A field exists in time as well as in space. Applying the ideas of Whittlesey,[6] we may say it has a time dimension as well as space dimensions and that the

---

2 Eric Fischer, "On Boundaries," *World Politics*, I (January 1949), 169–222. The final paragraph on page 197 is a good description of the conditioning process.

3 Benjamin E. Thomas, "Boundaries and Internal Problems of Idaho," *The Geog. Rev.*, XXXIX (January 1949), 99–109.

4 Karl W. Deutsch, *Political Community at the International Level: Problems of Definition and Measurement*, Organizational Behavior Section, Foreign Policy Analysis Project, Foreign Policy Analysis Series No. 2, Princeton University (September 1953), pp. 30–31.

5 Deutsch, *op. cit.*, pp. 37–62 and 70–71.

6 D. Whittlesey, "The Horizon of Geography," *Annals Assn. Amer. Geogrs.*, XXXV (March 1945), 1–36.

time dimension has three derivatives: velocity, pace, and timing. Highway patrols produce a field, as was mentioned above, but obviously it is important for both law-breaker and law-enforcer to know when the patrolmen operate as well as where. The effective scheduling of their patrol is a problem in timing. The whole of traffic and of traffic regulation can be considered a space-time field. Warfare and traffic are alike in this respect as in some others.

APPLICATION TO POLITICAL AREAS

Application of this theory to a case of one new national state is fairly simple: zionism is the idea, the Balfour Declaration the conspicuous decision, permitting migration and other movements. A field of settlement, governmental activity, and war leads to the state of Israel. Such telegraphic brevity oversimplifies history, but the theory seems to fit. For a state with a longer and more complicated evolution, history could not be so readily compressed. The theory provides a path between geographical and political study, but not necessarily a shortcut. It does not reduce political geography to five easy steps. It does not permit world politics to be shown on a chart in five columns headed "idea," "decision," and so forth. It may, however, provide some intellectual clarification and it may prove a handy way of working back and forth among historical, political, and geographical ideas and data.

Karl Deutsch has recognized eight uniformities in the growth of nations from other political forms of organization.[7] Five of these are clearly "field" phenomena: the change from subsistence to exchange economy, the growth of core areas, towns, and communication grids, and the concentration of capital and its effect on other areas. The seventh and eighth are "iconographical," but have "field" connotations: the growth of ethnic awareness and its relation to national symbols and to political compulsion. The sixth item, the rise of individual self-awareness, is more difficult to relate directly to a field though decisions made in a framework of an increasingly individualistic philosophy would lead to changes in established fields. In short, the process of national integration, whether looked at by geographers, like Hartshorne or Gottmann, or by a political scientist, like Deutsch, can be interpreted as a process of changing fields. Conceivably the outlines of the political area may not change. The former colony of Burma is perhaps en route to becoming a true national state without change of boundaries or capital, but a study of the political fields would show changes.

One virtue of the field theory is that it is not confined to politically organized areas. It is applicable without difficulty to an unorganized area like the Mediterranean, which is undoubtedly a political field. As William Reitzel showed, decisions may affect the Mediterranean as a whole and may create or control movement over the entire sea.[8] The ideas may vary: Mussolini's dream

---

[7] Deutsch, "The Growth of Nations: Some Recurrent Patterns of Political and Social Integration," *World Pol.,* V (January 1953), 168–195.

[8] W. Reitzel, *The Mediterranean: Its Role in America's Foreign Policy* (New York, 1948).

of a new Roman empire, Britain's concern with sea command, the American strategy of the containment of communism. Reitzel showed how American policy in the Mediterranean evolved as the cumulative result of small decisions taken first with the idea of winning specific military campaigns. These decisions, and the successful military movements that resulted, involved the United States in political and economic administration. The Soviet Union replaced the Axis as the rival Mediterranean power, Britain slumped down the power scale, and the United States found itself deeply embedded in Mediterranean politics. The Truman Doctrine of support to Greece and Turkey was an outcome, indicating the unity of the Mediterranean sea-power field. The accumulation of decisions created a field, the sea conditioned it.

In the case of administrative areas, a political area may arise from a decision with little or possibly no intervening movement. A new governmental agency may lay out its field service areas before it actually engages in any actions. In some cases, analysis will show that these field service areas reflect pre-existing fields, such as the areas used by other branches of government or known fields of economic activity, and in many cases existing boundaries will be followed. It is possible, however, that an administrative area might spring directly from a decision and reflect no existing field. TVA may be an example unless we say a field had been created by river boatmen, hillside farmers, hydrographic surveyors, and so forth. This seems far-fetched; rather it seems that the Tennessee Valley was proclaimed a political area and that a field of activity resulted. It should be noted, however, that the field spread beyond the limits of the drainage basin, once electricity began to circulate.

There is nothing deterministic about the idea-area chain. A given idea might lead to a variety of areas. Pelzer's study of Micronesia under four rulers demonstrates this point.[9] Although the area ruled was not identical in all four eras, it was basically the same. The number of possible uses for these small islands was limited. Nevertheless, the four rulers—Spain, Germany, Japan, and the United States—made different choices. Their fields were different in kind and intensity. If one insists (which the dictionary does not) that a theory must be able to predict specific behavior, then the field theory may not deserve its name.[10] With no theory whatsoever, a well-informed person with some map-sense could have predicted many American problems and decisions in Micronesia. As a guide to study, however, the field theory is applicable to such cases.

STUDIES OF NATIONAL POWER

Studies of national power may also be fitted into the field theory. Lasswell and Kaplan define power as "participation in the making of decisions."[11] If power

---

[9] Karl J. Pelzer, "Micronesia—A Changing Frontier," *World Pol.,* II (January 1950), 251–266.

[10] The definition of "theory" most appropriate to the present paper is: "The analysis of a set of facts in their ideal relations to one another," *Webster's Collegiate Dictionary,* 5th ed., 1947.

[11] Harold D. Lasswell and Abraham Kaplan, *Power and Society: A Framework for Political Inquiry* (New Haven, 1950), p. 75.

is participation in the making of decisions, if power is necessary before an idea can produce movement, then we can easily fit power into our theory. Hartshorne distinguished between political geography and the study of power.[12] He felt a geographer might sometimes tackle the question of "how strong is a state?" if no one else had done so, but that in so doing he was "migrating into a field whose core and purpose is not geography, but military and political strategy." That power is linked with decision supports Hartshorne, to the extent that geography has been more closely associated with the other end of the chain, but our aim is to pull political science and geography together, not to separate them. If power is more concentrated in the basin of decision, it is by no means absent in the others.

BOUNDARIES, CAPITALS, CITIES

The unified field theory fits boundary studies into the general pattern of political geography. A boundary is of course a line between two political areas, but it is also a line in a region, as was emphasized in Hartshorne's Upper Silesia study and in the present writer's books.[13] The boundary region is truly a field in which the line between the political areas conditions much of the circulation.[14] A boundary field may even be or become a political area as in the case of buffer states and frontier provinces.

Studies of capital cities also may be expressed in field-theory terms. Cornish listed the crossways, the stronghold, the storehouse, and the forward headquarters as characteristic situations for capital cities.[15] To these Spate added the cultural head-link.[16] There are other possibilities, such as compromise sites and geometric centrality. All of these words have meaning in terms of movement and field. The idea of, or need for, central administration leads to a decision on the site of the capital. The choice is conditioned by the field and in turn distorts or recreates the field. Once the capital is chosen and the field about it established, many further decisions and movements are conditioned, leading in most cases to the creation of a primate city much larger than any other in the country.[17]

Not only capitals, but other cities, may be brought into the scope of the theory. In Gottmann's terminology, many of the problems of a growing city

---

12 Hartshorne, "The Functional Approach in Political Geography," *Annals Assn. Amer. Geogrs.*, XL (June 1950), 125–127.

13 Hartshorne, "Geographic and Political Boundaries in Upper Silesia," *Annals Assn. Amer. Geogrs.*, XXIII (1933), 195–228. Stephen B. Jones, *Boundary-Making: A Handbook for Statesmen, Treaty Editors and Boundary Commissioners* (Washington, 1945). Especially Part I.

14 The pertinence of Eric Fischer's work on historical boundaries has already been mentioned.

15 Vaughan Cornish, *The Great Capitals, an Historical Geography* (London, 1923).

16 O. Spate, "Factors in the Development of Capital Cities," *The Geog. Rev.*, XXXII (October 1942), 622–631.

17 Mark Jefferson, "The Law of Primate Cities," *The Geog. Rev.*, XXIX (April 1939), 226–232.

arise from the fact that its circulation expands faster than its iconography. The metropolitan district outgrows the political limits, and vested local interests and loyalties make political expansion difficult. A sort of "metropolitan-idea" may develop, leading usually to functional authorities rather than to political integration. In a few words, the urban problem is to make the political area fit the field.[18] There are a number of choices possible such as annexation of suburbs, city-country consolidation, metropolitan districts, functional authorities, state assumption of local functions.

KINETIC AND DYNAMIC FIELDS

Since politics consists of conflicts and the resolution of conflicts (though neither conflict nor resolution need be accompanied by violence), these fundamental activities must be expressible in field terms. There are conflicts of ideas, but they do not amount to much until they are embodied in decisions that create or obstruct movement. (It may be wise to re-emphasize that "movement" includes such things of little bulk as messages and money. A restriction on foreign exchange is a restriction on movement.) Fields may be in contact, but not in conflict, may indeed overlap but not conflict, if the movement is merely kinetic. But if there is a dynamic aspect, conflict often will arise. For example, New York City's growing need for water forces its activity in this respect to be dynamic, bringing conflict with other claimants to Delaware River supplies. The international oil industry is inherently dynamic, since new sources must be discovered. The result is potential conflict, sometimes anticipated and resolved at least pro tempore. The relations of political dynamics to such fundamentals as resource needs and population pressures have of course been repeatedly studied,[19] and the present theory does little more than incorporate them into the concept of the field.

The general attitude of Americans toward world politics is that dynamic problems should if possible be reduced to kinetic situations by agreement, or in other words that dynamic fields should be converted to kinetic fields. The philosophy of communism, however, is in many respects the opposite, except for temporary tactical purposes. In its grand strategy, communism would like to convert kinetic fields to dynamic fields, with the pressure from the communist side, of course. (The Nazis held a similar philosophy.) The failure of the United States to understand this difference accounts for a number of American blunders in diplomacy. The notion of peaceful coexistence of capitalism and communism, sincerely held by millions outside the Iron Curtain and occasionally uttered, with what sincerity is not known, by major figures within the Curtain, expresses the belief that the fields of the ideologies can be merely kinetic in their relations, a belief that so far has little to support it.

---

[18] A.E. Smailes, *The Geography of Towns* (London, 1953), pp. 153–156.
[19] For example, by Frederick S. Dunn, in his *Peaceful Change* (New York, 1937); and by Brooks Emeny, in *The Strategy of Raw Materials* (New York, 1934).

There are no upper or lower limits on the magnitude of an idea. Man thinks easily of world government and can dream of space-ships and planetary empires. There are upper limits on decisions, movements, fields, and political areas, though these limits change with events (often, but not necessarily, upwards). Such ideas as the great religions, nationalism, liberalism, and communism have, in so far as they could produce decisions and movements, created fields. Whittlesey has shown how man's ideas of space have changed through primal and regional to worldwide conceptions, and how the third and fourth dimensions of the human habitat have been explored and put to use.[20] Ideas, fields of exploration, in some cases political areas, have expanded, reached above and below the earth's surface, and made better use of time. The idea of a Columbus, the decision of an Isabella, a voyage of discovery, a new field, a new empire—this progression might figuratively be compared to the idea of a chemist, the decision of an entrepreneur, an experiment, a new field of production, an economic domain.

Many of the most influential of ideas have been composite, or "culture-ideas." Western culture, for example, is more than just capitalism or democracy or Christianity—it is a composite of these and other factors. Toynbee holds that every culture tends to evolve its "universal state," a domain roughly coextensive with the culture.[21] If this is true, then we have another example of the chain from idea through a vast number of decisions (not necessarily consciously derived from the general culture-idea) and movements, creating a field and tending towards a political area which would be the universal state of that culture.

UTILITY OF THE THEORY

...Earlier...it was said that a valid theory, however minor, is at least three things: a compact description, a clue to explanation, and a tool for better work. If this theory merely provides nomenclature it satisfies the first requirement. Perhaps it goes farther than merely supplying words. It may reduce the apparent diversity of aims and methods in political geography, found by Hartshorne and his students. It may help to unify not only the theories of political geography, but political theories in general. It may help complete the tie between morphology and function, between region and process. It may show a relationship between "grand ideas" and the earth's surface.

This unified theory can provide no more than a clue to explanation, if it even attains that success. It can hardly provide an ultimate answer to any question. But to relate several disciplines, to show connections, may give hints. The user of this theory is at least sure to be warned against single-factor explanations and be led to seek contributions from sister sciences.

---

20 "The Horizon of Geography."
21 Arnold Toynbee, *A Study of History,* IV (London, 1939), 2–3.

It is as a tool for better work that I have the most hopes for this mental gadget. The chain of words in which the theory is expressed constitutes a sort of check-list ("check-system" might be better), by means of which one can orient oneself and tell where one should explore further. To return to the analogy of a chain of basins, one knows through which basin one has entered and where one can travel back and forth. If one begins with the study of a political area, ideas lie at the other end. If a study begins with movement, the scholar knows he should explore in both directions. For some of the basins one may need pilots from other disciplines, but at least one has a map of the chain. The theory tells students of geography and politics what (in very general terms) they need to learn from each other, what each has to add, but not how each fences himself off.

Another possible effect of this theory upon geographical work is that it may inspire the making of new types of studies and the compiling of new kinds of maps. Many maps either show or imply a field, but with the idea-area chain in mind, new sources of data suggest themselves: public-opinion polls, content analysis of publications, shipments of significant materials, movements of governmental officers, monetary transactions and so forth. The theory is "geographical" in that it makes mappable, through the concept of the field, the results of ideas and decisions that are themselves not mappable.

Conceivably the general plan of this theory can be extended to other than political studies. In fact, recent work in economic geography suggests a similar theory for that branch of our science. The idea-area chain may unite in one concept two main parts of geographical theory, the possibilist and regionalist views. Possibilism focuses on man's choices among environmental possibilities. Choices are decisions. They imply ideas and must lead to movements. The regional or chorological approach, beginning with the study of areas, can lead through movement to decisions and ideas.

Finally, the unified field theory may have utility outside academic circles. It seems possible that the concept can be used as an aid in evaluating diplomatic and strategic ideas and plans. This is an ambitious thought and may prove illusory. However, diplomacy and strategy begin with ideas, lead to decisions, result in movement, and therefore produce fields. In reverse, diplomacy and strategy are conditioned by the political areas and fields of the earth, which limit the possible decisions and practical ideas. No doubt such thinking goes on in high places unaided by our theory, but perhaps this bit of intellectual guidance will clarify some cases.

JAMES W. FESLER

The Reconciliation
of Function and Area

1

... Administrative areas ... fall into two types: governmental areas, in each of which a general or special unit of government collects funds and administers several functions or a single function; and field service areas, each of which is only a portion of the total area within which a department or bureau of a general government administers its functions. The fact that governmental areas rarely satisfy ideal specifications leads to the need for redrafting of governmental boundaries, horizontal coöperation among contiguous governmental areas, and redistribution of functions and vertical coöperation among the several levels of government. Field service areal patterns for individual functions pose the problem of selecting areas and headquarters cities that conform to dictates of natural areas and administrative efficiency. They also create a setting for consideration of decentralization of administrative authority. Departmental clusters of functions and the totality of functions of a government require that field service areas be geared not only to a single function but to coördinated management of functions in a common area. The clash between functional and areal lines of authority tests the administrative statesmanship of government departments and of the chief executive himself. Current experiments in areal coördination of departmental and governmental activities in a common area suggest new and promising approaches to the reciprocal adjustment of area and function.

There are two ways to reconcile function and area. One is by basic structural reform. The other is by perfecting coöperative techniques. The degree

From James W. Fesler, *Area and Administration* (Copyright © 1949 by University of Alabama Press), pp. 119–135. Reprinted by permission.

to which progress is made by one of these methods proportionately reduces the pressure on the other. Inter-areal, inter-functional, and inter-level coöperation ameliorates the awkwardness of governmental structural arrangements. To the extent that structure is improved, coöperation need carry less of the load of making government work.

Reconciliation of function and area through the regular machinery of government can take place only if we are clear on certain basic issues. Throughout American life there has developed an emphasis on specialization, segmentation, functional autonomy, and pluralism. It is reflected in education, in professional guildism, and in government, and it finds its epitome in modern industry. In government this emphasis has been expressed in the establishment of relatively independent and autonomous commissions, boards, corporations, code authorities, departments, and special units of government. It less obviously motivates the efforts of administrative bureaus and divisions to win immunity from effective control by department heads and the legislature. This they do through close alliance with interest groups, specialized legislative committees, and independent sources of political support. These developments threaten to carry functional specialization beyond the point of maximum returns to the people. Persons sharing concern over these and related developments need to devise an architecture that fits the parts into the whole—whether in education, the professions, government, or industry.

In government the architecture of the whole rests on two pillars—major function and area. In any government the many functions and subfunctions can be grouped into a few great clusters for coördinated direction by a top generalist. Through this device the virtues of functional specialization are maintained, but mutual adjustment of the specialties in the light of a major goal of government becomes possible. Those familiar with this device know that functional groupings are never perfect, that such obvious needs as a Federal department of transportation are resisted, that the generalist supervising a cluster of functions may be unable to establish firm control. They know also that, while grouping of functions modifies the extremes to which segmentation and autonomy may go, these clusters themselves are but a part of the whole and may mobilize segmental interests in society in support of programs oriented to those interests.

Area provides the other great foundation for the integration of governmental functions. Area provides the common denominator for the functions of the nation, the state, the county, or the town. Each of these governmental areas has a government that potentially can weave all its functions together so that they make a consistent pattern for the area in which they operate. Similarly, each area of the country, whether a river basin, a group-of-states region, or an existing governmental area like a state or county, provides a common denominator about which can be coördinated all or many field functions of the Federal government.

The problem of area and administration, therefore, is not a minor problem

of administrative mechanics worth attention only by administrative technicians. It opens up the fundamental problem of reconciling the parts and the
whole, of introducing coherence into an age of specialization, of keeping in
view the individual citizen on whom converge the multiple activities of
government.

Specialization may be functional or areal. Functional specialization is
greatest in higher levels of government and administration. Where a function
is performed by Federal, state, and local governments, it is generally true that
the Federal agency involved has a galaxy of experts organized in specialized
units that cannot be matched in state agencies. Similarly, state agencies in a
given functional field tend to be better equipped with specialists than the
run-of-the-mill local agencies. Only the great metropolises can match or exceed
functional specialization by the states. Moving downward through the hierarchy of governments, then, there is usually a decline in specialization and an
increase in generalization. The same observation holds for field service administration. A Federal department mobilizes centrally its highly specialized personnel, while nice distinctions among specialties tend increasingly to vanish
through the regional, district, and local levels of the department's field service.
In the lowest level of field service areas, the officials are perforce jacks-of-all-
trades. This phenomenon, whether in general government or in field administration, can be pictured as a local generalist backed up by a wealth of technical services at the higher levels. A basic problem of administration is to
channel these technical services to the local generalist so that he is not snowed
under by the volume of reading matter and personal visitations, so that he can
distinguish the wheat from the chaff, and so that he is not given conflicting
advice or directions on technical matters where his basis for judgment would
be inadequate. Much of the future of decentralization rests on our confidence
in administration by generalists, our willingness to sacrifice some specialized
knowledge at the local or district level, and our minimization of this sacrifice
by putting at the area generalists' fingertips the vast range of specialized knowledge available from higher administrative and governmental levels.

Area itself is a basis for specialization and, like functional specialization,
can emphasize the parts at the expense of the whole. The introverted nation-
state, serving values that have validity only for its portion of the earth's surface,
has long obstructed the development of a world structure that would relate the
parts to the whole. The coin bearing "regionalism" on its face carries "sectionalism" on its reverse side. States' rights can mask the stake of special interests in feudalistic practices and inequalities of opportunity that are condemned
by the nation's conscience. Local areas differ in their orientation toward public
policy issues, reflecting the differing social and economic interests of local communities. Even in field adminstration, each field service area may have a
partially different set of problems from the other areas, and its officials may
lose sight of the national departmental policy because of their sympathy with
the interests of the particular area. If, for example, materials or manpower are

to be allocated by field service area officials out of a national pool, there is danger of a competitive race to lower standards so as to get more than the fair portion for one's own field service area. Areal specialization is greatest at the lower levels in the governmental and administrative hierarchy, while the many competing particularisms tend to dissolve into greater generalization at the higher levels.

2

The emergent picture is of a tendency toward functional specialization and areal generalization at the higher governmental and administrative levels, and a tendency toward functional generalization and areal specialization at the lower levels. The fitting of functional parts into the whole of the governmental and administrative process might be expected to occur at the lower levels of government. The fitting of areal particularisms into the whole of national and state policies or departmental policies might be expected to be the task of the higher levels of government and administration. In a sense, it would appear that functions must draw together and abandon some of the niceties of specialization when brought face to face with the ordinary citizen in his local setting, and that areas must draw together and drop something of their particularistic approach when brought face to face with the shared objectives of all people in the nation or in the world.

There are legal and practical limits to the realization of these expectations. Lower levels of government and administration are poorly equipped to provide a structural integration of the many functions of Federal, state, and local governments, or even of the functions of, say, the Federal government alone. There is no machinery for continuous Federal-state-local integration of activities in a given area. Instead, the legal separation of the three levels forces emphasis on coöperation as the only cement for their common interests. Similarly, the Federal government has no field machinery with which to integrate fully its many activities in a particular area.

A major obstacle to the further development of inter-governmental and inter-agency functional coördination at lower levels of government is the lack of coördination at the centers of power. We have seen that areal coördination of the functions of a single Federal department must await the strengthening of the generalist department head at Washington. Similarly, the use of counties or cities as cores about which inter-governmental coördination can develop is severely handicapped by their failure to coördinate even their own functions, to expand their areas to sizes appropriate to modern functional demands, or to absorb the plethora of special, semi-autonomous . . . districts. Areal coördination of functions among governments and among a government's field agents must therefore await the development of adequate coördination within governments and within departments. Meantime, and perhaps indefinitely, the use of smaller areas to force reassessment of the relation of functional specialties to the whole governmental complex will have to proceed through the perfecting of techniques of inter-governmental and inter-agency coöperation.

Similarly, there are limits to the ability of higher levels of government and administration to modify the worst features of areal particularism. One of the principal obstacles is the assumption that we must choose between two alternatives. We need not choose between a strong Federal government and a strong state government, between absolute centralization and absolute decentralization, between bureaucratic regimentation and local self-government. The vice of such choices is manifold. Despite elaborate and repeated efforts of social scientists to marshal the advantages and disadvantages of each alternative, the choice is bound to be only pseudo-scientific. It forces us back on prejudices, the emotional symbolism of words, and sheer acts of faith. Once the choice between alternative positions has been made, there is set up an unscientific major premise that colors and distorts any attempt to apply scientific methods to the objective facts of governmental functioning. Instead, science is mustered simply to rationalize a foregone conclusion. The either-or approach precludes recognition of the fact that in the United States at least three magnitudes of governmental areas are needed—national, subnational, and local—and that the people have a stake in the efficiency and popular control of the governments at each of these three levels. In a field service the either-or approach neglects the need for finding a middle ground between central responsibility for results and for equitable treatment of all persons on the one hand, and on the other, adjustment of administration to distinct regional and local conditions. Both in government as a whole and in field administration we need a pragmatic approach that reflects institutional adaptability to space, time, and motion. The major premise of our thinking must allow for such adaptability.

Another obstacle to modification of areal particularism in its more extreme manifestations is the lack of a concerted effort by any higher level of government to take account of the problems of the lesser areas. The relation of the states to the Federal government is given continuous study at no single point in the Federal government. Nor in any state will there be found a point at which the problems of local areas are considered in a methodical, comprehensive fashion. In fact, the disorderly manner in which higher levels of government have handled their responsibilities toward the lesser areas accounts for much of the difficulty in which the lesser areas find themselves. This is less true of field administration. Departmental offices of field operations and the corresponding unit in the Bureau of the Budget provide foci for central consideration of the problems of field service areas.

3

Perhaps the most promising opportunity for reduction of areal particularism and achievement of a happy balance between centralization and decentralization lies in the perfecting of machinery for vertical coördination of a single function among several areal layers. Centralization of authority, it is clear, does not necessitate centralization of administration. Broad policy decisions can be made centrally for a vast area, while important but subordinate policy decisions and application of the policies to individual cases can be made at subcenters for smaller areas. Thus, national policies can be formulated to cover problems whose natural areas exceed state government areas or whose substantially diverse treatment would clash with minimal concepts of equality of opportunity. Yet administration may be decentralized either to Federal field service areas or to the states, counties, and cities.

When should the Federal government administer a Federal function through field service areas and when through states and local governments? The gulf between the two alternatives is illustrated by Paul H. Appleby and David E. Lilienthal. Appleby has written:

> If a program is Federal and if the responsibility is Federal, the authority should be Federal and the administering bureaucracy should almost always be Federal. Only thus can national purposes be served; only thus can there be popular control; administrative mechanisms not controllable by a Presidentially appointed top executive are not manageable by the people. The ends hoped for through delegation to the states can be and should be sufficiently attained through decentralization that is wholly Federal. To assume that decentralization and delegation to states are one and inseparable is to assume too much.[1]

Lilienthal takes the opposite tack, in these words:

> There are of course many instances where the facts appear to support the claim that good administration of national concerns cannot be obtained through the co-operation of local agencies. Local politics, ineptitude, lack of interest and experience in public matters and in administration, brazen partisanship, even corruption—all these stand in the way. I am sure these hazards exist. I am sure, for we have encountered most of them in this [Tennessee] valley. But what are the alternatives? Fewer citizens participating in governmental administration. Less and less community responsibility. More federal employees is the field armed with papers to be filled out and sent to Washington for "processing," because only there is "good administration" possible. The progressive atrophy of citizen interest. An ever wider gulf between local communities and national government, between citizens and their vital public concerns. Such are the alternatives.[2]

Decentralization to governmental areas has several disadvantages under particular circumstances. From the areal standpoint, there are certain functions for which the states are too small as administrative areas. Drainage basin development is an example; the Tennessee Valley Authority, which Lilienthal headed, was a wholly Federal instrumentality, not a coöperative state agency operating under a broad Federal statute. From the standpoint of operational technique, decentralization to governmental areas is probably most effective

---

[1] Paul H. Appleby, *Big Democracy* (New York: Alfred A. Knopf, 1945), pp. 87–88.
[2] David E. Lilienthal, *TVA: Democracy on the March* (New York: Harper, 1944), p. 162.

under substantial-grant-in-aid programs. The right of the Federal government to withhold or withdraw the grant-in-aid is the principal sanction through which that government can make the states adhere to standards of administrative efficiency and conform to the national policies for the particular function. What is involved is a double factor. The function, because it involves substantial flowing of national funds into the state area, is one that the states rather eagerly embrace. And the possibility that the grant may be suspended by Federal administrators protects the Federal government against lack of state conformity to Federal standards and instructions. This double factor in grant-in-aid programs is lacking in non-grant Federal-state programs, in programs where the grant is too small to affect state self-interest, and in grant programs where the Federal standards clash too sharply with state interests and attitudes.

. . .

. . . Federal-state programs are appropriate for those many functions where the Federal government is making up for the fiscal inadequacy of some states by channeling funds to them to maintain national minima; or where the state has legal authority over certain aspects of a function and the merging of this authority with that of the Federal government promises a more integrated administration from the citizen's standpoint; or where local governments have important legal and administrative authority which a state agency is in the best position to mobilize for support of a joint Federal-state program. In the last type of situation, the state's participation may be limited to the passing of enabling legislation, so that what results is a joint Federal-local administrative operation.

. . .

The reconciliation of function and area, we have suggested, can come about in part through basic structural reform. Such an approach is bottomed on the fact that the national, subnational, and local governments must be made satisfactory vessels for those functions or parts of functions that have respectively a predominantly national, subnational, or local character. Fiscal adequacy, general governmental efficiency, and popular control, though they now weigh heavily, should not be the factors on which allocation of specific functions depends. They merely distort the effort to assign individual functions to the governmental areas that can provide the closest approximations to natural areas for those functions and that are peculiarly in a position to give efficient administration to those functions. To remove from the picture the distorting factors calls for a number of actions.

Basic readjustment of governmental areas is important if we are to have areas that can assure fiscal adequacy and general efficiency and qualify for the discharge of functions that currently fall to higher-level areas only by default. I rule out readjustment of state boundaries, for we are not constructing a utopia. But readjustment of local government areas is urgent, for the smallness of such areas directly accounts for much of the local units' fiscal inadequacy, general inefficiency, and inability to provide able administration of the particular functions appropriate on other grounds for local governments. Readjustment of local areas has traditionally been a matter for local action. Yet in the past generation local action to consolidate counties and annex suburbs to cities has been almost nil. If we are not to continue to see local government wane, the state governments must be induced to establish local areas appropriate to modern needs. True, this is centralization of a sort, and the emotional advocates of local self-government will vehemently protest. But I am convinced that only by decisive state action to provide the areal setting necessary for healthy local government can the real values of decentralization be preserved. A precedent is set by the British establishment in 1945 of a Local Government Boundary Commission, which can recommend to Parliament the moving of municipal boundaries and the consolidation of local government units.[3]

Action to meet the problem of fiscal adequacy must go beyond mere readjustment of governmental areas. Enlargement of such areas will not answer the problem of cities and counties located in economically weak sections. Again the answer seems to be resort to the next higher level of government. Through shared-revenue and grant-in-aid programs the states can backstop the poorer local governments. A vertical relationship designed along fiscal aid lines has overtones of centralization, but seems in its ultimate values to offer promise of strengthening rather than weakening state and local government. It is in many cases the only alternative to wholesale transfer of functions to higher levels of government or toleration of low and disparate standards of government service. Fiscal aid, of course, should not be used, as it sometimes has been, to perpetuate weak local areas that could be strengthened by consolidation with neighboring areas.

While assurance of areal and fiscal adequacy should do much to strengthen local units, the general efficiency of such units might be further promoted by state prescription of minimal standards in such matters as budgeting, accounting, debt incurrence, and personnel selection techniques. Here, too, a degree of centralization is advocated in order that decentralization may flourish.

---

3 Coleman Woodbury, "Britain Begins to Rebuild Her Cities," *American Political Science Review*, XLI (October 1947), 907; Winston W. Crouch, "Trends in British Local Government," *Public Administration Review*, VII (Autumn 1947), 256–57. The drafting of comparable legislation in this country will call for a high order of skill. Incentive to action must be provided (*cf.* legislative inertia on reapportionment of legislative representation), yet the legislature should not be tempted to use its powers in punitive fashion against local areas controlled by rival political parties or factions. An alternative to decisive state action reshaping local areas is state passage of enabling legislation that weights the scales in favor of consolidation and annexation. A state law authorizing local voting on annexation of a suburb by a city can call for merging of the votes cast in the city and suburb, with the majority of the total determining whether annexation will take place. Contrast this with the customary requirement that the city and the suburb must each separately vote in favor of annexation for it to be consummated.

VINCENT OSTROM, CHARLES M. TIEBOUT,
AND ROBERT WARREN

The Organization of Government
in Metropolitan Areas:
A Theoretical Inquiry

Allusions to the "problem of metropolitan government" are often made in characterizing the difficulties supposed to arise because a metropolitan region is a legal non-entity. From this point of view, the people of a metropolitan region have no general instrumentality of government available to deal directly with the range of problems which they share in common. Rather there is a multiplicity of federal and state governmental agencies, counties, cities, and special districts that govern within a metropolitan region.

This view assumes that the multiplicity of political units in a metropolitan area is essentially a pathological phenomenon. The diagnosis asserts that there are too many governments and not enough government. The symptoms are described as "duplication of functions" and "overlapping jurisdictions." Autonomous units of government, acting in their own behalf, are considered incapable of resolving the diverse problems of the wider metropolitan community. The political topography of the metropolis is called a "crazy-quilt pattern" and its organization is said to be an "organized chaos." The prescription is reorganization into larger units—to provide "a general metropolitan framework" for gathering up the various functions of government. A political system with a single dominant center for making decisions is viewed as the ideal model for the organization of metropolitan government. "Gargantua" is one name for it.[1]

From *American Political Science Review*, LV (December 1961), 831–842. Reprinted by permission.

[1] The term is taken from Robert C. Wood, "The New Metropolis: Green Belts, Grass Roots or Gargantua," *The American Political Science Review*, Vol. 52 (March 1958), pp. 108–

The assumption that each unit of local government acts independently without regard for other public interests in the metropolitan community has only a limited validity. The traditional pattern of government in a metropolitan area with its multiplicity of political jurisdictions may more appropriately be conceived as a "polycentric political system."[2] "Polycentric" connotes many centers of decision-making which are formally independent of each other. Whether they actually function independently, or instead constitute an interdependent system of relations, is an empirical question in particular cases. To the extent that they take each other into account in competitive relationships, enter into various contractual and cooperative undertakings, or have recourse to central mechanisms to resolve conflicts, the various political jurisdictions in a metropolitan area may function in a coherent manner with consistent and predictable patterns of interacting behavior. To the extent that this is so, they may be said to function as a "system."

The study of government in metropolitan areas conceived as a polycentric political system should precede any judgment that it is pathological. Both the structure and the behavior of the system need analysis before any reasonable estimate can be made of its performance in dealing with the various public problems arising in a metropolitan community. Better analysis of how a metropolitan area is governed can lead in turn to more appropriate measures of reorganization and reform.[3]

. . .

I. THE NATURE OF PUBLIC GOODS AND SERVICES

The conditions which give rise to public rather than private provision of certain goods and services are examined in this section. Three views of these

---

122. Wood defines gargantua as "the invention of a single metropolitan government or at least the establishment of a regional superstructure which points in that direction." We do not argue the case for big units *vs.* small units as Wood does in his discussion of gargantua *vs.* grass roots. Rather, we argue that various scales of organization may be appropriate for different public services in a metropolitan area.

2 We use this term for want of a better one. An alternative term might be "multinucleated political system." We do not use "pluralism" because it has been pre-empted as a broader term referring to society generally and not to a political system in particular.

Polycentric political systems are not limited to the field of metropolitan government. The concept is equally applicable to regional administration of water resources, regional administration of international affairs, and to a variety of other situations.

3 By analogy, the formal units of government in a metropolitan area might be viewed as organizations similar to individual firms in an industry. Individual firms may constitute the basic legal entities in an industry, but their conduct in relation to one another may be conceived as having a particular structure and behavior as an industry. Collaboration among the separate units of local government may be such that their activities supplement or complement each other, as in the automobile industry's patent pool. Competition among them may produce desirable self-regulating tendencies similar in effect to the "invisible hand" of the market. Collaboration and competition among governmental units may also, of course, have detrimental effects, and requires some form of central decision-making to consider the interests of the area as a whole. For a comprehensive review of the theory of industrial organization see Joe S. Bain, *Industrial Organization* (New York, 1959).

conditions can usefully be distinguished: (1) public goods arising from efforts to control indirect consequences, externalities, or spillover effects; (2) public goods provided because some goods and services cannot be packaged; and (3) public goods consisting of the maintenance of preferred states of community affairs.

The control of indirect consequences as public goods

The basic criterion traditionally offered for distinguishing between public and private affairs was formulated some years ago by John Dewey: ". . . the line between private and public is to be drawn on the basis of the extent and scope of the consequences of acts which are so important as to need control whether by inhibition or by promotion."[4] The indirect consequences of a transaction, which affect others than those directly concerned, can also be described as "externalities" or "spillover effects." Those indirectly affected are viewed as being external to the immediate transaction. Some externalities are of a favorable or beneficial nature; others are adverse or detrimental.

Favorable externalities can frequently be recaptured by the economic unit that creates them. The builder of a large supermarket, for example, may create externalities for the location of a nearby drugstore. If the builder of the supermarket also controls the adjacent land, he can capture the externalities accruing to the drugstore through higher rents or by common ownership of the two enterprises. From the builder's point of view he has "internalized"[5] the externalities.[6]

Where favorable externalities cannot be internalized by private parties, a sufficient mechanism to proceed may be lacking, and public agencies may be called upon to provide a good or service. A privately owned park, even with an admission charge, may not be able to cover costs. If the externalities in the form of the dollar value of a better neighborhood could be captured, such a park might be profitable.

Unfavorable spillovers or externalities are another matter. The management of a refinery which belches out smoke has little incentive to install costly equipment to eliminate the smoke. Control or internalization of diseconomies usually falls upon public agencies. A function of government, then, is to internalize the externalities—positive and negative—for those goods which the producers and consumers are unable or unwilling to internalize for themselves, and this process of internalization is identified with the "public goods."

---

[4] John Dewey, *The Public and Its Problems* (New York, 1927), p. 15.

[5] John V. Krutilla and Otto Eckstein, *Multiple Purpose River Development: Studies in Applied Economic Analysis* (Baltimore: The Johns Hopkins Press, 1958), p. 69 ff. Krutilla and Eckstein develop the concept of "internalizing" external economies as a criterion for determining scale of a management unit in the administration of water resources.

[6] In practice, shopping centers may also give favorable rents to large supermarkets as "traffic generators." This recognizes the externalities they create.

Not all public goods are of the same scale. Scale implies both the geographic domain and the intensity or weight of the externality. A playground creates externalities which are neighborhoodwide in scope, while national defense activities benefit a whole nation—and affect many outside it. Thus, for each public good there corresponds some "public." As John Dewey has formulated the definition, "the public consists of all those who are affected by the indirect consequences of transactions to such an extent that it is deemed necessary to have those consequences systematically provided for."[7] The concept of the public is important to later considerations in determining the criteria of scale appropriate to public organizations.

Packageability

Public goods and services and, in turn, the functions of governments in metropolitan areas can be distinguished from private goods by a criterion commonly used by economists. A private good must be "packageable," *i.e.,* susceptible of being differentiated as a commodity or service before it can be readily purchased and sold in the private market. Those who do not pay for a private good can then be excluded from enjoying its benefits. This notion is formulated by economists as the "exclusion principle."[8] In contrast with Dewey's formulation of the nature of public goods, the exclusion principle focuses attention on the practicability of denying benefits. National defense, for example, will not be provided by private firms because, among other reasons, the citizen who did not pay would still enjoy the benefits. Furthermore, if citizens understate their preferences for defense—as by failing to build bomb shelters—on the assumption that it will be paid for by others, the result will be an inadequate provision for defense.

Most municipal public goods such as fire and police protection, or the abatement of air pollution, are not easily packageable either; they cannot be sold only to those individuals who are willing to pay.[9] This suggests two problems for public organizations.

First, private goods, because they are easily packageable, are readily subject to measurement and quantification. Public goods, by contrast, are generally not so measurable. If more police are added to the force, output will presumably increase. But how much is a question without an exact answer. Moreover, when factors of production can be quantified in measurable units of output, the production process can be subject to more rigorous controls. A more rational pricing policy is also possible. With quantifiable data about both input and output, any production process can be analyzed and the performance of different modes of production can be compared for their efficiency.

---

7 John Dewey, *op. cit.,* pp. 15–16.
8 Richard Musgrave, *The Theory of Public Finance* (New York, 1959), esp. Ch. 1.
9 Charles M. Tiebout, "A Pure Theory of Local Expenditures," *Journal of Political Economy,* Vol. 64 (October 1956), pp. 416–24.

Rational control over the production and provision of public goods and services therefore depends, among other things, upon the development of effective standards of measurement; this gets into the allocation of joint costs as well as of joint benefits.

A second, closely related problem arises in the assessment of costs upon persons who can benefit without paying directly for the good. Only public agencies with their taxing powers can seek to apportion the costs of public goods among the various beneficiaries. The scale criterion of political representation, discussed below, takes account of how this difference between private and public goods affects the organization of public agencies.

Public goods as the maintenance of preferred states of community affairs

The exclusion principle provides a criterion for distinguishing most public goods from private, but it does not, as commonly stated, clarify or specify the conditions which determine the patterns of organization in the public service economy. However, by viewing public goods as "the maintenance of preferred states of community affairs," we may introduce a modified concept of packageability, one that is amenable to some measurement and quantification, and that therefore may be more helpful in clarifying criteria for the organization of public services in metropolitan areas. The modification consists in extending the exclusion principle from an individual consumer to all the inhabitants of an area within designated boundaries.

The concept can be illustrated on a small scale in the operation of a household heating system which uses conveniently measurable units of inputs. However, the household temperature it maintains is a joint benefit to the family and a marginal change in family size will have no material effect upon the costs of maintaining this public good for the family. Yet since the family good derived from it is effectively confined to the household, outsiders are excluded and there are no substantial spillover effects or externalities for them. The family good is not a public good in the larger community. So household heating is treated as a private good in most communities. Similarly, a public good on a neighborhood or community scale can be viewed as "packaged" within appropriate boundaries so that others outside the boundaries may be excluded from its use. In this way, in some communities adjacent to New York City, for example, the use of parks and beaches is restricted to local residents whose taxes presumably support these recreation facilities.

Wherever this is practicable, the analogy of a household as a "package" for an atmosphere with a controlled temperature may be generalized and applied to the maintenance of a desired state of affairs within particular local government boundaries. Just as the temperature and the cost of heating can be measured, so it may be possible to develop direct or closely approximate measures both of a given state of community affairs resulting from the production of many public goods and services and also of the costs of furnishing them. An air pollution abatement program, for example, may be measured by an index of quantities of various pollutants found in air samples. Given costs of abatement, some preferred tolerance levels may then be specified.

Similarly, any community has a "fire loss potential," defined as the losses to be expected if no provision for fire protection is made. The difference between this potential and the actual fire losses is then the output or "production" of the fire protection service, and the net fire loss can be termed the "state of affairs" in that community with respect to fire losses. Fire protection, of course, does not eliminate but only reduces fire losses. Any effort at complete elimination would probably be so expensive that the costs would greatly exceed the benefits. The "preferred" state of affairs is some optimal level of performance where benefits exceed costs. The provision of a community fire department as a public good can thus be viewed as the maintenance of a preferred state of affairs in fire protection for that community, and the benefits can ordinarily be confined to its residents.

Police protection can be regarded in the same way. The traffic patrol, for example, operates to optimize the flow of traffic while reducing the losses to property and injury to persons. Even if perfect control were possible, the costs would be so great that the preferred state of affairs in police protection would be something less.

It must be acknowledged, however, that in the case of police protection and many other public services, in contrast, say, with garbage collection or air pollution abatement, the performance level or net payoff is much more difficult to measure and to quantify. Proximate measures such as the gross number of arrests for different types of offenses per month or per 10,000 population annually have little meaning unless considered in relation to various conditions existing in the community. Decision-makers consequently may be forced, for want of better measurements, to assume that the preferred state of affairs is defined as a balance between the demands for public services and the complaints from taxpayers.

While the output of a public good may not be packaged this does not of course mean that its material inputs cannot be. The preferred state of affairs produced by mosquito spraying is enjoyed by the whole community, while spraying supplies and equipment are readily packageable. Mosquito spraying, that is to say, can be produced by a private vendor under contract to a public agency.

This illustrates an important point, that the *production* of goods and services needs to be distinguished from their *provision* at public expense. Government provision need not involve public production—indeed, at some stage in the sequence from raw materials to finished products virtually every public good, not already a natural resource, is of private origin. So, a public agency by contractual arrangements with private firms—or with other public agencies—can provide the local community with public services without going into the business of producing them itself.

When the desired performance level or the net payoff can be specified by a measurable index, an element of rigor can be introduced to assure substantial production controls in providing a public good, even where the production itself is the function of a separate agency or entrepreneur. The producer can be held accountable for maintaining affairs within certain tolerances, and the agency responsible for providing the service can ascertain the adequacy of performance. Advances in the measurement and quantification of performance levels in the public service economy will consequently permit much greater flexibility in the patterns of organization for the production and provision of public goods and services.

If Dewey's definition is extended to include "events" generally rather than being limited to "acts" or to "transactions" among actors, his formulation is consistent with the conception of public goods as the maintenance of preferred states of affairs.[10] Public control seeks to internalize those events, viewed as consequences which impinge directly and indirectly upon diverse elements in a community, in such a way that adverse consequences will be inhibited and favorable consequences will be promoted.

In the final analysis, distinctions between private and public goods cannot be as sharply made in the world of human experience as this analysis might imply. In part, the technical character of specific goods influences the degree of differentiation or isolability that characterizes their distribution and utilization. Vegetables and landscapes cannot be handled in the same way. Many private goods have spillover effects such that other members of the community bear some portion of the benefits and losses, whatever the degree of public regulation. In every large community most people philosophically accept some of the costs of bigness—air pollution, traffic congestion, noise, and a variety of inconveniences—on the assumption that these are inevitable concomitants of the benefits that derive from living in a metropolis.

II.   SCALE PROBLEMS IN PUBLIC ORGANIZATION

Viewing the boundaries of a local unit of government as the "package" in which its public goods are provided,[11] so that those outside the boundaries are excluded from their use, we may say that where a public good is adequately packaged within appropriate boundaries, it has been successfully internalized. Where externalities spill over upon neighboring communities, the public good has not been fully internalized.

In designing the appropriate "package" for the production and provision

---

10 *Op. cit.,* pp. 4–5. Dewey's use of the terms "acts" and "transactions" implies that only social behavior is contemplated in public action. But physical events, *e.g.,* floods, may also become objects of public control.

11 See the discussion of "district boundaries and the incidence of benefits" in Stephen C. Smith, "Problems in the Use of the Public District for Ground Water Management," *Land Economics,* Vol. 32 (August 1956), pp. 259–269.

of public goods several criteria should be considered. Among these are control, efficiency, political representation, and self-determination. Needless to say, they are sometimes in conflict.

The criterion of control

The first standard applicable to the scale of public organization for the production of public services requires that the boundary conditions[12] of a political jurisdiction include the relevant set of events to be controlled. Events are not uniformly distributed in space; rather, they occur as sets under conditions such that boundaries can be defined with more or less precision. Rivers flow in watershed basins, for example. Patterns of social interaction are also differentially distributed in space and boundaries can generally be defined for them too. In other words, all phenomena can be described in relation to specifiable boundary conditions and the criterion of control requires that these be taken into account in determining the scale of a public organization. Otherwise the public agency is disabled in regulating a set of events in order to realize some preferred state of affairs. If the boundaries cannot be suitably adjusted, the likely result is a transfer of the governmental function to a unit scaled to meet the criterion of control more adequately.

Pasadena, for example, is subject to severe smog attacks, but the city's boundary conditions do not cover an area sufficient to assure effective control of the appropriate meteorological and social space that would include the essential variables constituting the "smogisphere" of Southern California. None of the separate cities of Southern California, in fact, can encompass the problem. Instead, county air pollution control districts were organized for the Los Angeles metropolitan community. The failure even of these counties to meet adequately the criterion of effective control has led the California state government to assume an increasingly important role in smog control.

The criterion of efficiency

The most efficient solution would require the modification of boundary conditions so as to assure a producer of public goods and services the most favorable economy of scale, as well as effective control. Two streams with different hydrologic characteristics, for example, might be effectively controlled separately; but, by being managed together, the potentialities of one may complement the other. This has certainly been the case in Los Angeles' joint management of the Owens River and the Los Angeles River by making one the tributary of the other through the 300-mile Los Angeles Aqueduct, skirting the Sierras. Joint management permits a greater joint payoff in recreational facilities and water and power production.

---

12 The boundary conditions of a local unit of government are not limited to the legally determined physical boundaries but should include reference to extra-territorial powers, joint powers, etc.

Other factors such as technological developments and the skill or proficiency of a labor force can bear upon efficiency as a criterion of the scale of
organization needed. If machinery for painting center stripes on city streets
can only be efficiently used on a large scale, special arrangements may be
required to enable several small cities to act jointly in providing such a service.
The same may be true in the utilization of uncommon and expensive professional skills; and it accounts for the fact that mental institutions and prisons
are apt to be state rather than municipal undertakings.

The criterion of political representation

Another criterion for the scale of public organization requires the inclusion
of the appropriate political interests within its decision-making arrangements.
The direct participants in a transaction are apt to negotiate only their own
interests, leaving the indirect consequences or spillover effects to impinge upon
others. Third-party interests may be ignored. Public organizations seek to take
account of third-party effects by internalizng the various interests in rendering
public decisions and in controlling public affairs. Specification of the boundary
or scale conditions of any political jurisdiction is important in determining the
set of interests which are to be internalized within the organization.

In considering the political design of a public organization three elements
of scale require consideration. The *scale of formal organization* indicates the
size of the governmental unit which provides a public good. The *public*, as
noted above, consists of those who are affected by its provision. The *political
community* can be defined as those who are actually taken into account in
deciding whether and how to provide it. Those who are affected by such a decision may be different from those who influence its making. An ideal solution,
assuming criteria of responsibility and accountability consonant with democratic theory, would require that these three boundaries be coterminous.
Where in fact the boundary conditions differ, scale problems arise.

If both the direct and indirect beneficiaries of a public transaction are
included within the domain of a public organization, the means are in principle available for assessment of the cost of public control upon the beneficiaries.
Except where a redistribution of income is sought as a matter of public policy,
an efficient allocation of economic resources is assured by the capacity to charge
the costs of providing public goods and services to the beneficiaries.[13]

The public implicated in different sets of transactions varies with each set:
the relevant public for one set is confined to a neighborhood, while for another
the relevant public may be most of the population of the globe. Between these
two extremes are a vast number of potential scales of public organizations.
Given certain levels of information, technology, communication, and certain

---

[13] This factor might be separately characterized as a criterion of equitable distribution of
costs and benefits, but we have chosen to consider it here in the context of political representation.

patterns of identification, a scheme might be imagined which had an appropriate scale of public organization for each different public good. As these conditions and circumstances change, the scale of the public for any set of transactions should be altered correspondingly. If it is not, what then?

Where the political community does not contain the whole public, some interests may be disregarded. A city, for instance, may decide to discharge its sewage below its boundaries, and the affected public there may have no voice in the decision. On the other hand, where the political community contains the whole public and, in addition, people unaffected by a transaction, the unaffected are given a voice when none may be desired. Capricious actions can result. The total political community in a city of three million population may not be an appropriate decision-making mechanism in planning a local playground.

Nevertheless, the statement that a government is "too large (or too small) to deal with a problem" often overlooks the possibility that the scale of the public and the political community need not coincide with that of the formal boundaries of a public organization. Informal arrangements between public organizations may create a political community large enough to deal with any particular public's problem. Similarly, a public organization may also be able to constitute political communities within its boundaries to deal with problems which affect only a subset of the population. It would be a mistake to conclude that public organizations are of an inappropriate size until the informal mechanisms, which might permit larger or smaller political communities, are investigated.

Seen in relation to the political community, the scale of formal public organizations merely specifies the formal boundaries. Since the feasible number of governmental units is limited when compared to the number of public goods to be provided, a one-to-one mapping of the public, the political community, and the formal public organization is impracticable. Moreover, the relevant public changes. Even if, at one time, formal public organizations, political communities, and the publics were coterminous, over time they would become dislocated. As a result, public organizations may (1) reconstitute themselves, (2) voluntarily cooperate, or, failing cooperation, (3) turn to other levels of government in a quest for an appropriate fit among the interests affecting and affected by public transactions.

The criterion of local self-determination

The criteria of effective control, of efficiency, and of the inclusion of appropriate political interests can be formulated on general theoretical grounds, but their application in any political system depends upon the particular institutions empowered to decide questions of scale. The conditions attending the organization of local governments in the United States usually require that these criteria be controlled by the decisions of the citizenry in the local community, *i.e.*, subordinated to considerations of self-determination.

The patterns of local self-determination manifest in incorporation proceedings usually require a petition of local citizens to institute incorporation proceedings and an affirmative vote of the local electorate to approve. Commitments to local consent and local control may also involve substantial home rule in determining which interests of the community its local officials will attend to and how these officials will be organized and held responsible for their discharge of public functions.

Local self-government of municipal affairs assumes that public goods can be successfully internalized. The purely "municipal" affairs of a local jurisdiction, presumably, do not create problems for other political communities. Where internalization is not possible and where control, consequently, cannot be maintained, the local unit of government becomes another "interest" group in quest of public goods or potential public goods that spill over upon others beyond its borders.

The choice of local public services implicit in any system of self-government presumes that substantial variety will exist in patterns of public organization and in the public goods provided among the different local communities in a metropolis. Patterns of local autonomy and home rule constitute substantial commitments to a polycentric system.

III.   PUBLIC ORGANIZATION IN GARGANTUA

Since all patterns of organization are less than perfectly efficient, responsive, or representative, some consideration should be given to the problem of organizing for different types of public services in gargantua, in contrast to the problems in a polycentric political system. This brief discussion will only touch on theoretical considerations involved in organizing diverse public services in the big system.

Gargantua unquestionably provides an appropriate scale of organization for many huge public services. The provision of harbor and airport facilities, mass transit, sanitary facilities, and imported water supplies may be most appropriately organized in gargantua. By definition, gargantua should be best able to deal with metropolitanwide problems at the metropolitan level.

However, gargantua, with its single dominant center of decision-making, is apt to become a victim of the complexity of its own hierarchical or bureaucratic structure. Its complex channels of communication may make its administration unresponsive to many of the more localized public interests in the community. The costs of maintaining control in gargantua's public service may be so great that its production of public goods becomes grossly inefficient.

Gargantua, as a result, may become insensitive and clumsy in meeting the demands of local citizens for the public goods required in their daily life. Two to three years may be required to secure street or sidewalk improvements, for example, even where local residents bear the cost of the improvement. Modifications in traffic control at a local intersection may take an unconscionable amount of time. Some decision-makers will be more successful in pursuing their interests than others. The lack of effective organization for these others may result in policies with highly predictable biases. Bureaucratic unresponsiveness in gargantua may produce frustration and cynicism on the part of the local citizen who finds no point of access for remedying local problems of a public character. Municipal reform may become simply a matter of "throwing the rascals out." The citizen may not have access to sufficient information to render an informed judgment at the polls. Lack of effective communication in the large public organization may indeed lead to the eclipse of the public and to the blight of the community.

The problem of gargantua, then, is to recognize the variety of smaller sets of publics that may exist within its boundaries. Many of the interests of smaller publics might be properly negotiated within the confines of a smaller political community without requiring the attention of centralized decision-makers concerned with the big system. This task of recognizing the smaller publics is a problem of "field" or "area" organization. The persistence of bureaucratic unresponsiveness in the big system, however, indicates it is not easily resolved. Large-scale, metropolitanwide organization is unquestionably appropriate for a limited number of public services, but it is not the most appropriate scale of organization for the provision of all public services required in a metropolis.

IV. PUBLIC ORGANIZATION IN A POLYCENTRIC POLITICAL SYSTEM

No *a priori* judgment can be made about the adequacy of a polycentric system of government as against the single jurisdiction. The multiplicity of interests in various public goods sought by people in a metropolitan region can only be handled in the context of many different levels of organization. The polycentric system is confronted with the problem of realizing the needs of wider community interests or publics beyond the functional or territorial bounds of each of the formal entities within the broader metropolitan region. The single jurisdiction, in turn, confronts the problem of recognizing and organizing the various subsidiary sets of interests within the big system. It is doubtful that suboptimization in gargantua is any easier to accomplish than supraoptimization in a polycentric political system.

The performance of a polycentric political system can only be understood and evaluated by reference to the patterns of cooperation, competition, and conflict that may exist among its various units. Cooperative arrangements pose no difficulty when joint activities produce a greater return to all parties concerned, if the appropriate set of public interests are adequately represented among the negotiators. A contractual arrangement will suffice. As a result, this discussion of the behavior of a polycentric political system will focus upon the more difficult problems of competition, of conflict, and its resolution. If a polycentric political system can resolve conflict and maintain competition within appropriate bounds it can be a viable arrangement for dealing with a variety of public problems in a metropolitan area.

Competition[14]

Where the provision of public goods and services has been successfully internalized within a public jurisdiction, there are no substantial spillover effects, by definition. In such circumstances there need be no detrimental consequences from competition in the municipal services economy. Patterns of competition among producers of public services in a metropolitan area, just as among firms in the market, may produce substantial benefits by inducing self-regulating tendencies with pressure for the more efficient solution in the operation of the whole system.

Variety in service levels among various independent local government agencies within a larger metropolitan community may give rise to a quasi-market choice for local residents in permitting them to select the particular community in the metropolitan area that most closely approximates the public service levels they desire. Public service agencies then may be forced to compete over the service levels offered in relation to the taxes charged. Such competition, however, would only be appropriate for those public goods which are adequately internalized within the boundaries of a given political jurisdiction.

Conditions amenable to competition normally exist among local units of government where a number of units are located in close proximity to each other and where information about each other's performance is publicly available. Information can lead to comparison and comparison can lead to pressure for performances to approximate the operations of the more efficient units. Where more than one public jurisdiction is capable of rendering service in a single area, further competitive tendencies may develop. Contractual arrangements among public jurisdictions for the provision of specific public services have long provided a competitive alternative to each jurisdiction which might otherwise produce its own services.

The separation of the *provision* of public goods and services from their *production* opens up the greatest possibility of redefining economic functions in a public service economy. Public control can be maintained in relation to performance criteria in the provision of services, while allowing an increasing amount of competition to develop among the agencies that produce them.

With the incorporation of the City of Lakewood in 1954, Los Angeles County, for example, expanded its system of contracting for the production of municipal services to a point approaching quasi-market conditions. Newly incorporated cities, operating under the so-called Lakewood Plan, contract with

---

14 This analysis is confined to competition between units of government and makes no reference to competitive forces within a unit of government. Competition among pressure groups, factions, and political parties is a fundamental feature of the democratic political process, but is not within the primary focus of this paper and its concern with the polycentric system.

the county or other appropriate agencies to produce the general range of municipal services needed in the local community.

Each city contracts for municipal services for the city as a whole. Services beyond the general level of performance by county administration in unincorporated areas are subject to negotiation for most service functions. Each city also has the option of producing municipal services for itself. Private contractors too have undertaken such services as street sweeping, engineering, street maintenance and repair, and related public works. Some contracts have been negotiated with neighboring cities. As the number of vendors increases, competition brings pressures toward greater responsiveness and efficiency.

By separating the production from the provision of public goods it may be possible to differentiate, unitize, and measure the production while continuing to provide undifferentiated public goods to the citizen-consumer. Thus Los Angeles County has, under the Lakewood Plan, unitized the production of police services into packages, each consisting of a police-car-on-continuous-patrol with associated auxiliary services. A price is placed on this police-car-on-continuous-patrol package, and a municipality may contract for police service on that basis. Within the local community, police service is still provided as a public good for the community as a whole.

Problems of scale arising from possible conflicts between criteria of production and criteria of political representation may be effectively resolved in this way. Efficient scales of organization for the production of different public goods may be quite independent of the scales required to recognize appropriate publics for their consumption of public goods and services. But competition among vendors may allow the most efficient organization to be utilized in the production, while an entirely different community of interest and scale of organization controls the provision of services in a local community.

The separation of production from provision may also have the consequence of turning local governments into the equivalents of associations of consumers. While Sidney and Beatrice Webb viewed local governments as associations of consumers, the dominance of production criteria in American municipal administration has largely led to the subordination of consumer interests.[15] However, cities organized to provide the local citizenry with public services produced by other agencies may be expected to give stronger representation to consumer interests. Among the so-called Lakewood Plan cities in Los Angeles County, for example, the local chief administrative officer has increasingly become a spokesman or bargainer for local consumer interests.

In this role, the chief administrative officer is similar to a buyer in a large corporation. Recognizing that the greater the number of vendors of public services, the greater the competition, the local chief administrative officer may seek to expand the number of his potential suppliers. As competition increases, vendors become more sensitive to the consumer demands he negotiates.

---

15 Sidney and Beatrice Webb, *English Local Government: Statutory Authorities for Special Purposes* (London: Longmans, Green and Co., 1922), pp. 437 ff.

The production of public goods under the contract system in Los Angeles County has also placed considerable pressure upon the county administration to become more responsive to demands of the public service clientele organized through their local cities. Important changes in operating procedures and organizational arrangements have been introduced into the county's administration of police protection, fire protection, library services, street maintenance, building inspection, and engineering services in order to increase efficiency and responsiveness.

Under these circumstances, a polycentric political system can be viable in supplying a variety of public goods with many different scales of organization and in providing optimal arrangements for the production and consumption of public goods. With the development of quasi-market conditions in production, much of the flexibility and responsiveness of market organization can be realized in the public service economy.

Several difficulties in the regulation of a competitive public service economy can be anticipated. Economic pricing and cost allocation are dependent upon the development of effective measurement of municipal services. Since the preferred states of affairs in a community cannot be converted to a single scale of values such as dollar profits in a private enterprise, it may be more difficult to sustain an objective competitive relationship in a public service economy. Although costs of contract services from different vendors of a public good may be the same, objective standards for determining the value of the benefits are needed, and may be hard to come by; otherwise the latitude of discretion available to the negotiators may limit the competitive vitality of the system and shift the competition to side-payoffs.

Without careful control of cost allocations and pricing arrangements, funds from non-competitive welfare functions might be used to subsidize the more competitive service areas. In Los Angeles County, close scrutiny of cost accounting practices and pricing policies by the grand jury has helped to prevent funds from being so transferred.

Any long-term reliance upon quasi-market mechanisms in the production of public goods and services no doubt will require more of such careful scrutiny, control, and regulation than has been applied toward maintaining the competitive structure of the private market economy. The measurement of cost and output performance may become an essential public function of the state in the administration of metropolitan affairs if continued reliance is placed primarily upon a polycentric system in the government of metropolitan areas.

Reliance upon outside vendors to produce public services may also reduce the degree of local political control exercised. The employee is subject to the control of the vendor and not directly to the control of the municipality. In contrast to the more immediate lines of responsibility and communication between local municipal employees and city officials, reliance upon vendors to provide municipal services may also restrict the quality and quantity of information about community affairs that are provided to the city's decision-makers. This constraint on information might reduce the degree of their control over public affairs.

This discussion merely indicates some of the considerations to be examined in an analysis of the effects of competitive arrangements in providing public services. As long as the particular contracting agencies encompass the appropriate sets of public interests no absolute impediment to their use need exist. With appropriate public control, competitive arrangements may afford great flexibility in taking advantage of some of the economies of scale for the production of public services in a metropolitan area, while, at the same time, allowing substantial diversity in their provision for the more immediate communities, based upon political responsibility within local patterns of community identification.

Conflict and conflict resolution

More difficult problems for a polycentric political system are created when the provision of public goods cannot be confined to the boundaries of the existing units of government. These situations involving serious spillover effects are apt to provoke conflict between the various units in the system. Arrangements must be available for the resolution of such conflicts if a polycentric political system is to solve its problems. Otherwise, competition and conflict are apt to become acute.

No community, on its own initiative, has much incentive to assume the full costs of controlling adverse consequences which are shared by a wider public. The competitive disadvantage of enforcing pollution abatement regulations, for example, against individuals and firms within a single community, when competitors in neighboring communities are not required to bear such costs, leads each community to excuse its failure to act by the failure of other similarly situated communities to act. In a polycentric system this is especially serious where many of the public "goods" involve the costly abatement of public nuisances.

Concerted action by the various units of government in a metropolitan area is easier to organize when costs and benefits are fairly uniformly distributed throughout the area. By way of example, this has been done under contractual agreements for mutual aid to assure the mobilization of greater fire-fighting capability in case of serious conflagrations. The random and unpredictable nature of such fires causes them to be treated as a uniform risk that might occur to any community in the larger metropolitan area.

Similar considerations apply to efforts to control mosquito infestations or air pollution. Leagues of cities, chambers of commerce, and other civic associations have frequently become the agencies for negotiating legislative proposals for the creation of mosquito abatement districts, air pollution control districts, and the like.

More difficult problems for the polycentric political system arise when the benefits and the costs are not uniformly distributed. Communities may differ in their perception of the benefits they receive from the provision of a common public good. In turn, a community may be unwilling to "pay its fair share" for providing that good simply because its demands for provision are less than in neighboring communities. These situations call for effective governmental mechanisms which can internalize the problem. If necessary, sanctions must be available for the enforcement of decisions.

The conflicting claims of municipal water supply systems pumping water from the same underground basins in Southern California, for example, have uniformly been resolved by recourse to legal actions in the state courts. The courts have thereby become the primary authorities for resolving conflicts among water supply agencies in Southern California; and their decisions have come to provide many of the basic policies of water administration in the Southern California metropolitan region. The state's judiciary has played a comparable role in conflicts among other local government agencies in such diverse fields as public health, incorporation and annexation proceedings, law enforcement, and urban planning.

The heavy reliance upon courts for the resolution of conflicts among local units of government unquestionably reflects an effort to minimize the risks of external control by a superior decision-maker. Court decisions are taken on a case-by-case basis. The adversaries usually define the issues and consequently limit the areas of judicial discretion. This method also minimizes the degree of control exercised following a judgment. California courts, in particular, have accepted the basic doctrines of home rule and are thus favorably disposed to the interests of local units of government in dealing with problems of municipal affairs.

The example of municipal water administration may be pursued further to illustrate other decision-making arrangements and their consequences which bear upon the resolution of conflict in a polycentric political system.[16]

While litigation may be an appropriate means for resolving conflicts over a given supply of water, local water administrators in Southern California have long recognized that lawsuits never produced any additional water. Organization for the importation of new water supplies was recognized as the only means for solving the long-term problem.

Los Angeles built the first major aqueduct to import water into the area on its own initiative. This water supply was used to force adjoining areas to annex or consolidate to the City of Los Angeles if they wished to gain access to the new supply. The condition for the provision of water required adjoining areas to sacrifice their identities as separate political communities. To get that one public good they were forced to give up other public goods. This provoked sufficient opposition to block any new developments which were not based

---

16 For further detail see: Vincent Ostrom, *Water and Politics* (Los Angeles, Haynes Foundation, 1953), esp. Chs. 3, 6, and 7.

upon consent and cooperation. The mechanisms for the resolution of subsequent conflicts were required to take on new forms.

The importation of Colorado River water was later undertaken by a coalition of communities in Southern California formed through the agency of the southern section of the League of California Cities. The League afforded a neutral ground for the negotiation of the common interests of the City of Los Angeles and the other cities in the metropolitan area which shared common water problems. After satisfactory arrangements had been negotiated, including provision for the formation of a new metropolitan water district and endorsement of the Boulder Canyon project, a Boulder Dam Association was formed to realize these objectives. In due course a new agency, the Metropolitan Water District of Southern California, was formed; and the Colorado River aqueduct was constructed and put into operation by this new district.

More recently, the Southern California Water Coordinating Conference, meeting under the auspices of the Los Angeles Chamber of Commerce, has been the agency for negotiating regional interests in the development of the California Water Program. The Metropolitan Water District was not able to represent areas in Southern California which did not belong to that district; and the rise of a variety of special municipal water districts precluded the League of California Cities, which represents cities only, from again serving as the agency for the negotiation of metropolitan interests in municipal water supply.

These illustrations suggest that a variety of informal arrangements may be available for negotiating basic policies among local government agencies in a metropolitan area. Such arrangements are vital in negotiating common interests among them. The larger public is taken into account in an informally constituted political community. These arrangements work effectively only so long as substantial unanimity can be reached, for formal implementation of such decisions must be ratified by each of the appropriate official agencies, including the state government when changes in state law or administrative policies are involved.

Higher levels of government may also be invoked in seeking the resolution of conflict among local governments in metropolitan areas. Again recourse is sought to a more inclusive political community. Under these circumstances, conflict tends to centralize decision-making and control. The danger is that the more inclusive political community will not give appropriate recognition to the particular public interests at issue and tend to inject a variety of other interests into settlements of local controversies.

Appeal to central authorities runs the risk of placing greater control over local metropolitan affairs in agencies such as the state legislature, while at the same time reducing the capability of local governments for dealing with their problems in the local context. Sensitivity over the maintenance of local control may produce great pressure for the subordination of differences while conflicting parties seek a common position approximating unanimity. A substantial investment in informal negotiating and decision-making arrangements can be justified from the perspective of the local authorities if such arrangements can prevent the loss of local autonomy to higher levels of government.

Ironically but logically, this effort to avoid recourse to conflict and the consequent centralization of decision-making tends also to reduce the local autonomy or degree of independence exercised by the local governing boards. Pressure for agreement on a common approach to some metropolitan problem limits the choices available to any particular local government. However, this range of choice may still be greater than that which would result from a settlement by a central authority. Negotiation among independent agencies allows the use of a veto against any unacceptable position. Agreement must be negotiated within the limits of the various veto positions if the alternative of recourse to an external authority at a higher level of political jurisdiction is to be avoided.

To minimize the costs of conflict to their power positions, administrators of local government agencies in metropolitan areas have tended to develop an extensive system of communication about each other's experience and to negotiate standards of performance applicable to various types of public services. Professional administrative standards may, thus, operate to constrain the variety of experience in local government agencies. Information about areas of difference and of potential conflict tend to be repressed under these circumstances. The negotiations about common problems through informal agencies are apt to be conducted in secrecy, and careful control may be developed over sensitive information.

These pressures to avoid the costs of conflict and seek agreement about metropolitan problems reflect the importance to local governments of resolving general public problems by negotiation at the local level in a metropolitan community. To the extent that these pressures are effective, the patterns of local government in a metropolitan area can only be understood by attention to the variety of formal and informal arrangements that may exist for settling areawide problems.

Contrary to the frequent assertion about the lack of a "metropolitan framework" for dealing with metropolitan problems, most metropolitan areas have a very rich and intricate "framework" for negotiating, adjudicating and deciding questions that affect their diverse public interests. Much more careful attention needs to be given to the study of this framework.

ALFRED DE GRAZIA

Local Institutions

. . . How does the study of levels of government relate to the study of political behavior and of the internal branches of the government? First, it adds a
new dimension, a new and important viewpoint to the study of political materials; it is a new way of cross-sectioning political events. Second, it introduces a
whole new group of generalizations or principles that pertain to political organization on a given level—local, federal, or international.

We should emphasize, however, that the study of the *levels* of government
derives a great many principles of value from the study of *political behavior*
and of the *internal political organization* of governments. The elements of
political behavior may be found throughout political events. We have not
hesitated, for example, to observe city bosses as well as presidents in our study
of leadership. Also we have considered the main levels of government in our
study of the legislative, executive, administrative, and judicial processes and
have found similarities in these processes on all levels of government. For
example, we have found that the legislative process of the state legislatures and
city councils has much in common with that of the national Congress, and the
judicial process operates in many ways the same whether we scrutinize it in the
commune, in the highest national court, or in an international tribunal.

. . .

FROM TRIBE TO METROPOLIS

Universal nature of local government

Man is bound to the earth, to geography, and from birth is with few excep-

Reprinted with permission of The Macmillan Company from *The Elements of Political
Science*, Volume II by Alfred de Grazia. © Alfred de Grazia 1962.

tions part of a territorial organization covering not more than a few miles. Whether or not the locality in which one is born maintains its primacy among his loyalties or influences exclusively his thoughts, it is rarely deserted completely by him in favor of competing political organizations. It is rarely forgotten, and always leaves an imprint on his character. A man is marked by "where he comes from." Furthermore, wherever he goes, he finds a new locality and a new local political organization about him. The national government or international order under which he lives may remain the same throughout his movements from one locality to another; Cass County, Peoria, and New York City all fly the same flag. But even if there were no national or international order, there would be a local order, as centuries of history have demonstrated. The past is laden with the importance of local government. The typical organization of mankind before the era of writing was the tribe. The first empires of the Near East and China sprang from aggressive and expanding cities. The climax of ancient history, from one point of view, was the attempt of the Persian Empire to destroy the city-states of the Greeks. The medieval cities nurtured the commerce and arts of the Western world for centuries and the folk of the country were attached firmly to small principalities, highly organized and isolated from the larger world.

The subjection of independent cities to nations

National government is the dominant form of the organization of political power in modern times. Sometimes this condition is laid to the development of wider markets, the increased movement of individuals, greater efficiency of government, and other reasons that assume that local sovereignty is incompatible with material progress. The fact is, however, that the unification of peoples into large nations that ushered in the modern period of Western history was not accomplished solely in the service of material progress. Venice, Florence, Genoa, Cologne, Amsterdam, Hamburg, and other medieval city-states lost their independence to greater states, not because of their poverty, their restriction of trade, or their incompetence, but, to the contrary, *because* they were tempting targets of aggrandizement to the most powerful nobles and kings. Hence we conclude that no "natural law" of efficiency directed the process by which cities became subordinate to nations.

More likely, the source of the pressure towards national unity in the nations of Europe, and thence America and Asia, came from an effective organization of rural localities. That is, as rural governments became well organized, their chiefs compelled the cities to form part of a national unity. When the kings improved the administrative and mechanical means of integrating and ruling large tracts of land, they could easily assemble the means to influence or conquer the independent cities.

The loss of local sovereignty to the nation frequently does not signify a great loss of power. This is especially true after the initial period in which a city-state becomes part of a large empire or national domain. Athens lost its sovereignty to the Roman Republic towards the end of the pagan era, but many Athenians became powerful Romans. Dutch cities lost their sovereignty to Spain in the sixteenth century, but economically they flourished and therefore constituted within the greater empire a political aggregate of considerable scope and influence. The same process occurred in the nineteenth century when the free city of Frankfort was joined to Prussia. Hence, we conclude that localities may lose sovereignty (symbolic and ultimate power) but increase their scope of power and retain many powers previously possessed.

Regionalism and localism remain strong

These glimpses of the colorful history of local government should prevent an exaggerated notion of how all-embracing nationalism has been or can be. It should also inform us that history does not move uniformly and that at any period of history, one can find tribes, city-states, and empires or other colossal human aggregations existing side by side. Among the cities and within the empires and nations one finds many differences of organization and varying degrees of independence of outside authority. The study of local government among contemporary political scientists is confined principally to localities that subsist under the aegis of a national government. This practice is in accord with the important facts of politics, for no great city or important local organization today is "free" in the sense that ancient Athens, Sparta, or Rome were free.

Yet national boundaries obscure many important internal differences and many examples of the great power of cities. For example, nationalism is weak in China where the village is the true community and strong in Germany where the Reich is the true community. But even this statement must be carefully guarded. The Chinese are not all localistic; many are Westernized or Sovietized nationalists; and some Bavarians, for instance, have always resisted German nationalism.

Also we include in localism attachments to territorial divisions larger than cities or rural neighborhoods. Many Americans are first Californians, first New Yorkers, first Texans. Italians and French are strong in regional sentiments; very often the Sicilian and the Florentine, the Breton and the Marseillais feel that national policy does not solve many regional issues. But under modern conditions, the tendency of politics seems to be to reinforce the national state and the first order or first level local government as centers of community sentiment. Internal political regionalism, be it in China or in the American South, seems to be declining as a source of political energy, and as a basis for political movements.

Administrative regionalism versus political regionalism

However, like the receding tides, political regionalism leaves behind a clutter composed of remaining sentiments, surviving structures of governments, and vested interests of people in jobs and status. Meanwhile, a new kind of regionalism—administrative in nature, technological in origin, and efficient in motive—is developing, and this new kind of regionalism cannot move far in the direction of governmental reorganization because it is blocked by the remains of the older regionalism, among other things.

Let us glance at the central concerns of the new regionalism and appraise briefly its prospects. Giant states like China and the Soviet Union have within them many divisions which may be called regions whether one defines the term for political, economic, physiographic, or cultural purposes. Even small nations like England and Belgium have within them surprising diversity in all these respects. A regional map of the United States can be constructed from different physiographic, economic, and social viewpoints. Figures 1–3 present three types of such regions.

But politics cannot coincide with any regional boundaries save in a general way. For one thing, regionalism, like the principle of self-determination, if pressed to its ultimate conclusions would result in dozens of unmanageable tiny areas in even a modestly sized country. The American South is a "natural" region and many political consequences emanate from that condition; yet, for example, Virginia differs in many significant ways from Texas or Arkansas. Then too, regions overlap. A region may be "natural" for one purpose but not for another. The inhabitants on one bank of a river may present a different

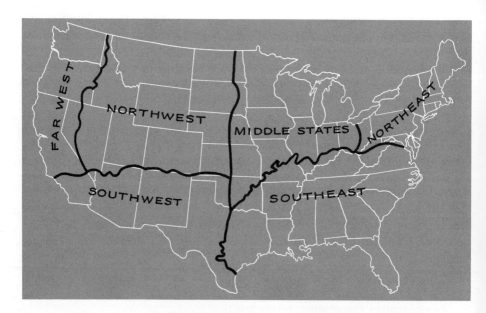

FIG. 1   Regions of socio-economic homogeneity; *showing the boundaries as they would probably be if state lines were disregarded.*

culture from those on the opposite bank, although both share important common problems. So too may be the case with an upriver and downriver region; for example, Minnesota and Louisiana that are both on the Mississippi River differ strikingly from each other. The best sort of regional boundaries for a forest conservation program may not at all coincide with the optimum limits of a hydroelectric power district. A civil defense district may hardly relate to natural physiography.

So regionalism can never be a standard for the construction of human boundaries that will please everyone. Administrative regionalism may be best defined as an attempt to assemble in appropriate limits as many common

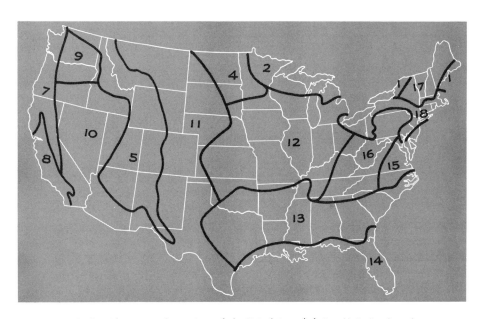

FIG. 2   Major geographic regions of the United States* (after M.C. Stark and D.S. Whittlesey).

1. Maritime Canadian Region	11. Semi-Arid Region
2. Region of Extractive Industries	12. Interior Mixed Farming Region
4. Spring Wheat Region	13. Cotton Region
5. Region of Rocky Mts. and Plateau	14. Southern Coastal Region
7. Pacific Cordilleran Region	15. Chesapeake Mixed Farming Region
8. California Region	16. Appalachian Upland Region
9. Columbia Plateau Wheat Region	17. New England Upland Region
10. Arid Region	18. Eastern Urban Region

* National Resources Planning Committee, *Regional Factors in National Planning and Development* (Washington, D.C.: United States Government Printing Office, 1935), pp. 174, 177. Note: two regions (3 and 6) are omitted from the map as developed by the N.R.P.C.

natural and cultural qualities as possible. Nor is this attitude granted free play, for practically everywhere we find that history has left eccentric tracings on men and places, burdening the present with political considerations of many generations past. Witness the difference in size of Rhode Island and that of Texas. Their boundaries are not wholly "natural" and seem anachronistic to the perfectionist and to the foreigner because of the rapid growth of communications and interstate industry.

Every nation has a cultural geography that does not conform in a high degree to political jurisdictions and political demands. Even great revolutions have failed to eradicate the individual cultures of regions. The Bolshevists, conscious at first only of the overpowering identity of interest among the "toiling masses," eventually began to encourage regional diversities of a cultural sort. So also did the French revolutionaries who thought initially only of the equality of all men and who sought mathematically to delimit provincial boundaries. Reacting to such excessive zeal for conformity and uniformity, an influential "regionalist" movement grew up in France in the nineteenth and twentieth centuries.

Still we find, in America and in most countries of western Europe that have been reorganized politically over the last century and a half, that present polit-

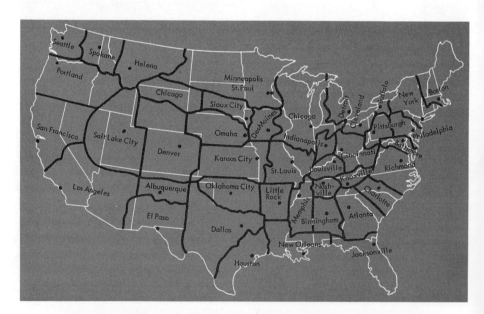

FIG. 3   Metropolitan regions in the United States as defined by daily newspaper circulation, 1929 (after R.D. McKenzie). Each heavy line encloses all cities or towns receiving 50 per cent or more of their metropolitan circulation from the given center. Note: The morning daily having the most extensive circulation was chosen for each center.

ical and administrative boundaries have tended to replace the customary boundaries. The French provinces of the *ancien régime* were replaced after the Revolution of 1789 by *départements* (for administration and elections) and *arrondissements* (chiefly for electoral purposes). The historic English counties (52 in number) have lost heavily in functions to the new administrative counties (62). The Italian republic of 1870–1922 created a number of administrative provinces out of the fewer historic regions of Italy, and the Fascist State carried farther the process of disregarding historic conditions by erecting a structure of *corporazione* for representing occupations regardless of their geographic location.

Administrative districts

In all countries, modern administration has by-passed traditional boundaries, including political ones, in performing its new functions. Certain of these new districts are created for ease and convenience of administration alone. Such would be election districts, judicial districts, tax collection districts, police precincts, fire protection districts, and school districts. Other kinds of districts are of far-reaching importance, for they perform tasks of great complexity and influence. Examples would be the districts formed in the United States by the Interstate Commerce Commission, or the Tennessee Valley Authority region that is almost a socio-economic world in itself and yet spreads over several "sovereign" state boundaries, making and carrying out policies that affect all the people in those states. The Port of London Authority and the Port of New York Authority are other examples of governmental bodies set up to determine and administer policy affecting the lives and fortunes of people governed by different local governments.

Units of government

The districts we have just described are purely administrative in the sense that their officers are selected for the performance of particular tasks and are not chosen by elections. The number of such districts is great. The United States alone may have a million such districts; and we may define units of government more strictly and still reach, according to the calculations of William Anderson and the Bureau of the Census, a total of 155,067 in 1942. Anderson defines a *unit of government* as "a resident population occupying a defined area that has a legally authorized organization and governing body, a separate legal identity, the power to provide certain public or governmental services, and a substantial degree of autonomy including legal and actual power to raise at least a part of its own revenues." There are more than a thousand such units in the metropolitan region of Chicago, and even more in the New York region. There are a great many overlapping police, fire, and other political jurisdictions. Extensive duplications of budgets, expenditures, and revenue collections occur. The complexity and prolixity of governing units together with the grave social problems of the rapidly growing cities have produced political problems of the first magnitude.

Urbanization

Indeed we might say that the great complexity of governmental units has been at least partially due to rapid urbanization. For example, the United States began as a preponderantly rural country: in 1790, only about 5 per cent of the population of four millions lived in what might be termed urban centers. The important forms of local government in those days were the county and the town, both essentially rural forms of government that have left their impression on local government to this day. Today most persons live in places of 2500 or more inhabitants or in the immediate shadow of metropolitan centers; only 20 million individuals live in truly rural places. The same process of urbanization has occurred in the countries of western Europe and, to a smaller extent, in other parts of the world. The proportion of people living in the cities is still increasing throughout the world, though in Europe the rate of increase is not so rapid as it was during the late nineteenth and early twentieth centuries. The Soviet Union, which has undergone its period of rapid industrialization later than the western European countries, is an exception; its rate of urbanization is still high.

Urban and rural societies

The differences between the city and country as centers of human activity give rise to important differences in the government and politics of the two types of human environment. The city presents a great problem of engineering; its public works, huge private buildings, great streams of traffic, ceaseless flow of production, commerce, and consumption bewilder the mind and demand ingenious and complex economic and physical arrangements. Its large expenditures and revenues present political and administrative difficulties of the first order. The wide range of needs, demands, and expectations of a heterogeneous population gives urban politics a color and complexity that does not occur in most rural communities.

From a sociological viewpoint, there is also a great contrast between urban and rural life. The farmer in his work does not deal with men so much as with the land and its products. The city worker constantly encounters other people and works in close association and competition with them. Life in the village and country is "close" and "familiar," and the human contacts are informal and "primary," as the sociologists say. City life is "distant" and "strange," and the human contacts are formal and "secondary."

As Park and Burgess have described the contrast:

> The neighborhood or the village is the natural area of primary contacts. In primary association individuals are in contact with each other at practically all points of their lives. In the village "everyone knows everything about everyone

else." Canons of conduct are absolute, social control is omnipotent, the status of the family and individuals are fixed. In secondary associations individuals are in contact with each other at only one or two points in their lives. In the city, the individual becomes anonymous; at best he is generally known in only one or two aspects of his life. Standards of behavior are relative; the old primary controls have disappeared; the new secondary instruments of discipline, necessarily formal, are for the most part crude and inefficient; the standing of the family and of the individual is uncertain and subject to abrupt changes upward or downward in the social scale.[1]

To say that this contrast is evident at all times and in all places would be incorrect. For instance, the rapid electrification of rural communities in America, the coming of the radio, motion pictures, and automobiles, the always restless mobility of the American people ("the frontier spirit") make the contrast at times dim. In Europe, Latin America, and Asia, the contrast between country man and city man is more striking, often showing itself in at least apparent differences in physical stature and other features.

Political problems arising from these various differences are profound and sometimes direct. The urban-rural debates over apportionment of representation in American state legislature are full of invective against one or the other mode of life. Hitler and the Nazis, mentally recoiling from modern urban sophistication and "strangeness," wished to remake Germany into a "folk state" in which everyone would feel that he "knew" everyone else and that all were "blood brothers."

The internal complications of local society

Beyond the differences normally occurring in urban as against rural societies, are significant internal social differences found in both kinds of localities. Whether we study the aborigines of Australia or the inhabitants of a New England town, citizens of old Athens or those of New York City, we find that the social structures of the societies account for numerous political situations.

Looking at a modern city, for example, one perceives two general configurations of the population, one geographical and based on the neighborhood, another social and based on social class. The significant social-geographical configurations found in the city may be called its ecology. Professor Park discovered that most cities grew up similarly in recent times. The center of the city contains its main business district, communication centers, large offices, hotels, and railroad terminals. The next belt or circle around the "downtown" area holds the poor, shifting population, the factories, and newly arrived workers from the country or abroad. Next comes the area of workers' homes, and then the belt of middle class residences of clerks, more skilled workers, and older immigrant groups. Finally one reaches groups having higher incomes and

---

[1] Quoted with permission from Robert E. Park and Ernest W. Burgess, *Introduction to the Science of Sociology*, 2nd ed. (Chicago: University of Chicago Press, 1924), pp. 285–286.

more education, including the bulk of professional and managerial personnel and the oldest residents of the community. An increasing number of the last category commute long distances to work and live in suburbs outside the legal jurisdiction of the city government.

The different sociological areas of the city produce different demands on government. For example, certain wards of Chicago contain a high proportion of all Chicagoans who receive direct public assistance to relieve the effects of poverty. Other wards contain a high proportion of people who are well-to-do. Each kind of area produces different kinds of voting behavior, different types of leaders, and generally a different political process.

Linked with the ecological divisions of the city and their political consequences may be the composition of the social classes within the city. A number of sociologists and cultural anthropologists have given us detailed studies of the social structure of various cities and rural communities. Among such writers, one may name especially Robert and Helen Lynd, Lloyd Warner, Paul S. Lunt, John Dollard, Clyde Kluckhohn, George P. Murdock, James West, and Alison Davis. Lloyd Warner and his associates, for example, studied a town of 17,000 in New England over a period of years and were able to show that in a number of ways the political attitudes and political associations of an individual varied in kind and extent with his position in the class structure of the town. In "Yankee City," as the town under discussion was termed, the authors examined the social position of the 136 officeholders in 1930-31 and concluded:

> Although the voters among the three lower classes far outnumbered those in the three higher, they had a disproportionately small percentage of officers in the political hierarchy. . . . Indeed, as the importance of the political offices increased, the proportion of upper-class officeholders increased.[2]

Also, the studies indicated a point that the authors did not fully develop, but which had previously been developed by Roberto Michels: in a representative government with universal suffrage, *politics is one of the most important points of contact between the various social classes.* Thus, James West made a study of "Plainville," a farm village nestled between North and South in the central part of the United States. In describing the social classes that existed in this rural area, he recited the exceptional case of a man who rose in class position quickly. "Ora Bell, who died recently, was the son of 'one of the biggest and worst and most ignorant families in town.' He was 'bright in high school,' 'worked every chance he got,' 'showed himself to be absolutely reliable,' 'kept away from all bad company except his family,' married a 'good, moral girl' (from the upper edge of the lower class), bought a home, saved his money, made many friends and finally ran for one of the county offices and won.

---

2 From W. Lloyd Warner and Paul S. Lunt, *The Social Life of a Modern Community* (New Haven: Yale University Press, 1941).

('People give Ory lots of credit for what he done, and they helped him. He showed what anybody can do what'll try.')"

The preceding remarks suggest that the study of local government is only half-done when the formal structure of government is mastered. The social organization and the political behavior of the population must also be studied. A striking fact (encountered rather early in a political career) is that city and country government are always meshed with the social structure of the locality at many points. If one studies the old English shire without understanding the connection between the local gentry and the public officers, if one studies modern Swiss cities without realizing the importance of the ancient and haughty families of the community, if one is concerned with the American scene and misunderstands the extent to which economic power and social prestige enter into the relations among citizens and politicians, one performs purely formal exercises and starves his own cause.

Stuart Chase was so impressed by studies such as those of Warner that he urged their consideration by all who work with local government. He wrote:

> The information already available ... in these books and monographs cannot fail, as Wissler said, to be helpful to all who direct the affairs of American towns—mayors, selectmen, city managers, chiefs of police, welfare commissioners, housing authorities, city planners, social workers, police court judges, traffic officials, school boards.[3]

Local attachments vary among individuals

While it is true that everyone in a local community is affected directly or indirectly by the government, the politics, and the social conditions of the locality, it is patent that individuals vary greatly in the extent to which they *feel involved* in the events of the locality. It will be remembered that we defined "community" in the first volume as the habitual relations or communications among people reaching a stipulated scope and degree of intensity. We left it up to each student to declare what particular community he was referring to in any particular case. Now so complex is modern society that, while one person may be obviously part of a national community in a psychological sense, a neighboring individual may be psychologically part of a local community only. Psychologically, the latter is more involved in immediate local affairs; his perspective is local; his interests are viewed locally; he becomes excited mostly about local questions.

We have already commented on the fact that a world community hardly can be said to exist save by the Hydrogen Bomb test: everyone may be blown up together. So far as identifications and psychological involvements go, the overwhelming majority of men and women are not members of such a community. What is not so often appreciated perhaps is that, in many countries,

---

[3] Quoted with permission from Stuart Chase, *The Proper Study of Mankind* (New York: Harper and Brothers, 1948), p. 135.

most people are first members of local communities and only secondarily, if at all, members of the national community—again speaking psychologically rather than physically. Furthermore, a considerable number of individuals identify most strongly with the smallest city precinct or unit of government—if they may be said to have any political identifications at all.

Local proximity groups

Such "proximity-bound" individuals form a myriad of little communication pools or interaction clusters. They constitute informal political action-reaction units. These groups may be compared with the "work group" found in large-scale functional organizations. The member of such work groups are tied to one another technologically by the task to be done and psychologically by the social relations arising from the contacts of their personalities and their operations. Proximity-bound individuals may also be compared with the army squad that has its own perspectives, morale, and group purposes, and that has only a rough and somewhat unconscious understanding of the vast plans of the army. But, unlike the work group and the squad, the proximity-bound political group is normally purposeless with relation to any great plan of the nation, party, or even the formal side of local government. Also, its communications are voluntaristic, sporadic, and not geared to any significant extent, by consciously designed machinery, to the grand issues of local—much less national and international—politics.

Too rarely does the observer of national and international issues turn to contemplate the politics of an urban or rural neighborhood. When he does he must perceive that the problems he regards as important are as nothing to a good part of the people he encounters. Many of the cultural practices of the people are bound up with decisions in the local sphere that directly affect them. A good part of the vote in elections everywhere is motivated by local interests, the voters in no lively sense being impelled by international, national, state, or even city-wide interests. The present writer's own experience would indicate that the vast majority of all contacts between people and government occur on neighborhood matters—matters concerning streets and alleys, schools and playgrounds, disputes over minor property rights, zoning and housing regulations, jobs and contracts, personal friendships and political grudges, and other concerns directly interesting to a handful of people. In certain nations, England and the Soviet Union for example, neighborhood matters may be of less importance in government than in the American republics or in France or Italy, but they are always of momentous consideration in the study and practice of politics.

It is also interesting to note that a large proportion of people are closer in the sense just described to their local governments than to their governments at a higher level, *even though they may trust* the officials of the higher government to a greater degree. Closeness is a product of frequency of interaction and the intensity of interest with which the interaction takes place. The teachers a child has, the policemen he observes going about their work, the cleanliness of the streets and alleys, the ordering of traffic, the removal of snow and debris, the inspection of facilities, the guidance of his recreation, and many other influences help to account for his political actions as an adult. The manner in which the most august political leaders debate in the United Nations Security Council and on the floor of Congress, and the manner in which such leaders operate the agencies of the administrative establishment invariably reflect their childhood experiences with local government.

High physical mobility in America

Moreover, in America at least, much of this local interest is not directed at the general problems of local government, but at immediate personal needs alone. To cite the complaint of many reformers, this great localism is directed at the wrong objects and therefore does not profit the locality as a whole. Local government in America would undoubtedly be the focus of more conscious and informed attention than at present, if it were not for two phenomena of modern life.

The first cause of "wrong" focusing is the high physical mobility of Americans. About 20 per cent of the population changes residence each year. One-quarter of this group moves between counties or countries abroad and America. (Of course, some people move more often than others.) A large part of the urban population of the United States has come from the country and many from states other than the one in which they presently live. Thus, Detroit, with its automotive industry, has attracted thousands of workers from the South, both white and Negro. It is difficult for a mobile population to immerse itself immediately in the interests and needs of its new urban home. The same is true of many of the immigrants who came to America throughout its history. They could hardly become involved immediately in the affairs of the strange cities into which they moved. And groups with more education and higher incomes are almost as mobile; an upper-income family may dwell in three or four cities during one generation.

The suburban problem

A second phenomenon that reduces the involvement of Americans with their local governments is the suburbs of the twentieth century. Whereas until World War I, by far the greater part of those who worked in a city lived in it, by 1940 one out of every six Americans resided in a suburb. Consequently, millions of Americans with high incomes and high education are involved neither in the civic life of the suburb, which is their dormitory, nor in the city itself, which is their place of work.

The suburban problem, unlike the first factor of long-distance physical mobility, produces many problems in addition to the highly important fact of a low degree of psychological involvement and participation. For the suburbanites, who have much of the personal wealth of the metropolitan area, cannot be taxed as easily by the city as those who live within the city boundaries. Yet the city must continue to provide the suburbanite with water, fire protection, paved streets, police protection, traffic control, and other expensive services while he is in the city. And, as the tax burden on those who remain in the city becomes higher in order to support the services to nonpaying suburbanites, more people move from the city to the suburbs and the problems become progressively more grave.

To a lesser extent, the great European cities are faced by the same problem of suburbanism. European cities, however, are not so grossly unplanned as American cities. (Sinclair Lewis once said the latter were so unplanned that they appear to have been planned that way.) Within the limits of the European standards of living, their cities are relatively "livable." Furthermore, European cities, for many reasons, are less subject to exploitation by private political interests than American cities. Their need for expansion and special governing institutions has been more favored by the governing legislature or executive.

HOWARD W. ODUM
AND HARRY ESTILL MOORE

Exploring the Region:
The Political Scientists

It would be difficult to find a more trenchant dictum with which to introduce the regional aspects of political science and to tie in the present American
situation with the classical political theory than the statement of Marshall E.
Dimock that "Federalism remains the most difficult problem of the American
constitutional system."[1] The special point which he is emphasizing here is that
"in a country as vast and varied as ours, there is needed an intermediate level
of administrative co-ordination and planning authority midway between the
states and the Federal Government." This need has been accentuated, he
thinks, by the growing fear that too much federal control would result in a
paralyzing over-centralization and loss of democratic participation in government and that the remedy is to be found somewhere within the bounds of
regional decentralization and planning. Yet this very timely characterization
of current situations finds its theoretical background well integrated into the
whole fabric of human society from the early tribal origins of the state on up
to classical theories of sovereignty and its territorial aspects. Since this present
treatise on regionalism seeks primarily to see the problem as a broad societal
one, it will be well to point up the governmental aspects, first from early
society, and, then, catalogue some of the concepts and theories of the political
scientists.

From *American Regionalism: A Cultural-Historical Approach to National Integration*, by
Howard W. Odum and Harry Estill Moore. Copyright 1938 by Holt, Rinehart and Winston,
Inc. Copyright © 1966 by Anna K. Odum and Harry E. Moore. Reprinted by permission of
Holt, Rinehart and Winston, Inc.
1 "Political and Administrative Aspects of Regional Planning," *Planning for City, State,
Region, and Nation*, p. 111.

Ralph Linton in *The Study of Man* points up the same issues of sovereignty in relation to regional groups in the states which evolved in the principles of confederation. If we substitute the term "states" for "tribes" we might well apply his text to the federalism of the United States. Thus, confederacies of tribes . . .

> . . . owe their origin to a community of interest, even if this is of a very limited and specific sort. The function of the central authority is that of directing and co-ordinating the voluntary activities of the federated tribes. It derives its powers from the consent of the government, and any attempt to coerce the tribes is promptly resented. However, the presence of common interests makes it possible for the central authority to perform its functions with a minimum of machinery and of delegated powers. Since the component tribes are always jealous of their rights, the government of a confederacy must be democratic in fact if not in theory.[2]

Professor Linton does not hesitate to bring this problem of sovereignty up-to-date. He concludes his chapter on the "Tribe and State" by pointing out that

> In spite of some 6,000 years of experimentation, the problems of organizing and governing states have never been perfectly solved. The modern world, with the whole experience of history to draw upon, still attacks these problems in many different ways and with indifferent success. One thing seems certain. The most successful states are those in which the attitudes of the individual toward the state most nearly approximate the attitudes of the uncivilized individual toward his tribe. If the members of a state have common interests and a common culture, with the unity of will which these give, almost any type of formal governmental organization will function efficiently. If the members lack this feeling of unity, no elaboration of formal governmental patterns or multiplication of laws will produce an efficient state or contented citizens. How such unity may be created and maintained in great populations and especially in fluid ones where the individual's close, personal contacts are reduced to a minimum is probably the most important problem which confronts us today.[3]

Before pointing out something of the place of regional factors in historical political theory it may be well to recall that historically the problem of local units versus centralization has a distinguished history in the United States as well as in the societal evolution of states. We have cited many times over the historical factors in the form of sectionalism and conflict between the several regions and especially Turner's treatises on the significance of sections in American history. A part of Turner's explanation was in terms of politics and political alignments and he was constantly warning of the dangers which might come from conflict between what might become sectional states in conflict with the nation. We have also pointed out the sectional emphasis by such historians as Beard, Adams, Schlesinger, Dodd, Buck, and others. It is, however, important to note the more nearly purely political aspects of these areal problems

---

2 Ralph Linton, *The Study of Man,* pp. 241–242.
3 *Ibid.,* p. 252 (Quoted by permission of D. Appleton-Century Company.)

and there is no one perhaps who could symbolize both the problem and its contradictions better than Thomas Jefferson himself. For Jefferson even until his last days was deep in the contradictions of federal and state authorities. Before his tasks as President drew him into the difficulties of union, he was a strong states' rights advocate. So also he was until the end. In practice he was constantly on the verge of centralized federalism, either seeking through experiment to find equilibrium, or forced by exigency to go further in practice than his theories would justify. Then as now what to do and how to do it was the question.

Wirth has pointed up the fear of overcentralization and the desire for liberty within sovereignty as the factor which led Jefferson to be overzealous to prevent the encroachment of a powerful centralized government upon the local units, the states. Distribution within consolidation or decentralization within federalism might be termed the Jeffersonian principle. Thus he wrote:

> But it is not by the consolidation or concentration of powers, but by their distribution that good government is effected. Were not this great country already divided into states, that division must be made, that each might do for itself what concerns itself directly, and what it can so much better do than a distant authority. Every state again is divided into counties, each to take care of what lies within its local bounds; each county again into townships or wards, to manage minuter details; and every ward into farms, to be governed each by its individual proprietor. Were we directed from Washington when to sow, and when to reap, we should soon want bread. It is by this partition of cares, descending in gradation from general to particular, that the mass of human affairs may be best managed, for the good and prosperity of all.[4]

It would seem fairly easy to trace with considerable continuity this mooted problem from the present back through the nation's history and before that in the political theories which constitute the basis for sovereignty. Thus Merriam in his *History of Political Theories, Recent Times* interprets this relational factor of sovereignty as one of the chief subjects discussed since the turn of the century, from which point we may take the trail back through Dunning's earlier three volumes on the history of political theories. Up to the end of the first third of the twentieth century, however, Merriam finds no satisfying agreement among the political scientists. Thus his appraisal of recent theories seems to give the perfect background for such notable discussions as those of Gaus, Dimock, Renner and others in *Regional Factors in National Planning and Development*.

Merriam's summary estimates that

> One of the outstanding features of the time was the development of federalistic theories of the state. The political theory of federalism, based largely on geographical isolation, had developed in the earlier part of the nineteenth century, notably

---

[4] Quoted by Louis Wirth, "Localism, Regionalism, and Centralization," *The American Journal of Sociology*, XLII, No. 4, 496.

in the United States and in Germany, and had found expression in a definite form of political organization; but with the consolidation of such states, both the theory and the practice of federalism had tended to fall into a decline. Economic federalism, however, had also developed in the early part of the nineteenth century, notably in the theory of Proudhon. With the sharper division of classes on an industrial basis, and of professional and vocational groupings, attention was again directed toward the federalistic doctrine as a means of political association and organization. Again and again, especially toward the end of this period, recurred the problem of the organization of the state upon the basis of economic or professional groups rather than upon a geographic or an ethnical basis, or upon some combination of ethnogeographic factors.[5]

Continuing the Dunning historical thread, it is helpful to follow Dunning back to Bodin and Montesquieu. It is interesting to note the similarity between Giddings' theory of *causation* in which he related physical factors to psychic factors of state and the theories of Bodin in which he magnifies "the influence of the physical environment [which] makes the subject of a long and careful investigation in both the *Method* and the *Republic*." Professor Dunning interprets Bodin to estimate "national characteristics" such that "northern peoples excel in bodily, physical strength, southern peoples in craft and genius," while "the peoples between the extremes" are better adapted to "control politics and maintain justice."[6] So, too, Montesquieu features the influence of physical environment upon political institutions holding that "Institutions ... vary ... according to the characteristics of the people," which in turn are affected by "the energy and activity which are produced by the colder climates and the indolence produced by the warmer."[7]

Professor Dunning thinks that

> It is the relation between the climate and liberty that constitutes the most important feature of this whole subject for political philosophy proper. Summarily stated, [Montesquieu's] theory is that every species of liberty is favored by the colder climates, and slavery by the warmer.... Another influence that promotes the distinction between the two continents in respect to political liberty is the fact that in Asia the natural geographical divisions, as determined by river systems, mountain ranges, etc., are of vast extent, and, therefore, according to the principle already noted, promote despotism, while in Europe the natural divisions are small and therefore favor the compact communities to whom liberty is normal.[8]

Professor Dunning says further,

> The net result of all the speculation that has been noticed was that some relation between geography and the nation was recognized, but the character of the relation was not made at all definite. And such remained the situation throughout the fierce

---

[5] C.E. Merriam and Harry Elmer Barnes, *A History of Political Theories, Recent Times*, I, 29–30. (Quoted by permission of The Macmillan Company.)

[6] William Archibald Dunning, *A History of Political Theories from Luther to Montesquieu*, II, 113.

[7] *Ibid.*, p. 419.

[8] *Ibid.*, pp. 420–422.

controversies of the mid-century over the rights and wrongs of nations and of nationalities. For none of the concrete problems as to boundaries could a scientific
formula furnish an acceptable solution. The mountains, deserts, seas, rivers and
other features of the earth's surface that had seemed to be natural marks of separation for communities of men either were lacking where need for them was greatest, or, when present, actually furnished additional incentives to strife in the rivalry
for occupation and control of them. Nor could the limits indicated by geography
be made to coincide with the limits indicated by language. A Germany that fulfilled
the glowing demand of Arndt for unity *so weit die deutsche Zunge klingt* would
outrage every canon of geographic theory, and would present many points where
geography could find nothing whatever to offer as a boundary. And there in the
heart of Europe lay the Swiss—a stout and respected nation, defying every rule of
both language and geography in its national life.

No more in the facts of physical environment than in those of blood and language, therefore, did the political theory of the early nineteenth century find an
objective criterion of nationality that would suffice to still the insistent clamor of the
democratic liberalism for recognition of the human will as the paramount factor.
Through the growing precision of geographic science as wrought out by Humboldt
and Ritter, and through the rise of ethnology and anthropology and comparative
philology, the influence of heredity, environment and speech on the evolution of
human societies was more justly apportioned and balanced, and political science
defined the nation in terms that gave due weight to each, while assigning to the
will and feeling of living men a part that was far from the least.[9]

Professor Dunning himself made one of his most distinctive contributions
through his interpretation of the sectional conflict between the North and
South. Epochal and pioneering were his treatments, through his graduate doctoral dissertations of reconstruction in the South, forerunner of later notable
books such as Paul Buck's *The Road to Reunion*, Claude Bowers' *The Tragic
Era*, W.E.B. Du Bois' *Black Reconstruction*, George Fort Milton's *The Age
of Hate*, and a long list of critical treatises on the South, even prior to the
popularity of books by and of southerners. These studies promoted by Professor Dunning must be accredited a big place in the literature of reintegration
of an ostracized section needing to come fully into the greater union of states
and regions. Professor Dunning's contributions, however, were not limited
either to his history of theory or of the southern section. His keen and pene-
trating sense of political development led him like Turner to interpret the
sectionalism of the country often in terms of delicate satire and humor. Thus
describing the clamor of partisan strife between the Federalists and Republicans he pointed up a continuity of conflict in which "Then as now, the commercial and financial regions stood opposed to the agricultural; then as now,
the regions where the Blacks were numerous stood opposed to those where they
were few; and then as now—but even more than now—New England stood
opposed to everything else—a thing *sui generis*."[10]

---

9 William Archibald Dunning, *A History of Political Theories from Rousseau to Spencer*,
III, 319–320. (Quoted by permission of The Macmillan Company.)
10 William Archibald Dunning, *Truth in History and Other Essays*, p. 46.

Returning now to the concept of sovereignty and liberty with which we began this chapter it is interesting to trace the concept of areal or territorial relationships to government in the United States as expounded by American political scientists. Here again the earlier theories and the present dilemmas run, now side by side, and now in widely diverging streams. It is possible to take as text the orthodox theories of sovereignty and argue for the increasing functions of the central governments over the states and it is possible to see in the encroachment of Federal Government the nullification of local autonomy and liberty. So, too, it is possible to find in the *trends* of both theory and practice bases for arguments both ways. It is in the harmonizing of such apparently justifiable authentic differences of opinion and conflict that regionalism finds its chief service in government. For without doubt the principle of national sovereignty makes it possible to nullify much that has been traditionally the sphere of the state.

The key to this situation is that of sovereignty and the distinction which Willoughby makes between the real federation of states in the United States and the contrariwise confederation of states. Thus he thinks one of the most important points involved in the

> nature and indivisibility of sovereignty is the distinction between what is known as a Federation or a Federal State, though this latter term is, as has been pointed out, an improper one, and a Confederation or, as the Germans express it, the distinction between a *Bundesstaat* and a *Staatenbund*. Both are made up of a grouping of large political units. In both the performance of the functions of the state is entrusted to two sets of governmental machinery, a general or central government which acts for all the units and a special government acting for each of the units independently of the others.
>
> Notwithstanding this similarity, the two are, from the political standpoint, fundamentally different. The former is a single State, the latter is composed of as many separate States as there are units composing the grouping. This difference arises wholly from the differences in respect to the location of sovereignty in the grouping. In the true Federation or *Bundesstaat,* sovereignty resides in the combined population of all the units. This population has, purely as a matter of practical expediency, decided to make use of two sets of governmental machinery for the performance of its functions: a central government to attend to matters which it is believed concern all, or should receive single generally-binding determination; and special machinery for each of the great geographical divisions into which the country, for historical or other reasons, is divided. Each of these governments is equally but the instrument through which the single State acts.[11]

John W. Burgess pointed out that a "State" such as one of the states in the United States Government is a kind of local government and under the federal system it is "a local self-government, under the supremacy of the Constitution of the United States, and of the laws and treaties of the central government

---

[11] W.F. Willoughby, *An Introduction to the Study of the Government of Modern States,* pp. 22–23. (Quoted by permission of Doubleday, Doran & Company, Inc.)

made in accordance with that Constitution, republican as to form, and possessed of residuary powers—that is, of all powers not vested by the Constitution of the United States exclusively in the central government, or not denied by that Constitution to the 'State.' "[12] Yet this is only one form of local government and, as Merriam has pointed out so often, there is the emerging city-state local self-government and others, so that Burgess' further analysis of the subjectivity of the state to the federal Constitution has considerable bearing upon the increasingly complex problem of the United States, states' rights, constitutionality and regionalism.

Burgess continues,

> Such being the nature of a "State" of the Union and such the method of its creation, what reason is there for speaking of the "States" in a system of federal government as indestructible? As they emerge from the status of Territories under the exclusive power of Congress, upon having attained certain conditions, why may they not revert to the status of Territories upon having lost these conditions of "State" existence; nay, why may they not revert to the status of martial law by having lost all the conditions of civil government? The dictum "once a State always a State" in a system of federal government has no sound reason in it. Under the Constitution of the United States, every "State" of the Union may through the process of amendment be made a province subject to the exclusive government of the central authorities. . . .[13]

Conflict and contradiction abound not only in political theories and in the practical implementation of these theories but in the historical development of the states and regions in the United States. Already we have pointed out many times the definitive contributions of Turner concerning the political sectionalism of the nation and we have noted something of the loyalties, priorities, and autonomies of the states, which themselves grew from a small number that were historically conditioned to a larger number which grew up through gradually shifting national frontiers. Yet it is important once again to have this politico-historical fact presented in the words of the political scientists. The conflict comes here between the principle of local government over against that of central sovereignty and between the historical traditional habits and patterns which grew up in each community and the encroaching technology and centralization tendencies.

Willoughby reminds us that

> The local-governing areas that exist within the states of the American Union were, in most instances, artificially marked out and created by the central authorities of those states, but in cases this was done only after the principle had become well established in American political philosophy that, so far as practicable, each locality is entitled, as a moral right, to have its purely local interests determined by its own inhabitants, and satisfied according to the methods that they may think best. The

---

[12] John W. Burgess, *Reconstruction and the Constitution, 1866–1876*, p. 2.
[13] *Ibid.*, pp. 3–4.

result has been the carrying into practice in the American states of many of the same principles, and much of the same spirit, as are found in English local government bodies. . . . The only merits that the American system of administrative and local government control is supposed to have are that it prevents the growth of rigid bureaucracies which are out of touch with and often disregardful of the wishes and interests of the people, and that it tends to give to private individuals a reasonably secure protection against arbitrary and oppressive acts upon the part of their rulers. The first result it probably secured, although at the expense of considerable administrative inefficiency, but it is very doubtful indeed whether, in actual practice, private rights are any better secured in America than they are under the systems of administrative centralization and of administrative courts that exist in France and Prussia.[14]

The trend here, as in most of the ways of current civilization, is more and more away from the power and entity of the states toward federal centralization. All along the line—business, commerce, education, management—and in state governments themselves there is everywhere the strong tropism toward centralization. Here again the evolution of the conflict seems to be somewhere between the two extremes and in accord with such expediency and equilibrium as must generally characterize the practices and policies of modern administration. This trend has been admirably stated by the authors of *Regional Factors in National Planning and Development;* and their viewpoints will be presented at length. Yet it is important to note the earlier trends as background for their conclusions.

Merriam reviews the trend in the early twentieth century:

Both the institutional and the theoretical developments regarding the area or unit of government were notable. The general tendency was toward nationalism as against the state in accordance with the decision reached in the Civil War and with the economic and social tendencies of the time. Broader powers were conferred upon the nation by the Fourteenth Amendment to the Constitution, and these powers were often broadly construed by the courts, while the state lagged behind in ideals and organization. The state was no longer the rival of the nation, but tended toward the position of a subordinate though powerful agency. Powerful social and industrial forces constantly worked in the direction of the national unit as against the state. Commerce demanded a greater degree of uniformity in the commercial code, and a general sentiment urged the need of uniformity at many points. The theory of national supremacy was more sharply formulated than ever by Burgess and others who assailed the commonwealth as a unit of government. There were some *post-bellum* statements of the state sovereignty doctrines, but these were more in the nature of historic justifications of the "lost cause" than serious advocacy of living principles of political action. The devotion to local self-government, notable in earlier years, declined during this period. It revived around the municipality, but even here the sentiment was by no means unanimous. Local self-government as a fundamental and necessary guarantee of liberty was not much

---

[14] W.W. Willoughby and Lindsay Rogers, *An Introduction to the Problem of Government,* pp. 448–449. (Quoted by permission of Doubleday, Doran & Company, Inc.)

in evidence, except for that development of the idea of local autonomy centering around the demand for broader powers of self-government for the city. Nor were these municipal powers asked as guarantees against some dangerous and centralized power, but as desirable means for the self-development and self-expression of communities with distinct local interests. Liberty was no longer regarded as primarily local in character, in danger of losing its soul if extended over too broad an area. Conceptions of liberty, justice, democracy were to a large extent interpreted in terms of the nation, rather than of the state or the city or the rural local government. . . .[15]

There were abundant sources to support this theory of the trend away from states, in addition to the epochs of the Civil War and Reconstruction. Merriam quotes Goodnow and Burgess pointing to the *nation* as the road to advance. Goodnow thought that if we were framing a new nation we should undoubtedly give the national government greater powers than the present constitution allows. Colonel Roosevelt in his "New Nationalism" was cited as glorifying the nation as the chiefest instrument for social and political progress, and he expounded the doctrine of interstate relations by insisting that there must be no neutral ground "to serve as a refuge for law breakers."[16] Yet, once again it seemed possible to find distinguished authorities who saw in this trend great dangers. Even Professor Burgess himself, in later years, as interpreted by his friend and adviser, William R. Shepherd, complained of the process of deterioration which enabled the government more and more to encroach upon the legitimate domain of individual rights and wrote that "it is high time for us to call a halt in our present course of increasing the sphere of government and decreasing that of liberty."[17] Thus his doctrine of increasing sovereignty of the federal power over the states appears to lead directly to the thing he does not want to happen.

One other example may be cited to indicate perhaps the more favorable position taken by Woodrow Wilson in his view of the states. Says Merriam,

> Possibly the best presentation of the importance of the state in our system of government was made by Wilson. He urged the importance of the state as an experiment station in which new plants might be tried. "Every commonwealth," he declared, "has been a nursery of new strength; and out of these nurseries have come men and communities which no other process could have produced. Self-government has here had its richest harvest." If our system of states had not come to us "by historical necessity, I think it would have been worth while to invent it." Local affairs are not uniform, and cannot be made so by compulsion of law. What we seek is co-operation, but not the strait jacket. Variety will not impair energy, if there is genuine cooperation.
>
> Our states have not been created: they have sprung up of themselves, irrespon-

---

15 C.E. Merriam, *American Political Ideas,* pp. 456–457. (Quoted by permission of The Macmillan Company.)

16 Quoted by C.E. Merriam, *ibid.,* p. 236.

17 Howard W. Odum (editor), *American Masters of Social Science,* p. 43.

sible, "self-originated, self-constituted, self-confident, self-sustaining, veritable communities demanding only recognition." The remedy lies, not merely in changing
the division of powers between state and nation, along lines of actual alteration
of interest, but in reorganization of the state from within. Instead of upsetting
an ancient system, we should "revitalize it by reorganization." "Centralization is
not vitalization," said he, and the atrophy of the parts will result in the atrophy
of the whole.[18]

Perhaps we have cited enough of the backgrounds within political theory
to indicate the general consensus of opinion on many aspects of the relation of
area to government in general and in the United States in particular. It seems
clear that in both the organic relationships between governments and areas
and between sovereignty of a centralized federation and the United States that
while there are abundant theories and discussions there is as yet little agreement among scholars or administration. So, too, there appears to be a similar
parallel in the case of the political geographers and students of government.
Here again there is a great deal of evidence couched in plausible theories in
many varying contributions, yet little of definitive agreement. As between
Bowman's problem approach to political geography and Haushofer's func-
tional-natural approach in Geopolitik there is a great chasm of difference. Yet
in either case, whether in seeking harmony of international relations through
the understanding of the habitats of men or seeking to find the nature and
origin of nations through regional natural environments, the areal factors are
fundamental. . . .

More important and immediate are the distinctive contributions of the later
current political scientists to the general concept, theory, and practice of regionalism or its related topics of sectionalism in politics, federalism and states, uniform state action, and regional administrative arrangements. . . .

W.Y. Elliott writes that

> The answer to the . . . question . . . of appropriate political machinery . . . assumes
> that the new role of the state requires, more than ever, an efficient administrative
> mechanism and a permanent non-political bureaucracy. . . . It is clear that so long
> as we duplicate bureaucracies by a federal centralization that overlaps the functions
> of the individual states, we have a wasteful system of government. A reduction of
> the number and functions of local (particularly county) government areas is cer-
> tainly indicated. The same reasoning applies to the states. They should be sup-
> planted, except as administrative areas or as convenient electoral districts, by
> geographically appropriate regions. As a suggestion I have termed these regions
> *commonwealths* and indicated an approximation of the present Federal Reserve
> districts, with perhaps one additional western commonwealth, as a more rational
> basis for our federal structure. . . . Federalism continues to exist in the United
> States only in the difficulty of formally amending the Constitution, in the extra-
> ordinary overrepresentation of small states in our powerful Senate, and in the

---

[18] C.E. Merriam, *American Political Ideas*, pp. 239–240. (Quoted by permission of The
Macmillan Company.)

unnecessary multiplication of jurisdictions and of bureaucracies. The domain of state control over finance, labor conditions, farming, manufacturing, mining, etc., has been almost obliterated by the avalanche of federal acts dealing with unemployment relief, national industrial recovery, agricultural adjustment, and codes and public-works programs.... The readjustment of economic life, particularly as international trade disappears through efforts at national self-sufficiency, demands coordination by the state. That may mean as thoroughgoing a revision of our system as was Solon's for Athens. That means planning and, where necessary, coercion. ...Planning of this drastic type is an executive function....[19]

Professor Elliott thinks that the states would have to be retained for some administrative units such as the English counties have, for centers of cultural differentiation, and for other purposes. His new regional commonwealths would become autonomous units for local functions but subject to one jurisdiction for courts. Quite a different viewpoint is that of Austin F. MacDonald who sees the solution more nearly in some adequate implementation of federal aid. This, of course, according to the broader premises of American regionalism, implies regional arrangements as minimum essentials.

The right of the Federal Government to give to the states land from the federal domain and money from the federal treasury has never seriously been questioned. ...But only within the last two decades has the Federal Government adopted the policy of purchasing with federal funds a considerable measure of supervision over numerous governmental activities not mentioned in the Constitution, and therefore presumably left in the hands of the states. Most of the money now appropriated by Congress for state use must be spent in a manner approved by the Federal Government.... For most purposes state boundaries have ceased to exist. But in the field of government state boundaries still play a very significant part. State railway commissions, industrial commissions, public utility commissions, insurance commissions, banking commissions, health commissions and a multitude of others are applying their local regulations to nation-wide enterprises with devastating results. The line of demarcation between national and state powers is very little different today than at the close of the Civil War. Forty-eight states are attempting to solve national problems in forty-eight different ways, most of them equally unsatisfactory. State constitutions, state laws and state judicial decisions have produced a bewildering patchwork of policies and counter-policies concerning matters of national importance. The demands for at least a measure of federal control have been insistent, and Congress has found a way to meet these demands in the newly developed system of federal subsidies.... Because it unites so skillfully the principles of local initiative and central supervision, federal aid is an important phase of American administration. The old line of divison between state and national powers is manifestly unsuited to present-day conditions. Local authorities find themselves powerless to cope with problems that have become national in character.... But men are loath to sacrifice the autonomy of the states. They know the dangers of excessive centralization. They realize that central control of government activities means the crushing of all local initiative. The real need is for some

19 W.Y. Elliott, *The Need for Constitutional Reform*, pp. 9, 185, 186, 190–191.

device that will combine state control with national leadership. Federal aid meets that need. . . .[20]

. . . W. Brooke Graves suggests that uniform state action might be the "way out" of the dilemma of overcentralization. This he believes more feasible than new regional governmental units. He sees uniform state action as a means of securing uniformity in such matters as insurance, divorce, marriage, child labor, corporation charters, motor traffic regulations, etc., and also in "matters which are of common concern only to a particular region, such as river and harbor control, control over oil production, flood control, et cetera."[21] "All are agreed," he says, "that uniformity is urgently needed in many fields of state government activity, but many object to achieving it by federal action. The author wishes simply to make clear a point which has not heretofore been properly recognized—namely, that we have here a practical workable alternative if we desire to use it. . . ."[22]

Another important contribution is that of A.N. Holcombe in which he emphasizes the trend from *sectional politics* to *class politics*. Although recognizing the past America as one which featured the struggle between geographic sections he concludes that, due to urbanization and industrialization, this is now giving rise to class politics. His work here is also of considerable significance in the area of urban and rural culture.

> American politics was originally rustic politics. Its character was determined by the interests and attitudes of the rural population. In the field of national government the struggle for power took the form of a conflict between the geographic sections into which the country was divided. The national parties were founded upon alliances between sectional interests, and the sectional interests were at first mostly agrarian interests. . . . The passing of the frontier and the growth of urban industry have shaken the foundations of the old party system in national politics. The old sectional interests are changing and the old sectional alliances are breaking down. . . . The character of the new party politics will be determined chiefly by the interests and attitudes of the urban population. . . . There will be less sectional politics and more class politics. . . . That rustic politics in the field of national government should have taken the form of sectional politics was also the necessary consequence of the original condition of the people. The essential fact was that "the agricultural interest" was by no means uniform throughout the country. . . .[23]

. . . The authors of the notable work on *Regional Factors in National Planning and Development* have not only made a significant and comprehensive contribution to the new field but . . . their conclusions are based on an extraordinarily wide range of inquiries. . . . Thus they interpret the regional problem as it relates to federal activity in the United States as being twofold.

---

[20] Austin F. MacDonald, *Federal Aid*, pp. 1, 2, 4, 12.
[21] W. Brooke Graves, *Uniform State Action*, p. 9.
[22] *Ibid.*, Preface, vii–viii.
[23] A.N. Holcombe, *The New Party Politics*, pp. 11, 13–14.

First, there are needed divisions of the country suitable for the carrying out, in the field, of administrative control from Washington. Second, subnational units of area are needed in order to accomplish actual decentralization of powers and activities of the federal agencies, particularly where planning and policy making are involved.

The first phase of the problem has been met by designing many different regional systems, wherein the individual regions are usually larger than a state and more nearly uniform in size than are the states. The second phase of the problem has been met, at least in a few instances, by devising systems of regions wherein each areal unit is more closely related to the function or object dealt with, than are the states or even the general run of federal administrative regions.

The bureaus of the federal departments have in most instances adopted regions simply to effect greater efficiency and convenience in administering their activities in the field. The significance of federal regions, however, transcends mere considerations of efficiency and economy in administration. The whole issue of regionalism is involved, or at least implied, and this is increasingly being raised by students of polity, geography, and social science. These students have demonstrated that most internal political boundaries exhibit slight conformity to natural physical areas, or to the social, economic, and political problems which are closely related to such areas. They have demonstrated further that such things as literacy, crime, birth rates, urbanization of population, differentiation in agricultural production, problems of reclamation or reforestion (sic), are definitely regional in character and occurrence. It is fairly obvious, therefore, that these can be treated most effectively, not by direct handling from Washington, but by a regional approach....[24]

Since natural regions do not coincide with states and since our government is based on a division of powers between one federal and forty-eight state governments, there is manifestly a no-man's land in which we have failed to provide machinery for action. However, this does not mean that regions have not made themselves felt in our governmental affairs. The United States has often been compared to a congress of nations, the emphasis being placed on the *States* rather than on the *United*, and the plural form of the national title stressed. This may lead to regionalism; in the past it has most often led to sectionalism. In fact, most of the discussions by historians and political writers of the past have stressed the separateness of the regions, or sections, rather than their integration into a national picture of distinctive but interdependent entities. Regionalism stresses integration, but not standardization.

We must repeat that this distinction between sectionalism and regionalism is of the utmost importance, but it is often ignored or not understood. Much of what has been written on sectionalism is regionalism, a considerable portion of what has been called regionalism is sectionalism. We have pointed out the fact that the fundamental distinction between the concepts is that sectionalism sees the nation from the point of view of the differing areas; regionalism sees the differing areas from the point of view of the nation. And it is important to

---

[24] Adapted from National Resources Committee, *Regional Factors in National Planning and Development,* December 1935, p. 31.

re-emphasize the fact that the difference is not one of mere academic interest "but is of the greatest possible significance in the formation of new policies and in the probabilities of participation in new national and regional planning programs by any and all regions" in order to avoid "A revivification of the older sectionalism rationalized in terms of the 'new regionalism.' "[25]

This is exactly what Turner feared. He wrote,

> I think it not too much to say that in party conventions as well as in Congress the outcome of deliberations bears a striking resemblance to treaties between sections, suggestive of treaties between European nations in diplomatic congresses.[26]

To this point of view, the regionalist would oppose facts and arguments to support the proposition that, though it is true that there has been sectionalism such as is here described and that such sectionalism may well continue, the emerging new regionalism offers a better, more workable solution of the problems arising from the complexity of American life. Recent efforts of the national government toward solution of such problems as those arising from farm tenancy, agricultural production control, population and income redistribution all have distinct regional applications and implications, but were approached from the point of view of national rather than sectional advantages.

The significance of economic interests is usually apparent in sectional political interests and is the basis of the need for regional realignment of areas. Plans for regional organization of districts served by power transmission lines, as the Tennessee Valley, to take the outstanding example, by rail systems, as illustrated in freight rate territories, by shipping facilities as demonstrated in the combination of ports into customs districts and the regulation of freight rates to these outlets, are obviously economic in their origin. No less so are the recurrent political movements, such as the opposition to the tariff by agrarian sections, demands for an inflated currency by debtor sections, interest in racial legislation by the South and the Pacific Coast regions, etc.; though the economic basis of the latter is often rationalized in purely political and social terminology. . . .

But the central issue of political regionalism seems to be that of centralization versus some degree of decentralization. Under our working theory of division of power between state and federal governments, we are faced with the alternative of suffering existing evils or of transferring more and more power to the Federal Government. Usually we choose the latter alternative in our desire for relief, so that centralization constantly increases. But actually, we are faced with many problems, such as those centering about Boulder Dam, for example, which affect regions. "They are problems too big for any single state, yet not big enough for the nation as a whole. They should not be loaded upon an already overburdened Congress, yet they are obviously beyond the compe-

---

[25] Howard W. Odum, *Southern Regions of the United States*, p. 253.
[26] Frederick Jackson Turner, *The Significance of Sections in American History*, p. 41.

tence of any single state legislature. They belong by right to regional governments, if we had such things."[27]

Not only is some such arrangement needed to meet the actual problems of
government which are rapidly multiplying, but also to develop vigorously
regional distinctiveness as a counterpoise to mass action and mob psychology,
the tendencies toward which are much stronger than the provincial spirit will
ever be able to challenge.[28] Students are well agreed that it is neither possible
nor desirable to establish absolute uniformity of governmental agencies over
a nation of such differing regions as are found within the United States. They
are equally agreed that there must be co-ordination and supervision to a measurable degree to maintain union. They are led thereby to a consideration of
regional organization as a means of practical attainment of the end sought.
Such organization is already under way in many of the governmental functions, and has been for decades, of course. Such a form of organization is
"natural" in that it meets conditions growing up naturally as a result of geographic and social forces.

. . .

The larger problem goes somewhat beyond the dichotomy of federalism-
states' rights. It is estimated that there are some 175,000 governmental units
within the United States; a multiplicity of units which inevitably makes for
huge duplication of effort and confusion of function.

> Our costly experience with devastating public confusion, with waste of all kinds,
> with projects inadequately investigated and planned—with political scandal, with
> inartistic outcomes . . . indicates the urgent need of prompt steps in the direction
> of more effective concert of action. Even the most rugged individualist cannot insist
> upon the general freedom of spending involved in such unlicensed liberty to build.
> There is nothing in the American situation, except inertia, to stand in the way of
> far closer relationships on the part of public works authorities. We may realize far-
> reaching advantages from the comprehensive view of the whole field, from the free
> interchange of information and experience, from the pooling of technical knowledge
> and facilities, from mutual consideration of credit situations, from such general
> advice and supervision as is not inconsistent with the requirements of vital self-
> government.[29]

Further, it is argued that such readjustment would be of the greatest benefit to those small governmental units and those poorer regions which now are
unable to secure adequate advice and supervision for the proper carrying out
of their functions since they would be enabled to participate in general funds
of knowledge and techniques. Thus, to them would be allocated functions and

---

27 W.B. Munro, *The Invisible Government*, pp. 153–154.
28 *Ibid.*, pp. 159–164.
29 National Resources Board, *Report on National Planning and Public Works in Relation
to Natural Resources*, December 1934, p. 65.

powers along with the ability to operate successfully, through relationships with other units.[30] Normally the initiative for such action would come from the locality, more keenly alive to its needs and opportunities than a central organization could be; the advantage coming from advice and co-ordination by the larger unit. "It is in a skilled balance between the overhead role of the Federal Government and the role of the localities and regions that wisdom lies. It cannot too often be reiterated that national planning does not involve or permit the centralization of all planning at the center, but presupposes a free flow of ideas, experiments, experiences from circumference to center and back again to the circumference."[31]

Actually, a system much like that described above is in actual operation in the case of the highway work of the national and state governments. Here the procedure is for the State Highway Commission to draw up plans and specifications for particular pieces of roadway construction and then to submit them to the *Federal Highway Bureau* for approval. By this system there is left a wide range for experimentation by the various states in efforts to meet local conditions and needs, while the wider experience of the Federal Bureau serves as a check upon local ideas and fits state plans into a national system. . . .

Hope for progress toward regional organization is to be found in the activities of such semi-official regional organizations as the New England Regional Planning Commission, an outgrowth of the older New England Council; and the Pacific Northwest Planning Commission, operating in widely differing regions and under differing types of organization; the one based on historical sentiment and economic unity while the other is based on unity of a drainage system and the resultant economic and social problems. Neither has authority to enforce its recommendations, being forced to rely upon the voluntary action of the states concerned. The Tennessee Valley Authority, in contrast, has large measure of authority within its region as concerns the direct objective it seeks. This is due to its character as a corporation. Another type of regional authority which is gaining great vogue at this time is the interstate compact. Because its advocacy is more recent and because in some respects it holds out greater promise, a short discussion of this form of interstate co-operation is essential to any study of political regionalism.

The mere fact that during the period extending from the formation of the republic to 1918 the interstate compact was used only 24 times, while, during the period of 1918 to 1931, 31 such agreements were called into being, argues that there have been changes in our governmental problems demanding some authority between the levels of the state and the federal governments. It is argued that bodies created by such means might receive public grants for pub-

---

[30] National Resources Board, *Report on National Planning and Public Works in Relation to Natural Resources,* December 1934, p. 65.
[31] *Ibid.,* p. 87.

lic work construction, for soil erosion, reclamation, forestry, etc.[32] But it is objected that such a device lends itself to almost interminable delays; that the compacting states can usually refuse to follow their agreements with impunity; that action through such compacts may be taken without due regard to its incidence on the remainder of the nation; that the legal basis for such compacts views each state as a sovereign power equal in all respects to the other compacting states when actually such a condition almost never exists because of differences in resources, population, and similar factors; compact making is likely to become a matter of horse trading, in which each compacting state uses every device available to promote its own particular interests rather than those of the region or nation.[33]

.   .   .

Finally, we come again to the conclusion that none of the types of regional organization in common use has been found altogether satisfactory in all cases; the field is still one in which experimentation promises the evolution of theories of greater value in actual practice. It appears that differing regions and differing functions demand different types of organization, and will probably continue to do so. For the immediate present it seems wise to limit the statement of theory to the observation that the old state-federal conflict ignores the existence of many problems which are certainly neither intrastate nor national in character, and that, therefore, there is a real need for some political unit equipped with powers of initiative and administration on a level between the two. The exact form of such a unit can best be left, perhaps, until further experimentation and experience have somewhat clarified the problems.

---

[32] National Resources Committee, *Regional Factors in National Planning and Development,* December 1935, p. 47.

[33] *Ibid.,* pp. 47–52.

IV

SYSTEM AND AREA:
THE POLITICAL COMMUNITY

DAVID EASTON

Objects of Support: The Political Community

THE BASIC POLITICAL OBJECTS

If we are to understand the function of support, we must begin by clearly recognizing that a system consists of numerous subsystems and aspects, some of which are more important and some less so from the point of view of support. . . . The task now is to conceptualize the various components of a system in such a way that we may handle economically the problems arising from possible stress due to the decline of support below a minimal level.

What elements of a system are most relevant to its capacity to persist in the face of a threatened loss of support? The search for answers to this question will lead us to identify and categorize those aspects of a system with respect to which support may vary independently and with respect to which fluctuations in the level of support may stimulate stress in different ways. These in turn may provoke differential coping responses on the part of the members of a system.

The relevant aspects of the system I have already identified as three basic political objects: the authorities, regime, and political community. Now, however, I shall develop these objects more fully so that we may see exactly what aspects of a system are involved in them. Thereafter, I shall indicate the kinds of responses through which systems have typically sought to inculcate and reinforce supportive attitudes and behavior to maintain minimal levels of input.

Change of a system will turn out to mean change of one or another of these objects and only where all objects change simultaneously can we consider that the former system has totally disappeared. Conversely, a system may persist *in toto* or only with respect to one of its basic objects. It will also become apparent that modification in one or another of the objects may represent a fundamental way through which systems are able to cope with stress from the environment and to keep some kind of political system in operation for the particular society.

ALTERNATIVE USES OF THE CONCEPT "COMMUNITY"

In speaking of the persistence of a political system, it is impossible not to imply at the very least that the members of the system show some minimal readiness or ability to continue working together to solve their political problems. Otherwise there could be no expectation of compliance with any authoritative allocation of values. This notion lies at the heart of that aspect of a system that I have been calling its political community and which will now be explored in detail for the first time.

To avoid any misunderstanding about the meaning of this concept, much more than a word or two needs to be said about its use by others. Although the idea "political community" itself rarely appears, the concept "community" is probably about as overworked a term as any that occurs in both the lay and professional lexicons. In lay terms, as well as in much professional discourse, it frequently appears as an ideological tool, a "practical concept"[1] intended to arouse and strengthen the affective bonds of a member for the political system or the society of which he is part.[2] But if we confine our scrutiny for the moment to the idea of *political* community, this immediately shrinks to a mere handful the number of cases in which it is used, at least in a technical or scholarly sense.

Two recent and well-developed applications of the concept, in the work of Deutsch and Haas, bear special attention as an aid in clarifying the implications of the special meaning that will be adopted in this analysis. Although the use by these authors falls into the general area of international relations, this in itself need not interfere with its relevance for our purposes. From my point of view, an international system is just another system at a different level of organization. But in all other respects it is amenable to investigation through the same conceptual apparatus that is being developed in this volume with respect to what we normally call domestic political systems.[3]

---

[1] "By a practical concept I mean a concept whose primary function is to guide action, direct and redirect attitudes, and to state commitments of one sort or another. A practical concept is contrasted to a theoretical concept, which is used to refer to and to describe various kinds of objects." J. Ladd, "The Concept of Community: A Logical Analysis," in C.J. Friedrich (ed.), *Community* (New York: Liberal Arts Press, 1959), pp. 269–293, at p. 270.

[2] For a recent survey of the meaning of the concept "community" and research relating to it see G.W. Blackwell, "Community Analysis," in R. Young, *Approaches to the Study of Politics* (Evanston, Illinois: Northwestern University Press, 1958), pp. 305–317.

[3] As D. Singer has pointed out, one needs only to keep his level of analysis straight. See "International Conflict: Three Levels of Analysis," 12 *World Politics* (1960) 453–461; and "The Level of Analysis Problem in International Relations," 14 *World Politics* (1961) 77–92.

Definition of the concept by Deutsch

Unfortunately, as the concept "political community" has been employed in the international sphere, it cannot be conveniently adopted for the identification of that aspect of a political system which we must isolate for an understanding of the effects of the input of support. In the work of Deutsch, for example, two different but related meanings appear, each of which were certainly appropriate for the specific context in which they were employed but neither of which is quite suitable for the more general theoretical analysis under way here.

In one piece of research, Deutsch finds it advantageous for the specific purposes of seeking to create indices for the measurement of the growth of a community, to adopt an approximation of the classic distinction between community and society prevalent in sociological and anthropological literature. He describes a society as "a group of individuals connected by an intense division of labor and separated from other societies by a marked drop in this intensity."[4] Community, on the other hand, he sees as "people who have learned to communicate with each other and to understand each other well beyond the mere interchange of goods and services."[5] By this he refers largely to the cultural integration of a people, culture consisting of those symbols, ideas, and artifacts transmitted from generation to generation. Since the focus of the work in which these concepts are defined is on communication, the utility of this kind of distinction is transparent.

In another work, however, where the emphasis of Deutsch's research on integration spreads to include aspects of political life other than communication, a considerably different, even though related concept appears. The generalized notion "community" now becomes more specific. It is transformed into the specific idea of political community. However, in pouring more concentrated political content into the concept, one might have expected that the term would have become somewhat narrowed in its meaning. But, in fact, in one sense it is broadened even further. It no longer seems to refer just to those components of social life that are communicable across the generations—that is, culture—and to interacting persons as they engage in the process of communicating it. The meaning of political community is now extended in a way that converts it if not into a synonym for, at least into an approximation of what I have been calling a political system.

Thus Deutsch describes a political community as "a community of social interaction supplemented by both enforcement and compliance." In this sense, it is a community of persons in which common or "coordinated facilities for the making of decisions and the enforcement of commands are supplemented by habits of compliance which are sufficiently widespread and predictable to

---

[4] *Nationalism and Social Communication* (New York: Technology Press of Massachusetts Institute of Technology and Wiley, 1953), p. 61.

[5] *Ibid.*, p. 65.

make successful enforcement in the remaining cases of noncompliance probable at an economically and culturally feasible cost."[6] And this definition is repeated in subsequent works so that it seems to have achieved some stability.[7]

One cannot cavil with this use of course. It is a forthright statement of a possible meaning for the concept and a meaningful one in that it is directed toward understanding a central problem: the way in which groups of people gradually link together, particularly internationally, to form units that are able to solve their problems peacefully, either in a unitary or in a federated system. But from our point of view, the reason Deutsch finds it helpful to select a meaning for political community that makes it equivalent to what I have been calling a political system is that in fact he is seeking to understand the processes underlying the initial formation of societies and political systems associated with them. Yet, since we are not in need of a special concept for this purpose but do seek one that will point up only one aspect of a political system to which members typically extend support, the definition of the concept as proposed by Deutsch will not serve our purposes.

Definition of the concept by Haas

Haas presents us with a second case in which the concept appears in a carefully delineated context. Haas adopts the term to describe a condition in the relationship among political groups such that "specific groups and individuals show more loyalty to their central political institutions than to any other political authority, in a specific period of time and in a definable geographic space." It is a condition "towards which the process of 'political integration' is supposed to lead."[8]

If we disregard the author's intention to formulate an ideal or model political unit, a norm against which other coalescing groups en route might be measured, his description of a political community comes very close to Deutsch's second usage. In fact, the specifications by Haas tend to fuse the idea of political community with those of a *modern* political system and therefore to restrict it somewhat more narrowly than in Deutsch's usage. Since he views "loyalty to their central political institutions" as a key ingredient, it signifies that the acceptance of a single superior set of authorities as the significant variable constitutes the most important variable in the emergence of a common political life. Even more so than in the case of Deutsch, he is apparently seeking to describe, not the communal aspect of a geographically based group but the total set of political relationships in which members may engage, which I have been calling a political system.

---

6 K.W. Deutsch, *Political Community at the International Level* (Garden City, New York: Doubleday, 1954), p. 16.

7 "We are dealing here with political communities. These we regard as social groups with a process of political communication, some machinery for enforcement, and some popular habits of compliance." K.W. Deutsch, S.A. Burrell, *et al.*, *The Political Community and the North Atlantic Area* (Princeton: Princeton University Press, 1957), p. 5.

8 E.B. Haas, *The Uniting of Europe* (Stanford: Stanford University Press), p. 5.

The dual implications of political community
as a concept

It appears that in at least these two cases, where the concept "political community" is introduced as a carefully and deliberately selected tool of analysis, it tends to be employed in a way that makes it a synonym of some kind for political system. It is important to recognize this because I now wish to give the term an alternative content, if only because in "political system" we already have a concept for the most inclusive set of interactions that can be called political. I wish to reserve "political community" for the special purpose of identifying only one particular aspect of a political system, as one of a number of basic political objects toward which support may be extended or from which it may be withdrawn.

This new way of looking at this concept will not estrange it completely from the implications it already bears for Deutsch and Haas. It is not accidental that they and others have seized upon the concept "political community" to help understand the phenomenon through which previously independent or separate groups coalesce into one political system. The peculiar value of the concept is that it conveys the latent notion that, underlying the functioning of all systems, there must be some cohesive cement—a sense or feeling of community amongst the members. Unless such sentiment emerges, the political system itself may never take shape or if it does, it may not survive. Whether it is defined as a bond created through common traditions built up in the communication processes within and across generations or as ties created out of loyalty to a common set of central institutions, in each case the emphasis is upon the essential ingredient of affective solidarity for the existence of something that resembles what I have been calling a political system.

It is understandable that those concerned with the conditions under which a peaceful international system might arise should temporarily, at least, isolate the community aspect of political life and elevate it to the point where it threatens to become the sole or dominant aspect. To common sense it is not immediately evident that new political formations are likely to take shape and achieve long-range stability either without the prior growth of community-like sentiments or their subsequent emergence. Feelings of community with one's fellows are so noticeable an ingredient in domestic political systems that it can easily lead the investigator, searching for the function that communal sentiments play, to substitute the communal aspects of political life, at least temporarily, for the whole.

To capture and retain the contribution that the idea of political community has for an understanding of the functioning of political systems, it will be necessary to break it down into the implications inherent in it. In the first place, it contains the suggestion that a group of persons are for one reason or another joined together in a common political enterprise. If this idea were not implicit, there would be little reason for turning to the idea of a community at all. Community suggests cooperation of some sort. In the second place, it also implies that the way in which the common enterprise is conducted may vary with respect to the degree of cohesion or sense of community the members feel. A community is usually something more than just an aggregate. It is a group that may be bound by the subtleties of sentiment.

The first implied notion I shall characterize as the *political community*. It represents an object toward which support may or may not flow. The second, I shall identify as a sentiment to be called the *sense of community*. This will represent a measure of the extent of support for the political community and will only be a possible characteristic of a political community, not an essential part of the meaning of the term. I shall examine each notion in turn.

THE POLITICAL COMMUNITY: DEFINITION

This concept . . . will refer to that aspect of a political system that consists of its members seen as a group of persons bound together by a political division of labor. The existence of a political system must include a plurality of political relationships through which the individual members are linked to each other and through which the political objectives of the system are pursued, however limited they may be.[9] In confining the idea of political community in this way, I do so in order to focus not on the form or structure of political processes but rather on the group of members who are drawn together by the fact that they participate in a common structure and set of processes, however tight or loose the ties may be.

For the moment it does not matter whether the members form a community in the sociological sense of a group of members who have a sense of community or a set of common traditions. The members of a political system who are participating in a common political community may well have different cultures and traditions or they may be entirely separate nationalities. The cultural and psychological distance among these component plural groups may well be increasing rather than declining.

Participation in a common division of political labor need not under all circumstances conduce to strengthening the sentiments of mutual identification; witness the comments already quoted with regard to the Habsburg Empire. It was never able to develop potent psychological bonds among its many nationalities to underpin the support coming from the loyal administrative services and other selected groups. But regardless of the degree of cohesion among the members of the system, as long as they are part of the same political system, they cannot escape sharing in or being linked by a common division of political labor. This forms the structural connection among the members of

---

9 Cf.: "A human community is a body of people sharing in common activities and bound by multiple relationships in such a way that the aims of any individual can be achieved only by participation in actions with others." R. Firth, *Elements of Social Organization* (London: Watts, 1951), p. 41.

the system that gives minimal linkage to political activities that might otherwise be isolated or independent.

A member of a system will be said to extend support to his political community insofar as he stands ready to act on behalf of maintaining some structure through which he and others may play their part in the making of binding decisions or is favorably oriented towards its perpetuation, whatever form it may take from time to time and however insignificant the role of the average member may be in the division. A group of people who come together to draw up some kind of constitution to regulate their political relationship—as in the case of the thirteen colonies in America—thereby indicate their intention to share a division of political labor. The particular structure of the relationship may change, the members of the system may be ranked, subdivided and rearranged politically so that the structural patterns are fundamentally altered. But as long as the members continue to evince an attachment to the overall group in which the changing interrelationships prevail and through which demands in a system are processed, they will be supporting the existence of the same and continuing community.

From the point of view of the existence of the political community, the extent of the sharing in the division of labor is immaterial. At the one extreme, we might conceivably find a system in which each member has an explicit and highly active role in the regulation of conflicting demands or the authoritative allocation of values. Every adult may be expected to show some interest in politics, participate at least to the extent of casting a vote and discussing the issues. At the other pole, it will be enough if a person sees his role as one of complete passivity and acceptance of the absolute authority of others over him. In this case, the member's part in the division of political labor is entirely that of owing a duty to accept his subordinate status in political life.

But if a person could not locate himself anywhere in the political division of labor in a system, was not able to relate himself to anything else that occurred in the system, even to the extent of feeling it was his obligation to obey a superior or abide by some vaguely apprehended tradition, one of two conditions might exist. Either he would not be part of the system or his ties to the political community would be in imminent danger of being severed. To avoid any ambiguity as to who is or is not a part of this division of labor, each system provides criteria of membership through territorial presence, legal definition, blood, subjection, kinship, or the like.

SYSTEMIC AND COMMUNITY CHANGES

Not all changes in a political system need affect the political community. This is why there will always be residual ambiguity if we describe a political system as having changed and yet fail to specify the basic objects with regard to which the change has occurred. Authorities typically come and go, regimes or constitutional orders may change. In both cases the community may remain quite stable. If we take metropolitan France alone as an example, in its community aspects it has experienced little change since the French Revolution aside from minor fluctuations at its geographic boundaries. But this is not equally the case for France's regimes which have undergone innumerable drastic transformations. Governmental changes, if not at the administrative, at least at the leadership level, have been too numerous to count easily.

But political communities are capable of changing. This occurs at moments when the membership undergoes some internal subdivision indicating that whole groups have withdrawn their support from the pre-existing division of political labor. The American Civil War, like any political fission, illustrates concretely what occurs with the cessation of the input of support. The war itself offered evidence that the members of the American political system could or would no longer contribute together to the prior division of political labor through which binding decisions had been made for the society. Their attachment to the most inclusive group in and through which the tasks necessary for the processing of demands to authoritative outputs were performed, was destroyed.

It was no longer a question in the United States of whether the South would support one or another alternative government, or whether it could envision its demands being satisfied through the normal procedures of the regime. The issue turned on whether the members could conceive of themselves continuing as a group that was part of and subject to the same set of processes for arriving at political decisions and taking political action. Support for such a group, which shared a division of political labor, had temporarily crumbled.

In principle, in addition to the kind of subdivision sparked by civil strife, a political community may lose its support, and thereby be destroyed, in several typical ways. Through emigration, if permitted, individuals may withdraw from a political community. If the trend is sufficiently pronounced as in the case of an informal but large-scale separatist movement, it could well affect the size, composition, and structure of the political community. The longing of some 60,000 members of the Ras Tafari sect in Jamaica to return to Nigeria or Ethiopia indicates the consequences of disillusionment with the benefits to be gained from continued participation in the Jamaican political community. In effect the poorest and most alienated blacks are saying not only that they dislike the authorities and regime of the whites and browns, but that they no longer have any feeling left for contributing by their presence to a common political structure with the whites and browns. They are choosing to share their labors, in resolving political differences, with the Nigerians or Ethiopians, the regime and governmental forms being left open-ended.

Perhaps the most decisive indicator of the withdrawal of support from a political community consists of group separation. By collective action a subgroup may hive off to join some pre-existing political community, in this way transferring support from one shared division of political labor to another, or to found an entirely new political system. In some systems, it is possible for such hiving off to take place without the type of regime itself being seriously influenced. In the case of many traditional tribal systems in Africa it was the accepted and ethically unrestricted custom for members of a lineage segment to break away from the parent stem in order to found a new chiefdom or kingdom under a purposefully selected leader.[10] The new system might retain the identical kind of regime that prevailed in the old system of which it had been part but out of which two new societies and political communities had been created.

LEVELS OF POLITICAL COMMUNITIES

Loss of support may therefore lead to different kinds of ruptures in the political community. But lest it appear that only those political units we call nation-states and some disappearing tribal political systems display community aspects or that nationalism is the one significant ideological expression of support for a political community, we need to generalize our discussion more clearly. As I have indicated elsewhere,[11] political systems may be identified at different levels of inclusiveness, from the parapolitical system of a voluntary organization to a municipality, province or state, national unit, and various kinds of international systems.

Some systems are independent of others in the sense that one cannot be included as a subsystem of the other. The United States and France represent such mutually exclusive systems. Some nest within others; that is to say, a given system may be alternately viewed as a separate system coordinate with others at the same level of analysis—two national units, for example—or as a subsystem of a supra-system of which it is part, as the United States is a subsystem of an international political system such as NATO or the United Nations.

In like manner, we can visualize an extensive nesting relationship beginning with a small municipality, say in the United States. It will be included in an ascending order of more comprehensive political systems, and each lower system in the hierarchy will be a unit in the higher one and, therefore, a subsystem of it. The municipality will be a subsystem within a township perhaps, the latter will constitute a subsystem in the political system of the county, this, in turn, a subsystem within a state and the state a subsystem within the national unit and so on up to the most comprehensive international political system. Whether we choose to view any of these systems as subsystems of a broader system or as systems coordinate with others at the same level will depend solely on the level of analysis being undertaken.

This conception has immediate relevance for the identification of political communities. It follows that just as the scope of a political system will vary

---

10 See the reference to this kind of separation in my essay, "Political Anthropology in B.J. Siegel," *Biennial Review of Anthropology 1959* (Stanford: Stanford University Press, 1959), pp. 210–262.

11 *A Framework for Political Analysis,* Chapters II–IV.

with the systems level, so will the scope of the political community. It is just an aspect of the system to which we may be referring. We may range from the local to the broad international community. For a person to say that he is a Parisian, a Frenchman, and a European indicates three different levels of political community to which he simultaneously adheres. Each of these communities stands at a different systems level, with each lower community nesting within its next higher supra-system. In every case, however, we find a different division of labor for the fulfillment of political processes at that level.

If we broaden our systems to include NATO and the United Nations in ascending order, it may appear that the more inclusive the group to whose division of labor we are referring, the lower must be the degree of political cohesion or integration. In those we have specified, this may well be the case. But there is no necessary connection between the level of analysis and the degree of cohesion. We may find tightly or loosely knit communities at all system levels; in principle all political communities, including those at the same systems level, may differ with respect to cohesion. Just as the European community may be low in integration compared to one of its subunits, each of the coordinate subunits will usually differ from the other along the same dimension.

But aside from the matter of its integration, from whatever level of systems we select our political unit, we can distinguish each one from the other through the fact that it will display a different, even if at times overlapping, division of labor for the negotiation and regulation of political problems. The most inclusive group at the given systems level to which a particular structure applies constitutes the political community at that level.

It is clear that, in its theoretical status, political community is an analytic concept. It refers not to the total human being as such or even all of his political interactions but to an aspect of his political behavior. We are looking at him as he is related to others as a member of a group that shares a political structure, however much or little any member may be emotionally attached to the group for the fulfillment of his political purposes. We can appreciate, therefore, how a person may be able to offer support to two or more communities simultaneously. Different causes may trigger his input or withholding of support with regard to the various communities toward which he may be oriented. For example, he may withdraw his support from NATO or the United Nations, if he is at all oriented toward either one, and yet increase his input to the French political community. Indeed, at the present juncture, it is Gaullist policy to require just that.

SOCIETY, COMMUNITY, AND POLITICAL COMMUNITY

In describing the political community as an object of attachment in this way, I have abandoned the classic sociological conceptual distinction between society and community.[12] In that view, society describes the instrumental or associative aspects of a group. It draws attention to the formal ties among the members, those that link them through the need to live and work together and to exchange goods and services. Community, on the other hand, is a concept that identifies the affective aspects of group relationships, those resting on personal and informal bonds and expressed through shared feelings, values, and knowledge or all cultural symbols that reflect and contribute to sentiments of solidarity. In Weberian terms, a community exists when there are actions that are "oriented to the feelings of the actors that they belong together."[13]

In order to separate clearly my use of the concept "political community" from the meaning such as this, typically attributed to it for other purposes, I shall refer to the sociological use as the *social* community in contrast with my concern with the *political* community. The differences implied in these two conceptions of the term "community," I shall explore in a moment. But it is clear now that, however helpful it may be, for purposes of general social analysis, to differentiate between society and community—or what I am calling social community—for our analysis of political life this kind of dichotomy holds little value. Nor does it make much sense, solely for the sake of keeping a uniform vocabulary, to try to force ourselves to develop an exact parallel with respect to the political system.

If we did, we would want to be able to distinguish what we might call a political society from a political community: the formal political relationships from the informal solidary bonds. It is true, the creation of such conceptual categories would not present an insurmountable hurdle, if it were necessary or useful to do so. But if we are to treat the canon of simplicity in analysis seriously, we would lose little and gain much in clarity if we find it possible to retain only one term, that of political community. This can incorporate what for other purposes and in other areas of analysis we might find necessary to divide into the societal and communal aspects of a group.

A simplified conceptualization has much to commend it. It will permit us to distinguish unambiguously between the political division of labor as an object of support, which I shall continue to call the political community, and the strength of feelings associated with this attachment, which I shall designate as the *sense or feelings* of community. This sense of community or these feelings of mutual identification will offer a possible measure of attachment to the political community.

It is important to bear in mind this distinction now being made between the political community and the sense of community. The latter is a dimension

---

12 For the classical distinctions, see the well-known discussions by Ferdinand Tönnies and Max Weber. For recent commentaries, see C.J. Friedrich (ed.), *op. cit.*

13 H.H. Gerth and C.W. Mills (eds.), *From Max Weber: Essays in Sociology* (New York: Oxford University Press, 1946), p. 183.

of the former, the affective aspect. It may or may not be present; and when present, it may appear in different degrees. It will reflect the varying cohesiveness of the political community. This is decisively different from the juxtaposition of society and (social) community in sociological literature. In that context, the concept "community" refers not to a *quality* of a common set of relationships but to a *different* set of relationships entirely. Each set must exist in every social group.

In the meaning with which I am using the term "political community" as against "a sense of community," the group that shares a political division of labor may or may not have developed a sense of community. Hence, a feeling of community need not always be present, and if it is, this sense may appear in varying degrees. Although, as we shall see, the utter and total absence of a sense of community may not be a frequent phenomenon, it is in principle possible. In this conceptualization, therefore, we shall always be able to keep clearly in mind the difference between the existence of a group with a common division of labor—the political community—and the degree of solidarity, if any, that it may possess—its sense of community. These feelings of community will indicate the extent to which the members support the continuation of the existing division of political labor, that is, of the existing political community.

THE SENSE OF POLITICAL COMMUNITY

Sense of social community versus sense of political community

What is this sense of political community which will form an indicator of the degree of cohesion in the division of political labor and thereby one measure of attachment for the political community? To clarify its meaning and appreciate its significance, the first point to note is that it does not represent the same thing as the sense of community often referred to with respect to the social community. If we speak about society at large, the idea of a sense of community is frequently used almost as a synonym for the feelings of solidarity already incorporated in the concept "(social) community" itself. As the affect involved in the idea of social community, a sense of community may be described in Deutsch's terms to be "much more than simply verbal attachment to any number of similar or identical values. Rather it [is] a matter of mutual sympathy and loyalties; of 'we-feeling,' trust, and consideration; of at least partial identification in terms of self-images and interests; of ability to predict each other's behavior and ability to act in accordance with that prediction. In short, it [is] a matter of perpetual attention, communication, perception of needs, and responsiveness."[14]

This describes the communal sentiment of people generally with regard to

---

[14] K.W. Deutsch, S.A. Burrell, *et al., op. cit.,* p. 129.

working and living together in a society to fulfill all their individual and social needs. It is an indication of the cohesiveness of *society*, what has already been identified as the social community. But as in the rest of our analysis, we are concerned only with the political aspect of society and here it is represented in the political community—that aspect of a group of persons as represented in those acts through which they contribute to a common political division of labor. The we-feeling or sense of community which indicates political cohesion of a group of persons, regardless of the kind of regime they have or may develop, consists of the feeling of belonging together as a group which, because it shares a political structure, also shares a political fate. Regardless of the dissimilarities of customs, religion, socio-economic status, nationality, and the like, to the extent that there is a *feeling* of political community, the members will possess mutual sympathy and loyalty with respect to their participation in a common political unit.

It is a mutual identification that may be expressed in many ways. We are the men of a great chief; we are subjects of the king; we are the citizens of this democracy. Often to say that we are Americans, British, Jamaicans, is to point less to the social and cultural differences than to the political bonds that unite a group of persons, even though the non-political overtones are never entirely removed. At least in modern societies, especially where cultural diversity prevails, national identification does have a strong political coloring, of necessity. Nevertheless, in every society the common political structure shared by the members tends to create minimal affective political bonds and it is to these that the concept "sense of political community" will be applied.

The level of communal affect

As has already been implied, this approach does not compel us to postulate that before a political system can exist or even if it is to persist, a sense of political community must first rise to some specified level. Although we may adopt the degree of mutual identification as one kind of measure of the input of support for the political community, it is conceivable that for considerable periods of time, the sense of political community may be low or non-existent. Support may be derived through means other than mutual feelings of belonging together. Not only is this conceivable; there is ample evidence to demonstrate the relative independence for considerable periods of time of political communities from the feelings of community among the members. It is possible for a political structure to bind a group together before feelings of mutual identification have emerged.

We may go further. Frequently the imposition of a common division of political labor has itself made possible the slow growth of sentiments of political solidarity; this reverses normal expectations of the significance of sentiments of solidarity as a pre-condition for the emergence of a political community. A political community may precede and become a condition for the growth of a sense of community.

This has been the experience on the part of most systems that have been brought into being through force, in part or in whole. In the early modern European period, the princes or absolute monarchs drew a geographic area into a political unity through force, frequently before any sense of belonging together had begun to emerge. Only slowly thereafter, through vigorous policies on the part of the political elite, was it possible to merge the members, who were compelled to support the existing political community, into a relatively homogeneous political unit with a high sense of political solidarity. Initially, support had to be generated through coercion, fear of sanctions, or the seduction of material rewards; subsequently these could be supplanted or reinforced by a continuing sense of belonging together.

Coercion may be only one of the sources of support for a political community. In other cases, especially where a group has come together voluntarily, the hard fact of participating collectively may help to arouse and sustain interest in and support for the new political community. A point such as this has been made with regard to the possible development of a more cohesive European political system. It has been suggested that the entrenchment of the habit of working together in a political division of labor sometimes derives less from the pre-recognition of common political interests and traditions than from the convergence of divergent but complementary aims. This is what has been found at the international level and which underlies much so-called functional thinking about the sources of a world or European community.[15] As persons are able to work out their specific problems successfully, the common political institutions through which differences are negotiated and regulated will help draw them together. Transnational institutions may help build up support for supra-national ones.

To generalize this idea, we may say that the prior acceptance of a participation in a division of political labor will help to generate and strengthen other kinds of bonds. Members develop vested interest in the mutual advantages of the ongoing pattern of relationships. In other words, instrumental ties and aims may well keep a group working together while affective bonds have a chance to mature.

But if a sense of community fails to emerge and deepen over time, as a source of support, it may leave a system extremely vulnerable to stress. The collapse of the Austro-Hungarian Empire under the blows of military defeat is a good example. Prior to the nineteenth century, the Habsburg monarchy survived for centuries. Yet traditional particularistic sentiments of the multiple constituent nationalities flourished, varied social, cultural, and economic practices made unity impossible, and large segments of the membership were constantly on the verge of open rupture. Here, coercion and material rewards plus inertia were effective ways of inducing the external trappings of minimal participation in and support for the division of labor necessary to enable the

---

[15] E.B. Haas, *op. cit.*

political system to function.[16] But in the long run, the input of support was insufficient to hold the political community together as a unified political system when it came under the stress of military defeat.

The Austro-Hungarian imperial system illustrates both the success and ultimate failure of structural integration under conditions in which strong affective solidarity is absent. A sense of political community is relevant, not to the possibility of a political community but to its duration under stress, a point to which we shall return when we come to consider possible responses to low inputs of support.

To some extent today, developing systems too have taken shape with low feelings of mutual responsiveness on the part of the participating tribal or other plural groups and although a common political structure may exist, an increase in the level of support will have to wait upon the slow stimulation of a sense of political community. But its present absence or low level does not indicate that the input of support for the political community is below the minimal level necessary for its persistence, even though undoubtedly without a gradual increase in feelings of political solidarity it is not likely that the community could endure.

The idea that it is possible to participate in a division of political labor in developing systems, even before the growth of sentiments of political solidarity, is supported by some students of developing systems in Africa. "Whereas in homogeneous societies," writes M.G. Smith, "it is society that constitutes law, in plural societies, such as those of Africa, there is evidence that law may serve to constitute society. Thus law both derives from and may establish society.

"In the first instance the social milieu is typically homogeneous, ethnically and culturally, and the basis of society is primarily consensual; in this situation law may express organic institutional relations. In plural societies, on the other hand, the social milieu is heterogeneous in cultural and ethnic constitution and coercive in base, and the law that seeks to constitute it and serves to regulate it is essentially sectional. In the culturally homogeneous society, the state—that is, the central political institutions—is, like law, a derivative, expressive, and secondary structure. In the evolution of plural units the state preexists society, and provides the legal framework within which the new society may or may not emerge...."[17]

The differences in terminology ought not be allowed to conceal the relevance of the ideas being advanced in this quotation. It confirms the point that structural participation or instrumental ties under some conditions may precede the growth of sentiments of solidarity in society. With the necessary changes in concepts, the same ordering of events could be said to apply to the

---

16 R.A. Kann, *The Habsburg Empire: A Study in Integration and Disintegration* (New York: Praeger, 1957), p. 111.

17 M.G. Smith, "The Sociological Framework of Law" in Helda and Leo Kuper, (eds.), *African Law: Adaption and Development* (Berkeley and Los Angeles: University of California Press, 1965), p. 26.

political community or group participating in a common division of political labor and the underlying supportive sentiments which may exist in varying degrees.

It is quite possible, therefore, that in the formation of new societies and associated political systems, a sense of belonging together politically may normally follow rather than precede the emergence of a political community. If this is so, there could be little doubt that a political community is phenomenally independent, at least in its initiation, from the feelings of solidarity that are usually considered to be a major pre-condition.

By fusing the politically relevant components of the sociological concepts of society and community into a single concept, "political community," we have succeeded in identifying and defining one of the major components of a political system. The idea of persistence and change of a political system will make sense only if the context indicates whether or not the reference is to the political community. Systems may change in many ways but where there is a decline of support below a certain level for the political community, there the system will be threatened with stress.

By adopting the concept "sense of community" to identify the affective, cultural aspects of the political community, we have been able to devise an analytic approach that provides us with a major indicator of support for the political community. It is true, under certain conditions, the virtual absence of such feelings need not in itself prove that the political community lacks the minimal support necessary to avoid stressing the essential variables. Nevertheless, since over the long run it is unlikely that many systems could persist without the development of a rather high sense of political community, or withstand severe crises, it does represent a significant measure of support.

The criterion by which political community has been selected as one central focus of support has been the probability that loss of support for it would prevent the system from continuing to process demands through to binding outputs. Using the same criterion, we shall now be able to identify the regime as a second major component of a system, no less significant than the political community for a full appreciation of stress due to loss of support and responses related to it.

WALKER F. CONNOR

Myths of Hemispheric, Continental, Regional, and State Unity

One of the more enduring and consequential myths of human relations is the assumption that groups who dwell on a single land-mass share certain common interests and traits because of that territorial contiguity, even though the groups in question may be separated by great distances.[1] An illustration of this phenomenon is offered by the phrase popularly ascribed to United States relations with Latin America in the post-1933 period, "the Good Neighbor Policy." By the term "neighbor," U.S. leaders were obviously implying the existence of a special relationship based upon a concept of relative proximity. Among the neighbors were the so-called "ABC" states of Argentina, Brazil, and Chile. Beyond the pale of the neighborhood were such states as the United Kingdom, France, Germany, Italy, Liberia, and the U.S.S.R. Yet, in navigable distances, each of these states was closer to the United States than was any of the "ABC" group.[2] Contrariwise, Argentina and Brazil were closer to Europe than they were to the "colossus of the north."

Reprinted with permission from the *Political Science Quarterly*, Vol. 84, No. 4 (December 1969), pp. 555–567, 570–582.

[1] For an earlier article concerned with this myth, see Eugene Staley, "The Myth of the Continents," *Foreign Affairs*, XIX (1941), 481–494. Staley's analysis was essentially limited to the Western Hemisphere, and his primary aim was to counter the tendency, prevalent in the period prior to the attack on Pearl Harbor, to stress a hemispheric concept of defense at the expense of European ties. For a still earlier reference to the myth as applied to the Western Hemisphere, see William Stevens and Allan Wescott, *A History of Sea Power* (New York, 1920), p. 2.

[2] The statement is based upon the distance between New York City and the major port of each of the other states. It holds true for both sea and air travel. To anticipate a possible objection it might be noted that the ports of Chile are closer to New York than they are to United States west-coast ports. Argentina is the farthest from New York, comparing unfavorably in this regard even with Turkey and the UAR.

In terms of its basic assumption that a special relationship exists among all of the states of the Western Hemisphere due to geography, the Good Neighbor Policy did not represent a departure from earlier attitudes, but rather furnished testimony to the tenacity of a myth which had been prevalent at least since the first stirrings of independence movements in Latin America. Thomas Jefferson, for example, noted in private correspondence in 1811:

> The European nations constitute a separate division of the globe; their localities make them a part of a distinct system; they have a set of interests of their own in which it is our business never to engage ourselves. *America has a hemisphere to itself. It must have its separate system of interests;* which must not be subordinated to those of Europe. *The insulated state in which nature has placed the American continent,* should so far avail that no spark of war kindled in other quarters of the globe should be wafted across the wide oceans which separate us from them and it will be so.[3]

In a similar vein, Henry Clay declared on the floor of the House of Representatives a few years later:

> There cannot be a doubt that Spanish America, once independent, whatever may be the form of governments established in its parts, *these governments will be animated by an American feeling, and guided by an American policy. They will obey the laws of the system of the New World,* of which they will compose a part, in contradistinction to that of Europe.[4]

Both statements predicate a mystical bond arising from an equally mystical proximity. From their sharp differentiation between Europe and all that is European on the one hand, and the New World and all that is "New Worldly" on the other, it is evident that both men had assumed a direct relationship between physical geography and contemporary human affairs. The oceans were viewed as constituting barriers to human relations, and the landed interconnection between the United States and the states to the south was viewed, at least by contrast with the oceans, as constituting a cultural and political bridge.

This same a priori assumption underlay the clarion of "Manifest Destiny," which called upon Americans to conform to Nature's law by making their political-cultural domain coterminous with the land-mass. While president, John Q. Adams found "it a settled geographic element that the United States and North America are identical." He was followed by others who pursued the logic of the concept of "natural frontiers" (ocean borders) to its conclusion. In 1845, for example, a congressman from Illinois prophesied on the floor of the House that the Speaker would soon recognize not just the gentleman from Oregon, but the one from Canada, from Cuba, from Mexico, "aye, even the

---

3 From a letter to his friend Alexander von Humboldt. Quoted in Dexter Perkins, *A History of the Monroe Doctrine* (Boston, 1963), p. 22 (emphasis added). It is assumed that the statement can be considered an accurate reflection of Jefferson's convictions, since it was not intended for publication.

4 Speech of March 24, 1818, cited in *ibid.*, pp. 3–4 (emphasis added).

gentleman from Patagonia." And he was supported in his prophesy by Stephen A. Douglas, who made clear, however, that he "did not wish to go beyond the great ocean—beyond the boundaries which the God of nature had marked out."[5]

Although the United States was later to settle for something far less territorially ambitious than the Arctic and the Straits of Magellan, the idea of the hemispheric bond was to remain the ideological nucleus of United States–Latin-American policy. From the espousal of the Monroe Doctrine in 1823 to the Alliance for Progress, the United States has steadfastly assumed the existence of special ties between itself and all of Latin America (1) because of their common separation from Eurasia by oceans and (2) because of their landed interconnection. Considering again that the United States and some of the South American states are closer to Europe than they are to each other, how else is to be explained the words of the Monroe Doctrine: "With the movements in this hemisphere we are of necessity more immediately connected, and by causes which must be obvious to all enlightened and impartial observers"? Or Secretary of State Olney's 1895 contention that "the States of America, South as well as North, *by geographic proximity,* . . . are friends and allies"?[6] Or Theodore Roosevelt's 1904 denial that the United States wanted anything in the Western Hemisphere other than "to see the *neighboring countries* stable, orderly, and prosperous"?[7] Or Franklin Roosevelt's reference to "good neighbors"? Or the official wording of the congressional rationale for the Alliance for Progress: "It is the sense of the Congress that the historic, economic, political, and *geographic* relationships among the American peoples and Republics are unique and of special significance . . ."?[8]

It is evident that this "unique" and "special" relationship is based upon the sharing of a single land-mass, for the United States shares little else with all of the states of Central and South America. Surely not culture, for the United States is a predominantly Anglo-Saxon, English-speaking, Protestant culture while its neighbors to the south are predominantly Latin, Spanish-Portuguese-speaking, and Catholic. Economically, some of the states of Central and South America have been important providers of raw materials to the United States, others have been essentially unimportant to the United States economy, and still others, such as Argentina, have been competitive with the United States.

But how important has the fact of sharing a common land-mass actually been? The reality, of course, is that relations with all states south of Mexico have been conducted as though they and the United States were distinct islands.

---

5 Frederick Merk, *Manifest Destiny* (New York, 1963), pp. 16, 28.

6 Perkins, p. 149 (emphasis added).

7 Annual Message from President Roosevelt to the United States Congress, December 6, 1904, in William Williams (ed.), *The Shaping of American Diplomacy* (Chicago, 1956), p. 530.

8 Foreign Assistance Act of 1962, Title VI—Alliance for Progress, sec. 251, par. (a) (emphasis added).

And this is true of the most important relations between Mexico and the United States as well. The "land-bridge" represented by the Isthmus of Panama is, in fact, a barrier (containing mountains and tropical jungle, and not completely crossed by a single north-south highway), which has been bypassed rather than utilized by man in his north-south travels. The major importance of the Isthmus in the relations among the states of the Western Hemisphere has been due to its man-made, east-west severance at Panama, rather than to its north-south continuity. Intercourse between the United States and other American states to the south has been conducted primarily by sea or, so far as passenger service in recent years is concerned, by air, but practically not at all by land. Yet, would the United States have been apt to postulate a "unique" and "special" relationship between itself and, say, Argentina, if the two states had been "separated by ocean," rather than "connected by land"?

I

The prevalence of the myth of landed relationships is not limited to the Western Hemisphere. There exists a common tendency, when looking at a world map, to conceive of the blue-painted oceans and large seas as chasms and voids, effectively separating the land masses—particularly Eurasia, Africa, and the Americas—into inward-looking, intrarelated wholes. Meaningful relations, it follows, end at the water's edge. As a formula this conception would read: *Two points, connected by land, are closer than two points, equally distant, but separated by water.*

The formula admittedly possessed validity prior to the late fifteenth century, if two points separated by water meant two points separated by a wide expanse of open ocean. But even in prehistoric times man had discovered and put into practice what his successors have continued to practice while often failing to perceive, that water poses less of a barrier to movement and to trans-communication than does land.

The socio-political consequences of the comparative advantage of water travel are manifest in the arterial role which navigable rivers have played throughout history. Thus, the first political integration of a large territory and population occurred in Egypt, where even today almost 99 per cent of the inhabitants dwell in that 4 per cent of the territory which stretches along the Nile. Other early societies developed along the Tigris-Euphrates, the Indus, and the Yellow Rivers.[9]

This integrating influence of rivers possesses great significance for contemporary South Asian politics. In the case of Burma, for example, an examination of the linguistic and relief maps illustrates that the Burmese-speaking people are limited essentially to the Irrawady and Sittang River Valleys, their deltas,

---

[9] There is some evidence that the Tigris-Euphrates civilization may antedate that of the Nile.

and a stretch of coastal plain. In Thailand the Siamese-speaking element is essentially restricted to the Chao Praya Valley. In Vietnam the Vietnamese-speakers are restricted to the Red and Mekong River Valleys, their deltas, a thin coastal strip, and the river and canal-infested Cochin-China plain. It is therefore evident that the rivers and off-coast waters have been the main passageways for cultural and economic intercourse throughout South Asian history. People separated by great distances along a navigable river or sea coast are very often culturally interrelated and, what is of key political importance, are conscious of that interrelationship because it has been nourished by continuing contacts. By contrast, people only short distances away (for example, the Karens, Kachins, Mons, and others in Burma; the mountain tribesmen of the north, and the Lao-speaking people of the northeast in the case of Thailand; the "montagnards" in the case of Vietnam) have been comparatively isolated from the dominant people within the political state in which they now find themselves. Many of the major problems of contemporary South Asia are the *in tandem* consequence of the attempt to combine within single territorial-political units what have hitherto been effectively separated highland and riverine-coastal culture groups.

Coastal waters have also served as intercontinental avenues since early times. The key role that was played by the Mediterranean in a number of ancient civilizations is impressed upon all "Western" schoolchildren. What is seldom emphasized in children's history books, however, is that "the cradle of Western civilization" actually consisted of the intertwined civilizations of Asia and Africa, as well as Europe. Moreover, even prior to the Christian era, goods from monsoon Asia regularly reached the Mediterranean by way of the Indian Ocean, the Red Sea, and the shortest possible overland route across the Isthmus of Suez. Similarly, a thriving ocean trade between east-coast Africa and the Indian subcontinent existed long before Vasco de Gama rounded southern Africa. The advances in navigational devices and shipbuilding which made possible "the Age of Discovery" represented, therefore, only an evolutionary, albeit a giant step in the pattern of human relations. Transocean voyages did not herald a radical departure from earlier patterns.

Significant overland movements have also occurred, of course. Overland migrations of people, covering great distances, are quite common facts of history; caravan routes for the carriage of goods long existed between the Orient and the Mediterranean and between the north and south Sahara; there have been empires such as the Khanate of the Golden Horde, which were based primarily upon overland relationships. But three points are evident: (1) Where navigable waters are available man, throughout history, has utilized them in preference to overland routes. In the conduct of relations beyond the immediate proximity, navigable waters have been a more important avenue than has land. (2) Both quantitatively and qualitatively, overwater relations have proved more pervasive than have overland relations. Thus, the historic overland migrations tended to be single-shot in nature; their routes did not form the channel

for continuing cross-fertilization of the cultures located at the originating and
terminal points of the migration. Similarly, the overland empires, such as that
of the Golden Horde, proved to have little enduring impact upon the peoples
of their further reaches.[10] The Chinese cultural impact remained confined to
the river valleys and coastal plains, but had little impact upon the peoples of
southern China, Tibet, Sinkiang, and Mongolia. Portuguese and Spanish culture had an enduring impact upon the variegated coastal-oriented people of
South America, but much less a one upon those of the interior. Indeed, the
influence of Castilian culture upon the coastal and riverine people of those
territories in South America once controlled by Spain has been greater than it
has been upon the Basques and Catalonians of territorial Spain. It is apparent,
therefore, that the interrelationship which was noted between water transport
and acculturation in South Asia is not unique to that region. (3) Important
overwater contacts have been conducted, often without distance having any
discernible impact, while territorially adjacent areas frequently have experienced little intercommunication.

II

The impact of technology upon "meaningful distance" has been a great and
an accelerating one in quantitative measure. But has it altered or merely mag-
nified the comparative disadvantage of land travel? An answer requires that
one differentiate distance in terms of transportation, communications, and
military strategy.

The continuous erection of road, rail, and pipeline networks is certainly
evidence of man's progress in overcoming barriers to overland transportation.
Nonetheless it remains the case that the water-transport of bulk items is by far
the most efficient method. As but one illustration, consider the cost ratio of
various forms of bulk-oil transport within the United States as compared with
ship transport: movement by pipeline is four times as expensive; by railroad,
twenty-two times; and by truck, seventy-five times more costly.[11]

Despite the proliferation of networks of other forms of surface transport
such figures make evident that water transport, wherever available, would be
the preferred method for the movement of bulk goods.[12] Illustrative of this

---

10 If, as it has long been assumed, the early Incas were not seafarers, the Inca empire would
be an exception. But recent discoveries of pottery raise serious doubts about this assumption.
See Walter Sullivan's article in the *New York Times*, June 1, 1969, and a description of a
voyage by reed boat from Peru to Panama in the *New York Times*, June 22, 1969.

11 John Alexander, *Economic Geography* (Englewood Cliffs, N.J., 1963), p. 347.

12 The distance, of course, must be sufficiently great to offset the cost and inconvenience of
transloading goods from truck or train to ship and vice versa. If the trip is relatively short
the advantage of direct rail- or road-transport from source to final destination will counter
the lesser ton-mileage expense of ship transport. This fact accounts for the great loss in the
relative importance of intrastate shipping within many states in recent years.

preference is the fact that 70 per cent of all tonnage shipped in and out of United States ports represents intra-United States trade. Similarly, in functional though not in political terms, there is justification for considering the Panama Canal an internal waterway; one-sixth of all shipping through the canal is merely en route from one United States coast to the other. San Francisco is closely tied to New York by water transport, despite the fact that the navigable water distance between the two is more than twice the overland distance, is greater than the distance from New York to Rio or Istanbul, and is greater than the distance from San Francisco to the port of Japan and Korea. The same comparative advantage explains why the transport of goods between Alaska and the group of forty-eight states south of Canada is conducted essentially as though each were an island. And it lends a measure of truth to the occasional slip of writers and speakers when they refer to the forty-eight states as "the continental United States," in contradistinction to the Hawaiian and, inferentially, the Alaskan Islands. It also explains why the Alaska Highway, constructed during World War II for strategic reasons, has been of negligible economic importance. Where alternate sealanes are available, lengthy roads such as the Alaska and the still uncompleted Pan American Highways are only of tourist, psychological, and highly localized economic value.

Air freight is also at a disadvantage. Its importance is still limited to those classes of goods which enjoy a high value-to-volume ratio, to situations in which rapid delivery is important, and to situations in which alternate methods of transport are unavailable.

The role of water travel relative to passenger transport is, of course, vastly different; and it loses primacy to air travel, and to land travel where adequate roads and railways are available. The pattern is not a simple one, however. While air travel is quite obviously the most important means of traversing long distances between important urban areas, it remains an inadequate means of reaching destinations of lesser import. Tales concerning the need to expend more time in reaching a relatively nearby airport than in traveling between two distant cities are now common ingredients of American lore. Since commercial intercontinental flights have long been a reality, such tales emphasize once more the inherent danger of assuming "land connects, water divides." They also raise the far broader question of the degree to which personal travel possesses significance for intercultural relations.

Capitals of "third world" states may be hours from Paris or Washington, and days, or even weeks, from points within their own states. As a result, the impact of air travel upon the great majority of the world's people has been negligible. Indeed, even in the case of states which possess a good intrastate transportation system, the direct impact of personal travel upon the society is minute. The average American, Frenchman, or Russian is not significantly affected by the coming and going of interstate travelers at New York, Paris, or Moscow airports; nor is his culture. On the other hand, if one is talking about the simultaneous visits of a foreign element in sufficiently large numbers to have a cultural impact,[13] then one could contend that the presence of the foreigner in such numbers is at least as apt to give rise to cultural isolation characterized by ethnocentrism and xenophobia. Intercultural person-to-person contacts, unless the necessary concomitant of some mutually desired function (trade or the prosecution of a military alliance in the face of a mutually recognized threat, for example), are apt to prove either unimportant or pernicious.

To contend that the impact of transcultural person-to-person contacts is probably not very great is not to be blind to the evidence that most societies today are culturally less isolated than formerly, and, therefore, more closely reflect one another in current tastes in music, dress, movies, architectural and structural design, student riots, and so forth. But two points should be noted. The first is that this transstate acculturation has not been due to personal contacts but to (1) the greatly increased interchange of goods, including such particularly pertinent items as machine tools, films, and technological and popular journals, (2) more efficient transcultural communications, and (3) the proliferation of multistate corporations such as General Motors, Uniroyal (formerly U.S. Rubber), and the International Business Machines Corporation, which facilitate the unencumbered intracorporate, interstate exchange of research results, style design, production methodology, and patents.[14] The second point is that the degree of this transcultural impact varies tremendously among states. Its most highly developed manifestation is most commonly held to be the recent impact of the United States upon the states of Western Europe—a transocean, not a transland relationship!

Technology appears to be reinforcing the primacy of water as an intercultural connector. Super-tankers, container-cargoes, proportionately smaller crews, nuclear propulsion advances, artificial, deep-draft harbors, increasing mechanization of unloading and loading processes, and more powerful ice-breakers are all increasing the relative efficiency of sea transport. Investments in such developments by industry, and the continued emphasis by governments upon improving water travel, indicate their expectation of the indefinite paramountcy of sea transport. The current plan of the government of the Soviet Union, for example, calls for increased outlays for inland waterways, and its efforts to make the "northeast passage" along the Arctic coast utilizable during longer periods of the year continue to have a high priority. Farther west plans are now underway to connect the Baltic and Black Seas via the Rhine and

---

13 Recent illustrations might include Allied occupation forces following World War II, population transfers of Russians and Ukrainians into Kazakstan and other Asian areas of the Soviet Union, similar Chinese settlement in Sinkiang and Tibet, and the United States presence in South Vietnam and Thailand.

14 For a report of an interesting speech on multistate companies by the chairman of a large British concern, see the *Christian Science Monitor*, April 25, 1969. The speaker referred to such companies as "the decisive business institution of our time" and cited a prediction that "by 1988, the free world's economy will be dominated by some 300 large companies responsible for most of the world's industrial output."

Danube Rivers. United States interest in improving the Saint Lawrence Seaway and in creating a larger canal across the Isthmus of Panama offer still additional evidence of the optimistic future anticipated for water transport.[15] The advent of the "Air Age" and, more recently, the "Space Age," have not signified the deathknell of the "Sea Age."

The concept of communications-distance offers a number of parallels with what has been said concerning air transport. Principal urban areas of the world are interconnected by communication channels without regard to distance or intervening oceans, while it is often much more difficult to make contact between those urban areas and nearby hinterlands. Despite some past technical problems in developing underseas telephone cables, the tendency for interstate channels of communication to be determined by demand rather than by distance or the intervening physical medium is evidenced by the often publicized fact that telephonic communication between South American capitals travels through New York, and two African points are in many instances telephonically joined only by a European detour.[16] The significance of such routes is in the lie they give to concepts of continental insularity and solidarity.

Recent technological developments and projected advances in the use of telecommunication satellites will bring all states, without regard to location, closer together in communicative distance. Intelsat satellites are even now available for the commercial use of telephone, telegraph, radio, and television transmission, and a vast extension of services is contemplated.

By itself, however, such a globe-girdling system will not affect areas otherwise poorly serviced by communications facilities. Continents will be more closely joined, capitals will be more closely joined, but sections of many states may remain essentially incommunicado.

Much publicity has been given in recent years to the integrating impact which the spread of the inexpensive transistor radio is having upon the less accessible areas of the states of Africa and Asia. Two warnings are appropriate, however. The first is that very little is known concerning either the degree or the nature of the impact of one-way communications. The phrase "meaningful monologue" is yet to be coined. Secondly, if the basic language, dialect, and colloquialisms common to the transmitting area are indistinguishable from those in the receiving area, then the two areas have long enjoyed an intensive, intracultural relationship. In such case, radio is merely augmenting an existing interrelationship, not creating a new one. If, on the other hand, language or

---

15 Perhaps the most publicized recent example of faith in the future of sea transport was offered by a private corporation, the Humble Oil and Refining Company, when in 1969 it supported a $30,000,000 venture in order to prove the feasibility of a year-round sea-route along the northern coast of the North American continent. The venture was justified on the grounds of the immense savings which could be obtained by complete ship transport of the oil on the Alaskan North Slope to United States east-coast ports. It was estimated that the alternative of moving oil to ships by a north-south trans-Alaskan pipeline would jump the total delivery price from $.96 to $1.81 per barrel. See the *New York Times*, August 18, 1969.

16 See, for example, Albert Wohlstetter, "Illusions of Distance," *Foreign Affairs*, XLVI (1968), 248.

dialect differs, then the announcer, even assuming that he can be understood, risks drawing attention to divisive rather than to common traits. If the programmers decide that it is best to make announcements in the local dialect or language, the question arises whether communications are strengthening intercultural contacts or cultural self-awareness. The transistors scattered among the tribes of northern and northeastern Thailand have been the means by which Peking and Hanoi draw attention, in the local dialect, to the distinctions and divisions between the listeners and the ruling Thais. Bangkok counters by broadcasts in the local tongues. In such a situation can one safely speak of transistorized assimilation? Or is it safer to note that cultural distance is being increased by the shortening of communications distance?[17]

III

The concept of strategic distance may appear anachronistic. In programming targets for ICBM's distance is immaterial, and it is also inconsequential whether the target be overland or overseas. Submarine-launched, intermediate-range missiles, however, continue to play an important role in the strategic planning of nuclear powers, so it might be noted that ocean relationships between potential enemies do affect vulnerability. Here again water connects and land separates, for the only meaningful measurement in this context is the distance of a target from the nearest major body of ocean-connected water. Again it is within this context that Omaha is one of the least vulnerable spots within the United States.

. . .

An examination of economic, communicative, and strategic distance . . . leads to the conclusion that distance is either meaningless—ICBM distance or intercapital communicative distance, for example—or that overwater distance is less segregative than overland distance. The forementioned formula should therefore be amended to read: *If distance is a meaningful consideration, then two points connected by water are closer than two points equally distant but separated by land.* Inexactitude, however, has not prevented the broadscale acceptance of the uncorrected formula, as manifested in popularly held myths of hemispheric, continental, regional, and state unity. All such myths contain two potential fallacies: (1) that the particular unit, whether a hemisphere, continent, region, or state, is somehow integrated and (2) that significant interests are not shared with those beyond the land borders of the unit.

IV

Hemispheric myths

Enough has been said concerning the so-called "Western Hemisphere"

---

[17] This subject is treated in greater detail below.

to indicate that geographic misconceptions concerning hemispheric relations underlie many important political decisions. There is a fallacy built into the division of the world into two parts and in assigning to each half a title such as "Western" and "Eastern" or "Northern" and "Southern." It lends a sense of naturalness to a dissection that is in fact totally arbitrary, and it posits the existence of intrahemispheric relations which may be absent to the exclusion of interhemispheric relations which *are* present. Even if cultural distances could be measured in actual mileage—which they cannot—it should be evident that two points immediately on either side of a mythical hemisphere-dividing line are closer than either is to the geographic center of its respective hemisphere. Perhaps televised views of earth from space flights will ultimately rid man of one of his favorite myths, for even while he watches the earth is offering to his vision an uninterrupted series of hemispheres. When man at the subconscious level comes to realize that the number of hemispheres is infinite he will perhaps also realize that the number of possible interhemispheric relations of a cultural and political nature are likewise infinite. The patterns of intercultural relations have little to do with hemispheres. British and United States cultural ties are, at least in this period of history, more pervasive than those between the United States and Mexico. Similarly, Australia and New Zealand are closely tied to Britain and the United States despite an intervening equatorial line which demarcates northern and southern hemispheres.

Continental myths

It is in continental myths that the "land connects, water divides" fallacy most commonly manifests itself. African continentalism, perhaps because it is the most youthful, has recently been the most vehemently articulated. African cohesion has been an a priori assumption of a number of statesmen such as Touré, Nkrumah, and Nyerere, and the assumption has been institutionalized in the Organization of African Unity. One of its more colorful articulations was made by Gamal Abdal Nasser in 1953:

> If we consider next... the continent of Africa—I may say without exaggeration that we cannot, under any circumstances, however much we might desire it, remain aloof from the terrible and sanguinary conflict going on there today between five million whites and 200 million Africans. We cannot do so for an important and obvious reason: we are *in* Africa. The peoples of Africa will continue to look to us, who guard their northern gate, and who constitute their link with the outside world. We will never in any circumstances be able to relinquish our responsibility to support, with all our might, the spread of enlightenment and civilization to the remotest depths of the jungle.[18]

The quotation is interesting as an example of how one who, according to the most common anthropological taxonomy, is a caucasoid may nevertheless iden-

---

[18] Gamal Abdal Nasser, *Egypt's Liberation: The Philosophy of the Revolution* (Washington, 1955), pp. 109–10.

tify himself with non-whites by stressing a geo-racial relationship; it is also a declaration of what might be termed "the Arab man's burden," which has been thrust upon him because some of the Arabs live in Africa. But for present purposes it is most interesting because it raises the question: In what way does Egypt or the entire northern littoral of Africa represent "the link with the outside world" for Dakar, Lagos, Cape Town, Cape Elizabeth, Dar es Salaam, and others?

Even a cursory glance at the transportation map of Africa will dramatize the absence of interconnecting facilities among the widely separated, important pockets of population. There is no African hub from which roads and railways emanate outward. Rather, the pattern of the transportation system, including navigable rivers, caravan routes, roads, and railways, consists of a number of seldom interconnected inward thrusts, usually short, from various points on the coast. South Africa is the only state whose interior could be said to be adequately serviced by a transportation system. There is no transcontinental railroad from north to south and, north of Rhodesia, none from east to west. The transportation map makes clear that economic and cultural ties among non-adjoining sub-Saharan African states have been practically non-existent. Most societies of interior Africa have been essentially culturally isolated, while those riverine, coastal, and railroad-neighboring peoples who have been affected by othe societies have been most affected by ones outside Africa.

The case of South America is similar. The area has indeed merited the epithet "the hollow continent," for climate and topography have combined to orient the important enclaves outward—that is, the key societies have had their backs to the continent. The dominance of a common Latin culture in most of the states is not denied, but this same culture is shared by the peoples of many of the islands of the Caribbean and the Iberian Peninsula. By itself, then, the common culture does not prove continental solidarity. More instructive is the persistence of the more indigenous Indian cultures which dominate most of the interior and separate the Latin enclaves. Only in recent years has there been a real attempt by many of the capitals to make highway and cultural contact with the interior. That interstate relations have occurred among Buenos Aires, Bogotá, and Lima is fully acknowledged, but their landed relationship has quite evidently been relatively insignificant.

The Asian pattern is also characterized by a number of major cultural pockets, each oriented to the periphery rather than to the interior. Contacts between the steppe- and highland-dwelling peoples on the one hand, and the riverine- and coastal-dwelling peoples on the other have been insignificant, as shown, for example, by the rather meager impact that Han-Chinese culture has had upon the peoples of non-coastal, peripheral China. Moreover, transcontinental relations often have been more significant than intracontinental, as signified by the impact of British culture upon the language and political institutions of the subcontinent. Finally, it might be noted that while the phrase is geographically incorrect the relative absence of overland contacts does cause references to the Chinese of South Asia as "overseas Chinese" to acquire a measure of cultural accuracy.

Of all the expressions conveying continental unity one would anticipate "European" to be the most meaningful. For generations "the Continent" has meant mainland Europe, and to be "continental" has been to display cultural mannerisms common to Europe. A large measure of cultural integration would certainly appear consonant with the often publicized common Greco-Roman heritage. But how is one to reconcile this concept of "Europeanness" with the history of that area for the past two hundred years? No area of similar size has offered so drastic an illustration of divisiveness, reflecting strong national jealousies and rivalries. There is no reconciliation because a single European culture is a fiction, and a multiplicity of languages, dialects, religious denominations, and other cultural manifestations is the fact. The smallest of the multistate continents is incredibly diverse; a land connection has not made the German more French or vice versa. Emphasis has been on the particular cultural unit, and "Europeanness" has been only a myth. Attempts to unify Europe (1) have not been the result of a "natural" growth of contacts but of coercive superimposition; (2) have been undertaken not in the name of Europe, but in the name of a particular national group; and (3) have been defeated by the stout resistance of groups desirous of cultural and political autonomy.

With the notable exception of Charles de Gaulle few have spoken of European unity in the post-World War II period, because of the Communist—non-Communist division. On each side of that line, however, there has been a subsequent attempt at regional integration. By increasing economic contacts, both the EEC and CEMA hopefully envisage the unification of six states. Though the total area of each represents only a small segment of all of Europe, the problems with which each has been confronted due to competing nationalisms are instructive. At the minimum they can be said to illustrate the fallacy of automatically assuming historic common interests and characteristics among even adjoining states.

The illusory nature of continental concepts is perhaps best illustrated by a question with which scholars and orators have grappled for centuries: Where does Asia end and Europe begin? The fictitious bifurcation of the land mass is an acknowledgment that overland contacts between its Pacific and Atlantic shores have been unimportant, but the attempt at geographic division is, in essence, the attempt to determine a line on one side of which all the immediately local people look westward while, on the other side, they look eastward. Such an inanity would hardly warrant consideration were it not for the impact that it continues to exert on human convictions. De Gaulle, for example, often spoke of a Europe for the Europeans, stretching from the Atlantic to the Urals, as though the Soviet Union were prepared either to divest itself of its holdings east of that mountain range or were able to differentiate between the interests of its European and Asian components. A physical watershed need not be a human one.

The problem of differentiating Europe and Asia does not end with the Soviet Union. Is Turkey, with territory on either side of the straits, to be considered Asian? The matter is further complicated by the fact that the Ottoman Turks came originally from central Asia, but at least since the time of Ataturk have considered themselves European. Does Europe stop even at the eastern border of Turkey? Turkic peoples stretch almost uninterruptedly from Turkey to western China. Moreover, how is one to explain the exclusion from Europe of the Indo-European language area of Iran, West Pakistan, and northern India? Cultural contacts and political borders have shown a remarkable disregard for continental divisions.

The term *continent* derives from *continere*, meaning to hold together, to repress, to contain. The expression, therefore, least applies to Europe, because culture groups of that region can claim a greater global impact for idea and customs than can be claimed for the cultures of any other region. "The Sea Age," "The Age of Discovery," "The Age of Imperialism," "Colonialism," "Neo-colonialism," and the prevalence of French, Spanish, Portuguese, and English in the most widely scattered regions are all testaments to the fact that Europe was certainly not a contained unit. Myths need not accord with reality, but it is particularly ironic that a recent French leader should have opposed an Atlantic community, denying a role to the United States with regard to the states of Europe simply because the United States is not European. Conveniently ignored were such matters as early French interest in the exploration of North America; France's alliance with the United States in the Revolutionary War; the United States-French transaction involving the Louisiana Territory; the United States-French alliances of World Wars I and II; de Gaulle's own interest in Quebec; and France's continued control of the trans-Atlantic islands of Saint Pierre and Miquelon, Guadeloupe, and Martinique, and of the trans-Atlantic mainland territory of French Guiana.

V

Regional myths

As in the case of hemispheres one can postulate as many regions as imagination permits. "Latin America," for example, is larger than a single continent, although regional terms are usually employed in reference to an area smaller than a continent but containing a number of states. The minimal implication is that the peoples of the region possess a number of important characteristics in common, which justifies its treatment as a distinct and separate entity. Seldom, however, do regional terms warrant such an unqualified ascription. Although it always possessed the danger of obscuring essential distinctions, the phrase "Latin America" was, until recently, a convenient shorthand expression for all of the independent states of North and South America plus the neighboring islands, minus Canada and the United States. The acquisition of statehood by Guyana, Jamaica, Trinidad-Tobago, and Barbados, as well as the anticipated statehood of British Honduras, however, antiquates the expression and again emphasizes the dangers of indiscriminately relating culture and location.

Other regional expressions are seldom more satisfying. Their arbitrariness is evident by the great variations in their geographic definitions over different periods and among authors in any given period. Changes in political borders and the relative knowledge of the complexities of the societies within the region help account for the geographic disparities in their descriptions. The region of the Near East, for example, is defined in the third edition of *Webster's New International Dictionary* as follows: "used originally of the Balkan States, later of the region included in the Ottoman Empire, and now often of all the countries of southeastern Europe, entire area extending from Libya or Morocco, Ethiopia, and Somalia to Greece, Turkey, Iran, Afghanistan, and sometimes India." One is tempted to ask: Inclusive or exclusive? The task of giving definition to the multiple definitions of such terms merits only sympathy, not criticism, and one can readily excuse, therefore, the oversight concerning Turkish territory in southeastern Europe; Greece's exclusion from southeastern Europe is more perplexing.

The incredible lack of precision in such terms would be humorous were it not for their tendency to evoke stereotyped images predicated upon the myth of cultural homogeneity. The images, in turn, hamper proper analysis.

The phrase "Southeast Asia" in most texts refers to Burma, Thailand, Malaysia, Singapore, Laos, Cambodia, the Vietnams, Indonesia, and the Philippines. The usual pattern of restricting regional groupings to landed relationships is broken here by the inclusion of Indonesia and the Philippines. Indonesia, which stretches some three thousand miles from west to east, reaches farther east than the farthest of the Far East states, Japan. Australia, which is excluded, is only a few miles across the Torres Strait from Indonesian territory. The Philippines, although also close to Indonesia, are markedly farther from the southeast Asian mainland than they are from China and Taiwan. The inclusion of the archipelagoes is due, of course, to the common ethnic heritage of the dominant group of mainland Malaysia with that of the Philippines and Indonesia. In the case of the Philippines this approach stresses early history, and, by contrast, ignores the fact that since 1500 Spain and the United States have had a greater cultural impact on the Philippines than have intraregional contacts, as evidenced by the prevalence of Catholicism and the widespread use of English. Moreover, it overlooks the fact that the dominant culture of Java is not the dominant culture of all of the Indonesian islands, including the two largest in terms of territory. But what is more important, if dominant culture is to be the criterion of membership, the off-African island of Madagascar (the Malagasy Republic) should have been included because of its Malay heritage. And Singapore, because of its dominant Chinese culture, should be considered part of the Far East, not Southeast Asia. So, too, should that area populated by the Vietnamese. The puzzled responses evoked by the political activism of Buddhist monks in Vietnam would have been less common if there were broader awareness that Vietnamese culture is much more a reflection of the cultures to its north than it is of those to its west, and that the northern, Mahayana Buddhism, common to China, Korea, Japan, and Vietnam, differs from the more pacifist Theravada (Hinayana) Buddhism of Burma, Thailand, and Cambodia.

Two points are clear. Southeast Asia, just as the Far East, the Middle East, the Near East, Western Europe, Sub-Sahara Africa, and other such geographic regions, is a highly diversified area, and it is the distinctions rather than common characteristics which are usually of key political importance. Second, regional categorization is dangerous not only because it tends to obscure important distinctions, but also because it tends to ignore important interregional relationships.

State myths

Of all the territorial concepts—hemisphere, continent, region, and state—it is the last which most resists generalization in terms of the degree of cultural, economic, and political integration. Some states, such as Japan, are quite thoroughly fused; others, such as Nigeria, are characterized by marked heterogeneity and centrifugal tendencies. Perhaps such discrepancies should be expected in confronting a unit which is found in such disparate territorial sizes. Canada, for example, is larger than Europe, and the Soviet Union is two to three times as large as either; at the other extreme, the Maldive Islands are approximately one-tenth the size of Rhode Island. Yet, from earlier statements, it should be evident that more important than the area is the distribution of population in relation to ease of intercommunication.

It is likely, however, that one must further differentiate between "natural" avenues of easy access, such as rivers and coasts, and artificial, man-made avenues, such as railroads and highways. There is little question that a highly intensive, modern transportation and communications network indicates extensive economic interrelationships, but its intercultural impact is less certain. Granted, it is a truism that centralized communications and increased economic contacts help to dissolve sectional cultural distinctions within what is fundamentally a one-culture state such as the United States. On the other hand, if one is dealing with two distinct cultures is it possible that increased contacts are apt to perpetuate and perhaps exacerbate nationalistic proclivities and particularism? Problems between the Walloons and Flemish of Belgium, the French-speaking and English-speaking Canadians, the Serbs and Croats of Yugoslavia, and the Czechs and Slovaks of Czechoslovakia have increased with increased contacts.

The fact is that very little is known concerning the assimilation process. Because its essence is psychological, involving self-acceptance, it is very conceivable that programs designed for its accomplishment are doomed to failure;

or, to put it more positively, that successful assimilation may best be achieved by contacts which are not made for that purpose. The Arab trader who in the midst of the busy bazaar of a sub-Saharan city quite unself-consciously prostrates himself on his prayer rug may exert greater cultural magnetism than the dedicated proselytizer. The Soviet Union, despite a half-century of ethnic plans and programs, is still plagued by "the national question." The failure of India and Pakistan to achieve their formal, constitutional commitment to have their varied peoples accept Hindi and Urdu respectively is also pertinent. So, too, is Franco's failure to Castilianize the Catalans and Basques. Such examples of resistance to governmental programs of assimilation could be multiplied. Programmed assimilation appears to produce an opposite effect. Assimilation is apparently most apt to be achieved as an accidental byproduct, not by design.

A related factor is that assimilation probably requires a period of great duration, extending well beyond a generation. More intensive contacts, whether by design or accident, may not only fail to telescope the process, but may well arouse a psychological barrier. Variations in tempo of intercultural contacts may not be merely a matter of degree, but may represent a qualitative consideration which determines whether a people move toward assimilation or ethnocentrism. The assimilation of all of the riverine people of China into the Han culture was accomplished only over many centuries. The post-1949 Chinese attempt to bring its remaining minorities into the state's cultural mainstream through greatly expanded contacts has resulted in substantial intergroup antagonisms.[19] Many contemporary states, indeed most of the states of Africa, Asia, and Latin America, contain large areas which have hitherto not been connected by arteries of transportation and communication. Such isolation is expected to alter rapidly, but the nature of the cultural result may be very different from that which is usually envisaged. Cultural integration cannot be assumed.

It is also probable that assimilation involves not only the question of duration but of chronological time as well. At least in "assimilationist time" the telephone, radio, train, and motor vehicle are very recent introductions and, what is of greatest importance, postdate the advent of the age of nationalism. The people who succumbed to foreign cultural inroads prior to the eighteenth century were not aware of belonging to a developed, competing civilization, in which they had hitherto taken great pride. By contrast, peoples everywhere today are much more apt to be aware of their membership in a group possessed of a history, customs, beliefs, and perhaps a language which distinguish it from other ethnic groups.[20] There are many reasons for this increase in ethnic consciousness, a major one of which has been the great increase in the frequency,

---

[19] For some remarkably frank admissions concerning this matter by the Chinese Deputy Chairman of the Commission of Nationalities, see Liu Chun, *The National Question and Class Struggle* (Peking, 1966), particularly pp. 18–22.

[20] See Walker Connor, "Self-Determination: The New Phase," *World Politics*, XX (1967), 30–53.

the scope, and the type of intra- and intercultural contacts. But regardless of its cause such cultural awareness is apt to hamper seriously any movement toward assimilation, and intercultural contacts are apt to strengthen the ethnic bond. It has been broadly assumed that an excellent communications and transportation network throughout a state has been a contributor to the cultural integration of all affected parts. While granting that such a network has tended to neutralize minor regional distinctions, it is more likely that the growth of an arterial system has occurred within what was already a fundamentally homogeneous cultural unit. Communications and transportation connections often strengthen common ties. But does this not portend an Iboland rather than a Nigeria, a Kurdistan rather than an Iraq, a Tibet instead of present China, a true Ukraine State rather than the U.S.S.R., a Flanders instead of a Belgium? *The "Age of Nationalism" may have heralded the end of assimilation.* And the end of assimilation portends increasing demands for the radical redrawing of most of today's political borders.

The matter is of the greatest importance, for the majority of states are multiethnic. Growing ethnic consciousness translated into self-determination movements is already challenging existing political structures without regard to hemisphere, continent, or region. Myths of unity to the contrary, even most states are culturally divided. The growing demand today, for good or evil, is to make reality approximate the myth of state unity by redrawing borders to reflect ethnic unity.

VI

Myths vary greatly in the degree to which they accord with fact. Regardless of their factual basis, however, myths engender a reality of their own, for it is seldom *what is* that is of political significance, but what people *think is*. If United States leaders have believed that a special relationship has existed between the United States and the states of South America because of their landed connection, then special ties do in fact exist, regardless of the questionability of their underlying assumption. Why, then, refute myths of unity? Surely a misconception which gives rise to a conviction of a transstate mutuality of interests, thereby promoting harmony, deserves cultivation not criticism.

The response must be that while myths of unity have a capacity for engendering harmony they also have a capacity for accentuating division. And the myths are invoked more often for the latter. The notion of "Africa for the Africans" is the result of a fallacious belief in intracontinental relations which never existed. It has also been the justification for expelling people of Asian heritage from East Africa, despite (1) the fact that the expellees were in most instances born in East Africa, and (2) that East Africa has had interrelations with Asia going back thousands of years, while its relations with the African interior have been virtually non-existent. Any geographic myth of unity, short of global scope, presupposes exclusivity.

Basing one's assumptions on myths also hampers logical analysis and can lead to questionable judgments. For example, it has long been accepted that colonialism per se is bad. But implicit in the popular definition of colonialism is the myth "water separates, land connects." Thus only if salt water flows between the mother country and the territory is it colonialism. The Soviet Union and China are seldom castigated for perpetuating colonialism, despite the fact that each contains huge areas, residues of an imperial age, which are populated by distinct minorities.

Another illustration of a questionable conclusion predicated upon the "water separates" myth is the concept of "spheres of influence." Its most recent manifestation is the position which holds that United States involvement in South Asia violates geographic logic. It is "natural," according to this school, for the Chinese "colossus of the north" to exert predominance throughout the region. As has been noted, however, the premise is not historically correct. Moreover, as long as freedom of the seas is observed the United States advantage in sea transport places the coast of South Asia, including that of South Vietnam, closer to the United States than to China.

Myths of geographic unity not only obscure important interunit relations but also tend to obscure important intraunit distinctions. It is what divides men and not what they have in common which is the catalyst of political history. Surely tribal nationalism is a more momentous fact of the politics within Africa than is African harmony. Ethnic nationalism may well be the most explosive challenge to the survival of the Soviet Union. Proper analysis, therefore, requires that one differentiate myth from fact.

It is not one world but a highly variegated world. The same is true of hemispheres, continents, regions, and most states. The patterns of distinctions and similarities, of shared and competing interests, are incredibly complex and kaleidoscopic in their dynamism. Although no set of relations is truly global, attempts to restrict a description of human relations to any subdivision of the globe are intrinsically unsatisfactory. A knowledge of the geographic backdrop is essential to an understanding of contemporary world politics, but it is seldom a sufficient explanation and often a deluding one.

BENJAMIN I. SCHWARTZ

The Maoist Image
of World Order

Are "The Chinese" prepared to accept the nation-state system that governs the international life of the West or are their images of the world and of China's place in it still governed by cultural habits derived from the remote past? It will be noted that this statement of alternatives leaves completely out of account a third category that dominates the discourse of the present Chinese Communist leadership itself—Marxism-Leninism and the "Thought of Mao Tse-tung." The latter is explicitly presented as marking a decisive break with both the culture of the past and the arrangements that govern the world of "capitalism and revisionism." Mao Tse-tung's present response to the above question no doubt would be a resounding rejection of both alternatives. We have, however, been educated by the profundities of the social sciences and depth psychology to discount conscious verbal behavior (at least on the part of others) in favor of larger "underlying" impersonal and unconscious forces. Nevertheless, in the following discussion the evolution of Communism in China will be treated as a third independent variable on the perhaps naïve assumption that what people say must be considered as at least one factor in explaining their behavior.

In dealing with non-Western societies we easily slip into the vulgar cultural anthropological mode. The notion that there is one easily defined and unchanging Chinese image of world order and that any given Chinese will embody this image is not likely to meet much resistance on the part of a Western audience. Just as any given Navaho chief is presumed to be a typical case of the unchanging patterns of Navaho culture, so Mao Tse-tung may be thought of as the incarnation of a uniform Chinese cultural response. In dealing with this question we have chosen to focus our attention on Mao Tse-tung not merely because he has obviously played a decisive role in recent Chinese history, but precisely in order to underline the fact that he is not the incarnation of a "Chinese image of world order" but one complex individual whose responses to many of the situations he has confronted have been signally different from those of other Chinese. As of this writing, we are indeed acutely aware that Mao's perceptions of many matters may differ most markedly even from those of some of his closest associates in the Chinese Communist leadership. Furthermore his life, like that of many of his contemporaries, illustrates not cultural stasis but the enormous cultural crisis that China has experienced in the twentieth century.

TRADITIONAL CHINESE IMAGE OF WORLD ORDER

Before dealing with Mao Tse-tung we must say something about the "traditional" Chinese image of world order. It must be stated candidly that those now making a serious effort to understand the history of Chinese culture tend to be profoundly uneasy about the simple and static generalizations which find such ready acceptance in these matters. In the West every generalization that we hazard about our international order must run the gauntlet of historians, specialists in international law, political theorists, and others, whereas generalizations about the millennial history of China still resound grandly in the vast cavern of our comparative ignorance. As our study of the Chinese past deepens, we will no doubt find that all of our present descriptions of the traditional order will undergo more and more qualification. Nevertheless, an attempt must be made.

In trying to discover the persistent features of the traditional image of world order, we find, first of all, the Chinese culture-area (*tien hsia*) conceived of as the center of a higher civilization that is ideally associated with a universal state governed by a universal king occupying a unique cosmic status. All surrounding states and principalities are ideally parts of this universal order and hierarchically subordinate to it in terms of tribute relationship. Of course such claims are not unique to China; they were made in ancient Mesopotamia, in Egypt, and in the Persian and Roman Empires. The uniqueness of the Chinese case lies in the persistence of such claims into the twentieth century. The Chinese universal kingship does not disappear from the scene until 1911.

The uniqueness of the Chinese experience does not necessarily spring from a particular cultural arrogance. It was in part due to certain contingent, external circumstances of Chinese history. In the ancient Middle East the absolute claims of Mesopotamian and Egyptian culture and universal kingship soon confronted each other. This fact may not have shaken Egyptian or Mesopotamian cultural confidence, but must certainly have done something to diminish the aura of these cultural and political claims among the various peoples who lived in surrounding and peripheral areas. China, on the other hand, remained unchallenged in its immediate vicinity by any polity whose cultural claims it felt obliged to consider. The only possible exception to this generalization is provided by Indian Buddhism. On the whole, however, Buddhism did not become the bearer of Indian political claims nor did it seriously challenge the basis of the Chinese universal kingship. The Chinese were not only unchallenged, they were also conscious of the influence of their own culture on surrounding peoples such as the Japanese, Vietnamese, and Koreans. And, as we know, "barbarian" rulers of China did tend in the long run to accept the absolute claims of the Chinese universal kingship. Thus experience tended to reinforce their claims.

One may, of course, raise questions about the degree to which the surrounding peoples accepted their assigned roles in the Chinese world order. The Japanese accepted cultural influence but managed to evade Chinese political claims. The Central Asian nomads and the peoples of Turkestan and Tibet probably never really accepted Chinese claims even where they were forced to assume the role of tribute bearers. Furthermore, there have been cases in the long history of China when emperors and officials have found it expedient to mute their own claims of political ascendancy. Still, if one considers the history of China in the last millennium in its broad sweep, it can be stated that the Chinese image of world order remained fundamentally intact.

It nevertheless may be asked how much this traditional Chinese image of the world order explains about the history of the foreign relations of the Chinese Empire. Does it, for instance, throw light on the question of Chinese aggressiveness? Actually, it was compatible with an extraordinarily wide range of attitudes and practices in the field of foreign policy. Surveying the long history of China one must arrive at the rather banal conclusion that it was compatible with both pacifistic isolationist policies and with aggressive expansionist policies. Even the attitude toward "barbarians" could run the gamut from the idealistic Mencian view that barbarians could be easily "civilized" by moral influence to the view that most of them were little better than beasts who could only be restrained by force. If Mao Tse-tung does indeed view the world through the eyes of his imperial predecessors, this throws little light on the future course of his policies. One would have to know which predecessors provide his model.

The traditional image probably had its most fateful effect on Chinese behavior during the nineteenth century, when it prevented an adjustment to the remorseless assault of the Western international system. The Chinese ruling class confronted a West as firmly committed to the universal validity of its conception of absolute nation-state sovereignty as the Chinese Empire was to its own view. Indeed, this conception had been given added weight by the rise of nineteenth-century nationalism. The history of China during the last half of the nineteenth century was marked by what Western observers regarded as an obscurantist, obdurate, and at times comical effort to resist the normal patterns of international relations. In retrospect it appears that the imperial court's resistance was probably based on an obscure yet sound instinct. The Chinese monarchy was, after all, inextricably tied to a cosmology of universal kingship. Whether it could have survived the crumbling of this cosmology and been converted into a Western-style "national" monarchy remains a moot point.

CHINESE NATIONALISM AND THE WESTERN IMAGE

Despite this resistance, however, the striking fact remains that by the turn of the century many articulate Chinese had made the qualitative leap. They had come to accept the Western system with all its conventions and were prepared to think of China as one nation-state among others. Figures such as Yen Fu and Liang Chi-ch'ao, whose writings were to exercise an enormous influence on the generation of Chinese now in its seventies, were entirely prepared to jettison the traditional conception of China's place in the world as the price of China's survival as a political entity. They had not renounced China's greatness but were prepared to rethink it in terms of modern nationalism. This was true not only of nationalist revolutionaries such as Sun Yat-sen, but even of many of the intellectual leaders of the monarchist movement who had given up the commitment to universal kingship in favor of something like a national monarchy. For at least a small but decisive segment of China's population, the bases of the traditional conception of China's place in the world had decisively collapsed. Again, however, we must rid ourselves of the tyranny of cultural holism. This collapse did not necessarily involve a total break with the whole range of habits of thought and behavior inherited from the past. It was entirely possible for the same individual to accept the concept of China as a nation-state among others without abandoning other traditions. It was simply that this particular sector of the cultural heritage had proven itself peculiarly vulnerable to the assault of new experience. Traditionalists as well as Westernizers were committed to the survival of China as a political entity and were by now aware that its survival depended on the acceptance of the game as it was played in the West.

To be sure, even after the arrival of modern nationalism one can find a tendency among some Chinese intellectuals and politicians to speak of China's universal cultural contribution to mankind. Sun Yat-sen, a man without deep roots in the cultural heritage, became more and more insistent in his later years on China's universal mission and the contributions of Chinese civilization to mankind. Is such thinking to be regarded as a reversion to the Sinocentrism of the past or can it be explained as analogous to similar phenomena elsewhere? Nationalism everywhere displays a tendency to universalize the particular. The German will insist on the universal superiority of *Deutsche Kultur,* the French on their *"mission civilisatrice,"* and the Americans on the "American way of life." It used to be common to explain the transnational element in Soviet Communism in terms of Holy Russia's messianism and the doctrine of the third Rome. Admittedly, we are here in an area where the boundaries between all our well-defined categories become hazy. The only tangible method of dealing with this question, crude as it may be, is to ask whether the Chinese are prepared to play the game (loose and ambiguous as its rules are) in terms of the prevailing international system.

Chiang Kai-shek provides us with a good test case. Ever since the 1930's he has been much more insistent than Sun on the superiority of Chinese traditional values and their applicability to the problems of modern society. Whether this commitment is authentic or simply a manifestation of national pride—or both—I shall not presume to judge. Yet there is no evidence whatsoever that he has not accepted the nation-state system or not operated within its framework. His famous manifesto on "China's Destiny" (written under his imprimatur) is at once profoundly "traditionalistic" in tone and deep, even orthodox in its commitment to the principles of national sovereignty as defined in the West. In his conception of world order, he owes infinitely more to Bodin than to Confucius.

Turning to the biography of Mao Tse-tung, one can make a good case for the assertion that he has lived his life within a basically Chinese context, particularly if we hasten to add that the word "Chinese" refers not only to a changeless cultural heritage but to a twentieth-century China in crisis. The sensitive years of early childhood were spent in a rural society untouched by any direct Western influence, and his earliest view of the world was derived from Chinese sources. Again, it is important to note that these sources were by no means as homogeneous in their message as Westerners might think. The message he derived from his beloved Chinese epic novels was not precisely the same as that of the Four Books. One could even find in the heritage inspiration for rebelliousness. It will not do to speak of the traditional elements in Mao without attempting to define what these elements are. In spite of this "rootedness" in China, there is no reason to think that during his formative years of intellectual growth after 1910 Mao did not come to accept without reservation the Western image of world order. His knowledge of the world at large was wholly derived from the writings of Yen Fu, Liang Chi-ch'ao, and translations of Western writings, all of which simply assumed the premises of the nation-state system. The young pre-Communist Mao can be called a modern nationalist without the slightest reservation. Like many of his contemporaries he dreamt of China's resurgence, but of its resurgence as a great power in a world of great powers.

THE COMMUNIST DIMENSION

Mao Tse-tung was to be converted to Marxism-Leninism, however, and with Marxism-Leninism we confront a new and complicating dimension. The October Revolution, as we know, was designed to shatter the whole "bourgeois" nation-state structure. Marx belonged to a whole group of nineteenth-century thinkers who regarded the international system of their time as anachronistic and moribund, and while we are all aware of the transformations that Marxism experienced at the hands of Lenin, there is every reason to believe that Lenin genuinely shared Marx's transnational outlook. In this he reflected the cosmopolitanism of a large sector of the Russian radical intelligentsia, which was quite unable to identify with the national glory of the Tsarist state. Lenin genuinely expected the October Revolution to serve as the spark for a world revolution that would dissolve the whole rotten international structure.

It is true that as a practical politician Lenin had devoted more attention to the "national question" than anyone else in the Marxist movement. He had created doctrinal rationalizations for harnessing resentful "bourgeois nationalism" to the wagon of revolution, and he had a genuine insight into the future role of such resentful nationalism in Asia. Lenin approached "bourgeois nationalism" from the outside as a cold manipulator, yet many of the formulae of Marxism-Leninism as they existed at the time of Lenin's death were already available for nationalist purposes. As a matter of fact, many of the young Chinese who were attracted to Marxism-Leninism in the early twenties (Mao among them) were already Chinese nationalists and as such were particularly attracted by those aspects of the Leninist theory of imperialism that seemed to explain China's national humiliation. This does not mean that they were completely insensitive to the apocalyptic cosmopolitan message of Communism. Indeed, some converts to Communism in China belonged to that small company of Chinese intellectuals who were ready to leap from the universalism of the older Chinese system to the transnational universalism of the new cosmopolitan philosophies from the West. The young Mao did not, on the whole, belong to their company. Surveying the evolution of his thought from 1921 to the present, one feels that Communism did not displace his nationalism but rather supplemented and complicated it.

In dealing with the relationship between "world Communism" and nationalism, we must first of all realize that we are not dealing with abstract essences but with a dynamic, evolving drama that has still not ended. It is a drama, moreover, in which the Chinese Communists themselves have played a large and ambiguous role.

In accepting Soviet Communism the Chinese Communists, including Mao, had of course accepted the notion of a supreme source of spiritual and political authority lying outside of China—this despite their nationalist passions. Furthermore, when this authority became completely tied to the interests of one territorial state—the Soviet Union—most of them continued to accept this authority. Only a handful of Chinese Trotskyists rejected the theory of "socialism in one country," and the supremacy of Moscow's authority in the Communist world continued to be accepted in Mao's China until the very end of the 1950's.

All of this has led some to suggest that the Chinese Communists, including

Mao, in accepting the hierarchic superiority of the Soviet Union were in effect reverting to the hierarchic-vertical mode of thinking so characteristic of the traditional order and rejecting the unfamiliar Western notion of equally sovereign states. I find this notion difficult to accept. It is first of all quite clear, as we have noted, that the Western conception *had* been accepted without difficulty by many of the future members of the Communist Party. One of the main attractions of the Marxist-Leninist doctrine was that it provided a devastating critique of the arrogant imperialist West from a "modern" Western point of view. It provided an excellent way of dealing with the dilemma to which Mao referred retrospectively in his speech on "The People's Democratic Dictatorship" in 1949, namely, that "the teachers [the West] are constantly attacking their pupils." The young people who joined the party were probably much more conscious of the weapons it provided against Western *hybris* than of its implied subordination to Moscow.

There were, of course, other reasons why the formulae of Marxism-Leninism proved attractive. Its assumption of knowledge regarding the direction of history, its promise of a total solution of China's immense problems of poverty, corruption, and disorganization must all be given great weight. I doubt very much that the attractions of the hierarchic concept of world order played a very significant role. It was, after all, a hierarchic order that placed the Chinese not at the summit but in an inferior position. The traditional order was based not on a mere abstract notion that there ought to be a hierarchic order in the relations of peoples, but on the rather specific complacent belief that China ought to be at the summit of this hierarchy. It would perhaps be more accurate to say that the Chinese Communists accepted Moscow's authority not because of the hierarchic implications of Soviet Communism but in spite of them. Their faith in certain basic assumptions of Marxism-Leninism was sufficiently strong to override their nationalist resistance.

This is particularly true, it seems to me, of Mao Tse-tung. He had accepted from Marxism-Leninism, as he understood it, many of the categories in terms of which the world is described; and many of these categories have continued to govern his image of the world to this very day. Until very recently this acceptance also involved a genuine acknowledgment of Moscow's ideological authority and of the Soviet Union as a model of socialism. It is precisely in this area, it seems to me, that a tension has existed from the very outset between the nationalist and transnationalist elements in his outlook.

We know of course that once he achieved ascendancy within the Chinese Communist movement during the Yenan period, he began to project his image of himself as the man who was applying the universal truths of Marxism-Leninism to the particularities of the Chinese situation. And he was doing this at a time when the doctrine was still dominant in Moscow that the authority to apply Marxist-Leninist doctrine to particular national situations was the exclusive prerogative of the Kremlin. We know that the nationalist coloration of Chinese Communism intensified during this period. In retrospect it does not seem at all plausible to assume that Mao Tse-tung was simply an "international

Communist" manipulating Chinese nationalism from the outside. What is more probable is that he assumed that the aspirations of Chinese nationalism and of world Communism could be easily reconciled. He may have genuinely believed—even after 1949—that, whatever the difficulties, a Chinese Communist state would be able to maintain general harmony with the Soviet Union in terms of certain overriding shared beliefs, without renouncing any of its basic sovereign prerogatives as a nation-state. After Stalin's death, we know that the Chinese Communist Government did everything possible to encourage those tendencies in Moscow that favored greater national autonomy within the world Communist movement; and since the outbreak of the Sino-Soviet conflict, the Chinese have, on one side of their polemic, made themselves the spokesmen of the most orthodox doctrine of national sovereignty within the Communist world. It is the Chinese who have promulgated one of the most striking doctrines in the whole church history of Communism, namely, that the decisions of any given national party (including the CPSU) are binding only within the area under the jurisdiction of that party.

All of this, of course, is highly "dialectic" in intention. One insists on the national sovereignty of states within the Soviet orbit in order to undermine the authority of the Soviet Union. Presumably, in a future international Communist order centered in Peking there will no longer be such insistence on national sovereignty. The fact remains that the Chinese Communist movement has itself played a crucial role in the unfolding relationship of Communism to nationalism. Whatever Mao's subjective intentions may be, Chinese Communism has helped to bring about what seems to be the triumph of the nation-state system over the transnational claims of Marxism-Leninism.

To be sure, in Peking the transnational aspirations now seem more alive than ever. The center of Communist authority, in Mao's view, has now definitely shifted from Moscow to Peking. True Marxism-Leninism is now dispensed only from Peking. It is thus precisely since the Moscow-Peking rift that those who emphasize the traditional cultural bases of Mao's image of the world have felt their case vindicated. Once again the Middle Kingdom has become the center of the "Way," and like the emperors of old, Mao Tse-tung is the highest source of both political authority and spiritual truth.

It is very difficult either to prove or to disprove a proposition of this nature. I have tried to demonstrate that both China and Mao Tse-tung have gone through a most tortuous course during the period between the collapse of the older world order and the present state of affairs, and that during that period many Chinese (including Mao at one stage in his life) had come to accept the nation-state framework without any difficulty, whatever their relationship may have been to other aspects of the traditional culture. The cosmology on the basis of which Mao asserts his authority is not the cosmology that underlay the traditional kingship. It is a cosmology that includes constant appeals to the authority of two "barbarians" named Marx and Lenin. It is of course true that the "Thought of Mao Tse-tung" is acquiring more and more weight within the ideological framework. Yet in appealing for support abroad the Chinese continue to emphasize the purity of their Marxism-Leninism. It may well be that this latest development in Chinese Communism resonates as it were with certain aspects of the traditional image of world order; however, the crucial question here is not whether it resonates with the traditional image but whether it is determined by it. If China's international behavior is determined by cultural images that have their roots in pre-history, we need not expect any speedy adjustments to a world that does not fit this image. If it is shaped by the more recent history of China and by a doctrine that is itself in a state of crisis and flux, if it is even shaped by the personal vision of Mao Tse-tung, who can in no way be equated with China, we must be alert to the possibility of sweeping shifts in the future.

Even as of this writing—in the very throes of the "cultural revolution"—China's relations with the world operate on two levels. On one level we find Mao's "higher" vision, in which China will be the center of a resurgent, purified Communist world. On another level we find the Chinese carrying on conventional diplomatic and commercial relations within the accepted nation-state framework, and even pressing the principle of national sovereignty within the Communist world. The aging Mao, to be sure, is deeply committed to his grand transnational vision and seems quite willing to sacrifice the possibility of more conventional diplomatic successes to the achievement of that vision.

These hopes for the realization of the vision, however, are not based on a programmatic blueprint but on certain expectations regarding the future course of world history. If these hopes are not realized in the foreseeable future, if the nation-state system proves as recalcitrant to the transnational hopes of Mao Tse-tung as it has to the hopes of others, will China be able to adjust to the world as it is? We have argued here that China has since the beginning of the twentieth century already demonstrated its ability to adjust to this system and that the process of adjustment has continued even under the Communists. Paradoxically, Mao Tse-tung has himself played a fateful role in weakening transnational authority within the Communist world. He has failed to consider the possibility that in undermining the supreme authority of Moscow in the Communist world he may have simply undermined the very notion of such authority in that world. Finally, there is now more room than ever for doubting whether all of Mao's colleagues within the Communist movement share the full ardor of his transnational vision.

I do not mean to suggest that the Western international system is more deeply rooted in some eternal, metahistorical order of things than the traditional Chinese conception of world order. In a world where China must continue to confront two other formidable world powers; in a world where there is an overriding passion for local and regional political independence; and in a world where none of the prevailing transnational ideologies, religions, or cultures have been able to establish their universal claims, the Western international system will continue to provide a more acceptable framework of world order than anything else available.

LUCY MAIR

Government Without the State

...What does it mean to call people or their institutions primitive? The word has implied a good many different things from the time when people in western Europe first began to ask questions about the manners and customs of people in Africa and the Americas, and later the Pacific Islands. It is a fact of history that it was the European peoples who discovered the others, and in most cases established political domination over them, and not vice versa, and the reason is not difficult to find. The European peoples had ships and methods of navigation which enabled them to travel further, and weapons which generally enabled them to win any battles in which they were involved, and the inventions which began in the eighteenth century greatly increased this advantage. These peoples were organized politically in a manner which made it practicable to extend their authority over areas far wider than any controlled by peoples in the countries they discovered; and this was largely because they had writing as a means of communicating over distances and of keeping records, and because they had monetary systems as a means of organizing trade and production. That is to say, they possessed technical superiority in a number of fields; indeed, in the very fields in which the technical superiority of the Romans had enabled them some centuries earlier to extend their domination over the Mediterranean basin. In all these fields, the techniques of the peoples who came under European rule were rudimentary, and in consequence their systems of government might also be called rudimentary. This is one of the senses of the word "primitive," and it is the only sense in which a modern anthropologist would use the word.

...Do all primitive societies have government?...Some writers, particu-

From *Primitive Government* by Lucy Mair (Baltimore: Penguin Books, 1967), pp. 7–30. Reprinted by permission of Penguin Books Ltd.

larly in the nineteenth century, have thought that many of the institutions
which are fundamental to western society developed fairly late in the history
of mankind, so that we might expect not to find them among peoples who had
not advanced along the path of civilization as far as ourselves. Government and
law are among these, and if politics is defined as that which pertains to government, those who hold this view would consider that primitive societies
pursue no activities which deserve the name of politics.

But there is another way of looking at politics, according to which it indubitably does exist in primitive societies. One definition of politics is the struggle
for power; and even if one is not willing to agree that power is the only thing
that men struggle for, one must admit that in every society there are conflicts
which must somehow be reconciled if the society is not to split into separate
independent parts. Conflict and competition begin within the family, however little we care to admit it; in fact, this is recognized in such phrases as
"fraternal enmity." But every society has an ideal of family unity such that
disputes between kinsmen are expected to be settled without any outside intervention. So some anthropologists would hold that the sphere of politics begins
where that of kinship ends. In the case of primitive societies it is not always
easy to say where this line comes, for in such societies people trace the links of
kinship much further than they do in the western world. But what one can say
is that between people who are in close daily contact throughout their lives,
sentiments are expected to develop (and often do) which limit the expression
of conflict, whereas outside these narrow circles one cannot rely on sentiment
alone to reconcile conflicting interests. In these wider fields of social relationships there are always and everywhere persons with conflicting and competing
interests, seeking to have disputes settled in their favor and to influence community decisions ("policy") in accordance with their interests. This is politics.

The seventeenth century philosopher Hobbes contrasted the state of nature,
in which every man's hand was against his neighbor, with civil society, in
which authority had been surrendered to a sovereign ruler (not necessarily a
single man). This was a logical rather than a historical argument; it followed
from Hobbes's assumptions about human nature that if there were no supreme
authority there could only be a war of each against all. But he did refer to
"savage people in many places in America" whose condition he thought
approached this. . . . In a number of primitive societies fighting is recognized
as a legitimate means of obtaining redress for an injury, though in those cases
it is not, as Hobbes imagined, a means of dominating others. The question
whether societies of this kind can or cannot be said to have government or law
is an interesting one, and contemporary anthropologists have answered it in
different ways.

Many modern writers have assumed that government must be carried on
through the type of organization which we call the state—a body of persons
authorized to make and enforce rules binding on everyone who comes under
their jurisdiction, to settle disputes arising between them, to organize their

defense against external enemies, and to impose taxes or other economic contributions upon them, not to mention the multifarious new functions which
the state has undertaken in the present century. Some primitive societies have
this kind of organization, but others do not, and the question then arises
whether they can be said to have government.

· · ·

... When you see a parliament and a cabinet, or a congress and a president,
you know you are looking at a government, and it is this kind of government,
or the country which has a government of this kind, that is called a state.
Governments of this familiar kind make laws which they enforce within whatever territory comes within their authority. The whole world is divided today
between governments each exercising authority over a territory with its recognized boundaries (of course there are sometimes quarrels about just where the
boundaries are). . . .

The authority of a state, then, extends over a fixed territory. Some writers
have said that primitive societies did not recognize territorial authority, and
that the appearance of this idea, the idea of a ruler or a government controlling a territory and claiming obedience from all the people in it, marked an
important stage in the evolution of government.

According to this view, primitive peoples do not have any notion of a
"country" with laws that apply to everyone in it. In the early stages of society,
these writers suppose, people recognize that they have certain duties towards
their kinsmen wherever they may be, but they do not recognize a ruler whom
they must obey because they are in his territory. The first form of society, they
assume, is a "tribe" consisting of people who believe that they are all descended
from one ancestor. They may obey a chief or headman because they think of
him as the head of a family (which may be a pretty large family) but not
because he is the ruler of the land or makes the law of the land.

The most famous exponent of this theory was Sir Henry Maine, the founder
of comparative jurisprudence. He thought the change from the "tribe" based
on blood relationship to the state based on "local contiguity" was so important
that he called it one of "those subversions of feeling which we term emphat-
ically revolutions."[1]

The question that Maine is considering here is what a body of people
accept as a reason why they should all obey the same laws. In primitive conditions, he says, the only reason is that they are *really* brothers, or at least cousins;
or they think they are. Later on it comes to be regarded as a sufficient reason to
obey "the law of the land" that you are in the land.

Maine points out that where the first of these principles is the basis of
common citizenship, the belief in common descent is by no means always true.
The different divisions of a people may have legends telling how they joined

---

[1] *Ancient Law* (Everyman Edition, 1959), p. 76.

its original members at some point in time. Many primitive peoples are indeed organized on the principle that everyone can be theoretically fitted into a genealogical tree, though some got there by adoption and not by birth. Maine calls this "the earliest and most extensively employed of legal fictions," and adds that "there is none to which I conceive mankind to be more deeply indebted. If it had never existed, I do not see how any one of the primitive groups, whatever were their nature, could have absorbed another, or on what terms any two of them could have combined, except those of absolute superiority on one side and absolute subjection on the other." But later, says Maine, "probably as soon as they felt themselves strong enough to resist extrinsic pressure, all these states ceased to recruit themselves by factitious extensions of consanguinity. They necessarily, therefore, became Aristocracies, in all cases where a fresh population from any cause collected around them which could put in no claim of community of origin."

.   .   .

... Those peoples who believe that they are all kin do not have the type of political structure that we call the state. The state itself in its simplest form entails the recognition that *one* body of kin have an exclusive claim to provide the ruler from among themselves. This can happen among very small populations; we can observe societies where certain kin groups have a privileged position (are aristocrats, if you like), but their privileges are so slight that it is difficult to speak of them as ruling, as aristocrats are supposed to do. The examples to be quoted seem to suggest that states arise when such privileged kin groups are able to command the services of followers through whom they can impose their will on the rest of the people. But, at any rate in some instances, this process has begun on such a small scale and developed so gradually that it does not seem realistic to speak of a revolutionary change in ideas.

A contemporary writer, MacIver,[2] goes further than Maine and argues that membership of primitive polities is based *solely* on kinship, and that in this respect, "tribal government differs from all other political forms." Its "territorial basis is not sharply defined." "Not sharply defined" is a rather slippery phrase. People who cannot write do not draw maps, and so they may not know where their boundaries are until there is a fight about them. But they may still have a strong conviction that certain territory is theirs and nobody else's. Schapera, who used the phrase "political community" to mean any body of people who have laws, rulers, or government in common, has shown that the smallest and simplest political communities have their recognized territory. Moreover, even these small communities do not consist entirely of people descended from one ancestor. In all primitive societies the rules of marriage forbid people to marry close relatives. So, in a very small political community where all the men are actually kinsmen, all their wives must be women who

---

2 *The Web of Government* (1947).

have been brought in from other communities. But of course these women become part of the community into which they marry and subject to its authorities, whoever they are; and the converse of this is that when a woman marries she loses her political allegiance to the group in which she was born. In larger political communities people who believe they had a common ancestor in the distant past are divided into *exogamous* lineages. The members of each such lineage must find their wives in other lineages; they believe that their common ancestry is too far back to be a bar to marriage. But these larger communities do not usually suppose that *all* their members have a common ancestor.

This is a convenient place to examine how the word "tribe" can be useful in discussion. It has come to be used by people who consider that they are civilized, as a way of describing societies which they do not regard as civilized and so it is very naturally thought to be an offensive word by educated members of the peoples who are called tribes. But when anthropologists use it, they are not concerned at all with levels of civilization. In writing about Africa they use it to describe political divisions of certain large populations which call themselves by one name and speak one language, but do not recognize one common chief or other type of government. These larger populations could be called nations; but today more and more of them are, politically, divisions of still larger populations, each with an independent government which is seeking to make a single nation out of all the people under its authority.

Nevertheless, we seem to be driven at present to use the word "nation" in two ways. In the first sense the Tswana of southern Africa, the Nuer of the southern part of Sudan, and the Ibo of the Eastern Region of Nigeria are nations. The Nuer number about 200,000; they call themselves by a common name which distinguishes them from their neighbours; they have a common language; their "culture"—the way they get their living, their rules of conduct, their religion—is the same for all Nuer. But all Nuer never act in common. They are divided into sections each with its own territory, which act independently and are often engaged in actual fighting. The Ibo are a much larger nation, numbering over four million. They too are divided into territorial units, independent of each other and often hostile. It is units of this kind which anthropologists call "tribes." In the case of the eight major divisions of the Tswana in Bechuanaland, each of which has a chief formally recognized by the Protectorate government and a territory allotted to it by this government, the word "tribe" is an indispensable part of the official language of the Protectorate. But anyone who wants to use it as a technical term, and not a term of abuse, should be clear that it simply means an independent political division of a population with a common culture.

The nations in the second sense are the new ones which have attained independence in this century by the rejection or withdrawal of colonial rule. In each of these new nations there are many sub-divisions, each with its own language and culture, which cannot be called nations without confusion, and indeed are not seeking to be independent nations. For them too the word "tribe" is convenient, though one can often avoid it by saying "people," which is actually vaguer.

The political community, then, has its own territory whether or not it is organized in the form of a state. Next, we have to ask whether we can say that those political communities which are not states have, or do not have, government or law. Now that we are talking about political communities that do not have any of the institutions by which we are used to recognizing a government with, we must ask the question differently. Instead of saying "What ought a government to look like?" we must ask "What does a government do?" or "What is government?" From there we can go on to see whether the *functions* of government, or at any rate some of them, may not be performed in simple societies even though they do not have the institutions of the state.

What then does government do? It protects members of the political community against lawlessness within and enemies without; and it takes decisions on behalf of the community in matters which concern them all, and in which they have to act together.

A collection of studies was published in 1940 by two anthropologists, Fortes and Evans-Pritchard, . . . called *African Political Systems*. This made the first attempt to answer the question whether there were in Africa any societies which could not be said to have political systems. The answer, of course, depended on what a political system was taken to be. The authors said the political system of any society was concerned with the regulation of the use of force. Every political community (though they did not use that phrase) recognizes some rules about when force may legitimately be used and when not, and this is what makes it a political community. But though all societies have political systems, some, they said, do not have governments. In the societies without government, the people were divided into groups based on kinship, which were independent for most purposes (but, unlike Maine's "tribes," these kin groups had their own land, and this was perhaps the most important thing that they had in common). The head of a lineage, as these corporate kin groups are called, might have the right to give orders to members of the lineage, but nobody could give orders to him. If a man was wronged, his lineage supported him in seeking redress by force. When they got tired of fighting they invited an influential man to mediate between the two sides. An outsider who arrived at the right moment might well take such a situation as a manifestation of Hobbes's war of each against all. The classical example of such a society is the Nuer. . . . There are other influences to make people keep the peace—or enough peace—in societies which have no policemen. For instance the people described by Fortes in *African Political Systems*—the Tallensi in Ghana— believed that their land could not prosper unless all were at peace when it was time for them to join together in their great religious festivals, and at these times they felt compelled to make up their quarrels.

The writers who contributed to that book were concerned particularly with the function of government in maintaining law and order. They did not consider the question who took communal decisions or what such decisions were about. Schapera, in a survey of the peoples (or tribes) of South Africa, has shown that in that region the smallest community, with the most rudimentary technical knowledge—the Bushman bands of ten to thirty men with their families, living by hunting small animals and gathering wild plants—recognizes that certain of its members have authority to take communal decisions. This, in Schapera's view, is enough to count as government. In some of the larger populations who are described in *African Political Systems* it might be harder to identify the persons who could be called the government. . . .

How do we know whether people have law? If there is no law that is not expressly enacted, very few, if any, nonliterate peoples have law, for enactments which are not recorded are apt to be forgotten, or at best become matter of dispute. The chiefs of the Tswana of southern Africa are said to have legislated for their people before the introduction of writing, but few of these earlier laws are remembered.

To Hobbes, where there was no law there must be anarchy, and the Nuer have been described by Evans-Pritchard, to whom we owe our knowledge of them, as living in an "ordered anarchy." Even a casual observation of actual primitive peoples shows that they are not constantly engaged in internecine fighting; that they recognize rules of conduct which they can state, and that these rules are obeyed sufficiently often for people to know what they are entitled to, and can expect of others, in any of the recurrent situations of life. Why? One popular explanation has been that primitive peoples are too dull-witted, or else too superstitious, or nowadays the more romantic word is "community-minded," to question the rules of conduct which they learn as they grow up, and so the force of "custom" is sufficient to maintain the social order. This interpretation was finally exploded by Malinowski's work in the Trobriand Islands off the coast of New Guinea. Malinowski lived three years in a Trobriand village, and so had plenty of opportunities of seeing people who were angry because their rights had been infringed, and of watching what they did about it. From his day anthropologists have studied quarrels with particular interest for the sake of the light that they throw on the reaction of a society to breaches of its rules.

It is agreed, then, that there is no society where rules are automatically obeyed, and that every society has some means of securing obedience as well as of dealing with offenders. The question remains, however, whether all ways of dealing with offenders are to be described as legal, and if not, what rules are to count as laws and what procedures are to be considered legal.

Floods of ink have been wasted on this subject. No writer has gone so far as to say that every rule which a person feels constrained to obey is a legal rule; the rules of etiquette, for example, obviously fall in a different category. Malinowski, however, would have brought nearly everything else under the heading of law; he hated formal definitions, and he regarded as formal the definition which says that laws are rules enforced by the authority of the state. A "functional" definition, seeking for the type of contribution which an institution makes to the totality of social life, would in his view have found law in every society, and he offered several such definitions.

Malinowski's leading contemporary, Radcliffe-Brown, in the introduction to *African Political Systems*, described law as "the application of direct or indirect penal sanctions . . . the settlement of disputes and the provision of just satisfaction for injuries." He would not, therefore, refuse to find law where there were not courts or judges. He gave as an example of legal action the "lynching" by the whole community of a heinous offender, which used to occur among some Kenya tribes. But he would not give the name of law to what he calls "regulated vengeance" or feud, in which one section of a community, with the approval of the rest, fights another section because a member of it has injured one of their members. Radcliffe-Brown recognized that the right to resort to feud supports the law against killing, since people will separate men who are quarrelling if they can, so as to prevent a feud from starting. But he would not consider the feud as a legal action.

Radcliffe-Brown's definition of political organization, which is followed in *African Political Systems*, is intended to apply to all societies, whether or not they have a state form of government. He says it is "that part of the total organization which is concerned with the maintenance or establishment of social order, within a territorial framework, by the organized exercise of coercive authority through the use, or the possibility of use, of physical force." The wider definition given by Schapera[3] is "that aspect of the total organization which is concerned with the establishment and maintenance of internal cooperation and external independence." This definition covers both the means of maintaining the order on which cooperation depends, and also the organization of cooperation itself.

.   .   .

. . . The ways in which people are distributed on the ground must obviously affect the way in which their government is organized, particularly when they have no means of long-distance communication. The "pattern of settlement," as it is sometimes called, is rather different in the case of each of these four peoples, and the differences show how important for peoples of simple technology are slight differences in the geographical environment. It would be wrong to assume that differences in settlement patterns are the most important reasons for differences in political systems. But they are particularly important in the case of pastoral peoples living in an environment which obliges them to be constantly moving their herds. Such peoples cannot live an ordered life at all unless they can move in peace through certain territory, and live at peace

---

[3] *Government and Politics in Tribal Society* (1956), p. 218.

when they are gathered together around the limited sources of water. The kind of arrangements by which peace is secured among them depend very much on how far the herdsmen have to move and in what conditions numbers have to congregate together.

Nuer country is all savannah. The Nuer build their villages on sandy ridges out of reach of the flood water; this is obviously necessary for people and houses, even if the houses are only huts of wattle and daub with roofs of straw thatch, and it is equally important for cattle, because cattle become sick if their feet are constantly wet. The villages are built on the tops of these ridges, strung out over a mile or two, with grazing land on one side and fields of millet or maize on the other, for the Nuer do grow grain, although they regard it as an inferior kind of food; they also catch fish in the pools which are left when the floods recede. In the dry season they have to leave the villages so as to be within reach of water and of grazing for their cattle. As the water sinks lower, more and more people have to gather together within reach of the pools that have not dried up. They congregate at these places in camps of grass huts. People who live in the same village do not necessarily go to the same cattle camp, so that different sets of people are in constant contact at different seasons of the year. In the wet season it is the people of neighboring villages who need to be able to count on peaceable relations among them if normal life is to be carried on; in the dry season it is a much larger number of people. During the time when the cattle are being driven across the country in search of water, what is important is that the herdsmen should be able to count on being able to travel without being attacked by other people moving through the same country.

The Dinka surround the Nuer on the north, south, and west. Like the Nuer they are herdsmen who supplement the meat and milk of their cattle with grain and fish. Their country is very like Nuer country, but less of it is under water in the rainy season. Whereas the Nuer villages in the rains are isolated on their ridges, the Dinka herds can still move about, though they have to keep to higher ground. Just as the pools get fewer in the dry season, so the dry ground gets less in the wet season; and for the Dinka the important concentrations of population are those of the wet season. The same people expect to finish the wet season every year at the same camp, on higher ground in the savannah forest. These are the herdsmen of a division of a tribe (sub-tribe) who also organize a number of other activities together. Because they join together in the wet-season camp, they think of themselves as forming the body within which peace ought to be preserved. But the size of such a body is limited in a way that the concentration of people at a dry-season camp is not. The wet-season camps are places where cattle can be tethered for the night on well-drained ground. If there are too many cattle, some herdsmen will find, as the floods rise, that there is nowhere to tether their herds except on ground that is waterlogged. Then they may decide to move away and find camping-ground somewhere else. A group of kinsmen who herd their cattle together will break off and look for a new camping site where they, as first occupants, will claim the highest ground. As time goes on and their numbers increase they will be recognized as a new sub-tribe, and no longer feel any particular obligation to maintain peace with the rest of their original sub-tribe. This kind of division seems to be the reason why the Dinka have spread over such an immense area. But in the dry season, when herds have to range more widely, a sort of truce is made between sub-tribes who would expect to treat one another as enemies at other times.

The Anuak live further up the same rivers which water the eastern part of the Nuer country. They depend for livestock on sheep and goats rather than cattle; they have cattle, but, as they themselves admit, they slaughter them for food with reckless disregard for the maintenance of the herd. Also, between 1932 and 1939 a large number of cattle were taken from them as a collective punishment for a raid on a neighboring people. In the western part of the country the rivers flood in the rainy season. The Anuak build villages which are out of reach of the floods, but some of these places in the dry season are short of water even for drinking. When this happens the villagers move to the edge of the marshes and camp on mounds which seem—like those beloved of archaeologists in the Middle East—to have been built up out of the rubbish left by many generations. A village may be from five to twenty miles from its nearest neighbor, and those that have to move in the dry season go independently, each to its own mound. There is no problem here of peaceful passage for herdsmen in territory where they may meet others. The villages are completely self-contained as far as the necessities of economic life are concerned. Of course marriages are often made between people of different villages, and there are other friendly contacts. But a village in western Anuakland is a distinct political community. There is also often fighting between villages.

In the extreme east of the country, where the forest begins, the river banks are higher and the land is never flooded. The villages are built close together on the river banks, with their cultivated land carved out of the forest behind them. They are protected from surprise attack by impenetrable growths of tall reeds on the riverside, and by the forest on their other sides, as well as by strong stockades. But it is never impossible to travel from one village to another.

Eastern Anuakland can be said to form a single political community; but this has come about not as a result of any actual need for peaceful cooperation between the villages, but because the greater ease of communications has made it possible for all to combine in a single system.

The Shilluk live along the west bank of the Nile to the north and south of Malakal. At this point the ground rises fairly steeply from the river, and houses can be built at a height which is permanently out of the reach of floods. Moreover, the Shilluk do not keep many cattle—a circumstance which leads their neighbors to despise them—and so their lives are not centered in the quest for water and grazing. If the cattle have to be moved in the dry season, boys take them to islands in the river or to pools in dry water-courses. The bulk of the population live all the year round in houses that stretch almost continuously along the river bank, with their cultivated land behind them. The Shilluk recognize a division of their country into eleven "settlements," each under its own head, but these are not clusters of houses with spaces between them. It is not usually easy to see where one settlement ends and the next begins. In the rainy season it may be difficult to get about on land, but people can always travel by river, so that no part of Shillukland is ever isolated from the rest. Some people think this is why the Shilluk are sufficiently united to recognize a single king; they are the only Nilotic people to do so. Even the Shilluk king does not have much authority. His capital is almost in the middle of the long line of settlements.

SYDEL F. SILVERMAN

The Community-Nation Mediator in Traditional Central Italy

One of the most strategic yet formidable problems in the anthropological study of complex societies is the relationship of the parts to the whole of such societies. Most attempts to tackle this problem have been concerned primarily with those parts which are localized social systems, or communities,[1] inter-dependent with though analytically separable from the whole, a national social system. The community and national levels of sociocultural integration of Steward (1955:43–63), the discussion of tensions between pueblo and state by Pitt-Rivers (1954:202–210), the community-oriented groups and nation-oriented groups of Wolf (1956), and the local roles and national roles of Pitkin (1959) are only a few examples of this recurring contrast, the social analogue of the great-tradition/little-tradition approach to complex cultures. Such a model immediately sets the task of formulating the interaction between the two systems.

One of the more promising efforts to describe this interaction has been the

From *Peasant Society, A Reader,* Jack M. Potter, May N. Diaz, George M. Foster, eds. (Boston: Little, Brown and Company, Inc., 1967), pp. 279–293. Reprinted by permission.

This paper is an abridged version of "Patronage and Community-Nation Relationships in Central Italy," which appeared in *Ethnology,* Vol. IV, No. 2 (April 1965). Reprinted by permission of the author and the publisher. That article deals with changes in the community-nation linkage with passing time. Field work was carried out in a rural community of Central Italy from August, 1960 to September, 1961. The project was supported by a predoctoral fellowship (MF-11, 068) and grant (M-3720) from the National Institute of Mental Health, United States Public Health Service. A more detailed description of the community is given in my doctoral dissertation (Silverman, 1963).

[1] The boundaries of the local system are not precisely coextensive with the community, since a local system may include regular relationships between members of different communities and since any community in a complex society has within it some representation of the national system. However, this paper will follow the common practice of using the term "community" interchangeably with "local system."

concept of the "mediator," an individual or group that acts as a link between local and national social systems. Wolf introduced the idea of the cultural "broker" in a discussion of data from Mexico, defining as "brokers" the "groups of people who mediate between community-oriented groups in communities and nation-oriented groups which operate through national institutions" (Wolf 1956:1075). The mediating functions which Wolf emphasizes are economic and political, and he traces a succession of three phases in the post-Columbian history of Mexico during which these functions were carried out by different groups in the society. In his review of peasant-society research published the same year, Redfield (1956) observed that a recurrent phenomenon in many societies is the existence of a "hinge" group, administrative and cultural intermediaries who form a link between the local life of a peasant community and the state of which it is a part. The concept of the mediator is relevant to many studies of "part-societies" which exist within a larger encompassing whole. It describes the pivotal chiefs within colonial nations, whose positions derive from earlier periods of tribal autonomy, as well as the elites looked up to by peasants, deriving from a historical balance between two stable classes; the formal agents of national institutions, who penetrate into communities from distant capitals, as well as the upwardly mobile villagers who move into positions in national institutions.

In the analysis of material collected during field work in a Central Italian community, the concept of the mediator proved to be most pertinent for understanding the relationship of the community to the larger society during a particular period. However, it was found that if this relationship is followed over time, not only are there changes with regard to the groups which perform mediation functions, as Wolf (1956) showed for Mexico, and the roles through which mediation is effected, as Geertz (1960) showed for Java, but there are fundamental changes in the structuring of links between community and nation. These changes suggest that the concept of the mediator is most useful if defined narrowly and thus restricted to a particular form of part-whole relationship.

The concept refers to a status which functions as a link between a local system and a national system. In interactional terms, the mediator may be seen as one to whom action is originated from the national system and who in turn originates action to the local system; to some extent, the direction is reversible, the mediator still being the middle element. However, if the mediator were to be defined merely as anyone who acts as a means of contact between the systems, it would include such a wide range of phenomena as to become virtually meaningless. Moreover, such a definition would obscure the important differences between various kinds of contacts which may exist.

Wolf (1956:1075) referred to the "brokers" as persons who "stand guard over the critical junctures or synapses of relationships which connect the local system to the larger whole." By taking Wolf's terms in their full implications, it is possible to arrive at a more precise definition. First of all, the functions which those who are defined as mediators perform must be "critical," of direct importance to the basic structures of either or both systems. For example, a person who brings awareness of a new fashion in clothing from the national into the local system would not by virtue of this function alone be considered a mediator, even though he does act as a communicational intermediary. Second, the mediators "guard" these functions, i.e., they have near-exclusivity in performing them; exclusivity means that if the link is to be made at all between the two systems with respect to the particular function, it must be made through the mediators. As a result, the number of mediator statuses is always limited. To the extent that alternative links become available, so that the mediators lose their exclusive control of the junctures, they cease to be mediators. These two criteria, critical functions and exclusivity, limit the extension of the concept. Persons who provide contact between the two systems but who do not necessarily fulfill both criteria will be referred to here as "inter-mediaries." While the terminology is clumsy, it is felt that there is an important distinction which needs to be made between the broader category, "intermediary," and the special kind of intermediary, the "mediator."

It seems to be general that there is a rank difference between the mediator and the other persons in the local system who are involved in the mediated interaction. The mediators may take on their function because of previous possession of a higher rank, or they may achieve a higher rank as a result of assuming the mediator role. In either case, the relationship between the local and the national system assumes a "vertical" form.

The concept of the mediator emerged out of the study of particular kinds of societies, those to which anthropologists first turned when they began to move beyond the primitives, namely complex societies which still retain a strong "folk" element. That it is within such societies that the concept finds its widest applicability suggests that it may represent a form of part-whole relationship peculiar to the preindustrial state society. It is obvious that in a society at a prestate level of integration there would be little necessity for mediators. On the other hand, the existence of mediators implies that the local units are separate from each other and from the larger society to the extent that a limited group can have exclusive control over the connections between part and whole—a situation associated with preindustrial societies.

This paper attempts to develop the "mediator" concept as an element of a particular kind of part-whole relationship, which is found at a particular level of development in complex societies. To this end, it examines the traditional mediators—in this instance a patron group—in the Central Italian community of Colleverde.

THE COMMUNITY

Colleverde (a pseudonym) is an Umbrian *comune* near the geographical center of Italy, about 50 kilometers from the provincial capital, Perugia, and approximately 150 kilometers north of Rome. The medieval castle-village which is the functional center of the community is situated on a hilltop overlooking the valley of the Tiber. The countryside of the comune covers a wide range of environmental variation, from a strip of level plain along the banks of the Tiber (about 150 meters above sea level), through a region of low and medium hills, to the woods, meadows, and wasteland of a high-hill zone (up to 650 meters). In 1960, Colleverde parish (one of two parishes in the comune, each of which may be considered a separate community) had a population of 1,885 in 465 households. About one-fifth of the inhabitants live in the village, the remainder on dispersed farms in the surrounding countryside.

About 80 per cent of the active population are agriculturalists. The majority work self-contained farmsteads, most of which comprise between two and fifteen hectares. Except for minor variations due to altitude, each farm produces the entire range of local crops and animals: wheat, olives, wine grapes, maize, a variety of minor crops grown for human and animal subsistence and for renewal of the land, meat calves (which since the advent of tractors after World War II have been rapidly eliminating the work oxen which were formerly raised), pigs, a few sheep, and barnyard fowl. In addition, industrial crops (tobacco, sugar beet, and tomato) have been introduced on a small scale in the irrigated tracts of the plain. Of these products, only the wheat, calves, and industrial crops are raised primarily or exclusively for sale. At least two-thirds of the land is cultivated under the *mezzadria* system of share-farming, while the remainder is worked by peasant proprietors, tenant farmers, and a few wage-laborers.

The mezzadria system is based on a contractual association between a land-owner, who furnishes the farm (including cleared land, farmhouse, outbuildings, and livestock) and advances all working capital as needed, and a peasant family who provide labor and the minor equipment. All other expenses and the income of the enterprise are divided between them, theoretically half and half; in 1948 the peasant's share of the income was raised by law to 53 per cent. As compared with other sharecropping systems, the mezzadria is distinguished by three elements: the integrated farm, the family labor unit, and the active participation in investments and operation of the enterprise on the part of both owner and cultivators.

The integrity of the farm and the major dependence upon a family for its labor requirements imply a recurrent imbalance between the number of working hands and the size of the farm. Adjustment is made primarily by a movement of families among farms as major changes in family size occur. Partly because large households traditionally were advantageous to the mezzadri (enabling them to work a larger farm),[2] the ideal household consisted of a patrilocal extended family, in which all sons brought their brides to live in

---

[2] The upper limit of household size was about twenty members. The average size, based on estimates from a population register covering the period 1881–1907, was seven or eight. Today, the average mezzadria household consists of about six members.

their father's household and in which authority and economic control were vested in the family head. Although during the past few decades the largest households have been breaking up, more than half the mezzadria families still have at least one married son residing in the parental household. In the community as a whole, however, only a third of the households consist of extended families, and the predominant form is the nuclear family.

The community is economically and socially heterogeneous. The fundamental principle of settlement pattern, the segregation of village center and countryside, demarcates the most pervasive social division, the people of "inside" and those of "outside." This cleavage is occupational: those who do not work the land (landowners and administrators of agricultural properties, professionals, clerks, merchants, artisans, and laborers) as against those who do. It is the major correlate of social-class differentiation: the *signori* (the local upper class) and a middle group consisting of the working people of families resident in the village for generations, as against the great lower class. It describes, in general, political party alignments within the community: the Right and Center as against the Left. To some extent it parallels a difference in the spirit of religious participation: the "cynical" (in the view of the Colleverdesi) as against the devout. It is also a cultural division, for the village is regarded as the seat. of civilization surrounded by rusticity, bringing *civiltà* (that which is "civilized," in the sense of "citified") to the countryside and bestowing the aura of civiltà on the whole community.

PATRONAGE IN COLLEVERDE

Until the recent postwar period, the mediation of relations between Colleverde and the larger society was the function of a patronage system. Before discussing this function, it will be helpful to describe the general features of traditional patronage in the community. Patronage patterns are familiar to all the older contemporary Colleverdesi, whose recollections (supplemented by local historical documents) were the basis for the following reconstruction. However, only vestiges of them remain today.

Patronage as a cross-cultural pattern may be defined as an informal contractual relationship between persons of unequal status and power, which imposes reciprocal obligations of a different kind on each of the parties. As a minimum, what is owed is protection and favor on the one side and loyalty on the other. The relationship is on a personal, face-to-face basis, and it is a continuing one.

As is the case in other cultures where a patron-client relationship receives explicit recognition, patronage in Central Italy is not coterminous with all the meanings of the term for "patron" (cf. Kenny 1960:14–15; Foster 1963:1282). In Colleverde, the term *padrone* is applied to: (1) the legal owner of something, for example a house or a dog; (2) one who controls something, such as the mistress of a household, or one who has self-control; (3) an employer, when reference is made to him by or to an employee; (4) the grantor of a mezzadria farm, whether or not he is actually the landowner and whether or not there is anything more than minimal contact with the cultivators; (5) a guardian deity; and (6) a patron in a patron-client relationship.[3] However, all of these usages which refer to one person as the padrone of another describe potential bases for the formation of a patron-client relationship.

The most important patron-client relationship in Colleverde was that between the parties to the mezzadria arrangement. The relationship developed informally, by extension of the formal terms of the contract. A peasant might approach the landlord to ask a favor, perhaps a loan of money or help in some trouble with the law, or the landlord might offer his aid knowing of a problem. If the favor were granted or accepted, further favors were likely to be asked or offered at some later time. The peasant would reciprocate—at a time and in a context different from that of the acceptance of the favor, in order to de-emphasize the material self-interest of the reciprocative action—by bringing the landlord especially choice offerings from the farm produce, by sending some member of the peasant family to perform services in the landlord's home, by refraining from cheating the landlord, or merely by speaking well of him in public and professing devotion to him.[4] Or the peasant might be the first to offer his "favors," in anticipation of those he would later have to ask of the landlord. Whether or not a true patronage relationship developed from the mezzadria association depended upon the landlord's inclination, his need of support, and his place of residence (or the length of an absentee owner's yearly sojourn in Colleverde).

The mezzadria association was particularly conducive to the development of a patronage relationship, for the institution had the effect of bringing land-lord and peasant into long and personal contact with each other. The minimum duration of the contract is one year, but typically it persists for several years, and traditionally it was common for a farm to be occupied by the same family for many decades and even for generations. The landowner's role as director of the enterprise requires his continuing interest and his physical presence much of the time. Some proprietors employ managers (*fattori*), who range from unskilled foremen and commercial agents to highly trained agricultural technicians, but traditionally even when this was the case the landlords main-

---

[3] In the third, fourth, and sixth instances, the term may also be used for address. Alternatively, the padrone may be addressed in the respectful form of using the given name preceded by *Sor* or *Signora* (rarely, *Sora*). In Colleverde, as in Foster's community, there is no specific term for "client."

[4] Until the reforms of recent years, the mezzadria contract required a number of "extra" obligations of the peasant to the landlord, including gifts of fowl and eggs in specific quantities at different times of the year and various forms of unreimbursed labor in the land-lord's household. Thus it is not always apparent whether a peasant's offering was the fulfillment of the formal mezzadria contract or part of a voluntary patron-client relationship. However, the essence of the latter was that the quantity or value of the goods and services given exceeded the formal requirements.

tained close contact with their farms. In contrast to the typical situation in southern Italy, the landowning class throughout the mezzadria area has a strong tradition of active interest in agriculture; for example, many receive higher education in fields which equip them for the management of their property. There is, in fact, a marked tendency to glorify their attachment to their land and "their" peasants.

Until recent years, the owners of Colleverde's land were the nucleus of the village population, constituting a local upper class. In other communities of the area, those proprietors who did not reside in the rural centers lived in the nearby towns and small cities and often retained part-time residences near their land. Thus the landlords were accessible. Moreover, close and continuing contact between landlord and peasant was encouraged not only by the necessary interaction related to the operations of the farm but also by the cultural definition of the mezzadria relationship. The association was ideally a personal and affectionate tie ranging far beyond the formal contract covering the enterprise, a tie between two families, one the protector and benefactor and the other the loyal dependent. To the peasant, the landlord was the most immediately available person to turn to for economic aid or for knowledge about the world outside. To the landlord, a patronage relationship was at the least a great convenience. It provided a check against being taken advantage of, a check that was cheaper, more reliable, and in any case a useful supplement to supervision by fattori. It facilitated contacts with the peasant and contributed to the day-to-day efficiency of the enterprise. Finally, it was a means of controlling potentially disruptive influences from the outside. It is significant that the paternalism of the mezzadria landlords has often been pointed to as a factor in delaying the spread of labor agitation to the Central Italian hill region for several decades after its onset in many agricultural areas of the nation about 1870 (Bandini 1957:77–78).

A peasant whose own landlord was unavailable or who was unable or unwilling to dispense favors occasionally turned to other landowners. More common was the formation of a patron-client relationship between lower-class persons who were not mezzadri and a local landlord or other local person of high status and power. The potential client would approach one of the signori with a request, or he might attempt to establish the relationship first by presenting him with some small gift or by making himself available to run errands or help out in various ways. Such relationships, although they did not center about common participation in an agricultural enterprise, resembled and may be said to have been patterned after the landlord-peasant relationship.

The patron-client relationships in Colleverde differed from those which Foster observed in Mexico in one important respect. An essential aspect of such relationships in Tzintzuntzan is that they are dyadic; they can exist only between two individuals: "Ego conceptualizes his obligations and expectations as a two-way street, he at one end and a single partner at the other end" (Foster 1963:1281)). In Colleverde, however, the dyad was not the only or even the most frequent form. When the relationship was formed between mezzadria landlord and peasant, the landlord became patron not to an individual but to an entire household. His obligations automatically extended to all members of the peasant family, unless some member specifically rejected his own obligations as client. On the other hand, the wife of the landlord became *la padrona*, and she was expected to adopt the role of patroness, especially toward the women of the peasant family. To a lesser extent, other members of the landlord's family were also treated as patrons and sometimes accepted the obligations of patronage. These extensions of the patron and client roles to whole households were not the result of independently established contracts; they were more or less automatic, although the other persons were not strictly bound to accept the role.

Furthermore, there was in Colleverde the concept of an individual (or a married couple or family) becoming patron to a group made up of unrelated persons. Traditionally, there were several community associations and organized projects (an important example was the 40-member band) which were initiated and/or maintained by local signori, who were considered their patrons. Such persons gave economic support and political protection to these groups (not to their members as individuals). Similarly, certain signori regarded themselves and were generally regarded by others as patrons of the community, with the responsibility to provide benefits for the community as a whole. One way in which this was done was by leaving a will providing that part of their patrimony be used in specific ways by the community. Such endowments were a major source of public funds and community charities.

THE PATRON AS MEDIATOR

The descriptions of patronage systems in various cultural settings suggest that one of the most important aspects of the patron's role is to relate the client to the world outside the local community. Pitt-Rivers (1954:141) emphasized this point in his analysis of an Andalusian village: "It is, above all, [the patron's] relationship to the powers outside the pueblo which gives him value." In Andalusia, a structure of patronage links the authority of the state to the network of neighborly relations and balances "the tension between the state and the community" (Pitt-Rivers 1954:154–55). Kenny (1960:17–18), writing about Castile, observed that the patrons are validly described as "gatekeepers," for "they largely dominate the paths linking the local infrastructure of the village to the superstructure of the outside urban world." In general, the patrons described from recent times in Spain and Latin America, and those of traditional Central Italy, are mediators in the full sense of the definition adopted here. Their functions are critical ones, for they have an essential part in the basic economic and political structures of the society. Moreover, persons become patrons precisely because their capacity to perform these functions is virtually exclusive.

It would appear, in fact, that patrons are particularly well adapted to performing the function of mediation between the local and the national system. The patron usually has a distinctly defined status in both systems and operates effectively in both. Furthermore, the relationship between patron and client is stable and durable. As Foster has pointed out, continuance of the relationship is assured by never permiting a balance to be achieved between the obligations of the parties; the account is never settled, but rather each constantly wins new credits which will be redeemed at a future time or incurs new debts which must later be paid. Stability of the patron-client tie is reinforced by its patterning after a kin relationship, the patron becoming "like a father" in obligations to and respect due from the client (as the close connection between "patronage" and "paternalism" suggests). Personalized terms of address are used, there generally are affective overtones to the relationship, and frequently there is a denial of utilitarian motives and an insistence instead upon the non-priced demands of "loyalty," "friendship," or being "almost like one of the family." (One Colleverde woman explained her economically advantageous relationship with her patroness with the statement, "We are old friends, so we always ask each other for favors.") In societies where social mobility is limited and where kinship therefore cannot function as a link between the local and the national system (cf. Friedl 1959), patronage provides a close, highly sanctioned, and self-perpetuating relationship between different social strata as a link between the systems.

Nevertheless, the data from Colleverde suggest that this aspect of patronage is a fairly recent acquisition. Until the unification of Italy in 1860, mediation of the client's dealings with the outside was only a minor aspect of the patron's role. The patronage system had its basis in the peasant's dependence upon the landlords, who historically were the peasants' sole recourse to physical protection and economic aid. However, under the domain of the States of the Church, the community had only tangential relations with the larger political unit, and for most Colleverdesi the sphere of social interaction extended no farther than the nearby market towns and a radius of neighboring communities within which there were cycles of fairs and religious festivals. Certainly for the lower classes extra-local contact was minimal, and there was little necessity for mediation.

After 1860, however, the new nation began the task of knitting together the separate regions and communities. The degree of contact between the national and the local system increased steadily, and more and more the nation encroached into the lives of Colleverdesi of all classes. The governmental bureaucracy entered the community, bringing to the peasants the bewildering demands of official papers and legal codes and occasionally offering equally bewildering economic benefits. New roads and railroads brought outsiders into the community and took Colleverdesi out. Obligatory military service and temporary labor opportunities in other areas took men to distant parts of the nation. To some the developing national institutions meant potential jobs,

both within the community and outside it. In order to deal with their expanding world, the lower-class Colleverdesi needed help. The peasants turned to
those who had always aided them. Persons who had no landlord, or whose landlord was unwilling or unable to help, sought other sources.

Of the functions performed by the patrons during the period from 1860 to
1945, some represent a continuity with the earlier role of the landlord: lending
money or guaranteeing loans, giving employment, helping to provide dowries
for the daughters of the client families, providing medicines and helping to
obtain medical services. However, to these were added many new functions,
involving the mediation of contacts with the world outside the community.
The patron filled out the papers which were required at every significant step
in the individual's life, and he spoke to bureaucrats on his client's behalf. As
government benefits were introduced, the patron was needed to obtain them.
For example, Sra. M., whose husband was killed during World War I, tried in
vain for months to collect a government pension for war widows, and only after
her patron spoke of her case to the appropriate officials did she succeed in getting it. The patron interpreted the law to his client and offered advice. If there
were trouble with the authorities, the patron would intervene. Many cases
could be cited of persons who were arrested by the *carabinieri* and released
after intervention of the patron, and of others who were sentenced to prison
and for whom the patron obtained pardons.

If a client had to go out of the community for any purpose, the patron
would recommend him to some acquaintance at the destination. In fact, all
dealings with institutions or persons outside the local system required personal
recommendations from a mediator.[5] When M.'s grandfather tried to get the
local tobacco concession, when R. applied to a military specialists' school, when
F. took his deaf sister to a physician in Rome, when P. as a young man went
periodically to the coastal plain to seek work, when T. took his bride to Perugia
to choose a coral necklace—all would have considered it foolhardy to do so
without a recommendation from a respected contact, and to get a recommendation a patron was needed. As jobs in the national institutions expanded, access
to them was also a matter of recommendations, and this remained no less true
even after adoption of the *concorso* system, an open competition for available
jobs based on examinations.

In the patronage patterns of traditional Colleverde which were vividly
recalled by older informants, the mediation functions were, in fact, the major
importance of the patron. For example, the most valuable patron was neither
the wealthiest nor the most generous, but the one with the best connections.

---

[5] The recommendation, the importance of which has diminished only slightly though the
channels have changed, is a request for a personal favor to the recommender, and it is not
at all concerned with the qualifications of the person on whose behalf it is made. The value
of a recommendation depends first upon the status of the recommender, second upon the
closeness of his connection to the addressee, and third upon the closeness of the connection
between the recommender and the recommended.

Yet this aspect of the patron's role was elaborated only in the late nineteenth and early twentieth centuries. It was only after the community became incorporated into a complex nation, a nation which made demands upon and offered opportunities to individuals and which required extensive contact between the local and the national system, that the dominant features of "traditional" Colleverdesi patronage emerged.

In general, the patrons of Colleverde in the 1860–1945 years can be characterized as a small group of local signori, no more than a dozen heads of households at any given time. Most were mezzadria landlords, owning as little as two or three small farms or as much as several hundred hectares of land. Some of the landlords also occupied professional or administrative positions of authority in the community, as schoolteachers, pharmacists, physicians, tax collectors, priests, and elected administrators. In addition, some of these positions were held by non-landed members of local landowning families, who also formed part of the patron group. The non-landowning patrons also included a few bureaucrats and professionals (the comune secretaries, two of the pharmacists, a physician, and some of the priests), who came to Colleverde from other towns in Umbria.

The patrons were not an aristocratic group, although a few landowning families traced remote kinship ties to Umbrian nobility. New members were recruited from the commercial class of the towns and cities of the region, for it was this class that throughout Umbria was taking over the holdings of the traditional landowners and educating its sons for the burgeoning bureaucracy and the professions. There was little mobility into the patron group from the lower classes of Colleverde, for the sons of the prosperous peasants and artisans who were able to purchase land, even those who acquired substantial holdings, were not accepted as "true" signori, nor were they likely to possess the connections with signori in other communities which were an important foundation of patronage power. Despite their ties and sometimes their origins outside the community, the patrons were fully a local group. They lived in Colleverde, and their identification with it was strong.

Each patron performed a wide range of mediation functions, the same individual often being for his clients at once the economic, political, social, and ideological link to the larger society. As a group, the patrons controlled virtually all the critical junctures between the local and the national systems. Colleverde's economic relationships with the rest of the nation were for the most part the concern only of the major landlords. This follows from the duality of the traditional mezzadria economy: only the landowners sold produce on the market, while the peasants' share was consumed for their own subsistence. Direct participation in the political life of the nation was limited to the patrons. The mayor and the administrative council of the community were selected from this group; they were elected, but until well into the twentieth century few persons other than the signori were eligible to vote. Moreover, it was primarily members of this group who acted as local representatives of the state, for local jobs in the bureaucracy were passed from one member of the elite to another. Even the religious ties of the community to the Universal Church were to a large extent in the hands of the patrons. Not only were the priests of Colleverde themselves often part of the patron group (as major landlords holding the several Church-owned mezzadria farms and usually as members of landowning families), but the patrons constituted the lay leadership of the local Church, and many had kin connections with Church officials throughout Umbria and in the Vatican.

The patrons had numerous social relationships based on kinship and friendship extending beyond the community, and they practiced frequent intercommunity visiting. The peasants, in contrast, maintained only rare ties of closest kinship outside the immediate area. Finally, because the patrons were long the only literate persons in Colleverde, they were the carriers of the national culture, and values and ideas filtered down through them to the rest of the community. In sum, this group were mediators precisely because they had, almost exclusively, direct access to the nation and because they occupied those formal positions which were the links between the local and national systems. In turn, this control of the mediation functions was the primary source of their power to exert patronage.

Looking outward from the community, the mediators' relationships with the national system were of two kinds. First, the local patrons had extensive ties with near and distant kinsmen, friends, and business associates—social and power equals to themselves—in other village centers, in towns, and in cities of the region. These were continuing relationships based on reciprocal, equivalent obligations. Second, the Colleverdesi patrons, as well as their equal numbers in other communities, were themselves clients to more powerful, higher-status patrons. These higher patrons did not function at the village level but belonged to the spheres of town and city. Thus, through a hierarchy of patronage (cf. Kenny 1960:22–23; Gillin 1962:37), Colleverde was linked to the higher units of organization within the nation.

The structure of the traditional relationship between Colleverde and the larger society may now be summarized. A small group of local upper-class families, the nucleus of which were the major landowners of the community, functioned as mediators. Although they considered themselves as Colleverdesi and were active in community life, they were also participants in the national society. Within the local context they acted out the national culture, creating —of a village of only 300 inhabitants—an urban-like, "civilized" center in the rustic countryside. Interaction between the mediators and those in the community for whom they mediated was based on a continuing and intimate patron-client relationship, which was an extension of the landlord-peasant relationship defined by the land-tenure system. Because of the nature of this relationship and the constant presence of the patrons, the clients were strongly aware of a wider social sphere without direct participation in it. Thus, the countryside was linked to the village (and the village lower class to its upper class) by the vertical bond of patronage, while the village was in turn linked to the outside through the patrons' participation in two kinds of networks: horizontal ties with equivalent members of other communities and vertical ties through hierarchies of patrons operating at progressively higher levels of national integration.

This description is an example of only one form that a part-whole relationship through mediators can take. Such a relationship varies significantly in at least five different ways. First, there is a tie between the mediators and those in the local system for whom they mediate, which need not be one of patronage. Not only are there other mechanisms by which the connection with a mediator may be established (such as kinship, ritual kinship, employment, or political appointment) and other cultural rationales for maintaining the connection, but the mutual rights and obligations and the kind of interaction involved may be different. The relationship may be limited to specific areas rather than as wide-ranging as the patron-client tie; the interaction may be sporadic rather than fairly continuous; and the quality of the relationship may be more or less emotionally intense than that between patron and client in Colleverde.

Second, the nature of the mediators themselves may vary greatly—their history, their traditions, and the manner in which they are recruited and replaced. For example, a mediating group recruited from economically successful peasants would be quite different from the patrons of Colleverde, a landowning class with quasi-aristocratic traditions.

Third, there is variation in the particular functions which the mediators perform and in the way in which these functions are combined. A political functionary whose main business is the collection of taxes is a mediator of a very different kind from the Colleverdesi patrons, whose functions touched every aspect of life. In the case of Colleverde, all mediating functions were combined and performed by the same group, but at the opposite extreme there might be a separate mediator for each function.

Fourth, the size of the mediating group may vary, determining a smaller or larger number of channels into the local system. In Colleverde there were multiple channels, intermediate between the extreme possibilities of a single individual as mediator and a situation in which each household has its own links to the national system.

A fifth dimension of variation is the kind of relationship of the mediators to the local system and the degree of their integration into it. The patrons of Colleverde were fully a part of the local system and locally resident. However, mediators may also be part of the local system yet not reside in the community, they may reside locally but remain detached from the local system, or they may be outsiders with only tangential relationships to the local system.

CONCLUSION: THE FATE OF THE MEDIATOR

Since World War II, a new kind of relationship between Colleverde and the larger society has developed. The patrons have been pushed out of the strategic link positions. Yet their control of the "critical junctures" has not passed to newly emerging groups in the society or to persons occupying different roles. New groups and new roles have appeared through which persons act as intermediaries, but the junctures can no longer be "guarded." Diverse, competing intermediaries, as well as an increase in direct participation by individuals in the national system, have replaced the mediators. It appears that the mediator represents a general form of community-nation relationship which characterizes an early phase in developing nation-states, and which regularly gives way as integration of the total society advances.

REFERENCES CITED

Bandini, M. 1957. *Cento Anni di Storia Agraria Italiana.* Roma.

Foster, G.M. 1963. "The Dyadic Contract in Tzintzuntzan, II: Patron-Client Relationship." *American Anthropologist* 65: 1280–1294.

Friedl, E. 1959. "The Role of Kinship in the Transmission of National Culture to Rural Villages in Mainland Greece." *American Anthropologist* 61: 30–38.

Geertz, C. 1960. "The Changing Role of Cultural Broker: The Javanese *Kijaji.*" *Comparative Studies in Society and History* 2: 228–249.

Gillin, J.P. 1962. *Some Signposts for Policy. Social Change in Latin America Today,* pp. 14–62. New York.

Istituto Nazionale di Economia Agraria. 1956. La Distribuzione della Proprietà Fondiaria in Italia, v. i: Relazione generale, a cura di Giuseppe Medici. Roma.

Kenny, M. 1960. "Patterns of Patronage in Spain." *Anthropological Quarterly* 33: 14–23.

Pitkin, D.S. 1959: "The Intermediate Society: A Study in Articulation." *Intermediate Societies, Social Mobility, and Communication,* ed. V.F. Ray, pp. 14–19. Proceedings of the 1959 Spring Meeting of the American Ethnological Society. Seattle.

Pitt-Rivers, J.A. 1954. *The People of the Sierra.* London.

Redfield, R. 1956. *Peasant Society and Culture.* Chicago.

Silverman, S.F. 1963. *Landlord and Peasant in an Umbrian Community.* Unpublished Ph.D. dissertation, Columbia University.

Steward, J.H. 1955. *Theory of Culture Change.* Urbana.

Wolf, E.R. 1956. "Aspects of Group Relations in a Complex Society: Mexico." *American Anthropologist* 58: 1065–1078.

AMOS H. HAWLEY
AND BASIL G. ZIMMER

Resistance to Unification
in a Metropolitan Community

The rise and development of the metropolitan community is one of the major social trends of the twentieth century.[1] The accumulated data bear out and surpass the forecast of N.S.B. Gras concerning the replacement of the town based economy by a metropolitan economy in the western world.[2] Bogue's allocation of the entire territory and population of the United States to metropolitan areas probably is no exaggeration of the prevailing situation.[3] Virtually every collective activity in which people engage today is encompassed in the organization of a metropolitan center.

Students of metropolitanism work with two conceptions of the metropolitan community. One is cast in theoretical terms, the other is a rough operational formulation of the former. Theoretically, the metropolitan community embraces the total population, together with the area it occupies, which carries on its daily life through a common system of relationships administered from a given central city. In view of the dynamics of modern life, a unit defined in this way has no stable boundary. The boundary shifts and changes with gains and losses of transportation advantages as between neighboring central cities and with alterations of the competitive balance. Nor does the boundary often fall on the lines which divide the political units used for the reporting of

[1] R.D. McKenzie, *The Metropolitan Community*, New York: McGraw-Hill, 1933; Donald J. Bogue, *The Structure of the Metropolitan Community: A Study of Dominance and Subdominance*, Ann Arbor: University of Michigan, 1949; Amos H. Hawley, *The Changing Shape of Metropolitan America*, Glencoe, Ill.: The Free Press, 1955.

[2] N.S.B. Gras. *An Introduction of Economic History*, New York: Harper and Bros., 1922.

[3] Donald J. Bogue, *op. cit.*

official statistics. Hence, for purpose of comparative analysis and description a more manageable principle of delineation is needed, even though it may mean sacrifice of accuracy. The concept of the standard metropolitan area has been developed in the U.S. Bureau of the Census as an operational definition of the metropolitan community.[4] It denotes an aggregate of at least 1,000,000 including a central city of 50,000 or more population, and the county containing the central city, together with all contiguous counties which are economically and socially integrated with the central city.[5] The standard metropolitan area admittedly is an approximation of the metropolitan community. But its serviceability outweighs many of its descriptive defects. Even on this modest basis, the 168 standard metropolitan areas recognized in the 1950 census contained over three-fifths of the total U.S. population, though only 4.3 per cent of the land area.

The pre-eminence of the metropolitan community in the settlement pattern and organization of American society notwithstanding, it is still a somewhat disconnected and incomplete social unit. Change, in this as in so many other instances involving complex social units, has moved forward unevenly in what has seemed to be a serial or wave-like manner. For analytical purposes, it is convenient to treat change as having certain identifiable components or phases. Thus, we shall deal with metropolitan development in terms of a number of phases which may or may not occur in any necessary temporal order.

The phases may be listed in the following order: (1) the growth of a large central city on the basis of interregional exchanges; (2) the improvement and extension of local transportation and communication routes into the hinterland; (3) the reorientation of the hinterland population toward a closer interdependence with the central city; (4) the rapid accumulation of urban population and urban land uses in the hinterland; (5) the adaptation of social and administrative systems to the territorially expanded community.

The growth of a large city is a necessary condition for the subsequent development of a metropolitan community. For it is only a large city that can provide the array of services and opportunities required to focus attention upon a particular place. Conversely, the large city has, or is capable of developing, the instrumentalities for organizing and integrating the diverse activities scattered over a wide area. But a city attains large size primarily on the basis of a substantial export function vis-à-vis other regions. Its growth, therefore, is based on those local advantages which foster its participation in the interregional economy rather than on its function as a local service center. At the outset, then, the city which later becomes a metropolitan center grows more or less independently of events in the many minor civil divisions scattered about it.

4 Henry S. Shryock, Jr., "The Natural History of Metropolitan Areas," *The American Journal of Sociology*, 43 (1957), 163–170.
5 *Census of Population: 1950.* Vol. II: *Characteristics of Population*, Washington, D.C.: U.S. Government Printing Office, 1952, XIV–XV.

But as a city grows larger it accumulates facilities for the attraction and mediation of trade and other activities in the surrounding area. It soon becomes necessary to extend and improve local roads and communication lines sufficiently to give full play to the central city's service facilities. As direct lines of access are pushed into the hinterland, the partial isolation of village and farm populations is destroyed. Freed from exclusive dependence on slow and roundabout movement over interregional routes for their contacts with the outside world, they can turn directly to a local metropolis for their daily requirements. Within the enlarged universe of daily interchange, the large city becomes a convenient point for the centralization of many functions formerly scattered widely over the area.

The developments which make possible the attachment of the occupants of an enlarged hinterland to a central city also reduce the necessity for a dense concentration of the population and industry in the central city. Accordingly, in response to the enlarged range of locational choice, urban residents and urban activities spread over the adjacent areas, first along the thoroughfares but subsequently into the interstitial zones. While the growth of urban occupancy of lands outside the central city's boundaries may begin as a centrifugal movement from the city, that growth is soon supplemented by accretion from without. Thus, what was once a relatively compact urban community contained within the municipal boundaries of a single city gives way to a diffuse community distributed over numerous locally governed areas.

The last phase in the maturation of the metropolitan community is the integration of the whole in a social and an administrative, as well as an economic, unity. This phase may be expected as an inevitable consequence of the preceding developments. Yet, although it has been taking form bit by bit here and there and always in a piecemeal fashion, it is the one uncompleted phase remaining even in the most highly developed metropolitan communities. To the extent that the several phases are separated in time, frictions develop. For the onset of one phase seems to imply the next, and if the next phase is not promptly forthcoming the effect of the preceding events is to produce imbalance, disorder, and confusion. These consequences have emerged in most acute form in connection with the delay of the last phase. The distribution of the members of an organization, i.e., the metropolitan community, over a number of semi-autonomous political or administrative units impedes, when it does not prevent, joint action in dealing with the day-to-day requirements of collective life. Moreover, it invites inequities and infringements of various kinds. Residents of one administrative area, for example, may use the facilities of another adjacent one without contributing to their maintenance, or they may so manage their affairs as to create a health hazard or other nuisances for the occupants of the adjacent area. Every administrative area is exposed to such difficulties, though the risks and the costs usually fall most heavily on the ones that have the greatest investment in public facilities and services. For this reason, the central city is especially vulnerable to the effects of dense populations residing on the periphery of its jurisdiction. On the other hand, satellite residents contribute to the wealth of the central city, but do not share in the tax revenues from industry and commerce. Consequently, locally raised revenues for services must come largely from residential properties. When industry expands in the hinterland, the tax wealth is lost to the central city but the growing population in the satellite areas places an increasingly heavy burden on the central city services, thus adding to the costs of government in the latter area.

We may view the metropolitan community that has yet to complete the final phase of its development as involved in a situation of diffused and unorganized power. Let us look upon the metropolitan community as a social system. Conceptually a social system is an organization adapted to the performance of a set of functions. Organization is the means of mobilizing and co-ordinating the power required to execute one or more functions. In large social systems, the principal parts are sub-systems each of which is also an organization of power for the conduct of a more or less specialized function. But the sub-system derives its power from two sources: from its own organization and from the parent system in which it is supported. A community is in effect a sub-system set within the larger systems represented by the state and the nation. It is, of course, an organization which engages in certain functions and presumably it has the power required for the purpose. It has the power, that is, to operate systematically in the production and distribution of goods and services of all kinds. But it also possesses a degree of administrative autonomy within a prescribed territory by virtue of power delegated to it by the state government.

Now it should be apparent that the emergence of the metropolitan community imposes an organization upon a constellation of territorial units (cities, villages, townships, school districts) each of which derives certain powers directly from an outside or non-local source, i.e., the state. The one basis of power is not, therefore, co-ordinate with the other. So long as that disparity obtains, the metropolitan community cannot operate in a coherent or effective manner.

Metropolitan communities throughout the nation are confronted with this situation of divided and incompletely organized power. Although the problems resulting from the lack of integration are most serious in the large communities, they are encountered in some degree in virtually all sizes of metropolitan communities. Efforts to accomplish the political or administrative unifications have met with almost uniform failure. A deep pessimism that full integration will ever be achieved has settled upon most responsible observers of metropolitan phenomena.[6] Consequently, attention has shifted to the devising of partial and expedient resolutions of the anomaly.

The problem, then is: What are the roots of the resistance to the establish-

---

6 See "A Symposium on Metropolitan Regionalism: Developing Governmental Concepts," *University of Pennsylvania Law Review,* 105, 1957.

ment of a single municipal government over the entire metropolitan community? What factors make for the persistence of an obsolescent governmental structure? It is unlikely that there is a simple answer to the questions. The explanation of any aspect or circumstance in a social system as complex as the modern metropolitan community must certainly involve manifold "causes." The best that can be done in the present state of knowledge is to advance a number of propositions as a means of isolating the possible "causes." Some combination of the several propositions may constitute the explanation of the failure of governmental unification to take place.

First, assuming that the metropolitan community has actually developed a unity in all respects except for its governmental organization, it may be that the frictions and unmet needs resulting from administrative disunity have not advanced far enough to have made action looking to a solution seem necessary. If this proposition is not supported in fact, there is the possibility that ameliorative action is prevented by a lack of consensus among residents as to the proper course action should take. That division of opinion may arise from social class cleavages. Or it may result from unwillingness on the part of substantial numbers of residents to pay the increased taxes improved service would require. It is also possible that there is a deep suspicion of the competence and the responsibility of centralized government. Finally, the knowledge of government and of what to expect from it may be so deficient that residents are really unable to act intelligently in the resolution of their problem.

These propositions will be examined with data pertaining to the metropolitan area of Flint, Michigan. Since a study of an individual metropolitan area is hardly adequate as a basis for generalizations concerning all such areas, no satisfactory test of the hypothesis can be realized. An analysis of their application to a specific case, however, will illuminate the situation in Flint and should be suggestive of guidelines for later research involving the population of metropolitan areas.

The following discussion draws freely on the accumulated works of Research Fellows and the teaching staff who have been participants over the past twelve years in the Metropolitan Community Seminar of the University of Michigan. The latter part of the discussion deals intensively with the contemporary situation. As will become evident, data for this part of the report have been obtained from a series of field surveys based on probability samples of residents in the area. Unfortunately, the boundary of the area is not constant throughout the report. It has been adapted to the requirements of various research undertakings.

METROPOLITAN EMERGENCE

The manufacture of vehicles has been the main economic base of the city of Flint since the 1880's. On the strength of its national leadership in the production of carriages, Flint by 1900 had attained a population size of 13,103. Its industrial organization, skilled labor force, accumulated capital, and transportation access to the principal markets facilitated the transition to automobile production in the years immediately following 1900. The Buick Motor Company was founded in Flint, in 1906, and two years later the General Motors Corporation was organized there. Flint's population rose to 38,550 during the first decade of the century, to 91,599 by the end of the second decade, and to 156,492 by 1930. The period of dramatic population increase ended in 1930. Thereafter growth was erratic and relatively slow. We shall return to the matter of population increase in a later connection. The first event of major consequence so far as metropolitan development is concerned was the rapid growth of the city.

Just as Flint's growth was based on the rise of the automobile industry, the automobile in turn revolutionized the pattern of local life in and around Flint. Whereas at the turn of the century Flint, as a prosperous small city, existed more or less independently of its hinterland, the motor vehicle converted it into the functional center of an expanding metropolitan community. That effect was not immediate, however, Adapted at first primarily to intracity use, the automobile had to await the development and surfacing of rural roads before its potentialities as an agent for change could be realized.

The impact of efficient highway transportation on outlying settlements is illustrated by the case of Linden, a village situated on the extreme southern edge of Genesee County in which Flint is located.[7] A farm service and shipping center in 1900, Linden was linked to Pontiac and Detroit by the railroad. It had infrequent exchange with Flint, which was but 17 crow-flight miles to the north. A round trip to Flint by passenger train, via Holly or Durand at which a change of trains was necessary, required a full day. Freight shipments from Flint seldom consumed less than two days. Accordingly, only one business establishment of some forty or more in Linden drew its supplies from Flint wholesalers. The village served as a link between the national economy and the farms scattered over an area within a team-haul distance of the village. Hence the tempo of local life varied with the weekly and seasonal rhythms of farm activities.

With the coming of the improved roads and the motor vehicle, Linden was brought within less than an hour's travel time of Flint. As a result the village underwent a profound reorientation and transformation of its economy. Farmers were no longer dependent on the produce marketing agencies in Linden. They could deliver farm products with their own vehicles to buyers in Flint and on the same trip shop for their consumer needs in a much larger retail market than a village could offer. Linden declined as a farmer trade center. As this was taking place the residents of the village were also responding to the new accessibility of Flint. Daily newspapers published in the larger city began to circulate in Linden. Retail merchants turned to Flint for their wholesale purchases. Even more important, Linden workers were absorbed into

---

7 Samuel A. Pratt, "Metropolitan Community Developments and Economic Change," *American Sociological Review*, 22 (1957), 434–440.

the Flint labor force. In 1900 employment in Flint on the part of Linden residents was impossible without a change of residence. But in 1930 twenty-nine workers, 14 per cent of the gainfully employed, commuted daily to Flint by motor vehicle. That proportion increased to 46 per cent by 1950.

Thus Linden was drawn into and made a part of an enlarged community having Flint as its service and administrative center. In the process, the village has become a suburban residence for the families of workers employed in the industries of the metropolitan center. The experience of Linden was repeated, with local variations in the time of beginning and the rate of transition, in virtually all of the village centers scattered over the country.

· · ·

The growth of both population and of industry in the hinterlands of Flint are indicative of a large-scale invasion of rural lands by urban uses. More than one-fourth of the 400,000 acres of farm land reported in the Census of 1900 had

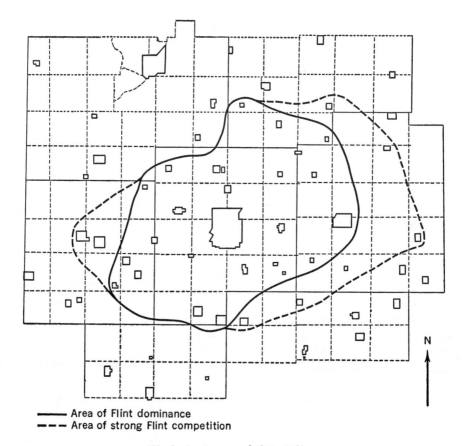

——— Area of Flint dominance
— — — Area of strong Flint competition

FIG. 1   Service area of Flint, Michigan.

been converted to urban uses by 1950. The process began slowly in the first decade of the century, gradually accelerated in the next decade, and reached a crescendo in 1920–30, when some 75,000 acres passed from farm to urban uses. A large part of that was annexed to the city of Flint, but much of it was removed from farm use for suburban residential development. In the depression years of the 1930's, the trend was reversed and 1200 new farms were created. Virtually all of the new farms, however, were farms only by courtesy of census definition, for their average size was less than 13 acres. Apparently many urban workers living outside of the central city planted their small acreages in garden crops to supplement curtailed wages and salaries. In any event, the possession of farm lands by urban activities was resumed after 1940. And by 1950 farm acreage had reached a new low figure of 293,000, despite the use by the Bureau of the Census of a more liberal definition of a farm.

The projection of Flint's influence over the surrounding area brought all of Genesee County and parts of the counties adjoining it on the east, north, and west within Flint's trade area. Figure 1 shows the boundary of the area within which Flint department store sales, women's apparel store sales, and newspaper circulation predominate over those of competing centers, that is, Detroit, Grand Rapids, Lansing, Saginaw, and Port Huron.[8] The area is that in which the resident population daily turns to Flint for its principal retail services, its recreation and entertainment, and much of its employment. Approximately the same area of influence as that shown in Figure 1 was obtained in an analysis of 1953 traffic flow data.[9] This involved plotting traffic gradients along trunkline thoroughfares and linking their low points with straight lines.[10]

. . .

Despite the significant enlargement of the scope of the Flint community to metropolitan proportions that has occurred since 1900, only minor changes in the territorial distribution of local government power have been effected. A series of annexations of township lands to Flint, between 1901 and 1919, increased the size of the central city from 6.3 square miles to 16.7 square miles.

---

[8] Marion E. Dunlap, *The Urban and Metropolitan Status of The City of Flint*, Social Science Research Project Reports; University of Michigan, 1948.

[9] Robert B. Reynolds, "Central Places of Flint Metropolitan Community." Unpublished Social Science Research Report, University of Michigan, June 1954.

[10] A further measure of the growth of Flint's importance as a focal point is observable in the changes in the ratio of workers in the major industrial installations in the central city to resident population of satellite urban places at differing distances between 1936 and 1950. During this period there was a 38 per cent increase in the ratio of industrial workers to resident population in the city. However, in the area five to fourteen miles distant from Flint the ratio increased by over 125 percent, whereas in the next distance zone there was more than a four-fold increase. That Flint's influence was rapidly extending in the hinterland is evident by the particularly large increases which occurred in the more distant locations. These data, it should be noted, pertain to village and urban satellite places. Doubtless a similar pattern obtains in the unincorporated areas as well. See Leo F. Schore, "The Separation of Home and Work in Flint, Michigan," Social Science Research Project, University of Michigan, June 1954.

The last and most substantial annexation was accomplished in 1920, increasing the city's scope to 29.4 square miles. Except for the losses through annexation in the central city, the townships in Genesee County have remained unchanged since 1900. The greatest change has occurred in the boundaries of school districts. Numerous consolidations reduced the number of school districts in the county from 137, in 1920, to 36, at present. All of the consolidations, however, have taken place outside of the four townships immediately adjacent to the central city. The sixteen school districts within those four townships today were present in essentially the same form in 1900. Other minor changes have appeared as two small special service districts for water supply purposes. This chaotic political and administrative situation persists with a vigor that is hardly affected by the expansion of the community.

In recapitulation, it seems that metropolitan development in the Flint area has followed the proposed sequence fairly closely. Rapid population growth began in the middle of the first decade of the present century and continued to about 1930. The improvement and extension of local transportation routes was inaugurated some ten years after the onset of rapid central city growth and was brought to its present state in 1934. The orientation of activities in the outlying area to Flint began with, and followed upon, the improvements of roads, moved ahead rapidly during the 1930's, and has continued down to the present. Although population growth in the outer area accelerated in the 1910–20 decade, not until the 1930–40 decade did population increase in the whole of the Standard Metropolitan Area outside of the central city exceed that within the central city. The diffusion of industry from the central city began between 1929 and 1939, but moved ahead most rapidly after 1947. There is no doubt that the population and activities in the city of Flint and in the surrounding area to a distance of some 15 or 20 miles have become integrated in a single functional entity. But the political sub-division of the territory involved has remained virtually as it was in 1900. The last stage in the sequence, political and administrative unification, has not taken place. . . .

. . . A possible basis for the reluctance to join the central city may exist in suspicions and doubts regarding the integrity, the responsiveness to citizen's needs, or other optimal qualities of large city government. Most fringe residents, in fact, felt that the size of government affects the efficiency of its operation. Of course, it is not improbable that such a view is simply conventional: were the issues to be presented in a different light more discriminating judgments might be elicited. For example, comparative evaluations of township and central city governments with reference to a number of specific attributes might circumvent the categorial commonplaces which are exchanged in casual conversation. This approach was employed and the results are set forth in Table 1. It should be remembered in reading this table that three-fourths of the fringe residents formerly lived in the central city. They have had some experience, in other words, on which to base comparative judgments.

On most attributes the township governments received a larger number of

TABLE 1   Per Cent Distribution of Comparative Evaluations of Township and
Central City Governments by Fringe Residents

| | | | Comparative Evaluation | | |
Attributes of Government	More in Twp.	About Same in Both Areas	More in Central City	No Opinion or No Answer	Total
Relative lack of economic burden-someness of government	47.2	30.3	15.5	7.0	100.0
Extent individual is free of government controls	40.0	40.2	9.9	9.9	100.0
Relative value of talking to officials	39.2	34.1	15.7	10.0	100.0
Extent government is free of influence from special interest	37.5	37.8	13.3	11.4	100.0
Extent officials are aware of problems in neighborhoods	34.9	44.8	14.0	6.3	100.0
Extent officials are concerned with the individual	33.4	43.8	14.3	7.4	100.0
Extent people have a say in running government	31.5	48.7	13.6	6.3	100.0
Relative interest of officials in neighborhood	24.7	40.7	25.7	9.0	100.0
Relative competence of government officials	12.6	64.6	13.8	9.0	100.0

favorable appraisals than did the central city government. But in no instance does the distribution of comparative judgments indicate unqualified support of township government. Although 47 per cent felt that township government was economically least burdensome, almost as many (45 per cent) asserted that either there was no difference between the two areas in this respect or that the central city government was least burdensome. On all other attributes the favorable appraisals of township government are clearly in the minority. But the central city government was viewed even less favorably on most of the items. The large proportions who could make no distinction between townships and central city governments are worthy of note, especially in the matter of competence of officials. This finding would be instructive, if we could assume that it represented well-reasoned judgments. Unfortunately, such an assumption would be very dubious. The "about the same" response probably was given by many unobservant and apathetic citizens. This interpretation finds some support in an analysis of citizens' knowledge of government.

Knowledge of local government

In an attempt to measure knowledge of government, fringe residents were queried about the number of offices in the townships to which they elect officials and the names of persons presently occupying those offices. The responses to these questions are shown in Table 2. It is noted that two-fifths of the residents were unable to name a single official position and only about one-third

TABLE 2   Per Cent Distribution of Household Heads by Number of Elective
Offices and Elected Officials of Township Government Identified

| | *Identification* | |
Number Mentioned	Elective Offices in Township	Name of Officials Holding Office
None	40.0	35.1
1 or 2	23.7	40.7
3 or 4	25.9	16.9
5 or more	7.7	3.6
No answer	2.7	1.6
Total	100.0	100.0

could name more than two offices. That two-thirds of the household heads
could name no more than two offices to which they elected persons indicates
limited familiarity with local governmental structure. Such a lack of knowledge
is strong supportive evidence against the popular interpretation that residents
are "close" to their government in the township areas. Further support of this
is found in the responses to the question regarding persons presently occupying
elective offices. Even when the 40 per cent who were unable to identify an
office are excluded, one-third of the remaining household heads were unable to
name any of the elective officials and three-fourths of the respondents were able
to name no more than two persons presently holding an elective office.

As a further measure of knowledge of government as well as participation
in local government, questions were asked about knowledge of the meeting
place of various governmental bodies and attendance at meetings of the bodies
during the past two years. Responses to these questions are shown in Table 3.

TABLE 3   Per Cent of Household Heads Who Know Place of Meeting and
Who Attended Meeting of Selected Groups

| | *Knowledge of*
Meeting Place | | | | *Attendance at*
Meetings | | | |
Type of Group	Know	Not Know	No Answer	Total	Have At- tended	Have Not At- tended	No Answer	Total
School Board	49.4	49.4	1.2	100.0	11.6	86.9	1.5	100.0
Township Board	45.3	53.8	1.0	100.0	14.5	84.3	1.2	100.0
Zoning Board	29.5	70.0	1.5	100.0	8.0	90.3	1.7	100.0
Board of Supervisors	22.5	75.5	2.2	100.0	3.4	95.4	1.2	100.0

As noted earlier the fringe area is divided into many small school districts,
yet it is observed that only half of the residents knew where the school board
meets, and only slightly more than one in ten had attended a meeting of this
body during the past two years. An even smaller proportion were familiar with
the meeting place of the township board, but attendance at meetings was
higher. Less than one-fourth were aware of the meeting place of the County

Board of Supervisors and only 3 per cent had ever attended a meeting of that body.[11]

Attendance at meetings is related to length of residence at present address. But, the proportion who have attended a meeting does not exceed 25 per cent in any length of residence category and that proportion is attracted only by the township board. It is also noteworthy that more of the respondents who evaluated the township government most favorably knew the elected offices of their governments than did those who were less favorable in their evaluations. On the other hand, those who felt the township governments compared unfavorably with the central city attended meetings of local government bodies more frequently. Perhaps meeting attendance is largely for purposes of protest on the part of otherwise distinterested persons. Protest, and certainly unsatisfied protest, would be associated with a deprecatory view of township government.

Although the governmental units in the fringe area are small, the evidence of knowledge about local government and participation in government is far from impressive. Central city residents demonstrate more knowledge and more participation in local government.

Still further comparative evidence between the two areas is to be found in the proportion registered to vote and in the proportion who reported that they have voted in at least one of the last two local elections. In both areas approximately four-fifths of the household heads claim that they are registered voters. However, a larger proportion of the central city residents reported that they voted in local elections than was found among fringe residents.

The available data on knowledge about local governments are admittedly crude. Nevertheless they raise a reasonable doubt concerning the ability of fringe residents to think constructively about solutions to service problems.[12] This has been suggested, too, by some of the inconsistencies among expressed opinions. Ignorance may be but part of the answer. There may also be a lack of local leadership from which to obtain definitions and clarification of issues. If such leadership were present, however, it might encounter difficulty in gaining access to the population. For, less than one-fourth belong to any formal organization other than a labor union or a church. The corresponding proportion in the central city is in excess of two-fifths. Thus, it seems that fringe

---

[11] As compared with the knowledge of the meeting place of the township board on the part of the fringe residents, it was found that in the city of Flint a much higher proportion knew where the city commission held its meetings and a larger proportion had attended a meeting of this body. City residents were also more familiar with the meeting place of the country board of supervisors and equaled the fringe residents in the proportion who attended a meeting of this group. City residents, however, had a large proportion who did not know the meeting place of the school board and attendance at such meetings was also lower in the fringe.

[12] Morris Janowitz, Deil Wright, and William Delaney, in their study of *Public Administration and The Public—Perspective Toward Government in a Metropolitan Community*, Michigan Government Studies, No. 36. Institute of Public Administration, University of Michigan, 1958, also found a relatively low level of knowledge prevailing in a random sample, even in respect to a matter that bears directly on individual welfare—the social security system.

residents are relatively inarticulate as well as inaccessible to leadership. This is especially true of the supporters of annexation: six of every seven of them belong to no organization. But it is also the non-members who, on the one hand, have the most unfavorable opinions of township government, and, on the other hand, know least about township government. Were it not that the total number of organizational members is so small, the non-members would appear to be a disaffected category of residents. The fact is, many other non-members share the opinions held by members. Organizational membership seems merely to be a symptom of the preference for the status quo.

Preferred solution related to evaluation of needs

Part of the resistance of fringe residents to governmental unification as indicated earlier may be due to their inability to assess correctly local needs and attributes of local government. Thus, this leads us to a more direct inquiry into the relationship between evaluations and attitudes concerning governmental reorganization. Before doing so however, it is noted that objective observers are generally critical of the rural type township government in densely settled fringe areas. There is general agreement among them that such areas have the same problems and needs as central city areas. Consequently there is a need for more government. In respect to the latter, they view annexation as an effective means whereby fringe area service problems could be economically solved.

We have already observed that fringe residents generally lack knowledge of local government on which to base mature judgments. Pursuing this further, we find that fringe residents, who view the needs of their area as would an objective observer, are much more likely to favor governmental reorganization. These data are shown in Table 4. The residents who do not see a need for more government, in large proportions (72.1 per cent), prefer to continue under the existing township. Only 6 per cent prefer annexation. Support for annexation comes largely from residents who express a need for more government. Resistance to annexation is strongest among residents who feel that no more government is needed. These data further suggest that resistance to governmental reorganization is due to lack of knowledge of the needs of the area.

TABLE 4   Preferred Solution to Fringe Problems by Need for More Government

Need for Government	Township as is	Township Become City	County	Annex	No Answer	Total Per Cent
More government needed	44.6	9.1	18.2	26.8	1.3	100.0
More government not needed	72.1	5.5	15.6	6.1	.7	100.0

*First choice only.

In Table 5 we again find that support for annexation comes largely from residents who assess local needs realistically. Residents who express a need for more government are four times as likely to support annexation as those who report that more government is not needed. Resistance to annexation is staunchest among those who feel that there is no need for more government. Among the latter more than 92 per cent are opposed to annexation in that they would not vote for it if placed on the ballot at the present time. By contrast one-third of the residents who want more government would vote in support of annexation.

TABLE 5   Vote for Annexation by Need for More Government

| | Annexation Vote | | Total |
Need for Government	Yes	No	Per Cent
More government needed	33.3	66.7	100.0
More governmet not needed	8.3	91.7	100.0

In Table 6, it is noted that the supporters of annexation are much more critical of township officials than are residents who oppose such an approach. Three times as many of those who support annexation report that township officials are less aware of neighborhood problems than is found among the opponents of annexation. Similarly, those critical of the relative competence of township officials are four times as large among the supporters of annexation. The inability to distinguish the relative competence of township officials is particularly marked among the opponents of annexation, but we note the large proportion of fringe area residents who express no real difference between the officials of the two areas.

TABLE 6   Comparative Evaluations of Attributes by Vote for Annexation

| | Evaluation of Attributes | | | | |
Vote for Annexation	More in Town-ship	About Same in Both Areas	Less in Town-ship	No Opinion No Answer	Total Per Cent
	Official Awareness of Problems				
Yes	21.6	44.3	27.8	6.2	100.0
No	40.7	44.3	9.7	5.3	100.0
	Relative Competence of Officials				
Yes	6.2	57.7	32.0	4.1	100.0
No	15.0	67.3	8.3	9.3	100.0

Although the fringe residents are clearly opposed to annexation as a solution to their problems, among many, this is only a temporary resistance....

The expected advantages and disadvantages of annexation are found to be important influences on how residents would vote on such an issue [Table 7].

TABLE 7   Vote for Annexation by Advantages and Disadvantages
of Annexation

Vote for Annexation

Advantages and Disadvantages of Annexation	Would Vote Now or Later	Would Never Vote For	No Opinion No Answer	Total Per Cent
Total	46.2	48.4	5.3	100.0
Advantages				
Better services and facilities	63.7	33.8	2.5	100.0
Other	46.4	48.8	4.9	100.0
Don't know any	26.5	67.4	6.1	100.0
No answer	16.7	61.1	22.2	100.0
Disadvantages				
Higher taxes	42.1	55.9	2.0	100.0
Other	35.7	57.1	7.1	100.0
Don't know any	77.6	14.9	7.5	100.0
No answer	31.0	41.4	27.6	100.0

Thus, among residents who report better services and facilities as an advantage of annexation, nearly two-thirds would vote favorably either now or later. This pertains to nearly half of the fringe respondents. However, among the approximate one-third who report that there wouldn't be any advantages gained by annexation, more than two-thirds would never vote for it. The large proportion in the no opinion and no answer category again is worthy of note.

In respect to the expressed disadvantages of annexation, the high proportion of favorable votes in the higher taxes category is of particular interest. Although three-fifths of the fringe residents report that higher taxes would be a disadvantage of annexation, more than two-fifths of this group would vote favorably, now or later. This is a higher proportion than among those who list other disadvantages. This lends further support for our earlier interpretation that resistance to governmental unification is not based on fear of increased costs to individual taxpayers which might follow. Support for annexation is particularly marked among the small minority who report that there wouldn't be any disadvantages. Here too, we find support for reorganization among those residents whose evaluations are comparable to those of an objective observer. Conversely, resistance is most pronounced among those who are incapable of making such judgments. It is noted, however, that the latter group contains a large proportion of the total residents, whose combined voting strength at the polls would outweigh the supporters of annexation in the fringe area.

CONCLUSION

The development of the Flint metropolitan community clearly has drawn the area immediately adjacent to the central city, to say nothing of more outlying areas, into such intimate relations with the central city that for all practical purposes they constitute a single unit. That unity would be complete had governmental unification followed in the normal course of events. Since it did not, the immediately adjacent or fringe area has languished in an underdeveloped condition. It is deficient in virtually all of the services required for reasonably efficient and sanitary urban living. This, despite the accumulation there of a relatively dense residential population most of which resided formerly in the central city and is therefore urban in origin as well as in the character of its settlement. Nor is this judgment of the fringe merely that of an outside spectator equipped with standards alien to the locality. The residents are themselves aware of, and highly critical of, the service inadequacies in their neighborhoods. They, moreover, indicate a readiness to act toward a solution of the problem. They recognize a need for the enlargement of governmental functions, and they are prepared to pay higher taxes.

The readiness to act, however, does not contemplate the merging of the fringe with the central city. More than three-fourths of the sample interviewed were opposed to such a proposal, preferring to rely on an alternative path to the solution of the service problem. Most wished to proceed through the township government in its present form. This involves something of a contradiction; for it is not possible both to retain the township government as it is and to expand greatly the number and scope of its activities. But apart from that, continued reliance upon the township gives no assurance of an efficient solution. Many of the service problems overreach township boundaries. Hence, serious efforts to deal with them would result in a melange of intergovernmental arrangements.

On the surface, it would appear that the most rational and simple manner of resolving service inadequacies is to consolidate the fringe and the central city under a single municipal government. This could be done by annexation. Why then, is this means not adopted, or rather, why is it actively resisted? The question gathers force from the comparative evaluations of township government. These indicated considerably less than enthusiastic support for the townships, contrary to the expressed preference for the development of needed services by townships. On the other hand, the knowledge of local government possessed by fringe residents, as revealed by certain gross indicators, seems extremely meager. It raises a question of their competence either for deciding upon a solution for service inadequacies or for making comparative appraisals of local governments. In this may lie a large part of the explanation of the large number who judge township and central city governments as about the same.

We are brought to the conclusion, at least tentatively, therefore, that the resistance to governmental unification rests largely in ignorance of government and what to expect of it. Support for annexation, it will be recalled, was concentrated among the most highly educated respondents and those whose perception of local needs and evaluation of attributes of government closely resembled those of objective observers. The conflicting opinions expressed by the bulk of the population raise doubts as to whether the connotations of annexation are generally understood. One can hardly avoid the suspicion that annexation has become an invidious term. It appears to call forth an unreasoned response, a response which defeats the objectives of the persons concerned. Whether this is a correct surmise or not, it seems clear that further work on the problem dealt with here should give careful attention to the kind and amount of knowledge about local government possessed by the population in question. This should include an exploration of the folklore gathered about semi-technical terms and the legal and administrative processes they denote.

In the meantime fringe residents hold the balance of power in any effort at governmental unification, though they constitute but a third of the total population involved. Barring the development of a legal means for circumventing their autonomy, the only promise of success would appear to rest in a process of education in the meaning and processes of government.

ROGER E. KASPERSON

Toward a Geography
of Urban Politics:
Chicago, a Case Study

Although the interest of the urban geographer has been channeled into diverse approaches to the city, one important dimension—the political geography of the city—has remained grossly neglected. Indeed, despite the incontestable importance of public decision-making for a wide variety of urban functions, a researcher is hard-pressed to unearth more than a handful of geographical studies upon this subject. There are surely a number of reasons for this neglect, but one may well cite the association of urban geography with economic geography and the focus of political geography upon the national state as leading factors. The conviction that our understanding of urban problems would be greatly augmented by a fuller realization of their political attributes has generated the present research.

.   .   .

PROBLEM

Within most American cities, there are certain areas in which political support and opposition are concentrated. The cores of these conflicting areas may be apparent, but their boundaries are blurred and in a constant state of flux. Indeed, the very flexibility of the zones plays an influential role in the politician's decision-making process. Moreover, since there is a constant struggle for political support in many of these areas, this competition has far-reaching implications for the politician's very existence in public life. To maintain or

---

From *Economic Geography*, Vol. 41, No. 2 (1965), 95–107. Reprinted by permission of the author and editor.

further his position, he must strive to maximize his political power at the expense of his opponents.

The way in which city issues are decided, then, operates within a spatial framework that is too often overlooked by the political scientist and the geographer. Can areas of conflict be determined and systematically arranged in a study of the geography of urban politics? What are the implications to the decision-making process of the existence of such areas?

ASSUMPTIONS

Several factors are assumed in the following analysis. First, by politicians is meant those politicians who function on a city-wide base of power (i.e., a mayor or city treasurer), as opposed to those who operate on a more localized base of power (i.e., a ward alderman). The second assumption is that each politician, when faced with alternatives, chooses the one which he believes will return him the greatest benefits in terms of political advantage and the realization of certain goals. In actual situations, this choice will not always be conscious and such a rational maximizing of benefits and costs oversimplifies the decision-making process. The assumption is necessary, however, for an initial assessment of the role of geographical differences in urban politics. Finally, when discussing the characteristics and political implications of the voting zones, it is assumed that zones are discrete and homogeneous units, though this is clearly not the case in reality.

ELECTORAL BACKGROUND AND ZONAL DELIMITATION

With its fifty wards (Fig. 1), Chicago typifies the "small-ward" American city, a characteristic which has important ramifications for Chicago politics. Chicago aldermen, elected from relatively small wards of 20,000–70,000 registered voters, have direct contact with a sizable number of their constituents. In addition, the coincidence of the location of wards with comparatively homogeneous ethnic and economic groups reinforces this link between the aldermen and the electorate.

In terms of formal governmental structure, Chicago's 50 aldermen comprise the ruling force in the city's politics.[1] Each is an independent representative of his own ward and is elected for a four-year term. Since he is elected from a localized base of power, his first duty is to the welfare of the population of his ward. City-wide issues are of secondary importance to the alderman. This decentralized governmental structure doubtlessly would produce an ineffectual political system if informal controls were not present to centralize this dispersed

---

[1] Martin Meyerson and Edward C. Banfield, *Politics, Planning and the Public Interest: The Case of Public Housing in Chicago* (Glencoe, Ill., 1955), pp. 64 ff.

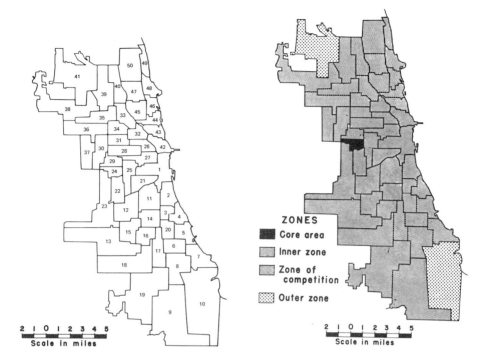

ZONES

■ Core area

▨ Inner zone

▦ Zone of
  competition

▧ Outer zone

FIG. 1   Chicago is typical of the "small-ward" American city. Source: Board of Election Commissioners, City of Chicago.

FIG. 2   Zones are based on the mayoral election of 1951. Source: Board of Election Commissioners, City of Chicago.

power. Meyerson and Banfield recognize two chief sets of such informal control. First, a handful of powerful Democratic aldermen, usually working with the mayor, effectively control the City Council when key issues are at stake. This is accomplished largely by controlling committee assignments, especially those of the important Finance Committee. Second, the presence of the ward committeeman, the party leader in the ward, forces the alderman to toe the line. The ward committeeman decides who will run on the party's ticket in the ward, appoints and dismisses precinct captains, and distributes patronage.

By means of this informal integration, the Democratic machine has sustained itself in power since 1931. During the late 1940's, however, the machine under Mayor Kelly underwent heavy fire from a number of reform-demanding civic groups. Widespread scandals and corruption had convinced party leaders that some internal changes were mandatory. In 1947 Martin Kennelly, a Democratic businessman, was chosen to run for Mayor on the understanding that he would not become party leader. His subsequent election ushered in the politics of the 1950's.

To interpret the spatial aspects of the politics of this decade, voting returns have been mapped by wards and grouped into political zones based upon consistency of voting habits. Returns for the mayoral elections of 1951, 1955, and 1959 serve as data bases. Two principal considerations determined the choice of 1951 as the base year: (1) between the 1947 and 1951 elections, a major change was made in the distribution of wards, and (2) 1951 touched off a decade that has been characterized by urban politics as being of a nature different from that of the preceding two decades. The flagrantly corrupt administration of the traditional Chicago machine had become increasingly incompatible with the ethics of a modern American metropolis.

Based upon an analysis of area voting patterns for the three election years, Chicago can be divided into four political regions. The *core area* includes the wards in which the Democratic Party obtained over 80 per cent of the votes cast. The *inner zone* contains those wards in which 60–80 per cent of the electorate cast its vote for the Democratic Party. The *outer zone* consists of the wards in which the Republican Party received 60 per cent or more of the votes cast. The crucial area between the outer and inner zones is the frontier *zone of competition*, where no party received 60 per cent of the vote. The critical limits of these regions were chosen arbitrarily, but minor alterations would not seriously affect the over-all results of the study.

The voting patterns that led to the re-election of Mayor Kennelly in 1951 are shown on Figure 2. The chief area of Democratic support was centered in the populous heart of the city with an important sub-center in the Calumet area. The frontier zone of competition was composed largely of the outlying wards north and south of the inner zone. Despite Kennelly's re-election, the Democratic machine increasingly came to regard him as a liability.[2] His drive to strengthen the civil service system had incurred a loss of important sources of patronage. In addition, Kennelly's role as a "ceremonial" mayor with weak leadership encouraged factional quarrels which threatened the internal coherence of the machine. With these and other grievances, 1955 ward leaders nominated Richard Daley as their mayoral candidate. Kennelly contested the primary with strong support from the newspapers and good-government groups, and Daley's victory shifted much of Kennelly's former support to Robert Merriam, the Republican candidate. Nevertheless, receiving strong support from the key Democratic wards of the core area (Fig. 3), Mayor Daley won the election. The inner zone reveals the divisive effects of the election and the loss of the Calumet sub-center.

When Mayor Daley assumed office, there was a widely-held suspicion that Chicago was destined to return to the machine politics of Mayor Kelly. Daley, however, incorporated a number of reform programs into his administration and operated under the slogan "good government is good politics."[3] Public approval of this shotgun wedding may be inferred from Figure 4. In the elec-

---

2 James Q. Wilson, *Politics and Reform in American Cities* (Reprint Series, Joint Center for Urban Studies of the Massachusetts Institute of Technology and Harvard University, 1962), pp. 44–45.

3 *Ibid.,* p. 45.

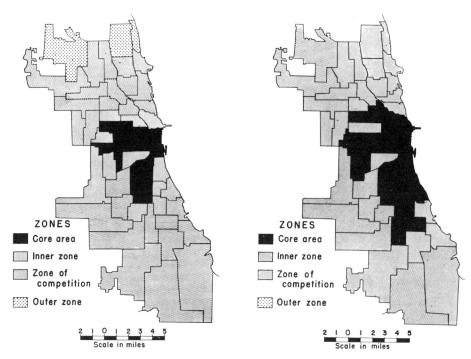

ZONES
■ Core area
▨ Inner zone
□ Zone of
  competition
▨ Outer zone

2 0 2 3 4 5
Scale in miles

FIG. 3 The zones are based on the mayoral election of 1955. Source: Board of Election Commissioners, City of Chicago.

ZONES
■ Core area
▨ Inner zone
□ Zone of
  competition
▨ Outer zone

2 0 2 3 4 5
Scale in miles

FIG. 4 Based on the mayoral election results of 1959. Source: Board of Election Commissioners, City of Chicago.

tion of 1959, Mayor Daley faced weak opposition and garnered the support of newspapers, good-government groups, and prominent business and civic leaders. The core area expanded from seven to 19 wards, while all but three of the remaining 31 wards fell into the inner zone. The outer zone disappeared, for in no ward did the Republican candidate receive 60 per cent of the vote. The flexibility of the voting zones in these three elections is immediately apparent, and its significance will be examined later in the study.

For purposes of analysis, it was necessary to arrive at a composite set of regions from the three elections. The most satisfactory method of regionalization, though admittedly imperfect, was to delimit the wards of the core area and the inner and outer zones according to the aforementioned percentages for all three elections. For a ward to warrant inclusion in the core area, then, its electorate must have cast over 80 per cent of its votes for the Democratic Party in all three elections. The overlapping area which resulted was delegated to the frontier zone of competition, to which it more correctly belonged. The composite map (Fig. 5) thus constructed enabled the researcher to examine the social and economic characteristics of the zones and to evaluate them in relation to the urban politics of Chicago.

POPULATION CHANGE IN
CHICAGO, 1950-1960

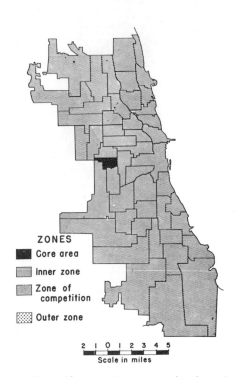

ZONES

■ Core area

▨ Inner zone

▢ Zone of
   competition

▦ Outer zone

2 1 0 1 2 3 4 5
Scale in miles

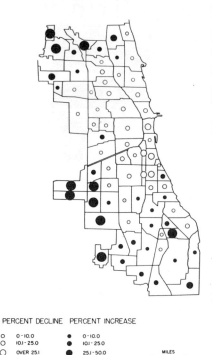

PERCENT DECLINE   PERCENT INCREASE

○	0-10.0	●	0-10.0
○	10.1-25.0	●	10.1-25.0
○	OVER 25.1	●	25.1-50.0
		●	OVER 50.1

MILES
0 1 2 3

FIG. 5 The composite zones are based on the
results of the mayoral elections of 1951, 1955,
1959.

FIG. 6 Population changes are shown by com-
munity area. Source: Chicago Commission on Human
Relations, as taken from Advance Table PH-1, *1960
Census of Population and Housing.*

SOCIAL AND ECONOMIC CHARACTERISTICS

The concentric character of the voting zones is readily apparent in the electoral
maps. The pattern immediately suggests a possible relationship to Burgess's
concentric zone theory of land use.[4] In 1950, the beginning of the period in
question, most of the core area and inner zone, corresponding roughly to
Burgess's transition area and zone of independent workingmen's homes, had
a median income per family of less than $3000, as compared with the city mean
of $3956. These zones also contained large immigrant and Negro minorities.
A low percentage of owner-occupied housing units and a high population density per dwelling unit are also characteristic of the inner zone. In contradistinction to these characteristics are those of the frontier zone of competition and

---

4 Ernest W. Burgess, *The Growth of the City*, Robert E. Park, Ernest W. Burgess, and
Roderick D. McKenzie, eds.: The City, (Chicago, 1925), pp. 47–62.

the outer zone, which generally correspond, respectively, to Burgess's zone of better residences and zone of commuting. Higher income per capita, lower population density per unit, better housing conditions, and a higher percentage of native-born whites all combine to distinguish these zones from the core area and the inner zone. This general pattern is confirmed by the census tract data for 1960.

A final significant zonal distinction revealed by a comparison of 1950 and 1960 census data is the character of population change within the city. Figure 6 indicates community areas registering population increases and decreases between 1950 and 1960. Clearly, the core area and inner zone have experienced serious population declines, often in the order of 10–50 per cent of the total population of the community area. During the same period, community areas in the zone of competition and the outer zone revealed markedly smaller population losses, and many areas, particularly in the western portion of the city, experienced relative increases in population. These demographic changes hold far-reaching implications for Chicago politics.

The differing social and economic features of the voting zones are not to be interpreted as determinants of voting behavior. The spatial distinctions do contribute, however, to explanations of the varying types of appeals with which politicians court the zones, of the different interests in city issues, and of varied conceptions of the public interest on the part of the electorate of the zones. Finally, they provide an ecological setting against which the interplay of urban politics becomes more meaningful.

IMPLICATIONS FOR PUBLIC DECISION-MAKING

The relative importance of each zone is constantly changing. The population changes shown on Figure 6 are increasingly forcing the politician to rely upon the zone of competition and the outer zone for support. The political efficacy of the core and inner zones, the traditional areas of Democratic support, is constantly being undermined by the population losses in these areas and by the rapid population increase in the outer areas of the zone of competition. These demographic changes find expression in the changes in voter registrations over the past decade (Fig. 7). The core area and inner zones showed major declines between 1950 and 1960, whereas the chief increases occurred in the outer ring of wards encompassing the city. The vital statistics are summarized in Table 1. The entire city showed a decline of 7 per cent in voter registrations, but the losses did not occur uniformly in all sections of the city. The core area and inner zone showed a drop of 13 per cent, whereas the frontier zone of competition had only 4 per cent fewer registered voters in 1960 than in 1950. Because of these geographical changes in registrations, the Democratic politician is increasingly torn between his obligation to the core and inner zones and the need to capture votes in the zone of competition. This conflict is creating far-reaching changes in the character of Chicago politics.

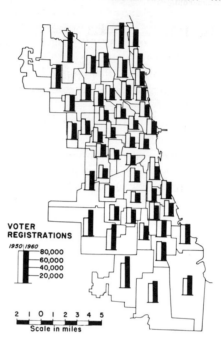

VOTER REGISTRATIONS

1950 1960
—80,000
—60,000
—40,000
—20,000

2 1 0 1 2 3 4 5
Scale in miles

FIG. 7   Changes in voter registration show a marked decline in the central portions of the city. Source: Board of Election Commissioners, City of Chicago.

With the increase of voting power in the frontier zone of competition, middle class ethics and values are becoming more influential in determining public policy. Here resides the politically conscious electorate which views government as a means of enacting general principles which should be of city-wide rather than of local neighborhood scope. Here the political process is conceived as necessitating farsighted planning rather than factional dispute and political bargaining. In short, this is the citadel of good government policy, urban planning, social welfare groups, and public reform. Because of such concerns, these areas are characterized by a responsiveness to the mass media. In fact, many of them have been dubbed, rather derisively, "newspaper wards" or "silk-stocking wards."[5] Professional politicians are acutely aware of the influence of the press in these areas and seek to maintain cordial relations with reporters and editors.

The inner zones, by contrast, shun many of the programs espoused by the outer zones and are less sensitive to the mass media. Here greater value is placed on neighborhood needs, material gifts and favors, and family and ethnic ties. In the past, politicians capitalized on the poverty-stricken and more tran-

_____

[5] Meyerson and Banfield comment that in the newspaper wards "voters usually split the ticket in the way a newspaper advised. The alderman in the 'river wards' could afford to be contemptuous of the newspapers; in their wards editorials were words wasted." Meyerson and Banfield, *op. cit.*, p. 75.

TABLE 1   Changes in Voter Registrations, 1950–1960

	Year						Percentage change
Zone	1950	1952	1954	1956	1958	1960	1950–1960
Core area and inner zone	526,216	522,733	457,324	454,263	420,320	429,807	−13
Zone of competition	1,561,354	1,648,062	1,473,883	1,539,428	1,427,730	1,506,167	− 4
Chicago total	2,087,570	2,170,795	1,931,207	1,993,691	1,848,050	1,935,974	− 7

Source: Board of Election Commissioners, City of Chicago.

sient population of this area to erect a political machine with its accompanying corruption.[6] Significantly enough, good government groups, such as the League of Women Voters, continue to post observers at polls in these wards in an attempt to eliminate possible electoral manipulations. Even with observers, however, it is noteworthy that most of the accusations of voting irregularities in the 1960 Presidential election were directed at these wards. Special objects of attention have been the so-called "river wards," located along the Chicago River in the core area and inner zone. A cultural antagonism exists between these zones which is more fundamental than voting data reveals.

The zonal differences in social and economic values have partially contributed to different methods of assembling political support in Chicago. To secure maximum support, the politician often varies his type of voter appeal to suit the values and interests of the particular ward. In the frontier zone of competition and in the outer zone, public support tends to rely more effectively on good government and reform programs than on patronage. This type of appeal can be termed intangible as opposed to tangible.[7] Tangible appeals are more widely used in the core area and inner zone where the electorate has a low per-capita income and material benefits have real value. As the wife of one machine committeeman put it, "The system for becoming a leader is based on the number of favors a politician can do for the people in his ward. Needy people can't turn to their bank account, and they're appreciative of small things. In a silk-stocking ward, there's not much a politician can do except keep the streets clean. The people don't need small favors and so they have a different kind of politician."[8] Thus, political support in the inner zone is maintained by a system of carefully distributed city jobs and local favors. Even

---

6 Harold F. Gosnell, *Machine Politics: Chicago Model* (Chicago, 1937). For a colorful and informative portrait of one such ward, see William Braden and Art Petacque, "The Wayward First Ward," *Chicago Sunday Sun-Times*, February 10, 1963.

7 This distinction is based upon the discussion of material and immaterial incentives in Chester I. Barnard, *The Functions of the Executive* (Cambridge, 1956), pp. 142–160.

8 Mrs. Florence Pacelli, quoted in Braden and Petacque, *op. cit.* Another ward committeeman said, "What I look for in a prospective captain is a young person—man or woman—who is interested in getting some material return out of his political activity. I much prefer this type to the type that is enthused about the 'party cause' or all 'hot' on a particular issue. Enthusiasm for causes is shortlived, but the necessity of making a living is permanent." Meyerson and Banfield, *op. cit.*, pp. 70–71.

retribution of a tangible nature can be, and is, employed—fire inspections, police investigations (or lack thereof), and city ordinance enforcement.

The danger of adopting any one approach is that it may well boomerang on its originator. A politician's adoption of a particular appeal for one area may well create repercussions in other wards throughout the city. Consequently, the politician must weigh the relative areal benefits he will receive against the drawbacks incurred. In some situations, the methods of obtaining support in different zones is not irreconcilable. A particular appeal which generates nearly maximum support in one area may simultaneously appeal to a certain strata or segment in another. A controversial political issue recently resolved in Chicago exemplifies some of the spatial overtones of public decision-making.

Since the establishment of the Chicago Undergraduate Division of the University of Illinois in 1946, there has been considerable interest in establishing a Chicago campus. The subsequent struggle over the location of the campus reveals the interplay of geography and politics in public decision-making. Miller Meadows, a county forest preserve in a western suburbs, was one of the earliest sites under serious consideration. Strongly recommended by a real estate research organization which had been hired to recommend sites, its chief advantages were that it was inexpensive ($.29 per foot with a total cost of $3 million) and had reasonable accessibility (55.4 per cent of the potential students were only an hour away by public transportation). Furthermore, Miller Meadows boasted the added attraction of scenic beauty. On June 27, 1956, in the face of powerful opposition from the Advisory Committee of the Board of Forest Preserve Commissioners, the Board of Trustees of the University of Illinois selected Miller Meadows as the site for the new campus.

Legal difficulties and political opposition persistently hamstrung plans for this location, however, so that in early 1959 the Board of Trustees concluded that the adjacent Riverside Golf Club should be the site. At this juncture, Mayor Daley intervened. At a meeting of the Board of Trustees on February 23, 1959, he announced that the City of Chicago would defray any extraordinary cost arising out of the selection of alternative sites in Chicago as compared with the cost of the Riverside Golf Club location. In effect, this action allowed for a large number of alternative sites which were formerly economically unfeasible. A proposal to use Meigs Field was rejected because the city wanted to retain its services as an airport. When the Board of Trustees selected Garfield Park, Mayor Daley again countered with a successful proposal to locate the campus on Chicago's near west side.

In terms of political benefits, the near west side location possessed several important advantages. Strong support for this site was provided by local business interests, such as Sears-Roebuck Company, whose main plant was threatened by neighborhood deterioration. Second, inhabitants of the core area and inner zone gained the advantage of a sizable new source of employment and ease of accessibility for attending the University. Finally, the approved plan pleased many voters in the frontier zone of competition and the outer zone because the plan included an extensive urban renewal and conservation plan which would eliminate the city's worst slum district and supplant it with an intellectual center. Moreover, two-thirds of the financing necessary for the project would be provided by federal sources.

Mayor Daley's adroit political maneuverings serve to illustrate the effectiveness of the politician's tools. To obtain a favorable decision on his proposal of the near west side site, his administration took the following actions. First, the city arranged for the University to secure more than twice the amount of frontage along the Congress Expressway than was originally planned (Fig. 8). In addition, elimination of a portion of the site originally proposed prevented the campus from being split by a major thoroughfare. Second, the city administration and the Chicago Land Clearance Commission pledged a new urban renewal program for the provision of new private apartment buildings in the area. Third, Mayor Daley guaranteed that city housing agencies would "push" a large community conservation program to the west of the campus. Finally, Mayor Daley's proposal conveniently received support when prominent business and civic groups announced that the city would contest the legality of the alternative area (Garfield Park). A visible grain of truth can be found in the angry remark of Sam K. Lenin, President of the Garfield Park Chamber of Commerce. "Our Garfield Park site has been overpowered by the downtown money interests and outmaneuvered by the Chicago politicians."[9]

While the politician is concerned with the potential voting capacity of a particular area, he must also consider its flexibility. If one ward is relatively inflexible, the politician can profitably risk alienating some of his support there in order to realize larger gains in another, more flexible ward. An examination by ward of zonal voting characteristics for all three elections affords some understanding of the variation among wards. It was found that the frontier zone of competition showed greater flexibility than the inner zone and core area.

The significance of this flexibility is illustrated in the 1959 election. Mayor Daley mobilized the Democratic machine to its fullest capacity and produced an overwhelming endorsement of his administration. In so doing, he gathered the support of the usually recalcitrant opposition press, voluntary associations, prominent business and civic leaders, and other typically Republican groups. It is not insignificant that his most impressive gains occurred in the zone of competition, not in the inner zone and core area (Fig. 4). In fact, some wards of the inner zone betrayed signs of a possible upper voting limit.

Another variation among voting zones may be related to the different types of appeals made. In the inner zone, rigid party control through patronage compels the ward alderman to toe the line. In the outer zones, however, the

9 *Chicago Daily Tribune*, February 11, 1961.

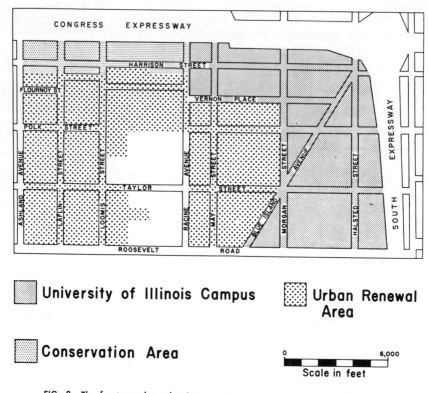

University of Illinois Campus   Urban Renewal Area

Conservation Area

0   6,000
Scale in feet

FIG. 8 The frontage along the Congress Expressway represents more than twice the amount than was originally planned. Source: Community Conservation Board, City of Chicago.

alderman is less dependent upon the political machine for patronage votes and more dependent upon his ability to appeal to mass media and local voters. Thus, there may well be a weakening of party loyalties in various areas which will confront the city-wide politician with labyrinthine problems. By garnering more total votes through intangible appeals, he is less and less likely to have a loyal and disciplined party of aldermen.

The spatial aspects of politics are implicit in a number of other city issues. For example, Mayor Daley is appointing more and more "blue-ribbon" candidates to public office, Police Superintendent Wilson being one the more recent of a large number of academic and professional figures. With every "blue-ribbon" appointment, one more patronage job, and perhaps indirectly more, is lost to the party. Another issue is the entire activity of urban planning and urban renewal. Urban planning receives much of its impetus, drive, and personnel from the frontier zone of competition and the outer zone, while the core area and inner zone often vehemently oppose it. The fact remains, however, that city politicians are increasingly recognizing the advantage of city planning in assembling and maintaining political support.[10] Doubtlessly, this is one important reason why the 1951–1961 decade has witnessed more political support for planning than have past decades, even though the cultural background of the politician himself may motivate him to oppose the general philosophy embodied in urban planning.

---

10 See Norton Long, "Planning and Politics in Urban Development," *Journ. of the Amer. Inst. of Planners*, Vol. 20 (1959), pp. 163–169.

ROBERT A. NISBET

The Political Community

From Rousseau comes most of the intellectual devotion to the State that has made the political mentality so influential in social and moral thought during the past century and a half. "I had come to see," he wrote in his *Confessions*, "that everything was radically connected with politics, and that however one proceeded, no people would be other than the nature of its government made it." And in his discourse on *Political Economy*, he declared: "If it is good to know how to deal with men as they are, it is much better to make them what there is need that they should be. The most absolute authority is that which penetrates into a man's inmost being, and concerns itself no less with his will than with his actions. . . . Make men, therefore, if you would command men: if you would have them obedient to the laws, make them love the laws, and then they will need only to know what is their duty to do it. . . . If you would have the General Will accomplished, bring all the particular wills into conformity with it; in other words, as virtue is nothing more than this conformity of the particular wills with the General Will, establish the reign of virtue."

Establish the reign of virtue! This was the moral imperative that was to capture the visions of men of good will everywhere in nineteenth-century Western Europe. But establish it how? Establish it through the sovereign power of the State! Man is born free and good, yet everywhere he lies fettered and corrupt, the product of repressive institutions. Not through kinship, class, church, or association can man be freed, for these are the very chains upon his existence. Only by entering into the perfect *State* and subordinating himself completely to its collective will will it be possible for man to escape the torments and insecurities and dissensions of ordinary society. The redemptive

---

Abridged from *Community and Power* (originally published as *The Quest for Community*) by Robert A. Nisbet. Copyright 1953 by Oxford University Press, Inc. Reprinted by permission.

power of the sovereign State—this was Rousseau's burning slogan for the modern world.

In ancient Athens the State had come to take on this guise of community during the period following the disastrous wars with Sparta. Many a reflective mind in that dark period could see in the intensification of the political bond among individuals the sole hope for the recovery of order in the *polis*, for the establishment of a new stability that would forever dispense with the old, but now distracting, ties of family, class, and association. Plato was but one of the more enlightened of those who saw in the power of the State not repressive force but the very basis of moral life, the prime source of true individuality and virtue. In Plato's view, the State, properly conceived, was the most holy of sanctuaries, a refuge from the torments, frustrations, and iniquities that had come to plague Athens as the consequence of spiritual factionalism. "Let this then be the law," declared Plato in *The Laws*: "no one shall possess shrines of the gods in private houses, and he who performs any sacred rites not publicly authorized, shall be informed against to the guardians of the law." Spiritual faith and the State must be as one, else there will be incessant conflict between the two, and man will be, even as he now is, torn by uncertainty and doubt.

It is not surprising to learn from Rousseau that, of all influences upon his mind, Plato's was greatest. In the visions of both philosophers we are given a political structure that is nothing less than community itself, with all its social and spiritual anodynes. In the warming atmosphere of the benign, omnicompetent State man will be able to discard his distractive, conflict-engendering social allegiances. Then, freed of old burdens, will he find surcease from uncertainty and disquiet. He will know at last the meaning of secure status, clear function, and ineffable spiritual release. He will know these in the pure State.

After Rousseau, the State would be regarded by many men as the most implicative of all forms of association. Inevitably the charms of kinship, religion, and cultural association would pale before the brilliance of the new State. No longer would the political relationship be regarded as but *one* of society's bonds. It would be seen as synonymous with society, as the culmination of man's long struggle for a just social order. The new State would be more than an abstract legal framework of rights and duties. It would be community itself, the Political Community.

What is the political community? It is an idea system, and, I believe, the most potent of all idea systems in the complex nineteenth century. We shall not often find it in its fullness in the writings of any single person or in any single pattern of events in the nineteenth century. We must await the twentieth-century totalitarian State for the full realization of the idea of the political community. But we are nevertheless able to descry this system of ideas running throughout the nineteenth century in one or another form, in one or another degree of intensity. It is a kind of brooding omnipresence, giving force and direction to a variety of visions of social redemption. It touches the foundations of modern popular democracy, especially on the Continent; it gives sub-

stance and appeal to cultural nationalism; it becomes the context of the socialist movement before the century is ended; it becomes the matrix of the most
successful schemes of humanitarianism; it becomes, at times, the context of
Christianity itself. In a diversity of ways we see the idea of the political community making its inroads into the minds and acts of the new men of power in
the nineteenth century, the men for whom power was but the other face of
humanitarian redemption.

Fundamental to the political community is the belief that the normal
plurality of authorities and functions in society must be supplanted by a unity
of authority and function arising from the monistic State. The power of the
State must become the context of the realization of all man's aspirations, even
as the Church formed this context in the Middle Ages. There is, second, the
view of the people, not as diversified members of social groups and cultural
associations, but as an aggregate of atomized particles needing the absolute
State for protection and security. Man, in this view, is a timid, insecure, and
lonely being apart from his membership in the omnipotent, all-benign State.
The power of the State must not be regarded as repressive force. What separates the political community from earlier forms and visions of the State is its
insistence that only through absolute, unitary power can man find freedom,
equality, fraternity, and virtue. Freedom becomes freedom *from* other institutions, freedom *to* participate in Leviathan. Equality is the mechanical equivalence of talents, functions, and ideas engendered by the State's leveling influence upon all other associations and statuses, and enforced by the iron mold of
law. Fraternity is the bond of political brotherhood that must rule out, as its
very condition, all other brotherhoods based upon interest, place, or belief.
And virtue, what is it? Virtue is, in Rousseau's words, "nothing more than the
conformity of the particular wills with the General Will." Power is not power
if but formed in the alembic of political imagination; it is freedom, equality,
brotherhood, virtue. It is community.

In practical terms, what Rousseau's ideas pointed toward was a two-fold
emancipation: first, of the individual from his traditional associative chains;
and, second, of the State itself from the mass of feudal customs which, everywhere, limited its real efficacy. For only by extricating the State, the *ideal* State,
from the mass of intrusive localisms and partial allegiances descended from
the past would it be possible to use its power to emancipate man from these
same prejudices and entanglements. What was demanded was a revolutionary
liaison between the individual and the omnipotent State. Between the challenge of atomistic individualism and the militant power of the central State,
dedicated to human welfare, it would be possible to grind into dust all intermediate associations, reminders and nourishers of the despised past.

It was in a real sense a necessary affinity, for all major social movements are
a combination of radical individualism and authoritarian affirmation. New
structures of belief and authority cannot be introduced until human beings have

been alienated, in one way or another, from the old. Hence the insistence upon individual release from old institutions and social groups, and upon man as the natural embodiment of all virtues. Hence also the emphasis upon the State as the area of reassimilation and upon political power as the instrument.

This affinity between social individualism and political power is, I believe, the most fateful fact of the eighteenth and nineteenth centuries. It forms the very substance of the ideology of the political community; it comprehends the majority of ideas of political humanitarianism. It is impossible to understand the massive concentrations of political power in the twentieth century, appearing so paradoxically, as it has seemed, right after a century and a half of individualism in economics and morals, unless we see clearly the close relationship that prevailed all through the nineteenth century between individualism and State power and between both of these together and the general weakening of the area of association that lies intermediate to man and the State.

It was the French Revolution, following hard upon Rousseau's clamant prophecy, that served to translate so many of the adjurations of the *Social Contact* into hard administrative reality and to bring forcibly to the attention of intellectuals throughout Europe the new perspective of redemption through political power. However minor Rousseau's influence may have been upon the *causes* of the Revolution, his influence upon the *course* of the Revolution became great. "Hitherto," wrote Sébastien Mercier in 1791, "the *Social Contract* was the least read of all Rousseau's works. Now, every citizen broods over it and learns it by heart."[1]

The tremendous value of the *Social Contract* to the men of the Revolution lay, first, in its extraordinary flexibility. It could serve the authoritarian demands of the Revolution as easily as it could provide an apologetics for the corrosive individualism of the early phases. But its greatest value lay in its ingenious camouflaging of power with the rhetoric of freedom, and in its investment of political power with the essence of religious community. Rousseau had succeeded in *spiritualizing* the political relationship and, in so doing, had removed the State conceptually from the ordinary realm of political intrigue and force. "How are you to know a Republican?" asked Barère late in the Revolution. His answer to his own question might have been taken from the chapter on the Civil Religion. You will know him when he speaks of his country with "religious sentiment" and of the sovereign people with "religious devotion."[2]

. . .

What the spectacle of the Revolution emphasized to many minds in the

---

[1] Quoted by C.E. Vaughan in his Preface to his edition of *Du Contrat Social* (Manchester, 1918).

[2] Cited by C.J.H. Hayes, *Historical Evolution of Modern Nationalism* (New York, 1931), p. 68.

decades following it was a truth known to every great political leader from
Cleisthenes to Napoleon. The State that would become powerful must become
identified with the people; it must become *absolutely* identified. The State
becomes powerful not by virtue of what it takes from the individual but by
virtue of what it takes from the spiritual and social associations which compete
with it for men's devotions.

    It is in these terms, indeed, that the phenomenon of nineteenth-century
nationalism becomes intelligible. All serious students of nationalism are agreed
that, in its contemporary form, nationalism is the child of the French
Revolution.

    ... The loss of older statuses could not help but turn men's eyes to the
status of *citizen*. The loss of older memberships could not help but be followed
by a growing willingness to make the State itself the primary area of association. "A State becomes a nation," A.D. Lindsay has correctly written, "when
instead of its members being primarily divided between sovereign and subjects,
government and citizenship become a common task, demanding not passive
citizenship but active cooperation from all."[3]

    The modern State is not the offspring of the nation. It is far more correct
and relevant to say that the nation is the offspring of the State. Nationalism, in
the form that has become triumphant in the last century and a half, is no mere
development, as is so often argued, of folk ties of tribe, locality, or region.
Doubtless the emotional elements which earlier populations found in kinship
and region, in local community and church, have been transferred, so to speak,
to the nation. But the logical continuity of symbolic transference should not be
made the basis of assuming any continuity of social development in this
instance. Modern nationalism, as a state of mind and cultural reality, cannot
be understood except in terms of the weakening and destruction of earlier
bonds, and of the attachment to the political State of new emotional loyalties
and identifications.[4] It cannot be understood, that is, apart from those rents and
clefts in the traditional structure of human loyalties, caused by economic and
social dislocation, which left widening masses of human beings in a kind of
psychological vacuum. And it cannot be understood except in terms of the ever
more hypnotic appeal exercised by the political association in the hands of men
who saw the State as the new and final enclosure of human life and purpose.

    ... The medieval Church had been strong because of what it did for its
members. The State must do no less. The medieval Church had sought to bind
man spiritually as well as economically, culturally as well as politically, into an
undiversified unity of membership that would leave nothing outside it. The
State must similarly seek to make itself the harmonious co-ordinator of all
human interests, being no less sensitive to the economic, the charitable, the
communal, and the symbolic needs of the people.

---

    3 *The Modern Democratic State* (London, 1943), Vol. 1, p. 151.
    4 Hans Kohn in his *Idea of Nationalism* (New York, 1944) has made emphatic this relation
of nationalism to earlier forms of social unity. See his comments in the Introduction.

Thus Fichte, in the addresses he gave at Berlin after Napoleon had humbled the Prussian people, made unquestionably clear the relation that must prevail between a government and its people if the government would be powerful. The State must assume humanitarian and educative functions; it must create a meaningful ethical bond between itself and the people. In every previous system of government, Fichte declared, "the interest of the individual in the community was linked to his interest in himself by ties, which at some point were so completely severed that his interest in the community absolutely ceased." What is now necessary is "to find an entirely different and new binding tie that is superior to fear and hope, in order to link up the welfare of her whole being with the self-interest of each of her members." This new tie would be the State based upon the people, the political community, successor to the Church in its inclusion of all human needs, desires, and hopes. If only we have the will to create such an order, Fichte concluded, we shall be able to produce "an army such as no age has yet seen."[5]

The motives behind the vision of the nation-community could vary from militarism to humanitarianism to those of what Matthew Arnold in England called sweetness and light. For in the structure of the political State, properly conceived, Arnold could see the only real hope for the cultural redemption of Western society. For a long time the "strong feudal habits of subordination and deference continued to tell," but now "the modern spirit has almost entirely dissolved these habits, and the anarchical tendency of our worship of freedom in and for itself . . . is becoming very manifest." What, then, "if we tried to rise above the idea of class to the idea of the whole community, *the State*, and to find our centre of light and authority there? . . . We want an authority, and we find nothing but jealous classes, checks, and deadlock; culture suggests the idea of *the State*."[6]

The Revolution was distinguished by the triumph of the political relationship and of man's political status over all other relationships and statuses in society. Thus the term "citizen" reached a degree of prestige that threatened all older titles of status in society, and political functionaries enjoyed a new merit. There were many conflicts and resistances, of course. The edicts and enthusiasms of Paris were not easily communicated to other parts of France. But we may say, nevertheless, that the most momentous aspect of the Revolution, in psychological terms, was its systematic depreciation of all the statuses that had characterized traditional French society, and its calculated celebration of the personal qualities and statuses that arose from man's membership in the

---

5 *Addresses to the German Nation*, translated by R. Jones and G. Turnbull (Chicago, 1922), pp. 10, 11, and 190.

6 *Culture and Anarchy*, edited by J. Dover Wilson (Cambridge University Press, 1935), pp. 76, 94, and 96. "We have not the notion," Arnold laments, "so familiar on the continent and to antiquity, of *the State*—the nation in its collective and corporate character, entrusted with stringent powers for the general advantage, and controlling individual wills in the name of an interest wider than that of individuals."

political order. Not economic man, nor religious man, but *political* man was, in a very important sense, the key figure of the Revolution.

. . .

In power lay popular unity. But this was an old reflection. What was now so exhilarating was the realization that in political power lay, also, *equality, virtue, justice,* and *freedom* itself. To use the absolute, centralized power of the State against religious and economic tyrannies—was this not a transcendent way of making men good and free? All of this Rousseau had argued brilliantly. All of this had been demonstrated to the admiring gaze of the nationalist, the democrat, and the humanitarian alike, by the incomparable Revolution. Whatever else the Revolution may be, in the various perspectives of historical interpretation, it would be folly to overlook the fact that it was *power*—power in a form hardly known since the days of Caesar and his admiring multitudes.

"After the Revolution," Lord Acton has written, "the purpose of the continental governments formed on that pattern is not that the people should obtain security for freedom, but participation in power." The characterization is apt, but it is highly important to see that, for a growing number of intellectuals and politicians, and even for the masses themselves, such participation in power, with its attendant properties of centralized administration, carried with it implications of joyous release. Of all the subtle alchemies of thought performed by Rousseau and by the guiding spirits of the Revolution, the subtlest and the most potent was the conversion of absolute power into the illusion of mass freedom.

What was new, and profoundly exciting, was the sense of achieving freedom through absolute identification with the will of the majority, a will expressed relentlessly and single-mindedly by the government. During the Revolution freedom had come to mean, increasingly, the freedom not so much of individuals taken singly or in small groups but of the *whole* people. The emancipation of the entire people from the tyrannies exercised by church, class, family, and local custom—this was the most potent and revolutionary conception of freedom. And the key to the reality of this conception of freedom lay in the centralizing, absorptive work of governments. When Robespierre announced to the National Convention that the will of the Jacobins was the General Will, he could have cited Rousseau in support of his position. After all, were not the Jacobins motivated by justice? Were they not dedicated to the common weal, to virtue. Were they not, in Rousseau's words, "well-intentioned"? And who else but Rousseau could have prepared the minds of the Convention to accept credulously Robespierre's ringing declaration that the "government of the Revolution is but the despotism of freedom against tyranny"?

This conception of mass participation in power, with its corollary of mass power as mass freedom, has proved to be the most revolutionary of all political doctrines in the modern world. If the power of government is but the reflection of the will of the masses, or, rather, of the interests of the masses, and if the General Will is merely a means of forcing individuals to be free, then does it not follow, as the Jacobins held, that every increase in governmental authority, every increase of *political*—at the expense of religious, economic, and kinship—authority is, *ex hypothesi*, an increase in real freedom for the people?

. . .

We are familiar enough with the idea of the political community, with its elements of redemptive power, in the writings of the nineteenth-century zealots of nationalism. The names of such men as Jahn, Wagner, Mazzini, Maurras, and Treitschke come readily to mind. But the major channels of the idea of the political community are to be found in writings and movements which were not, in intent at least, nationalist at all. The idea of political power was most successfully disseminated, not by the writers who saw national power itself as the primary goal, but by those who saw in political power the sole means of realizing cherished social and moral objectives connected with popular welfare.

This is the point that is crucial. The modern State and the whole ideology of the political community have become significant, influential, not through worship of naked power but because of the promise which seemed to lie in political power for the salvation of man—for the attainment of moral goals that had eluded mankind for thousands of years. Not to the writings of power worshipers or reactionaries must we look for the source and diffusion of the ideology of the political community in the nineteenth century, but to those men who, like Bentham and Marx, were eminently rational and whose goals were the release of mankind from its long bondage to oppression, misery, and ignorance.

. . .

The State as conceived by Bentham, Halévy has written, "is a machine so well constructed that every individual, taken individually, cannot for one instant escape from the control of all the individuals taken collectively."[7] Here, indeed, is the essence of the General Will. But, as in the writings of Rousseau and in the speeches of the Jacobins, what is central and directive is not the primary worship of power. Rather, it is the principle, so fundamental in Bentham's political theory, that only *because* of the control exerted collectively is it possible for each individual to be taken individually. Only through the elevation of political power to the point where it supersedes all other powers and constraints, to the point where it becomes the sole power in men's lives, is it possible to create that scene of rational impersonality demanded by the needs of individual liberation. It is no contradiction to be reminded of Bentham's

---

[7] The dependence of my treatment of Bentham upon Halévy's *The Growth of Philosophical Radicalism* will be apparent to all who have read that great work. In addition I must express my appreciation to the anonymous writer in the *Times Literary Supplement* (21 February 1948) for his keen analysis of Bentham.

hostility to many of the existent political and administrative structures of his time, of his incessant zeal for the liberation of individual reason. Granted the supremacy of the individual in Bentham's ethics and granted also his relentless opposition to many aspects of the English State, his larger system of thought nevertheless seems unified only when we see that the prime object of his endeavors is the discovery of that political system in which such irrationalities as the common law and the rotten boroughs can be eliminated, and in which the individual, emancipated from all his institutional fetters, can achieve the life of perfect reason.

Quite apart from his early reflections on the possible moral achievements of political legislation, the idea of the centralized administrative State logically becomes central in Bentham's thought when he finds it necessary to supplement "natural" and "sympathetic" identifications of interest by recourse to what he calls "artificial" identification. The first two are based upon the principles of hedonistic psychology. But the third is the direct reflection of the vision of the political community, the community rationally and impersonally organized, omnipotent and monolithic. It may be true, as some unkind critic has suggested, that whereas Bentham began with self-evident natural interest he was forced to conclude with the policeman and the penitentiary. But the fact remains that for Bentham, as for Rousseau, the policeman and penitentiary were but means of "forcing individuals to be free."

Behind Bentham's constantly developing reliance upon the omnipotent, benevolent political community lay always the vision of a society in which men would be freed from the tyrannous and stultifying traditions that had come down from the Middle Ages. Hence his almost fanatical desire to see exterminated not only the rotten borough and the functionless aristocracy but also the Inns of Court, the Church, the common law, the semi-public corporations, such universities as Oxford and Cambridge, the jury system, the parish, and even the traditional family.

. . .

. . . In the writings of Karl Marx the vision of omnicompetent power in the service of human welfare becomes almost blinding. Despite the predominantly economic cast of Marx's analysis of society and his philosophy of history, there is much reason for insisting that Marx's greatest importance lies in his willingness to translate the moral values of socialism into the structure of the centralized, political power. Whatever else Marxian socialism may be in ethical and historical terms, it is plainly a significant chapter in the history of political collectivism.[8]

The extreme collectivism and centralization of contemporary Soviet Russia

---

[8] This section on Marx owes much to A.D. Lindsay's essay, *Karl Marx's Capital* (Oxford University Press, 1925), to the recent work by Martin Buber, *Paths in Utopia* (London, 1949), and to some of the writings of the nineteenth-century anarchists.

are by no means distortions and corruptions of the Marxian philosophy of power. They are clearly rooted in the ideas of strategy and tactics that Marx and Engels were led to formulate in anticipation of revolutionary demands. The anarchists and French socialists against whom Marx and his followers fought so savagely were well aware of this aspect of Marx, and the words Bakunin first applied to Rousseau—"the true founder of modern reaction"— were as often applied to Marx himself by later anarchists.

Much has been made of the asserted Marxian disavowal of the State. It has been widely supposed that Marx held the State in disdain, that he regarded it and its power as a purely transitory phenomenon, dependent wholly upon the economics of exploitation. With the disappearance of capitalist classes, there would then be no need for the anachronism of the State and its machinery. Engels declared that "the authority of the government over persons will be replaced by the administration of things and the direction of the processes of production. The state will not be 'abolished,' it will wither away." But Engels prefaces these words with the statement: "The first act of a State in which it really acts as the representative of the whole of society, namely the assumption of control over the means of production on behalf of society, is also its last official act as a State." From this curious piece of reasoning it would appear that what disappears is not the State, in any sense that has had significance since the eighteenth century, but a special form of *government*. What Marx and Engels chose to label the "state" was actually a form of government that the French Revolution and subsequent nationalism had made largely obsolete —the simple vertical relation between an institutionally remote government and the people.

The unpopularity of the idea of the State, especially among the anarchists and the followers of Proudhon, led Marx and Engels, as a means of broadening their own popular following, to borrow some of the terminology of the anarchists, all the while combating vigorously both the anarchist and syndicalist movements. The "withering away of the State" was in part a terminological trick by which to steal some of the anarchist thunder and, in part, a piece of self-deception which resulted from confusion between the legal state as a centralized structure of power, and a particular form of state regarded for tactical and definitional purposes as part of the exploitative apparatus of the capitalists. As more than one student of Marx has been forced to conclude, Marx was never above letting tactical necessities influence his description of the universe itself.

Marx's own summary toward the end of the *Manifesto* of action to be taken and of the political significance of that action is instructive in this connection. "The proletariat will use its political supremacy to wrest by degrees all capital from the bourgeois, to centralize all instruments of production in the hands of the State, i.e., of the proletariat organized as the ruling class; and to increase the total of productive forces as rapidly as possible." In his list of the steps that will be a necessary part of the Revolution in "the most advanced" countries, the following are included: "Centralization of credit in the hands of the State, by means of a national bank with State capital and an exclusive monopoly. Centralization of the means of communication and transport in the hands of the State. Extension of factories and instruments of production owned by the State; the bringing into cultivation of waste lands, and their improvement. . . . Establishment of industrial armies, especially for agriculture. Combination of agriculture with manufacturing industries; gradual abolition of the distinction between town and country, by a more equal distribution of population over the country. . . . When in the course of development, class distinctions have disappeared, and all production has been concentrated in the hands of a vast association of the whole nation, the public power will lose its political character. Political power, properly so called, is merely the organized power of one class for oppressing another. . . ."

If we consider the State in terms which were made perfectly familiar by Hobbes and Rousseau and in light of the institutional realities of organized political government in the nineteenth century the final words have an almost naïve ring. It would appear in fact that what is terminated is not the State but merely "the organized power of one class for oppressing another"—a quite different thing. To suppose that the public power would lose its political character when all production had been "concentrated in the hands of a vast association of the whole nation" was to miss entirely the nature of the political State that was developing in Marx's own time. Subsequent socialists have been all too willing to follow the reasoning by which a powerful, centralized, "vast association of the whole nation" could be declared bereft of political character simply because, like Rousseau's General Will, it reflected in theory no domination by a privileged social class minority. Marx's goal is the political community, centralized and absolute.

·   ·   ·

Marx had as little use as Rousseau or Robespierre for the natural pluralism of society, for the difference between town and country, for localism, for autonomous association—whether religious or economic—and for the family. For Marx, as for the Revolutionary democrats and the Philosophical Radicals, differences of locality, religion, and grouping must be abandoned in favor of a rational, centralized society. The practical result, as A.D. Lindsay has written, is that society is treated by Marx as though it had but a single center. "The smaller associations within the State are treated not as subordinate forms in which the general will finds expression but as rivals to it."

·   ·   ·

The nineteenth century has been called the Century of Great Hope. Innumerable historians have characterized its dominant qualities in the words of progress, democracy, freedom, and the liberation of reason from the shackles of superstition and ignorance. There is no need to quarrel with any of these characterizations. The nineteenth century was each and all of them. But it was something else, too, something that touched upon and, in one way or another, involved all of these moral values, something that we are only now beginning to understand clearly.

It was the century of the emergence of the political masses: masses created in widening areas by the processes of social destruction bound up with the increasing penetration of political power into all areas of society; masses created by the impact of a factory system that, in the essentials of its discipline, frequently resembled the military State itself; masses devoid, increasingly, of any hope for relief from the established, traditional institutions of society— family, church, and class.

Between the State and the masses there developed a bond, an affinity, which however expressed—in nationalism, unitary democracy, or in Marxian socialism —made the political community the most luminous of all visions. In it lay salvation from economic misery and oppression. In it lay a new kind of liberty, equality, and fraternity. In it lay right and justice. And in it, above all else, lay community.

What gave the vision of the political community added brilliance was the fact that so many of its elements—rational centralization of authority, the mass electorate, equality, political participation, unity, and so forth—could seem to be the elements of inexorable progress. Diversity, localism, regionalism, administrative decentralization—were not these the central elements of the despised Middle Ages, elements that were, as Michelet once insisted, being expunged remorselessly and eternally by the beneficent hand of Progress? All that did not serve the interests of the emerging new State, its unity and centralization, could be treated scornfully as unrealistic, as unprogressive, as an outcropping of the past. "Reactionary" and "Utopian" became, in equal degree, the appropriate epithets for all the ideas that did not begin with recognition of the historic inevitability of the political community and its dominant values.

KARL W. DEUTSCH

Nationalism and
Social Communication

POPULATION CLUSTER, COUNTRY, AND ECUMENE

Cultures and societies appear to the human geographer as settlement patterns on a map, connected by natural or man-made facilities for transportation. The effects of the facts of physical geography vary with the technologies and social institutions which are brought to bear on them: whether an ocean functions as a barrier or as a highway may depend on the technology of shipping and of the resources allocated in a given society to its development. In this fashion the barriers of the Swiss Alpine passes were turned into major highways in the thirteenth century by improvements in roads and bridges.

Regions of settlement are held together by facilities for transportation and separated from each other by relative discontinuities in their effectiveness. Settlement patterns are thus found to consist of local and regional clusters. . . . Such clusters and transportation facilities are not evenly distributed. Within each "country" of the political geographer there stands out a nuclear area or ecumene: "The ecumene of each state may be thought of as the region or regions which are well peopled and given internal coherence by a network of transportation lines. It is distinguished from sparsely populated or uninhabited parts of the same country, penetrated only here and there by routes."[1] Related to this approach is the human geographer's notion of a capital city or principal

Nationalism and Social Communication (Cambridge: M.I.T. Press; New York: John Wiley & Sons, Inc., 1953), pp. 23–30, 70–74, 78–70. Reprinted by permission.

[1] D. Whittlesey, *The Earth and the State* (New York: Holt, Rinehart and Winston, Inc., 1939), p. 10: "The term 'Ecumene' is Mark Jefferson's who defines it as the land within ten miles of a railroad. . . . To define the ecumene as it exists in all parts of the earth and in the long view of human history, every type of transportation route in being should be included. The zones in effective contact with the routes, be they wide or narrow, in conjunction with the areas of densest population, approximate the ecumene. . . ."

456

city, which need not be identical with the administrative center of the area where it in fact predominates.

A variety of this is found in the relationship of key cities or key areas or nodal areas to the often much larger regions of hinterland which they may dominate in terms of transportation, strategy, or economics. Typical examples of key areas are harbors and river mouths which may dominate much larger river valleys in matters of trade and transportation. Control of such key areas by members of one nationality gives them power over the lives of the members of other peoples in the hinterland so that the simpler notions of "national self-determination" become difficult to apply.[2]

Units of human geography are bounded by relative discontinuities in settlement and transportation; transportation discontinuities involve not necessarily a drop in the quality and number of roads but rather in the density of traffic moving over them, although in practice the two will often be related. Nevertheless, each discontinuity will apply to some particular operation or group of operations; we may expect to find, therefore, not sharp and simple borders but rather bundles of borders; if enough of these are close enough together we may speak of boundary zones.

Such zones may bound a country, that is, a relatively larger area within which observation shows a markedly greater degree of transportation and economic interdependence than with any other area.[3] Several such countries may show markedly greater interdependence among each other than with the rest. To these sometimes the term "great space" (*Grossraum*) has been applied. There is currently a significant degree of transportation interdependence between the most developed areas all over the world, and the concepts of world transportation and "world ecumene" are therefore meaningful.[4]

SPEECH COMMUNITIES, STANDARD LANGUAGE, AND DIALECTS

Where the anthropologist may look for communities of culture, and the human geographer for communities of transportation, the student of language deals with communities of speech. A community of language is a community of infor-

---

2 Cf. Deutsch, "Problems of Justice in International Territorial Disputes," in *Approaches to Group Understanding* (New York: Harper & Row, Publishers, 1947), p. 251.

3 G.P. de T. Glazebrook, "Nationalism and Internationalism on Canadian Waterways," *Essays in Transportation*, H.A. Innis, ed. (Toronto: University of Toronto Press, 1941), pp. 2–3.

4 "No accurate world-map superimposing transportation zones on population density has been constructed...." Whittlesey, *op. cit....* Transportation between particular areas may, of course, drop off sharply for social or political reasons, despite unchanged geographical and technological conditions. This happened in the shifts of trade routes during the Mohammedan, and later the Mongolian, Conquests; still later in the closing of Japan to foreign commerce in the Tokugawa period; and it might happen in the years to come in the "cold war" which might destroy the world ecumene for some time, much as the ecumene of the Mediterranean was destroyed for a time by the split between Moslems and Christians. Any major shift of this nature might in the turn promote some shifts in the areas of greatest density of population.

mation vehicles: most words of the language, or at least the words most frequently used, will be recognized and spoken by most members of the group,
with identical or closely similar denotations. As regards less frequently used
words, or their connotations (i.e., the amount and kind of memories evoked by
them), the effects of the community of language may be modified by the effects
of the community of culture. Ties of transportation, economic intercourse,
social stratification, cultural similarity, and similarity in already existing speech
habits, as well as relative barriers and discontinuities in all these respects will
all have their effects in determining what the actual speech community will
be at any one time. Philologists have imagined maps of such speech communities, on which each speech contact would be represented by a single line, so
as to show their relative densities of speech traffic over a period of time. Such
a map could perhaps be accurately constructed for small samples, using such
measuring techniques as the concept of message unit from communications
research. However, it might be important to distinguish between several major
kinds of speech communication: the number of times a newsboy says "five
cents" to his customers is not equivalent to the number of times he talks things
over with his friends.

Within almost any major language we find regional divisions into dialects
and social divisions of linguistic stratification. We find again language centers
and leading groups; these groups in these centers set the standard language
both in its colloquial and its written form. Thus Francien, the dialect of the
Ile de France and to some extent of the Champagne region, came to set the
national standards for both literary and colloquial French, particularly after
the influence of the Langue d'Oc dialect had been reduced by relative economic
decline and military defeat of these regions in the thirteenth century. . . .

Examples of the manner in which the speech habits of the linguistic centers
and elites have been imposed on a variety of local dialects, and have thus
brought about a sharper delimitation of language areas, have been cited from
Romance philology, from the history of Dutch, and from the history of Serbian
and Bulgarian.[5]

The history of China offers a striking example of the interplay of the geographic distribution of fertile land, waterways, and settlement patterns on the
one hand with early language centers and later patterns of linguistic integration and differentiation on the other. Standard Mandarin Chinese as well as
its related spoken dialects seems to have been derived from the language of the
populous Northwest, which was settled early and connected by relatively efficient transport facilities with other parts of China. The separate spoken dialect
or language of the Canton region developed in an area which was well connected internally, but marked off in just these respects from most of the rest of
the country. . . .[6]

Language is preserved by special techniques and institutions: language

---

5 H. Paul, *Principles of the History of Language* (New York, 1889), pp. 30–31, 34–35.
6 Cf. Percy M. Roxby, "China as an Entity," *Geography* (March 1934), pp. 1–20.

standards, grammars, dictionaries, schools, printing, and radio. Yet it continues to change. Where a previous community of intercourse has ceased to exist, a formerly common language will slowly develop into increasingly different dialects which may in the end become mutually incomprehensible. Language communities are therefore bounded by barriers of dialect and language, geographically between regions, sociologically between strata, and historically in time. Attempts have been made to grade the effectiveness of language barriers to communication.[7]

Several different standard languages may belong to a language family, although this has little practical effect on communication between the more remote members of such families. A "world language" has been often proposed, and actual language for specialized types of communication over entire cultural areas have existed in the past, such as Latin or Church Slavic. In the most successful case of such unification, that of the Arabic-speaking peoples, the original "foreign" language eventually has been adopted by the descendants of a number of "non-Arab" peoples in North Africa and the Near East.

. . .

The community which permits a common history to be experienced as common, is a community of complementary habits and facilities of communication. It requires, so to speak, equipment for a job. This job consists in the storage, recall, transmission, recombination, and reapplication of relatively wide ranges of information; and the "equipment" consists in such learned memories, symbols, habits, operating preferences, and facilities as will in fact be sufficiently complementary to permit the performance of these functions. *A larger group of persons linked by such complementary habits and facilities of communication we may call a people.*

The test of *complementarity* of any set of communications equipment is communicative effectiveness. How fast and how accurately do messages get through? How complex and voluminous is the information that can be so transmitted? How effectively are operations on one part of the net transmitted to another? The extent of complementarity for any set of facilities, or any community, will be indicated by the answers to these questions.

Complementarity or communicative efficiency is a function, an overall result. The same or a closely similar result may be reached by several different combinations of elements, or even by the entire replacement of some elements by others. This is obvious in the simple examples from communications engineering which were cited earlier, but it also applies to social communication. The communicative facilities of a society include a socially standardized system of symbols which is a language, and any number of auxiliary codes, such as alphabets, systems of writing, painting, calculating, etc. They include informa-

---

7 Stanley Rundle, *Language as a Social and Political Factor in Europe* (London: Faber & Faber Ltd., 1946), pp. 42–44 with map and table.

tion stored in the living memories, associations, habits, and preferences of its members, and in its material facilities for the storage of information, such as libraries, statutes, signposts, and the like; and a good deal more. Some of these facilities, individual and social, also deal with the treatment of information, its recall from storage or memory, its transmission and recombination to new patterns. Taken all together, they include, therefore, in particular the elements of that which anthropologists call culture. If these elements are in fact sufficiently complementary, they will add up to an integrated pattern or configuration of communicating, remembering, and acting, that is, to a culture in the sense of the citations quoted earlier in our discussion; and the individuals who have these complementary habits, vocabularies, and facilities are what we call a people.

It is now clear why all the usual descriptions of a people in terms of a community of languages, or character, or memories, or past history, are open to exception. For what counts is not the presence or absence of any single factor, but merely the presence of sufficient communication facilities with enough complementarity to produce the overall result. The Swiss may speak four different languages and still act as one people, for each of them has enough learned habits, preferences, symbols, memories, patterns of landholding and social stratification, events in history, and personal associations, all of which together permit him to communicate more effectively with other Swiss than with the speakers of his own language who belong to other peoples.[8] "I found that my German was more closely akin to the French of my (French-Swiss) friend than to the likewise German (*Ebenfallsdeutsch*) of the foreigner," says the editor of a prominent German-Swiss paper in his reminiscences. "The French-Swiss and I were using different words for the same concepts, but we understood each other. The man from Vienna and I were using the same words for different concepts, and thus we did not understand each other in the least."[9]

What is proposed here, in short, is a functional definition of nationality. Membership in a people essentially consists in wide complementarity of social communication. It consists in the ability to communicate more effectively, and over a wider range of subjects, with members of one large group than with outsiders. This overall result can be achieved by a variety of functionally equivalent arrangements.

This function of nationality differs from the old attempts to specify nationality in terms of some particular ingredient, somewhat as modern technological trends towards evaluating materials in terms of their performance differ from the older practice of evaluating materials in terms of their composition. In both cases, "composition specifications" are replaced by "performance tests," based

---

8 Cf. Max Huber, "Swiss Nationality," *Modern Political Doctrines,* Sir Alfred Zimmern, ed. (London: Oxford University Press, 1939), pp. 216–217.

9 Ernst Schuerch, *Sprachpolitische Erinnerungen* (Bern: Paul Haupt Verlag, 1943), pp. 36–37.

on more detailed analysis of the functions carried out.[10]

Peoples are held together "from within" by this communicative efficiency, the complementarity of the communicative facilities acquired by their members. Such "ethnic complementarity" is not merely subjective. At any moment, it exists as an objective fact, measurable by performance tests. Similar to a person's knowledge of a language, it is relatively independent of the whim of individuals. Only slowly can it be learned or forgotten. It is a characteristic of each individual, but it can only be exercised within the context of a group.

Ethnic complementarity, the complementarity that makes a people, can be readily distinguished by its relatively wide range from the narrow vocational complementarity which exists among members of the same profession, such as doctors or mathematicians, or members of the same vocational group, such as farmers or intellectuals. Efficient communication among engineers, artists, or stamp collectors is limited to a relatively narrow segment of their total range of activities. In most other things they do, in their childhood memories, in courtship, marriage, and parenthood, in their habits of food and drink, in games and recreation, they are far closer to mutual communication and understanding with their countrymen than with their fellow specialists in other countries.

The facts of social class may change this picture. But if and where they change it, they will do so not because of anything in the theory but because they are facts, and to the extent that they are facts. Where workers in industry are cut off from the rest of the community, from better housing on the "right side" of the railroad tracks, from conviviality and intercourse, from education and careers, from comforts and income, from security and prestige—there Disraeli's word of the "two nations . . . the rich and the poor" may express a real state of affairs. Under such conditions, men may discover more similar experiences and greater mutual understanding with their fellow workers in other countries than with their "own" well-to-do countrymen who will see them only at the servant's entrance.

At certain times and places the barriers of class may thus outweigh the ties of language, culture, and tradition. Wage earners may then deliberately seek to advance their fortunes in a competitive society by seeking international class alignments; or they may choose to press for improvement of their lot along national lines, trying to keep out cheaper foreign labor, and to secure for themselves some share in the national prosperity of their employers.

Where, on the other hand, wage earners have more ample ties with the rest of the community, and fuller opportunities, not merely in words but in substance; if they find not merely factories and slums but schools, parks, hospitals, and better housing; where they have a political and economic "stake in the country" and are accorded security and prestige, there the ties to their own

---

10 Cf. J.K. Roberts and E.L. Gordy, "Development," *Research in Industry, Its Organization and Management*, C.C. Furnas, ed. (New York: D. Van Nostrand Co. Inc., 1948), pp. 32–34.

people, to its folkways and living standards, education and tradition, will be strong in fact. There will be a greater stock of common experiences, a greater flow of social communications across class lines, more conviviality and informal social association, more vertical mobility and intermarriage, and, as a result of all these, probably far more effective complementarity of social communication within the people than across its borders. Social reforms, as Bismarck knew, many knit a people more closely; high wages, as Lenin observed, may tend to assimilate the outlook of workers to that of their middle-class compatriots; and periods of democracy and social progress, as Otto Bauer predicted, may leave different peoples more unified internally, but more sharply marked off from each other.

The critical facts of social communication and intercourse can be surveyed, tested, and to some extent measured, before political decisions must be taken. "To the blind all things are sudden."[11] But for enlightened statesmanship it should be possible to do systematically what some men, like Disraeli himself, did in a rough and ready way: to appraise the many specific channels of communication within a people, and between its different classes, so as to be able to estimate how such a group will respond to a strain. Will India's Hindus and Moslems form in the long run one nation or two, and what are the chances for an eventual reunion between India herself and Pakistan? Will French workers turn right or left in politics? With careful investigation of the elements which go into the making of these social decisions, their outcome could at least be guessed at more intelligently before policy finds itself overtaken by events.

Even where we have one people, the range and effectiveness of social communication within it may tell us how effectively it has become integrated, and how far it has advanced, in this respect, toward becoming a nation. "That universal circulation of intelligence," Arthur Young noted on the eve of the French Revolution, "which in England transmits the least vibration of feeling or alarm, with electric sensibility, from one end of the kingdom to another, and which unites in bands of connection men of similar interests and situations, has no existence in France."[12]

The notion of complementarity might be extended so as to include the actual or probable communicative efficiency of individuals over a range of different social arrangements. In this sense complementarity would be lower if it permitted efficient communication between individuals only in a very few relationships, such as, perhaps, only in the context of their familiar native village,

---

11 Alexander H. Leighton, *The Governing of Men: General Principles and Recommendations Based on Experience at a Japanese Relocation Camp* (Princeton: Princeton University Press, 1946), p. 258.

12 Arthur Young, *Travels During the Years 1787, 1788, and 1789* (London, 1792), pp. 146–147; cited in H.A. Innis, *Empire and Communication* (Oxford: Clarendon Press, 1950), p. 198. The rapid spread of the Revolution through much of France suggests that by 1789 there may already have been more effective "circulation of intelligence" among the French people than Arthur Young surmised; but the principle of his test—which he had no means of carrying through with any thoroughness—seems to have been sound enough....

or of their familiar economic institutions. Burke and Disraeli assumed such a limited type of complementarity when they prophesied that Frenchmen or Englishmen would cease to be a people if they should lose their traditional aristocratic social institutions, and that in such an event they would have to take "many a weary step" before they could regain "a true political personality."

Complementarity is greater if it permits individuals to communicate efficiently no matter how often they change their residence or their occupations. In this sense complementarity may be that elusive property of individuals which, in the words of Dr. Hermann Finer, "makes society cohere,"[13] or which in our terminology makes it a community, perhaps even despite considerable variations in external circumstances. This, on the whole, has been the experience of the American nation. Men could move from the theocracy of Massachusetts Bay to the freedom of Rhode Island, or from the established institutions of the tidewater regions to the new conditions of the frontier, and yet retain their capacity to cooperate and form a nation. "A nation well regulated," Benjamin Franklin wrote, "is like a polypus: take away a limb, its place is soon supplied, cut it in two, and each deficient part shall speedily grow out of the part remaining. Thus, if you have room and subsistence enough . . . you may, of one, make ten nations, equally populous and powerful; or, rather, increase the nation tenfold in strength."[14]

Peoples are marked off from each other by communicative barriers, by "marked gaps" in the efficiency of communication. Such gaps are relative. In geography, divides between river basins are effective, not by their absolute heights or steepness, but the difference between their opposite slopes. Similarly barriers to communication are more or less effective not only according to the difficulty of communication across them but also according to the relative ease and attractiveness of alternative channels of communication available to the individual.

.   .   .

In the age of nationalism, a nationality is a people pressing to acquire a measure of effective control over the behavior of its members. It is a people striving to equip itself with power, with some machinery of compulsion strong enough to make the enforcement of its commands sufficiently probable to aid in the spread of habits of voluntary compliance with them. As the interplay of compliance habits with enforcement probabilities, such power can be exercised through informal social arrangements, pressure of group opinion, and the prestige of national symbols. It can be exercised even more strongly through formal social or political organizations, through the administration of educational or

---

13 Herman Finer, in *Goals for American Education,* L. Bryson *et al.,* eds. (New York: Harper & Row, Publishers, 1950), p. 108.

14 Benjamin Franklin, "Observations Concerning the Increase of Mankind" (1751), par. 23; in L.M. Hacker, *The Shaping of the American Tradition* (New York: Columbia University Press, 1947), p. 113.

economic institutions, or through the machinery of government. Whatever the instruments of power, they are used to strengthen and elaborate those social channels of communication, the preferences of behavior, the political (and sometimes economic) alignments which, all together, make up the social fabric of the nationality.

All group power thus acquired by members of the nationality leads them to ask for more. Formally or informally, dissenters find themselves pressed into line, while a significant part of the members of the nationality begin to demand control of the state or part of it.

Once a nationality has added this power to compel to its earlier cohesiveness and attachment to group symbols, it often considers itself a *nation* and is so considered by others. In this sense, men have spoken of a Polish, Czech, or Irish nation, even after these groups had lost their earlier political states, or before they had yet acquired control of any state at all.

In all these cases, nationalities turn into nations when they acquire power to back up their aspirations. Finally, if their nationalistic members are successful, and a new or old state organization is put into their service, then at last the nation has become sovereign, and a *nation-state* has come into being. At this moment, if not earlier, the successful nation may face a new immediate problem: how to use its new panoply of power against the claims of other nationalities. The more successful it has been in promoting its own members into privileged or controlling positions in society, the more it will now have to fear from the rise of other peoples and other nationalist movements.

At the end of this road a successful career of nationalism might turn a nation into a class. All its members in that event would become members of the privileged strata of society, and none would have to stoop to humbler occupations, for other peoples would be made to furnish the drawers of water and the hewers of wood. The national channels of communication would no longer even in part cut across the barriers of society; on the contrary, the barriers of class would become reinforced by the barriers of nationality, language, and culture. Something of this was implied in the vision of some British empire builders towards the end of the nineteenth century, and it found its extreme expression in the Nazi idea of a German *Herrenvolk*. But every step toward this goal has to be paid for with an increase in danger. Ever more remote from fundamental economic production, ever more cut off morally and politically from the majority of mankind, the would-be "master race" would of necessity become the obvious target for all social and national processes of revolt and of destruction. Nationalism, which set out to make the nation strong, may at this point begin to make it potentially weaker and more vulnerable. Whether men and women will follow nationalist leaders to the end of this path, or whether they will be able to break the fatal cycle may well depend on the availability of alternative leadership, and perhaps even more on the nature of their own experiences and aspirations drawn from their everyday life. . . .

ERNST B. HAAS

The Challenge of Regionalism

I

The organization of the world's ... states into various systems of competing and overlapping regional associations has now been a fact of international relations for over ten years. It cannot be said that as a fact it has gone unnoticed. On the contrary, regionalism has given rise to a floodtide of literature bitterly critical of the development or determined to justify it as a necessity for world security and a support for a sagging UN structure.[1]

. . .

The most interesting challenge inherent in the study of regionalism lies in the potentialities of the field for insights into the process of community formation at the international level. Regional relations, meetings, decisions, administrative devices, bureaucracies, and inter-ministerial, inter-expert, and inter-parliamentary institutions provide a mass of data on the process of "denationalization" of normal government functions with their delegation to regional decision-making units. While it is true that universal institutions can be used for precisely the same kind of study, it is likely that the data will prove more

---

From *International Organization,* Vol. XII, No. 4 (1958), 440–458. Reprinted by permission of the author and the World Peace Foundation.

1 See Norman J. Padelford, "A Selected Bibliography on Regionalism and Region Arrangements," *International Organization,* November, 1956 (Vol. 10, No. 4). For a comprehensive critique of the assumptions underlying regionalism see Edgar S. Furniss, Jr., "A Re-examination of Regional Arrangements," *Journal of International Affairs,* 1955 (Vol. 9, No. 2). Economic regionalism is sharply challenged by Gunnar Myrdal, *An International Economy,* New York, Harper & Bros., 1956. Extra-UN regional military arrangements are treated critically by the Commission to Study the Organization of Peace, *Regional Arrangements for Security and the United Nations,* Eighth Report, June 1953. Ernst B. Haas, "Regionalism, Functionalism and Universal Organization," *World Politics,* January, 1956 (Vol. 8, No. 2); "Regional Integration and National Policy," *International Conciliation,* May 1957.

instructive at the regional level, if only because of the greater bulk of activity.
I shall take advantage of the recently published pioneering work of the Princeton Center for Research on World Political Institutions by stating its conclusions and the context to which they apply.[2] While the authors derive their
information from a study of closed historical cases in the Atlantic area, they
also seek to project them in an assessment of the North Atlantic Treaty Organization (NATO). I shall then proceed to discuss the possibility of generalizing
these propositions by applying them to the study of supranational economic
integration in contemporary Europe and to state the lessons to be derived from
this regional experience. . . .[3]

II

On the basis of an examination of ten closed cases of successful and unsuccessful unions of states in Europe and North America the Princeton study advances
a series of general and specific findings on how "security-communities" are
attained.[4] A "security-community" is a "group of people which has become
integrated" and "integration" is defined as the "attainment, within a territory,
of a 'sense of community' and of institutions and practices strong enough and
widespread enough to assure, for a 'long' time, dependable expectations of
'peaceful change' among its population." For practical purposes, however, the
study proceeds in terms of two sub-types of security-community permitting of
greater institutional specificity. Integration may be achieved through an "amalgamated" security-community, which implies the creation of a governmental
structure, whether that of a unitary, federal, or personal union type of state
being immaterial. Roughly, the concept of the amalgamated security-community corresponds to the kind of regional arrangement which provides for a

---

[2] Karl W. Deutsch, Sidney A. Burrell, Robert A. Kann, Maurice Lee, Jr., Martin Lichter-
mann, Raymond E. Lindgren, Francis L. Loewenheim, and Richard W. Van Wagenen,
*Political Community and the North Atlantic Area: International Organization in the Light
of Historical Experience,* Princeton, N.J., Princeton University Press, 1957. The conceptual
and methodological principles applied in this study are treated in Karl W. Deutsch, *Nationalism and Social Communication,* New York, Wiley, 1953; and Karl W. Deutsch, *Political
Community at the International Level,* Garden City, Doubleday, 1954. . . .

[3] Ernst B. Haas, *The Uniting of Europe: Political, Economic, and Social Forces, 1950–57,*
London, Stevens & Sons; and Stanford, Stanford University Press, 1958. The otherwise un-
documented empirical material on group behavior in western Europe which appears in Part
IV of this article is presented in detail in this book. The theoretical conclusions derived from
this material, however, appear in print here for the first time.

[4] The study abstracts its findings from the examination of these cases: United States, 1789–
1877; England-Scotland, middle ages to 1707; England-Ireland, until 1921; German unification, early 19th century until 1871; Italian unification, early 19th century until 1860;
Hapsburg monarchy, middle ages until 1918; Norway-Sweden, 1814–1907; Switzerland, 13th
century until 1848; England-Wales, late middle ages; English unification, middle ages. The
cases were selected to include both pluralistic and amalgamated security-communities, successful and unsuccessful attempts at unity. The authors assumed all their cases to be "closed"
historically.

heavy dose of central decision-making, whether "federal" in the more restricted legal sense or not. On the other hand, integration may also be achieved through a "pluralistic" security community, any arrangement in which no true central decision-making unit is created and in which the constituent states retain their independence but which nevertheless provides for the kind of social interaction thought conducive to integration.

With commendable caution, the authors eschew a rigorous statement of which factors or conditions must be considered "necessary and sufficient" to bring about integration. They doubt that the successful isolation of a number of recurrent historical themes amounts to a truly "scientific" statement of a process. "When we call certain conditions 'essential,'" they note, "we mean that success seems to us extremely improbable in their absence. Though essential, they also seem to us insufficient: even if all of them were present, we do not know whether any other conditions might be required which we may well have overlooked. A similar consideration applies to those conditions that we call *helpful* but not essential: we found that integration occurred in their absence, and might well recur this way in future cases."

Within this methodological context, the general findings are as follows. Pluralistic security-communities are easier to attain and maintain than more formal unions, provided that the central aim is merely the preservation of peace among the participants. This conclusion is not true if socio-political aims other than peace predominate. However, the actual attainment of either type of security-community cannot be judged readily by the passage of some "threshold" of integration. Successful integration is attained when the subjective criterion of certain elite expectations is met: if the expectations of key elites in the region converge toward demands for peaceful change and other benefits thought to be obtainable only through the union, integration is underway. Objectively speaking, integration can be considered achieved when the states in the region cease to prepare for war against one another, a condition which can be easily verified from military statistics and plans.

A range of conclusions was derived from the concept of social communication. First of all, successful integration is held to depend on the prevalence of mutually compatible self-images and images of the other actors participating in the process of unification. This involves first and foremost successful predictions on the part of one nationally identified elite of the behavior pattern of other elites active in the region. It is this type of sympathy-feeling among the crucial actors which is held to be of importance, not verbal commitment to common symbols and propositions, such as "freedom," "peace," or "welfare." Further, successful integration tends to take place around a "core area," a region possessing superior administrative skills, military power, economic resources and techniques, as well as capacity for receiving and assimilating the demands of other regions so as to satisfy them. Actors in the weaker areas look to the core area for leadership and help in the satisfaction of their demands; sympathetic response on the part of the elites active in the core area then begets progressive integration without in the least implying any 'balance of power" among participating units. A great deal of stress is placed on the "capacity" of the administrative system and the attitudes prevailing in the core area actively to respond to the needs expressed by others.

The Princeton authors note that successful integration for both types of security-community is more likely if improvement of the communications network takes place before the actual burdens are spelled out in terms of political demands. They note also that war among the participating actors should cease to be a respectable mode of policy before the achievement of political union. Further, the nature of the elite structure is singled out as being of crucial importance. It is desirable for successful integration that in each political unit, before the act of union, rigid social stratification be weakened and that mass participation in public life be increased. But it is equally desirable that "international" contacts among elites of similar status and outlook in all the political units be made to flourish. Hence internal democratization was a prerequisite for the successful integration of Switzerland, Germany, Italy, Canada, or the United States; but close "international" ties among poiltical parties, trade associations, labor unions, religious organizations, and the like are essential for larger regional integration. Put another way, the conditions and consequences associated with democracy and pluralism in modern western society emerge as crucial elements in the process of international integration.

"Take-off," a concept adapted from the theoretical literature on economic development, is a central point in this explanation of growing regional unity. Whenever a given doctrine associated with integration has been adopted by a politically crucial elite as its own and thus lifted from advocacy initially confined to literary and philosophical circles, integration has acquired a momentum of its own; it "has taken off." Under what conditions does this happen historically? The Princeton authors argue that it happened in the cases they studied whenever a young generation developed aims implying a "new way of life" (e.g., the attainment of individual freedom and civil liberties), the realization of which was thought to depend on a revolutionary change in established governmental institutions and on similar action by like-minded groups in neighboring states. Often such visions include claims for new governmental services which cannot, for administrative and ideological reasons, be satisfied by the established structure. Naturally such developments imply the prevalence of mutually compatible images among the internationally allied elites, complementary values, a skill for compromise and for de-emphasizing issues which might strain the alliance. The use of force is more often an obstacle than an aid, and the movement profits if its leaders de-emphasize integration for its own sake and present it merely as a means to other, more immediately desired, ends.

Such are the general findings applicable to regional integration, irrespective of institutional refinements. For "amalgamated" security-communities, the authors also argue that certain additional "essential" requirements could be isolated. Some of the initial expectations of elites—though by no means all—have to be satisfied to anchor the union. Some concrete "bonuses" may have to be paid to "persuade" hesitant elites to identify themselves with the union, usually specific financial or economic rewards. Administrative and economic growth in the core area must continue in order not to disappoint initial expectations. Leadership groups must continue to practice skill in de-emphasizing divisive values and in stressing common aspirations, in advancing successful mutual prediction of behavior patterns and to facilitate easy interchange in group and personal roles in common tasks. And a generous range of all kinds of inter-personal, inter-group, and international transactions (mail, trade, meetings, etc.) must continue to multiply non-national contacts, eventually implying a larger measure of institutional standardization.

As for essential requirements for successful "pluralistic" security-communities the authors stress merely the need for compatibility among the major value systems involved, the attendant capacity to receive, understand, and sympathetically deal with demands of allied governments and elites—mutual responsiveness—and the need for successful mutual predictions of behavior patterns. Diplomacy by *fait accompli,* shifts in policy without consultation, or unilateral threats and warnings are all incompatible with this requirement for successful regional growth among states retaining their independence.

These conclusions were drawn from historical cases outside the social context in which we live today. The revolution in weapons technology making possible total war with a minimum of manpower had not occurred. Involvement in all corners of the globe for most of the participating units was less pronounced. The world was not divided into warring camps in disagreement on almost every aspect of life and thought. The industrial revolution had not yet affected equally most of the states in question. Mass democracy and mass participation in politics were only a factor at the very end of the historical period under study and the concern with the welfare state was still to come. The "mass man" had not yet been discovered as an important political figure, and the refinements of manipulation associated with totalitarian government were confined to the literature of political philosophers. In view of the difference in variables governing the Princeton cases and our own period, can we assume the validity of the conclusions for the study of regionalism in our time? For instance, the Princeton authors note, *inter alia,* that unions based on initially non-political aims do not necessarily lead to political security-communities, thus throwing some doubt on the Mitrany thesis of functional international organization leading to peace and order;[5] elsewhere they affirm that the existence of an external military threat may be a helpful condition to aid in regional

---

5 David Mitrany, *A Working Peace System—An Argument for the Functional Development of International Organization,* London, National Peace Council, 1946, pp. 9 and 51; also David Mitrany and Maxwell Garnett, "World Unity and the Nations," London, National Peace Council, n.d.

integration, but that it is certainly not essential. If these conclusions apply to our own era, much of the logic underlying contemporary regional organizations and efforts seems misapplied if not fallacious. Without arguing dogmatically that the presence of the variables just listed *must* beget different conclusions, I suggest that the difference in context is sufficiently striking to make checking of these conclusions a necessity in the contemporary setting.

III

In our effort to check these historically derived findings in the context of contemporary efforts at regional integration it is first essential to raise a number of methodological points. One of these refers to the problem of *time*. When must mutual responsiveness among the interacting elites and actors come into existence? Before, during, or after the onset of integrating relations? When must core area capability be well developed, before or during the "take-off" period? Is an increasing flow of mail, trade, migration, and personal contacts the cause or the result of integration? The question of *when* these conditions are thought to come about is vital when we seek to set up a rigorous conceptual scheme to explain the causes of integration. Especially in relation to indicators hinging on social communication we must know whether the transactions measured prevail among the elites to be integrated before the process starts or whether they come about as a result of events which characterize the region after the process has gone on for some years. If the latter is the case, we have merely defined an already functioning political community in terms of communications theory, but we have not explained the steps through which it had to proceed before getting there.

Another fundamental question refers to the hierarchical *level* at which social action relating to integration is thought to take place. Does successful mutual responsiveness, communication, and the de-emphasis of divisive issues rest on mass participation in politics or on its minimization? Are numerically small groups of economic, industrial, administrative, and military elites the crucial actors, or must the analytical focus be put on political parties and their constituencies? What is the role of doctrine, ideology, and mere issue-oriented pragmatic rationality in the inter-group contacts relating to integration?

These problems of analytic method are exemplified in a paradox patent in the field of international organization: ambitious institutional structures exist, but there are few obvious integrative consequences flowing from them. Are such structures the cause or a result of integration, or perhaps even unrelated to the process? Do they represent consensus at some elusive elite level or do they correspond to mass aspirations? Are they one of the background conditions from which community may develop, do they channel the process, or are they irrelevant to this whole range of inquiry? The North Atlantic area, singled out by the Princeton authors for a contemporary application of their historical findings, illustrates the difficulty.

There can be no doubt that the physical existence of NATO coincides in time with the prevalence of a *de facto* pluralistic security-community among the major member states: since 1948 these countries have been more closely united in the pursuit of the totality of policy aims than any other recent regional conglomeration and there has been no use of force in the settlements of disputes among them. However, when tested against the findings summarized above, the NATO score is poor.

Thus, while there is an adequate compatibility of major national values (with the exception of Portugal), the pattern of mutual responsiveness is pockmarked with complaints of inadequate attention by the United States, France, the United Kingdom, West Germany, and Turkey to each other's and their allies' objectives. If the Marshall Plan was the highpoint of United States responsiveness, a fairly consistent deterioration has set in since. Nor is there unambiguous evidence that the demand for a new way of life uniformly characterizes the younger generation in most of the member countries. Such a way of life may be made up of concurrent demands and expectations relating to growing welfare services, rationality, and constitutionalism in government, applying the lessons of the sciences to social relations and technology, forswearing war among the members as a practical means to settle disputes, and admitting that military defense solely by the national state is impossible and too costly in terms of competing welfare commitments; but if it is, Greece, Portugal, Italy, and Spain would probably have to be omitted from the membership list. The core area requirement is met in part by the Canadian-United States complex; but its responsiveness is open to doubt. Among other background conditions held out as helpful for pluralistic security-communities, but essential for the amalgamated variety, the authors note a very great range of mutual transactions at all levels of inter-group relations, with the exception of personal mobility. National social mobility seems to be growing and interchanges take place on an increasing scale horizontally, though the Princeton study is uncertain whether actual horizontal communication links among like-minded groups in separate national settings are adequate for continuing community development.

The inferences to be drawn from this picture are thus uncertain. The institutional structure of the North Atlantic area and the overall context of international relations within it satisfy the formal requirements of a pluralistic security-community. The social processes isolated as being historically of significance in the development of such a community, however, are only imperfectly represented in it. Further, if effective decision-making is introduced as a criterion of community, it could be argued that in the military realm at least, and perhaps also in the relations of the NATO countries with the Soviet Union in Europe, the members of the alliance adhere to centrally made decisions with remarkable fidelity. But according to the social processes thought productive of community relations, this should not have been expected. A final incongruity of NATO as a regional community is that the scope of total interpersonal and inter-group relations and responsiveness is probably greater in it than in several of the other historical situations studied, situations which led eventually to political amalgamations. But who would predict such an outcome for NATO after the decline in inter-allied consensus since 1956?

What, then, is cause and what is effect? Was it mutual responsiveness or something else which led to the conclusion of the Atlantic Pact, to the establishment of Supreme Headquarters, Allied Powers, Europe (SHAPE), to the common infrastructure program, the annual review, and all the other institutional evidence of community? It was indeed mutual responsiveness, but a responsiveness limited to one factor: a common perception of an outside threat. This made possible extensive common planning and standardization of national habits and institutions as long as the participating actors were essentially members of the military elite. It could go on as long as the conflicts between NATO military planning and welfare commitments were explained with reference to the external threat. It could remain non-controversial and removed from the mainstream of national politics because the issues in question were treated as being severely technical. It required few of the major social communications variables isolated in other contexts. But it is condemned to failure if the common perception of the external threat gives way to dissident assessments.[6]

This methodological digression into the NATO experience, as seen in the focus of the Princeton findings, illustrates that lessons of the past should not be automatically applied to contemporary situations. It suggests that the "background" and "process" factors be identified, separated, and sorted according to a time sequence and that the social groups thought to be carriers of the movement toward integration be specified. To my mind, the true challenge of regional studies lies in the establishment of causative relations between these aspects of the political process and the institutions through which they are channeled. The results, far from invalidating the findings of the Princeton group, will nevertheless enable us to restate these in the context of modern social conditions. I shall attempt to do this by analyzing supranational economic integration among the "six" continental European countries, seeking to combine institutional and behavioral indicators.

IV

In identifying the background factors found to be directly related to continental European economic integration, emphasis will be focused on those ideologies, attitudes, and expectations of articulate organized groups which

---

6 On the basis of a series of different behavioral propositions, Harold Guetzkow comes to the same conclusion. See his "Isolation and Collaboration: A Partial Theory of Inter-Nation Relations," *The Journal* of Conflict Resolution, Vol. I, No. 1 (1967), 64–67. The motivational hypotheses presented by Guetzkow in his *Multiple Loyalties: Theoretical Approach to a Problem in International Organization*, Princeton, N.J., Center for Research on World Political Institutions, 1955, are strikingly borne out by my findings.

prevailed between the end of World War II and 1950, the date of the first official federative proposal, Schuman's call for the European Coal and Steel Community (ECSC). Expectations will include "identical" aims, implying identical reasoning patterns regardless of the nationality of the group. These will be contrasted with "converging" expectations, i.e., aims based on a reasoning pattern peculiar to a given national group but sufficiently similar in aim to result in support for integrative proposals. Converging expectations make for regional unity instrumental in nature rather than being based on principle. Identical and converging expectations must finally be contrasted with aims of groups opposed to integration.

Thus we find that certain voices in all countries concerned advocated closer unity or federation because division of Europe was held responsible for military, cultural, and political weakness, dependence on the United States, inferiority to the Soviet Union, and therefore inability to deal with internal aspects of the Communist threat to established and generally held European values. The same voices tended to define a "third force" doctrine for a future United Europe and to preach economic revival through a regeneration of competition in a larger continental market, including the abolition of trade barriers and the destruction of cartels. Still others, sometimes identical with the groups just summarized, and sometimes not, equated a United Europe with a general economic, social, and cultural regeneration, achieving a new synthesis beyond the old issues of national hatreds, wars, and class conflict.

These expectations were identical throughout the continent. They were defended by the dedicated federalists, for the most part intellectuals and professional people *not* overlapping with practical politics, industry, labor, agriculture, or other entrenched elite groups. Among the political parties, only certain Christian-Democrats and a few Socialists subscribed to these ideas, including some Christian-Democrats but no Socialists in leading positions. It is fair to say that identical expectations united only certain politically peripheral persons. While they included the organized federalists of all religious and secular persuasions, it cannot be demonstrated that these people influenced the actual course of integration unless—as in the case of Adenauer, Schuman, Monnet, De Gasperi, Beyen, and Pella—they were also active as politicians and negotiators.

Background conditions were otherwise when we focus on converging expectations. Here we find that German trade associations, trade unions, and political parties—except the Socialist Party (SPD)—were one in favoring economic unification *if* this were the means for regaining German economic equality, i.e., if remaining occupation controls were removed simultaneously, including the ban on cartels. But we also find certain French trade associations, trade unions, and the political parties of the center and moderate right embracing economic federalism as a means for controlling an economically resurgent Germany, maintaining in force allied decartelization and deconcentration measures under "European" auspices, and assuring for French industry nondiscriminatory access to German coke and the southern German export market. All non-Marxist Italian parties and trade unions favored closer European unity, because they saw in it the possibility for capital imports, unhampered exports of goods which could find a ready foreign market, and above all the right for Italian workers to migrate. The general argument of freer trade appealed to organized business in Belgium, Holland, and Luxembourg, but a very specific economic "bonus" was necessary to create a pro-integration bias among certain Belgian and Italian industrialists who feared extinction in a free, larger market.

Opposition to economic federalism characterized trade associations convinced that without the protection of national tariffs and subsidies they would decline. It also applied to right-wing political parties (the Rassemblement du Peuple Francais in France) whose attachment to the militarily independent national state is an important ideological tenet and applied to left-wing parties (the SPD and many of the Belgian Socialists) who saw in economic federalism merely a regionally cartelized but otherwise unreformed capitalism, whose impact on the national working class and national welfare was thought to be harmful. Opposition also characterized all major groups in industry, agriculture, and politics in the United Kingdom for reasons too well known to require recapitulation.

The major conclusion on background expectations is one which Princeton authors also discovered: a marked fragmentation in national attitudes prior to the initiation of the process of integration. The United Kingdom showed little disunity, and hence non-participation in ECSC negotiations was not very controversial.

Fragmentation into opposing group opinions in each nation facilitated the *eventual* establishment of close links on a regional basis of communication among ideologically allied political and economic elites. In contrast to the Princeton findings, however, it must be stated that with the exception of the close ties among a few important Christian-Democratic politicians, the growth of this now striking communications network was the *result* of the establishment of federal institutions and not its cause. Contacts among trade unionists, industrialists, administrators, and parliamentarians certainly existed before 1950; but they were lacking in intensity, in concrete programs, in consensus, and in results. The background requirement in inter-elite responsiveness, of mutuality of values, and of willingness to de-emphasize clashing aspirations was in evidence only among a very narrow group of administrators and certain key politicians; it was not then a general phenomenon of regional inter-group relations.

My findings support the argument that the existence of a "core area" can be a vital consideration in regional unification. However, in the European context this meant a desire to unify in order to *control* such an area—the Ruhr—not to rely on it. On the other hand, many supporters of unification regarded the United Kingdom as a sympathetic "core area" around which unity should develop; their disappointment in the United Kingdom's refusal to accept this role was important in defeating EDC, but not in stopping regional integration in the economic field.

Nor do my findings support another key conclusion of the Princeton authors, the notion of the "new way of life." If the "new way of life" demanded by the younger generation is specified as a dedication to regional welfare economics, cultural regeneration, and political mediation between Moscow and Washington, such a strand of thought can indeed be isolated among the background conditions surrounding European economic federation. However, it is typical of federalists who are peripheral to the political process and therefore not consistently applicable to the policy-making elites. On the contrary, these seem often to have embraced unity as a device to protect an "old" way of life. If the "new" way be identified merely as a dissatisfaction with European international relations of the inter-war variety, however, then it becomes an important background factor, typical, however, of the old as well as the new generation.

These conditions and attitudes prevailing before 1950 clearly explain why Schuman's proposal for a federal approach to economic unity was eventually adopted. In view of the dominant national fragmentation of aspirations, the scheme was a direct way to realize a new dispensation for a few, and instrumental toward achieving some very concrete and immediate economic benefits to many others. A definite change, or a "take-off" did not take place until after the actual institutions of ECSC had been established. New modes of conduct and new channels of communication among elites did not develop until *after* the institutional constitutive act. It was then that a closer rapport among trade unions, trade associations, political parties, and senior civil servants began to develop, a process which eventually "spilled over" from the realm of coal and steel to the field of general economic unification—or the European Economic Community (EEC)—and acquired an independence momentum perhaps in 1955.[7] This finding re-enforces the proposition that institutions are crucial causative links in the chain of integration, a consideration inadequately singled out by the Princeton authors.

The new institutions were called upon to realize the benefits expected of a common market restricted to coal and steel, while being fully cognizant of the economic impossibility of acting meaningfully unless such related areas as foreign trade, taxes, wages, monetary policy, and counter-cyclical measures were also subject to regional regulation. In this setting each nationally organized group began to search for regional allies to aid in the implementation of a

---

[7] The briefest, and yet accurate, descriptions of the ECSC and EEC Treaty rules are to be found in John Goormaghtigh, "European Coal and Steel Community," *International Conciliation*, May 1955, and Serge Hurtig, "The European Common Market," *ibid.*, March 1958. The economic issues of the common market are analyzed by Raymond Bertrand, "The European Common Market Proposal," *International Organization*, November 1956 (Vol. 10, No. 4), and the political process of negotiation by Miriam Camps, *The European Common Market and Free Trade Area*, Princeton, Center of International Studies, 1957. See also the Economist Intelligence Unit, Ltd., *Britain and Europe*, London, 1957.

program for coal and steel considered beneficial to it. Interest groups coalesced in their efforts to influence the policy of the ECSC High Authority, as did the parliamentarians selected by national legislatures to control the High Authority in the ECSC Common Assembly. More important perhaps in the context of a "pluralistic" security-community, a special set of relations and a new code of conduct came to characterize the Council of Ministers and the Associated national administrators, the organ to which the High Authority often deferred and which came to exercise the fundamental decision-making role in the expansive aspects of ECSC. Unlike the pattern in the Organization for European Economic Cooperation (OEEC) and other inter-governmental organizations, a presumption developed toward reaching consensus at a higher level of central action than that favored by the least federally minded member government. This resulted in progressive inter-governmental compromise toward more and more central economic planning, entrusted often to the High Authority. Eventually the process produced the Messina Conference of June, 1955, and the Brussels Conference of Experts appointed to draft the EEC and Euratom agreements.

It could be argued, then, that a "take-off" mentality did develop when significant decision-makers and elites realized that more economic benefits than sacrifices would develop as a result of further federal unity, and when they sought to influence the central institutions accordingly. The "take-off" became an operational reality when groups previously indifferent or hostile toward integration turned to the advocacy of further unity by way of EEC, on the basis of their experience in ECSC institutions and with the effects of ECSC economic policy.

Successful "take-off" is a manifestation of a previously successful "spillover"; demands and expectations for further integrating measures are voiced as a result of performance in previously federated spheres of governmental activity. Performance is held inadequate because of an insufficient grant of powers or timid policy on the part of central authorities; hence the claim for new federal powers to achieve better performance is a direct outgrowth of the earlier institutional system and the realignment of group expectations produced through it. It becomes of the essence for the accurate statement of a regional process of political integration to state these realignments.

National trade associations affected by the initially created federal institutions may in principle persist in the positions analyzed in our discussion of the pre-federal background, but experience with European groups indicates that they adapt to new rules by changing policies, if not aims. Thus the initially anti-ECSC Belgian collieries became firm supporters of federal authorities merely because they expected a more sympathetic treatment from them than from their national government. Other trade associations initially hostile become conditional supporters of the new system as they realize that the supranational authorities may be instrumental in achieving certain of their aims. This is illustrated by the eagerness of the French steel and coal industries to use ECSC for purposes of sustaining cheaper access to German coke and for increasing German production costs by "equalizing" social security and wage payments. Still others subscribed to the free market implications of the ECSC Treaty but opposed any granting of manipulative or planning powers to the supranational organs. Five years later such groups—for instance, the Germans, Belgian, and Dutch steel industries—still favor the same principles and exert themselves politically to minimize public regulation of the free market, especially in opposing anti-trust and anti-cartel measures. Their commitment to this political action compels them to work through the federal authorities. As for a "spillover," these groups favored EEC if it created a general free market but opposed strong central institutions to assert political control over it. Trade associations opposed to the continuation of economic integration, i.e., the adding of EEC to ECSC, were easily identified as the industries dependent on national protection, just as in 1950; in France and Italy this included the bulk of medium and small-sized manufacturing establishments and the major national trade associations.

National trade associations experience the necessity to combine supranationally in order to achieve common political goals once the new institutions are installed. While such combinations have occurred on a massive scale in Europe since 1950, there is little evidence that the allied industrialists are consistently receptive to each other's needs, expectations, and values. Compromise occurs rarely; divisive aspirations are not usually de-emphasized successfully by leaders who emerge with a tacit mediating role; subordination of nationally-defined economic interests to common regional positions is not observable among industrialists after five years of experience in ECSC. The supranational alliances, then, remain *ad hoc* groupings for immediate tactical advantage. However, as EEC illustrates, integration is proceeding rapidly just the same.

But the picture is quite the reverse in the ranks of the trade unions. All non-communist unions were in favor of economic integration in 1950, though with varying degrees of enthusiasm and by no means unconditionally. One of the conditions was the dedication of the federal institutions to direct measures for raising living and working standards. As ECSC in practice devoted little effort to this aim, the unions were compelled to fashion themselves into a more potent political force in order to lobby more effectively; and in the process they had to achieve agreement on their aims. They successfully de-emphasized divisive aspirations on price policy, cartels, and migration by stressing the aims which unite them: regional collective bargaining for the standardization first of fringe benefits and eventually of wages and hours. Labor's radical supranational realignment and unity was obtained partly as a result of national economic demands pressing for a supranational equalization of cost factors and partly through the astute mediating role of certain key officials. Unlike the industrialists, the trade unionists display great mutual responsiveness and a good deal of role interchangeability in successfully combining alternating national leadership with consistent supranational compromise on common interests. What is more striking still, it can easily be demonstrated that these features developed rapidly over time and received a further decisive stimulus with the inauguration of EEC.

The process of integration since the debut of ECSC seems to have affected key political parties quite unevenly. The Christian-Democrats did not change in their unswerving support for integration. But about half of the Radicals in France abandoned their former instrumental and conditional support for economic federalism as their fear of Germany grew and their insistence on a French "national solution" hardened. On the other hand, many of the Moderates in France saw even more instrumental benefits in continuing integration than had been apparent in 1950; they supported EEC and even the expansion of ECSC powers—always on the assumption that certain French interests would thereby be favored. The German liberals, similarly, concluded that growing unity among the Six is an obstacle to German reunification and therefore voted against EEC after having favored ECSC—for anti-allied reasons. The striking changes, however, occurred in Socialist ranks. The SPD maintained its opposition to ECSC until 1954 and switched thereafter to become one of the most consistent and forceful advocates of a regional planned economy functioning through democratic federal institutions. The Section Francaise Internationale Organization, after overcoming its division on the EDC issue, now takes the same position, as does the Belgian Socialist Party which was split on ECSC and EDC. Finally the Nenni Socialists in Italy, who had opposed all European unity efforts, in 1956 aligned themselves with the, by then, general continental socialist position.

Doctrinal consensus on a trans-national basis has developed significantly as a result of activities in the ECSC Common Assembly (since 1958 the European Parliamentary Assembly, with control functions over ECSC, EEC, and Euratom). Largely as a result of the increased opportunities to criticize meaningfully and continuously the activities of a true administrative agency, the Socialist deputies of six nationalities began to function as a supranational political party, showing a consistent record of successful internal compromise, deference to each other's wishes, alternating leadership, and willingness to de-emphasize issues on which a unanimously endorsed doctrine proved unobtainable. Agreement reached by way of supranational activity proved highly significant in begetting the changed socialist positions in the home legislatures. Within the limits of the technical issues so far raised in the context of economic unification, the supranational group of Christian-Democratic deputies shows less doctrinal unity but functions smoothly as a general support for any "European" policy, exercising a role analogous to a national "government" party, whereas the Socialists tend to act as the "loyal opposition." The Liberal group shows no such unity and is rarely cohesive on concrete policy issues. Nevertheless, all three groups have developed into a permanent parliamentary elite conversant with the problems of integration and respected as such in their home legislatures. Again, however, this increase in trans-national communication and national prestige occurred *as a result* of the institutionalization of democratic parliamentary control functions at the regional level.

Realignments among governments are less patent. In essence, the positions of the three Benelux governments and of Italy are unchanged as compared to 1950: they still favor a maximum of economic unification and the creation of a sufficiently powerful federal political structure to administer the rules of the common market and to implement its welfare objectives. Many statesmen in these four countries are frank to admit that they see in economic federalism the precursor to a full political union. These positions were expressed uniformly in the negotiations which resulted in the EEC and Euratom treaties.

Things are otherwise in Germany and France. In 1950 these two governments agreed in favoring a maximum of political federalism for ECSC and a minimization of inter-governmental features. During the EEC negotiations, there was a tendency for the German negotiators to minimize institutions for the common market and to oppose the insertion of provisions facilitating economic planning. The French, by contrast, were concerned mostly with minimizing the federal aspect of EEC so as to permit them to continue unilateral policies inconsistent with the EEC rules. However, the fact that an agreement was reached which subordinates national demands for the relaxation of the rules to the consent of EEC organs indicates that the degree of mutual responsiveness in these inter-governmental dealings was extraordinarily high. But it also illustrates the general finding on the process of integration that once governments have committed themselves—for whatever reasons—to certain common measures of fundamental importance to the daily lives of their entire citizenry, they can resolve future problems of implementing the agreement only by means of further delegation of power to the center. This "administrative spillover" is an essential consequence of initial acts of integration in a crucial policy sector. Withdrawal from its implications is not possible—as in the case of NATO—when the external stimulant changes. Since the range of issues which gave rise to the initial step is woven completely into the contemporary preoccupation with welfare, withdrawal would imply a sacrifice of economic advantage—a step not taken lightly by elected politicians.

Given the background conditions we specified, given the initial act of institutional unification based on identical and converging aims and expectations, a realignment of political forces calculated by the actors on the basis of normal political expediency takes place. This realignment will result in the intensification of growth toward a regional political community *if the task of the center is expanded.* But the story of why the supranational task was expanded significantly in Europe since 1950 again confirms the earlier finding, stressed equally by the Princeton study, that demand for increased regional activity is based essentially on instrumental motives and only rarely on principle. If enough task expansion occurs, the eventual condition characterizing the region will be a federal or unitary state, or a "pluralistic" institutional setting in which central decisions of ministerial organs are always implemented because there is no meaningful alternative to them. The lessons derived from the analysis of the process leading toward task expansion can now be summarized:

1. Groups subject to a process of integration are not uniformly responsive to each other's claims even though the institutional pressures are such as to make concerted supranational action politically reasonable and practically desired by most.

2. In the modern European setting, groups previously exposed to active international value sharing find it easier to achieve this responsiveness. In practice, this has meant Socialist and Catholic labor and political groups.

3. Government negotiators and high civil servants working in isolation from political pressures and democratic accountability achieve mutual responsiveness more readily than groups resting on mass support.

4. Despite initial acts of integration, continuing rewards must be held out to participating groups in order not to alienate them. For labor this has meant the promise of an active welfare policy under EEC; for the French conservatives it has meant the "Europeanization" of investment programs in French Africa and the temporary waiving of some common market rules under EEC as applied in France; for Italy it called for creation of the "European Bank"; for French and Belgian industrialists it resulted in the promise of some measures for the "equalization" of costs of production through higher social security contributions in the Netherlands and Germany.

5. The contemporary process of integration need not include dedication to an inter-elite agreement on a "new way of life." On the contrary, it is my conclusion that integration is advocated as a means to defend some cherished aspect of an established way of life, even though this "way" may be transformed willy-nilly by the consequences of the integration process. Under modern socio-economic conditions, three types of attitude development can be identified, each of which implies merely the buttressing of previously advocated values in a new setting:

   a. High-cost industries move from initial opposition to integration to strong support of federal institutions with the aim of inducing the new authorities to adopt a protectionist and subsidizing policy for the industries in question. The same is true for trade unions in these industries. The political consequence is a tendency toward regional protectionism resting on firm supranational constituency pressure.

   b. Groups that consider themselves marginal in the nations undergoing integration will, after initial indifference toward or mild support for unity proposals, rally to the new central authorities and seek to induce them to adopt a comprehensive welfare and planning policy designed to protect the interests of the groups in question. They will also seek to penetrate the new institutions as a means for gaining equality and respectability at the supranational level, which was denied them in the national context.

   c. Low-cost industries initially favor measures of economic integration, provided no ambitious federal regulatory powers are created and industrialists are left free to complete or conclude "agreements" as they see fit. As soon as the federal authorities seek to control cartels and regulate the market, opposition to the *method,* but not necessarily the principle, of integration is voiced, hinging around the argument that standardization of economic rules and practices is not required in a common market. However, in the process of opposing the federal authorities, the dissident low-cost industries are involuntarily committing themselves to channelling their political aims through the new centers of power.

Whether because of growing positive expectations of the new central institutions or because of the negative aim of seeking to block institutional action at the center, the net result of the group realignment is an enhanced role for the center. The tendencies outlined here imply that all important groups are influenced in this fashion, that some opposition to integration is reconciled by its benefits while groups that continue to question central policy do so in the spirit of loyal opposition. This is the pattern uncovered in the five-year experience of ECSC. Whether it will prevail also under EEC is open to some doubt. Political parties consistently identified with the authoritarian Right and the pro-Soviet Left in all member countries have not changed their attitudes since 1950, continue to oppose integration and use their influence in connection with integrative tasks so as to sabotage them. However, these parties have little following among the groups who have been directly concerned with the work of ECSC, and no evidence of unrepentant opposition to integration has been found among the industrialists, trade unionists, and merchants associated with ECSC. We must remember, however, that so far, peasants, small retail businesses, artisans, and family-size manufacturing establishments have remained unaffected by the progress of economic unification. It is these groups which furnish the bulk of the authoritarian and fascist constituency in western Europe, utilizing appeals to exclusive national symbols and often rejecting supranational sharing of values on principle. Whether transitional economic protection and subsidies will suffice to woo these members of Europe's flourishing middle-class movements into the realignment pattern is by no means certain.

V

Our discussion shows that significant differences in background conditions, in the constituents of the process, in the kind and manner of elite participation can be discovered in the analysis of community formation at the regional level, depending on the historical setting and the functional preoccupation of the decision-makers. Lessons derived from pre-contemporary social contexts do not automatically apply to regional organizations now functioning, and findings derived from NATO, for instance, cannot be automatically carried over into organizations dedicated to a different kind of task even when they function in the same cultural and time setting. In addition to the cultural and functional differentials between regional organizations, we must bear in mind marked structural variations. Does the integrative impact produced by intergovernmental organizations compare favorably with the role of various kinds of supranational, federal, or confederate arrangements? To shed further light on these problems, the study of regionalism must be so generalized as to take account of the cultural, the functional, and the structural variants in the contexts to be examined.

One approach to the study of regional integration in non-western settings is to focus on the relation of existing regional institutions and legal rules to the underlying social structure. Past and present findings in the European context agree in stressing the importance of fluid social relations and fragmentation of opinion and groups as important background conditions for integration. Do similar conditions exist in the Western Hemisphere setting, in the Arab world, in Southeast Asia, or in the Caribbean? Or can the development of entities like the West Indian Federation be attributed to such forces? In all these regions international and federal institutions exist; but do they reflect merely the momentary aims of governments or are they tied to some basic social process whose nature could be studied by using the analogy of the European and Atlantic setting, at least as a point of departure?[8]

Existing institutions could serve a further research purpose. Our European lesson drives home the potential role of institutional forces in rechanneling and realigning previous group loyalties and expectations. Have Organization of American States (OAS) bodies, Southeast Asia Defense Treaty Organization (SEATO) meetings, Arab League conferences, and the like had similar consequences; or, since the answer is probably negative, why have no such consequences come about? The answer could reveal more information about the nature of background conditions in non-western settings as well as lead to insights on the relation between functional orientation and integrating results in regions other than the industrial-democratic setting analyzed so far.

For that matter, the differences in the growth of regional cohesion observable from the work of economic organizations with slightly different functional missions but operating in the same region are not yet satisfactorily explained. Why did the ECSC lead to EEC and Euratom, and therefore to greatly accelerated integration, and why did OEEC and the European Payments Union, operating in the same context but with different powers and larger memberships, fail to expand? Why is it possible to argue that integration advances more rapidly as a result of decisions made in private by senior civil servants in the ECSC/EEC framework, but that in OEEC the same technique yields no parallel consequences?[9] It might be suggested that all members of ECSC/EEC

---

[8] Research hypotheses on differences and similarities in political behavior among western and non-western systems are developed by G.McT. Kahin, G. Pauker, and L.W. Pye, "Comparative Politics of Non-Western Countries," *American Political Science Review*, December 1955 (Vol. 49, No. 4). I consider many of the variables discussed there as applicable to work on international organizations. The same is true of hypotheses and research designs put forward by comparative politics specialists concerned with western systems. See G. A. Almond, T. Cole, and Roy Macridis, "A Suggested Research Strategy in Western European Government and Politics," *ibid.*, December 1955 (Vol. 49, No. 4). Also Gabriel A. Almond, "Comparative Political Systems," *The Journal of Politics*, 1956 (Vol. 18).

[9] With very few exceptions, all discussions of OEEC are institutional or economic in scope and intent. Some indications of political process may be gleaned from Robert Marjolin, *Europe and the United States in the World Economy*, Durham, N.C., Duke University Press, 1954; Lincoln Gordon, "The Organization for European Economic Cooperation," *International Organization*, February 1956 (Vol. 10, No. 1); René Sergent, "Schritt für Schritt zum Gemeinsamen Markt," *Europa*, October 1955.

are marked by internal fragmentation and political movements looking for new solutions to old problems, whereas the United Kingdom and Scandinavia among the OEEC members are less plagued by this internal situation; but it would require more rigorous research into OEEC decision-making to substantiate this hypothesis.

The social background of the Arab effort at regional unity holds out fascinating questions for studies of this kind. It is here that the demand for a new way of life on the part of the younger generation might be demonstrated to be a background condition and a causative factor in the process of advancing and retarding regional political unity. Did the Arab League fail to produce unity because it was based on the negative consensus of groups identified with the *status quo*? Is Nasserism a more potent stimulus to unification because it self-consciously identifies itself with a new way of life castigating the foreigner and promising domestic abundance? Further, the Arab cultural heritage might offer insights into patterns of achieving mutual responsiveness among elites which have no exact counterpart in the western setting.[10] But systematic research into regional decision-making would be required before adequate answers become available.

In the work of OAS and its predecessor bodies the notion of the core area might be subjected to a rigorous non-European test. To what extent did inter-American cooperation receive encouragement from the help and sympathy which the Colossus of the North might mobilize? But it might also be asked to what extent OAS has its Latin *raison d'être* in a desire to achieve security *against* the United States by enmeshing the Colossus in a firm network of Latin-inspired legal obligations and institutional safeguards. In short, systematic research into the expectations entertained by Latin American elites with respect to OAS might reveal an anti-United States mutual responsiveness pattern which at the same time would imply a number of non-integrative consequences for the work of OAS. But if this can be substantiated in the legal, social, and economic aspects of the OAS program, would it explain the singular success of OAS efforts at maintaining collective security in the Western Hemisphere? In all likelihood a different range of factors would explain this strikingly integrative aspect of regional activity.[11]

Mutual responsiveness and the compatibility of elite aims could also be submitted to rigorous analysis in the study of SEATO and of the Baghdad Pact.

---

10 To my knowledge, no discussions of political processes in the Arab regional organizations have appeared in English. Much information, however, can be gained from the diplomatic record alone. See T.R. Little, "The Arab League: A Reassessment," *Middle East Journal*, Spring 1956; Paul Seabury, "The League of Arab States: Debacle of a Regional Arrangement", *International Organization*, November 1949 (Vol. 3, No. 4); B.Y. Boutros-Ghali, "The Arab League," *International Conciliation*, May 1954.

11 Very little discussion of political processes in OAS, as distinguished from institutional analyses and descriptions of actions in specific crises, is available. See, however, A.P. Whitaker, *The Western Hemisphere Idea*, Ithaca, Cornell University Press, 1954; and Martin B. Travis, Jr., "The Organization of American States: A Guide to the Future," *Western Political Quarterly*, September 1956 (Vol. 10, No. 2).

Is fear of the communist enemy the unifying factor in these alliances? Is it the hope for rewards unilaterally proffered by the United States in the realm of military and economic aid? Or is it some local issue, say Kashmir, which bears no intrinsic relation to the basic function of the alliance? A study of the processes compromising these aims in a setting of culturally heterogeneous members might prove instructive.

Generally shared expectations of economic gain are constituents of the process of integration found to recur with monotonous regularity. However, the degree of regional cohesion obtained through this expectation seems to vary sharply. True, in the ECSC/EEC setting it proved dominant and successful. The Princeton authors note that the disappointment of such expectations in the NATO framework may be partly responsible for the slow-down in Atlantic integration. But why did such expectations fail to yield a regional economic planning structure in the setting of the Colombo Plan? Why is their presence in OAS the subject of many words but of little action? Why have essentially military pacts like SEATO stressed economic aid and development more than armaments? The uniformity of economic expectations and policies to meet them varies with the regional setting and the functional preoccupation of the members, factors which themselves may be traced back to underlying conditions of social organization and communication.

Whatever the answers may be, they compel renewed attention to the phenomenon of regionalism as a fixed feature of our time. And to obtain them, there is no alternative to the systematic study of regional integration, combining institutional analysis with the study of political process. In doing so we may hit a rich lode of materials which might explain how nations cease to be nations, how they lose the self-consciousness which comes from having lived within the confines of a fixed set of frontiers, or how they develop loyalties extending over a broader geographic area, but which still display the earmarks of nationalism.

EDWARD W. SOJA

Communications and Territorial Integration in East Africa: An Introduction to Transaction Flow Analysis

In this paper, a technique known as transaction flow analysis is described and subsequently applied to the network of telecommunications in East Africa. The objectives of this exercise are to illustrate the potential contribution of a communications approach to the examination of the spatial aspects of territorial integration and to suggest an addition to the relatively bare quantitative tool kit of political geography.

Political geographers have long recognized that a primary function of any politically organized area is to integrate effectively its territorial components—to create a community of interests which accommodates innovation, sustains development, and promotes the general welfare of its adherents.[1] Nevertheless, there has been surprisingly little systematic research by geographers directly related to the analysis and measurement of political integration within a spatial context.

In recent years, however, a number of political scientists, borrowing from such relatively new and rapidly expanding fields as cybernetics, information theory, and systems analysis, have provided a fresh perspective on the fundamental processes which bind areas (and their populations) together.[2] This per-

---

Reprinted from *The East Lakes Geographer*, Henry L. Hunker, Editor, Vol. 4 (December 1968), 39–57, with permission of the author and editor.

[1] See, in particular, R. Hartshorne, "The Functional Approach in Political Geography," *Annals of the Association of American Geographers*, XL (1950), 95–130; and "Political Geography in the Modern World," *Journal of Conflict Resolution*, Vol. 4 (1960), 52–67.

[2] An excellent introduction to the basic concepts of the three closely associated fields of cybernetics, information theory, and systems analysis can be found in W. Ross Ashby, *An Introduction to Cybernetics* (London: Methuen, 1956). Other standard works include Norbert

spective revolves around the central role of communications in human behavior and has introduced into the social science literature several valuable concepts of relevance not only to the present discussion but to the methodology and approach of political geography as a whole. This paper attempts to explore these developments, and particularly one of the analytical techniques they have generated, with the intention of stimulating greater interaction between political geography and political science. It is hoped that, through increased interdisciplinary communications, the distinctive points of view of each discipline can mesh more effectively together to the general benefit of both.

The use of transaction flow analysis in the study of territorial integration must be considered within the broader context of what might be called a behavioral theory of communications. As previously mentioned, the growing acceptance of communications as a primary factor in human behavior has led to numerous attempts to extend the theoretical formulations of the related fields of cybernetics, information theory, and systems analysis into the various social sciences in the desire to provide new and more powerful interdisciplinary perspectives on problems of focal interest.[3] One of the leading figures in these developments has been Karl Deutsch, whose past works have proven of great interest to the political geographer and with whom the techniques of transaction flow analysis are most closely associated.[4]

Regarding the role of communications in the growth of integrated political communities, Deutsch has asserted that "The study of quantitative densities of transactions is the first step toward estimating the degree to which people are connected with one another."[5] A *transaction* may be defined as an exchange between units which always involves the communication of *information* and

Weiner, *Cybernetics: Communications and Control in the Animal, the Machine and Society* (Cambridge: MIT. Press; and New York: Wiley & Sons, 1948) and *The Human Use of Human Beings* (Boston: Houghton Mifflin Co., 1950); Colin Cherry, *On Human Communication* (Cambridge: MIT Press; New York: Wiley and Sons, 1957); Claude Shannon and Warren Weaver, *The Mathematical Theory of Communications* (Urban: University of Illinois Press, 1949); L. von Bertalanffy, "An Outline of General System Theory," *British Journal of the Philosophy of Science*, I (1951), 134–165; and J.G. Miller, "Living Systems: Structure and Process," *Behavioral Science*, Vol. 10 (1965). A brief review of the impact of these fields on political science is supplied by W.J.M. Mackenzie, *Politics and Social Science* (Harmondsworth: Penguin Books, 1967), pp. 96–120. References more specifically related to questions of political integration will be noted in later sections.

3 Two illustrations of this development include David Easton: *A Systems Analysis of Political Life* (New York: Wiley and Sons, 1965) and Richard L. Meier, *A Communications Theory of Urban Growth* (Cambridge: MIT Press, 1962).

4 Deutsch develops his views on the role of communications theory and cybernetics in political theory building in *The Nerves of Government* (New York: The Free Press of Glencoe, 1963). More direct inquiries into the role of communications in political integration can be found in his several contributions to P.E. Jacob and J.V. Toscano (eds.), *The Integration of Political Communities* (New York: J.P. Lippincott Co., 1964). Other works by Deutsch of interest to the political geographer include *Nationalism and Social Communication* (Cambridge: The MIT. Press, 1953 and 1966) and "The Growth of Nations: Some Recurrent Patterns of Political and Social Integration," *World Politics*, Vol. 4 (1953), 168–195.

5 "Communications Theory and Political Integration," in Jacob and Toscano, p. 51.

may represent a transfer of people, goods or services. R.L. Meier, in his stimu-lating volume, *A Communications Theory of Urban Growth,* describes a trans-action in the network of human relations as involving "discrete interaction over space, an adjustment to recent events and new opportunities, and a joint experience which accommodates the participants to the changing socio-economic system."[6]

Before moving further, however, it is necessary to return briefly to the more basic concept of information. In the theories of cybernetics—the science of com-munications and control—information is used in a highly specialized way. In simplest terms, it can be defined as "amount of order" and refers to that which is not random and can therefore convey meaning. Information has also been associated with *negative entropy,* where entropy is defined as disorder or more broadly as a process in which order (i.e., information) is gained or lost due to energetic transactions between parts of a system.[7] But rather than plunging further into the complex terminology of information theory—a very worthwhile exercise but one which cannot effectively be undertaken here—perhaps greater clarity can be provided by a short discussion of how these concepts have been applied within social science research with particular reference to the integra-tive process.

Information, as used by Meier, refers to the capacity to select from a set of alternatives. It involves knowledge concerning the physical and human envi-ronment and is related to a potential for control or regulation. Wherever infor-mation is concentrated, behavior is more ordered and predictable. The choices available can be more clearly discerned and the probable outcomes of these choices more easily identified and evaluated—hence the potential for system regulation and control.[8]

The exchange and conservation of information within a network of social relations provides the integrative glue enabling the network to survive and grow as a cohesive, organized unit. Essential, therefore, to an understanding of the integrative processes at work in any territorial community is a knowledge of the pattern and intensity of information flow in space, for it is this dynamic exchange between the component parts of a system that creates the bonds of mutual awareness and interdependence which promote integrative behavior.[9]

This brings us back to the transaction, which is the basic unit of informa-tion flow. Transactions between areas can be viewed as indicators of the flow

---

6 *Op. cit.,* p. 66.

7 See J.G. Miller, *op. cit.*

8 *Op. cit.,* pp. 150–152.

9 Ackerman, in discussing the role of systems analysis as a fundamental integrating concept in geography, has stressed the great importance of studying spatial interaction and informa-tion flow: "...to choose a research problem without reference to the connectivity of the system is to risk triviality. What space relations tell us of connectivity in the system is signifi-cant to the science as a whole. Areal differences are significant *only* insofar as they help to describe and define the connectivity or 'information' flow." Edward A. Ackerman, "Where is a Research Frontier?" *Annals of the Association of American Geographers,* Vol. 53 (1963), 437.

and concentration of information within a network of human relations in space, and consequently of mutual awareness and at least potentially integrative behavior. Charting the pattern and measuring the direction, intensity, and persistence of transaction flows in space thus offers an insightful window on the processes of territorial integration.[10]

There must be some threshold in the flow of transactions, however, beyond which two units become solidly locked together in a chain of interreactive behavior. Below this level, the flow of information from *A* to *B*, for example, may not be sufficient to sustain a close tie due to the flood of additional information being received by *B* from other parts of the system. One can easily accept the virtual inevitability of mutual awareness that would develop, once communications had been established and maintained, between two persons stranded on a small island, or to stretch the point somewhat further, between Adam and Eve. It would be difficult to imagine the behavior of one not being affected by that of the other. Add more people to the growing micro-community, however, and soon levels of mutual awareness become highly variable and the behavior of each individual may not necessarily involve a sensitivity to the presence and behavior of all others.

Identification of this important threshold has been operationalized in the concept of *salience*. Whereas transactions may be considered to convey images through the exchange of information, salience sustains these images through a significantly greater than normal flow of transactions. Salient units are not indifferent to each other's behavior for a significant level of interaction has been reached. Developing a measure of salience—the greater than expected flow of information used as an indicator of mutual awareness—is a primary aim of transaction flow analysis in the form discussed in this paper.

There remains, however, the problem of interpreting salience with respect to integrative behavior. Salience can lead to both positive and negative reaction, to community feeling as well as conflict, depending on the kinds of information being exchanged and consequently the nature of the images conveyed. Two noninteracting strangers are much less likely to do violence to one another than are a husband and wife!

In an attempt to solve this problem, one author has distinguished between those transactions which lead to positive reaction, or are "mutually-rewarding," and those which increase the chances of conflict, or are "mutually-depriving."[11] Before relating salience to the potentials for integration, therefore, the nature of the information being exchanged should be properly evaluated. Very often, however, the informational content of transactions cannot be clearly identified

---

10 It is interesting in this context to note the similar statement by Meier: "The use of an index of social communications representing the degree of interaction as *information* flow, and of knowledge as *information* storage, provides an important direct link to the other sciences. Advances in insight in any of them may now be translated quickly into implications for human organization, most particularly the culture of cities." *Op. cit.*, p. 152.

11 J.V. Toscano, "Transaction Flow Analysis in Metropolitan Areas," Jacob and Toscano, *op. cit.*, pp. 100–102.

and interpreted with respect to this distinction and furthermore the two may be extremely difficult to distinguish even if this were possible. This is one of several areas where a certain unresolved "fuzziness" enters into the analysis of transaction flows. Hopefully, these problems are symptomatic of the early stages in the development of an important analytical technique and will resolve themselves with further application and elaboration.

In summary, therefore, the use of transaction flow analysis as a tool for studying territorial integration is based on the following assumptions: 1) the greater the level of transaction flow between areas, the greater become the chances for salience; 2) salience is an indicator of a high level of mutual awareness; 3) the greater the level of transaction flow of the mutually-rewarding kind, the greater the likelihood for cooperation and integration; 4) an integrated territorial community is maintained by a complex pattern of information exchange which hinges upon a connected network of salient transaction flows encompassing all its major areal components; 5) existing and potential levels of integration between areas will be reflected in a mapping of salient flows. This approach to the study of territorial integration shifts the focus from an examination of the degree to which certain key characteristics (e.g., language, religion, levels of development) are shared by the population in an area to the more fundamental analysis of *interaction patterns*.

There are many kinds of transaction flows one can examine and an equally large variety of methods to apply.[12] Of some value, for example, are preoccupation ratios, which use the relationship between internal and external transactions as a gauge of community insularity. Simple gravity models have also been suggested as tools for examining the impact of distance and social or political boundaries on the flow of transactions.[13] One such model has been applied with interesting results by a geographer to interaction patterns within Quebec and between Quebec and surrounding regions of Canada and the United States.[14]

The method used here, however, involves the application of an indifference, or null, model to obtain expected transaction flows (given a number of assumptions) from which salience is measured. This model, which will be referred to hereafter as the transaction flow model, has been used most frequently in the analysis of international trading patterns, but is equally applicable to other types of transactions and to the national, region, and local levels as well.[15]

---

12 See Karl Deutsch, "Transaction Flows as Indicators of Political Cohesion," *ibid.*, pp. 73–97.

13 Karl Deutsch and Walter Isard, "A Note on the Generalized Concept of Effective Distance," *Behavioral Science*, Vol. 6 (1961), 308–311.

14 J. Ross Mackay, "The Interactance Hypothesis and Boundaries in Canada: A Preliminary Study," *The Canadian Geographer*, Vol. 11 (1958), 1–8.

15 See, for example, the interesting applications to integration within metropolitan areas in J.V. Toscano, *op. cit.*, pp. 98–119, as well as illustrations from other chapters in this stimulating volume.

As developed by Deutsch and Savage,[16] the transaction flow model is based on an assumption of origin-destination independence—that is, assumption that the specific character of the origin of a transaction will not affect its destination, and vice versa. All possible destinations have an opportunity to receive the transactions in proportion to their relative sizes. Put in another way, the model presumes that the number of transactions from area A to area B will reflect only some measure of what might be called the relative attractive power of B within the entire system. The most commonly used yardstick for attractiveness, and the one that is used in the illustrations which follow, is the proportion of all transactions made in the system which are received at a particular point (e.g., B), although other measures such as population size or wealth can be used, as can the relative figures for outgoing transactions.

As an example, let us suppose that Great Britain is the destination for 10 per cent of all international trade. Under the assumptions of the transaction flow model, France, the United States, Madagascar, and all other trading states should send approximately 10 per cent of their exports to Great Britain.[17] In other words, Great Britain will expect to receive essentially the same percentage of trade transactions from all parts of the international trading system regardless of their actual state of origin. Hence the idea of origin-destination independence.

Interaction, therefore, is considered to be indifferent to all other influences within the system except the relative size or attractive power of its component parts.[18] The model does not identify the largest generators of transactions nor does it help in charting absolute flows. These, in fact, are given. Instead, the model provides a statistical standard from which can be measured those flows which, for one reason or another, exceed what might normally be expected in a system with transactions reflecting only differences in size.[19]

In reality, of course, such forces as the friction of distance, political boundaries and cultural and economic influences affect very powerfully the patterns of communication flow. The model, however, by *not* initially incorporating these factors, provides a means for evaluating their relative impact within the system. It identifies those pairs of points or areas which are interacting at a higher

---

[16] I.R. Savage and Karl Deutsch, "A Statistical Model of the Gross Analysis of Transaction Flows," *Econometrica*, Vol. 28 (1960), 551–572.

[17] Actually the expected percentage will be slightly higher than 10 per cent, since an area is not permitted in the model to have transactions with itself. The predicted percentage of A's transactions to be sent to B will herefore be equal to the number of transactions received at B divided by the total number of transactions within the system *minus* the amount received at A.

[18] In some ways, the model describes a situation similar to the "steady-state" or "dynamic equilibrium" of open systems with an established pattern of hierarchical dominance.

[19] For a more detailed discussion of transaction flow analysis, its terminology, major concepts, and applications within political science, see S.J. Brams, *Flow and Form in the International System*. Unpublished Ph.D. dissertation, Department of Political Science, Northwestern University (June 1966); and, by the same author, "Transaction Flows in the International System," *The American Political Science Review*, Vol. 60 (1966), 880–898.

than expected level and challenges the investigator to discover the relevant variables most closely associated with these deviations. A properly selected index of salience is thus susceptible to the techniques of regression analysis to assess quantitatively these spatial associations.

To illustrate its use, the transaction flow model was applied to telephone traffic between 24 exchange regions in East Africa in 1961 and 1965.[20] The computer program used was a modification of the Deutsch-Savage model in which the origin-destination assumption is applied to predict the expected flows only for those units which actually have exchanges.[21]

Federal institutional structures such as the former East African Common Services Organizations have existed for many years linking the three states of Kenya, Uganda, and Tanzania,[22] and it was generally felt that the potentials for supra-national integration in East Africa were greater than those for any other cluster of African states. In the late 1950's and early 60's, Tanganyika and Kenya were in the forefront of the drive toward federation, and in 1960, the current President of Tanzania, Julius Nyerere, even stated his willingness to postpone Tanganyikan independence until Kenya and Uganda received theirs—on the condition that the three federate immediately. Nyerere apparently suspected that separate independence would foster national introversion and hinder the federal effort.

From 1961 to 1965, the three component territories of East Africa obtained their independence (Tanganyika in 1961, Uganda in 1962, and Kenya in 1963) and, as Nyerere had feared, the once bright prospects for their federation began to fade rapidly as each state turned increasingly toward problems of internal unity and nation building. During this period, Uganda appeared least in favor of federation and in the unsuccessful negotiations of 1963 was, as one author puts it, the "reluctant partner."[23] After these negotiations, however, Nyerere's Tanzania seemed to take the strongest steps toward nation building and weak-

---

20 The data were based on telephone trunk call censuses for East Africa which were made available to the author by the East African Posts and Telecommunications Administration, Nairobi. The 1961 census was recorded over a two-day period with a total recording time of nine hours, while the 1965 census involved a five-day period and thirty hours of recording time. In reference to the differences between the two censuses, see note 26.

21 This modification was suggested in L.A. Goodman, "Statistical Methods for the Preliminary Analysis of Transaction Flows," *Econometrica*, XXXI (1963), 197–208. Goodman's modification was the basis for S.J. Brams, "A Generalized Computer Program for the Analysis of Transaction Flows," which was used in this study. A write-up and listing of the Brams program are available from the Vogelback Computing Center, Northwestern University. If nonexistent exchanges were not ignored in the present illustration, the smaller regions would be salient with nearly every other region to which they made more than the absolute minimum of calls.

22 Tanganyika and Zanzibar joined together in 1964 to form the United Republic of Tanzania. Although Zanzibar was not included in the telephone censuses, Tanzania rather than Tanganyika will be referred to in the text when the 1965 data are discussed.

23 J.S. Nye, Jr., *Pan-Africanism and East African Integration* (Cambridge: Harvard University Press, 1965), p. 189.

ening her contacts with her neighbors to the north. As a result, by the end of 1965, the issue of political federation had been pushed into the background.[24] It was expected that the critical events of this period would be reflected in the changing pattern of salient telecommunications linkages, thus providing a propitious testing-ground for transaction flow analysis.

The solid lines on Figures 1 and 2 represent the pattern of salience which existed in 1961 and 1965 respectively. The primary measure of salience used is the Relative Acceptance (RA) Index, equal to the actual number of transactions between two regions, minus that expected from the indifference model, divided by the expected value:

$$RA_{ij} = \frac{A_{ij} - E_{ij}}{E_{ij}}$$

A positive value for the RA Index was not automatically considered to indicate salience, but instead $RA = .25$ was arbitrarily selected as the critical threshold. Thus, for two regions to be salient, the flow of transactions *in both directions* must be at least 25 per cent greater than expected from the model. Due to the arbitrariness of this threshold level, however, all positive RA values are shown on the maps, with dashed lines representing flows in which RA is greater than zero in both directions but less than .25 in at least one; positive flows in one direction only are indicated by arrows from the region of origin.

In addition, a minimum absolute deviation $(D_{ij} = A_{ij} - E_{ij})$, also set arbitrarily, was considered prerequisite to salience.[25] This absolute measure has been used in previous studies in the attempt to alleviate a sensitivity to above normal exchanges from small units which is inherent in the RA Index.[26] The RA Index alone would tend to "favor" very small regions in that a minor deviation from expected (e.g., $A_{ij} = 5$, $E_{ij} = 4$, $RA_{ij} = .25$) could produce a significant index. Thus, D_{ij} is used to achieve a balance by "favoring" larger regions.

As is evident, both indices have their built-in disadvantages and there is need for further refinement of the index of salience. But it should be stressed that any possible refinement must be made with full recognition of the conceptual connotations of salience within communications theory. In particular, this will require more extensive investigation of the comparative behavioral consequences of salience in large and small units.

It is difficult to draw many significant conclusions from an analysis of only

---

24 For a general geographical analysis of the potentials for integration in East Africa, see William A. Hance, "East Africa: A Study of Integration and Distintegration," Chap. 6 in Hance's *African Economic Development* (New York: Praeger, 1967). An excellent analysis of the political, economic, and historical background to this topic can be found in Nye, *ibid.*, and in Colin Leys and Peter Robson (eds.), *Federation in East Africa: Opportunities and Problems* (Nairobi: Oxford University Press, 1965).

25 The minimum *D* values used in 1961 and 1965 were one and three respectively.

26 See the works of Brams, *op. cit.*

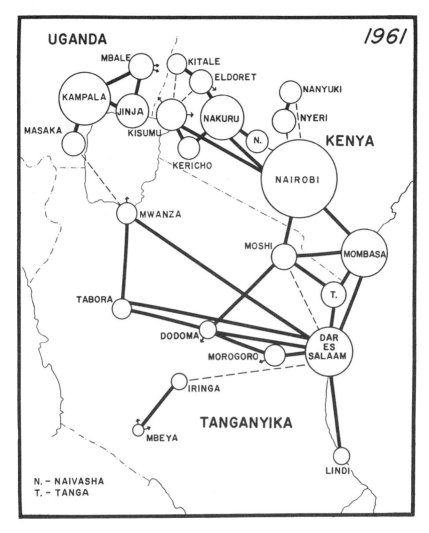

FIG. 1 Salient transaction flows in East Africa, 1961. Solid lines=RA<.25 and D<1 in both directions; dashed lines=RA<0 in both directions but >.25 at least one way; arrows=RA<0 in one direction only. Size of circles is in proportion to percentage of total trunk calls made between 24 exchange regions in East Africa.

one type of transaction flow, especially when it is not possible to evaluate the content of information being transacted.[27] Several different patterns (trade, postal traffic, passenger movements, perhaps content analysis of newspapers or

_____

[27] A difference in sample time for the 1961 (nine hours) and 1965 (thirty hours) censuses creates a potential source of distortion when comparing the two patterns of salience. Many

visits from government officials) and their interrelationship are more indicative of the realities of information flow through a communications network. Tele-communications offer only one window onto the larger picture.[28]

Furthermore, in a developing area such as East Africa, telephone calls are made almost entirely by a very small stratum of society and this restricts any attempt to extend interpretation beyond the economic and governmental elite. The confidence with which one can classify the flows as mutually rewarding or depriving is still another problem.

Nevertheless, telephone communications probably offer the best nexus within which to examine salience and its bearing on territorial integration in an area as large as East Africa. It is an extensive form of communications and consequently should provide more realistic patterns with respect to the assumptions of the indifference model than most other forms of information exchange. In addition, telephone traffic has been found elsewhere to be an excellent index of spatial interaction and social communications.[29] A more basic justification is that of all the types of detailed origin-destination data required for transaction flow analysis, at this scale, telephone traffic data is probably most easily available. All these reasons, however, do not eliminate the need to interpret the patterns revealed in the present illustration with appropriate caution.

Returning to the example at hand, an examination of Figures 1 and 2 clearly reveals that the most striking feature of salient transaction flows in East Africa is their marked degree of national clustering. Although distance and other variables are important, the impact of national boundaries seems to be the major factor causing divergence from the indifference model and producing the pattern of salient links.

The salient flows of the four Uganda regions, for example, form a network isolated from the rest of the East African system. No reciprocally significant links exist across its borders and moreover there appears to have been an increase in Ugandan isolation from 1961 to 1965. In the earlier year, there existed a reciprocally positive flow between Masaka and the Tanganyikan lake

---

regions had a larger number of partners in 1965 than in 1961 simply because of the longer time period sampled. This had the effect in some cases of reducing the expected flow predicted by the model for the 1961 partners, thus increasing the RA indices in 1965. This possible distortion was carefully considered when interpreting the changes in the salient flow pattern and no observations have been made which were not supported by trends identified in an analysis of the 1962 and 1963 censuses, which were also based on nine-hour samples but have not been included in this study.

28 An interesting review of the role of mass communications in the developing countries is given in Wilbur Schramm, *Mass Media and National Development* (Stanford: Stanford University Press, 1964).

29 For example, see Mackay, *op. cit.*, and J.D. Nystuen and M.F. Dacey, "A Graph Theory Interpretation of Nodal Regions," *Papers and Proceedings* of the Regional Science Association, Vol. 7 (1961), 29–42. Telephone traffic has also been widely used in diffusion studies to estimate the local range of private communications. See T. Hägerstrand, "On Monte Carlo Simulation of Diffusion," in W.L. Garrison and D.F. Marble (eds.), *Quantitative Geography*, Part. I: Economic and Cultural Topics (Evanston: Northwestern University Studies in Geography, Number 13, 1967), 1–32.

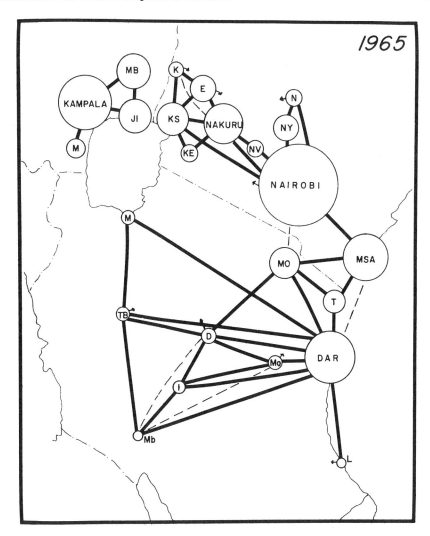

FIG. 2   Salient transaction flows in East Africa, 1965. Symbols
are the same as in Fig. 1.

region around Mwanza, and positive one-way flows from Mwanza to Jinja;
from Mbale to Kitale and Eldoret in Kenya; and from the Kenya lake region
around Kisumu to Mbale. At this time, the seeds of an interstate circulatory
system in the Lake Victoria basin appeared to exist, with the potential perhaps
to develop into a major centripetal force for an East African Federation.[30] In

---

[30] An interesting discussion of the potential role of the Lake Victoria basin in the development of East Africa is found in T.J.D. Fair, "A Regional Approach to Economic Development
in Kenya," *South African Geographical Journal*, Vol. 45 (1963), 55–77.

1965, however, all these positive flows disappear and the Uganda network of positive linkages becomes totally isolated.

There is a similar national focus in Tanganyika (now Tanzania after the incorporation of Zanzibar in 1964) and Kenya, but several salient relationships did exist cross-nationally, the highest and most permanent of which—between Mombasa and Tanga—probably reflects the persistence of an important circulatory subsystem along the long-settled East African coast. But again, these cross-national flows are weakened significantly from 1961 to 1965, while the intranational network becomes much more dense.

Two isolated cells which appeared in 1961, one north of Nairobi and the other in southwestern Tanganyika, establish salient links with their respective national networks in 1965. The new salience with Mbeya and Iringa is indicative of the greater attention being paid by the government of Tanzania in Dar es Salaam to its isolated and underdeveloped southwest and may be a precursor of more intimate relationships with neighboring Zambia.[31]

Another interesting intra-national change is the increase of salient links for the Kisumu region of Kenya. The new links are all with sections of the former White Highlands, most of which is now being turned over to African farmers in a large-scale resettlement program. This increase in salient links mirrors the growing importance of the Kisumu region in independent Kenya.

The only salient international flows which remain in 1965 are between Mombasa and the Tanga and Moshi regions of Tanzania. But perhaps most revealing are the changes which occurred in the Moshi region itself, which includes the two important towns of Moshi and Arusha. While the average RA Index for Nairobi-Moshi dropped from .62 in 1961 to .26 in 1965, the figure for Moshi-Dar es Salaam increased dramatically from .26 to 1.42. A comparison of the Moshi-Mombasa and Moshi-Tanga links shows similar but much smaller changes, which in combination appear to signify a pronounced reorientation of this fertile and densely populated region on the slopes of Mt. Kilimanjaro, hitherto very closely tied to parts of Kenya, to the national communications grid of Tanzania.[32]

In late 1967, however, the town of Arusha—once considered as a site for the capital of an East African Federation—was selected as the administrative headquarters for the new East African Economic Community (EAEC) and a num-

---

[31] The *New York Times* in its review of economic conditions in Africa (January 27, 1967), made the observation that Zambia was transformed in 1966 from the northernmost section of Southern Africa to the southernmost section of Eastern Africa! This referred particularly to the increased ties between Zambia and Tanzania created after the unilateral decision of independence by Southern Rhodesia forced Zambia to seek new avenues for its imports and exports.

[32] The Tanzanian government has fostered this reorientation in several ways. A toll, for example, was levied at the major border crossings, the two most important of which lead to Moshi and Arusha. In addition, the government has urged exporters based in the Moshi-Arusha region to use the Tanzanian port of Tanga rather than Mombasa, which is actually closer by rail.

ber of institutions for interterritorial cooperation formerly housed in Nairobi, or, to a much lesser extent, Dar es Salaam and Kampala, are now being shifted to it. It will be most interesting to chart the changes in the communications pattern in East Africa that might be generated by these developments.

The patterns of salience represented in Figures 1 and 2 also appear to indicate that information flow in Tanzania is more heavily concentrated in its capital region than is true in Kenya. Dar es Salaam, for example, was salient to every other Tanzania region in 1965 and also had the largest number of salient linkages of any exchange region. Kenya, in contrast, had three major nodes of salience, Nairobi with six links and Kisumu and Nakuru with five. (The small number of exchange regions in Uganda makes a similar assessment much more difficult.)

It is tempting to interpret these patterns as reflecting the differences between Kenya and Tanzania with respect to their internal problems of national integration. Kenya, on the one hand, has been plagued by ethnic and regional rivalries both before and since independence, while Tanzania has faced far fewer problems of such a nature but has instead been more concerned with developing its much poorer system of transport and communication to avoid regional isolation.

But before extending this interpretation further, it should be noted that salience in the examples being examined is based on the sending and receiving totals of regions throughout East Africa. The pattern would be very different if the analysis were applied to only Kenya or Tanzania. Whereas the actual number of calls between Dar es Salaam and Dodoma, for example, may produce salience within the East African system, the same number may not do so when only interregional calls within Tanzania are being considered.[33]

To illustrate some of the modifications which occur when the East African system is broken down into its component parts—essentially a reduction in the scale of examination—a separate analysis was run on the ten exchange regions of Tanzania and the ten for Kenya in 1965 (Figs. 3 and 4). The most evident result is a large reduction in the number of salient flows due primarily to the reasons stated above. The role of distance becomes more important, with nearly all the regions in both Kenya and Tanzania being salient only with other nearby regions. These changes result in a marked reduction in the degree of focus on the two national capitals, both of which stand isolated from the remainder of their networks in terms of salient linkages.

Nairobi is now salient only with Mombasa, and Dar es Salaam only with Morogoro and Lindi. Except for the importance of Dodoma, the Tanzanian network of salience is rather simple and indicative of the relatively poor development of communications in the country and the absence of a dominant interregional focus. In Kenya, however, a distinct split into two subsystems is

---

[33] This is because the relative attractive power of Dar es Salaam and Dodoma is much greater within the Tanzanian communications system than within that of all East Africa.

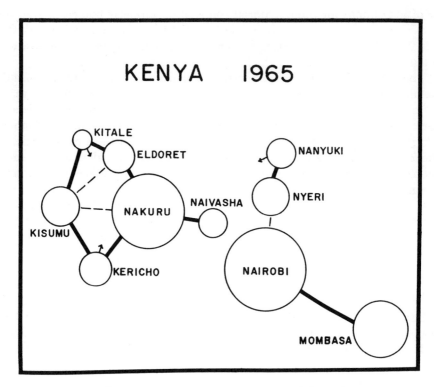

FIG. 3   Salient transaction flows in Kenya, 1965. Symbols are the same as in Figure 1. Size of circles in proportion to percentage of total trunk calls made between 10 exchange regions in Kenya.

evident, one focusing on Nairobi and encompassing much of central Kenya and the coast, the other centered on Kisumu and Nakuru and showing signs of becoming very tightly interconnected.

In another work, the present author has discussed the potentially critical role of Nakuru in tying together the two major population clusters of Kenya (in the eastern highlands and the Lake Victoria basin) to prevent the growth of a disintegrative form of regionalism.[34] But in terms of the salient links existing in 1965, it appears that this has not been achieved and many of the events in Kenya since independence—particularly the emergence of a powerful opposition party with its primary support in the Kisumu area—reflect the problems of effectively integrating these two populous regions.

Summarizing briefly, transaction flow analysis of telephone calls in East

---

[34] Edward W. Soja, *The Geography of Modernization in Kenya* (Syracuse: Syracuse University Press, Geographical Research Series, No. 2, 1968), Chap. IX.

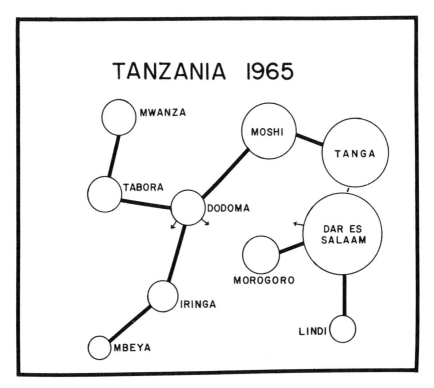

Fig. 4 Salient transaction flows in Tanzania, 1965. Symbols are the same as in Figure 1. Size of circles in proportion to percentage of total trunk calls made between 10 exchange regions in Tanzania (Zanzibar excluded).

Africa has shown that the primary factor shaping the patterns of salient relationship between regions was the existence of international boundaries which compartmentalize information flow within three distinct communications subsystems. This compartmentalization, moreover, appears to have increased from 1961 to 1965 paralleling the progressive introspection of the three newly independent states and dissipation of the potentials for effective political federation. If the behavioral implications of salience are accepted, one must conclude that interterritorial communications have not been sufficiently well-developed to support a tightly-knit East African Federation. In a behavioral sense, there are virtually no "East Africans," just Kenyans, Ugandans, and Tanzanians.

Most isolated within the framework of interterritorial communications has been Uganda—the "reluctant partner." Despite the physical proximity of much of Uganda to parts of Tanzania and Kenya, its national boundaries have acted as formidable barriers to interaction. This barrier effect has prevented the growth of intensive interaction in the Lake Victoria basin, shared by all three states and located in or near the most densely populated and productive sections of East Africa. The success of the newly formed East African Economic Community will depend largely on its ability to stimulate increased transaction flow within this important focal area.

Closer relations exist between Tanzania and Kenya, particularly along the coast and between the coast and the interior regions of Moshi-Arusha and Nairobi. Although weakened between 1961 and 1965, this international network remains much stronger than that in the Lake Victoria region and will probably intensify further with the development of Arusha as headquarters for the EAEC.

Whereas the political subdivision of East Africa is the major factor structuring the patterns of salience at the international level, physical proximity becomes most important within the three states. This relationship was brought out most clearly in the separate transaction flow analyses for Tanzania and Kenya. These analyses, in addition, indicated that the networks of salience at the national level are not as dense as might be inferred from the East African maps. The Tanzanian network is almost at minimum connectivity, while that for Kenya is significantly split into two subnetworks reflecting internal ethnic and political divisions. These observations further emphasize the fact that the measurement and interpretation of salience is bound to the particular system under examination. Thus the associations between salience and the potentials for territorial integration at the East African level cannot be directly applied to the national situation.

In conclusion, therefore, the application of transaction flow analysis to telecommunications in East Africa, even on such a generalized and exploratory basis, has revealed a number of important patterns of interaction which are directly relevant to the study of territorial integration. The maps of salient relationships, for example, can be viewed as representing a set of behaviorally significant linkages within the communications system of East Africa, a subnetwork of intensive contacts indicative of the degree of mutual awareness existing between various sections of the larger region. As such, the measures of salience provide valuable estimates of the *behavioral distance* between subregions with respect to the potentials for territorial integration. In this study, only the most obvious factors affecting salience (i.e., political boundaries and physical proximity) have been mentioned, but the need has been recognized for more rigorous examination of these and other variables which influence the quantitative densities of transaction between areas.

There remain many additional problems and questions involving the use of transaction flow analysis in geography which have barely been touched upon here. For example, is the assumption of origin-destination independence a realistic one with respect to all forms of transaction flow? Should a measure of physical distance be incorporated into the method for predicting the expected flow between units? If so, how will this change the patterns of salience and how can these changes be interpreted? What does asymmetry—a "lopsided" flow between regions—indicate? Of what significance is a large number of salient links? An evenness of transaction flow (i.e., few if any very salient links)? How can the information content of transactions be evaluated and measured, particularly with respect to mutually-rewarding vs. mutually-depriving characteristics? Are reductions in the amount of deviation from the indifference model, as one author suggests, a sign of increasing integration?[35] What are the most revealing kinds of transactions to examine? Can measures of salience contribute more realistic frameworks for the use of diffusion models?

These questions point out the great need for further application and refinement of the technique, particularly in conjunction with studies of communications and behavior at the local level. It is hoped, however, that this study has not only suggested an interesting new tool, but has also opened up new avenues for research into the behavioral aspects of communications which can contribute to a more theoretical, quantitative, and spatial political geography.

---

[35] Brams, *Flow and Form in the International System*, p. 123. Divergence from the model involves the Percentage Discrepancy Statistic (P), which represents the percentage of transactions which would have to be moved from one cell to another to make the model fit the data perfectly. The P-values for East Africa were 43.8 in 1961 and 44.8 in 1965, a very small change but one towards weaker integration if one accepts the initial assumption.

J. S. NYE

Patterns and Catalysts
in Regional Integration

I

Is it possible to integrate states into larger unions without the use of force?
Should we think of a continuous "federalizing process" in which economic integration is a first step?[1] Are there certain conditions under which economic integration of a group of nations automatically triggers political unity?

Since in most historical instances of political union, political and economic integration developed more or less simultaneously, it is not surprising that an apparent exception from recent history has attracted considerable attention. The European Economic Community (EEC) has had a strong impact both on statesmen from other areas of the world and on theorists concerned with international organization. Although a great number of questions remain unanswered about the process of European integration, scholars have begun to explore the question of the extent to which theories developed primarily upon the basis of European experience can be generalized to other parts of the world.

As yet we have far too few cases to be able to make very sound generalizations about comparative regional integration. Some scholars are not even sure whether the similarities between integration processes in industrial and non-industrial contexts are sufficiently greater than the differences between the two contexts to justify a comparative approach.[2]

From *International Organization*, Vol. XIX, No. 4 (Autumn 1965), 870–884. Reprinted by permission of the author and the World Peace Foundation.

[1] See C.J. Friedrich, "International Federalism in Theory and Practice," in Elmer Plischke (ed.), *Systems of Integrating the International Community* (Princeton, N.J.: Van Nostrand, 1963), pp. 126–137.

[2] Ellen Frey-Wouters, "The Progress of European Integration," *World Politics,* April 1965 (Vol. 17, No. 3), 461.

A suggestion worthy of detailed critical attention as to how to go about comparative study of regional integration has been made by Ernst Haas and Philippe Schmitter.[3] These authors suggest a pattern of nine variables[4] whose interrelations may remain unknown but which seem likely to intervene more or less consistently between economic and political unions. By hypothesizing this pattern, Haas and Schmitter lead us to seek possible functional equivalents for variables which may be missing in particular cases.

The value of the Haas-Schmitter approach is limited, however, by difficulties concerning two of their underlying concepts and by a related ambiguity which results from their failure to spell out the relationships between their variables. The questionable concepts are the idea that "the relationship between economic and political union had best be treated as a continuum" and the characterization of integration as "gradual politization of the actors' purposes which were initially considered 'technical' or 'noncontroversial,' " resulting in an outcome of "automatic politization" where

> all other things being roughly equal, a "high" scorer in our categories is likely to be transformed into some species of political union even if some of the members are far from enthusiastic about this prospect when it is argued in purely political terms.[5]

How accurate is it to conceive of an integration process in the case of developing areas as a continuum? And is the nature of the process really "politization"? The idea that there may be discontinuities in the integration process—gaps which call for some extraneous *deus ex machina* to overcome—has been suggested about the European process. The distinction tends to be made not so much between economics and politics as such as between "high" and "low" politics. "High" politics is symbol laden, emotive, and based on attitudes characterized by greater intensity and duration than "low" politics which is consequently more susceptible to the rational calculation of benefits associated with economic problems. Whether the distinction is phrased in terms of high and low politics, *gemeinschaft* versus *gesellschaft*, or Edmund Burke's nation versus

---

[3] See Ernst B. Haas and Philippe C. Schmitter, "Economics and Differential Patterns of Political Integration: Projections About Unity in Latin America," *International Organization,* Autumn 1964 (Vol. 18, No. 4), 705–737; and Philippe C. Schmitter and Ernst B. Haas, *Mexico and Latin American Economic Integration* (Berkeley, Calif.: Institute of International Studies, 1964), pp. 1–39. The Haas-Schmitter scheme is concerned with that aspect of the spectrum of integration in which increasing interdependence is sufficient to support political institutions. This might also be called unification. To avoid confusion, my usage of "integration" in this article follows theirs. "Federation" refers to a particular institutional form of political union.

[4] *Background conditions*: 1) size of the units, 2) rate of transactions, 3) extent of pluralism, and 4) elite complementarity; *conditions at the time of economic union*: 5) governmental purposes, 6) powers of union; and *process conditions*: 7) decision-making style, 8) rate of transaction, and 9) adaptability of governments. See the table on p. 510.

[5] Haas and Schmitter, *International Organization*, Vol. 18, No. 4, 707, 717.

trading company, the essential point seems to be that what is true about integration in the one sphere may not be true in the other.[6]

We do not know yet whether the alleged discontinuity will prove crucial in Europe. Intense and durable (*gemeinschaft*) loyalties tend to follow and coexist with associational or instrumental (*gesellschaft*) attitudes after some period of time. The crucial variables determining whether the alleged discontinuity disrupts an integration process would then be the length of the "period of vulnerability" before less durable and intense instrumental loyalties are reinforced by more durable and intense communal loyalties and whether the integration process is confronted with a grave crisis that would cause actors to reverse decisions on instrumental grounds during the "period of vulnerability." It is conceivable that if the European Economic Community is not threatened by a depression or similar grave crisis before durable loyalties are established, the gradually rising price of disruption may make the theoretical discontinuity between the two types of politics irrelevant, as the Haas-Schmitter approach suggests.[7]

In many underdeveloped areas (and probably among Communist countries), however, much that in the European context would be simple welfare politics becomes tinged with emotion and symbolic content that is usually associated with national security politics.[8] One consequence of this is that there is less opportunity for autonomous bureaucrats to go quietly about the business of integration in "non-controversial" spheres.[9] The major problem then is not, as in Europe, whether some crisis will make the theoretical discontinuity between the two types of politics relevant. It is as though the integration process had already reached the "high" politics area before the benefits from the welfare politics of integration had become great enough to encourage the learning of new behavior. If the problem in most underdeveloped areas is one of premature "overpolitization," then it is not helpful for comparative study to conceive of the integration process as "gradual politization." If we wish to continue to conceive of integration as politization, then we must add the concepts of "depolitization" (possibly a corollary of the growth of political pluralism which might accompany economic development) and eventual "repolitization." Since this

6 See Stanley Hoffmann, "Discord in Community: The North Atlantic Area as a Partial International System," *International Organization*, Summer 1963 (Vol. 17, No. 3), 521–549; Karl Deutsch, "Supranational Organization in the 1960's," *Journal of Common Market Studies* (Vol. 1, No. 3), 212–218; and Edmund Burke quoted in Arnold Zurcher, "The European Community—An Approach to Federal Integration," in Plischke, pp. 87–88.

7 For evidence that this is occurring, see Leon N. Lindberg, "Decision Making and Integration in the European Community," *International Organization*, Winter 1965 (Vol. 19, No. 1), 56–80.

8 The content of "high" politics may vary with the context. In some instances, economic problems like location of industry may show more of the aspects of "high" politics than a subject like defense which is usually associated with "high" politics in Europe.

9 The almost impossible problem of avoiding political entanglement is described in detail by Albert Tevoedjre, former Secretary-General of the Union africaine et malgache (UAM), in *Pan-Africanism in Action* (Cambridge, Mass., 1965).

would probably involve a time period of generations, we might prefer to alter the characterization of integration as politization to allow us to be more discerning in the shorter run.

If everything tends to be "high" politics, then the image of a continuum and the theoretical discontinuity between two types of politics are not relevant to an integration process in this type of an underdeveloped context. Nonetheless, we might wish to speak of "institutional" discontinuities in such a context. In theory, we can conceive of a whole spectrum of possible institutional arrangements between economic and political union. But in some underdeveloped areas, parts of the theoretical institutional continuum may not be politically relevant. For instance, given a politics of strong personal control of state and party machinery, institutional arrangements which do not promise sufficient immediate centralization of power to attract key political leaders to the new center may be unviable. The possibilities suggested by the concept of a continuum may not exist in practice.[10]

The other major problem with the Haas-Schmitter approach is their failure to be more specific about the relationships between their variables. Is their list of nine variables merely a handy checklist like others which have been published,[11] or is it designed to tell us more? For instance, are high scores (or functional equivalents) on all nine variables a sufficient condition for "automatic politization" even in an underdeveloped or Communist area where a small, contrary-minded elite is in complete control of the political machinery? And are each of the variables (or functional equivalents) a necessary condition for automatic politization? If one or more of the variables, say high elite complementarity in conditions of high transactions, is sufficient in the political context of an underdeveloped area, of what value then is the rest of the scheme? When must we find functional equivalents and when need we not bother? Finally, the term "functional equivalence" tends to imply the existence of system or interdependence, yet it is precisely this aspect which is absent from the Haas-Schmitter scheme.

The best way to illustrate both the value and the problems of the Haas-Schmitter scheme as an approach to integration in underdeveloped areas is to apply it to what once appeared to be one of the most promising cases in the underdeveloped world, the attempts of East Africans to form a federation on the basis of their economic union in 1963.

---

10 It is possible to conceive of bridges for this institutional gap, for instance, the allowing of key leaders to hold office in their territorial bases and at the new central level simultaneously. However, this may be difficult in practice.

11 See, for instance, the ten variables listed by Karl Deutsch and others, *Political Community and the North Atlantic Area: International Organization in the Light of Historical Experience* (Princeton, N.J.: Princeton University Press, 1957), pp. 123–154. For an example of their limited value in an African context, see Chapter 11 of the excellent study by William Foltz, *From French West Africa to the Mali Federation* (New Haven, Conn: Yale University Press, 1964). Haas is aware of this problem and helped to call it to the author's attention.

II

The states of former British East Africa (Kenya, Tanzania, and Uganda) constitute an area the size of Western Europe. However, in 1963, they had a combined population of only 25 million and a gross domestic product (GDP) the size of that of a European city (£550 million). The East African states provide a particularly interesting example of the problems of creating political unions in Africa not only because their three leaders met in June 1963 and pledged that they would federate before the end of that year (a pledge not fulfilled) but because so many of the conditions for successful federation between states existed in East Africa. Using K.C. Wheare's criteria, the East Africans enjoyed geographical neighborhood, prior political association, and roughly similar colonial political institutions. They were motivated by desires to gain and maintain their independence, to gain economically, and to have a stronger defense through federation.[12]

Moreover, the East Africans had a considerable degree of social integration. Not only do the East Africans have a common elite language (English), but Swahili serves as an indigenous lingua franca in Tanzania, most of Kenya, and parts of Uganda. Nairobi, the capital of Kenya, serves as a commercial center of East Africa, and Kenyan newspapers are read in the other two countries. Many members of the elites of the three countries, including 40 per cent of the cabinet ministers, attended Uganda's Makerere College and, at the other end of the social spectrum, a number of Kenyan workers (and a lesser number of Ugandans and Tanzanians) travel to the other countries for labor.

East Africa is connected by more than 4,000 miles of railways, the capitals are within a long day's drive of each other over all-weather roads, and East African Airways (EAA) schedules flights to nearly all parts of the area. Though a large majority of the population of each country is rural and illiterate and communications cannot compare with those in Europe, the beginnings of impressive social integration—of the growth of transnational society—exist. Certainly, in transportation, language, education, telecommunications, and news media, the East Africans are more socially integrated among themselves than they are with any other countries.

Colonial rule bequeathed an impressive degree of functional cooperation to the East African states. By 1927 the United Kingdom had created an East African common market, and in the 1930's various common services such as postal and telecommunications administration, meteorology, locust control, air service, and higher education were established. After the Second World War, a central bureaucracy and legislature were established for the common services. This organization, the East Africa High Commission, was only reluctantly

---

12 See K.C. Wheare, *Federal Government* (3rd ed.; London: Oxford University Press, 1953), p. 37. Although Kenya is involved in a territorial dispute with its northern neighbor, Somalia, Uganda has disproportionately large neighbors to the north and west, and Tanzania harbors refugees from Portuguese East Africa to its south, none of the East African states felt an absolutely compelling need to federate for the sake of defense.

accepted at first, but, with the coming of independence to Tanganyika in 1961, farsighted African leaders arranged for the maintenance of the organization in slightly altered form as the East African Common Services Organization (EACSO).

EASCO consists of an "Authority" composed of the heads of government which decides specified matters on a unanimous basis, a Central Legislative Assembly (CLA) indirectly elected by the three territorial legislatures and limited in jurisdiction areas of EASCO competence, four ministerial committees including one cabinet minister from each territory which meet four times a year to oversee the administration of the various services, and a bureaucracy which includes a Secretary-General and some 300 senior civil servants with headquarters in Nairobi.[13] This executive is not as strong as the Commission of the European Economic Community, and there is neither a detailed treaty governing the common market nor a jurisdiction to try infringements of the cooperative arrangements as there is in Europe.

EASCO plays a large role within the underdeveloped East African economy. It has nearly 21,000 full-time employees (including unskilled labor) and accounts for nearly 8 per cent of the GDP, but most of this is accounted for by its three most important services, the self-financing communications services (East African Railways and Harbors [EAR&H], East African Posts and Telecommunications [EAP&T], and East African Airways). EASCO also administers (but does not set the rates of) income and excise taxes, meteorology, and civil aviation and runs eleven research institutes.

In their common market the East Africans enjoyed almost free movement of goods as well as labor and capital. Major exceptions were certain agricultural products. Transactions were made easier by the existence of a common currency although this involved the monetary rigidity of a currency board since there was no central bank. Although interterritorial trade was about one-fifth of external exports, trade between the East African territories grew more rapidly after World War II than did their trade with the outside world. In particular, Kenya's exports of light manufactures to the rest of East Africa grew rapidly. When this caused loss of customs revenue to the other partners, a distributable pool (based on 40 per cent of company income tax and 6 per cent of customs and excise revenue) was established to help compensate Uganda and Tanganyika.[14]

Despite adjustments, it has not been so easy to separate high politics from technical economic cooperation in the context of economically underdeveloped countries whose political leaders are interested in using government power for

---

13 Some services and research institutions have headquarters outside Nairobi.

14 For a detailed description of EACSO, the East African common market and the frictions involved, see Joseph S. Nye, Jr., "East African Economic Integration," *Journal of Modern African Studies*, December 1963 (Vol. 1, No. 4), 475–502. See also *East Africa: Report of the Economic and Fiscal Commission* (Cmd. 1279) (London: Her Majesty's Stationery Office, 1961); and Benton Massell, *East African Economic Union* (Santa Monica, Calif.: RAND Corporation, 1963); pp. 1–89.

rapid economic and social change. Frictions developed between the three countries in the coordination of foreign economic policies, in the coordination of
development plans, in the tendency for new industries to cluster in Kenya, and
in the reluctance of Ugandans to have Kenyans compete in the Ugandan labor
market given the general conditions of unemployment in East Africa. Disputes
also arose over the distribution of the benefits of various services. The rigid
monetary policy caused interterritorial problems, and there was no agreement
over what powers should be given to a central bank.[15] Finally, in 1964, Tanganyika, long the strongest and most ideologically committed advocate of
cooperation and federation, threatened to withdraw from the common market
and from some of the common services and to establish a separate currency.
After hastily convened talks, an arrangement was reached which allows East
African countries to protect certain of their industries against each other's competition—the first major breach of the common market. In addition, the East
Africans agreed that of six new industries, three would locate in Tanganyika,
two in Uganda, and one in Kenya. Even this agreement has failed to remove
the sources of friction.[16]

The East African experience suggests that in the political and economic setting of the new African states, a high degree of economic integration spills over
into political integration or spills back. To a considerable extent, Tanganyika
accepted a number of compromises on functional cooperation as a first step to
federation. In June 1963, when the East African leaders announced their intention to federate, it seemed that this policy of sacrifice and restraint on full
exercise of sovereignty had borne fruit. After a few weeks of discussion, however, talks on federation bogged down and, by the end of the year, Tanganyikan
enthusiasm and patience had been severely sapped. Many observers attributed
this failure in the federal negotiations to the dissimilarity of political institutions, in particular to the continued strength of the separatist Buganda area in
Uganda. Actually, this was only a minor factor. It was those Ugandans who
had previously been most committed to the idea of federation (and to the ideology of Pan-Africanism) who became reluctant to surrender their control over
the power to reshape their local society.

In part, personal fears contributed to Ugandan hesitation—it is sometimes
said that no executive agrees to a merger if it means the elimination of his
position. But the Ugandan concern was not something that could be solved
simply by insuring that a few jobs went to the right people. The Ugandans
balked at economic and institutional issues which affected Ugandans' power
over such matters as monetary reserves, public debts, location of industry, and

---

[15] In 1963 Erwin Blumenthal of the Deutsche Bundesbank suggested a two-tiered banking
system in a report to the Tanganyikan government, but it has not been implemented. See
The Present Monetary System and its Future (Dar es Salaam, Tanganyika: Government
Printer, 1963).

[16] See *Kampala Agreement* (Dar es Salaam, Tanzania: United Republic Information Service, 1964).

location of the capital. As representatives of the smallest and landlocked state, Ugandans opposed those provisions of the draft constitution which provided for a powerful presidency, a weak upper house, and central government power over Ugandan resources.

On the other hand, any compromise weakening the proposed constitution would have meant that the proposed federation would not have had sufficient power to redistribute industry and resources from richest Kenya to poorer Tanganyika in order to satisfy the latter state. In short, Tanganyika was dissatisfied with the status quo for economic and ideological reasons and strongly favored a centralized federal pattern. Uganda, for political reasons, preferred the status quo to a centralized federal pattern. Kenya, which gained most from the status quo economically, was interested in any compromise which preserved its economic gains but leaned toward Tanganyika in political preferences. As the prospects of federation faded, Tanganyika became less willing to compromise on functional integration.[17] In the aftermath Kenya has become somewhat disenchanted with its concessions on industrial location, Uganda has announced plans for establishing its own central bank as well as its intention of withdrawing Makerere from the University of East Africa, and Tanzania has promoted arrangements that will terminate the common currency. Whether these indications of further spillback will prevail, as seems likely, or whether alternative positive indicators such as plans to establish a common shipping line and to extend functional cooperation to include Zambia will result in stability, the prospects for spillover into political union have enormously weakened since 1963.

III

A minor difficulty in applying the Haas-Schmitter framework to East Africa (see the table on p. 510) is that East African economic union began much earlier under British colonial rule. Nonetheless, given the commitment of the new elites, we can take 1961 as a second starting point. Turning first to the background conditions, in 1961 the comparable size and power of the units judged in terms of the "specific functional context of the union"[18] was somewhat unbalanced in favor of Kenya which sold more than twice as much to its partners than it bought from them. The effects of this imbalance, however, were not unfavorable to further politization and indeed served as a positive stimulus for Tanganyika. Imbalance in size did contribute to the failure of politization in 1963, but not imbalance in terms of the specific *functional* context of the union. Uganda was willing to maintain the imbalanced status quo. It was its smaller population (seven million compared with Tanganyika's ten and Kenya's eight and one-half) in the context of *political* union which caused its elite to

---

17 For details on these problems, see Joseph S. Nye, Jr., *Pan-Africanism and East African Integration* (Cambridge, Mass: Harvard University Press, 1965).
18 Haas and Schmitter, *International Organization*, Vol. 18, No. 4, 711.

Comparison of Economic Unions[a]

	Eec	*Eacm*[b]/- *Eacso*	*Lafta*
Background Conditions			
1. Size of units	mixed	mixed−	mixed
2. Rate of transaction	high	mixed+	mixed
3. Pluralism (modern)	high	low	mixed
4. Elite complementarity	high	high−	mixed
Total Judgment	high	mixed	mixed
Conditions at Time of Economic Union			
5. Governmental purposes	high	mixed+	low
6. Powers of union	high	mixed−	low
Total Judgment	high	mixed	low
Process Conditions			
7. Decision-making style	mixed	mixed	mixed
8. Rate of transaction	high	mixed+	mixed
9. Adaptability of governments	high	mixed	mixed
Total Judgment	high	mixed	mixed
Chances of Political Union	good	possible	possible-doubtful

[a] Adapted from Haas and Schmitter, *International Organization*, Vol. 18, No. 4, p. 720. I have used Haas' judgment of scores for the European Economic Community and the Latin American Free Trade Association (LAFTA) but have used new scores for East Africa and suggested the alternative outcome of "political union" rather than "automatic politization."

[b] East African common market.

fear loss of control of the nation-building, resource-allocating governmental machinery.

Parenthetically, there may be a limit beyond which increasing disproportion of size in both functional and political contexts enhances the prospects of political union. It can be argued that the formation of Tanzania in 1964 depended in part on the fact that Tanganyika was 360 times the size of its tiny, defenseless, island neighbor, Zanzibar. We will return to this point below.

The rate of transactions in 1961 was high by African standards even though the proportion of intramarket trade to total trade was about half that of the EEC. In elite complementarity, the common educational and political background of most East African leaders—at Makerere College and through participation in the Pan-African Freedom Movement of East and Central Africa (PAFMECA)—should give East Africa approximately as high a score in this regard as the postwar European leaders of the EEC.

The major background condition in which East Africa received a low score was on the existence of modern (functionally specific) groups. The underdeveloped economies did not generate the full range of economic interests, middle-level managers to articulate and organize them, or pluralist ideologies to protect them that industrialized European economies generate. In theory, traditional groups might serve as a functional equivalent. In certain cases, tribal ties across borders facilitate political integration. However, a stronger case can be made for the proposition that strong traditional pluralism generally increases the insecurity of a modern African political elite and makes it more reluctant to enter political unions with countries whose leaders are more firmly in control. The strength of traditional groups in Uganda hampered the development of a single party system comparable to that in Tanganyika and thus contributed to the fear on the part of the Ugandan political elite that they would lose political power in a larger union.

We can find a more plausible functional equivalent in the broad sense in which Haas and Schmitter saw the *"técnicos"* with their UN Economic Commission for Latin America (ECLA) ideology as performing an analogous function with respect to initiation of LAFTA that modern groups converging in a pragmatic calculus of benefits did for the EEC.[19] The small political elites with their ideology of African unity very nearly served as a functional equivalent in the heady period following the May 1963 Addis Ababa Summit Conference of Independent African States (which established the Organization of African Unity [OAU]). But when the Ugandan elite later felt threatened by its earlier commitment, the dominant position of the small elite proved a sufficient condition to prevent spillover and the ideology was sufficiently diffuse to allow of reinterpretations to fit this new attitude of the elite.

Moreover, as Ernst Haas and Philippe Schmitter note about the Latin American Free Trade Association, such a functional equivalent may be adequate for creation of a union but inadequate for its maintenance. What is more, it may even hinder its maintenance. An East African federation might have encountered the problems of the Mali Federation in West Africa. Small political elites committed to African unity were a functional equivalent for the missing convergence of modern groups in the formation of the Mali Federation, but the same ideology blinded the Sudanese leaders to the concessions they would have to make to Senegal to maintain the Federation.[20]

On the conditions at the time of the African confirmation of the economic union in 1961, East Africa gets a "mixed-plus" rating (the only doubt concerned part of the Ugandan elite) for having converging economic aims with a strong political commitment to eventual political union. On the powers or strategy of the union, East Africa received only a "mixed" score. Despite the existence of a supranational bureaucracy disposing of nearly 8 per cent of the GDP (or more than the governmental budgets of Tanganyika or Uganda), there was no firm timetable for the dismantling of obstacles, and voting formulas emphasized unanimity. Moreover, non-partisan regional bureaucrats were in a poor situation to take independent action in the highly politicized atmosphere of East Africa.

As for the process conditions, East Africa received a "low-mixed" mark on decision-making style. Some committees of uninstructed experts worked well, particularly in the financial and communications fields. Others, particularly in

---

19 Schmitter and Haas, *Mexico and Latin America Economic Integration,* p. 33.
20 Foltz, pp. 118–165.

the politically sensitive fields of commerce and industry, were reduced to lowest common denominator solutions.

The score was "mixed-plus" with regard to the rate of transactions after union. On the one hand, East African trade compared with trade with the outside world increased in importance for each of the three countries, and infrastructure was improved. On the other hand, mobility of labor and educational interchange tended to decrease.

As for learning or adaptability of the governmental actors and their ability to use crises for redefinition of aims at a higher level of consensus, East Africa receives a "mixed" score. Awareness on the part of governmental actors of the serious problems in their economic union contributed to the abortive attempts to create a federation. When this failed, the Tanganyikans precipitated a crisis which the East Africans used as a stimulus for working out a compromise solution which involved some infringement of the market but forestalled at least for a while its total disruption or the disruption of the services. Something better than a low score is deserved for attempts to use crises to redefine aims at the *highest level politically possible* rather than allowing spillback to proceed unchecked—even if the attempts prove futile in the long run.

IV

Although the Haas-Schmitter framework directs our attention to many of the relevant variables, it does not always lead us to ask the right questions about them. Moreover, since the relationships between the variables are not spelled out, it treats them all equally, whereas there is reason to believe that relations between the elites is by far the most important variable. One of the basic problems with the Haas-Schmitter framework as a starting point for the comparative study of regional integration is that this "revised functionalism" still places too little emphasis on conscious political action.[21] The concept of "automatic politization" smacks too much of the functionalist preference for "the administration of things"—at least for application to developing areas like Africa. This is not based upon supposed irrationality of Africans. Careful calculation of welfare benefits and economic interests when making decisions makes sense only when the political framework within which interests interact can be taken for granted. Most African states are still involved in determining and changing the structure within which interests work. In such conditions, the primacy of politics makes sense.

In East Africa a small political elite in each country is intent on using the powers of the captured colonial state to create a national community; the prevalent ideology, influenced by the need for unity in the struggle for independence is more centralist than pluralist; and the underdeveloped economies do not

---

[21] See Ernst B. Haas, *Beyond the Nation-State: Functionalism and International Organization* (Stanford, Calif.: Stanford University Press, 1964), Chapter 1.

generate the full range of economic interests or the middle-level managerial skills to organize what specific interests do exist. The resulting dominance of the political elite can in certain conditions be sufficient for achievement of political union; but it also means that the transition from economic union to political union is more visible and correspondingly more easily disrupted. Functionalist theory seems to rely on a certain invisibility of integrating forces, due either to the complexity of industrial society or to a fit of absentmindedness on the part of political leaders. Neither condition is likely in the highly political atmosphere of new African states.

It is true that the East Africans often tended to become caught up by the "either-or" aspects of their situation and failed to explore all the institutional possibilities.[22] But it would not be wise to attribute the East African failure to unique conditions. As we suggested earlier, many developing countries have small elites whose impatience, insecurity, or concern with nation building leads them to allow their prestige to become involved in even technical matters. This makes institutional compromise difficult and provides grounds for our view that interim arrangements between economic and political unions may fail to attract the critical political leaders to the new center if too much power is left with the component states. This seems to have been a problem in the West Indies where the important Jamaican politicians remained primarily concerned with Jamaican politics and were ready to sacrifice West Indian union for the sake of success in Jamaica.[23] Similarly the French West African Federation was not strong enough to attract the critical leaders to Dakar, particularly after the changes of 1956.[24] Presumably, this difficulty is not limited to poor areas, and political involvement in technical matters in centrally planned, Communist Party-controlled countries makes it equally difficult to conceive of the integration of the Council for Mutual Economic Assistance (COMECON) areas as a problem of increasing politization.[25]

Another reason that the Haas-Schmitter scheme is not adequate as a framework for the comparative study of regional integration is that it diverts attention from extraneous factors which cannot be fitted within the nine variables. Yet a "catalyst" may be almost a necessary condition for integration in underdeveloped areas.

.   .   .

---

[22] In November 1963, two political scientists attending a university conference on federation in Nairobi submitted a memorandum which brought to the attention of East African leaders the number of alternatives available. See A.H. Birch and R.L. Watts, *Alternative Ways of Distributing Authority Within Federation* (Nairobi, mimeographed, 1963).

[23] See Hugh W. Springer, *Reflections on the Failure of the First West Indian Federation* (Cambridge, Mass.: Harvard University, Center for International Affairs, 1962).

[24] See Foltz, *From French West Africa to the Mali Federation,* and Ruth Schachter Morgenthau, *Political Parties in French-Speaking West Africa* (Oxford: Clarendon Press, 1964), Chapter 8.

[25] See Andrzej Korbonski, "Comecon," *International Conciliation,* September 1964 (No. 549), 3–62; and Kazimierz Grzybowski, *The Socialist Commonwealth of Nations* (New Haven, Conn.: Yale University Press, 1964).

More attention must be paid to the external environment of world politics in which an integration process takes place. Even European integration was helped by its initiation in an environment in which Europe had (as a result of war) undergone a drastic change from autonomous actor to pawn in a bipolar power struggle. The importance of factors outside the economic integration process is suggested by the comparative success of political unions formed in developing areas while the colonial power was still present (or played a large part) and the relative absence of successful political unions of underdeveloped countries after independence.[26] Nearly all successful political unions in Africa, for example, have either occurred before independence and/or involved United Nations actions (Ghana-British Togoland, Somalia-British Somaliland, Cameroun-British Cameroons).

One exception to the rule is the still uncertain union of Tanganyika and Zanzibar as Tanzania. If anything, the great disproportion in the size and strength of the two partners suggests the partial relevance of the Bismarck model which Haas and Schmitter exclude from their concern. Similar circumstances might arise between Senegal and Gambia or some of the other West African enclaves. But the model is Bismarckian with severe limitations. Because of the existence of international organizations which dampen open conflict, the disproportion must be so great that it allows a Goa-like *fait accompli* if open force is used, or else there must be severe internal confusion if subversion is used. In other words there are great limits on the use of military force as a catalyst in today's environment, but the possibility is not entirely excluded, particularly if military force is held partly in abeyance and is used to limit the number of alternatives available to a small country.

Another possible catalyst in today's environment might be economic aid. Most African countries are highly dependent on outside aid and in principle this might allow donors to provide the extra conditions needed to supply the political will for bridging discontinuities which might arise in an integration process. In a world of competitive aid giving and with countries extremely sensitive to infringement of new sovereignty, it is uncertain how effective a catalyst this can be, but it could be important if potential "federalizers" chose to use their power for this purpose.

My concern here is not with the source of catalysts (if any) for African integration, but with the need for some concept like "catalyst" to supplement the conditions established in Haas' nine variables. To state that a catalyst is a necessary condition for spillover from economic to political union in an underdeveloped setting may be too strong. We would need only a single case to disprove this. Though this case does not yet exist, it seems reasonable to allow for its possibility by merely stating that in studying regional integration in an underdeveloped setting, one should focus not only on the process variables but also look for possible *dei ex machina*.

---

26 Of course I am not arguing that formation under colonial rule is a sufficient condition for success of a political union.

This formulation leaves open the possibility of purely voluntary regional integration in developing areas, while it also prevents scholars from allowing a preference for "peaceful" integration to divert them from the full range of relevant factors. Moreover, even if a catalyst is stated to be a necessary condition, whether this makes "peaceful" or "voluntary" integration impossible depends on the definitions of those terms and the type of catalyst involved. What degree of outside limitation on the range of choices available to integrating elites is necessary before we call a process "involuntary"? "Voluntary" is a relative term which can be applied in at least a qualified sense so long as some alternatives remain. Similarly, if the catalyst is a qualified "Bismarckian" type such as we discussed above, we might hesitate to call the process "peaceful." However, what if the catalyst is a consortium of aid donors?

To answer these questions we may wish to elaborate the concept of catalyst although by its nature it will remain to some extent ambiguous. We might, for instance, wish to distinguish passive environmental catalysts from active catalysts which we might term "federalizers" or "unifiers."[27] We might distinguish between catalysts or unifiers which involve military force and those which do not; those indigenous to a region and those foreign. We might distinguish between catalysts which are effective only for the initiation of an integration process and those which can be effective at various stages in the process. With more empirical work we may be able to develop generalizations between types of catalyst, types of discontinuities, and types of setting as described in the Haas-Schmitter pattern variables. My main concern in this article, however, has been to establish that the Haas-Schmitter scheme is not yet the framework which we need for a comparative study of regional integration both because of problems with its underlying concepts and its ambiguity about relations between the variables; and to suggest that any suitable framework must provide for attention to outside environmental factors of world politics.

---

[27] C.J. Friedrich has suggested that "integrating federalism" may call for a "federalizer." See *New Tendencies in Federal Theory and Practice,* A Report Given at the Sixth World Congress of the International Political Science Association (Geneva, mimeographed, 1964).